EMBRACE ^{AN} ANGRY WIND

BOOKS BY WILEY SWORD

Shiloh: Bloody April (1974)

President Washington's Indian War, the Struggle for
the Old Northwest, 1790–1795 (1985)

Firepower from Abroad: The Confederate Enfield
and the LeMat Revolver (1986)

Sharpshooter: Hiram Berdan, His Famous
Sharpshooters and their Sharps Rifles (1988)

Embrace AN Angry Wind

THE CONFEDERACY'S LAST HURRAH:

SPRING HILL, FRANKLIN,

AND NASHVILLE

Wiley Sword

HarperCollins*Publishers*

In memory of my father,
Winfield E. Sword, 1905–1985

Within his soul tossed a certain restlessness, like the gathering
ripple of a morning breeze across the meadow grasses.
For he endeavored, by climbing that one additional step, to
see what was beyond—and how far two uncertain legs
might carry him.
Despite life's hard knocks he remained a compassionate man,
as beneath that worldly facade he understood our
common clay.
He was considerate and giving, knowing that all want of
others, if only for understanding.
Although his flesh is gone, his spirit endures. It burns brightly
within me, and will remain with my children and in their
offspring for time eternal.

HarperCollins books may be purchased for educational, business, or sales promotional use. For information, please call or write: Special Markets Department, HarperCollins Publishers, Inc., 10 East 53rd Street, New York, NY 10022. Telephone: (212) 207-7528; Fax: (212) 207-7222.

FIRST EDITION

Designed by Cassandra J. Pappas

Library of Congress Cataloging-in-Publication

Sword, Wiley.
  Embrace an angry wind : the confederacy's last hurrah : Spring Hill, Franklin, and Nashville / by Wiley Sword. — 1st ed.
    p. cm.
  Includes bibliographical references (p.) and index.
  ISBN 0-06-016301-1 (cloth)
  1. Franklin (Tenn.), Battle of, 1864. 2. Nashville, Battle of, 1864. I. Title.
E477.52.S85 1991
973.7'37—dc20   90-55554

92 93 94 95 96 CC/RRD 10 9 8 7 6 5 4 3 2 1

CONTENTS

Acknowledgments — vii

Preface — ix

I. A Sharp Wind Is Blowing — 1

II. A Cupid on Crutches — 6

III. Dark Moon Rising — 14

IV. The President's Watchdog — 23

V. Too Much Lion, Not Enough Fox — 30

VI. Affairs of the Heart — 36

VII. Courage versus Common Sense — 42

VIII. Words of Wisdom — 51

IX. Who Will Dance to Hood's Music? — 63

X. Old Slow Trot — 75

XI. In the Best of Spirits and Full of Hope — 87

XII. Playing Both Ends Against the Middle — 99

XIII. The Spring Hill Races — 110

XIV. Listening for the Sound of Guns — 124

XV. A Hand Stronger than Armies — 140

XVI. Do You Think the Lord Will Be with Us Today? — 156

XVII. One Whose Temper Is Less Fortunately Governed — 170

XVIII. Tell Them to Fight—Fight like Hell! — 185

XIX. The Pandemonium of Hell Turned Loose — 197

XX. Glorified Suicide at the Cotton Gin — 214

XXI. Where Is the Glory?   232

XXII. There Is No Hell Left in Them—Don't You Hear Them Praying?   245

XXIII. The Thunder Drum of War   258

XXIV. Forcing the Enemy To Take the Initiative   272

XXV. Gabriel Will Be Blowing His Last Horn   286

XXVI. The Sunny South Has Caught a Terrible Cold   300

XXVII. Let There Be No Further Delay   308

XXVIII. Matters of Some Embarrassment   319

XXIX. Now, Boys, Is Our Time!   331

XXX. I Shall Go No Farther   345

XXXI. Mine Eyes Have Seen the Glory   357

XXXII. Where the Grapes of Wrath Are Stored   369

XXXIII. Crying Like His Heart Would Break   381

XXXIV. A Retreat from the Lion's Mouth   392

XXXV. The Cards Were Damn Badly Shuffled   404

XXXVI. The Darkest of All Decembers   423

XXXVII. Epilogue: The Twilight's Last Gleaming   434

Order of Battle, Confederate Army of Tennessee   444

Order of Battle, Federal Army   448

Reference Notes   452

Bibliography   485

Index   493

ACKNOWLEDGMENTS

A PROJECT OF the scope and complexity of the 1864 Confederate invasion of Tennessee requires a significant amount of help and cooperation in attempting to tell the full story. Many persons and institutions were indispensable in locating and providing research materials, the loan of rare books, and generally uncovering potential sources of information.

For the help of the following I am particularly grateful:

Bill Mason, Morehead City, N.C., and the late Mil Lent, Redford, Mich., were most helpful in supplying various books and documents from their personal collections.

Tom Cartwright, Curator of the Carter House, Franklin, Tenn., provided many materials and documents. Mrs. Virginia Bowman, also of Franklin, Tenn., was of great help with local historic sites and data.

I wish to especially thank Don Troiani, Southbury, Ct., for the superb painting of Opdycke's Charge used on the dust jacket.

Many individuals provided assistance in research and often contributed their time or materials in their possession. Listed in alphabetical order, they are:

Tom Broadfoot, Wilmington, N.C.; William C. Davis, Harrisburg, Pa.; Jill Garrett, Columbia, Tenn.; Betty L. Krimminger, Chapel Hill, N.C.; Bill MacKinnon, Bloomfield Hills, Mich.; Bill Matter, Harrisburg, Pa.; Mike Miner, Sevierville, Tenn.; Bob Smillie, Northville, Mich.; Dr. Richard Sommers, Carlisle Barracks, Pa.; Bob Younger, Dayton, Ohio; Dave Zullo, Gaithersburg, Md.

Of the many libraries, historical societies, museums, firms, and other entities who contributed various materials, the following are particularly noteworthy. Their valuable assistance is gratefully acknowledged. In alphabetical order, they are:

The Carter House, Franklin, Tenn.; the Huntington Library, San Mareno, Calif.; Kennesaw Mountain National Battlefield Park, Georgia, Dennis Kelly; J. B. Leib Photography, York, Pa.; Library of Congress, Manuscripts Division, Washington, D.C., David Wigdor; the Museum of the Confederacy, Richmond, Va.; the National Archives, Washington, D.C.; the National Museum of Health and Medicine, Armed Forces Institute of Pathology, Washington, D.C.; the Saturn Corporation, Spring Hill, Tenn., Bruce MacDonald, Vice President; the United States Army Military History Institute, Carlisle Barracks, Pa., Dr. Richard Sommers, Michael J. Winey; the University of Michigan— Bentley Historical Library, Ann Arbor, Mich.; the University of Michigan—William L. Clements Library, Ann Arbor, Mich.; the University of North Carolina Library, Chapel Hill, N.C.; the University of the South, Sewanee, Tenn.

I would like to thank Ilene Stone, my office manager, for her help with the reams of correspondence. I am indebted to my agent, Jeff Herman, and especially to M. S. "Buz" Wyeth, Vice President and Executive Editor, and Daniel Bial, my editors at HarperCollins, for making this project a reality.

Last but not least, I would like to thank my wife, Marianne, for her patience and understanding during the many long hours of research and writing.

WILEY SWORD

PREFACE

THE AMERICAN Civil War, long recognized as perhaps the nation's supreme crisis, endures today in the minds of many, reflecting a fascination that recalls past glory and manliness; it was an adventure of the greatest magnitude. In large measure, the great disunion crisis has been extensively portrayed as a heroic war, the first of the modern and last of the romantic conflicts. It freed the slaves and saved the Union. There was an abundance of brilliant leaders on both sides; Robert E. Lee, "Stonewall" Jackson, U. S. Grant, and William Tecumseh Sherman are household names, even today. If many of their men fought and died, it was in essence a worthy death, suffered in the cause of liberty or a cherished ideal.

Popular history has a way of obscuring some of mankind's ugliest scars, as a matter of both perspective and proportion.

Perspective reflects little more than the interpretation of reality. Yet perspectives generally vary from reality, because they incorporate attitudes, largely influenced by the extent of our experience and knowledge. Historical proportion is equally difficult to grasp. It involves somewhat of a refined perspective, incorporating balanced judgment, knowledge, and perception.

Today we endure as a society extensive tragedy much as a daily routine. We despair at the death of several hundred persons in the crash of a commercial airliner, or the loss of individuals in a fatal fire or gruesome highway accident. The pages of newspapers are filled with accounts, and countless hours are devoted to investigating, reporting, and explaining these varied disasters. It is entirely proper that much public attention is focused on such incidents, if only to learn from particularly calamitous mistakes. Yet as a matter of proportion all such tragedies pale in comparison with the American

Civil War. Then it was not hundreds of casualties that lay stricken on various sites across the nation, it was thousands.

Of the more than 2.5 million men who fought in the Civil War, about 620,000 lost their lives. As statistics, these numbers are so intimidating that the essence of the personal meaning is often missed. Imagine one of our largest football stadiums—the Rose Bowl, for example—filled to capacity. If every single person in the crowd represented an American who died in the war, it would take more than six entirely full Rose Bowl Stadiums to hold the extent of our Civil War dead. Or, if each dead American from the Civil War were laid end to end, theoretically they would stretch beyond the distance from Chicago, Illinois, to Atlanta, Georgia.

Yet even these figures are misleading as a full measure of tragedy, for beyond these deaths were the more than 500,000 additional men who were shot but survived, many suffering the amputation of arms or legs. The proportion of tragedy is staggering. It was the costliest war as measured by American deaths in our nation's history. In fact, the total of American military deaths from all other wars combined barely exceeds the total of our Civil War dead.

As a matter of perspective, however, these grim statistics are perhaps the less important part of the story. It has been estimated that within the Confederate army the average individual was shot, stricken with disease, or otherwise disabled six times during his term of service. In personal terms, this meant suffering of unprecedented levels. To the common soldier, often in his early twenties with his health at its most vigorous peak, participation in the Civil War was really a continual test of survival. It was an arduous task just to cope with the ongoing challenges of the battlefield, unsanitary camp conditions, and infectious outbreaks of disease. Moreover, due to the difficult communications of the era, these men often endured their ordeal without full public awareness or understanding of their extraordinary plight. Even their own leaders often failed to grasp the personal meaning beyond the military results. That is why many veterans, both blue and gray, who saw and suffered were drawn together after the war in a common bond; only they truly knew what it was like. They were the ones who had paid in pain and torment. This was the hidden side of the war, the personal insight that came only from experience. Try as one might, there was no way to adequately convey in personal terms to another who was not there the full meaning.

At Franklin and Nashville, two of the most devastating personal experiences of the American Civil War, the superficial accounts both contemporary and in later memoir form were inadequate to fully depict one of the most extraordinary and compelling of human experiences. Lost forever was the full experience as witnessed by the participants. Today we can only approximate their ordeal and estimate their emotions. Yet, from a technical perspective, the historian has the advantage of utilizing source material not readily available at the time, and relating the part to the whole in analytical context. What emerges is an approximation of the reality, as carefully reported and crafted with as much verisimilitude as the recorded facts allow. Were any of the veterans alive today to read this account, they would undoubtedly learn of events and incidents which as individual participants they had missed.

Fortunately, the story that emerges today through comprehensive research is quite clear and detailed. It is a powerful tale, one worthy of being remembered as a particularly revealing episode of the sacrifices endured in our nation's past. Though long obscured and often overlooked, it is a tragic and important story, one of the most dramatic of the American experience.

In fact, the invasion of Tennessee in the winter of 1864 may have been the dramatic pinnacle of the American Civil War. To draw a historical parallel, the battles of Franklin and Nashville may well represent the Civil War equivalent of the World War II atomic bombing of Hiroshima and Nagasaki. As surely as the nuclear devastation of these two Japanese cities led to the surrender of Japan, the destruction of the Confederate Army of Tennessee became the real basis for the demise of the Southern Confederacy. With the devastating loss of the Confederacy's second most formidable army, not only was one of the most vital productive regions of the Deep South stripped of essential military protection, but thereafter an overwhelming concentration of Northern armies was imminent against Robert E. Lee's Army of Northern Virginia. The Confederacy had suffered a fatal wound. It was an end to reasonable hope for Southern independence. What had begun as a bold campaign, an invasion to restore a disastrously lost military balance, had instead become an ultimate disaster.

Beneath the surface of this all-pervasive defeat on the battlefield lingers a supreme drama involving some of the greatest personal travail and emotional upheaval of a generation. Vivid in the tangled web of the Southern Confederacy's death throes were the intense personal experiences that changed forever the lives of some of the era's most prominent personalities. Beyond the agony of the common soldier, the South's key leaders were made to suffer and despair as never before. Who today can understand the inner anguish that caused the Confederate commander to months later stare intently into the fire, livid spots mottling his face, perspiration beading his forehead, bitter memories of an all-pervasive disaster tormenting his mind? Or can we know the emptiness and heartbreak of a young woman who had just learned her fiancé had needlessly met the cruelest of deaths on the battlefield at Franklin? Time does not efface such scars, it only distances the agony.

Today these compelling events reflect a uniquely astounding American story. More than 125 years after the tragedy it is as yet difficult to write about—not in recounting the events, but in conveying an essence of the full meaning, from the emotion of the moment to the anguish that followed.

May we therefore consider the uneasy silence of the long-ago dead and remember with understanding their deeply moving ordeal, one that forever changed a generation and its legacy.

WILEY SWORD
Birmingham, Michigan

CHAPTER I

A Sharp Wind
Is Blowing

THE WEATHER, noted a longtime resident of mid-Tennessee, was absolutely
"wretched." It began to snow briskly by midmorning. At least half an inch
of snow carpeted the frozen ground before noon. Adding to the misery was
the wind, sharp and cutting, which blew directly from the north. The freezing
temperatures, the rough, nearly impassable roads—rutted and scarred by
nearly two weeks of rain—and the icy wind made for a vicious, cruel day to
travel, this November 21, 1864.[1]

Yet it was a day long anticipated, and later so well remembered. To the
officers and men of the Confederacy's Army of Tennessee this day was as
much as a new beginning. That morning at dawn the men had been called to
arms. Their regimental commanders had told them of the forthcoming offensive: they were going into enemy-occupied country, into Tennessee, they
said. The army would leave its present camp near Florence, Alabama, and
march in the direction of Nashville. There would be a lot of hard marching
and some fighting ahead, so it was presumed. Yet their commanding general
had assured them that there would be little risk of defeat. He would not
choose to fight a battle in Tennessee unless the advantage was all on their
side—where the numbers were no worse than equal, and the choice of the
ground was theirs. If only they could at times endure short rations they might
earn a redeeming victory over the despised enemy.[2]

The great invasion thus had begun. Slowly, ponderously, the army had
arisen from its scattered camps and pushed north. By sunrise that frigid
morning most of the regiments and artillery batteries were in motion. A spirit
of confidence prevailed throughout the army. "The ground is frozen and a
sharp wind is blowing," noted an observer, "but as my face is towards

Tennessee, I heed none of these things. God in mercy, grant us a successful campaign."[3]

Soon thereafter the state line between Alabama and Tennessee was reached. Here there was a sign, crudely made, that some soldier had fashioned and hung over the road. It read: TENNESSEE, A GRAVE OR A FREE HOME. Nearby, the exiled Confederate governor of Tennessee, Isham G. Harris, shook hands with the army's commander and bade him a formal welcome to the state. Everybody seemed to agree that it was an affecting scene, and optimism prevailed among the men, many of whom were once again returning to their former homes.[4]

Less than fifty miles away at Pulaski, Tennessee, an apprehensive and fretful Federal private, noting the forbidding and ominous weather, wrote in his diary: "This is a very rough day, [it has] snowed and blowed all day." He had spent the morning on picket duty, and in the afternoon there was word of an impending move. Said one of his division's brigade commanders at the time: "The Rebels have been threatening for some time to transfer the war to the banks of the Cumberland and Ohio [rivers], and I should not be surprised if they attempted it. They seem disposed to cross the [Tennessee] river now, but . . . if they try this new move they will find it hard to get back to Georgia and Alabama." Noting that the Union army had been at Pulaski for about two weeks and was well fortified against attack, he concluded that the enemy might think "that he will catch us now with a small force, and try to carry out a favorite purpose to transfer the war to the [Kentucky] border." Should this happen, he continued, the Rebels would be greatly mistaken, for the Union forces would soon have "an army of 70,000," enough to whip the Rebels "and have something to spare."[5]

II

The Confederate genesis was desperation. By the autumn of 1864, the Civil War was nearly lost for the Southern Confederacy. The great hope of Southern independence burned ever lower, flickering like a solitary candle in the gathering breeze.

Despair in the South had progressively risen to full tide. Prospects for a negotiated peace had died aborning. The Lincoln administration had denied the Confederacy's peace initiative by declaring that the only basis for negotiations would be an unequivocal return to the Union and the emancipation of slaves, both unacceptable conditions to Southern leaders. Any beneficial foreign recognition of the Confederacy was stalled in the resolutions of neutrality that had followed the failure of "cotton diplomacy," and military reverses such as Antietam and Gettysburg. Even the prospect of Abraham Lincoln's defeat by the "Peace Democrats" in the general election of 1864 had proved unrealistic. Heavy recruitment of new Union soldiers to replace the veteran regiments whose three-year term of enlistment was expiring was in full swing.[6]

The South's politicians thus seemed more outspoken, and talked increasingly of the North's overwhelming resources in manpower and materials. Nearly three million men comprised the North's total military strength; little over one million might be counted on to serve for the South. On the actual rolls at the beginning of 1864 there were about 860,000 Union soldiers, whereas the South had only 481,000 military men. Now, in November 1864, the disparity was even greater—about 950,000 Federals, and perhaps 450,000 Confederates.[7]

In material resources the perspective was equally grim. Prior to the war, almost 90 percent of the United States' industrial firms were located in the North. Two states, New York and Pennsylvania, each had more industrial capacity than the entire South. More than 92 percent of the prewar nation's gross national product of $1.9 billion originated in the Northern states. The agrarian South had too much cotton and too few guns in 1861. In 1864 the circumstances had changed. Said Confederate President Jefferson Davis in an impassioned speech that year: "Once we had no arms, and could receive no soldiers but those who came to us armed. Now we have arms for all, and are begging men to bear them." The North's overwhelming numbers, their seemingly inexhaustible resources, even their technology—repeating rifles and ironclad warships—after more than three exhausting years of warfare seemed to be an insurmountable obstacle. Or were they? Davis and various other war leaders still exuded optimism.[8]

The essential basis of survival for the Southern Confederacy in late 1864, the Southern military leaders foresaw, was not military conquest, it was at best a prolonged standoff. Demonstrating to the Northern public their government's folly in maintaining an unwinnable and unpopular war, exacerbating its costliness and catering to the profound longing for the war to cease— this was the sole remaining practical means of independence for the South.

The will to win, or at least to persevere until the object was gained, combined with dwindling if yet adequate resources in men and materiel, might yet enable the South to weary the populace of the North into abandoning the struggle. "This Confederacy is not yet . . . 'played out,' " intoned Davis. "Say not that you are unequal to the task. . . . I only ask you to have faith and confidence."[9]

It was an interesting thought: that the will of the people, unless broken, could see the Confederacy safely through all of the imposing obstacles. "Brave men have done well before against greater odds than ours," said Davis in urging a heightened effort. Stating that "two-thirds of our men are absent [from the army]—some sick, some wounded, but most of them absent without leave," the president admonished, "If one-half the men now absent without leave will return to duty, we can defeat the enemy." It was the battle for the minds and will of the Southern people that Davis foresaw as the key to overcoming the present adversity. The resolve of the populace at large, their morale and perspectives, would be either the means of sustaining the cause or the basis for ultimate defeat. How the Southern people saw the war would determine the further effort they would make.[10]

Yet Davis knew that popular support for the war turned upon some cause for hope or basis of optimism. "Victory in the field is the surest element to a peace. . . . Let us win battles and we shall have overtures soon enough," he asserted. To that end he foresaw that there must be some reversal of the widespread despondency following the general retreat of the Confederate armies and the loss of large segments of the South.

Davis already had endorsed a plan to atone for recent disasters such as the naval defeat at Mobile Bay and the fall of Atlanta: "We must march into Tennessee—there we will draw from twenty thousand to thirty thousand to our standard; and so strengthened, we must push the enemy back to the banks of the Ohio." He told a milling throng at Macon, Georgia, "Let no one despond. . . . [If] genius is the beautiful, hope is the reality." At Montgomery, Alabama, the president urged, "The time for action is now at hand. There is but one duty for every Southern man. It is to go to the front." To an enthusiastic audience at Columbia, South Carolina, he proclaimed, "Within the next thirty days much is to be done, for upon our success much depends."[11]

Noting the dire threat of Union General William T. Sherman's consolidated armies at Atlanta, poised to strike deeper through the vulnerable heartland of the South, an aroused Davis warned that "we must beat Sherman, we must march into Tennessee." This time and place, urged the president, would be decisive. "We are fighting for existence, and . . . you must consult your hearts."[12]

One of Jefferson Davis's most interested and attentive observers fully agreed in principal. Reading in various newspapers of Davis's plea for a united resolve and of plans to carry the war northward, he must have chuckled over Davis's philosophy. From his own perspective he had some equally specific ideas to implement: "The time has come now when we should attempt the boldest moves . . . because the enemy is disconcerted by them. . . . We are not only fighting hostile armies but a hostile people, and must make old and young, and rich and poor, feel the hard hand of war as well as their organized armies."[13]

His name was William Tecumseh Sherman, and he perceived that the underlying key to waging successful war was psychological as well as physical. Defeating the enemy's will to persevere was crucial. Thus he had bold, unconventional plans in this regard—a strike at the very heart and soul of the Confederacy—a march through their vast public granary to wreak total devastation. With his victorious forces, the conquerors of Atlanta, Sherman's "bummers" would set a new precedent in the meaning of war. It was Davis's concept reversed. Instead of relying on the defeat of the enemy's armies as a means of public support and ultimate victory, Sherman would act directly against enemy popular opinion. The grizzled forty-four-year-old Federal commander saw this clash for the minds of the populace as crucial to winning an early peace. "You cannot qualify war in harsher terms than I will," he told a delegation of Southern citizens. "War is cruelty, and you cannot refine it; and those who brought war into our country deserve all the curses and maledictions a people can pour out." Warning of the forthcoming policy he would pursue, Sherman wrote, "If the people raise a howl against my barbarity and cruelty, I will answer that war is war, and not popularity seeking. If they want peace they . . . must stop the war."[14]

They were grim, unrelenting words from a calculating mind and a determined foe. At the very time the Confederate Army of Tennessee was preparing to march for Tennessee, Sherman's men had begun their sixty-mile-wide swath through the heart of Georgia. "It surely was a strange event," Sherman later observed, "two hostile armies marching in opposite directions, each in the full belief that it was achieving a final and conclusive result in a great war."[15]

In the rear of Sherman's southward-bound columns Atlanta lay smoldering in ruins, a pall of black smoke hanging high in the air over the desolate landscape. Gun barrels glistening in the sunlight from long blue lines of infantry stretched as far as the eye could see. A passing band struck up "John Brown's Body," and Sherman admired the moment. "The day was extremely beautiful," he wrote, "clear sunlight, with bracing air, and an unusual feeling of exhilaration . . . a feeling of something to come, vague and undefined . . . full of venture and intense interest."[16]

Only a few weeks earlier he had written to several prominent Southern citizens: "Now that war comes home to you, you feel very different. You deprecate its horrors. . . . I want peace . . . and I will ever conduct war with a view to perfect and early success."[17]

The war of wills—one to be sustained and perpetuated, the other to be broken—had been joined. The stakes were higher than ever before: outright survival for the Confederacy, and an early end to an unpopular war for the Federal government. An extraordinary cast had been assembled for the contest, and it only remained for the actors to play their parts with a skill and verve that would determine the nation's, as well as their own, uncertain fate.

CHAPTER II

A Cupid on Crutches

THEY CALLED HIM "SAM," a nickname he picked up at West Point. At six feet two inches tall, muscular in physique and broad-shouldered, he looked a bit like some backwoods lumberjack masquerading in the uniform of a Confederate general. Only thirty-two years of age in early 1864, his striking appearance belied his youth: a full, tawny beard and heavy mustache so elongated his face as to make it appear of outlandish size. He had the look of an old crusader, something out of *Don Quixote*, thought Richmond socialite Mary Boykin Chesnut. His entire appearance seemed to her to suggest "awkward strength."[1]

The ladies of Richmond, Virginia, who knew of his reputation as a hell-for-leather fighter and a leader of the "wild Texans" serving with Lee's army, seemed at first shocked by his shy, almost self-deprecating manner. From his first presence amid the Southern capital's high society, there was something deeply fascinating if not compelling about the man.[2]

His sad, blue eyes with a furrowed brow, downcast mouth and long, straight nose made his normal expression almost hangdog—like a melancholy yet playful bloodhound. Despite his rough-hewn appearance, close observers noted his light auburn hair, and especially his small, finely shaped hands. Women always seemed attracted to him; indeed, they often found him captivating. Perhaps that was but part of the mystique, and a manifestation of the many contrasts and quirks noted in his background and personality.[3]

John Bell Hood was not at all what many regarded him to be. First of all, he was not a Texan. The son of a prosperous young Kentucky doctor, Hood had grown up in the lush bluegrass region near Mt. Sterling as an ill-mannered hellion. Unlike his older sister and brothers, a streak of wildness and nonconformity was evident in young Hood. His indifference to social customs and academics kept him frequently in trouble, and even when he entered West Point through the influence of his uncle, then a U.S. congressman, there was the prospect of failure. "If you can't behave, don't come home," his father reportedly admonished. "Go to the nearest gate post and butt your brains out."[4]

Hood had barely managed to prod and squirm his way through West Point with the Class of 1853, accumulating in his senior year 196 demerits, four short of expulsion. His grades were low, particularly in mathematics, and when he graduated as a brevet second lieutenant in July 1853, he stood forty-fourth in his class of fifty-two. Part of the problem may have been a lackluster education at a "subscription" school in rural Kentucky. Thanks to this bare-bones high school equivalency, Hood appeared to be relatively simplistic in his thinking and was not regarded as having a refined or calculating mind. Moreover, his meager academic foundation provided a disadvantaged background for any future association with the sophisticated and elite, a matter he seemed later to well understand.[5]

Certainly, if there was not mental brilliance, there was a strong measure of physical courage evident in John Bell Hood. Happily, his regular-army duty assignments had resulted in service with and under some of the most promising military figures of the era, including Albert Sidney Johnston, Robert E. Lee, William J. Hardee, and a dusky-bearded major, George H. Thomas. As a member of the famed 2d U.S. Cavalry, a unit later described as "the greatest aggregation of fighting men that ever represented the United States Army in the Old West," Second Lieutenant Hood had led a mounted foray against raiding Indians during July 1857. Following a sudden ambush of his twenty-five-man detachment, Hood's courage and leadership became crucial as his men fought off a larger number of Comanches. Lieutenant Hood had been wounded during the onslaught, an arrow piercing his left hand and lodging in his horse's bridle. Hood merely broke off the shaft, freed his hand, and continued to fight.[6]

Promotion to first lieutenant followed in 1858, and with the beginning of the Civil War he resigned on April 16, 1861, to fight for the South. Because of his native state Kentucky's divided politics, it seemed evident that there was little prospect of a Confederate commission soon forthcoming from that region. After journeying to Montgomery, Alabama, then the Confederacy's capital, Hood was commissioned first lieutenant in the regular cavalry (credited to his "adopted state"—Texas), but was soon ordered to report to General Robert E. Lee in Richmond, Virginia.[7]

By good luck and opportune timing, whereby his dash and ardent fighting spirit quickly came under high notice, within the span of three months Hood had become a lieutenant colonel. Again, little more than a month later, on September 30, 1861, he was commissioned colonel of the 4th Texas

Infantry. This was in large part due to President Jefferson Davis's notice of Hood's role in a minor skirmish during mid-July.[8]

Hood's new command, formed of wild and unruly Texans whose skilled frontier experience made them among the finest raw material in the Confederate army, was a perfect match in assignment and temperament. Soon a strong bond had developed between the men and their colonel. Pride and soaring morale produced one of the most revered fighting units in the entire army, an elite brigade that soon came to be known as Hood's Texas Brigade.[9]

Hood's extraordinary luck had resulted in his promotion to brigadier general on March 3, 1862, and command of the Texas Brigade following the resignation of their original commander, former U.S. Senator Louis T. Wigfall of Texas, who was returning to a legislative career. Hood had jumped over several officers who held seniority as colonels, and already there was talk among some officers about the rough-hewn "Texan" who seemed to be moving up too rapidly.[10]

Yet the days of glory for John B. Hood had only fairly begun. His first exposure to widespread notoriety came at the Battle of Gaines' Mill on the Virginia Peninsula, June 27, 1862. Personally ordered by Robert E. Lee to lead a frontal assault against a formidable Federal line that had already repulsed several attacks, Hood was eager for the chance. There were severe obstacles: a creek bed at the foot of the enemy-held Turkey Hill, strong entrenchments, and an abatis, all protected by glowering batteries of artillery and several lines of blue infantry bristling with bayonets. Worse still, the ground was almost entirely open over the span of perhaps a mile. No matter. Hood's Texans went forward with a will, moving at a quick step, with Hood leading them. Their instructions were not to fire until ordered to do so—"I knew full well that if the men were allowed to fire they would halt to load, breaking the alignment, and, very likely, never reach the breastworks," Hood wrote years later. Without firing a shot the Texans pressed onward into a storm of bullets and shell. Hood's ranks were shot to pieces, colors went down, and there was the maddening terror of not being able to fire in reply. With leveled bayonets Hood's Texas Brigade swept on, men dropping at every step. The first Federal line was met. Here erupted the ugly, muffled sound of hand-to-hand combat with clubbed muskets and plunging bayonets. Finally, a sharp volley exploded from the Texans' guns. The first blue line began to flee. Then the second. A loud cheer. On the crest only a few enemy gunners remained, and the Texans burst among the cannon, engulfing them. There, amid the swirling smoke, wild cheering suddenly erupted. Hood's Texans had won the day. The tide of battle was turned. Reinforcements swept through the breech in the enemy lines. Instead of a devastating defeat, Gaines' Mill had become a crucial Confederate victory.[11]

Hood, miraculously, was unscathed. Amid the wrecked guns and carnage he looked around. Nearly an entire Federal regiment, the 4th New Jersey, had been captured, and fourteen pieces of artillery were taken by his men. It was a sight and thrill he never forgot. Valor and courage had won the fight. It seemed to be a keen lesson well learned. Praise was heaped upon him by no less than two ultimate heroes, Thomas J. "Stonewall" Jackson and Robert E. Lee. Soon, although only a brigadier, he was placed in charge of a division. Above all else, Hood had gained a new confidence. Even a year later his staff officers would reflect about the fierce, almost surreal light that burned in his eyes during the height of battle. Those sad, soft blue eyes had suddenly blazed with fire and all of hell's fury. He was a man transfigured. Even the incomparable Stonewall had paid him high tribute. Here, truly, was a fighter, a man to be reckoned with—at least on the battlefield.[12]

"Sam" Hood, whom Lee had sent on that fateful charge at Gaines' Mill with the solemn words "May God be with you," seemed to bear such a charmed existence that it appeared he just might be destiny's darling. Not only had Hood passed through subsequent battles without a scratch, but in the midst of the bloodiest day of the war, at Antietam, where his command was such a key factor in staving off defeat, Hood's reputation continued to brighten. At the cost of virtually his entire division Hood had bought precious time for Lee and saved the army's entire left flank. Stonewall Jackson was effusive in his praise for Hood and wrote to the War Department requesting his promotion to major general. "His duties were discharged with such ability and zeal as to command my admiration," wrote Jackson. "I regard him one of the most promising officers of the army."[13]

By early November 1862, Hood was a major general and basking in the glory of it all. Whereas little more than a year ago he had been a junior field officer, he now commanded a large division, more than 7,000 officers and men, and was a key figure in Lee's high command. Even Richmond was beginning to take such notice that his corps commander hesitated to write a candid report about Hood's alleged carelessness at Fredericksburg, because he was in such "high favor with the authorities" that criticism was not prudent. After the victory at Fredericksburg and a brief detached foray to Suffolk, Virginia with Lieutenant General James Longstreet's command, John Bell Hood seemed to stand on the crest of new heights. He even boldly asserted his ideas to the high command. A letter to his "friend" Robert E. Lee suggested that smaller-sized army corps might be beneficial. Perhaps Lee might favor Hood with such a command? Ambition began to burn brightly in the back of the young general's mind.[14]

Then came Gettysburg. Hood's division served with Longstreet's Corps, and Longstreet's performance at Gettysburg on July 2d seemed substantially less than what was desired in Lee's eyes. Hood had spearheaded the famous flanking attack in the vicinity of Little Round Top which ultimately failed. Further, early in the action Hood was severely wounded in the left arm and had to leave the field. There was scant praise for Hood in the official reports, save for a perfunctory remark by Longstreet complimenting his division commanders.[15]

Hood had been wounded by shell fragments that injured his left hand, forearm, elbow, and biceps, and his arm remained in a sling for months to come. The young South Carolina surgeon on his staff, Dr. John T. Darby, had been able to prevent amputation, but thereafter his left hand was mostly paralyzed. It had been a sudden, unexpected turn of fortunes. Perhaps Gettysburg was merely a brief if ugly aberration. Yet Hood had recently met an attractive and daunting young lady. Was it possible this and his stroke of bad luck might be somehow interrelated?[16]

II

The gay parties of Richmond and bustle of the wartime capital seemed fascinating to John Bell Hood. Open receptions at the Executive Mansion provided a chance to mingle with the prominent and influential. The whirl of social life and a dazzling number of pretty ladies became a strong temptation.[17]

During a brief sojourn in Richmond during the spring of 1863 Hood had met Sarah (Sally) Buchanan Preston. Of all the fashionable and refined young ladies on the Richmond scene, there were perhaps few more beguiling and tempestuous. Everybody knew her as "Buck"—a revealing appellation derived from her middle name. Buck was of the sort that flirted and fluttered about with both innocence and sensuous mischief. She was always trying her hand. Coy and demure, she seemed to play the part of wanting men to fall in love with her, but never quite giving herself in return. "She had a knack of being fallen in love with at sight," wrote her close friend Mary Chesnut. Sweet and lighthearted, Sally Preston played the Richmond scene like a goddess. If not quite beautiful, she was lovely and had a voluptuous figure. Her soft blue eyes twinkled when she talked, seemingly changing in hue with her moods, and there was an air of mysterious elegance. Educated in Paris, bilingual, and always dressed in the most stylish clothes, at age twenty Buck Preston was a captivating if elusive young woman.[18]

Hood fell spellbound almost from the start. His surgeon, John Darby, had first brought him to see the lovely Preston girls. There was Mary ("Mamie"), and Susan ("Tudy"), but from the beginning Hood had his eye on Buck.[19]

At their first meeting, on March 18, 1863, as Hood's division marched through Richmond en route from the Rappahannock line, the general had admired her elegant profile and told John Darby she stood "like a thorough-bred." After the ill-fated Suffolk campaign in April, Hood had returned to Richmond on May 5th to do some serious courting. Yet the Gettysburg campaign had interfered.[20]

Following his wounding on July 2d, Hood had remained at Staunton,

West Virginia, in the Shenandoah Valley until early August. When he returned to Richmond it was much as a wounded hero. Despite his crippled left
arm, Hood kept up a heavy pace in his pursuit of Buck. Ordered to Chattanooga, Tennessee, in early September 1863 along with two divisions of
Longstreet's Corps to reinforce Bragg's army, Hood had taken leave of Buck
with great reluctance. On his way to board the train at Petersburg, Virginia,
he had proposed to her. "She would not say yes, but she did not say no," said
Hood a few months later. "At any rate, I went off saying I am engaged to
you." Buck, however, was coy and coquettish, saying she was not engaged
to Hood, but would think about it.[21]

In her heart there may have been an alluring twist of emotions following
the blush of Hood's courtship—the flattery of his affection, his attentive,
patronizing ways, and the celebrity and stature of his success. Yet Sally
Preston was truly a flirt, always testing and probing to see what might be, not
willing to settle for less than that of an ultimate passion. Too, such a commitment would be a burden of dire social implication. Wasn't it better to be
pursued by many men than captured by one? With Buck's youth, wit, and
attractiveness there was always no end of men in love with her.[22]

Yet there was a darker side to Sally Preston that already was the talk of the
town. Her many lovers, wrote Mary Chesnut, seemed to have been afflicted
with a deadly "spell." So many had been killed or died of wounds that Sally
appeared to have been continually in mourning. Colonel William Ransom
Calhoun had been mortally wounded in a duel with another officer in September 1862. Lieutenant Colonel Braddy Warwick of the 4th Texas, Hood's
old regiment, had been killed in action during the Seven Days' battles around
Richmond. Also there was Claud Gibson, shot at Fredericksburg, and several
others. When asked if he too might be succumbing to Buck's charms, one
young Richmond officer protested: "I dare not. I would prefer to face a
Yankee battery. They say so and so is awfully in love with Miss S[ally]
P[reston]. Then I say look out! You will see his name next in the list of killed
and wounded."[23]

If Hood scoffed at the thought, he soon might have reconsidered. He too
fell a bloody victim within a few days of their parting. Arriving by train from
the East just as the crucial Battle of Chickamauga was about to begin, Hood
hastened into the fight. On September 20th, while leading a furious assault
that was to send the Union army to the brink of disaster, Hood was struck
in the right leg by a rifle ball. It was an ugly wound, the bone being shattered
only a few inches below the hip. Immediate amputation was deemed essential, and Dr. T. G. Richardson of New Orleans, the Army of Tennessee's chief
medical officer, performed the operation. Hood was horribly disfigured by
the amputation, retaining but a four-and-a-half-inch stump. It was the greatest physical trauma of his entire lifetime, but Hood's robust physique and
strong will to live pulled him through. Despite having been originally re-

ported as dead in the Richmond papers, by mid-November he was back in Richmond, marked for promotion to lieutenant general and very much a war hero for the South.[24]

III

Mary Chesnut described the apprehension as Hood was carried from his carriage and placed on her sofa with a blanket thrown over his lower body. Everyone felt like crying and all the talk was about his missing leg, she said, but Hood wishfully watched the door—in vain—for the appearance of Sally Preston. Matters had not been going well between the two of them since his return. Was he to be scorned as less than a man with his missing leg and crippled arm?[25]

Hood soon attempted to resolve the issue in characteristic fashion—with a forthright and aggressive personal offensive. At Christmas he was found despondent—it was the hardest battle he had ever fought in his life, he said, and he had been routed. Buck told him there was no hope and had said no, he complained glumly; it was all over.[26]

Yet in January 1864 there was a sudden change of heart. They were frequently found together, Buck and the wounded knight. As they both traveled in the same social circles and shared mutual friends, there was ample opportunity for flirtatious chats. She soon had his star hat pin with the diamond center. Then, in early February, there was a spat; he had angrily ranted at her carriage driver, who clumsily caused the general to slip as he dismounted. Also Hood seemed to drink too much, and often failed to use proper pronunciation.[27]

Buck, however, again seemed to play the part of the fickle temptress. She told him that if her parents didn't oppose the match she would care for him. On February 8th they went riding. He held out his hand. "Say yes or say no," he insisted. Cy, her driver, was riding behind them. "What could I do?" she later confided. "So I put mine in his. Heavens, what a change came over his face. I pulled my hand away by [force]." Hood insisted on seeing her father to ask for her hand. John S. Preston made no formal opposition at the time. Later both parents wept in despair. They told Buck not to publicly announce her engagement, hoping a "thousand accidents of life to come between [them]."[28]

Hood was also working against time. Slated to return to an active war role and a special assignment, he had precious few days to press his affections. In an aside to Mary Chesnut, Buck confided how an engagement in Richmond meant so little. Further, she would never disobey her parents, she proclaimed. At a party several nights later she was overheard denying her engagement and flirting with the guests. Said a partygoer, the farce was not "the devil on two sticks," it was "Cupid on crutches." A close friend of Hood's remarked how eager he was for the general to return to the army.

"These girls are making a fool of him," he said. Yet Hood seemed to remain oblivious to the many snide remarks. To Mary Chesnut he commented, beaming, "I am so proud. So grateful. The sun never shone on a happier man! Such a noble girl—a queen among women!" Said Mary Chesnut, "He did not notice that I answered never a word."[29]

CHAPTER III

Dark Moon Rising

Major general pat cleburne had several ideas on how to save the Confederacy. By the end of 1863 he had begun to see the prospect of failure for the South and became convinced that drastic corrective action must be taken if their cause was to prevail. As a matter of greater morale and inner resolve, he originated and formally proposed the idea of a secret order of Southern soldiers, Comrades of the Southern Cross, a society with semi-Masonic overtones dedicated to uniting the minds and hearts of the Confederacy's soldiers. Cleburne felt such an organization might help win the war by achieving a unity of action. Perhaps among the first political action groups, it sought the power of an effective lobby. The intent appears to have been to utilize the society as a persuasive force for correcting injustice, and providing an internal political leverage for effective management of the war. Despite the formation of several chapters, the pressing duties involving the modern phase of continuous campaigning that the war was then entering left little time for widespread organization. Cleburne's secret society never flourished.[1]

Cleburne's other idea for saving the South was even more controversial. Well aware that the North was organizing blacks for active military service, Cleburne developed a proposal for enlisting Negro soldiers in the Confederate army, guaranteeing freedom to those who thus fought. This idea of using slaves as soldiers, Cleburne recognized, was drastic action. It was not a new idea, having been variously proposed by a few individuals on scattered occasions. Yet no one had brought the issue to full debate; no influential or prominent champion of the idea had come forth. In December 1863 Pat Cleburne had discussed his ideas with several ranking army officers, many of whom were willing to endorse his formal proposal.[2]

At Dalton, Georgia, on January 2, 1864, Cleburne resolutely stood in front of a specially assembled meeting of the corps and division commanders of the Army of Tennessee and read his proposal.[3]

These were brave words from a man who had only first stepped on United States soil at New Orleans on Christmas Day 1849. The third child of a moderately prosperous Cork County doctor, Patrick Ronayne Cleburne had been born on St. Patrick's eve, 1828, an omen, so some said, of greatness. His mother had died only nineteen months later, and when his father breathed his last in November 1843 Patrick withdrew from school to help the family in its financial hardship. Twice rejected for admission to Dublin medical school, and feeling he had thus disgraced his family, in February 1846 he had joined the British 41st Regiment of Foot as a private. The tenuous and austere life within the ranks of the British army was a harsh lesson in reality. Two months in the hospital after being stricken with acute rheumatism following prolonged guard duty in subzero weather convinced him of the wisdom of a brighter future. Despite his promotion to corporal in July 1849, two months later he purchased his discharge with twenty pounds inherited from the family estate and made arrangements to sail for the United States on November 5, 1849.[4]

Shy with the ladies, Patrick Cleburne had been laughed at as a clumsy Irish bloke when he attended a dance at his new hometown of Helena, Arkansas. A clerk in a drugstore, his thick Irish brogue an impediment, Cleburne seemed to have prospect of little more than a staid, mundane existence in a far-off corner of rural America in 1851.[5]

Little more than ten years later, in 1862, Cleburne was a Confederate brigadier general and not only an acknowledged commander of extraordinary military ability, but an exalted community leader. Beneath the plain-spun facade this man was a tenacious fighter in the face of adversity. Moreover, he had a driving zest for success in life, and a flair for achievement. Determination was Cleburne's byword. Laughed at for his awkwardness on the dance floor, he took dancing lessons and was soon a skilled participant. His speech became so polished after joining the debating society, he studied for the practice of law. When he had been dumped in the mire by a thoroughbred after first attempting to ride, he practiced so long and often that within weeks he became a proficient horseman. Beset by diminished financial means, he saved enough money from his meager salary to make a $400 down payment and buy an interest in the drugstore. By 1853 Pat Cleburne was a self-made success. Elected master of his masonic lodge, the handsome bachelor sold his ownership in the drugstore in 1854 and for two years studied law. Cleburne's admission to the Arkansas bar in January 1856 marked his rise to full prominence in the community.[6]

While appearing to be an unassuming man of modest and quiet temperament, within the soul of Pat Cleburne burned a passion for achievement. Blessed with talent, ability, a keen mind, and ample common sense, he had before him the brightest of futures. He gained wealth from land speculation in the years before the Civil War, and his growing involvement in civic and legislative affairs ensured his prominent role as a community leader.[7]

In 1860 Cleburne had foreseen the approach of the dark storm clouds of Civil War. During January 1861 he had written to his brother about the coming conflict, saying that if a peaceable separation of the Southern states was denied, he was "with Arkansas in weal or in woe." "I never owned a Negro and care nothing for them," he told his brother Robert, but these Arkansans had been his friends and had stood by him on all occasions. He was thus "with the South in life or in death, in victory or defeat."[8]

As captain of the local volunteer rifle company, the Yell Rifles, Cleburne had been so moved with emotion when presented with a Bible by well-wishers at the Episcopal church that he could scarcely speak prior to leaving for the war in April 1861. Elected colonel when the consolidated companies met in May 1861 to form the 1st Arkansas Infantry (later reclassified as the 15th), Cleburne at age thirty-three was quickly marked for important command.[9]

"I know nothing of the future," wrote Cleburne at the time, "but I suppose I will have a conspicuous share in the events approaching." This was destiny foreordained. As for his younger brother Joseph in Cincinnati, about to align himself with the Federal government, Patrick told Robert to tell him "my honor forbids me from further correspondence with him during the war." It was heavy irony. Pat Cleburne all too well foresaw the grim prospects ahead. Recognizing that "I may die in this conflict," he told the family, "I hope we shall one day meet again, if not on earth, in heaven." The issue of defending Southern rights had from the onset meant a brother's war, and even perhaps his own life. Yet Cleburne hesitated not a moment. "I have seldom been a false prophet," he uttered in explanation. "An honest heart and a strong arm should never succumb."[10]

II

Pat Cleburne, wrote a member of his staff, seemed born to greatness. A rather dull, impassive figure when at ease, in the fury of battle he was a man possessed. At Shiloh, his first battle, the newly promoted brigadier general had been thrown from his unmanageable horse in attempting to traverse a swamp during the initial attack. Covered from head to foot with mud, Cleburne had emerged from the morass to lead his brigade in prolonged fighting that ultimately cost more than 1,000 casualties from his brigade of 2,750.[11]

His loss in killed and wounded was heavier than that of any other brigade in the army, noted his friend and commander, Major General William J. Hardee. With praise from Hardee for conspicuous gallantry and "persevering valor," Cleburne's star was shown to be rapidly on the rise.[12]

At Richmond, Kentucky, in August 1862 and at Perryville that October,

Cleburne was lauded by his superiors, Lieutenant General E. Kirby Smith terming him "one of the most zealous and intelligent officers of the army." Even the austere Braxton Bragg paid Cleburne high tribute in recommending him for promotion to major general in late 1862. The young, ardent brigadier was exceedingly gallant yet "sufficiently prudent," said Bragg. "He is the admiration of his command as a soldier and a gentleman."[13]

By now Cleburne had come under the favorable notice of even Jefferson Davis, who was visiting the Army of Tennessee at the time. According to Hardee, the president personally ordered the Irish brigadier's promotion and assignment to division command. In later years Davis would be fond of characterizing Cleburne as the "Stonewall Jackson of the West."[14]

For all of his dash and glory, Cleburne continued to labor under a lingering sense of ill presentiment. Dogged by fatalistic thoughts and hampered by bad luck at inopportune moments, he had been often compelled to resort to a rigid mental discipline in confronting adversity. At Helena, Arkansas, in May 1856 he had been seriously wounded by a pistol ball during an ambush following a political squabble that involved his friend Thomas C. Hindman. The shot evidently had been meant for Hindman, and struck Cleburne in the small of the back, ranging upward at a forty-five-degree angle to lodge under the skin near his lungs. After mortally wounding one of the assailants, Cleburne was carried to a nearby room above a drugstore, where he hovered between life and death for nearly a week. Attended to by his former partners at the drugstore, Doctors Charles E. Nash and Hector M. Grant, Cleburne slowly regained his health.[15]

Six years later at the Battle of Richmond, Kentucky, he had been shot in the lower left jaw, the bullet knocking out two teeth and lodging in his mouth. Thereafter, Cleburne was prone to wear a short, well-trimmed mustache and beard to mask the scar. Again at Perryville, only two months later, he was painfully wounded near the ankle by a shell which killed his mount. Yet Cleburne's unflinching courage and resolute attitude had seen him through. Asked by a friend why he had further risked his life to return his adversary's fire after being shot in the Hindman episode, Cleburne had replied with grim humor, "I had either to defend myself or run, and I was trained in a school where running formed no part of the accomplishments."[16]

Despite the physical trauma, if there was a dark moon rising in Cleburne's life, it was too often an inability to reach his ultimate potential. There were virtues, not vices, that kept getting in his way. Temperate and modest in social circles, his easygoing personality failed to attract attention. Then, being unwilling to compromise principle or personal dignity for political expediency, he ran afoul of army politics. That he acted solely upon what he knew was right was all that mattered to Pat Cleburne. In his mind's eye there seemed to be only black or white, with very little gray area for compromising one's judgment.

Cleburne's true ordeal was that of the soul; it began with the alienation of his former benefactor, Braxton Bragg. Bragg's incompetence was notorious throughout the army. Following the botched combat at Stones River near Murfreesboro, Tennessee, Bragg had requested a frank opinion from his principal subordinates about his conduct of the campaign. Instead of receiving the support he expected, Bragg was astounded to learn from Cleburne, among others, that he did not "possess the confidence of the Army." Again, following the lost opportunity of Chickamauga, Bragg was the object of derision. A formal petition was sent to Richmond by many of the Army of Tennessee's ranking officers asking for his removal. Cleburne, who harbored no personal ill feeling against Bragg, knew all too well of his defective generalship, and had signed the petition. When an aroused Jefferson Davis visited the army to resolve the crisis in October 1863, Cleburne was further required to condemn Bragg's leadership. The shake-up in army command that followed left Bragg in control and many of his detractors transferred. Davis had entirely sustained his friend Bragg, and Cleburne soon learned that he had generated much animosity for his criticism of the commanding general. In November 1863 his division virtually saved the army's artillery and transportation on the retreat from Missionary Ridge by a determined six-hour stand that turned back repeated enemy attacks. Yet Cleburne profited little. Despite receiving the formal thanks of the Confederate Congress for his action, the second such vote he had been honored with (the first was for the battle at Richmond, Kentucky), Cleburne remained in limbo within the army's hierarchy.[17]

As the year 1863 drew to a close, there was much to pause and reflect about for Cleburne. Recognized as perhaps the ablest division commander in the entire army, Cleburne was idolized by his men, and as a special mark of recognition had been allowed to retain for his division their distinctive blue flags with a large white moon in the center. Regulations issued May 1, 1863, required use by all Confederate units of the "National Flag," the famous St. Andrew's Cross red flag. In the Army of Tennessee only Cleburne's division was permitted to carry their old flags.[18]

Cleburne had termed his proposal to enlist blacks in the Confederate army a "concession to common sense." Three years of bloody warfare had all but depleted the white manpower resources of the South, a "fatal apathy" was manifesting itself within the Confederate ranks, he said, and dire measures were needed to prevent subjugation. Slavery, from a military standpoint, Cleburne insisted, was the Confederacy's greatest weakness. By enlisting slaves and emancipating all Negroes who remained loyal to the South, this would reverse their armies' numerical inferiority and provide ultimate superiority over the enemy's armed masses. It would further deny the North the very same source of manpower, and encourage foreign nations to recognize a South that had divested itself of the hated "peculiar institution." Apart from all other considerations, Cleburne pointed out that the necessity of obtaining more fighting men was crucial. The South could only accomplish this, he said, by utilizing the Negro and setting free the whole race as a fair incentive.[19]

Cleburne was unprepared for the storm of controversy that immediately followed. Those present were bitterly divided over the merit of the proposal, and the Army of Tennessee's new commander, General Joseph E. Johnston, decided to table the matter as more political than military in nature. Yet one of the most outspoken critics of the idea at the meeting, division commander Major General W. H. T. Walker of Georgia, on the following day sought a copy of the proposal to forward to President Jefferson Davis. Believing that Walker's unintentional service in bringing the matter before the administration was of importance, Cleburne provided a copy and anxiously awaited what he knew must be a decisive reply from the president.[20]

When it was suggested to Cleburne by his staff that Walker would surely defame the document and it might cost Cleburne a chance for promotion, the taciturn Irish general replied that at worst he would be court-martialed and cashiered. If that was the case he might enlist as a private in his old regiment, the 15th Arkansas, and still do his duty.[21]

At the time, the prospect of censure seemed to be remote and highly improbable. General Braxton Bragg finally had been removed from command at his own request after the debacle at Missionary Ridge. On the same day that he had been relieved, Bragg wrote that Cleburne deserved the special notice of the government for his stand at Ringgold Gap on November 27th. Moreover, there was a vacancy in corps command following the removal of Lieutenant General Daniel H. Hill in the aftermath of Jefferson Davis's October visit. Perhaps even more promisingly, General E. Kirby Smith, as commander of the Trans-Mississippi Department, had requested a new commander for the District of Arkansas, Cleburne's home state. Smith had listed Cleburne as one of his three choices. Cleburne's promotion to lieutenant general had been well earned on the battlefield, and at long last the politics of his alignments within the army made him the obvious choice.[22]

There was further pleasant news. His close personal friend William J. Hardee had been temporarily assigned overall command of the Army of Tennessee, and Hardee had asked Cleburne to be his best man at his wedding, planned for January 13, 1864.[23]

III

If Cleburne thought his bold idea for saving the South would be objectively assessed in Richmond, he had sadly misread the character and beliefs of Jefferson Davis.

Noted for his strong convictions, and long besieged by influential politicians, skeptics, supporters, detractors, and all manner of persons with an object to gain, Davis had relied in the final analysis on a select few friends for advice, but mostly on his intuitive judgment. As the president of the Confederacy, Davis was especially tough when it came to being maneuvered into what he considered a distasteful or wrong decision. His deeply ingrained, intense personal pride and a rigid code of honor had resulted in a certain stubbornness that had proved to be both a blessing and a damning curse to the Southern Confederacy. Furthermore, his stoical and austere manner only accentuated the strong-willed arrogance that seemed to characterize his official conduct. Extremely sensitive to criticism, the prideful Davis habitually turned within when set upon by adversity. On the surface there was too often visible only a facade, his sphinxlike stoicism. Within lay the burning turmoil of a thousand emotions, churning and twisting amid a granite-firm sense of honor and pride.[24]

When practiced within the realm of something the president thought of as his expertise, such as in military matters, this self-defeating stoicism had the broadest implications. An 1828 graduate of West Point, Davis considered himself perhaps foremost a military man. His Mexican War service had brought him fame and success as colonel of the 1st Mississippi Rifles, "the hero of Buena Vista." Close friendships and character judgments formed at the academy and during the Mexican War were frequently the basis for Davis's wartime decisions when it came to appointments of personnel. Often perceptive and logical in his value judgments, many of his assessments were sound, as in the case of Albert Sidney Johnston. Yet others were so bad as to prove ultimately ruinous. As the war progressed increasingly unsatisfactorily, it was Davis's decisions about his generals and their campaigns that perhaps contributed the most to the ultimate defeat of the Confederacy. If Jefferson Davis was strong-willed in supporting what he considered to be an unjustly criticized commander, he too often was a terrible judge of his generals' abilities. Among the worst such scenarios were those of Braxton Bragg and John Bell Hood.[25]

Bragg was the quidnunc of the Confederacy and the weakest link in the hierarchy of the upper-echelon generals. A North Carolinian with an emaciated look and a sour disposition, the forty-six-year-old former West Point officer had served with Davis during the Mexican War and came to prominence only by accident—when General P. G. T. Beauregard left his command on sick leave without notifying Richmond. Given permanent command of the discredited Beauregard's forces, Bragg had ultimately proved lacking both as a strategist and a combat general. The defeats or bungling leadership at Perryville, Stones River, Chickamauga, and Chattanooga had so disgraced Bragg in the eyes of much of his army that even Jefferson Davis acceded to his resignation from command of the Army of Tennessee on November 30, 1863.[26]

Because of Bragg's adept organizational abilities and his strong discipline, Davis admired him and had long retained him in command in the face of intense criticism. Embittered by the suggestions of incompetency from his own subordinate generals, and disgraced by the formal petitions for his removal, Bragg left the army in December 1863, retaining harsh memories of those whom he felt had conspired against him. Although finally disenfranchised from the Army of Tennessee, Bragg had so factionalized the western command structure that deep-seated personal antagonisms and rival cliques remained in his aftermath. Although perhaps the most despised general associated with any Confederate army, he was soon given another influential assignment—special military adviser to President Jefferson Davis. Davis's stubbornness in the Bragg matter provided a revealing insight to one of the president's most glaring weaknesses: he simply would not allow himself to be proven wrong in his judgments. Having endured enormous pressure and abusive criticism for his pro-Bragg decisions, he flaunted Bragg's prominence by calling the embittered North Carolinian to his side as a close military confidant. "The power to assign Generals to appropriate duties is a function of the trust confided in me by my countrymen . . ." admonished Davis in a similar situation, "[and] while I hold it nothing shall induce me to shrink from its responsibilities or to violate the obligations it imposes." In early 1864 Bragg was thus on the scene in Richmond and of key influence when several of the most far-reaching decisions to affect the war effort in the west were made.[27]

When Cleburne's proposal to enlist slaves in the Confederate army reached Richmond about the third week in January 1864, it was accompanied by an acerbic cover letter from the outraged W. H. T. Walker, who asserted, "My strong conviction [is] that the further agitation of such sentiments and propositions would ruin the efficiency of our army, and involve our cause in ruin and disgrace."[28]

Jefferson Davis was shocked. He not only agreed with Walker, but was equally astounded by Cleburne's suggestion. Wasting little time in responding, Davis wrote a private note thanking Walker on January 23rd. In it Davis observed that it was an injury to the public service that such a subject should even be discussed among high-ranking generals or officials. In directing the entire suppression of the matter, Davis ordered that all discussion cease, lest the public obtain knowledge of the matter. "If it be kept out of the public journals," urged Davis, "its ill effects will be much lessened."[29]

Due to the removal by Jefferson Davis of Lieutenant General Daniel H. Hill from command of his corps following the post-Chickamauga Bragg controversy, an important vacancy remained to be filled in the Army of Tennessee. Cleburne's old friend, Major General Thomas C. Hindman, who also had been shot in the 1856 political incident at Helena, Arkansas, was in temporary command. Yet Hindman had been wounded at Chickamauga and was closely aligned with Lieutenant General William J. Hardee, one of Bragg's detractors.[30]

Bragg and Davis conferred. A new, prestigious face seemed to be needed to restore confidence in the West. Pat Cleburne appeared to be the ablest general, yet Cleburne had written that damning proposal about arming the slaves. There was also the matter of his siding with Bragg's detractors. Discredited in Davis's eyes and regarded much as a traitor by Bragg, Cleburne was quickly and summarily passed over.[31]

Instead of Cleburne the Army of Tennessee obtained as a new corps commander John Bell Hood. It was to prove one of the most fateful decisions ever made by Jefferson Davis. Set in motion was a bizarre sequence of events destined to seal the very fate of the Confederacy.[32]

CHAPTER IV

The President's
Watchdog

Sᴀᴍ ʜᴏᴏᴅ had become all too well known in Richmond circles following his Chickamauga wound. Hood had found adulation, accommodation, and social prominence of undreamed-of proportions. Everywhere the one-legged general went, he was accorded a hero's welcome. There were receptions in his honor, theater parties, dinner parties, and other gala public appearances. A Hood "mania" seemed to possess the capital, observed one modern historian, and he was feted and catered to as were few others. "Chickamauga is the only real victory we have had since Stonewall Jackson," said Mary Chesnut in explanation, "and this man is the hero of Chickamauga."[1]

Of particular significance was Hood's burgeoning friendship with Jefferson Davis. Davis well remembered the combative leader of the Texas Brigade and the effusive praise he had received for his aggressive fighting qualities. The president and Hood were frequently seen together and became involved in an extensive dialogue, both in public and during private discussions. Hood's intense, combative spirit had earned the president's admiration, and Davis sought the thirty-two-year-old Kentuckian's confidential advice about the war. Hood, when taken into the president's confidence about the faults of some senior commanders, allegedly replied, "Mr. President, why don't you come and lead us yourself? I would follow you to the death."[2]

Feeding Jefferson Davis's ego was just the sort of political protocol that so ingratiated Hood to the president. Here was a demonstrated fighter and an acclaimed war hero not only willing to support the president's policies, but expressly attuned to his aggressive military thinking. It was an ominous melding of mind and spirit.

Davis conferred with Hood on long carriage drives, held a reception in his honor, and even was observed arm in arm assisting Hood slowly down the church steps after a Sunday service. Hood responded by favoring Mrs. Davis at social occasions and was seen conversing with her at supper long after the other guests had departed.[3]

Instead of a handicap, Hood's missing leg seemed to be a badge of honor and the basis of much respect and sympathy—very much an entrée into coveted political circles. It also seemed to awaken a deeper hunger within Hood, a burning ambition to clamber to the very top within the army.

With Braxton Bragg on the scene and a significant influence as military adviser to the president, Hood was the beneficiary of a most fortuitous combination of political and practical circumstance. The Army of Tennessee seemed to be plagued with dissension, inordinate difficulties, and ill luck. Bragg's resignation after Missionary Ridge had resulted in a distasteful appointment by Jefferson Davis, that of General Joseph E. Johnston to command the Army of Tennessee. Davis's difficulties with Joe Johnston went back to the fall of 1861, when a serious clash over seniority of rank led to hard feelings and much bitterness. Then in November 1862, when Johnston had been made commander of an enlarged department embracing the entire area between the Appalachian Mountains and the Mississippi River, he had, in Davis's eyes, proved to be most ineffective. Johnston declined to take personal command of the Vicksburg army and seemed reluctant to fight to prevent surrender of that key citadel. Yet Davis's decision to reappoint Johnston to active command of the Army of Tennessee on December 16, 1863, was based on the limited selection of senior generals available—Robert E. Lee refused to go west, and P. G. T. Beauregard was discredited by his earlier behavior. Johnston had strong support in Congress, moreover, and many in the army favored his appointment when General William J. Hardee, the temporary commander, refused to accept the responsibility of permanent command. Because of the threat to Atlanta, the Confederacy's great rail center, Davis was particularly anxious about the spring 1864 campaigns.[4]

William Tecumseh Sherman, with a Federal army estimated at 100,000, was known to be preparing for active operations against the Army of Tennessee. President Davis feared that Johnston would allow the enemy to seize the initiative, thus risking the loss of further vital territory. The government's position, especially that of Davis and Bragg, was that the Army of Tennessee must prevent further penetration of Confederate territory by assuming the offensive. This meant carrying the war northward into Tennessee and Kentucky.[5]

Bragg, who seemed to believe that the Army of Tennessee was still his own special provenance, continued to hold a great animosity toward several of that army's generals whom he considered to have jealously conspired in his removal. In early 1864 he was thus bristling with advice. Hood was an obvious favorite of Davis's. Having praised Hood in his Chickamauga report, terming him "the model soldier and inspiring leader," Bragg now fully endorsed him for the role of corps commander under Johnston. Apparently there was an ulterior motive in mind—that of not only pleasing Jefferson Davis but thwarting the anti-Bragg factions in the Army of Tennessee.[6]

Davis strongly favored Hood's promotion to lieutenant general for a variety of reasons. As early as October 29, 1863, he had indicated his intention to promote Hood to that rank. Of even more significance, Davis evidently sought to establish a major conduit of information, as well as an indirect measure of control over Johnston's operations, by the assignment of Hood to the western army. Hood, being generally unrecognized as an "administration man," would be in a key position to keep his eye on the Army of Tennessee and advise Richmond behind the scenes of Johnston's compliance with the policies and objectives of the president. Much as a covert but highly placed watchdog, Hood might warn the administration of Johnston's failure to act, and relate the true circumstances of the army's condition and capabilities. It was an important assignment in a most crucial area. It was also highly unethical and improper.[7]

The secret correspondence that Hood later carried on with Bragg, Davis, and others at Richmond provided candid information on Johnston's policies and conduct. As might be expected, it also proved to be highly distorted and lacking in objectivity. Hood, aware of Davis's distrust of Johnston and his concern about the impropriety of waging a defensive campaign, was soon portraying Johnston in unfavorable terms. The die could not have been cast in a more ominously dark metal.[8]

John Bell Hood, much a physical wreck but now the president's man in the west, rose almost unnoticed as a star and key personality in the overall waging of the war. The ambition that burned so brightly in Hood's mind had flared and intensified. In all that he had accomplished, his method of simple, straightforward aggressiveness—of attacking and overwhelming—had been vindicated. From Sally Preston to the lieutenant generalcy, and even to his elevated importance as the president's confidant, he had succeeded by direct, assertive action. It was his code and credo.[9]

If audacity alone could win so much, what new laurels might the future bring? Hood intended to soon show the world.

General Johnston was enthusiastic about the arrival of Hood to command a corps in the Army of Tennessee. "We want you much," he advised Hood prior to Hood's arrival at Dalton, Georgia, on February 25, 1864. In fact, wrote Johnston to Senator Louis T. Wigfall about a month after Hood's arrival, his greatest comfort since taking command was Hood's presence with the army.[10]

Johnston had been misled. Within a few weeks Hood was secretly corresponding with Jefferson Davis, Braxton Bragg, and even James Seddon, the secretary of war. Hood reported on the strong condition of Johnston's army and its commander's lack of aggressive plans, as far as he knew. The offensive that the government favored had not been seriously considered by Johnston, Hood confided, despite his doing "all in my power to induce [Johnston] . . . to move forward." Correspondence flowed back and forth between Richmond and Hood, while Johnston, of course, remained oblivious of the entire matter. Hood continued to convey to Davis and Bragg much self-serving propaganda, such as telling Bragg that instead of a major threat in the western theater, the enemy appeared to be preparing for a greater effort against Richmond and would probably send heavy reinforcements from the west to the east. This in so many words was pointed criticism of Johnston's failure to assume the offensive, Johnston having asserted that the Federal buildup in the west would necessitate his remaining on the defensive.[11]

On April 13, 1864, in a letter to Bragg, Hood expressed his increasing frustration with Johnston, asserting that despite all of his efforts Johnston would not take the offensive, and that he was unaware when the army would be in better condition for an advance. Hood stated that he was thus full of regret, "as my heart was fixed upon our going to the front and regaining Tennessee and Kentucky." Otherwise, the new lieutenant general revealed his own personal ambition, telling Bragg on April 3rd that if it was found necessary to send reinforcements east from the Army of Tennessee, "I am fond of large engagements and hope you will not forget me."[12]

Hood's deception should have been obvious from the beginning. Sherman, with three armies whose combined numbers soon swelled to over 100,000 men and 254 cannon, was poised by late spring to march from Tennessee against Johnston's army. His objective would be the capture and destruction of Atlanta, little more than a hundred miles distant. The stakes during the crucial 1864 campaigns were enormous: the restoration of a divided Union or the survival of the Confederacy.[13]

With the war stalemated in the west and east during the spring of 1864, the prospect of a continuing enormous financial burden and thousands more maimed and dead sons and fathers had soured the populace, and frustration and complaint were rife throughout the North. Further, 1864 was an election year, and the strong Copperhead elements within the Democratic party had proposed a platform of peace at any cost. Failure of the government's military campaigns during the summer of 1864 would be certain to further stagnate the war effort and perhaps ensure the defeat of the Lincoln administration at the polls. Because many veteran Northern regiments' three-year terms of enlistment were due to expire during the summer, the potential loss of a significant portion of the existing Federal armies was a chilling prospect. These issues would be directly influenced by the extent of immediate, important success in the winning of the war.

II

With the combined operations of the Federal armies now being master-minded by a single military chieftain, Lieutenant General Ulysses S. Grant, the simultaneous Union offensives were to begin during the first week in May 1864. Major General G. George Meade and Sherman would lead separate primary assaults against the two major Confederate armies and the cities they guarded (Richmond and Atlanta). Following Grant's advance into Virginia's wilderness during the first week, by May 8th Sherman's columns were in motion and the Confederate Army of Tennessee was soon outflanked into retreat.[14]

From Rocky Face Ridge, near Dalton in northern Georgia, to Resaca, then on to Cassville, Joe Johnston's army had been outflanked by superior numbers. Within the span of a week Johnston had retreated nearly half the distance to Atlanta. A trap set by Johnston on May 19th to crush a segment of Sherman's advancing column under Major General John M. Schofield failed when Hood mistakenly abandoned his assigned position to confront a force of enemy cavalry. Although later prepared to fight from a strong defensive position astride the Etowah River, Johnston was dissuaded from the attempt by the arguments of Generals Leonidas Polk and Hood, who felt the Union artillery would enfilade their lines. While Hood continued to ardently advocate offensive operations in letters to Richmond, within the army during mid-May he was a spokesman for conservative action. In fact, said Major General Hardee a few months later, "Hood was of all others in favor of retreating. If General Johnston had followed his advice he would have crossed the Chattahoochee [River] two or three weeks before he did," confided Hardee.[15]

Johnston, thus counseled, retreated across the Etowah into the rugged Allatoona Range. Yet Sherman bypassed this strong defensive terrain by marching toward Dallas, Georgia, on a circuitous march designed to swing beyond Johnston's left flank before returning eastward and interposing his armies on the main rail route to Atlanta. Johnston astutely blocked Sherman's three columns at Dallas and New Hope Church on May 25th.[16]

Bogged down in the mud due to incessant rains, an impatient Sherman next attempted a costly and futile frontal assault against Johnston's position at Kennesaw Mountain on June 27th. When the rains stopped on July 1st, another flanking march around Johnston's left compelled a Confederate withdrawal to the line of the Chattahoochee River. Again, due to his large numerical superiority Sherman was able to send a column under Schofield upriver to outflank this new river line. Crossing the Chattahoochee in the direction of Roswell, Sherman's columns were able to destroy the Georgia Railroad from Stone Mountain to Decatur. By mid-July separate wings of Sherman's army were in motion south of the Chattahoochee, and Johnston had been forced to withdraw into the defensive fortifications around Atlanta.

So exasperated by the flanking marches of Sherman's army were the Confederates that a prisoner told his Federal captors that it was the general opinion in the Southern army "that Sherman came into the world by a flank movement."[17]

The Richmond officials were greatly alarmed by these continual Confederate withdrawals. Johnston's retreat beyond two barrier rivers and strong defensive terrain had sparked much controversy as to his intention to defend Atlanta. Intensifying the issue were Johnston's meager explanations for the withdrawals. His secretiveness as to his plans for halting Sherman's offensive, it was rumored, was rooted in Johnston allegedly having learned that a spy in the war office at Richmond was informing the enemy of his every move. "He dares not let the president know of his plans," offered a congressman in explanation. Johnston, instead, was said to be conveying to the administration innocuous generalities, such as that Sherman could never take Atlanta by siege due to the heavy losses he would suffer.[18]

The government's misgivings were accentuated when Hood sent his aide, Colonel Henry P. Brewster, to Richmond with his candid appraisal of the campaign in late May (following the retreat across the Etowah). Brewster's outright criticism of Johnston's strategy (so much senseless retreating), and his expression of Hood's frustration at Johnston's lack of aggressiveness, was like rubbing salt in an open wound. Indeed, Richmond society was soon abuzz with rumors that Johnston would be replaced. Jefferson Davis was particularly chagrined about reports that Johnston's army was demoralized due to the continual retreats, and he resented Johnston's continual appeals for reinforcements, which Johnston insisted were necessary before Sherman's vulnerable railroad supply line could be attacked.[19]

Due to the inveigling of Braxton Bragg, the confused situation in the west was soon an open crisis. Bragg reported to Davis that the disparity in numbers between Johnston's and Sherman's armies was then less than ever before. With so much controversy, Davis sent Bragg to Atlanta on July 9th to investigate and to confer with Johnston.[20]

Bragg arrived at Atlanta on July 13th, stayed until the 17th, and met with Johnston perhaps twice. Never disclosing the nature of his trip, Bragg asked few questions, offered no advice, and his presence seemed to be a mystery— perhaps only the unofficial visit of a functionary, thought Johnston's staff.[21]

Just how mistaken they were was revealed by Bragg's aroused correspondence, including his telegrams and lengthy letters to Jefferson Davis. Bragg began by advising Davis that a complete evacuation of Atlanta would take place, by all appearances. He noted that Johnston's army had lost 10,000 men since June 10th and was sadly depleted, thus there was little that was encouraging. Following his meeting with Johnston on the 13th he wired Davis that Johnston proposed no offensive operations—an outright lie, since at the time plans were being made to attack Sherman as he crossed Peachtree Creek. Further, Bragg implied that Johnston was adrift in a strategic inertia, saying he could not learn that "he has any more plan for the future than he has in the past."[22]

The whole matter was, of course, a charade. Bragg sought to fatally discredit Johnston, well knowing that general's future was on the line. Bragg, still embittered by the animosity of many in the Army of Tennessee toward him, apparently sought a measure of revenge. By manipulating affairs to his purpose, Bragg might pull the strings so as to at least ensure a successor of his choice. After meeting with two of his supporters among the ranking officers, Joe Wheeler and Hood, he had gathered the detailed information he needed for the coup de grace. Hood provided the most damaging evidence, writing in effect a poison-pen letter to Bragg that stated that Johnston would not strike a decisive blow by giving battle, or force the enemy to fight.[23]

On July 15th Bragg dispatched three telegrams and sent a lengthy letter by special courier to Jefferson Davis. From overestimating the enemy's forces to preparing to abandon Atlanta, Joe Johnston's generalship was condemned by Bragg as being weak and vacillating. At the same time, a further troubling report arrived from Senator Benjamin Hill that Johnston had told him he could hold Sherman north of the Chattahoochee for at least a month, only to have retreated the very next day. Added to a telegram from Johnston on the 11th that Federal prisoners at Andersonville should be relocated lest they be liberated by Sherman's men, to Davis all this was damning evidence that Johnston would not fight for Atlanta. Atlanta was the industrial hub of the west, and the gateway to a munitions region in Georgia (Athens, Augusta, Columbus, and Macon) that was essential to the Confederacy's survival. The people of Georgia seemed panic-stricken, and Jefferson Davis waited no longer.[24]

On July 17th a telegram was sent to Atlanta relieving Joseph E. Johnston of command of the Army of Tennessee.[25]

CHAPTER V

Too Much Lion,
Not Enough Fox

SALLY "BUCK" PRESTON, dressed in her flowing white dressing gown, was found by Mary Chesnut at the head of the stairs in the Preston home, "her blue eyes wide open and shining black with excitement." For months there had been reports that her fiancé, Sam Hood, was destined for greater fame and glory. His letters to Buck had been progressively less frequent as the campaign for Atlanta intensified. At first he would write her letters of thirty pages, but thereafter she rarely heard from him more than once a month, he was so busy.[1]

When a friend came and breathlessly spoke the news—"Johnston has been relieved from command of the western army; Hood replaces him. . . ."—the ominous words had hit Buck like a thunderbolt. Amid the smiles and congratulations of friends she stood transfixed. "Poor Sam," she said. "They have saved Johnston from the responsibility of his own blunders—and put Sam in," she murmured. Friends were aghast.

"Why, Buck, I thought you would be proud of it," said Mary Chesnut.

"No," uttered Buck. "I have prayed [to] God as I have never prayed [to] Him before since I heard this. And I went to the convent and asked the nuns to pray for him too," she said in earnest tones.[2]

Her friend Henry Brewster later summed it up: due to the "senseless retreating," Hood had been placed in a well-nigh "hopeless" position. Davis's mistake had been to keep Joe Johnston too long in command. Another friend urged Buck, "Go at once. Get Hood to decline to take this command. It will destroy him if he accepts it."[3]

Said Mary Chesnut of Buck following receipt of the news, "she did not sleep one wink that night nor the next, she told us."[4]

II

The Army of Tennessee, said an observer, was astounded by the sudden change within the army's high command. Johnston was relieved, he was told, as "you have failed to arrest the advance of the enemy to the vicinity of Atlanta . . . and express no confidence that you can defeat or repel him. . . ." Shocked by the administration's action, Johnston could but feebly protest that having been confronted by overwhelming numbers he had compelled the enemy to advance more slowly than had recently occurred in Virginia. Although the army seemed greatly demoralized by his removal—clusters of soldiers by the hundreds were talking open rebellion against all military authority, said an officer of Hiram Granbury's Brigade—by July 19th Johnston was on the train to Macon and out of the campaign. In a caustic remark, based on the surprise selection of his successor, the veteran campaigner Johnston chided Richmond, "Confident language by a military commander is not usually regarded as evidence of competency."[5]

Indeed, being little experienced in high combat command, John Bell Hood's selection as the new commanding general was an enormous surprise to the army. Having served as a corps commander for little more than a few months, and being an "outsider" to the Army of Tennessee, he was largely looked upon by the men with uncertainty and a lack of confidence. Hood wrote that he fully felt "the weight of the responsibility so suddenly and unexpectedly devolved upon me." In fact, he sent a telegram to Jefferson Davis stating that due to the campaign in progress it was dangerous to change commanders, and he felt it best not to make this change until the fate of Atlanta was decided. Davis ignored this perfunctory shunning of responsibility for the possible loss of Atlanta, and told Hood by return telegram that Johnston's defensive policy had proved disastrous, and his mind was made up that a change was necessary.[6]

Hood immediately began active moves to correct what only four days earlier he had said to Braxton Bragg was the bane of the army:

> We have had several chances to strike the enemy a decisive blow. We have failed to take advantage of such opportunities. . . . I deem it excessively important . . . that we should attack him even if we should have to recross the [Chattahoochee] river to do so. I have . . . so often urged that we should force the enemy to give us battle as to almost be regarded [as] reckless by the officers high in rank in this army, since their views have been as directly opposite. I regard it as a great misfortune to our country that we [have] failed to give battle to the enemy many miles north of our present position.[7]

John Bell Hood, maimed of body, controversial of intellect, but an ardent fighter, would now attempt to settle the burning question: Could Southern dash and courage defeat the Northern onslaught against Atlanta by forthright tactical means—aggressive, attack-oriented fighting? Jefferson Davis, in attempting to solve a complex military problem, had appointed a man who had ranked at the very bottom of his class at West Point in ethics, and nearly so in tactics.

The basis for selection of Hood as the Army of Tennessee's new commander provided an important insight into the administration's thinking. As early as July 12th Davis had asked the opinion of Robert E. Lee about Hood as a successor to Johnston. Lee's reply was ambiguous, stating that Hood was "a bold fighter, very industrious on the battlefield, careless off," but he was uncertain that Hood possessed some of the qualities necessary for a commanding general. Davis, who went through the motions of cabinet approval for removal of Johnston, also sought Braxton Bragg's recommendation of a successor. At the time there appeared to be only two practical choices: Hood and General William J. Hardee. Hardee was the senior corps commander in the Army of Tennessee, had temporarily commanded the army following Bragg's removal, and seemed to have Robert E. Lee's endorsement. Yet Bragg was distrustful of Hardee and considered him among the conspirators who had ardently sought his ouster. Hood, in private conversations with Bragg, portrayed Hardee as lacking in aggressiveness, and in the same mold as Joe Johnston. Bragg needed little persuading. On July 15th he wired Davis that Hood was the best man for the job, being "far better" than other officers of the army. In an aside, however, Bragg wrote that Hood was not a man of genius or a great general, possibly leaving the door open for Bragg's own reappointment. On July 17th Hood was promoted to the temporary rank of full general and urged by Davis on July 18th to do his duty to correct "a [defensive] policy which had proved so disastrous."[8]

The news was not received cheerfully in the Army of Tennessee. An observer noted how on July 18th "at all hours in the afternoon can be heard 'Hurrah for Joe Johnston and God Damn Jeff Davis.' " The next day he wrote in his diary that the noise and commotion continued, and "if Jeff Davis had made his appearance in this army during the excitement he would not have lived an hour." Said another of the suspicion that Hood might not prove to be the general for the job at hand, there was perhaps too much "lion" in the man, and not enough "fox." Indeed, wrote Georgia Colonel James C. Nisbet, Hood might have a "lion's heart,"[9] but there was also a deep suspicion he had a "wooden head."

Several miles distant, within the camps of Sherman's armies, an old classmate of Hood sat on the porch of the Howard House and reflected with William Tecumseh Sherman about the startling news, printed in an Atlanta paper that had just been brought through the lines by a citizen. James B. McPherson had known Hood well—they were classmates at West Point; McPherson had graduated at the top of the class of 1853, but Hood had been 8th from the bottom. "I inferred the change of commanders meant 'fight,' " said Sherman. McPherson agreed, and warned that Hood was a determined, rash man. John Schofield, also Hood's classmate, thought Hood bold even to rashness. "This was just what we wanted . . ." confided Sherman, "to fight in open ground, on anything like equal terms instead of being forced to run up against prepared entrenchments." Sherman had notice sent throughout the army of the change, and all commanders were cautioned to be constantly ready for battle.[10]

Major General Oliver O. Howard had been one year behind Hood at West Point, and summed up the general estimate of the new Confederate commander among the Federal officer corps in a letter to his wife. Howard minced few words in his remembrance of Sam Hood: "He is a stupid fellow but a hard fighter—does very unexpected things."[11]

III

General Hood soon realized what price he would pay for his sub-rosa intrigues in rising to the top of the army. The feelings of outrage within the high command, in fact, may have had much to do with the forwarding of a telegram to Davis on July 18th by the army's three corps commanders, Hood, Hardee, and Stewart. This terse telegram asked for the suspension of any change in commanders until the fate of Atlanta had been decided. Davis's refusal to comply only accentuated the bitterness that immediately spilled over. Hardee was devastated by the appointment of a junior officer to a post he considered as rightfully his. Within a few weeks Hardee requested a transfer to a new command, and a growing animosity between Hood and Hardee was soon the talk of the army. The army's chief of staff, W. W. Mackall, resigned in protest within the week. Division and brigade commanders generally expressed their dismay, and it was evident to Hood that he was now very much on the spot as an outsider, one of the Virginia faction so frequently sent west to correct matters—which so greatly aggravated the western officers. Worse still, he was no longer in a strategically strong position with Richmond as the administration's favorite-son Johnston critic. Instead, he was the responsible entity, the man who must now demonstrate the success of his theories and the merit of his bold criticisms.[12]

Hood began by utilizing a modification of Johnston's plan to strike Sherman's divided forces as they crossed Peachtree Creek. Confusion in tactical arrangements ensued when Hood was not present at the front line to direct proper alignment and attack coordination. The Confederate assault, ordered for 1:00 P.M. July 20th, soon miscarried. After a four-hour delay, the Federals were found to have crossed Peachtree Creek and had occupied high ground, throwing up entrenchments and rude breastworks. Attacks by Hardee's and Stewart's troops were annihilated by a withering fire. Hood's onslaught resulted in the loss of nearly 5,000 men, while the Federals suffered less than 2,000.[13]

Two days later, in Atlanta's eastern defensive zone, Hood ordered an assault by two of his best corps against the Federal column under Major General James B. McPherson. By sending Hardee's Corps on a roundabout fifteen-mile march beyond the enemy's southern flank, Hood hoped to smash the Federal column in front and rear. At the sound of the flank attack by Hardee, the corps in front, Major General Benjamin Franklin Cheatham's, would attack to ensure a complete victory. Yet Hood's plan went awry. Part of the flanking column took the wrong road, was blocked by a flooded mill pond, and had to be rerouted. Hardee's attack struck the refused flank units of McPherson's command, rather than beyond their defensive line as intended. Hood delayed in attacking with Cheatham's corps until late in the afternoon, and the uncoordinated assaults were beaten off in fierce fighting known as the Battle of Atlanta. Hood, who again was not present on the field, lost nearly 8,000 men, and the Federals less than half that, about 3,700.[14]

For the third time in eight days, Hood sent his troops forward to attack an advancing Federal column on July 28th at Ezra Church, west of Atlanta. Here McPherson's former command (he had been killed in the fighting of the 22nd) under Major General Oliver O. Howard, which had been shifted to the western zone, had time to entrench and throw up rude breastworks on high ground. Hood's uncoordinated and largely unsupported attacks were shattered at the cost of 5,000 casualties. His opponents suffered a loss of less than 1,000. Hood, who had remained in Atlanta throughout the fighting, had in little over a week squandered nearly 20,000 men in fruitless attacks that did little to halt Sherman's relentless advance.[15]

Left with little choice but to withdraw into Atlanta's extensive fortifications, Hood soon was advocating a new strategy—to operate with his cavalry against Sherman's railroad lines of supply, so as "either to force him to fight me in position, or to retreat."[16]

A month-long raid by 4,000 cavalry under Major General Joseph Wheeler that began August 10th failed to significantly interrupt Sherman's supply lines. Wheeler was often prevented from important successes by Federal detachments protected by blockhouses built on strategic sites. Moreover, the Confederate cavalry was so debilitated by the arduous rigors of continuous fighting and marching that they required extensive rest, refitting, and reorganization once they returned to their own lines.[17]

As August dragged on in siege warfare around Atlanta, Hood sought to protect his two remaining railroads approaching the city from the direction of West Point (Atlanta & West Point Railroad) and Macon (Macon & Western Railroad). Several Federal cavalry raids were beaten off, and damages were quickly repaired. Yet Hood badly miscalculated when Sherman boldly broke off the siege on August 26th and secretly marched southwest with nearly his entire command to seize these two remaining railroads.[18]

At first believing Wheeler's cavalry raid might have forced Sherman into a retreat, Hood carelessly allowed Sherman to seize the Atlanta & West Point Railroad, and also to gain a lodgment on the Macon road near Jonesboro before responding. Then, having on August 30th sent Hardee's and Stephen Lee's corps on a forced march to Jonesboro, Hood suddenly recalled Lee's corps a day later when another Federal column occupied Rough and Ready, a small village between Jonesboro and Atlanta. Believing the Federal thrust at Jonesboro was only a diversion while the main columns prepared to attack Atlanta from the south, Hood thus sought to get Lee's men back into position at Atlanta.[19]

Hood's bewilderment was soon demonstrated by the outright fall of Atlanta. Throughout August Sherman had sought to draw Hood out of his trenches, well realizing that Atlanta's fortifications were too strong and extensive to directly assault. "[I] have no fears of Hood. I can whip him outside of his trenches," asserted Sherman to General Ulysses S. Grant on August 19th. Having written only eight days earlier that he would risk a great deal to draw Hood out, Sherman moved to interdict Hood's two remaining railroads, in order to force him to evacuate Atlanta or come out and fight to save his vital supply routes.*

Having quickly seized the West Point road without a fight, then advancing with four corps en route to Jonesboro on August 31st, Sherman sought to close off Atlanta's last railroad line. Attacked by Hardee's Corps on August 31st at Jonesboro, the most advanced Federal troops beat off their assailants from behind rude breastworks. Although the Confederates fought valiantly, the absence of Stephen D. Lee's Corps on September 1st allowed Sherman to mass four corps on Hardee's front and decisively break the too-thin lines. Hardee withdrew south to Lovejoy's Station, severely beaten. Hood suddenly realized he had been badly duped. With the railroads gone and Sherman closing in, Hood hastily ordered the evacuation of Atlanta, barely escaping southeast with his demoralized army during an all-night march. To the thundering sound of twenty-eight rail car loads of ammunition blowing up at once—Hood's entire reserve supply—the sullen gray ranks trudged on through the oppressive darkness. Hood had waited too long to remove an enormous stockpile of ordnance, quartermaster's, and commissary stores. Together with vital manufacturing machinery abandoned or destroyed, the loss of critical war materiel at Atlanta cast a pall over the future of the Confederate Army of Tennessee.[21]

---

*Because Sherman's cavalry had failed to isolate Atlanta by permanently destroying these railroads, Sherman boldly moved with his entire army to accomplish this task.[20]

CHAPTER VI

Affairs of the
Heart

SALLY PRESTON WAS FOUND IN BED. She seemed despondent, noted Mary Chesnut. Poor Buck. When Buck learned of Atlanta's fall, the blow had been hard enough. Now the storm of indignation was at a fever pitch, resulting in the condemnation of Hood as a failure and an ignorant general for throwing away so many lives in those fruitless attacks. Even Jefferson Davis's sister-in-law ranted openly in society how Hood should be damned for not justifying the faith the president put in him. "[Oh] how she gave it to poor Hood," noted Mary Chesnut, who was so upset by it all that she couldn't sleep.[1]

When Mary had tried to prepare Buck for Hood's possible removal, she had "turned white as the wall" at the thought, said Mary. To add a further burden, Buck's own father, who remained deeply opposed to the match, had told a friend that Hood was a half-educated man, and he was totally in amazement that his daughter could fall in love with him.[2]

Buck sat in bed, toying with the diamond ring from Hood. It was not enough that his star was under a dark cloud. She had not heard from her general for about a month, and wondered if there was foul play with his letters.[3]

II

The expressions of outrage and heated debate that centered on the Richmond authorities had reached a new crescendo by mid-September 1864. With each report of staggering losses following Hood's unsuccessful attacks the outcry about Davis's actions in removing Joe Johnston had swelled and spilled forth in bitter criticism. With the outright fall of Atlanta, much of the Southern populace was infuriated. One-hundred-gun salutes were sounding throughout the Federal armies in honor of the great victory of Sherman's men, and the South was in despair. Demands were being made on Jefferson Davis to remove Hood and name a new commander in the west. Even the president's aide de camp, Custis Lee, was said to be urging Hood's dismissal in favor of Beauregard.[4]

Jefferson Davis was a man deeply troubled by the painful events of September 1864. Complaints of sagging morale in the Army of Tennessee were continually heard, as well as reports of bitterness and strife among the officer corps. Hood, asserting that he was heavily outnumbered by the enemy, was demanding reinforcements "to prevent this country from being overrun." Fearful that Sherman would liberate the 30,000 Federal prisoners at nearby Andersonville, he was further urging their immediate removal. Meanwhile, General William J. Hardee, complaining that Georgia and Alabama were in grave danger of being seized by the Federals, was adamant about not further serving under Hood. Added to Davis's intense embarrassment over these matters were the political consequences of Atlanta's fall—especially the public outcry for corrective action. As a political realist, Davis knew that some changes must be made.[5]

With a heavy heart the president had considered the professional criticisms of Hood's generalship. Indeed, he had gone so far in early August following the ruinous losses of the three Hood sorties as to instruct Hood that he must be more cautious in his fighting: "The loss consequent upon attacking him in his entrenchments requires you to avoid that if practicable," admonished Davis. With an eye toward his future options Davis in mid-September asked Robert E. Lee if Beauregard would accept a command in Georgia.[6]

Yet Hood had obtained the strong support of others, such as Braxton Bragg, who even lied about and made excuses for Hood's failings. In the midst of the Atlanta fighting Bragg wrote: "The moral[e] effect of our brilliant affair of the 22d [July] has been admirable on our troops. . . . He [the enemy] was badly defeated, and completely failed in one of his bold flank movements." Further, there were outbursts of sympathy for Hood from various sources. Governor Isham G. Harris of Tennessee wrote to Richmond that Hood "has won upon the confidence of the army—officers and men, steadily since he assumed command. . . . The officers, with very rare exceptions are giving him the fullest and most cordial support."[7]

Jefferson Davis well understood that he faced a most difficult situation. "The crisis was grave," he later wrote. While sympathetic to Hood's plight he remained undecided about what action to take. Due to the enormous consequences involved, and in order "to judge better the situation," Davis determined to personally visit Hood's headquarters at Palmetto, Georgia. There he would attempt to resolve the myriad problems besetting the army and threatening his presidency.[8]

Traveling only with two aides, including Colonel James Chesnut (Mary's husband), and without public notice, Davis arrived by train at Palmetto about 3:30 P.M. September 25, 1864. At stake, as Hood well knew, was his career as well as the army's fate.[9]

In Richmond, Buck Preston reflected about Hood's impending crisis. She thought about how much she would like to see him, and considered how much better it would be if he returned to Robert E. Lee's army, "where his men would fight," rather than to stay with that demoralized army which would never support him.[10]

III

Patrick Cleburne had been at first a very bashful young man, wrote a close friend who had long sought to introduce him to some of the attractive girls in Helena, Arkansas. "My wife could never get him in the parlor when young ladies were visiting us." He would invariably blush if one of them spoke to him, and it was only with time and practice that he overcame his shy awkwardness in the presence of young women. By the time of his entry into the war he had given the matter of marriage considerable thought, and wrote to his brother: "I am not married and this is not a time for marrying or giving in marriage. If . . . I was certain I would not be a permanent invalid [following the war], I would wish to marry." As for the prospect of his being maimed in the war, he added, "I sometimes think I will be, at other times I think my fears [are] unnecessary."[11]

What had happened thus seemed that much more difficult to explain. From the first moment their eyes met he was obsessed that this was to be the woman he would love and marry. They had met among the most storied of circumstances, at a spacious Alabama plantation amid the social whirl of a grand and famous wedding. Susan Tarleton, twenty-four, petite and demure yet witty and captivating, was the beguiling maid of honor. Major General Patrick Ronayne Cleburne, nearly thirty-six, frequently reserved in manner and often seen with a firm, war-worn countenance, was at once festive and caught up in the gala event. As best man he had celebrated the marriage of his close friend and commanding officer Lieutenant General William J. Hardee, forty-eight, to the beautiful twenty-six-year-old Mary Foreman Lewis of Marengo County, Alabama.[12]

For Cleburne it was the first time in more than two years he had been on leave from the Army, and his spirits were soaring. Amid the magnificence of the Bleak House plantation, several miles east of Demopolis, Alabama, he had suddenly become involved in a starry-eyed romance.

The Hardee wedding had been a stately beginning. On January 13, 1864, generals and staff officers in full dress uniforms were prominent among the pomp and panoply of a formal ceremony. Cleburne had worn his best uniform and the dress sword presented to him by the men of the 15th Arkansas, his old regiment.[13]

The day following the wedding ceremony, the wedding party had set out on a trip to Mobile via one of the three stately paddlewheel steamboats plying the lovely Tombigbee River. For twenty-four hours the boat gracefully glided on the picturesque river. Susan and Cleburne, Susan's sister Grace, and their close friends Sallie and Amelia Lightfoot were among the passengers. Sallie found romance with Susan's older brother Robert, whom she would marry ten months later. Henry Goldwaithe, who also had been at the wedding, fell in love with Susan's sister Grace. In all, it was such a romantic interlude for many that months later the men would jest about the fatal, romantic atmosphere of the Bleak House plantation. That location, they joked, seemed warranted to strike the strongest bachelor down in merely a few days.[14]

By the time Cleburne returned to the army he was deeply, wonderfully in love. Correspondence flourished across the miles. Cleburne would write to Susan every day if he had the chance. By the first week in March 1864 Cleburne had arranged for another furlough of twelve days to go to Mobile. By the 6th he was again in the city and with Susan. Already his close friends predicted news about a forthcoming wedding.[15]

The general himself, writing from the Battle House Hotel on March 11th, proclaimed with playful mirth to a friend the happy news—"I arrived here last Sunday. I took advantage of the lull [in fighting] . . . to come down and learn my fate from Miss Sue. After keeping me in cruel suspense for six weeks she has at length consented to be mine and we are engaged."[16]

Following his return to the army, Cleburne's letters were often full of playful sparks, teasing Susan about the brevity of her letters—saying she was taking all sorts of advantage of him by writing in large handwriting and leaving large intervals between the lines.[17]

Susan, at once happy and lovestruck, wrote at least twice a week, but found writing letters to the general severely taxing. She wanted to say just the right thing, to encourage him in his heavy responsibility when all was chaos and death in an army fighting for its life at Atlanta. She wanted him to be careful, not to expose himself needlessly. She wanted him to come back to her. Day after day, week after week, there were terrible, grim headlines from the front. Atlanta was about to fall. The flower of the army was being consumed in battle. Would this ghastly killing ever end? When could they be together again?[18]

IV

Pat Cleburne's return to the army following the Hardee wedding had been almost triumphal. On the way back to Tunnel Hill, Georgia, he had stopped in Atlanta and conversed with a Confederate congressman, Colonel A. S. Colyar, about his proposal to enlist slaves in the army. Cleburne was most animated in his enthusiasm, wrote the man, saying that if this action was taken now, relations for all time to come could be beneficially molded between the two races.[19]

On January 31, 1864, the day following his return to Tunnel Hill, Cleburne received a letter from General Joseph E. Johnston. It read in substance: A letter had been received from the Secretary of War expressing the president's conviction that the proposal relative to arming the slaves was unacceptable. In order to prevent any disruptive public debate, "officers high in the public confidence" were enjoined from discussing the matter, and such ideas were to be suppressed in entirety.[20]

Cleburne, while obviously disappointed, accepted the president's verdict without rancor. "After such an opinion . . ." he wrote to Congressman Colyar, "I feel it my duty to suppress the memorial and to cease to advocate the measures mentioned." Cleburne had his staff officers destroy all copies of the proposal except the one returned from Richmond. Thereafter he was careful to make no public mention of this matter, in full compliance with the president's wishes.[21]

Not only was Cleburne not promoted to lieutenant general and assigned to command of Hindman's Corps instead of John Bell Hood, but a few months later he again was denied promotion when Leonidas Polk was killed at Pine Mountain during the Atlanta fighting. Alexander P. Stewart, his junior in rank as a major general, but having ingratiated himself with Bragg, was promoted and assigned to lead Polk's old corps. With Hood's elevation to army command in mid-July, the vacancy for Hood's Corps was given to Stephen D. Lee, another junior major general whom Hood had known in the east. Perhaps the most distressing of all, when Hardee, Cleburne's friend and patron, was transferred in late September 1864, Benjamin F. Cheatham was assigned by Hood to take command of the very corps Cleburne had once temporarily commanded in Hardee's absence. Cheatham was notorious throughout the army as a hard drinker, if a stern fighter. The wisdom of these assignments was even commented on in the Northern press, the *New York Herald* reflecting that "Cheatham is only a fighter, not a general, and a better horse jockey than either [of these]." Cleburne was "perhaps the best man in Hood's army at this time," continued the *Herald*, "at least possessed of more of the sterling qualities of a man and experience as a soldier."[22]

Four assignments to corps command in the Army of Tennessee over the span of eight months, and Cleburne had been summarily passed over on each occasion. Davis's and Bragg's obstinacy had prevailed. Cleburne's staff officers had been right about the controversial January 1864 proposal costing him promotion. If not court-martialed, Cleburne had been effectively blacklisted from further promotion.[23]

At least there was Susan. At the end of September there was the sudden prospect of a furlough for Cleburne. Although Atlanta had fallen, the fighting had quieted and he would apply for a leave to go to Mobile. For Susan Tarleton the nearly six months of waiting, of holding her breath at every news dispatch, of keeping a brave face and suppressing a longing heart, would soon be at an end. At last they would be together and able to hold each other once again.[24]

CHAPTER VII

Courage versus Common Sense

DURING THE SUMMER OF 1864 the agony of the war had reached a new height for the soldiers of the Confederate Army of Tennessee. Under Joe Johnston the Atlanta Campaign had begun with defensive fighting, resisting the enemy's approach from behind entrenchments and strongly prepared works. Only when these positions were outflanked by the larger numbers of Sherman's wide-swinging columns were the Confederate ranks compelled to retreat. Yet in July the sudden change in commanders had brought a new combat philosophy. Featured was an aggressive, seek-out-the-enemy-and-attack concept that was designed to contest every foot of Southern soil.[1]

In contrast, for the Union infantrymen the campaign until mid-July had been a grueling ordeal of seemingly endless marches and constant fighting. Because the soldiers were fully resigned to facing strong defensive works at every turn, the prospect of making frontal attacks had proved ruinous to morale and had weighed heavily on the minds of the men. An Elgin, Illinois, youth serving with the 127th Illinois Volunteer Infantry, Private Eugene McWayne, wrote candidly to his family of his admiration for the skill of the enemy general. "Old Joe Johnston is sharp," he admitted. "He generally gets his men out of our traps, but if ever [we get] around him, we have him." Following a conversation with several captured Rebels in mid-July, he wrote: "They [Rebels] say that 'you uns flink our men so that they have to fall back.' Bully for the 'flink,' I say. It saves a great many hard fought battles after all."[2]

McWayne's wisdom was that of the front line, where tactical lessons had been too frequently learned proportionate to the quantity of blood spilled. At the beginning of the war courage and valor were deemed the essential qualities necessary for victory. No matter how severe the task, unflinching courage was presented as a sure means to win the day. The manly virtues of standing up face-to-face against the enemy with solid, unwavering ranks, flags flying, and a drum roll sounding—this was the ideal, patriotic conception of war.[3]

Reality came in the form of the rifle and its deadly, improved bullet, the minie ball. Until the advent of the Civil War the most widely used military small arms were of smoothbore, wherein the typically used round ball literally bounced down the barrel upon firing. The rifled bore, however, imparted a spinning motion to the minie ball, a cylindro-conical-shaped projectile with a hollow recess in its base. The trapped gases expanded the soft lead edges of the recess into the rifling grooves, imparting much greater velocity and improved accuracy. Instead of proficient combat accuracy at perhaps fifty yards for a smooth-bore musket, the deadly rifle musket with its minie bullet was a consistent killer at about 200 yards' range in skilled hands. Large quantities of Enfield rifle muskets were imported from England through the blockade to Southern ports, and by mid-1862 most of the armies North and South were generally armed with single-shot rifle muskets. The tactical consequences were enormous.[4]

Within the first year of fighting across the broad continent the effect of sweeping technological advances in small arms was readily apparent. The devastation wrought by these improved weapons at such battles as Shiloh, Second Manassas, Antietam, Fredericksburg, Stones River, and many others had convinced even the most skeptical private in the ranks that fighting in the open using Napoleonic battle tactics was a certain death warrant. Particularly obvious was the fact that a direct charge, the favorite tactic of many conventionally schooled generals, was unbearably costly against even hastily prepared enemy positions. The newly evolved nature of combat, incorporating advanced weapons, greater firepower, and obstructed, well-protected defensive positions, generally made the frontal charge futile. In fact, the resort to a direct assault almost invariably produced a bloody defeat.[5]

The key to understanding all of this was experience and the most precious attribute of all, common sense. Yet practicing wisdom in leading troops in battle had been a difficult and painful undertaking for the commanders on both sides. William Tecumseh Sherman had hurled his men at Joe Johnston's entrenched lines twice during the Atlanta Campaign, at Kennesaw Mountain and New Hope Church. Both cost Sherman thousands of casualties with little to show for the effort. The lieutenant colonel commanding the 127th Illinois was so disgusted with the lack of judgment on the part of a brigadier general that he flatly refused to obey orders to lead what would obviously be a suicidal frontal attack at Ezra Church.

Sherman had learned these lessons well. In a private letter to Henry Halleck, the Federal army's chief of staff, he wrote after the fall of Atlanta of his newfound respect for enemy entrenchments: "Atlanta was so protected by earth-works that I dared not assault. . . . Our men will charge the parapet without fear, but they cannot the abatis and entanglements, which catch them at close range."[6]

On the very same day, September 4, 1864, Sherman's opposite number, General John Bell Hood, wrote to Braxton Bragg of his dismay with the courage and ardor of his army: "There is a tacit if not expressed determination among the men of this army, extending to officers as high in some instances as colonel, that they will not attack breastworks." Following the Battle of Atlanta he had told his soldiers, "Experience has proved to you that safety in . . . battle consists in getting into close quarters with your enemy. [Captured] guns and colors are the only unerring indications of victory. The valor of troops is easily estimated . . . by the number of these secured." This was his inflexible credo—the Gaines' Mill syndrome, where disciplined valor had won the day. Hood, the ardent advocate of attack, thus repeated his commitment to direct assault despite the dramatic failure of this policy in the fighting for Atlanta. His inflexibility and inability to perceive the evolving lessons of the battlefield reflected perhaps Hood's greatest weaknesses—a lack of higher intelligence and common sense.[7]

Although not a general, Eugene McWayne, serving in the ranks of the Union army's 15th Corps, had already learned more about the tactical elements of the new era in fighting than had Sam Hood. Writing of the grisly aftermath of the Battle of Atlanta, he reported from personal experience of the change in Confederate tactics since Hood had taken command from Joe Johnston:

> We kill a great many Rebs in the fights now. More so than ever, because they come out from their works and charge our men, which is useless for them. For they do not do any good, only get their men slaughtered. Our men [began] the other day in burying the Rebs. They smelled so they got a rope and put [it] around their necks, and four or five [men] got a hold and start with him, drawing them up in line, just as they [do in] lay[ing] railroad ties. It looks rough. . . . You know how a piece of fresh meat would look all covered with fly blows. . . . We buried 2420 Rebs and sent over under a flag of truce to the Rebs 800 dead, which makes 3220 dead Rebs that we know of.[8]

On September 4th Sherman reported that his consolidated Union armies were "in magnificent heart" following their victorious experiences at Atlanta.[9]

In the Confederate capital about two weeks later, Jefferson Davis had to push through special emergency requisitions to pay the troops of the Army of Tennessee, based on Hood's "urgent appeals" to keep the men from deserting in crippling numbers. If the results were not then evident in the minds of the respective generals, the issue of attack or maneuver had been well settled in the soul of each army, as measured by morale.[10]

II

Following the loss of Atlanta, Hood had been at the mercy of newspaper editors and all manner of critics. He had responded by blaming others. His actions in dealing with Jefferson Davis were equally contrived.

The president arrived at Palmetto, Georgia, on September 25, 1864, and serious discussions that would decide Hood's fate and command of the Army of Tennessee were promptly begun. Hood evidently asserted that he had been given "an untenable" military position to assume, and as "comparatively a stranger" to the army he had acted "to abandon no more territory without at least a manful effort to retain it." His offensive operations, Hood insisted, were designed to correct the "timid defensive policy" which had cowed the army and caused the men to distrust him. He had fought for and held Atlanta forty-six days, whereas Johnston had retreated a hundred miles in sixty-six days, he told Davis.[11]

The widespread reports by Northern newspapers of his enormous losses and demoralized soldiers following the failed July sorties had been exaggerated, scoffed Hood. Further, "the wanton neglect of the chief quartermaster"—who was addicted to whiskey, he added—was cited as the reason for the crippling loss of so many munitions and much railroad stock during Atlanta's evacuation. As for the loss of the fight at Jonesboro which sealed Atlanta's fate, Hood had implied to Bragg on September 5th that it was all Hardee's fault—"a disgraceful effort," he said. This matter was expanded in the presence of Jefferson Davis to become a key element of Hood's defense. He announced, "according to all human calculations we should have saved Atlanta had the officers and men of the army done what was expected of them." He told Davis that "in the battle of July 20th we failed on account of General Hardee. . . . Our failure on the 31st of August, I am convinced, was greatly owing to him." To add substance to his accusations, Hood then virtually demanded Hardee's transfer to another department.[12]

Regarding the offensive as the best method—indeed, perhaps the only method—Hood outlined a proposal for Davis. As early as September 6th, four days after the fall of Atlanta, Hood had advocated a bold new plan, one that would cater to Davis's known wishes and offer the promise of such important success that it would negate many of the consequences of Atlanta's loss. Hood at the time wrote to Davis:

> I am of good heart and feel that we shall yet succeed. The army is in need of a little rest. After removing the prisoners from Andersonville, I think we should, as soon as practicable, place our army upon the communications of the enemy, drawing our supplies from the West Point and Montgomery Railroad. Looking to this, I shall at once proceed to strongly fortify Macon. Please do not fail to give me advice at all times. It is my desire to do the best for you and my country.[13]

Hood had learned from his earlier close association with Jefferson Davis that the best way to deal with the president was to flatter him and bow to his strong convictions. Repeatedly, in his clandestine correspondence with Braxton Bragg during the spring of 1864, Hood had lavishly praised Davis, well knowing the letters would be shown to the president. "I appreciate his greatness even more than before," wrote Hood on April 3d. Mary Chesnut had earlier appraised Hood's self-serving manner of blandishment and termed him "an awkward flatterer."[14]

Davis, of course, was desperately looking for an acceptable, practical solution. He had long sought to wage offensive warfare, even to carry the war into Tennessee and Kentucky. It was his burning hope at the beginning of the spring 1864 campaign, and had significantly and negatively impacted his relationship with Joe Johnston. Hood may have been less than brilliant as a general, but he knew his politics. Davis's stoicism was a mask that Hood plainly saw through. The president was an impassioned and emotional man whose pride was at the very root of his actions. By catering to his mania about always being correct in his judgments, Hood was playing to Davis's most vulnerable side.[15]

Hood's plan was deceptively simple. Rather than fight Sherman in a full-scale pitched battle, which had proven unprofitable despite his earlier assertions, Hood, with a depleted army, intended to seize the initiative by maneuver. Not strong enough to challenge Sherman's full command, but fully capable of doing great harm as a will-o'-the-wisp raider against the enemy's extended and vulnerable supply lines, Hood disclosed his intentions to Davis. By destroying much of the enemy-held Western & Atlantic Railroad from Chattanooga to Atlanta, Sherman's critical railroad line of supply would be broken. Thus, by swinging north, rather than remaining on the defensive in southern Georgia and Alabama, Hood might be able to force Sherman to withdraw to protect his communications. If, however, Sherman ignored this threat and moved south into Alabama or toward the Carolinas' coast, he would leave in his rear a dangerous enemy capable of raiding further north or swinging south in rapid pursuit. If Sherman followed Hood north, as fully expected, the Confederate commander might compel Sherman to attack him on favorable defensive terrain, thus negating much of the Federal numerical superiority.[16]

The alternative of remaining on the defensive, Hood seemed to realize, was impractical both politically and strategically. To delay would only allow Sherman to gather strength for an anticipated move into southern Alabama, where destruction of the Confederacy's vital war-making resources would continue. Further, it might well cost Hood his command.[17]

Hood's concept was thus offensive/defensive: to act against the enemy's lines of supply, which would, in essence, serve to protect the Confederacy's. To seize the initiative and force Sherman to react to Hood's movements would forestall any further major conquest of Southern territory in the region, which would be of great political value and was an important consideration to Davis. Further, by drawing Sherman away from Atlanta in pursuit of an evasive Confederate army, Hood might thwart Sherman with deft maneuvering. By simply withdrawing into rugged terrain or behind major rivers, Hood could, if he desired, avoid the costly battles which had so damaged his reputation.[18]

In fact, there is some evidence that during the Palmetto conferences Davis may have cautioned Hood about his earlier overly aggressive fighting. If so, Hood's plan offered an option of not fighting a pitched battle until the circumstances were deemed entirely favorable for the Confederates.[19]

The remaining issue at hand, the political necessity of appeasing the public by taking some remedial action following the loss of Atlanta, was discussed in a final, tense conversation between Hood and Davis prior to the president's 6:00 P.M. departure by train for Montgomery, Alabama, on September 27th. Although it appeared that Davis might be leaning toward retaining him, Hood remembered that Davis, after mounting his horse to ride to the station, had said that he might find it necessary to assign another commander. Davis later cited "the proposition confidentially mentioned" in "our closing conversation," which seems to have involved Hood's willingness to serve under a theater commander, if need be. Then, without making a final judgment, Davis boarded a train and sped off in the night, "anxiously reflect[ing]" about the crucial decision he must quickly make. Clearly, the matter rested on which general would be retained with the Army of Tennessee—Hood or Hardee.[20]

The army did not have long to wait. From West Point and Opelika, Alabama, the following day, September 28th, Davis wired his decision. It immediately became, as he foresaw, truly a controversial and momentous decree:

> West Point, Alabama, September 28, 1864, General John B. Hood, Headquarters Army of Tennessee: Relieve Lieutenant General Hardee from duty with the Army of Tennessee, and direct him to proceed at once to Charleston, S.C.[21]

III

John Bell Hood had won again. Hardee was off to a separate command, the Department of South Carolina, Georgia, and Florida, a secondary assignment. Hood, Davis's "very gallant and faithful" general, had thus been sustained in command of the Army of Tennessee. "You will . . . proceed as though no modification of existing organization was contemplated," said Davis in his telegram, giving Hood his full blessing for implementing the confidentially discussed "proposition." In jubilant reply, Hood wired to the president on the same day, "I commence to change my headquarters tomorrow [i.e., advance]. . . . I am very hopeful of good results."[22]

Hood's plan to operate on the enemy's lines of communications was, in Davis's words, an opportunity to "rescue Georgia, save the Gulf States, and

retain possession of the lines of communication upon which we depended."
Davis foresaw that if Hood was successful Sherman's Atlanta victory would
become barren, and he would be compelled to retreat toward Tennessee, "at
every mile of which he might be harassed by our army." If, however, Sherman ignored Hood and marched through Georgia to the coast, due to the
Confederates' better knowledge of the country and a superiority of cavalry,
he might be prevented from foraging on the countryside. This, reasoned
Davis, would so delay Sherman's progress as to consume all of his provisions,
and "absolute want should deplete if not disintegrate his army." As for the
public outcry for a change in army leadership, Davis would circumvent
criticism by a ploy. By establishing a theater command to encompass Hood's
Army of Tennessee and Lieutenant General Richard Taylor's Department of
Alabama, Mississippi, and East Louisiana, full cooperation of both forces
would be secured "without relieving either of you of the responsibilities and
powers of your special commands," he told Hood. The entire matter would
thus be resolved practically and politically. On paper the theater commander
would be in control and responsible. Yet in practice there would be little
change in the actual operations of the army. The new theater commander
would command in person only if "present with either army," a circumstance not specifically anticipated by Davis during active operations.[23]

The entire matter would be contingent, however, upon the key accept-
ance of a ranking general willing to operate under these guidelines. The man
whom Davis had in mind from the beginning was just the sort of functionary
who had a popular following, yet had been largely disenfranchised by the
administration—General Pierre Gustave Toutant Beauregard.[24]

Beauregard, once considered the reincarnation of one of Napoleon's
marshals, had fallen on difficult times. Maligned and largely discredited following his removal from field command in the west during mid-1862, for the
past two years he had served in virtual exile as commander of the Department of South Carolina, Georgia, and Florida. While playing an active role
in the defense of Charleston, South Carolina, and other points along the
coast, he had been clearly snubbed by the administration. Linked to the
anti-Davis bloc of critics, Beauregard had been ignored in his repeated pro-
posals to reinforce the western armies from the east. Harsh feelings had
resulted over his frequent sarcasm and fault-finding, which further embittered Jefferson Davis against him. Then, when Beauregard became directly
involved in the defense of Richmond during mid-1864, he had been effectively removed from independent command even though a full general. Compelled to serve under Robert E. Lee as the Richmond operations moved south
of the James River, Beauregard was also under the close scrutiny of Bragg
and Davis. Finally, in mid-September, amid widespread rumors that Beauregard would soon replace Hood, Lee on behalf of Davis had approached him
about commanding in Georgia. Believing he might be called upon to super-
sede Hood as commander of the Army of Tennessee, Beauregard had indi-

cated his willingness to assume that position and anxiously awaited develop-ments. When Jefferson Davis summoned him to a conference at Augusta, Georgia, on October 3, 1864, Beauregard hoped to assume again an impor-tant field command.[25]

That Davis had another program in mind was quickly evident once their conversations began. Davis wanted Beauregard in the role of a theater com-mander, with little more than supervisory authority. That Davis needed Beauregard's assent for political purposes was quite evident, however, in the evasive outlining of his role as a commander once present with either army. Davis suggested an overseer's role for Beauregard, but said the general might assume direct command whenever the circumstances made it expedient.[26]

Beauregard was thus at first deceived by Davis's proposition. Believing he in fact was being assigned a crucial and significant role that would involve direct control of operations in his department, the Creole general hastened to the task at hand. First he resolved much of the ongoing difficulty with Governor Joe Brown of Georgia, who had long been fighting the Davis administration over such matters as control over the Georgia militia and recruiting and supplying the army. Beauregard, who was on friendly terms with Brown, journeyed to Milledgeville to obtain the governor's support. Beauregard then hastened on to join Hood's army, already in the process of carrying out the initial limited offensive against Sherman's communica-tions.[27]

When Beauregard finally caught up with Hood at Cave Spring, Georgia, on October 9th, his conference was quick and relatively easy. Beauregard had been informed by Davis of Hood's plan to operate against Sherman's vulnerable supply lines, and it appeared that Hood had been successful. Sherman was reported moving north with all but one corps, which was left to guard Atlanta, and Hood was excitedly talking of drawing Sherman "still farther north." Without any staff, horses, or baggage, and lacking specific knowledge of the terrain, Beauregard declined to take command and has-tened off to see Richard Taylor, who was commanding the other army in his department. Before he left, he cautioned Hood to be very careful in the forthcoming second phase of operations against Sherman north of the Oos-tanaula River. The movement was to be a raid in force against the railroad, advised Beauregard, and no battle was to be fought unless of dire necessity and with every advantage to the Confederate army. Beauregard also asked to be kept advised of Sherman's movements so he might rejoin the army in time for any impending battle. Beauregard then departed for ten days to arrange for a change in supply bases.[28]

By the time he returned, Beauregard began to have serious misgivings about Hood's operational concepts. Hood had shifted much farther west than anticipated, without crossing the Tennessee River. Beauregard thus demanded Hood's concise statement of his plans for future operations. Yet, being well aware of Jefferson Davis's posturing with Beauregard as a de facto commander with little real authority, Hood didn't bother to reply for four days.[29]

Thereafter, Hood rarely deigned to correspond with Beauregard or his staff, instead sending his communications directly to the Richmond authorities. On November 6th Hood wrote in detail to Jefferson Davis of his plans to cross the Tennessee River once adequate supplies were on hand, even saying, "General Beauregard agrees with me as to my plan of operations."[30]

By that time the thoroughly angry Beauregard had begun to perceive his naïveté in considering his position as one of command authority. Based on Davis's largely unfriendly relationship with him, Beauregard at this point must have realized that he had been assigned much as a figurehead in order to placate Davis's critics. When on October 17th he had assumed command of the newly created "Military Division of the West," Beauregard had said, "full of hope and confidence, I come to join in your struggle, sharing your privations, and with your brave and true men, to strike the blow that shall bring success to our arms." Only two weeks after issuing these words, they must have seemed a bitter prophecy indeed.[31]

IV

In Richmond Mary Chesnut sat commiserating with her friends over the fate of Sam Hood. Putting Beauregard over Hood was considered by the public as practically condemning Hood, thought Sally Hampton. Mary Chesnut was angered: "Poor J. B. [Hood]," she wrote in her diary, "after all he has suffered. And now that fool Creole [Beauregard] goes to take his credit from him. . . . I see the speeches of all the generals. I hang my head for my country. . . . Only brave old J.[ohn] B. [Hood] spoke like a man and a soldier—decently!"[32]

CHAPTER VIII

Words of Wisdom

THE CROWD WAS ENTHUSIASTIC BUT HUSHED. Mary Chesnut wrote that there was little standing room anywhere nearby. From an adjacent window she watched the throng as they struggled for a better place to see the speaker as he moved onto the front piazza of the Chesnut residence. Jefferson Davis, on his way back from the Army of Tennessee to Richmond, had stopped at Columbia, South Carolina, for an overnight stay at the home of his aide, Brigadier General James Chesnut. A band had come to play, the Arsenal Cadets were there, and Davis was looked upon for an impromptu speech. Speaking in low, eloquent tones, Davis admonished the crowd:

> Does any man imagine that we can conquer the Yankees by retreating before them? . . . The only way to make spaniels civil is to whip them. And you can whip them. . . . I have just returned from that army [from] which we have had the saddest accounts—the Army of Tennessee, and I am able to bear to you words of good cheer. That army has increased in strength since the fall of Atlanta. It has risen in tone; its march is onward; its face looking to the front. . . . General Hood's strategy has been good and his conduct has been gallant. His eye is now fixed upon a point far beyond that where he was assailed by the enemy. He hopes soon to have his hand upon Sherman's line of communications, and to fix it where he can hold it. . . . I see no chance for Sherman to escape from a defeat or a disgraceful retreat.[1]

Interrupted by bursts of applause, Davis spoke with growing fervor. "I believe it is in the power of the men of the Confederacy to plant our banners on the banks of the Ohio, where we shall say to the Yankee, 'be quiet or we shall teach you another lesson.' Within the next thirty days much is to be done, for upon our success much depends."[2]

At the end of Davis's nearly hour-long speech he was thoroughly exhausted, thought Mary Chesnut, and she had a refreshing mint julep ready for him. With an excited throng overflowing the house, the president's hand was nearly shaken off, she noted. Even Sally Preston was thrilled, especially as Davis had "stood up" for Sam Hood. "Buck said she would kiss him for that—and she did," observed Mary Chesnut. "He all the while smoothing her down on the back from the shoulders as if she were a ruffled dove." Hood was a gallant soldier and a noble gentleman, offered the president, and he had only appointed Beauregard over him because the "Macon clique" were undermining the presidency, and the public might be more satisfied by a name they better knew.[3]

Feted on sixty-year-old Madeira and boned turkey stuffed with truffles, Jefferson Davis was toasted and bade an affectionate farewell by the local Methodist minister, who fervently prayed, "May God bless the president, and save him!"[4]

Out on the back porch Mary Chesnut was "concocting dainties for dessert" and listening to Custis Lee talk about the war. Caroline Preston, Buck's mother, was present, and when the subject of Hood's forthcoming campaign came up, there was a sudden, awkward silence. Finally Caroline Preston spoke up, saying that some people talk so well that they can almost fool anyone into believing that they are right. What they do a woman's intuition regards as no less than madness, she said. "This movement of the western army is against common sense."[5]

II

William Tecumseh Sherman read with keen interest his spy's report of Jefferson Davis's recent speeches. Added to newspaper accounts and even a printed copy of Davis's speech of September 22d at Macon, Georgia, the message amused Sherman. "Davis seemed to be perfectly upset by the fall of Atlanta, and to have lost all sense and reason," he later wrote. Particularly of value was Davis's proclamation that the Kentucky and Tennessee troops would soon be treading their "native soil"—as Hood's army would operate against Sherman's communications at a point far beyond their present locations. Sherman was amazed that the Confederacy's president had attempted "no concealment of these vainglorious boasts." Deeming Davis's speeches of much importance, on September 27th Sherman wired a full copy of the Macon speech to the administration in Washington. With a wry smile and a bold imagination, Sherman soon began to formulate his forthcoming plans for his own campaign. Davis had given us "the full key to his future designs," said Sherman, who well remembered an old school adage: "To be forewarned is to be forearmed."[6]

III

Pat Cleburne had approached the headquarters of the commanding general on September 28th, expecting to obtain a leave of absence in order to visit his fiancée, Susan Tarleton. Hood said no. Instead of taking leave of the army, the very next day Cleburne was to lead his division across the Chattahoochee River with Cheatham's Corps and begin a new offensive, said Hood. Cleburne's gloomy letter written to Susan that day had arrived on October 2d and had sent her off "for a good cry." To a close friend, Susan wrote:

> This puts an end to his visit, and what grieves me more, [it] is but the commencement of another long and arduous campaign. I don't know how I am going to get through it, the past one has nearly used me up. Everyone is telling me how thin and badly I am looking. I believe I have had a regular fit of "the blues." . . . I think we have been badly used by fate . . . [but] "what can't be cured must be endured," so I suppose I can but wait patiently and keep up a brave heart.[7]

As Susan had read Cleburne's letter, her fiancé was at Powder Springs, Georgia, twelve miles from Marietta. The army was in motion, advancing northward to cut Sherman's lines of supply. A spirit of hope had been rekindled in the Army of Tennessee, and that evening some of Cleburne's men gathered at his tent to serenade him. The evening was warm and breezy, with just a hint of fall in the air. When the songs had ended, Cleburne felt moved to address the throng. The current offensive was of much importance, he said, and every man should do his whole duty. In Ireland the downtrodden masses had suffered from oppression, yet if the North prevailed the South's condition would be much worse. It was essential that their united ranks stand firm by the righteous cause they espoused. As Cleburne finished, an observer noted how he paused for a moment and turned his face toward the heavens. A resolute expression was chiseled on his firm features as if in granite, and in a fervent, impassioned voice he said: "If this cause that is so dear to my heart is doomed to fail, I pray Heaven may let me fall with it, while my face is toward the enemy and my arm battling for that which I know is right." It was one of the most soul-stirring of speeches, wrote a listener, and all had walked away visibly moved with emotion.[8]

IV

The men laughingly called them "Old Mrs. Lincoln's Hair Pins." It was difficult work, at first. With an axe the men would cut fence rails to the proper length. Then they would begin prying, using the leverage of their hardwood rails to force an end up. Slowly, and with great resistance, the first iron rail would be loosened, enabling them to then pop the entire length free. With one section of rail gone, removing the others was much easier. Next the wooden ties would be taken up and piled on the roadbed until stacked about as high as a man's head. Once the whole stack was set afire and a proper heat generated, the iron rails would be balanced on top of the pile. When the center sections were red-hot, two men on each end would take one rail at a time to a nearby stump or telegraph pole and bend it double by walking around this improvised anvil. It was all "great fun," said a soldier—this wrecking of Sherman's railroad line to Atlanta. For miles "Old Mrs. Lincoln's Hair Pins" were strewn along the roadbed, the twisted and bent rails looking like so much debris in the wake of a tornado.[9]

The Western & Atlantic Railroad had once been a major route of Confederate supplies, but now it was in enemy hands, and for Hood's men, destroying the railroad became a great frolic. Cutting off the Yankee army's supplies would be just the ticket, they said. For many miles the smoldering ruins of the devastated railroad stretched northward, adding to the disarray of wrecked bridges and downed trestles.

Hood's offensive against Sherman's supply line had begun on September 29th and 30th, when the Army of Tennessee crossed the Chattahoochee River on pontoons west of Palmetto, Georgia, and headed for the region north of Atlanta. At first there was little enthusiasm. This railroad raid had been nothing but "rain, rain, mud, mud, march, march," wrote a weary private in his journal.[10]

Yet on October 3d the divided segments of the army had struck hard at the vulnerable Western & Atlantic Railroad. Stewart's Corps had captured Big Shanty and its garrison of about 175 men. The next day Acworth, Georgia, surrendered with 250 officers and men, and Major General Samuel G. French's Division was sent northward to take Allatoona, with its large supply of provisions.[11]

The fight at Allatoona had been a spirited affair, with the Federal garrison attempting to defend the sixty-five-foot-deep cut in a ridge through which the railroad passed. Finally some outer redoubts were captured following several hours of hand-to-hand fighting on the morning of October 5th. The three Confederate brigades making the assault were about to press on toward the main redoubt when they were suddenly recalled about 1:30 P.M. Major General French had just received a report from a cavalry unit in the direction of Marietta that Sherman's infantry were entering Big Shanty, only about fifteen miles distant. French already had lost nearly 900 men from his attacking force of 2,000—severe punishment for the 200 Federal prisoners and two battle flags captured. Fearing that Sherman's troops might cut off his march to rejoin Hood's army, French ordered a retreat. After withdrawing westward, French wrote that the decision to retreat had been agonizing, since so many of his men had fallen. Even more distressing was the fiasco involving the captured Federal storehouse in Allatoona. The million rations therein were greatly needed by the Confederates, but due to the quick retreat French had ordered them destroyed. Belatedly sent to torch the building, French's men were unable to start the blaze. "The matches furnished would not

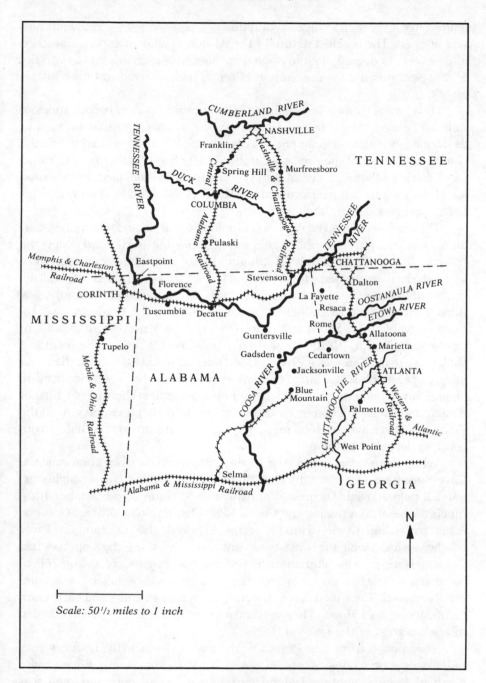

MAP 1   Theater of Operations—August–December 1864
Army of Tennessee
(Sources: O.R. Atlas, plates 149, 150)

ignite," wrote French in disgust, and due to a heavy enemy fire the attempt was aborted. The botched nature of the Allatoona affair was soon disclosed after it was discovered that the alleged advance of Sherman's infantry to Big Shanty was based on a false report. French had no need to break off his attack.[12]

Hood wasn't much disappointed. Having torn up twenty-four miles of railroad between Marietta and Allatoona, he was confident that his plan to devastate Sherman's supply line was working. When he passed a brigade resting by the side of the road on October 7th he had told them, "the Yanks [are] leaving Atlanta in a great hurry." The men had hallooed and shouted for Hood with loud hurrahs, noted a soldier. Hood, smiling, had raised his hat in acknowledgment and passed on.[13]

The army seemed to be rapidly rekindling its spirits, and when Confederate scouts had reported Sherman's infantry moving northward along the railroad line near Kennesaw Mountain, Hood had withdrawn westward some thirty miles to Cedartown, Georgia. Here Hood wired Bragg that he proposed to cross the Oostanaula River and destroy Sherman's communications from Kingston to Tunnel Hill. This, envisioned the Confederate commander, would force Sherman to continue to fall back northward in pursuit, or else move south. "If the latter, I shall move on his rear; if the former, I shall move to the Tennessee River." Hood later confided, "In truth, the effect of our operations so far surpassed my expectations that I was induced to change my original plan." In fact, he hoped to entice Sherman to further detach and divide his forces by drawing him into rough country near the Tennessee River, where Hood might have an opportunity to offer battle from a strong defensive position.[14]

When Beauregard concurred in this plan during a brief conference at Cave Spring on October 9th, Hood hastened to further carry out his expanded railroad raid. The march northward was resumed on October 10th, much of the army crossing the Coosa River that day near Rome, Georgia. After bypassing Rome, Hood's army followed the Oostanaula River northeastward along the west bank until, on the 12th, they approached Resaca. Here Hood's ultimatum to the Federal garrison of about 700 to surrender or face an assault where "no prisoners will be taken" was summarily refused. The Union commander, bolstered by rifle pits and earthwork fortifications, told Hood, "If you want it come and take it." Hood decided instead to go after the railroad.[15]

The railroad from near Resaca all the way to Tunnel Hill, about twenty miles, was soon aflame, wrote an observer. At Dalton, nearly fifteen miles north of Resaca, another Federal garrison of 751 officers and men was encountered inside a small redoubt. Major General John M. Schofield had been at the railroad depot in Dalton when Hood's troops approached. Barely escaping by train ahead of Hood's surrounding men, Schofield left behind the 44th U.S. Colored Infantry as the principal garrison. Hood's summons to surrender was the same as he had issued at Resaca: parole of all white officers and soldiers if a surrender was made, but no quarter if an assault became necessary. The garrison's commander, Colonel Lewis Johnson of the 44th U.S.C.T., nervously talked with Hood under a flag of truce. Aware of the anxiety of some nearby Confederates to get at the "niggers" of the 44th Infantry, Johnson feared for their lives. Cautiously, he asked if Hood would respect their rights as prisoners of war. Johnson could choose between surrender or death, answered Hood. Furthermore, Johnson must decide at once, continued Hood; he would not restrain his men.[16]

Johnson capitulated. Quickly the bewildered black soldiers were herded together, their pockets searched and all valuable belongings taken. Amid curses and insults, the more than 600 blacks were turned over to Major General William Bate's Division of mostly Tennessee troops. Bate appropriated the blacks' shoes for Confederate use, then marched them to the railroad, where they were forced to tear up about two miles of track. One soldier who refused to work was summarily shot on the spot. At least five others were executed when they were unable to keep up with the marching column. In all, the abuse "exceeded anything in brutality I have ever witnessed," later wrote Colonel Johnson. Bate was accused of being especially mean and vulgar, insulting of the white officers, and by Hood's directive had ordered the return of all soldiers identified as former slaves to their masters. Paroled at Dug Gap on the afternoon of October 15th, Johnson and his officers were relieved to escape with their lives. On the march to the rear they had been constantly threatened with massacre. Indeed, their lives were saved only by the guards' "greatest efforts" in holding back a taunting throng of gray soldiers, said Johnson. The Rebel army, he noted, was in good condition, well dressed, and very determined. Fifty pieces of artillery and an estimated 40,000 men were counted as they passed. Johnson was told by some Confederates that they next intended to go into mid-Tennessee.[17]

Throughout the night of October 13th Hood's army continued to tear up the railroad. That evening many of his soldiers dined on rations of crackers and flour captured from the Dalton storehouses. Yet by midday on the 15th the entire army was in motion, moving southwest along the Chattooga Valley to avoid Sherman's pursuit. Several additional small Federal garrisons had surrendered at Tilton and Mill Creek Gap, and with Wheeler's cavalry guarding their rear, Hood's sore-footed men marched with soaring spirits toward Gadsden, Alabama.[18]

Hood again had a decision to make. Once in the rugged mountain terrain he could await Sherman's approach and offer battle from a strong defensive position. Or he again might swing northward, cross the Tennessee River at Guntersville, Alabama, and strike the enemy's communications near Bridgeport. He hoped such a movement would force Sherman north into Tennessee to obtain supplies. This would, in effect, recover the territory lost during the

Atlanta Campaign which Jefferson Davis had so deplored. By October 19th Hood had made up his mind.[19]

October thus far had been a good month for Sam Hood. From the president's expression of confidence to the effective disruption of Sherman's supply line, the past three weeks had been a series of successes. Now, from Columbia, South Carolina, came even more pleasant news. Dr. John Darby, Hood's former surgeon who had saved the general's arm after Gettysburg, had married Buck's sister Mary in a prominent ceremony on October 1st. "Mamie," as Mary was fondly called, had worn a dress of tulle and blond lace, with diamonds and pearls. Darby, better known as "P.V.," because he had answered *"Perseverenta omnia vincit"* ("He who perseveres, conquers") after once being scornfully asked by Buck if he thought Mamie would marry him, was part of "the handsomest wedding party I ever saw," thought Mary Chesnut. John Darby was "the perfect figure," she wrote, noting how resplendent he looked in his handsome London-tailored uniform, brought back from Europe when he had purchased Hood's wooden leg in December 1863.[20]

In a storage trunk in the Carolinas was Sam Hood's own wedding uniform of the finest gray cloth. The sad fate of Buck's beloved brother, Major Willie Preston, who had been killed at Atlanta on July 20th during Hood's first sortie, seemed but a sad memory now. The Darby wedding had brought much joy to the Preston household, and there was more lively talk of "H" and "D" among the Prestons. As the crusty John Smith Preston explained, the initials did not "mean hell and the devil." He said, "They allude to my sons-in-law apparent—or expectant."[21]

V

As early as September 20th Sherman, with grim humor, had mentioned to Grant the prospect of capturing Savannah. "If you can whip Lee and I can march to the Atlantic I think Uncle Abe [Lincoln] will give us a twenty days' leave of absence to see the young folks." On the 25th of September, following information that Hood seemed to be shifting his army toward the west, Sherman was convinced that the enemy had left the door wide open to the interior of Georgia. However, with Hood evidently going on the offensive following Davis's well-reported visit, Sherman decided to wait and watch the enemy's movements. Later, when "all things are ready, I will take advantage of his opening to me all of Georgia," he wrote. Once "Hood shows his hand" as to which railroad he would operate against, said Sherman on September 30th, he would know how to proceed. "If we make a countermove I will go out myself with a large force and take such a route as will supply us, and at the same time make Hood recall the whole or part of his army," he asserted.[22]

On October 1st, with full confirmation of Hood having crossed the Chattahoochee River, Sherman telegraphed to Grant that he would attack Hood's army if he attempted to raid the Western & Atlantic Railroad south of the Etowah. Yet, said Sherman, if Hood went out of his reach, "why would it not do for me to leave [the defense of] Tennessee to . . . [reserve and detached units] and for me to destroy Atlanta, and then march across Georgia to Savannah or Charleston, breaking roads and doing irreparable damage? We cannot remain on the defensive."[23]

Grant at first objected to the idea of leaving both Atlanta and Hood's army behind and marching to the sea. He was joined in his concern by President Abraham Lincoln, who was afraid a misstep by Sherman would prove fatal to his army. The immediate result was that Sherman was forced to continue the ineffective, reactive style of defense that he was so anxious to avoid.[24]

Having dispatched his best subordinate general, Major General George H. Thomas, to take charge of protecting mid-Tennessee from Nathan Bedford Forrest's cavalry on September 29th, Sherman thought at first that his defenses were adequate, if scattered. Although he anticipated that Hood might attempt to follow up the success of Forrest's cavalry by moving northwest into mid-Tennessee, Sherman's pursuit of Hood's raid had been seriously delayed until October 4th. Sherman then was suffering from a lack of good intelligence. His cavalry and spies had failed him at a critical time. Forced to helplessly watch from Kennesaw Mountain as his railroad burned above Big Shanty on October 5th, Sherman could but belatedly send the Twenty-third Corps on a futile sortie to cut off French's retreat westward. Meanwhile, with his other four corps he continued marching northward along the railroad to restore order.[25]

Sherman's only solace had been the stout defense of Allatoona. By use of signal flags from Kennesaw Mountain, part of a brigade of the Fourteenth Corps had been summoned from Rome, Georgia, to the reinforcement of Allatoona. Aided by Henry sixteen-shot repeating rifles in the hands of the 7th Illinois Infantry, the assaults on the Federal redoubts had been repulsed with heavy Confederate casualties. The brigadier general commanding, John M. Corse, had suffered a nasty wound in the face during the fighting. Yet he triumphantly telegraphed to Sherman on October 6th, "I am short a cheekbone and an ear, but am able to whip all hell yet![26]

Sherman, however, remained in no mood for boastful banter. After elements of his army pursued the Confederates westward to the old battleground near Dallas, Georgia, Sherman marched north to Kingston on October 10th. Here he awaited Hood's next move, fuming over the destruction of more than eight miles of railroad that required 35,000 new ties and six miles of iron to repair. Ten thousand men were set to work, wrote Sherman, and in about a week the railroad was running again.[27]

Still, he telegraphed to Grant: "It will be a physical impossibility to protect the [rail]roads, now that Hood, Forrest, Wheeler, and the whole batch of devils are turned loose without home or habitation." Renewing his proposal to march to the sea, Sherman said it was useless to occupy Georgia. The proper move was "the utter destruction" of the state. Southern independence was at stake, he noted. "They may stand the fall of Richmond, but not all of Georgia." He warned, "By attempting to hold the roads, we will lose a thousand men each month, and will gain no result. I can make this march, and make Georgia howl!"[28]

Grant, again, was unsure. He seemed to vacillate in his opinion, debating the matter with the administration in Washington. Undaunted, Sherman kept up the pressure via telegraph.[29]

Grant finally yielded. In a terse telegram at 11:30 P.M. on October 11th he wrote, "If you are satisfied the trip to the sea coast can be made, holding the line of the Tennessee firmly, you may make it, destroying all the railroad south of Dalton or Chattanooga, as you think best."[30]

There was little solace for Sherman when he received this message on the morning of October 12th. Again, procrastination and delay had cost him the initiative. Hood had again struck rapidly and unexpectedly, forcing Sherman into another defensive maneuver.[31]

Sherman had misconceived Hood's plans, thinking that Hood, in keeping with Jefferson Davis's boasts, would move westward to threaten Bridgeport, and Decatur, Alabama, before striking for Kentucky or Tennessee. Thus, Sherman was shocked to learn on the 12th that Hood had begun another sortie against the Western & Atlantic Railroad, more than twenty miles north of Kingston.[32]

From Resaca, Georgia, came word on the morning of October 12th that Hood had advanced swiftly up the Oostanaula Valley, surrounded Resaca, and was demanding its surrender. Sherman was then at Rome, about twenty-five miles southwest. Immediately he rushed into another hasty and ineffectual pursuit. Being uncertain of Hood's motive, Sherman briefly thought that the Confederates actually might be moving against Rome. Moreover, he had been caught by chance with many of his troops marching westward from the vicinity of Kingston to Rome. In a confusing mishmash of garbled orders and tangled communications, many of the troops were kept at a standstill due to the crush of troops and wagons attempting to march and countermarch in various directions. For more than half the day on October 12th the Fourth Corps was idle because of the congested traffic.[33]

Although Sherman later stated that he acted in the belief that Hood would attempt to avoid a battle, rather than to aggressively cut off Hood's retreat via the Chattooga Valley, Sherman's initial response was defensive. Indeed, word was passed among his troops on the morning of the 13th that Resaca had fallen and Hood might move against Kingston. Belatedly, Sherman reconsidered and ordered all available units up the railroad to Resaca. Most of his troops finally reached Resaca on the 14th, two days late. The arrival at Resaca of Sherman's initial reinforcements on the morning of the 13th had found the garrison safe. Hood merely had threatened Resaca while moving farther north against the railroad from Dalton to Tunnel Hill. Pursuit thereafter was north and west, but despite marches of thirty-five miles in twenty-four hours by some Federal units, Hood escaped to the southwest along the Chattooga Valley on the 15th and 16th. Later Sherman offered the excuse that if he had moved aggressively to cut off Hood's retreat via the Chattooga Valley the Confederates would have merely moved eastward in escaping.[34]

In all, it was the type of war that William Tecumseh Sherman abhorred. This business of defending Atlanta and the region's outposts, he wrote, "was a harder task than to take them."[35]

By October 20th his columns were at Gaylesville, Alabama, watching Hood's army, about thirty miles distant at Gadsden. Here Sherman again began reflecting about his long-anticipated move to smash Georgia to pieces.[36]

Stating that he would not pursue Hood farther than Gaylesville, Sherman soon began earnest preparations for what he referred to as "my big raid." He instructed his chief commissary, "On the 1st of November I want nothing in Atlanta but what is necessary for war. Send all trash to the rear at once, and have on hand thirty days' food and but little forage. I propose to abandon Atlanta and the railroad back to Chattanooga, to sally forth to ruin Georgia and bring up on the seashore." In order to obtain all needed food and clothing, remove the sick and wounded, and bring out the surplus stores, the recently devastated railroad would be repaired before again being completely destroyed as Sherman departed Atlanta. For all of this to be done, Sherman allowed his staff ten days.[37]

Grant, "on reflection," had begun to think highly of Sherman's plan. He even surmised that Sherman might take surplus arms along and "put them in the hands of negro men." These semi-organized black auxiliaries, he inferred, might be of some use and contribute to Georgia's demoralization. Left unsaid was the prospect of a slave insurrection. Even Henry Halleck, the chief of staff, seemed to delight in Sherman's forthcoming march through Georgia. "Your mode of conducting war is just the thing we now want," he told Sherman. "We have tried the kid glove policy long enough."[38]

Sherman's soldiers didn't mind. An almost gleeful Illinois sergeant wrote from Gaylesville, "[We] have been living on the country for the last month and it suits me first rate. It is my best hotel." One of his regimental companions marveled at the amount of local food they foraged and wrote, "[We] have plenty to eat, such as yams, fresh pork, beef, mutton, and veal; also plenty of the feathered tribe, which is too numerous to mention; honey, molasses, dried fruit, and preserves—no end to them." Sergeant Andrew McCornack, in the Fifteenth Corps, shrugged off the chilly weather, writing to his parents that although they couldn't carry enough clothes to remain warm on all occasions, there was little problem. "Where there is plenty of rail fences there is no trouble in keeping warm," he reported. "The first thing [we do] after going into camp and stacking arms is to pile rails for a fire, and [gather] boards to sleep on. We make the houses and barns suffer."[39]

Hood's railroad raid had set a precedent in logistics. Even the twenty-four miles of torn-up and twisted track proved to be of little significance. On October 21st telegraphic communication was restored between Chattanooga and Atlanta. On the 27th the railroad was reported intact, and the next day trains began running regularly between these two cities. Hood's bold raid had shut down the railroad for exactly twenty-three days.[40]

Instead of cutting off Union supplies, noted Sherman with grim humor, Hood's efforts had resulted only in depriving Georgia's civilian populace as well as accustoming Union soldiers to living off the land. "We find [an] abundance of corn and potatoes out here [in the countryside]," he wrote. "They cost nothing a bushel. If Georgia['s soldiers] can afford to break our railroads, she can afford to feed us. Please preach this doctrine to men who go forth and are likely to spread it."[41]

CHAPTER IX

Who Will Dance to
Hood's Music?

P. G. T. BEAUREGARD was thoroughly shocked. He had just spent a difficult two weeks arranging for transfer of the army's supply base from the Atlanta vicinity to Jacksonville, Alabama. When he returned to visit Hood's army at Blue Pond, Alabama, on October 19th, he found that Hood had already moved twenty-seven miles farther southwest to Gadsden. Hood had not informed Beauregard of this move, nor did he seem much concerned about the consequences. Moreover, Hood had unilaterally decided on a new plan to force Sherman to pursue his army into mid-Tennessee. In fact, he had already ordered the transfer of his supply base more than one hundred miles farther westward to Tuscumbia, Alabama. This was necessary, said Hood, since he intended to cross the Tennessee River near Guntersville, Alabama, and swing northward against Stevenson and Bridgeport, on the Memphis & Charleston Railroad.[1]

The exasperated Beauregard and an adamant Hood sat down to resolve yet another major shift in equipment and planning during the night of October 21st. Poring over maps and arguing various points, the generals spent nearly the entire night in protracted debate. Hood argued that Sherman was short on provisions and forage and that the destruction of the Western & Atlantic Railroad had been so thorough during the recent raids as to require five or six weeks for repair. By moving the Confederate army into mid-Tennessee before Sherman completed the repairs, Hood reasoned that the Union general would have little choice but to pursue in order to obtain supplies.[2]

Beauregard pointed out that there was little time to properly arrange for a change in Rebel supply bases in the drive north. Further, there was uncertainty about the condition of the railroad running to Tuscumbia. More ominously, there was the matter of safely crossing—and recrossing in the event of a disaster—the Tennessee River, which was patrolled by Union gunboats.[3]

Hood argued that the Memphis & Charleston Railroad was said to be in fair running order, and that if necessary he could get ample supplies in Tennessee, including capturing those of the enemy. As for the gunboats, Hood said he would use his portable pontoon train to cross the Tennessee River at any convenient point, and that mined torpedoes and emplaced heavy artillery would keep the "tinclad" gunboats at bay.[4]

Beauregard remained unsure. Hood was rash and careless with operational details, that much was obvious from the events of the past few weeks. Yet he had been successful in drawing Sherman and his Yankee army back from Atlanta.

Hood spoke with insistence. Not only had Jefferson Davis supported his proposal to push the war northward into Tennessee, but Braxton Bragg had approved the general plan of operations, announced Hood.

Beauregard knew of Hood's close relationship with Davis. The politics of the matter were very evident in Hood's demeanor.

Beauregard agreed to the plan.[5]

Hood felt contempt for Beauregard's nitpicking and careful, conservative methods, but he needed the Creole general to work out the supply details that would provision his army. Thus, he agreed to several face-saving changes in cavalry assignments insisted on by Beauregard.

On the morning of October 22d the leading elements of Hood's army departed Gadsden, marching toward the Tennessee River in the vicinity of Guntersville, about forty miles distant. In his haste to leave, Hood left behind the pontoon train necessary to cross the Tennessee River. Beauregard had to make the arrangements for its transportation to the army. It was perhaps a strange omission for a general bent on beating a well-equipped adversary to the heartlands of Tennessee.[6]

II

En route to Guntersville, Hood learned that the crossing there was strongly guarded. Mindful of the possibility of Federal gunboats patrolling the river and playing havoc with his pontoons, he impulsively changed the army's destination to Decatur, more than forty miles west of Guntersville. Decatur, although garrisoned by Federal troops, was thought to be vulnerable to attack and was a strategic crossing point, marked by a Federal pontoon bridge at the site of the old Memphis & Charleston Railroad bridge. Upon arrival in front of Decatur on October 26th, Hood found about 3,000 Federal infantry defending an entrenched line that included two forts and 1,600 yards of rifle pits and defensive parapets. Two wooden gunboats were patrolling the river, and Hood spent the 27th getting his troops into position encircling

Decatur.[7] That night Beauregard arrived on the scene, very much disturbed that Hood had again changed his destination and plans without notifying him.[8]

On the 28th a dense fog enveloped the area and the Confederate skirmishers were pushed forward to a sheltered ravine within 800 yards of Decatur's main fortifications. By midday a Federal sortie from along the riverbank had driven the mixed line of sharpshooters and skirmishers out of the ravine with a loss of 120 men and 5 officers captured. Thereafter, Hood made plans to again push the army farther westward some forty miles, to Bainbridge, so as to effect a crossing below Muscle Shoals. The shoals would prevent the gunboats from dropping down to interfere, and Hood might be closer to his new base of supply at Tuscumbia.[9]

Beauregard, who had remained at Gadsden until the 24th, now began to fully perceive Hood's woeful indiscretion and careless planning in the management of his army. As revealed by the diary entries of the men, the supply system had all but broken down, the few shoes and clothes issued at Gadsden were insufficient, and the morale of the army was again plummeting. It began raining on the evening of the 27th, and an officer wrote of the march to Decatur: "The road was full of water and mud, and . . . we had to walk in the middle of the road. [In] some places the mud and water would be knee deep. [The night was] so dark we actually could not see an inch before us—still we kept going." At 10:00 P.M. the exhausted men had camped in the rain along the side of the road. On the following morning they marched the remaining four or five miles to Decatur, only to move off again the following evening. "We have had nothing to eat since the morning of the 27th," wrote a disgruntled captain, "and today a wagon drives through camp and issues two ears of corn to each man." There was so little meat that several privates from each company in the 20th Mississippi were detailed for squirrel hunting, and parched corn had become the army's regular staple. As they turned their backs on Decatur, a soldier noted with disgust that they were leaving without success or benefit. "[We] came away and left the U.S. flag flying in full view of us," said the man.[10]

III

Hood had changed his mind again. At the last moment he had been dissuaded from placing his pontoons at Bainbridge, and resolved to go still farther in the direction of Tuscumbia. Here, opposite Florence, Alabama, a combination pontoon/trestle bridge might be easier constructed utilizing the old, partially intact railroad trestlework. Protection from Union gunboats was assured by Muscle Shoals from above and Colbert Shoals from below.[11]

Although the new site was only about four miles removed from Bainbridge, Beauregard saw that Hood still had little conception of what his actual operations would be. In a curt note on October 30th, he had his chief of staff ask Hood for a brief summary of past operations and a concise statement of his future plans. Hood remained silent, ignoring this request for three days, while continuing to correspond only with the administration in Richmond about his plans and movements.[12]

Hood ordered the emplacement of pontoons at Florence, only a few miles from Tuscumbia on the north bank, and assigned the task of covering the movement to Stephen D. Lee's Corps. Lee was directed to move on the night of the 29th, and the following day he got three brigades across the nearly 1,000-yard-wide river at two sites, crossing in small boats despite opposition from John T. Croxton's brigade of Federal cavalry. Randall Gibson's Louisiana brigade charged the Federal position near the old railroad bridge embankment and drove Croxton's men from the town, aided by a barrage of artillery fire from across the river.* By the night of the 30th Lee had put across a bridgehead of two divisions and began to entrench while the pontoon bridge was being constructed. On November 1st the bridge was in place, trestled at both ends, and the balance of Stephen Lee's Corps crossed by November 2d. Hood then directed the remainder of the army to camp in the vicinity of Tuscumbia, pending the actual start of the offensive into mid-Tennessee.[13]

Beauregard, meanwhile, had been fuming about the callous treatment by Hood. On October 31st he telegraphed to Jefferson Davis, seeking to determine if he might actually run the forthcoming campaign. Beauregard posed the key aspect in the form of a query—was he to assume command upon being present with Hood's army? Davis's reply of the following day directed that while Beauregard was to command either of his armies when present, he should not relieve the army's commander—so as to retain "the contemplated freedom of motion" desired for what Davis obviously knew were forthcoming offensive operations. Beauregard got the message; Hood was still in strong favor.[14]

On the following day, November 3d, the two generals held a tense but momentous meeting at Hood's headquarters. The ill feelings harbored by both generals were muted by a mutually advantageous if uneasy practical agreement. Beauregard promised his support for Hood's plan, which was to invade mid-Tennessee, advancing against Pulaski or Columbia as the circumstances involving enemy movements might dictate. Nathan Bedford Forrest's cavalry would join Hood in mid-Tennessee, and the army would march forth on November 5th with fifteen days' rations. For his part, Hood would acquiesce in Beauregard's role as the nominal commander, keeping him informed of plans and movements. Thus, on November 3d Hood finally issued a note to Beauregard stating that his plans were to advance in a few days, and

*Federal units (brigades, divisions, corps) were assigned a numerical designation (e.g., Emerson Opdycke's brigade was the 1st Brigade, 2d Division, Fourth Army Corps). Accordingly, all references to the unit when listed by the commander's surname are shown in lower-case type. Confederate units, however, were officially known by their commander's name, hence the use of upper-case type for a specific unit designation (e.g., Cleburne's Division).

mentioning his "regret" that his busy schedule and his impaired health had caused him to be unable to prepare the reports earlier called for. Beauregard sent a syrupy note to Davis that day, saying that as Hood had conducted the present movement so successfully he (Beauregard) would not assume immediate command while present with the army.[15]

The whole matter proved to be a farce. Within ten days Hood was back to his usual routine of ignoring Beauregard except for the barest correspondence. Beauregard, having recently lauded Hood in his official letters, was caught in an untenable situation as far as complaining to Richmond. Again he endured callous treatment by Hood with smoldering resentment until finally another heated confrontation occurred.

Part of the problem involved the planned switch in cavalry. By Beauregard's insistence Joe Wheeler's troopers had been sent from Hood's army to watch Sherman's movements along the Georgia line. Forrest, who was to replace Wheeler with his division of mostly Mississippi, Kentucky, and Tennessee cavalry, had been operating in Richard Taylor's department from the vicinity of Corinth, Mississippi.[16]

By chance, when Beauregard changed cavalry assignments, Forrest had just begun a raid along the west bank of the Tennessee River toward a principal Union supply base at Johnsonville, Tennessee. Due to disrupted communications and a delay in sending orders through Richard Taylor at Selma, Alabama, it was the evening of November 1st before Forrest recieved instructions to report to Hood. As such, they were from Beauregard, being dated October 29th. Beauregard told Forrest to report to Hood near Bainbridge, on the Tennessee River, instead of in mid-Tennessee as had been at first contemplated. Because his command was scattered along the river, Forrest was unable to comply immediately. On the morning of November 3d Forrest again received verbal instructions, via Hood's courier, to report at Bainbridge. Hood, concerned about the absence of adequate cavalry to protect his vulnerable wagons of ordnance and stores, wanted Forrest present from the beginning of the march into Tennessee.[17]

Forrest, one of the Confederacy's most brilliant cavalry commanders, although not extensively educated or trained in military science, was caught in a dilemma. He had recently succeeded in capturing a Federal gunboat as well as three transports and barges laden with supplies. By November 3d he had just concentrated his forces opposite Johnsonville and was preparing to shell the depot and boats tied up at the wharf. Deciding to wreak as much damage as possible at Johnsonville before retiring, Forrest sent off a dispatch that day saying he would reluctantly comply as fast as the worn-out condition of his horses would allow. The same day he sent another dispatch to Hood reporting that he had no means of crossing the Tennessee River except on any flatboats which might be captured near Perryville. Further, the forage was all used up in mid-Tennessee, warned Forrest, and to subsist his command would be forced to travel along the line of the Duck River.[18]

On the following day Forrest shelled Johnsonville, destroying an immense amount of supplies and the transports at the wharf. By the light of the burning enemy depot Forrest withdrew during the night of the 4th. The weather continued to be wretched, with drenching rain and mud that bogged wagons and artillery at every step. Unable to travel rapidly, Forrest was prevented from crossing the rain-swollen river at Perryville due to a lack of boats. He then continued south along the west bank to Corinth, where his depleted command arrived on November 10th.[19]

Hood, meanwhile, had increasingly fretted about Forrest's absence. On November 2d he dispatched a telegram saying, "When can I expect you here? . . . I am waiting for you." Ten days later he told Jefferson Davis in a letter that he had not advanced for want of Forrest's cavalry to protect his wagon trains. Since Forrest would join him in a few days, wrote Hood reassuringly, he then would be able to move forward. Actually, Forrest's absence was being used much as an excuse for the delay, which Hood later expanded into a full-fledged indictment of Beauregard's management in ordering a shift of cavalry. That neither Hood nor Beauregard seriously considered delaying the advance for the arrival of Forrest's cavalry was evidenced by the Creole general's telegram of November 3d to Forrest ordering that commander to join Hood en route in mid-Tennessee, per the original plan. Hood concurred in this arrangement and wrote the same day that Forrest should be informed of the "certainty" of the army's advance movement on Saturday, November 5th. Of course, due to delayed communications and the inclement weather, this "en route" plan was impossible to implement, and Forrest's command was unable to move via Tuscumbia to join Hood's army until November 14th through the 16th.[20]

Despite completion of the pontoon bridge on November 1st, Hood's army had remained idle day after day as the overworked commissary officers struggled to obtain the twenty days' supply of rations Hood demanded. The entire army depended on food stores coming up the ramshackle Mobile & Ohio Railroad to Corinth, then being routed westward on the even more decrepit and little-used Memphis & Charleston Railroad. In fact, from Cherokee Station to Tuscumbia, about fifteen miles, the railroad was entirely destroyed. Of necessity, Hood's already overworked wagon train was compelled to haul all supplies overland from Cherokee Station to the army. This inefficient and sadly depleted supply system was barely able to supply the daily needs of Hood's men, much less accumulate a sizable surplus. Indeed, the meager rations provided often resulted in parched corn being the soldiers' daily fare. Hood became so disillusioned that he even considered a third change of supply bases.[21]

Contrary to his earlier assertion that he might find sufficient food in Tennessee, Hood repeatedly decided not to move without sufficient food stores. Frequently he had ordered commands to prepare to march across the river, only to countermand the orders shortly thereafter. It was November

13th before Cheatham's Corps crossed, and Stewart's men were delayed until the 20th in getting over the rickety pontoon bridge. Said Hood in later reflection, bad luck had begun to plague him, and it was a matter of concern that this "storm" promptly end.[22]

If there was anything prior to his forthcoming offensive to intensify Hood's acknowledged superstitious nature it was the weather. October had been a season of fair climate, with moderate rain toward the end of the month. November, however, had become a meteorological catastrophe. The rain that fell during the first few days of the month had continued, being interrupted only by a few brief periods of clearing skies over the span of four sodden weeks. There was mud everywhere, wrote a disgusted soldier forced to slosh through the mire at a cold and stark campsite with little to eat. There were so many rainy, disagreeable days that one dreary day seemed like the next. Even more ominous were the frigid nights, with bone-chilling temperatures that made sentries shiver in their all-too-thin uniforms. Of debilitating effect on Hood personally, the foul weather only accentuated the pain in his leg stump and the difficulty of moving about. Beyond the physical drain, the dire climate soured Hood's mood and he became morose with each new episode of failure and delay.[23] A daring raid by some of Union Brigadier General John Croxton's 2d Michigan cavalrymen against the pontoon bridge during the first week in November had resulted in the squandering of two days of good weather for repairs. Raiders floating down the river at night in improvised log canoes had cut a few pontoon tie ropes, effecting minor damage. Under the rush of high water and debris which followed the heavy rains, the flimsy bridge broke on the night of November 9th. Many of the pontoons were scattered and lost. Since replacement pontoons had to be sent from Corinth over the dilapidated Memphis & Charleston Railroad, then hauled by wagon from Cherokee Station, it was the evening of November 12th before the bridge was back in use.[24]

Of particular concern to Hood's commanders was the disastrous effect of the weather on railroad reconstruction. Both the Mobile & Ohio and the Memphis & Charleston railroads were in such disrepair that the rising waters from creeks and streams frequently swept away the flimsy bridges. Beauregard reported on November 15th that railroad construction to Tuscumbia had been greatly delayed and that it would require perhaps another fifteen to twenty days to complete. Yet, due to the rain, so many other points on the road were becoming impassable that he estimated the bad weather might extend the work possibly an additional two weeks. In all, the combination of bad weather, scanty supplies, and want of transportation had detained Hood's army in the vicinity of Florence, Alabama, for three weeks. Hood announced to Beauregard on November 17th that he had only a week's rations on hand and needed much more. Beauregard went to Corinth the next day and found that despite empty cars being located at several depots, there seemed to be no food stores en route. "Where are your supplies?" he abruptly demanded of Hood.[25]

Squarely at question throughout the entire three-week delay at Florence was Hood's lack of prior planning and judgment in supporting his offensive movements. Contrary to his hasty estimates when at Gadsden on October 21st—that the railroad was in fair running order and ample supplies might be obtained in Tennessee if needed—Hood had found only a few weeks later that these premises upon which he had based his offensive plans were woefully incorrect. As Beauregard had long since recognized, Hood's careless methods were the harbinger of further ominous difficulty.[26]

When Hood rashly suggested shifting supply bases again, this time to Purdy, Tennessee, Beauregard not only quashed the attempt, but determined to retaliate. On November 11th Beauregard ordered Stewart's Corps to parade the next day for his "informal review" without notifying Hood. Hood responded to the perceived challenge like a petulant child. In an acid-laced note to Beauregard he stated that "all orders" relating to his army "must pass through me." Furthermore, the propriety of a review, said Hood, "was more than questionable," since it afforded enemy spies an opportunity to estimate the army's strength.[27]

Beauregard had Hood's dander up, and he pushed even further. "You must have a low estimate of your wily adversary," he shot back, "if you suppose that at this late day he is ignorant of the position of your army and the strength of your corps." Furthermore, as soon as circumstances permitted, Beauregard said, he would separately review the corps of Cheatham and Lee. Then, to rub salt in Hood's wounds, he sent off another pointed note about alleged mistreatment of prisoners, asking Hood if the "negroes at work on the railroad . . . are the same captured by your command in Georgia, and if so, what arrangement has been made for medical attendance upon them."[28]

Hood was so exasperated that he transferred his headquarters from the south shore and across the Tennessee River to Florence without notifying Beauregard. The Creole general's staff officer had to chase after Hood on the 14th, finally locating him after a long search. Hood was told that due to information just received he was not to begin his offensive into mid-Tennessee until Beauregard had talked with him.[29]

Only the news of significant enemy movements prevented further bitter recriminations between the two generals. On November 15th Beauregard reported that heavy Federal troop movements had been observed on the Mississippi River. Yet before Beauregard could go to Corinth to inspect and prepare for the defense of that crucial railroad depot, another crisis loomed.[30]

Hood had been warned in early November by Joe Wheeler's cavalry that Sherman had divided his forces. Accordingly, Hood had wired Jefferson Davis on November 6th that should Sherman move with two or three corps south from Atlanta, it would be "the best thing that could happen for our general good." The gruff reply that Hood received on November 12th from an uneasy Jefferson Davis took him completely by surprise.[31]

"The policy of taking advantage of the separated divisions of Sherman's forces, by attacking him where he cannot reunite his army, is too obvious to have been overlooked by you," chided Davis. "I therefore take it for granted that you have not been able to avail yourself of that advantage during his march northward from Atlanta, and hope the opportunity will be offered before he is extensively recruited." Moreover, intoned Davis, "If you keep his communications broken he will most probably seek to concentrate for an attack on you. But, if as reported to you, he has sent a large part of his force southward, you may first beat him in detail, and subsequently without serious obstruction or danger to the country in your rear, advance to the Ohio River."[32]

Thus, Davis had criticized not only Hood's yielding of the initiative, but his lack of aggressiveness in fighting a divided enemy—the very strategy Hood had sought to implement for winning the war in the west. Hood, startled, replied immediately, offering Forrest's absence as the primary excuse for the delay in his offensive. As for not fighting Sherman in northern Georgia, "I did not regard this army in proper condition for a pitched battle," said Hood, adding, however, "it is now in excellent spirits and confident." Accordingly, Hood assured Davis, "you may rely upon my striking the enemy wherever a suitable opportunity presents, and that I will spare no efforts to make that opportunity."[33]

Hood had suddenly realized his predicament. Davis's patience was wearing thin. Beauregard was fuming at his indiscretions and the lack of results. To make matters worse, Wheeler soon reported several of Sherman's corps moving into mid-Tennessee. This evidently caused Hood to believe that Sherman was stringing out his entire army to protect Tennessee against the forthcoming Confederate offensive. Realizing that prompt action was necessary while the enemy was still divided, Hood had hurriedly rushed his preparations. His headquarters were transferred to Florence from the Tuscumbia side on the morning of November 13th. Cheatham's Corps marched across the river that day following a four-day delay, part of which had been due to a break in the pontoon bridge. Supply trains and cattle were put across on the 14th. Then it happened again—"Hood's luck" in bad weather.[34]

On the evening of November 9th the weather had cleared, and the skies thereafter remained bright for nearly a week. On the afternoon of the 14th, however, heavy storms had returned, with the wet weather extending for five of the next six days. The Tennessee River rose eighteen feet at Florence, reported an officer, and Hood's army virtually came to a standstill.[35]

The crowning touch to the horrendously frustrating initial weeks at Florence was Jefferson Davis's day of prayer. By Hood's order the entire day of November 16th was to be observed in accordance with the president's proclamation, and all officers and soldiers were requested to attend a place of worship. "I went to church today in Florence," wrote a diligently observant officer, "[and] heard a good sermon. About 700 men [were] present, and all seem[ed] to be quiet and attentive."[36]

Ironically, on this very day of prayer, with the Army of Tennessee idle, Sherman departed Atlanta on his soon-to-be-famous "March to the Sea." The sound of blaring band music greeted Sherman's ears, and long lines of marching infantry swept before his eyes. Having been given the time to make all preparations and burn Atlanta, Sherman sallied forth with 60,000 men, "well provisioned, but expecting to live chiefly on the country." The contrast in attitudes and resourcefulness was well reflected in the activities of the two army commanders on that day. Hood might pray, but Sherman was going on the offensive. By November 17th Sherman's men had cleared Atlanta, and only the swirling black smoke above a ruined and desolate city remained.[37]

"Time is of the utmost importance," Hood had urged more than two weeks earlier, yet on November 17th, the only entirely clear day of the week, his official army journal recorded, "nothing of importance has transpired today."[38]

It took several days for Hood and Beauregard to learn about Sherman's activities in destroying Atlanta and the railroad. On the 16th word was received suggesting that Sherman was about to march with three corps south from Atlanta to Augusta or Macon. The next morning news arrived that Sherman had, in fact, burned Atlanta and moved off toward Macon with a very large force. Based on Hood's confident estimation of Sherman's defensive dispositions near Atlanta of only a few days earlier, this was a heavy shock to the Confederate high command. What should they do?[39]

Beauregard had few doubts, and Hood was even more certain in his opinion. Rarely had they agreed so easily; Sherman had a head start that could not be overcome. Hood's army was out of position for pursuit, about three hundred miles west, with virtually impassable roads and overflooded creeks and rivers to cross. The railroads were in no condition to transport the men, nor even to support the movement with supplies. If Hood went in pursuit, the Union column gathering to defend Tennessee would be able to invade Alabama with impunity. There really was no choice.

While Beauregard urged Hood to "take the offensive" and strike the enemy while dispersed, thus "distract[ing] Sherman's advance into Georgia," he was far more circumspect to the authorities in Richmond. Soon called upon by Davis to explain why Sherman was virtually unopposed in Georgia, Beauregard avoided taking responsibility for what was likely to be an unpopular decision with the administration. Hood's reaction was certain, he having stated that his army was too small to divide. On November 19th Hood wired that he thought it best to take the offensive immediately, adding that he expected to move two days later.[40]

Caution had been the byword as late as November 15th, when Beauregard instructed Hood to guard his right flank and rear during the advance into Tennessee against Sherman's sudden foray from his supposed position in northeastern Alabama. Now, only a few days later, both Beauregard and Hood were desperately seeking to get the troops under way regardless of incomplete preparations.[41]

But the rain had begun anew, and the weather continued to deteriorate into freezing rain and snow as the third week in November drew to a close. Hood was more vexed than ever, being again plagued with his dire logistics. On November 18th the dirt road from Cherokee Station to Tuscumbia was described as almost impassable. The railroad had been extended only six miles in the direction of Tuscumbia, and another ten remained to be completed. Bridges were down, and there were few workmen. In exasperation, Hood ordered a new command of cavalry, slated to join Forrest, to instead raid into western Tennessee, where they would seize "all the mills within your reach . . . and put them to grinding at once." Forrest also was told to put his cavalry in motion on the 18th and "set all mills to work which can be found."[42]

Hood was concerned with Napoleon's dictum that an army travels on its stomach. Whereas Sherman was marching through a land of plenty, Hood's men would be going into an impoverished and all but ruined area, devastated by three years of active warfare. Accordingly, to his already impoverished army Hood issued field orders saying that on the march about to begin there "may be a scarcity of bread ration." Still, he expected the officers and men to bear up and meet this privation with "a cheerful, manly spirit." The meat ration would be temporarily increased, said Hood, and "the fruitful fields of Tennessee are before us." Should the men get hungry, they were to remember that the country they traversed was once a rich and bountiful land until wasted by the enemy. Any privation they endured should be "an incentive," not for murmuring, but for "determined patriotism." Hood's grim ploy was of crucial importance in dealing with the morale of the men. As he revealed to Beauregard, there were only seven days' rations on hand as of the 17th, and he wanted at least thirteen more.[43]

Beauregard was in little mood to listen. He was so livid about Hood having been delayed for three weeks at Florence that he began relentlessly badgering Hood about getting his men in motion—regardless of food, weather, or any other circumstance. On November 18th Beauregard had learned that instead of three Union corps being present with Sherman, a fourth, the Fourteenth Corps, had joined the march. Now he became most abrupt in his language. "Push on active offensive immediately," he telegraphed to Hood on November 20th.[44]

Hood, of course, was of an independent mind. His cavalier attitude toward Beauregard in doing only what he pleased despite orders spilled forth even more vituperative language. Although repeatedly ordered by Beauregard to send one or two brigades of Jackson's cavalry division to aid Wheeler in harassing Sherman, Hood had refused to comply, saying that these units "could not be now spared." Beauregard fumed that "it was indispensable" that at least one of Jackson's brigades be sent. It was of no use. Thereafter, Jackson's men remained with Hood, and Beauregard meekly reported to Richmond that the cavalry could not be spared from the Army of Tennessee.[45]

Frustrated, exasperated, and all but ignored by Hood, Beauregard left Corinth, Mississippi, for Montgomery and Macon on November 19th. There he would be able at least to work with Richard Taylor, who had been put in charge of defending Georgia from Sherman's bummers. By the 22d Beauregard was at Montgomery, and thereafter so little correspondence was exchanged with Hood that "No news from General Hood" became the standard byword in Beauregard's communications to the administration in Richmond.[46]

Hood, meanwhile, was virtually tripping over his foot in the rush to get his army moving northward. On the 18th Stewart's Corps, the last to be sent across the Tennessee River, was told to hold everything in readiness to cross at sunrise on the 19th. Due to the continuing heavy rains and the jam of supply trains on the narrow pontoon bridge, the order was countermanded only hours later. Stewart's crossing thus was delayed until the 20th.[47]

About the only direct action Hood was able to take prior to the 21st was to direct Major General Forrest on November 20th to at once send small parties forward to break the enemy's railroad and telegraphic communications north of Nashville. Why only small parties instead of a larger force? "We can't spare the larger ones," said Hood's acting chief of staff. It was perhaps a fitting end to the beginning of Hood's invasion of Tennessee.[48]

IV

Having read in the newspapers about the events then transpiring in northern Alabama, Mary Chesnut noted with interest that the Macon, Georgia, paper had said, "Hood's brilliant movement [against Sherman's line of supply] will free Georgia from Yankees." Wrote Mary in amazement, "No doubt. [It will] send them on their way, lighthearted and rejoicing, into the Carolinas. They say both Beauregard and General Lee counseled that strategic reverse waltz of Hood's, but his vis-à-vis [Sherman] would not dance to Hood's music." Now Sherman was marching from Atlanta with all the South open to him. "We are at sea. Our boat has sprung a leak," wrote Mary Chesnut in dismay.[49]

CHAPTER X

Old Slow Trot

During the Mexican War the citizens of Southampton County, Virginia, had proudly honored George H. Thomas for "military skill, bravery, and noble deportment." Now they called him a traitor. His family destroyed his old letters. They turned his picture to the wall. No mention of his name was made in society. His two sisters, Julia and Fanny, had been heard to say that if he ever came home they would use on him his fine 1848-dated presentation sword that remained behind the door. They even informed him that it was best if he would change his name.[1]

It might not have mattered so much if the man had not been one of the most gifted military leaders of his time. For the last three and a half years he had been one of the principal antagonists of the South. Thomas had never lost a battle; time and time again he had been the saving grace of his army. For staving off certain disaster at Chickamauga in September 1863 he had been dubbed the "Rock of Chickamauga."[2]

Thomas's most remarkable talents were his great sense of responsibility, solid competence, and keen perspective, the very qualities personified in his decision to remain loyal to the Union. The personal crisis he had confronted in April 1861 was to Thomas far more difficult than the problems and dangers of the battlefield. Many of his fellow officers in his regiment, among them Robert E. Lee and Albert Sidney Johnston, had resigned to fight for the South.[3]

As a major of the famed 2d U.S. Cavalry in 1855 he had been appointed by none other than Jefferson Davis, then the secretary of war. Virginia's strong political clout in Congress had assured Thomas of patronage commensurate to his reputation as one of the three foremost younger officers in the service. The brightest of futures was in the offing.

His decision to fight if need be against Virginia and the South in April 1861 was tantamount to political suicide. Because he was known as a Virginian and a Southerner in Washington, D.C., circles, his loyalty was at first widely suspect. Suddenly without any powerful congressional patron to champion his cause, Thomas had stood by, all but shunted aside as officers his junior in ability, experience, and rank were promoted over him.[4]

These ugly circumstances he knowingly accepted. Relegated to a minor assignment in western Virginia that summer under an aged and bungling general, Thomas was frustrated and disconsolate. After the Union fiasco at Bull Run, he was begrudgingly given a brigadier's commission in the reorganization of the army, but only after Sherman and his old West Point instructor, Robert Anderson, petitioned for his appointment.[5]

Finally offered the chance to demonstrate his ability and leadership in Kentucky, Thomas had responded with an important victory at Mill Springs in January 1862. Yet little official recognition was forthcoming until after the Shiloh campaign. Largely due to the failings of others, Thomas was at that time promoted to major general and assumed command of the Army of the Tennessee. Regarded by the former commander, Ulysses S. Grant, as somewhat of an interloper, Thomas voluntarily requested that he return to an active assignment as a division commander, and thus cleared the way for restoration of Grant to his old post.[6]

Thomas's strong character was evident when during a period where competent leadership was lacking in the west, he declined command of the Department of the Cumberland. He felt Don Carlos Buell's "hands had been tied" by bureaucratic interference. The Virginian's code of honor thus cost him the opportunity to lead the Army of the Cumberland during the Stones River campaign. William Starke Rosecrans was appointed after Thomas refused the command.[7]

Following Chickamauga, where Thomas's obstinate stand on Snodgrass Hill had saved Rosecrans's army when all seemed to have been lost, Thomas had reluctantly assumed command of the Army of the Cumberland in the reorganization that followed. Yet thereafter a new overall army organization had been implemented, resulting in an iron-willed theater commander for Thomas to report to—Ulysses S. Grant.

Thomas's difficult personal relationship with the rough-hewn and more youthful Grant was evidently founded upon the resentment Grant felt when he had been displaced and Thomas appointed in his place during the Siege of Corinth. These two generals were of widely varying temperament and personality. Neither liked the other, nor seemed even to trust the other's motives. Their cool relationship was accentuated by the arrival at Chattanooga during the siege of that city in October 1863 of Grant and his highly favored friend since Shiloh, William Tecumseh Sherman. Following the raising of the siege, despite Thomas's yeoman work in assaulting Missionary Ridge in late November, Grant got most of the credit.[8]

Called to the east as the army's commander-in-chief, Grant chose William T. Sherman, Thomas's junior in rank as a major general, to succeed him in command in the west. It was again a bitter disappointment to Thomas. Although commanding the Army of the Cumberland, which comprised nearly two-thirds of Sherman's entire force of three separate armies, about the only solace for Thomas after Missionary Ridge had been welcome revenge against an old army associate and former friend, Braxton Bragg. During the siege of Chattanooga a letter had arrived from the North with a request for Thomas to forward it through the lines to its intended recipient in the South. Thomas had appended a note to Bragg, under whom he had served so well during the Mexican War, asking him to forward the letter. Bragg, however, had returned the letter to Thomas endorsed, "Respectfully returned to Genl. Thomas. Genl. Bragg declines to have any intercourse with a man who has betrayed his state." Thomas had fairly exploded at the insult. "Damn him, I'll be even with him yet," he swore.[9]

Missionary Ridge had settled that score.

There were, however, many other conflicts to be faced, equally as vexing. During the Atlanta campaign, while not on unfriendly terms with Sherman, Thomas was frequently in disagreement with Sherman's decisions, particularly as to the wisdom of the costly frontal assault at Kennesaw Mountain. Sherman wrote Grant of Thomas's so-so performance, saying the Army of the Cumberland was "dreadfully slow," and "a fresh furrow in a plowed field will stop the entire column and all begin to entrench. I have again and again tried to impress on Thomas that we must assail and not defend . . . and yet it seems that the whole Army of the Cumberland is so habituated to be on the defensive that . . . I cannot get it out of their heads." Yet, when Atlanta had been won, Sherman confided to Henry Halleck, the chief of staff, "George Thomas, you know, is slow, but true as steel."[10]

Thomas, as Sherman's most reliable subordinate, had subsequently been detached in late September 1864 to take charge of a reserve force at Nashville, designated for the protection of Tennessee. Moving to Chattanooga in the wake of Nathan Bedford Forrest's raid into mid-Tennessee during late September and early October, Thomas had overseen the deployment of troops attempting to "clear out Tennessee" of Confederate raiders. Sherman had written at the time that he had little concern about Hood's infantry, but that the enemy's cavalry was to be feared. Indeed, Sherman had been correct. Forrest, crossing the Tennessee River at mile-wide Colbert Shoals on September 21st, had swiftly pounced upon the Federal garrison at Athens on the 23rd. The Union commander was intimidated into surrendering on the 24th, and 1,300 prisoners with a large quantity of stores and horses were taken. Hastening north to Pulaski, then eventually to Spring Hill, Forrest was able to destroy nearly all of the bridges and trestles on the Tennessee

& Alabama Railroad between Decatur and Spring Hill, including the 1,100-foot-long, 90-foot-high Elk River trestle. Hastening back to the vicinity of Florence in early October, Forrest got his command safely across the river by October 6th despite a heavy pursuit. Forrest reported a total of 86 Federal commissioned officers and 1,274 enlisted men captured, with 800 horses, and a vast quantity of property destroyed, all at the cost of 47 killed and 293 wounded of his 4,500-man force.[11]

Thomas, who had belatedly reached Nashville on October 3d, was exasperated by the bungled attempt to catch the brilliant Confederate raider. Yet there was little time to fret. Another heated crisis was then brewing. With the beginning of Hood's series of railroad raids along the Chattanooga line during the first two weeks in October, Thomas had to reposition his troops immediately to help Sherman thwart this movement. Two divisions of Sherman's forces hurriedly sent to Chattanooga arrived by rail to guard that region, while other troops under James B. Steedman and L. H. Rousseau were recalled from northern Alabama and rushed hither and yon.[12]

Hood had no sooner withdrawn into northeastern Alabama than "that devil Forrest" again appeared in western Tennessee. Forrest's arrival along the west bank opposite Johnsonville, and the enormous destruction at this depot on November 4th, caused Thomas to rush troops in that direction. They were too late, and again the overworked railroads creaked and groaned as Thomas's troops were rerouted back to mid-Tennessee. In all, it had become an exasperating six weeks for Thomas at Nashville. Sherman, hastening his preparations to march to the Georgia seacoast, had left behind for Thomas the essence of only two corps, scattered guard detachments, and new recruits. With this agglomeration Thomas was ordered to form an army and stop Hood's invasion of Tennessee, or else pursue the Confederates if Hood chose to follow Sherman through Georgia.[13]

The question about Thomas had always been his inner fire. Known as somewhat of a plodder, a methodical and careful general of great ability, Thomas had earned various nicknames among his men, including "Old Tom" and "Old Pap," from his fatherly image. If a man of high principle, he was unassertive and seemed almost phlegmatic in personality. His unassuming manner and stoic pride often caused him to suffer in relative silence while ensnarled in politics and the victim of injustice during his long army career. "I have taken a great deal of pains to educate myself not to feel," he glumly told another officer who complained that he had been badly treated.[14]

Although a man to be reckoned with and relied on in a fight, Thomas's advancing age of forty-eight accentuated his deliberate movements. He was square-jawed and thought by many to resemble George Washington, but his bulky six-foot frame had become corpulent in recent years. In shape he resembled a large A-frame tent. His neatly trimmed mustache and full beard were nearly all gray now. Older than many of his contemporary generals, Thomas was variously looked upon as stubborn and set in his ways.[15]

Yet the man was one of the best generals in all of the army. A born fighter with the heart of a lion, George H. Thomas was a man transfigured on the battlefield. Here his steel-gray eyes narrowed and burned with an intense ferocity. Above all else, his soldiers, the men who knew him best, offered strong opinions about "Old Pap." They thought about his clearheaded judgment and his careful concern for them. They had witnessed his subtle but profound greatness. He was their much-beloved commander. They knew he would never let them down.[16]

John Bell Hood thought otherwise. Thomas was once the austere instructor at West Point who had ranked Hood forty-fifth—seventh from the bottom— in artillery and cavalry proficiency. Later, Hood had to kowtow to Thomas, who was his senior officer in the old 2d Cavalry. Now they were on equal footing as army commanders, with both in crucial, career-making or -ending roles. It would be the pupil against the teacher, the new against the old, dash against common sense. Hood had maneuvered P. G. T. Beauregard out of the way; Sherman was going in the opposite direction; the principal central character who remained was "Old Slow Trot" Thomas. Hood may have remembered with relish how Thomas had earned that nickname. When on the cavalry exercise field at West Point the high-spirited cadet horsemen, ordered to trot, would forge ahead into a gallop, the bulky instructor Thomas would cry out, "Slow Trot, Slow Trot," so that he might catch up. Now it would be Hood's turn to gallop at full speed. Could Thomas keep up?[17]

II

Thomas had been emotionally wrought for weeks. There were too many unreliable reports, too many false alarms. Hood's intentions were unknown. The consensus was that Hood, when he learned that Sherman was marching south through Georgia, would withdraw from Alabama and follow the Federal column. Sherman repeatedly expressed this view, and on the very eve of his march he told Thomas that "public clamor will force him to turn and follow me." Thomas was attempting to evaluate the many reports of enemy deserters, spies, cavalry scouts, captured prisoners, and even escaped Union soldiers. Most suggested that Hood would advance into mid-Tennessee. Yet there was little physical evidence of such a move. Putting together the mosaic that would reveal Hood's intentions had become a perplexing problem. The basic difficulty was that Hood was showing few signs of going anywhere. Day after day reports were coming in from cavalry patrols of "nothing new," only the familiar status quo around Hood's positions at Florence.[18]

From the first appearance of Hood in the vicinity of Decatur during late October, there had been a flurry of activity at Thomas's Nashville headquarters. With the 4,000-man Federal garrison at Decatur penned in by Hood's army, at the time there was only a single brigade of depleted Union cavalry to watch the north bank of the Tennessee River for an enemy crossing.[19]

John T. Croxton, a youthful Yale-educated Union brigadier with considerable energy, had the job of guarding the river crossings between Florence and Decatur. Despite having four regiments, Croxton's combined strength was only about 1,000 men, less than that of a single regiment at the beginning of the war. Having spread his men over a twenty-four-mile span along the river, Croxton was at such a loss to locate the enemy on October 25th that he wrote to Thomas, "Where is Hood? It might be well for me to know."[20]

On the evening of October 29th the former Kentucky lawyer got a break. An old Negro waded, swam, and stumbled across Muscle Shoals after dark, a remarkable feat, bringing word that later that night Hood's men would attempt to throw pontoons across the Tennessee River at Bainbridge, four miles northeast of Florence. He was taken to Croxton, who then ordered one of his best regiments, the 2d Michigan Cavalry, to guard that crossing.[21]

The Michiganders forlornly waited there all night. On the following afternoon, however, they learned that they had been guarding the wrong crossing. Two Confederate brigades from Stephen D. Lee's Corps, selecting a point "never known or used as a ferry," had crossed that night on flatboats to an island three miles below Bainbridge. There they had remained concealed until preparations were completed to bring forward the army's pontoons. About 3:00 P.M. on the 30th, Lee's brigades suddenly emerged from the brush and struck for the north bank. Croxton's horsemen scrambled for their mounts and dashed to the site. They were too late. Despite the firepower from the 2d Michigan's Spencer carbines—seven-shot repeaters—Lee's men swept back the Union cavalrymen and easily secured a lodgment on the north shore. At Florence, on the site of the ferry, Randall Gibson's men had crossed without difficulty during the same day. Swiftly they had chased off about 200 raw troopers of the 12th Tennessee Cavalry, who were said to be "badly mounted and carelessly handled."[22]

Thereafter, Croxton lingered about Shoal Creek bridge, eight miles east of Florence, watching Hood's activities, and resorting to such devices as floating heavy timbered rafts downriver to smash into Hood's pontoons. Fortunately for the undermanned Croxton, by November 6th he had some much-needed help.[23]

Two brigades of Federal cavalry under Brigadier General Edward Hatch had been ordered to rejoin their parent command from Clifton, Tennessee, where they had been resting and refitting in preparation for Sherman's march through Georgia. Hatch's men had started to return to Sherman's army on October 29th, only to be halted en route on November 1st at Pulaski, Tennessee. Thomas desperately needed more "eyes and ears" to keep track of Hood, and a mobile force to hold back the enemy's cavalry. Using Sherman's permission to appropriate detached units, Thomas countermanded Hatch's orders and sent these horsemen south to aid Croxton. By virtue of his seniority in rank, Hatch, an up-from-the-ranks Iowa officer of much ability, assumed overall command of the cavalry operating in Hood's front. On the 6th Hatch's two well-mounted brigades had begun skirmishing with the outlying Confederate cavalry pickets near Florence, but were unable to develop significant new information.[24]

About the only other mounted troops in the area able to watch Hood were those under Horace Capron, an Illinois colonel with a ragtag brigade of 800 men, sent on November 1st west of Florence to look for any enemy movement in the direction of Waynesboro. Here Capron had fumed and fussed about inadequate food and forage, and accomplished little but to report on the activities of a few guerrillas in the area.[25]

In all, this dearth of reliable information had been very alarming to Thomas. His fears that Hood would swiftly advance once his pontoons were in place were fueled in early November by Croxton's reports that "a large infantry force" had crossed to the north side. Thomas told Robert S. Granger at Decatur to send out parties and chop down trees and obstruct crossings of the Elk River between Decatur and Pulaski. Athens was prematurely abandoned in haste, and there was concern that a swarm of Rebel cavalry would soon strike the Tennessee & Alabama Railroad.[26] Thomas's anxiety was only partially abated on November 2d. He then learned that Hood's advance elements were entrenching about Florence, a significant sign that a forward movement was delayed. Following reports from Croxton that Hood was out of rations, Thomas had briefly turned his attention to Forrest's raid in west Tennessee.[27]

By mid-November Thomas was more perplexed than ever about Hood's plans. The weather continued to be horrendous. Sherman had just begun marching south from Atlanta, and like Sherman, Thomas considered it probable that Hood would withdraw and pursue the raiding blue columns. Yet a steady flow of information kept trickling in that Hood would not go back to Georgia and was gathering supplies for an offensive into mid-Tennessee.[28]

Since Thomas was so concerned about Hood slipping away south after Sherman, on November 13th Croxton ordered an attack on the enemy's pickets along the main road to Florence. The intent was to get a prisoner. After a brief firefight, a lone private was captured from a Mississippi cavalry unit and was closely interrogated. From his effusive chatter Thomas learned that only one infantry corps was across the river and that another had attempted to cross, but Hood's pontoon bridge had broken. Forrest was en route to the army, said the man, and they had been told that Forrest would take them on a great raid as far as the Ohio River. Hood, he thought, was going to Nashville.[29] Thomas, thereafter, directed that the entire cavalry force be kept in front until it was known "whether or not Hood is moving."

On November 16th Thomas learned from Hatch that two new prisoners taken that morning had reported Cheatham's Corps then crossing the river, with a general advance imminent. This news was corroborated by an escaped prisoner, a lieutenant from the 2d Michigan Cavalry, who had seen an estimated 700-wagon supply train going to Hood's army from Cherokee Station.[30]

Soon there were ominous new reports of a greater number of campfires within the enemy lines. Then another notice from Hatch arrived at midnight on the 18th, stating that one of his reliable scouts had returned with news that a third enemy infantry corps would cross the river on the 19th. In all, it was substantial evidence that Hood was going on the offensive.[31]

Thomas, however, largely discounted these reports. He was convinced that one element alone would keep Hood from marching—the weather. Heavy rains were lashing the countryside, making it almost impossible to move infantry along the mud-choked, deeply rutted and quagmired roads. Any enemy movement, even if by cavalry, Thomas wrote Halleck on November 19th, "can be no more than a demonstration."[32]

Hatch soon thereafter dispatched two reports to cause Thomas to change his mind. The first told of a clash on the 19th with Forrest's cavalry, said to be advancing along the road to Lawrenceburg. The second, written on the morning of the 20th, reported that Confederate infantry had advanced that morning a distance of fourteen miles from Florence. Apparently they were moving toward Lawrenceburg. Hatch already had confirmed that Forrest's entire four divisions of cavalry, an estimated 10,000 horsemen, were present.[33]

Thomas was taken aback. There was no longer any doubt that the Rebels were advancing. But to what purpose? Was it only a raid of Forrest's cavalry, supported by infantry, against the railroad between Pulaski and Columbia? Thomas's principal in-field subordinate, Major General John M. Schofield, seemed to think so.[34]

The damnable rain, slosh, and low cloud ceiling kept scouting at a minimum. Good intelligence was lacking. There was so much befuddlement among the Union generals that even Schofield suggested on November 20th that Forrest merely might be moving north to encamp where forage was more abundant. "It seems hardly probable that he will attempt aggressive operations while the roads are so bad," wrote Schofield in second-guessing his hours-earlier estimation of a railroad raid.[35]

Hatch continued to press for information. On the 21st his scouts had observed Stephen D. Lee's Corps twenty miles north of Florence, going toward Lawrenceburg. Two other Confederate corps were detected to be advancing, and Cheatham's Corps was discovered on the road to Waynesboro. Hatch even provided a reasonably accurate estimate of the enemy's columns—30,000 to 35,000 infantry, plus 60 pieces of artillery, and 10,000 cavalry. "There is no doubt of their advance," warned Hatch in an urgent 8:00 A.M. message to Thomas.[36]

Thomas, although still skeptical, was forced to react. His telegram to Halleck that night advised that he had directed his troops to pull back "gradually" to protect Columbia before Hood could arrive, "if he should really move against that place." On the 22d Thomas finally learned that he had badly underestimated Hood's mounting desperation. Hatch's reports were confirmed. The brash Hood, after lying inactive for three agonizing weeks at Florence, was suddenly rushing north with his entire army, via Waynesboro and Lawrenceburg. Thomas and Hood were now pitted in a multifaceted race, replete with maneuver and strategy. Hood had gotten off to a rapid start against his former instructor, and "Old Slow Trot" would have to move at a much faster pace if he was going to stay ahead of the galloping Sam Hood.[37]

III

"We are having a pretty good time now, having but little to do," wrote a complacent Federal private on November 20th. Another soldier spent much of each day idly playing whist with his comrades, while an officer observed that they were pleasantly situated, with a plentiful quantity of supplies. "Indeed, we are living well; having for the first time . . . soft bread and potatoes," he informed his sister. Life at Pulaski had not been difficult for Thomas's soldiers despite the raw weather. "We have been here [since November 5th]" wrote Union Brigadier General Luther P. Bradley, "and are well fortified against attack."[38] On November 21st, with a raw wind howling amid swirling snow squalls, Brigadier General Jacob D. Cox sat in his tent playing chess and reading in order to dissipate the boredom. "We try to keep from suffering by fires [built] before each tent door," announced the comfortably situated Cox.[39]

At that very time Hood's army was on the march, his gaunt men arching their bodies forward against the wind and snow. By that evening word was received from Hatch of Hood's proximity to Lawrenceburg, less than twenty miles to the west. There soon was considerable commotion in the Pulaski camps. "We will have to move accordingly without much delay," Schofield wrote anxiously that night. It was a classic understatement.[40]

In a flurry of activity, Schofield ordered two of his divisions to march on the morning of the 22d to Lynnville, about twenty miles north in the direction of Columbia. The remaining two, under David S. Stanley, were to follow no later than the following morning. Thereafter, on the 23d, the withdrawal would continue to Columbia.[41]

Thomas already had ordered Schofield to concentrate in the vicinity of Columbia, and acknowledged, "I shall have to act on the defensive." He had too few men at present: only 12,000 of the Fourth Corps, 10,000 in Schofield's Twenty-third Corps, and, he thought, about 3,000 effective cavalry. Hood might have lost the initiative to Sherman, but it was now painfully apparent to Thomas that he had stolen it back from him.[42]

Witnessing the sudden activity in camp, an Illinois soldier wrote that something must be up, because there was much haste to get on the road.

Indeed, it was soon rumored they "were running a race with General Forrest."[43]

IV

Thomas needed more time. His army would have to be rebuilt, and reinforcements obtained. Hood's advance must be retarded, and every day gained was of importance.

As late as November 15th Thomas had suggested to Ulysses Grant that the situation was well in hand in Tennessee, saying in another telegram to Halleck that day, "[I] will take advantage of the first opportunity to strike him [Hood], if he exposes himself." Ten days later, confronted in mid-Tennessee by Hood's entire army, Thomas wrote to Grant that the enemy force "so greatly outnumbers mine at this time that I am compelled to act on the defensive."[44]

What had happened in that short span of little more than a week to so change Thomas's perspective?

The first and least imposing circumstance involved Thomas's woebegone cavalry corps. The clear superiority of the Confederate cavalry was common knowledge throughout Sherman's Military Division of the Mississippi. Hood was estimated to have 10,000 veteran horsemen, all operating under perhaps the best cavalry commander in either army, Nathan Bedford Forrest. Their opponents, Thomas's 4,300 troopers, were a hodgepodge of units, some usurped from other departments, others culled from regional remounting depots, and all hastily thrown together as a stopgap measure to confront Hood. The best horses in Sherman's department had been turned over to Judson Kilpatrick's division, which had accompanied Sherman on the March to the Sea. An estimated 10,000 potential cavalrymen were without mounts, and nearly all had been routed far to the rear for remounting. The equipment of the in-field units was deficient, particularly in improved small arms. Complete reorganization of the cavalry was necessary, and new, more competent commanders were quickly needed.[45]

The new chief of cavalry, Major General James H. Wilson, sent from the east in late October to spearhead reorganization of Sherman's depleted horse soldiers, had originally suggested to Thomas that the improvements would be implemented by November 12th. Yet on November 16th Wilson acknowledged "this force of cavalry is yet behind in its reorganization and equipment." The improved weapons ordered from New York were still en route, and so few new horses had been obtained that Thomas used the cavalry's deficiency as a primary reason why he would not advance to meet Hood's army. To further complicate matters, Wilson departed Nashville to take charge of active operations against Hood's advancing cavalry on November 21st, leaving his adjutant, a major, in charge of the ongoing replenishment program.[46]

By far the more serious difficulty perplexing Thomas throughout the month of November 1864, however, was the absence of 10,000 veteran troops of the Sixteenth Corps under Major General A. J. Smith. Sherman had promised to send Smith's men to Thomas as reinforcements back in October, yet more than a month later there was no word of their approach.[47]

Smith had been detached with two divisions from Sherman's army during the summer to operate in Mississippi against Forrest's cavalry. Temporarily transferred to Rosecrans's Department of Missouri during the crisis resulting from Sterling Price's invasion of that state in early October, A. J. Smith's troops had been sent on a harrowing march into the western regions of Missouri. Following Price's defeat at Westport on October 23d and his subsequent disorganized retreat, Smith's men were again available for service east of the Mississippi River.[48]

Sherman, on October 29th, telegraphed to Rosecrans, seeking their return as rapidly as possible due to the threatening movements of Hood toward Tennessee. Although Rosecrans promised his full cooperation, the Missouri River was so low, he said, that Smith could reach the Mississippi River sooner by marching overland. A. J. Smith, with two divisions of the Sixteenth Corps, then was ordered to rejoin Sherman's forces. It would take ten days to march to the Mississippi, estimated Rosecrans.[49]

When Smith received his marching orders on November 2d he was at Warrensburg, Missouri, about 200 miles west of St. Louis. Once he reached that point, he intended to quickly embark on transports for Tennessee. Based on Sherman's assurances, Thomas began looking for Smith's arrival about November 10th. On the 11th he wrote, "[I] am daily expecting him here."[50]

Thomas was grossly mistaken. At that time A. J. Smith was only then approaching St. Louis following an exasperating march. On the 14th he telegraphed to Thomas from that city that his troops were still en route from Western Missouri. The same wet weather plaguing Tennessee was holding Smith's men back. Flooded streams, washed-out bridges, and mud-choked roads had so hindered his troops that it was uncertain when they would arrive.[51]

By the 22d, with Hood confirmed to be on the march toward Columbia, Thomas, in the absence of further word from A. J. Smith, was "patiently waiting" for his arrival. Unknown to Thomas, on that day Smith still dallied in St. Louis. He would require another two days before leaving for the mouth of the Ohio River at Cairo.[52]

Everyone had surmised that it was going to be a "hard campaign," but no one among Smith's veterans seemed to understand that a crucial race for Nashville was then in progress. To add further difficulty to the rapidly deteriorating situation, telegraphic communications were frequently interrupted or delayed in and out of Nashville. What had begun three weeks ago as a routine troop movement had suddenly become a life-or-death gambit.[53]

Thomas had little choice but to hold on, gathering what manpower he could from wherever it might be found. Word that A. J. Smith would bring along another small division of 1,200 men from the Seventeenth Corps, then at Benton Barracks, was of small solace. Smith's swollen command of about 12,000 men would be of little value until present. With Hood sweeping northward into Tennessee, there seemed to be too many problems and but few advantages. Thomas must pull back his advanced posts and withdraw his outlying garrisons or risk their capture. Schofield would have to retard Hood's advance. Wilson had to keep Forrest away from the vital railroads. Somehow the cavalry must be remounted and reequipped. The in-field units must be provisioned and supplied. Raw, untested regiments would have to take an active part in the campaign. New commanders were taking over in crucial roles. The entire army was being formed in the midst of pending battle.

Suddenly the weight of a thousand worlds seemed to have been placed upon the shoulders of George H. Thomas. At 10:00 A.M. on Thursday, November 24th, A. J. Smith finally set out from St. Louis with the last division of his troops. It would require perhaps an entire week to get them to Nashville. On that very day Ulysses S. Grant, from his headquarters at City Point, Virginia, wired to Thomas, "Do not let Forrest get off without punishment."[54]

It was yet another burden. Misconceived circumstances and imperfect communication had become all too frequent at a distance of nearly a thousand miles. Grant, ever demanding, was looking for Thomas to take the offensive.

Whatever the day might bring, November 24th had been designated as a time of national rejoicing. In honor of the occasion, one of "Old Pap's" privates reassuringly wrote to his wife, "The prayers of the righteous avail much." George H. Thomas certainly hoped so.[55]

It was Thanksgiving.

CHAPTER XI

In the Best of Spirits
and Full of Hope

T HE 20TH LOUISIANA'S band was not much to look at, a few straggly privates with assorted horns, drums, and perhaps a fife. Their reputation was at a peak, however, in the fall of 1864. They were one of the better bands in service with the Army of Tennessee, having played for Jefferson Davis at Palmetto Station during his September visit. On November 13th, when Cheatham's Corps had crossed the Tennessee River at Florence, an awed observer had watched from a high bluff and listened to the strains of music wafting from the river. The pontoon bridge was the longest he had ever seen, stretching a mile and a half, he thought, and the sight was impressive. With the flat bridge being close to the water's surface, it appeared from a distance that the men were walking on the water. This seemed to be a once-in-a-lifetime sight, so many troops marching across by fours with a band playing ahead of each brigade. The weather was fine, and the town of Florence, with its railroad bridge in ruins and the shells of a few burned houses, stood stark against the shore. It was a strange and yet compelling sight. The Army of Tennessee seemed to be marching into the very ruins of war.[1]

There had been much gaiety during the next few nights. Various parties for the officers were held at the homes of several ladies in Florence, and on the night of the 14th the Tennesseans serenaded General Forrest, who had just arrived at Hood's headquarters from Corinth. Both Forrest and Hood gave short speeches, and all had enjoyed the merriment to the fullest. One of Hood's staff officers had noted his general's fondness for a party, and how Sam Hood was never one to shy away from tableaux involving "'galop and deuxtemps.''[2]

Hood was in good health and high spirits, wrote an observer at the time, and his physical disabilities seemed to have been largely overcome. He was "the finest looking man I think I ever saw," noted a surgeon. Indeed, despite his old wounds there was a certain charm about his appearance. Hood's stiff left arm was still bothersome, and his hand was paralyzed. Also, he had the choice of two artificial legs which had been carefully fitted to his right leg stump. There was the rather grotesque French contraption that Dr. John Darby had brought back from Europe in early 1864, purchased with funds contributed by Hood's old Texas Brigade from the Army of Northern Virginia. Also, Hood had what Mary Chesnut referred to as the "Charlottesville leg," a rather plain wooden or cork limb of more simple design. Although forced to use a crutch when walking, Hood wore a boot with a spur on each leg, and when mounted on horseback the prosthesis hung stiffly outward. Even though some of his men referred to him as "Old Pegleg," Hood had demonstrated his physical mettle by regularly riding horseback for fifteen to twenty miles without dismounting, even while strapped to the saddle. The carriage which he had brought up from Atlanta in the spring of 1864 had been sent back, and Hood would ride everywhere, his crutch jauntily slung from his saddle like some musician's violin case. Instead of a grueling disability, his missing leg had proved to be a noted cause. Mary Chesnut once heard him say in jest that so many people talked about him it seemed as if he were a centipede: his foot was in everybody's mouth.[3]

When his men saw him on that memorable Monday, November 21, 1864, he was the very embodiment of the bold, purposeful fighter—a general with a mission. His proclamation to the army issued that day had boldly announced: "You march today to redeem by your valor one of the fairest portions of our Confederacy. This can only be achieved by battle and by victory." His field orders for the campaign urged "a cheerful, manly spirit" and "determined patriotism" in meeting the expected hardships as they marched to repossess the "fruitful fields of Tennessee."[4]

Despite the threatening, raw weather, for that first day's march there had been the greatest enthusiasm. At roll call that morning the regimental commanders had addressed the men, telling them that a hard campaign was ahead, their base of supplies would be left behind, but by disciplined marching and fighting they would persevere. There would be no more fighting under the enemy's terms, they were told. Their adequate strength and the choice of ground would be assured before going into battle. As such, there would be little risk of defeat in Tennessee. "All this was very nice talk," wrote an officer, "for we all felt confident that we could always whip an equal number of men with the choice of the ground." Indeed, "every man felt anxious to go on under these promises from General Hood," he reported.[5]

The men were no sooner marching on the hard, frozen roads than it had begun to snow. A harsh wind was in their faces, and the bone-numbing cold chilled to the very marrow, yet it made little difference. "The ground is frozen hard and a sharp, cold wind is blowing, but as my face is towards

Tennessee, I heed none of these things," wrote an eager Tennessean, anxious to return home.[6]

By 10:00 A.M. Hood's headquarters was on the march, joining Cheatham's Corps on the road toward Waynesboro. Twelve miles were covered that day, and camp was made at Rawhide, near the Alabama/Tennessee border. Hood's three army corps were advancing along separate roads, each moving in a slightly different direction, with Stephen D. Lee's Corps well in the lead due to their advanced position before the march began. On the 20th Lee had moved ten miles north of Florence on a middle route, a backwoods country road known as the Pinhook. With Cheatham on the westernmost road, which led to Waynesboro, and Stewart, the last to cross the Tennessee River, traveling the shorter Lawrenceburg road on the right flank, an unobstructed path for each corps was assured. Forrest's cavalry had been divided to move in advance of the various columns, with Abraham Buford's and William H. Jackson's divisions going to Lawrenceburg, and James R. Chalmers's advancing toward Waynesboro. It was Hood's objective to place his army by rapid marches between Schofield's forces at Pulaski and Thomas's at Nashville.[7]

Yet from the beginning the march was plagued by extraordinary difficulty. A want of good maps caused delays in locating the proper country routes despite the presence of local residents in the army. The seldom-used backwoods roads that Stephen D. Lee's men were utilizing became almost impassable for artillery. The horses were soon jaded, and having been on short forage, they became progressively weaker. It was necessary at times for two regiments to move with the batteries in order to manhandle the guns and caissons through the mud holes and over the many knolls and hills. Even along Cheatham's route "the roads were in such a terrible condition that the men marched in the woods and fields to escape the mud," wrote one unit's commander.[8]

By pushing his men from sunrise to dark, Cheatham moved to within fourteen miles of Waynesboro on the 22d, traveling a difficult eighteen miles that day in intensely cold weather. Heavy skirmishing with detachments of Federal cavalry already had begun in front of the respective columns. Forrest's cavalrymen at first had been compelled to stay close to the infantry to screen their movements, but now they began to rapidly press back their outmatched opponents.[9]

On November 23d, a sunny but very cold day, Cheatham's men had reached Waynesboro by 4:00 P.M. The town was deserted, and a soldier observed that what had once been a very nice village had been largely ruined by the war. Houses were torn down, others had been burned, gardens were destroyed, and the hide-tanning yard had been gutted for timber. Since Cheatham's wagon train had broken down four miles in the rear, for many men that night there was the added misery of losing what few provisions

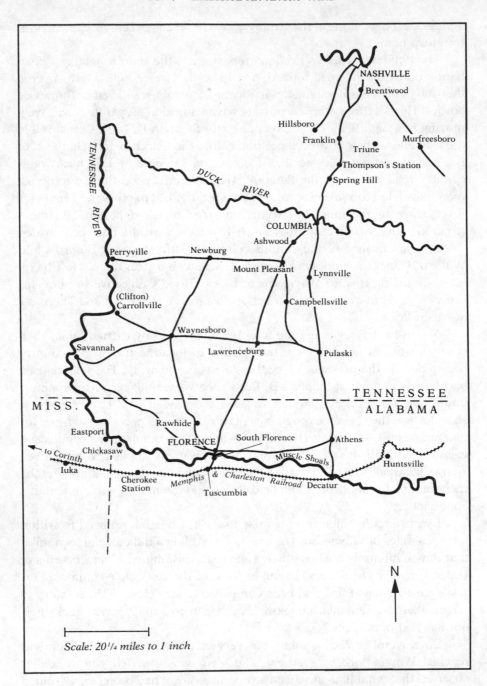

Map 2   Invasion Route—November 1864

were available. In fact, for the next few days many of the troops subsisted on a ration of three biscuits a day.[10]

By the 23d, Forrest's cavalry had raced far ahead in pursuit of the rapidly retreating Federal horsemen and were in the vicinity of Mount Pleasant. Forrest, riding with Chalmers's Division, that afternoon came within a fraction of a second of losing his life. The Confederate "wizard of the saddle" had pushed his men hard that day. In his front were the weakly resisting cavalrymen of Horace Capron's brigade. Capron's men were "considerably demoralized," many of his troopers having poor mounts and Springfield rifle muskets instead of breech-loading cavalry carbines. When driven beyond Henryville, in the gathering darkness of early evening Capron's men had made preparations to encamp near Fouche Springs, along the road to Mount Pleasant.[11]

Yet Forrest had planned a deadly trap. Leaving Edmund W. Rucker's Brigade to skirmish with the sizable enemy rear guard, Forrest had swung around the flank by a side road. Suddenly, at the head of his 80-man escort, Forrest charged through the unsuspecting camp of Capron's 800-man brigade. With pistols blazing, Forrest and his escort quickly stampeded the entire camp, their minimal strength being grossly overestimated in the confusion and gathering darkness. When Rucker's Brigade charged forward at the sound of Forrest's attack, the entire rear guard of Capron came galloping pell-mell down the road toward the camp. Forrest's escort, armed with captured Spencer repeating carbines, fired from ambuscade on these troops, creating the wildest confusion. It was nearly dark, and Forrest, riding next to his adjutant general, Major J. P. Strange, suddenly encountered a small party of horsemen moving up a side path. A challenge was shouted from among the party, but Forrest, perhaps thinking they were his own men, rode ahead. The horseman leading the squadron held a revolver at the ready. Too late, Forrest discovered that the man was a Federal officer. At point-blank range the man raised his pistol and pulled the trigger. Strange, at the last instant, lunged forward. The revolver was deflected, and the shot passed close by Forrest's body. In an instant some of Forrest's escort were on the scene and the Federals surrendered. A total of about sixty-five prisoners were taken during the day, along with many horses and even an ambulance. It was further evidence of the widespread superiority of Forrest's cavalrymen over their increasingly disorganized mounted foes.[12]

On a cool and dark Thanksgiving Day, the 24th, Hood's entire army had funneled back into the same roadway, the Waynesboro to Mount Pleasant pike. Despite the added congestion and greater difficulty with the single, badly rutted roadway, the weather had cleared and Hood wanted to avoid detection of his infantry. His swing to the west, away from the proximity of Pulaski and Lynnville, was thus a calculated maneuver. Hood was now about halfway to his initial destination, the quaint Tennessee town of Columbia. Lying along the Duck River, Columbia was about thirty-five miles north of

Pulaski, on the railroad running between Decatur, Alabama, and Nashville, Tennessee. Having placed his army on the western flank of Schofield's force at Pulaski, Hood, on the morning of the 24th, was only about forty-five miles south of Columbia. Accordingly, he looked upon the next few days as critical in an intensifying race to first occupy Columbia.[13]

That afternoon Hood suddenly learned that the race for Columbia was in earnest. Forrest's cavalry had entered Mount Pleasant that morning and learned that the enemy was hastily leaving Pulaski. Immediately, at 11:00 A.M., Forrest sent orders for most of Jackson's and Buford's divisions to rapidly move east to the railroad and cut off Schofield's retreat. If the enemy were found to be already past the point of interception, he urged both commands to pass on toward Columbia and press hard after the blue columns. Chalmers's most advanced units already were said to be within four miles of Columbia along the Mount Pleasant pike, and still driving the Federal cavalry. Although two Federal corps were reported en route for Columbia, it seemed unlikely that they would arrive before the disorganized Federal cavalry gave way in front of Chalmers.[14]

Forrest's plan for Jackson's and Buford's divisions miscarried. Their men had been skirmishing with Hatch's Federal cavalrymen since the 22d in the vicinity of Lawrenceburg. Hatch's three brigades had withdrawn east toward Pulaski on the 23d, with Jackson and Buford closely following. That evening, when within five miles of Pulaski, Hatch's men had suddenly turned north in the direction of Campbellsville. Therefore, on the morning of the 24th, Jackson and Buford had followed Hatch rather than proceed east toward Pulaski. At noon on the 24th they caught up with Hatch's division, strongly posted at Campbellsville, and a sharp fight ensued. Hatch escaped about sunset in the direction of Lynnville after a severe pummeling that cost him eighty-four prisoners and four stands of colors. Yet the two Confederate cavalry divisions remained at Campbellsville, moving on toward Columbia the following morning. Forrest's urgent instructions to intercept Schofield's infantry on the Pulaski–Columbia route had been received too late to be implemented. Thus, it remained for Chalmers's lone division to get past Capron's cavalry on the Mount Pleasant road and into Columbia before the approaching Federal infantry.[15]

Chalmers had begun early after daylight on the morning of the 24th with a rush at the remnant of Capron's men. Seven miles distant from Columbia, three Federal regiments attempted to make a stand. They had received urgent instructions that morning from their newly arrived division commander, Brigadier General Richard W. Johnson, to hold Mount Pleasant at all hazards. Since Capron's beleaguered men already had been driven beyond Mount Pleasant on the 23d, this was impossible. Yet Capron gamely attempted to further resist on the morning of the 24th. Their awkward armament of muzzle-loading rifle muskets inspired little confidence. "Our rifles after the first volley were about as serviceable to cavalry as a good club," wrote a major of the 14th Illinois Cavalry, who further complained that his men were unable to reload while mounted. Attacked in a narrow lane, with horses and men "in the highest state of excitement," their situation again was quickly out of control. When Chalmers sent Rucker's Brigade around both of Capron's flanks, the Federal retreat soon became a rout. By 7:30 A.M. Capron was fleeing hurriedly down the crushed gravel road toward Columbia, with Chalmers in full pursuit.[16]

II

Major General John M. Schofield had been up all night. He had written early that morning from Lynnville that it then appeared Hood was closer to Columbia than his own men were. At the time, the only Union troops present at Columbia were portions of three regiments, in all about 800 men under Brigadier General Thomas Ruger. Capron's 8:00 P.M. estimate that the enemy was in superior force and that he would be compelled to retreat to Columbia had caused Ruger to appeal to Schofield on the night of the 23d for more troops. Schofield issued a 1:00 A.M. order on the 24th for Cox's infantry division, then in advance ten miles beyond Lynnville, and also Stanley's two divisions, to march immediately to Columbia. Cox received Schofield's order at 4:00 A.M. and had his troops awoken at once.[17]

The footrace was on, and Cox, in the vanguard, had his men on the march at 5:00 A.M. "We [had] expected to get our breakfast," wrote one of Cox's sergeants, "[but] just as we were putting our coffee to heating the bugle sounded. . . . I well knew there was something in the wind." Briefly halting only once, Cox's three brigades hastened on with empty stomachs. The sun was about an hour high, remembered a soldier, when suddenly their command was ordered off the road. Abruptly they marched briskly westward along a side road, then across the fields toward the Mount Pleasant pike. Firing was heard nearly two miles distant, and with quickening heartbeats the men rushed hurriedly onward.[18]

His men were just in time, said Cox. Thundering down the road appeared Capron's horsemen, "in hasty retreat" with Chalmers's gray riders close upon their heels. Cox rapidly deployed his two leading brigades on either side of the Mount Pleasant road and with a few volleys brought the pursuit to a halt. The lieutenant colonel of the 15th Tennessee Cavalry was killed while trying to wrest a flag from a Federal color-bearer. With three batteries and two brigades in their front, Chalmers's men were unable to force their way across Bigby Creek and soon pulled back. The gaunt gray cavalrymen had to be content with seizing a nearby flour mill and sniping at Cox from long range.[19]

Hood had lost the race to Columbia. Later he learned that the contest hadn't even been close. Orlando Moore's Brigade of the Twenty-third Corps had arrived at Columbia at 2:30 A.M., following an all-night ride on the railroad from Johnsonville. Stanley's two divisions, marching rapidly from Lynn-ville, came up beginning at 10:00 A.M. and soon began entrenching next to Cox along the line fronting Bigby Creek. Hood's closest infantry at the time were well south of Mount Pleasant, being more than thirty miles distant. Even if Chalmers had managed to enter Columbia against the garrison troops, he soon would have been driven out by Schofield's reinforcements.[20]

Far from disappointed, Sam Hood was found on the afternoon of November 25th by Chaplain Charles T. Quintard as "in the best of health and spirits, and full of hope as to the results of the present movement." S. D. Lee's Corps had begun marching at early dawn, and by nightfall they went into camp just north of Mount Pleasant. Along the route they had encountered about forty Yankee prisoners, taken on the 23d, now glumly going to the rear. Everybody seemed to be in buoyant spirits, and Hood dispatched a message to Beauregard saying that the enemy had abandoned Pulaski and were moving toward Nashville. Plenty of mills were now in the Confederates' possession, said Hood, and there would be no further difficulty about supplies.[21]

Although the rain that began that night continued throughout the 26th, Hood's men pushed relentlessly on toward Columbia. The route was via the Mount Pleasant and Columbia pike, with a hard surface, and thankfully there was no mud to contend with, noted a Texas soldier. The lush countryside was in marked contrast to the scraggly, undergrowth-laced timber and impoverished land they had passed north of the Alabama border. This was "one of the gardens of the world," thought Captain F. Halsey Wigfall of Hood's staff. "The lands are very fertile, the plantations well improved, and the people before the war were in the possession of every luxury. . . . There has been no part of the Confederacy that I have seen which has been in [the enemy's] possession and has suffered so little." In an aside, he candidly noted that the lack of destruction apparently was due to the fact that many of the citizens had adopted a "twice serving policy"—of taking oaths "of all sorts" in order to keep their property inviolate.[22]

Five miles south of Columbia lay the magnificent Polk plantation. It was the site of four separate Polk residences, including "Hamilton Place," the home of Lucius J. Polk, the brother of the recently deceased Lieutenant General Leonidas Polk. The Polk family had donated for the use of the community their Gothic chapel, fashioned of red brick, with ivy-covered walls. Known as St. John's Episcopal Church, this elegant little structure stood amid a grove of tall magnolia trees, with the Polk family cemetery in the rear. For many it truly seemed to be God's acre, a beautiful spot replete with an Old World nostalgia and a deep, romantic atmosphere. It was "the prettiest place I have ever seen in my life," thought a soldier of Cleburne's Division who marched past on the 26th. In the drizzling rain, Pat Cleburne visited the spot, walking among the grave sites near the church. It reminded him of Athnowen churchyard in Ireland, his father's burial place, which had a similar charm. Cleburne was deeply affected.[23]

That evening John Bell Hood established his headquarters at the Ashwood Hall residence of Colonel Andrew J. Polk, across the road from St. John's Church. During the afternoon the Louisiana regiment's band had played for the local residents, even as Stephen D. Lee's Corps advanced to confront the busily entrenching Federals on the outskirts of Columbia.[24]

The following day, Sunday, November 27th, the rain continued at intervals throughout the daylight hours as the remainder of Hood's army moved into position around Columbia. It was an auspicious occasion. For the first time since October, Hood's entire army was again closely confronting a major enemy force. With Lee's Corps on the left, Stewart's in the middle, and Cheatham's on the right, the Army of Tennessee now completely encircled the fortified perimeter of Columbia. Forrest's cavalry, as a result, were relieved and sent beyond the right flank for some much-needed rest.[25]

Hood, during the 27th, transferred his headquarters to the home of Mrs. Amos Warfield, located on the Pulaski pike several miles closer to Columbia. When joined by Chaplain Quintard that evening, Hood was found to be in a pensive mood. His army at last confronted the enemy, and he realized that the time was at hand for decisive action. The Confederate commander had been thinking ahead—to the capture of Nashville. Confidentially, he told Quintard about his scheme of using 700 volunteers for what apparently would be a suicidal attempt to storm "the key of the works about the city." These 700 would be martyrs, the deeply moved Quintard recorded in his diary.[26]

It was, of course, a fantastic and unlikely scheme, typical of Hood's aggressiveness. Yet Hood had to first think of getting to Nashville ahead of Schofield's troops, who now defiantly blocked his way at Columbia.

There seems to have been little doubt in Hood's mind about what to do. Schofield's entrenched position at Columbia seemed too strong to easily assail. Taking a page from the hard-earned lessons of Sherman's campaign for Atlanta, the obvious way to reach Nashville ahead of Schofield was to go around him. Already Cheatham's Corps, on the right flank, had been ordered on the 27th to make preparations to cross the Duck River east of town. With the enemy entrenched along the south shore, and encumbered by wagons and artillery, it was apparent to Hood that they would have difficulty keeping pace with his men as they marched north toward Nashville. However, a major problem existed. The Duck River was so swollen from the recent rains that the many fords were now too deep to cross without a bridge. The pontoon train, en route from Florence, Alabama, was partially being drawn by Texas longhorn steers, so depleted was Hood's transportation system following October's forced marches. In place of horses and mules, the slower, more difficult to manage cattle had lagged far behind even the supply wagons. Thus, Hood would have to wait another day for the arrival of his pontoons.[27]

That night, said Quintard, Hood spent much of the evening talking about his religious convictions. He professed an earnest trust in God, and "such deep religious feelings that I could plainly discern the Holy Spirits work[ing] upon his heart," thought the chaplain.[28]

Amazingly, the following morning it appeared as if God's purpose might be moving to fruition through the plans of John Bell Hood. The enemy had unexpectedly evacuated Columbia during the night, passing to the north shore, where they had fortified along a ridge about a mile and a half beyond the river. The weather had finally cleared, and November 28th would be warm and bright. Even the rivers were falling. At first light, the men of Stephen D. Lee's Corps had occupied Columbia, bringing artillery forward to the high ground along the south riverbank. The people of Columbia seemed to be in a state of "the wildest enthusiasm," wrote an observer. Hood had the Yankees on the run.[29]

With the arrival that day of a telegram from General Beauregard, forwarded by courier, the campaign's success seemed to be foreordained. Beauregard reported from Macon, Georgia, on the 24th that Sherman's movements were progressing rapidly toward the Atlantic seacoast, "doubtless to reinforce Grant." The severely harassed Beauregard urged, "It is essential you should take [the] offensive and crush [the] enemy's forces in Middle Tennessee soon as practicable, to relieve Lee." Hood, now further aware that the government would be looking to his success for direct relief from the building pressure on Robert E. Lee, immediately wrote to Richmond with a copy to Beauregard that the enemy had evacuated Columbia, and "are retreating toward Nashville." His army was moving forward, wrote Hood reassuringly. The tenor of his entire message exuded the fullest confidence.[30]

There was good reason for his optimism. Hood had conceived what he later termed the most brilliant plan of his career. Fully remembering Sherman's successful Atlanta maneuvering, Hood now slightly revised his earlier plan to outflank the enemy's position. Since Schofield was on the north bank, the need for greater rapidity in movement was apparent. Hood had learned from the local residents in his army of the various accessible fords east of Columbia. The pontoon train was close at hand, and he would therefore "press forward with all possible speed" and "either beat the enemy to Nashville, or make him go there at a double quick." In order to outmarch Schofield, his troops would move in "light marching order," leaving nearly all of their artillery behind. Most of S. D. Lee's Corps also would stay at Columbia to demonstrate against Schofield's position and hold him in place as long as possible. Perhaps Lee's presence might even deceive the enemy commander as to Hood's movements. In order to clear the way for the infantry, Forrest's cavalry would drive back the Federal cavalry guarding the various Duck River fords.[31]

It was a bold plan, with its success dependent only on proper execution.

Many of Hood's men were now home. The "Maury Grays," Company H of the 1st Tennessee Infantry, had left Columbia in 1861 with 120 men. Now there were 12 left of that original number, and only 20 men comprised the entire company. Other local men had joined such units as the 24th and 45th Tennessee Infantry, and Jake Biffle's regiment of horse (9th Tennessee Cavalry). With home sentiment running at a fever pitch, a few men were allowed liberty to visit relatives, and portions of the 45th Tennessee were furloughed for a few days.[32]

That morning, November 28th, the Confederate army, led by two regiments, the 3rd and 18th Tennessee, had rushed into downtown Columbia before daylight. The impoverished and deprived status of the troops was fully evident in the indiscriminate pillaging that occurred before additional troops arrived. Soldiers broke into stores, destroyed property, and consumed liquor. At the Athenaeum School building the soldiers carried off bedding, and even school desks to burn for fuel. The Athenaeum's gutters were torn down and cut into short sections which were soon punched so full of holes that they resembled "nutmeg graters." They were used for grinding corn into meal, said a citizen, who noted that the men humorously called them "Arm-strong mills." Hood issued field orders condemning the plundering, but let the men off without punishment. His orders merely announced that if "example and moral suasion" were not productive of better behavior, "harsher means will be used."[33]

Other troops from Carter L. Stevenson's Division had rushed into the abandoned stone fort known as Fort Mizner and secured two siege howitzers left behind by the enemy. Their belated attempts to save the two end sections of the railroad bridge over the Duck River failed, however, and the flames cast an eerie glow over the countryside that morning.[34]

By midmorning, with orders for Forrest's cavalry to swing wide to the east and cross the Duck River, there was hasty movement in the cavalry camps. Forrest's men were sent via backwoods roads beyond the mouth of Fountain Creek to four separate fords along the Duck River. His gray troopers had to swim their horses due to the swollen river, but three crossings were made during the late afternoon of the 28th in the face of feeble resistance from the Federal cavalry. Jackson's Division got across at Carr's Mill, nine miles east of Columbia; Chalmers's men crossed at Holland's Ford seven miles east of the town, and Forrest, with Biffle's regiment, swam the river at Owen's Ford, about five miles east of Columbia. Only Buford's Division, meeting strong resistance from Capron's reinforced brigade, now about 1,800 strong following the arrival of two new cavalry regiments, was unable to force a crossing at Hardison's Mill on the Lewisburg pike.[35]

After riding eastward to cut off the Federal cavalry opposing Buford in the gathering darkness of evening, one of Forrest's brigades successfully scattered Capron's rear guard. The enemy force at the ford was then forced to cut their way through a line of blazing Confederate carbines in order to escape capture. Buford's men thereafter were enabled to cross, and by the morning of the 29th, Forrest had concentrated his entire command near Rally Hill, about thirteen miles northeast of Columbia. The route for Hood's infantry to cross the Duck River was now wide open. Even more importantly, Forrest had essentially removed the enemy's cavalry from its primary role as the eyes and ears of the Federal army.[36]

Earlier that morning, a local youth, Wash Gordon of the 1st Tennessee Infantry, had taken Hood's acting chief engineer, Lieutenant Colonel Stephen W. Presstman, to Davis's Ford, only four miles east of Columbia. Incredibly, Davis's Ford was unguarded. Evidently the enemy knew little of its former status as a crossing point for one of the two major thoroughfares of the region. Presstman was easily convinced of the practical nature of the ford and directed a unit of sappers and miners to clear the approaches for pontoons. Throughout the afternoon the work continued, and the pontoon train was ordered up from Columbia.[37]

Hauled by emaciated, plodding steers, the slow-moving pontoon train moved east from Columbia on East 9th Street and was easily observed as it passed Burns Spring from the Federal-held ridge north of town. Federal artillery opened fire on the slow-moving pontoons, but their fire was inaccurate and little damage occurred. By the evening of the 28th, Presstman's engineers were busily working on emplacing the pontoons, and before daybreak the bridge was ready for use.[38]

John Bell Hood appeared to have gained a decided advantage. Matters were going so well that he told Chaplain Quintard that night how in the morning he would "go through the woods" in order to beat the enemy to Nashville. Schofield, he thought, would withdraw from his position near Columbia before morning. It would probably be a close race. Tomorrow would be an important day in Hood's life, he seemed to realize, and he planned to rise well before daylight. At dawn his army would begin their advance.[39]

Remembering the fiasco involving Hardee's flanking march on July 22d at Atlanta—when his troops took the wrong roads—Hood had resolved to go personally with the advance on November 29th. He considered that he had learned his lesson well. Hood did not intend to leave such important matters for others to again mismanage.

In his uniform pocket was a regional map. His local guide was present. Nothing seemed to be left to chance.[40]

CHAPTER XII

Playing Both Ends
Against the Middle

JOHN MCALLISTER SCHOFIELD LOOKED the part of perhaps a rogue banker with the glint of evil in his eye. He was a stocky, ruddy-faced man with a decidedly dumpy appearance, and his short stature, long patriarchal beard, balding head, and beady, squinting eyes made him appear almost comical, if somehow sinister. A West Point graduate, Class of 1853, he had been John Bell Hood's classmate. Schofield had graduated seventh in his class of fifty-five, but ranked first in infantry tactics. The son and grandson of ordained ministers, Schofield was an adept politician with a flair for cultivating the right connections. Indeed, his army career reflected his polished social aptitude.[1]

After resigning his commission in 1860 to teach physics at Washington University in St. Louis, Schofield had rejoined the army at the outbreak of the Civil War. A few early campaigns in Missouri had resulted in his brigadier's star during November 1861. Then, after his promotion to major general of volunteers in May 1863, he assumed command of the Department of Ohio in February 1864 following extensive lobbying for the post. By further politicking through top officials, including his former commander, Henry Halleck, Schofield had arranged an assignment with Sherman's consolidated armies in 1864. As commander of the Twenty-third Corps (Army of the Ohio) during the Atlanta Campaign, Schofield had served with rather modest distinction.[2]

Vain and highly ambitious, the rotund thirty-three-year-old Illinois general had on November 14th assumed the in-field command over Thomas's two corps deployed in mid-Tennessee due to seniority in assignment. Since Schofield was a department commander, whereas David S. Stanley, the senior major general by date of rank, commanded only a corps, Schofield was given the overall command based on the interpretation of Schofield's friend, Halleck. Yet Sherman rated Schofield with only modest marks; he was "slow and leaves too much to others," said Sherman after Atlanta. He even had to mildly reprimand Schofield in late September for going home to Illinois when "you should be with your army."[3]

Schofield's combat experience was not extensive, and once present at Pulaski, Tennessee, in mid-November 1864, his nervousness was soon apparent. Since George H. Thomas's instructions required Schofield to delay the enemy as much as possible until A. J. Smith's troops arrived, he had sought to present a firm front despite his anxiety about the exposed position at Pulaski.[4]

An unpleasant surprise occurred on the morning of November 24th when it appeared that Hood had lunged ahead of Schofield's slowly retreating forces and was about to capture Columbia. On the 21st Schofield had resolutely told Thomas: "I do not believe Hood can get this far [Pulaski], if he attempts it, while the roads are so bad, and [A. J.] Smith may be able to join us before they get better. It will be well to avoid the appearance of retreating when it is not necessary."[5]

However, when advised of the enemy's rapid advance by Hatch's cavalry that same afternoon, Schofield quickly had secured Thomas's permission to evacuate Pulaski and concentrate at Columbia. On the afternoon of the 24th he predicted that an assault on Columbia by Hood's main force would occur, if at all, on the following day. Yet Schofield's information was woefully lacking. Hood's infantry actually was many miles behind and did not come up to Columbia until the 26th and 27th.[6]

Immediately following Schofield's arrival at Columbia about noon on the 24th, he rearranged the town's defenses. Cox's and Stanley's troops were busily entrenching along the Mount Pleasant pike, where the original perimeter had been established by Cox during that morning's action with the Confederate cavalry. Worried that there was too much ground to defend and not enough troops, Schofield, late that afternoon, ordered a new, "interior" line constructed to cover primarily the railroad bridge, two miles west of town. Further, he decided to cross all but 7,000 of his men to the north bank, to be "ready to move as necessary." With the fords above and below town well guarded, Schofield assured Thomas, "I think Hood cannot get the start of me."[7]

After learning on the afternoon of the 24th that only Confederate cavalry were present in front of his Columbia defenses, Schofield completely revised his estimate of Hood's movements for the third time in twenty-four hours. Following receipt of Hatch's 4:00 P.M. dispatch, and only forty-five minutes after having told Thomas he anticipated Hood's attack on Columbia during the following day, Schofield informed Thomas, "The indications are that Hood gave up his movement on Columbia this morning and is now going toward Pulaski."[8]

*   *   *

Schofield's men found Columbia much to their liking, despite being filled with troops and refugees from the Pulaski area. Due to the Confederate conscription law which required all men between the ages of seventeen and fifty to serve the government, a vast exodus of unwilling residents and a bewildered throng of Negro refugees had choked the roads for miles around. They swarmed everywhere, wrote a Michigan cavalryman, who took particular note of the procession of "darkeys." Each family seemed to be led by a "big buck" laden with household belongings, followed by the women and children carrying all manner of articles on their heads. "All [were] fleeing in terror from the advancing Rebel army as [if] from a pestilence," he noted.[9]

In Columbia the houses were appropriated for military use as needed. Several residences that became obstructions between the entrenched lines were burned down by Schofield's men, "due to military necessity." Other residents found their homes occupied by ranking Federal officers and their staffs. The fine home of Joseph H. James, Columbia's most prominent jeweler, was occupied on the ground floor by Federal officers, and the furniture and piano put out in the yard. For three days and nights the James family lived upstairs while the Yankees made firewood of their picket fence and even one piano leg. James had buried a large jar of his most valuable watches, rings, and gold jewelry under a small cherry tree at the corner of his house. Since the dwelling was within the principal Federal line of defense, entrenchments were dug in the yard during the night of November 24th. Sure enough, a Union soldier discovered the jar, and the following morning James sadly observed his loss.[10]

Schofield established his headquarters at the Athenaeum, near the Corinthian Hall building where Nathan Bedford Forrest had been seriously shot during an altercation with one of his own lieutenants in 1863. Although found to be "courteous and affable" by local residents, Schofield, like his soldiers, was said to be "looking for warm times."[11]

Schofield intended to cross most of the Fourth Corps to the north bank of the Duck River after dark on November 26th, leaving little more than two divisions in a beachhead about the railroad bridge. Yet the rain made the roads almost impassable, said David S. Stanley's chief of staff. Accordingly, it became "almost impossible" for wagons to move down the riverbank in the mud, water, and darkness. Even Schofield's personal baggage wagon was upset and his bedding thoroughly soaked. When two of the pontoon boats sank under the swirling, rising waters at midnight, the attempt to cross was called off.[12]

During the 27th Hood's entire army was observed moving into position at Columbia, confronting the weakened outer line. Only a single Union division, Thomas J. Wood's of the Fourth Corps, and Thomas J. Henderson's brigade of the Twenty-third Corps held the entire outer perimeter. His line had been "stretched out like an India rubber string" since the 25th, said

Wood, and he bitterly complained about having to cover an "enormous" front with a single rank.[13]

Due to interrupted telegraphic communications, Schofield had not heard from Thomas beyond his 11:20 A.M. wire of the 25th. A large number of guerrillas were said to be infesting the countryside between Franklin and Columbia, tearing down the wires. Beginning on the 26th a line of couriers was established between these sites to relay telegrams. The only message to get through on the 26th warned Schofield that if it was necessary to withdraw to the Duck River's north bank, Thomas wanted cavalry kept on the south side to delay Hood's apparent attempt to move eastward and strike the Chattanooga railroad. "If you can hold Hood on the south side of Duck River, I think we shall be able to drive him back easily after concentrating," said Thomas.[14]

Schofield pondered his situation. The rain was swelling the rivers to overflowing. Reports that all the Duck River fords were impassable except by swimming made it apparent that Hood would be delayed in any flanking movement. With Wilson's cavalry covering the eastern fords over the expanse of more than a dozen miles, it appeared he would have adequate warning of any enemy crossing. Nonetheless, early on the morning of the 27th Schofield became convinced that Hood was working eastward, intending to cross the Duck River as close to Columbia as possible. The source of this information was probably one of Capron's scouts. "Though not very satisfactory," it was strongly credited by Schofield.[15]

Heightening the Federal general's concern was the receipt that day of fresh information about Hood's strength and direction of movement, obtained from an unlooked-for source. Three Confederate privates of 1st Tennessee Infantry, furloughed on the 26th to visit their nearby homes, had paddled across the Duck River in a canoe and were picked up by Capron's cavalrymen near Davis's Ford early in the morning of the 27th. One of the men provided extensive data about Hood's army, revealing unit strengths, and that the right of the Confederate line would rest near Huey's Mill, about seven miles east of Columbia.[16]

Accordingly, Schofield became convinced before noon on the 27th that Hood "does not intend to attack [at Columbia]," but would go north across the Duck River via the eastern flank. In response, he devised a conservative plan intended to provide maximum flexibility. Schofield would concentrate his entire force north of Columbia, ready to contest "any attempt the enemy may make to cross," which is what Thomas wanted. Yet he would not greatly risk the defeat of his army.[17]

Amazingly, Schofield had made these decisions not only while Hood's infantry was still en route to Columbia, but evidently before the Rebel commander even had finalized his specific plans![18]

Anticipating that the abandonment of Columbia would greatly concern Thomas, who wanted Hood held south of the Duck River, Schofield rather apologetically telegraphed to his commander early on the morning of the 28th. "I regret extremely the necessity of withdrawing from Columbia, but believe it was absolute," said Schofield. "I will explain fully in time."[19]

Schofield was torn between his conservative inclination to risk little in a confrontation with Hood until reinforced, and Thomas's expectation that he would hold the enemy back, at least until the arrival of A. J. Smith. Yet playing both ends against the middle had its drawbacks, as John Schofield soon learned.[20]

Jacob Cox had cautioned him after crossing to the north shore early on the morning of the 26th that the peninsula of land opposite Columbia, with its much lower elevation, was not suitable for defensive purposes. Thus, the only nearby high ground on the north side, a ridge that ran about a mile and a half distant from and parallel to Columbia, was selected for the new main defensive line. The immense wagon train of supplies and ammunition, already having been sent across the river, was now at Rutherford Creek, about four miles north on the road to Spring Hill. Here they were safe from the enemy's guns firing from the bluffs at Columbia.[21]

With the Duck River falling on the 28th, Schofield realized that there were too many fordable places to prevent the enemy's cavalry from crossing. But Schofield, being preoccupied with details involving communications and the army's relocation, felt James H. Wilson's cavalrymen would "hold the crossings near us and watch the distant ones." Meanwhile, the sound of active skirmishing and occasional long-range artillery duels reverberated through the air in front of Columbia during the bright and clear morning of November 28th as Confederate infantry and artillery began moving into town and along the high southern riverbank.[22]

Shortly after 2:00 P.M. on the 28th Schofield had sudden word of enemy activity to the east. Wilson, at cavalry headquarters four miles east of Columbia, had just learned from Colonel Horace Capron that the enemy, presumed to be cavalry, were "crossing in force" above Huey's Mill. Schofield, already alarmed by an earlier report that Confederate infantry might be crossing the Duck River, ordered Wilson to investigate and report back. At 2:10 P.M. Wilson received another dispatch from Capron that his detachments sent to scout the south bank had been driven back across the river, and he was, at 11:20 A.M., fighting a heavy force at the Lewisburg pike crossing site. Wilson sensed a crisis brewing, and began moving his cavalry "in that direction."[23]

In fact, after confirming the presence of a large enemy force at the ford on the Lewisburg pike (Hardison's Mill), Wilson reacted decisively. He ordered the bulk of his entire cavalry corps to concentrate at Hurt's Crossroads, some five miles north of the Hardison's Mill ford. Both Croxton's brigade and Hatch's division had been watching the lower river crossings, and by midafternoon their troopers were at Hurt's Crossroads, where they erected barricades across the macadamized Lewisburg pike.[24]

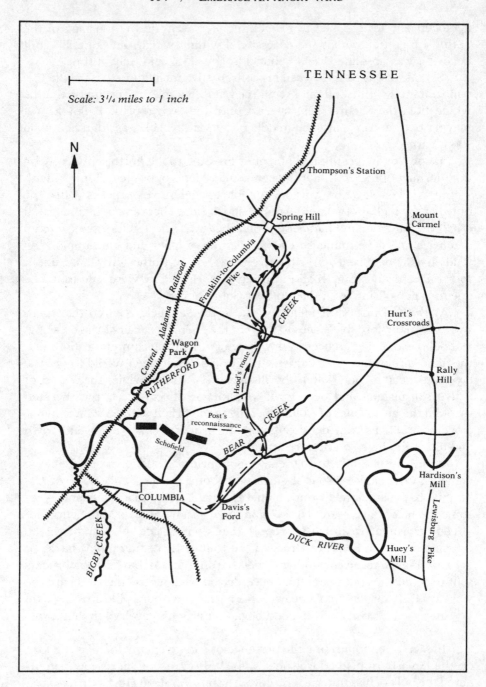

TENNESSEE

Scale: 3¹/₄ miles to 1 inch

N

Thompson's Station

Spring Hill

Mount Carmel

Franklin-to-Columbia Pike

Central Alabama Railroad

CREEK

Hurt's Crossroads

Wagon Park

Hood's route

RUTHERFORD

Rally Hill

Post's reconnaissance

BEAR

CREEK

Schofield

Hardison's Mill

COLUMBIA

Davis's Ford

Lewisburg Pike

BIGBY CREEK

DUCK RIVER

Huey's Mill

Map 3   March to Spring Hill—November 29

The brash twenty-seven-year-old Wilson had made a big mistake. The Federal cavalry having been pulled back from the Duck River fords west of Capron's position, during the late afternoon Forrest was able to cross three large units at the vacated fords without serious opposition. Lawrence S. Ross's Brigade of Jackson's Division was thereafter able to swing east unnoticed along the Shelbyville road and suddenly strike the reserve elements of Capron's brigade posted at the Lewisburg pike crossroads. Capron and a newly arrived regiment held in reserve there, the 7th Ohio Cavalry, were stampeded after "a spirited engagement." An entire company of the 7th Ohio Cavalry was captured along with several flags. Furthermore, although unknown to Ross's men, the remainder of Capron's brigade had been cut off at the Hardison's Mill ford.[25]

Major J. Morris Young, with the 5th Iowa Cavalry, had joined Capron's brigade only several days earlier. Having at midday repulsed the attempt of Buford's entire division to cross at Hardison's Mill ford, at 4:30 P.M. Young's men remained unengaged. The sun was setting, and across the river they could see Buford's cavalrymen building fires and killing hogs. Suddenly there was firing in the rear, and Young learned from several fleeing men that Capron with the reserves had been attacked and routed. Realizing that he was trapped, Young hurriedly formed his brigade and ordered a cautious retreat north along the Lewisburg pike. About 5:30 P.M. Young's men suddenly encountered Ross's full brigade, barricaded in the "outhouses and buildings" recently evacuated by Capron. At the head of the 5th Iowa Cavalry, Young immediately ordered the charge sounded and sent his men thundering over and past Ross's men with sabers flashing. It was a most gallant affair, wrote Young. "The groans and cries of the [enemy's] wounded, as we rode, cut, or shot them down could be heard distinctly above the noise and din of the charge." His loss, due to the darkness, amounted to only about 30 men from the 1,500 troopers present.[26]

The escape of Young's command hardly solved Wilson's growing problems. At sunset, with Hatch's and Croxton's men still barricaded at Hurt's Crossroads, it appeared to Wilson that Forrest's cavalry, having crossed west of the Lewisburg pike, were en route to Spring Hill. At 4:30 P.M. he sent an urgent message to Schofield saying "you had better look out for that place," and that he was still trying to collect his force together. Soon there was more grim news. After interrogating a prisoner—one of Forrest's cavalrymen captured that night along a road near Rally Hill—at 1:00 A.M. on the 29th Wilson sent Schofield new and dramatic information. Confederate infantry were reportedly poised to cross during the night on pontoons in the wake of the cavalry. The prisoner, said Wilson, had thoroughly described the building of the pontoons that evening, and said that the bridging was expected to be completed by 11:00 P.M.[27]

Wilson was both aroused and alarmed. The enemy's infantry certainly would be across between 1:00 A.M. and daylight, he warned. "I think it very clear that they are aiming for Franklin, and that you ought to get to Spring Hill by 10:00 A.M. I'll keep on this road [Lewisburg pike] and hold the enemy all I can." In closing, Wilson almost outstepped the boundaries of propriety, saying: "Get back to Franklin without delay, leaving a small force to detain the enemy. The rebels will move by this road toward that point."[28]

Somehow, either the original courier got lost or was turned back, and two hours later another dispatch had to be sent. By the time a second copy of the message was prepared and a new courier obtained, it was 3:00 A.M. On the outside of the envelope instructions were written to the courier: "Important, Trot!" Due to the roundabout route, he had to travel a distance of about twenty miles. About 7:00 A.M. the courier finally trotted into Schofield's camp.[29]

II

John M. Schofield had spent a very frustrating afternoon on November 28th attempting to make some sense out of the events then occurring. From his headquarters north of Columbia he had at first scoffed at the prospect of Confederate infantry crossing in Wilson's front, saying at 3:30 P.M., "The force is reported to be infantry, but I do not regard it as very probable." The enemy's infantry had been observed in Columbia since morning, and his artillerymen were busily emplacing batteries, signs that Hood was still in Schofield's front. Yet during the afternoon a Rebel pontoon train was fired on as it moved eastward out of Columbia. Schofield, anxiously waiting for further reports from Wilson, began to consider the option of a withdrawal should the Federal cavalry be unable to push Forrest's gray riders back. He queried Thomas about where he proposed to fight if Hood advanced, and asked him to replace the washed-out bridge at Franklin with pontoons. Obviously, Schofield was looking toward retreating beyond the Harpeth River, if necessary.[30]

Shortly after 5:00 P.M., word arrived from infantry Colonel Abel D. Streight, posted on the extreme left flank of the Fourth Corps line, that at least two regiments of Confederate cavalry had crossed the Duck River a short distance from his position. Brigadier General Thomas J. Wood, Streight's division commander, was astounded to learn that all Federal cavalry pickets had been withdrawn from the river. "As the country is open the whole Rebel army may be over on our left flank without hindrance," wrote the aroused Wood to his corps commander, David Stanley.[31]

Schofield, also having just learned of Wilson's cavalry's pull back, was upset. In an abrupt note to Wilson he chided his cavalry commander for withdrawing so many of his troopers, pointing out that the enemy's cavalry had crossed "very near the left of our infantry." Wilson was told to see to replacing these men. "The river in our immediate vicinity should not be left without cavalry pickets," he warned.[32]

Yet at 5:20 P.M. it was nearly dark, and for the moment there seemed to be little further danger. Schofield merely wrote a perfunctory note to Stanley about guarding the army's wagon train. However, with the arrival a few minutes later of Wilson's 4:30 P.M. dispatch, Schofield again became concerned. He wired Thomas telling him that the Confederate cavalry had seized Rally Hill, about a dozen miles distant to the east. Through Stanley, Schofield then ordered two of Brigadier General Nathan Kimball's infantry brigades to proceed to Rutherford Creek "without delay" and guard the army's vast wagon train park.[33]

Yet that was the extent of Schofield's response. He opted to wait for additional information before altering any major troop dispositions. Despite the apparent Confederate cavalry thrust on his flank, there was no report of enemy infantry involvement. His basic plan, in fact, remained unchanged—to move to confront Hood and prevent his crossing the Duck River only if a major movement was in progress, not merely a cavalry raid. Contesting a cavalry thrust was Wilson's responsibility.[34]

In order to clarify the nature of the present Confederate movement, however, Schofield ordered a reconnaissance patrol to go out and determine "whether anything can be seen of the enemy."

Again, the basis for Schofield's actions had been rooted in one of Thomas's communiques, just received at 6:00 P.M. Thomas wrote that A. J. Smith would certainly arrive at Nashville by December 1st, and that as U. S. Grant was pressing for the Federal forces to take the offensive, seemingly in three days "we will be able to commence moving on Hood."[35]

Thomas J. Wood was thoroughly exasperated. The hard-luck veteran regular who had become the unwitting scapegoat at Chickamauga for the fatal gap created due to Rosecrans's direct order was not willing to suffer another fiasco based on a superior's incompetence. In a candid note to Stanley he remarked: "It seems to me a little strange that General Schofield does not intimate what measures he proposes to adopt to protect ourselves and guard our trains, and still more strange that he does not initiate such measures at once, as the enemy, according to his own statement, has crossed the river in force. It is perfectly patent to my mind, if the enemy has crossed in force, that General Wilson will not be able to check him. It requires no oracle to predict the effect of the enemy's reaching the Franklin pike in our rear." Acting on his own responsibility, Wood thus ordered out two companies of the 51st Indiana regiment, a total of about 150 men, posting them about a mile beyond his line to watch for the enemy. Further, Wood told Stanley that two of Kimball's brigades should at once be brought eastward, to cover the open ground there. In the event of an attack, said Wood, as matters now stood, "we could not extricate our trains, [and] possibly not ourselves." Thereafter, Stanley rescinded the order for Kimball's second brigade to march north to

Rutherford Creek that night, saying they should wait until daylight on the 29th.[36]

By the time the reconnaissance patrol ordered by Schofield was ready to depart, it was 9:00 P.M. and too dark "to look for the cavalry that has crossed above us." Wood's 150-man outpost thus remained the only Federal unit sent east beyond the infantry's lines.[37]

That night at Schofield's headquarters there was little new information, only an ambiguous 8:30 P.M. report from Wilson stating that Confederate prisoners had reported "Hood is going to flank us on one side or the other."[38]

Shortly after 7:00 A.M. the following morning, November 29th, Schofield received an enormous jolt. Wilson's urgent 1:00 A.M. dispatch finally arrived! Schofield immediately gave Stanley orders to move two divisions promptly to Spring Hill. Also, he ordered the wagon train to proceed there from Rutherford Creek as rapidly as possible. Even Thomas Ruger's division of the Twenty-third Corps, posted near the railroad bridge site, was ordered at 8:00 A.M. to retreat at once to Spring Hill with all but one regiment, which was left behind to "guard the river."[39]

After conferring with Stanley and Wood, Schofield had no thoughts of moving to confront Hood. Instead, he was proceeding only as if to escape a possible trap.

Less than an hour after Wilson's message arrived, another came from General Thomas, dated 8:00 P.M. November 28th. Thomas had been so badgered by Ulysses Grant about taking the offensive that, with the prospect of A. J. Smith's troops being soon present, he decided to assume an offensive posture. Unaware of the events then transpiring near Columbia, Thomas telegraphed: "If you are confident you can hold your present position, I wish you to do so until I can get General Smith here. After his arrival we can withdraw gradually, and invite Hood across the Duck River and fall upon him with our whole force, or wait until Wilson can organize his entire cavalry force, and then withdraw from your present position. Should Hood then cross the river we surely can ruin him."[40]

The tenor of Thomas's message was unmistakable. He wanted Schofield to stay put unless absolutely compelled to fall back. A second and later dispatch from Thomas, received by the same courier, responded to the preliminary news of an enemy crossing. Thomas advised: "If Wilson cannot succeed in driving back the enemy, should it prove true that he has crossed the river, you will necessarily have to make preparations to take up a new position at Franklin, behind [the] Harpeth [River], immediately, if it becomes necessary to fall back."[41]

Although permission to withdraw was clearly at hand, the expectations of Thomas heavily weighed on Schofield's mind. The key to the matter seemed to be the necessity of falling back. Was Schofield absolutely sure Hood was moving with infantry across the Duck River?

Now there was a new development. Confederate artillery had just opened with a heavy and sustained barrage on the Federal positions north of Columbia. With the enemy's artillery and various units of his infantry clearly present in front, would Hood be so brash as to leave these behind during a major flanking march? Suddenly Schofield wasn't so sure what his former classmate, Hood, was attempting to do.[42]

Because Wilson's cavalrymen had been withdrawn or driven back, he had little basis for obtaining reliable information from that source. The reconnaissance ordered for the past evening had not advanced due to darkness. Although his cavalrymen were supposed to be the eyes and ears of the army, Schofield now had little choice but to use the slower-moving infantry. About 8:15 A.M. he ordered a new reconnaissance patrol from Wood's division, to leave as soon as possible and "learn the fact" as to any crossing by the enemy's infantry.[43]

Meanwhile, Schofield suspended the general orders to retreat, telling Ruger's division only to make preparations to leave. Although he allowed Stanley to continue getting ready to march to Spring Hill as an escort to the wagon train, he soon ordered Stanley's second division, Kimball's, to halt and wait at Rutherford Creek. At 8:20 A.M. Schofield telegraphed to Thomas that he would act according to his "instructions" received that morning. Thereafter, Schofield simply awaited the result of his infantry's reconnaissance.[44]

Inspired by the uncertain debriefing of a prisoner, yet put off by the compelling if unrealistic wishes of Grant and Thomas for an imminent offensive movement, Schofield's original decision to withdraw had developed into a bizarre scenario. If Hood's method was brash aggression, Schofield, Hood's West Point superior as a tactician, had begun to act more the part of a vacillating and indecisive commander. Unmindful that to wait for developments in a crisis was tempting fate, Schofield had strung out his army over a large expanse of country, violating the very instructions that Thomas had so insisted on, even as repeated in the soon-to-be-famous 8:00 P.M. November 28th dispatch—to "concentrate your infantry."[45]

Schofield's combat inexperience was showing. His forthcoming confrontation with destiny was rapidly becoming a matter of luck.

CHAPTER XIII

The Spring Hill Races

JAMES H. WILSON WAS NOT only one of the youngest major generals in the Union army, he was one of the most fortunate. His promotion to command of the cavalry in the Military Division of the Mississippi was due mostly to his mentor and close friend, Ulysses S. Grant. Between January and December 1863 Wilson, at the age of twenty-six, had been jumped from a regular-army lieutenant to a brigadier general of volunteers. Little more than nine months later he was a brevet major general. It was just the kind of success to feed Wilson's large ego and expand his growing ambitions.[1]

As one of Grant's staff officers in 1862, Wilson had evidenced a strong drive to succeed, was quick to make bold decisions, and had been known as a man who would "get things done." While often impatient with superiors and subordinates alike, Wilson's volatile personality matched his boundless energy, high intellect, and strong determination. To many, including Grant, Wilson appeared to be a dynamic and gifted officer of outstanding promise.[2]

Following his promotion to brigadier general, Wilson had administered the newly created Cavalry Bureau in Washington, D.C. His stern, forthright handling of scheming cavalry horse contractors resulted in eliminating much corruption and bureaucratic inefficiency. It further marked him as an officer rapidly on the rise. When Grant came east in the spring of 1864, he summoned Wilson to cavalry division command under Philip Sheridan, while others such as George Custer and Henry E. Davies remained as brigade commanders.[3]

Despite having Grant's confidence, Wilson's weaknesses were equally as glaring. Nicknamed "Harry" at West Point, young Wilson was often brash, took criticism with ill-concealed rancor, and sought to shun blame for his failures by shifting responsibility onto others. When his men suffered heavy casualties after being trapped behind enemy lines in the Wilson-Kautz Railroad Raid of June and July 1864, Wilson's ego was much bruised. "The upstart and imbecile" Wilson, said George Custer in a private letter, had been defeated through his "total ignorance and inexperience" in field command of cavalry.[4]

Despite Custer's criticism, following a brief stint in the Shenandoah Valley Wilson got the big break he so ardently coveted. Again, through the influence of U. S. Grant, he was handed a most significant assignment. Sherman, following Atlanta, had remained frustrated by the lack of important success of his cavalry. In Sherman's discussions with Grant concerning the need for an energetic, bold, and aggressive commander, Wilson's name came to the forefront. Wilson, said Grant, "will add fifty percent to the effectiveness of your cavalry."[5]

Promoted to brevet major general and put in charge of Sherman's entire cavalry corps, Wilson came west in October 1864 riding the crest of his reputation as a "get things done reformer."[6]

Wilson, however, was driven by the need to be successful in deed as well as position. His attempt to thwart Forrest's veteran horsemen had met with little success during the enemy's advance toward Columbia. Further, when confronted by Forrest's flanking movement on November 28th, he had without consultation pulled most of his 3,500 cavalrymen back from the north riverbank. Wilson hoped to stop the gray riders' progress by this concentration. Instead, the immediate result was a serious gap in intelligence about enemy movements. The pressure Wilson soon felt was reflected by Schofield's curt order of that evening to restore the mounted pickets at the Duck River fords. Due to delay in transit, the early darkness of that time of year, and the confusion surrounding Forrest's advance, Wilson found it impractical to do so. Accordingly, at first light on the morning of November 29th Wilson seemed to be even in a worse predicament, both with his commander and with the enemy.[7]

His barricaded position at Hurt's Crossroads, he readily perceived, would be little deterrent to Forrest. Accordingly, at 4:00 A.M. Wilson ordered a retreat along the Lewisburg pike to Mount Carmel, a small village about five miles north.[8]

At daylight on the 29th William H. Jackson's 2,800-man division attacked Wilson's rear guard, Croxton's brigade, and a running fight began. When Jackson pressed too closely, Croxton dismounted several regiments and hastily built a barricade of rails and logs to fight off their pursuers. Several attacks were easily beaten back, said a Federal officer, who observed that Forrest's men were rapidly becoming very shy of barricades.[9]

Unknown to Croxton, Jackson's men were operating with deliberate restraint. In fact, the entire pursuit was a ruse. Forrest had directed the commander of Jackson's leading brigade not to press the enemy too vigorously. He wanted Chalmers's Division to have time to pass around Wilson's flank and strike the head of his column from the north.[10]

Hatch's division was on the road, with Datus Coon's brigade leading the withdrawal, as they approached Mount Carmel about 9:00 A.M. Ahead, Capron's small brigade was already in the village, hastily erecting rail barricades and preparing for Wilson's pending occupation.[11]

Suddenly Chalmers's men, led by Forrest, burst out of the nearby cedars, yelling and screaming "like legions of wild Comanches." Coon's troopers, mostly Illinois veterans armed with Spencer repeating carbines, dismounted and opened with such an intense volume of fire that Chalmers's cavalrymen were held back until the remainder of Hatch's division came forward.[12]

Wilson hurriedly put Hatch's men into the Mount Carmel defensive perimeter, but they were hardly in place before Croxton's brigade, closely pursued by Jackson's men, dashed back through Wilson's lines, jumping their horses over the low rail barricades west of the road. Croxton's men quickly took position along a nearby garden fence, and all braced for the coming onslaught.[13]

Within minutes Forrest's command swarmed out of the cedar thickets and a sharp fight began. Wilson posted an artillery battery to cover the creek front, and their guns roared incessantly. Several of the nearby dwellings were set afire, and amid a scene of the wildest confusion women and children were seen running along the road. In the yard of one small log house, two little toddlers sat playing, oblivious of the danger, their mother being too terrified to run out and rescue them. Abruptly, and most unexpectedly, the fighting ended.[14]

The Confederates were seen quickly withdrawing into the cedars, and Wilson's men shouted at the top of their lungs in triumph. By 10:00 A.M. the firing had nearly ended, and Wilson's aide dashed off a brief note to Schofield, saying that while the Union horsemen had been driven back to Mount Carmel, there was no evidence of anything but cavalry in their front.[15]

Wilson by now was thoroughly vexed, if not rattled. Already he had decided to further withdraw and "turn the command off the [main] road." Prominent in his mind was the prospect of Forrest again outflanking his position. The skillful Confederate leader had stolen the march on him that morning, and by hard riding had passed ahead of most of the Federal column. Wilson wanted no repetition of such an embarrassing event.[16]

Of further concern, while preparations began for another withdrawal, the enemy's activity in front continued to dwindle. This was further evidence to Wilson that Forrest was again moving to gain Wilson's rear. Directing Hatch's men to withdraw slowly while dismounted, Wilson warily pulled back toward Franklin. By his order, Hatch's men remained on foot ready to meet an attack over the distance of two miles before they were allowed to remount.[17]

Little fighting occurred throughout the remaining morning hours, and by noon Wilson was at Nolen's plantation, four miles southeast of Franklin. The Confederates seemed to have disappeared. There was the distant rumble of gunfire in the direction of Spring Hill, heard since 11:00 A.M., but some Confederates had been recently observed on the adjacent Peytonsville and Bethesda road, and Wilson feared the worst. Remembering the enemy prisoners' reports from the previous evening about Forrest going to Nashville via Franklin, Wilson needed little convincing as to what had happened.[18]

At noon Wilson's adjutant wrote that in the opinion of his commander, "there is no doubt that he [Forrest] has gone to Nashville." Wilson promptly dashed off a series of urgent dispatches to Thomas and Schofield, his tone being that of befuddlement. "I am afraid now that we held on too long near Hurt's Crossroads this morning," he told Schofield. "Indications are very strong that while the enemy attacked us in force, he threw columns on the Bethesda and Peytonsville road." At 2:00 P.M. Wilson wrote to Thomas, "My impression is that Forrest is aiming for Nashville, via Triune and Nolensville," adding, "You had better look out for Forrest at Nashville tomorrow at noon." About all that the Federal cavalry commander could offer Thomas in the way of encouragement was, "I'll be there before or very soon after he makes his appearance."[19]

Having dispatched Richard W. Johnson with Croxton's and Capron's brigades eastward toward Triune to look for the enemy, at 2:00 P.M. Wilson pondered the distant heavy firing to the south. Had a part of the enemy's force cut back toward Spring Hill? Some of Wilson's officers were convinced "that Forrest has divided his forces, sending some up the Davis Ford Road [to Spring Hill]." Yet Wilson decided to remain where he was so as to cover the roads north. It was very evident that Wilson was preoccupied with only one concern—Forrest, and the threat to Nashville. Not until 10:00 P.M. did he inquire of Schofield about "your position and the result of the day's operations."[20]

That evening Wilson learned from a scouting detachment sent south toward Mount Carmel that only a single camp of enemy cavalry had been found. No other sightings of Rebel forces were reported from the direction of Triune. Thus, the perplexing question remained, nagging and tormenting an increasingly worried Wilson: If not moving toward Nashville, where had Forrest gone?[21]

II

John Bell Hood had arisen at 3:00 A.M. that morning. There was time only for coffee and Chaplain Charles Quintard to pray for God's "blessing, guidance, and protection." Hood responded, "Thank you, Doctor. That is my hope and trust." As he turned away he remarked to Quintard, "The enemy must give me fight, or I will be at Nashville before tomorrow night."[22]

An orderly supported Hood from behind, another held his crutches, and Hood raised his left foot into the stirrup. A third man raised the general's wooden leg over the saddle and emplaced the foot. Hood was strapped to the saddle, and horse and rider slowly moved off.[23]

Hood's grand, strategic movement was at last in progress. He had explained the basic plan to his key generals; their objective would be to cut off the Federal army from the direct route to Nashville. Two of Stephen D. Lee's divisions would remain behind to demonstrate in Schofield's front and prevent the enemy's rapid withdrawal. Meanwhile, Hood with the rest of the army would strike cross country for Spring Hill, the modest farm village some miles in the enemy's rear. Once in position, Hood could either block Schofield and force him to fight from a disadvantage—he being separated from his base at Nashville and positioned between two strong Confederate columns—or else race ahead of the trapped Union column and attack that city. In order to march speedily over the soft backwoods country roads, all but two artillery batteries and most of the army's wagons would remain behind with Lee. Lee's Corps would later cross the Duck River as Schofield withdrew and harass the enemy's retreat. Forrest's role would be to clear the Federal horsemen out of the way and seize Spring Hill in advance of Hood's infantry.[24]

The day had begun with the bright promise of success. Mild temperatures softened the breeze, and vivid streaks of dawn glowered on the horizon as the men from Patrick Cleburne's leading brigade, Mark Lowrey's, tramped across the pontoon bridge at Davis's Ford. The banks of the Duck River were piled with knapsacks and camp articles, left there by orders of regimental officers so that the men might march more rapidly. By 7:30 A.M. Cleburne's Division was across, and William Bate's men arose from the cedar forest where they had been waiting and joined in the march. About 9:30 A.M. the entire striking column, 19,621 effective infantrymen, was north of the Duck River.[25]

Hood rode with the advance of Cleburne's column. The sky was clear and bright, and it would be an almost balmy late autumn day, a good omen for the army's success. Twelve miles ahead by Hood's map lay Spring Hill and military immortality.[26]

About a mile north along the Davis's Ford road Hood drew to a halt. The map he had differed significantly from the route they were following. Hood summoned his local guide, John Gregory, and Pat Cleburne. Gregory, born and raised several miles north of Columbia, knew the region like the back of his hand. Dismounting, Gregory drew a map in the dirt with a stick, explaining that the Davis's Ford road twisted and turned generally along property lines. As a very crooked backwoods road that was one of the first in the county, it had been abandoned in places since 1860. Being soft and little used, "it was then one of the worst roads in Maury County." Gregory pointed out that while the straight-line distance from Davis's Ford to Spring Hill was a little over twelve miles, the actual distance by the Davis's Ford road was far greater (it actually was seventeen and a quarter miles). Cleburne's own personal guide, Jim Smith, also a local resident, confirmed the accuracy of Gregory's information.[27]

Hood was surprised. His map, likely drawn from the one left behind by Schofield in his room at the Athenaeum, had proved to be very inaccurate and misleading.* Evidently not having bothered to check with Gregory or other local guides prior to the actual march, Hood now foresaw that there would be a significant delay in reaching his objective, well beyond the time frame he had anticipated. As Cleburne sat making a hasty sketch on a piece of paper of Gregory's map in the dirt, Hood forlornly ordered the column to proceed.[28]

Soon there was another surprise for the Confederate commander. Major T. E. Jameson of the 48th Tennessee, also a local man, had been detached to go with the advance and report any difficulties encountered. About 10:00 A.M. Jameson dashed up to warn that his advance party had been fired on by Federal skirmishers occupying the site of Cooper's Mineral Well on Bear Creek. Hood's scout, Gregory, soon confirmed the report, adding that from a hill he had seen Federals deployed in line of battle along a small ravine.[29]

A shock wave must have raced through Hood's mind. Was it possible that Schofield had anticipated Hood's northward movement and was moving to attack the Confederate army from the flank? Or perhaps Schofield was merely protecting his own flank as he withdrew toward Spring Hill. Noting that the adjacent range of hills would screen his columns from view, Hood, now somewhat shaken, decided to continue on only after making a major alteration in the marching column. With the danger of a sudden enemy attack on his left flank uppermost in his mind, Hood directed that Cheatham's leading corps divide into two parallel columns. They would thus be in position to instantly form two lines of battle if attacked. While Cleburne's and Bate's men continued along the roadway, John C. Brown's Division was directed to march off the road about 400 yards to the east, being designated as the "supporting column." To further ensure against surprise, nearly two brigades were pulled from Brown's Division and sent as skirmishers beyond the flank of Cleburne and Bates.[30]

In all, said a disgusted Brown, the resulting march over the muddy, rough ground, through woods and fields, thoroughly exhausted his men. Soon they were "just dragging themselves along," remembered one of his soldiers, and the men became "weary and worn out."[31]

The confirmed enemy presence adjacent to his line of march made Hood nervous and was to have a profound effect on his thinking during the remainder of the day. By noon, when the column was briefly halted for lunch, Hood

*In the B. F. Cheatham Papers at the Tennessee State Library and Archives at Nashville is a military map of mid-Tennessee, marked "Copied from Federal Map/ Supposed Scale 3-1/2 miles = 1 inch/ E. G. Anstey, Dr[aughtsman]." This seems to have been the map copied for Hood and his corps commanders' use on the Spring Hill march. See Map 4.

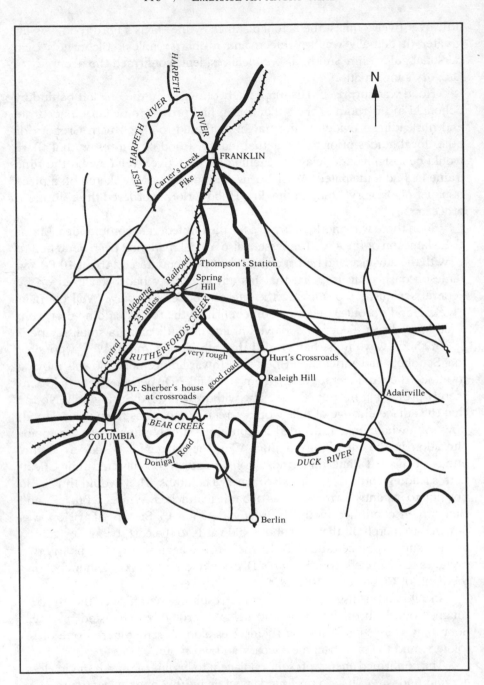

N

MAP 4 Facsimile of Confederate Military Map "Copied from Federal
Map—Supposed Scale 3½ miles = 1 inch—E.G. Anstey—Dr[aughtsman]"
(B.F. Cheatham Papers, Tenn. St. Libr. & Archives)

Scale of this version: 5 ¼ miles to 1 inch

was found no longer to be in buoyant spirits. Frustrated by the unlooked-for delays, he exchanged heated words with Brigadier General Hiram Granbury of Cleburne's Division.[32]

As the day progressed, the column crossed over a branch of Bear Creek and the mood of the men became more relaxed. A youth had some Negroes roll several hogsheads of tobacco from his parents' barn, and as the men marched by he cried out, "every one of you take a handful of tobacco, but leave plenty for those behind you." Another local woman began cooking "snacks" for the passing columns, including frying in skillets two fattened hogs for Cleburne's men. When Cleburne attempted to pay her, she refused and offered to cook him a fine turkey dinner that night. "No, ma'am," replied Cleburne, "we'll be too busy tonight, but tomorrow night I'll be back for it with many thanks."[33]

By 3:00 P.M. Hood's leading units were approaching Rutherford Creek, only a few miles southeast of Spring Hill. The crackle of small-arms fire echoed in the distance, and Hood suddenly ordered a halt.[34]

III

Nathan Bedford Forrest had spent a very profitable morning in pursuit of Wilson's Union cavalrymen. Forrest's ruse had worked to perfection. The Union cavalry commander had all too obligingly taken the bait offered by Ross's 600-man Texas brigade at Mount Carmel. Wilson had withdrawn toward Franklin, pursued by Ross, even as Forrest with the remainder of his command disengaged and marched unseen for Spring Hill, six miles west along the Mount Carmel road.[35]

Forrest had about 4,500 veteran horsemen with him and was confident of quick success. Moving rapidly, about 11:00 A.M. he was two miles from town when his advance suddenly ran into Federal pickets. Without bothering to dismount his men, Forrest ordered a charge by several of his best brigades, Frank Armstrong's Mississippians, with Edward Crossland's Kentuckians, and the 14th Tennessee Cavalry. With a yell they dashed headlong at the line of blue uniforms visible behind hastily erected rail barricades.[36]

Spring Hill had been quiet early that morning. The prosperous Tennessee community already had gained a certain notoriety during the war, being the site where Confederate Major General Earl Van Dorn had been fatally shot by an outraged husband in May 1863.* This morning the sleepy little village was garrisoned by the 12th Tennessee Cavalry, a new and untried Federal regiment fresh from Nashville. Most of its men had been detailed during the past few days to operate the courier line between Columbia and Spring Hill,

*Van Dorn was shot in the back of the head by Dr. George B. Peters, a member of the state legislature, following evidence that the general was involved in an affair with Peters's attractive 25-year-old wife, Jessie. Peters was never formally brought to trial.

and the 12th's commander, Lieutenant Colonel Charles C. Hoefling, had put most of his 200 remaining troopers on picket duty.[37]

About midmorning the quiet scene at Spring Hill had suddenly given way to turmoil. From the direction of Columbia appeared the leading elements of the army's vast wagon train. The road into Spring Hill was soon jammed with milling, bewildered animals and cursing teamsters. Four companies of the 73rd Illinois Infantry, who were to deploy north of town and halt stragglers, arrived just in advance of the slowly trundling wagons. Also present were about 240 men of the 103d Ohio Infantry, the regular escort for Schofield's headquarters' wagon train. With an agglomeration of cavalry, infantry, and noncombatants milling about on the streets, the scene at Spring Hill had become chaotic by 11:00 A.M.[38]

Suddenly there was word of danger from the east. Three of Hoefling's outpost companies were under fire from swarms of Confederate cavalry. Word of Forrest's menacing presence spread like wildfire. Everyone was frightened by the imminent threat to the vulnerable supply wagons. Hoefling dashed off an anxious note to Schofield at Columbia, warning of the danger and reporting that all communication with Wilson's cavalry had been cut off.[39]

It was apparent to Hoefling that he must have help if Spring Hill was to be defended. John H. Hammond's cavalry brigade at Franklin was supposed to be en route for Spring Hill by Schofield's specific order of the 28th. Yet Hammond had received a separate, conflicting order from Wilson to "move with rapidity" and join Wilson's force near Mount Carmel. Deciding that Wilson's order, being dated later than Schofield's, should be given priority, the Union brigadier had gathered his 900 men and about 9:00 A.M. began marching from Franklin in the direction of Mount Carmel. Hammond was thus moving obliquely away from Spring Hill, where time was running out for Hoefling and his men.[40]

Moving northward from Columbia along the Franklin pike that morning were the 3d Illinois Cavalry and three companies of the 11th Indiana Cavalry, en route to Spring Hill following Wilson's pullback order of the previous afternoon. These units had been guarding the Duck River crossings twelve miles west of Columbia, and were intending to join their newly designated brigade when it concentrated at Spring Hill. By chance they were approaching their destination at a most crucial time.[41]

Upon their arrival before 11:00 A.M. the Illinois cavalrymen learned they had blundered into a highly dangerous situation. Extricating themselves from the tangle of wagons and horses jamming the streets, the 3d Illinois Cavalry and the three Indiana cavalry companies rode eastward from Spring Hill along the road to Mount Carmel. After galloping nearly two miles from town, the veteran cavalrymen deployed in line of battle, hastily throwing up a barricade of rails and logs. Soon there was the crackle of skirmish fire from the vedettes in front, and the men crouched down behind their cover of rails in nervous anticipation. They knew they would not have long to wait.[42]

About 10:00 A.M. that morning a stray company of the 2d Michigan Cavalry, isolated and nearly cut off in the vicinity of the Duck River, had trotted into Spring Hill. Thankful not to have been captured by the many Rebel units observed on their flanks during the march, the Michiganders marveled at their narrow escape. The only explanation for such seemed to be that the enemy had thought the company one of their own units.[43]

Once within the Spring Hill lines, the captain commanding had alerted Hoefling about the enemy's threatening presence, and was later directed to move east of town and join the patchwork of cavalry outposts. With the sharp crack of carbine fire echoing in the distance, Company M of the 2d Michigan Cavalry grabbed their Spencer carbines and headed for the firing line.[44]

Forrest's men came on like a very whirlwind, said a participant. Armstrong's Mississippi brigade boldly rode straight at the Federal line, posted along the crest of a hill. Evidently expecting only moderate resistance, the Confederates were surprised by the volume of fire and the stubborn composure of the enemy's troopers. Some of the 3d Illinois' cavalrymen had breech-loading carbines, Sharps and Burnsides, but most had five-shot Colt Revolving Rifle Muskets. Further, they were combat veterans of two years' western service. Aided by many of the 12th Tennessee's inexperienced but well-armed troopers, the Union perimeter remained intact with a sustained volume of fire that threw back the mounted Confederate attackers.[45]

Forrest was undaunted. After re-forming his men, he ordered them dismounted for another attack by the full extent of his command then present. Greatly outnumbering the Union defenders, Forrest's cavalrymen worked their way forward and soon had the Union line outflanked. The blue line slowly began to withdraw, and Forrest moved toward the south with a portion of his men. Into their path moved Company M of the 2d Michigan Cavalry with their deadly Spencers. Firing on foot from skirmish order, the Michiganders put out a sustained barrage, holding their position briefly, then slowly withdrawing. This self-perpetuating, collapsing style of defense considerably frustrated Forrest, whose dismounted troopers had to continually root out the stubborn Union troopers from strong positions in the rolling, wooded terrain. Due to the Illinois and Tennessee cavalries' continued begrudging withdrawal on the Michigan company's flank, a considerable amount of time elapsed before Forrest's men approached the outskirts of Spring Hill.[46]

Once atop a high hill overlooking the Franklin and Columbia pike, Forrest saw a compelling target of opportunity. In plain view on the pike was a crowded column of Union wagons hurrying to reach Spring Hill. The sight caused Forrest to risk another mounted charge. Ordering up the 21st Tennessee of Buford's Division, Forrest put them in at a gallop, across an open field. Out in the open against the Spencers of Company M, this full regiment was cut to pieces by the single Michigan company. The 21st's commander was wounded three times, and Forrest's indiscretion had cost him more time.[47]

Having been pushed back to the outskirts of Spring Hill following about an hour of fighting, the beleaguered Michiganders were relieved to see the detachments of wagon guard infantry throwing up rude breastworks in their rear. The 73d Illinois' four companies were busily piling up rail barricades north of town, while detachments of the 103d Ohio Infantry had begun constructing a log and rail perimeter east of the village. With haste, the Union cavalrymen scrambled back behind the rails and girded for another attack.[48]

It was shortly after noon and Forrest studied the new and more imposing Federal line. A courier from Hood galloped up and delivered an urgent message. Hood had heard the firing at Spring Hill and told Forrest to hold his position "at all hazards." The advance of his infantry column, he said, was only a few miles distant and moving forward rapidly. Forrest ordered up Tyree H. Bell's Brigade to press the enemy. It seemed that Hood's infantrymen would soon be on hand to help exploit any break he might develop in the makeshift Union line.[49]

IV

David S. Stanley had been on the road to Spring Hill since midmorning. His assignment must have been less than inspiring, even perhaps somewhat demeaning: escorting a ponderous wagon train to the rear while the balance of the army stood toe-to-toe with Hood at Columbia. At best it was a lackluster job for the army's senior ranking major general, and seemed to be of significance only because of the threat of danger in the rear from roving Confederate cavalry.[50]

Stanley's lack of urgency in marching to Spring Hill was reflected by the nature of the march. Walter C. Whitaker's brigade of the 1st Division already was in advance at Rutherford Creek, four miles north along the road to Spring Hill. Instead of sending Whitaker on to occupy Spring Hill, Stanley directed that he stay in place until the entire corps had marched past, then bring up the rear. Although Schofield's order to march was given by 7:30 A.M., it was 8:45 A.M. before Emerson Opdycke's leading brigade got under way. The ponderously slow column of about 800 wagons and perhaps forty pieces of artillery was soon strung out along the pike for miles amid Stanley's two divisions. After halting at Rutherford Creek about 10:30 A.M., by Schofield's order Stanley's trailing division, Kimball's, was detached to remain there and guard against an enemy sweep along Rutherford Creek.[51]

By 11:30 A.M. the head of Stanley's column was still more than two miles from Spring Hill after having been on the road for nearly three hours over the distance of about seven miles.[52]

At 11:30 A.M. Stanley had gone into a roadside house with his staff, possibly for refreshments. Soon a rather frightened cavalryman was brought to see him. Buford's Rebel cavalry division, the man stammered, was halfway between Rally Hill and Spring Hill, and driving for the latter place. Promptly, a courier approached with an urgent dispatch for General Schofield from the garrison commander at Spring Hill, warning about the threatened attack on that village. Stanley opened and read the message. In the distance firing now could be heard east of town. Stanley immediately sprang into action.[53]

Emerson Opdycke's brigade by then was within a mile of the village. Alerted of the danger, Opdycke's men started for Spring Hill at a run. At 12:30 P.M. they sprinted past the road to the railroad depot and north beyond the village for a short distance. Ahead, a thin line of Confederate skirmishers had approached to within 400 yards of the parked wagon trains. Opdycke rushed two small regiments of skirmishers forward while his men formed in line of battle. Within minutes they advanced against the Rebel line, which swiftly gave way and soon disappeared. Opdycke now ordered a halt and deployed his men in a half-mile perimeter across the northern section of town.[54]

Ironically, Opdycke had hastened to a sector which was not seriously threatened. It was the eastern perimeter that had attracted Forrest's primary attention.

John Q. Lane's brigade was the second in line along the pike. Entering Spring Hill on the heels of Opdycke's men, they were directed to the right, and swung directly into the face of Forrest's approaching cavalrymen. As his men double-timed into line of battle, Lane threw out skirmishers from a Kentucky regiment, then ordered an advance against the Confederate line, visible on a low hill half a mile east of town. Passing the makeshift perimeter of cavalrymen and the wagon guard infantry, Lane's 1,666-man brigade went forward with a rush. Momentarily there was a flurry of fighting as Lane's men swept up the rising ground. When a portion of Jackson's Division attempted to countercharge, it "was repulsed with loss." In fact, following a half hour's fighting, Lane's men had cleared the hill of Forrest's cavalrymen, principally Frank Armstrong's Brigade of Mississippians.[55]

To Lane's south, Luther P. Bradley's brigade, the last in Stanley's column, had belatedly moved up to occupy a wooded knoll east of the pike. Bradley's men had been delayed by the passing of several artillery batteries, and came up following Lane's fight with Jackson's men. Bradley put his men to work building log and fence-rail barricades along a knoll about a half mile east of the turnpike. Since he was isolated from Lane's brigade, which had pushed farther north and east, Bradley put a single regiment in reserve, ready to move to any threatened point. He then, shortly after 2:00 P.M., advanced an entire regiment, the 64th Ohio Infantry, as skirmishers. They were soon observed fighting with a line of dismounted Rebel cavalrymen armed with Enfield rifles.[56]

Forrest by now had shifted about a mile and a half south of the Mount Carmel road with Bell's Brigade of Chalmers's Division, to the vicinity of the high hill overlooking the Columbia pike. Evidently he had been screened from viewing Bradley's advance as the Union infantrymen advanced to a wooded knoll in front. Yet, observing the approach of Union skirmishers, Forrest approached Chalmers and told him to "drive those fellows off." Chalmers seemed very reluctant, evidently having learned from his men that a strong Union infantry column had moved in front. Forrest chided Chalmers with a curt retort: "I think you are mistaken. That is only a small cavalry force." Prodded by Forrest's insistence, Chalmers agreed to try it with the men of Bell's Brigade.[57]

Moving forward against the enemy's skirmishers, Bell's dismounted cavalrymen rapidly pushed them back about a half mile. Soon they approached a woods where the 64th Ohio had just taken cover. Suddenly from the rear near the turnpike sounded the roar of artillery. Twelve-pounder fused shell and percussion shell from three-inch rifle cannon whizzed through the air. Amid the deafening explosions, Bell's men halted. Two Federal batteries, a total of four twelve-pounder Napoleons and six three-inch Ordnance rifles, were in place along the turnpike. Chalmers, who had gone in with Bell's men, was duly impressed. His command got no closer than 300 yards of the enemy line. After each battery had fired about twenty rounds, the Confederates began to fall back. When Chalmers returned to see Forrest, the veteran commander sheepishly remarked, "They was in there sure enough, wasn't they, Chalmers?"[58]

By now it was after 3:00 P.M. Forrest had been fighting the enemy at Spring Hill for four hours. Interrogation of several captured skirmishers from the 64th Ohio confirmed the presence of at least a portion of the Federal Fourth Corps. Forrest's men were running low on ammunition, and it was apparent that he could do little more than skirmish with the enemy until Hood's infantry came up.[59]

Forrest waited impatiently. News arrived of an important capture by his gray riders north of town, a Union courier carrying a dispatch for Schofield from Thomas. The message, dated 3:30 A.M. November 29th, was of profound importance, ordering Schofield to withdraw to Franklin. "I desire you to fall back from Columbia and to take up your position at Franklin, leaving a sufficient force at Spring Hill to contest the enemy's progress until you are securely posted at Franklin," read the message. Forrest now knew what Schofield did not: that the entire Union army must fall back rather than risk being cut off. While Franklin was intended to be the next Federal point of defense, the Union army was still south of Spring Hill. Schofield thus was virtually at the Confederates' mercy once Hood's infantry seized the turnpike to Franklin.[60]

Forrest had done his part skillfully and well. Now all he could do was watch in frustration as enemy officers "dashed back and forth" along the lines of thrown-down fence rails, erecting more barricades and hastening to get the steady stream of wagons, ambulances, and artillery into park at Spring Hill.[61]

The Confederate infantry should have arrived hours ago. The minutes continued to tick away. Where was John Bell Hood?

CHAPTER XIV

Listening for the Sound
of Guns

T HE PROLONGED FIRING HEARD ahead in the vicinity of Spring Hill convinced John Bell Hood that Forrest's cavalry, instead of occupying the village without difficulty, had encountered substantial opposition. Again, anxious thoughts raced through Hood's mind. Had Schofield anticipated his movement and somehow arrived at Spring Hill ahead of the Confederates? Was his army marching into a trap?

About 3:00 P.M., while at Rutherford Creek, two and a half miles from Spring Hill, Hood issued his first, fateful instructions. Major General Cheatham's three divisions would wade across the creek, push forward to join Forrest, and strike the enemy at Spring Hill. Stewart's trailing corps would advance only to Rutherford Creek and wait in line of battle on the south side, ready "to move down the creek, if necessary." Stewart later explained that Hood felt Cheatham's command might be "in great danger of being outflanked and crushed." Accordingly, Stewart's men were to remain in reserve, ready either to go to Cheatham's assistance or march down the creek to attack the enemy and block off their escape.[1]

While staff officers busily assisted in getting Cleburne's leading division across the small but swollen creek, Hood with his staff rode ahead to learn of the current situation. Cheatham remained behind in order to bring forward his second division, William Bate's, as a support for Cleburne.[2]

Hood, it appears, promptly went forward along the Rally Hill pike and rode atop the high hill where Forrest had earlier observed the Columbia-to-Franklin turnpike. Here he sat on his horse, watching "the enemy's wagons and men passing at double quick along the Franklin pike." Forrest was probably there, and the presence of what appeared to be "a general and his

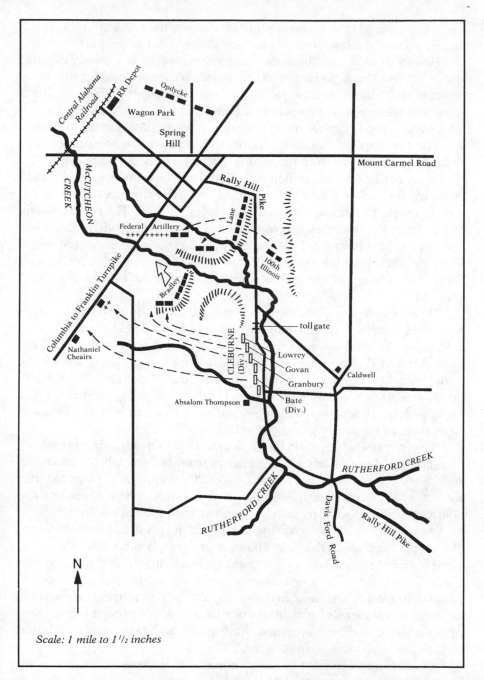

MAP 5   Confederate Attack at Spring Hill
November 29

staff'' was noticed by a Union commander across the rolling terrain. David Stanley soon had a few "complementary shells" fired at the party.[3]

Hood's fixation with the enemy along the turnpike was plainly evident, and as he rode back down the hill he began busily revising his plans. By personal observation, and perhaps from the assessment of Forrest, Hood knew that there was no prospect of a Federal attack. Yet, with the Yankee troops and wagons rapidly moving toward Spring Hill along the turnpike, Hood now anticipated that the real danger would come from the direction of Columbia, rather than from the troops defensively occupying Spring Hill.[4]

Many of Cleburne's men had pulled off their socks and shoes and rolled up their pants before wading Rutherford Creek. The troops were animated, and they rapidly marched north and west along the Rally Hill road, crossing McCutcheon Creek as they approached the base of the hill where Hood had just observed the turnpike. It was a beautiful afternoon, remembered one of Forrest's officers, and the sight of Cheatham's Corps marching forth, their battle flags waving in the mellow sunlight, sent a thrill through all who watched.[5]

When Hood met Cleburne along the roadway, he directed his most renowned division commander to deploy his troops, en echelon, in a cornfield along the road south of the toll gate, fronting westward toward the Columbia and Franklin pike. Cleburne put Mark Lowrey's Brigade on the right, Daniel C. Govan's in the center, and Hiram Granbury's on the left. Some of Forrest's cavalrymen, Tyree H. Bell's Brigade, formed on Cleburne's right as supports, although Bell's men had only four rounds of ammunition per man remaining after their day-long fight.[6]

The en echelon formation thus reflected Hood's newly revised plans. By staggering Cleburne's brigade alignments from left to right in ascending stair-step formation, the entire division would be in proper position to strike for the turnpike about a mile and a half due west, then wheel left and confront Schofield's troops marching up the road toward Spring Hill.[7]

As Cleburne's 3,000 troops swept boldly forward at about 4:00 P.M., Hood rode back along the Rally Hill pike and met William Bate's division, already forming in line west of the roadway. Following the instructions of his corps commander, Cheatham, Bate was positioning his three brigades to move in support of Cleburne, and also aligned them in echelon formation to conform to Cleburne's formation. Cheatham was not present when Hood approached Bate, Cheatham already having ridden ahead to watch as the last of Cleburne's brigades went forward.[8]

Cheatham and Hood at this point missed seeing one another. It was one of the great Confederate misfortunes of the day, and perhaps of the war. Hood told Bate "to move to the turnpike and sweep toward Columbia," which conformed to the plan he had just outlined for Cleburne. Yet Cheatham, having until recently remained at Rutherford Creek, was operating under Hood's earlier instructions—to form his divisions and attack northwest, toward Spring Hill. Cheatham never understood how Cleburne had seemingly misaligned his division in relation to the enemy's position at Spring Hill. Cheatham evidently had not talked with Forrest, who was then riding with Cleburne in the 4:00 P.M. advance.[9]

Soon thereafter, as Bate's men went forward toward the turnpike, Hood trotted farther south to the nearby farm of Absalom Thompson and its fine 1835 vintage home. Here he would stay for the remainder of the day, often being seen sitting by the roadside talking with officers and sending various messages. Cheatham, meanwhile, remained on the battle line conveying instructions to combat units which no longer reflected Hood's revised plans. Hood and Cheatham had virtually changed places and roles. Both were thinking of attacking and overwhelming the enemy, but there were two different tactical objectives in mind. Cheatham was seeking to strike the Federals at Spring Hill; Hood's objective was to drive back Schofield's column approaching from Columbia. This situation would soon set a new standard in command frustration.[10]

Cleburne's and Bell's men, said Nathan Bedford Forrest, went forward with "a promptness . . . energy, and gallantry which I have never seen excelled." The sun was rapidly setting, and behind the line of Govan's Brigade rode Cleburne on his dark bay, Red Pepper, directing the movement of his men with a drawn sword. Nearby, Forrest also rode behind the line near Brigadier General Govan.[11]

Cleburne's infantrymen had encountered only a few Federal skirmishers as they advanced over the rolling terrain. Yet as Lowrey's Brigade on the right flank swept down a hill, they passed through an extension of woods and into an open field. Unknowingly they had approached at a perpendicular angle a concealed line of Federal breastworks along the wooded knoll to their right. Suddenly there was a crashing volley, and Lowrey's men came under an intense fire from the close-by ranks of Stanley's infantrymen.[12]

Responding promptly, Lowrey swung his left regiments forward in a right wheel to confront this hidden enemy line. An observer watched with admiration as Lowrey's men, part of the best fighting division in the Army of Tennessee, came on with a rush. They pulled down the rims of their old hats over their eyes, bent their heads to the storm of missiles pouring upon them, and changed direction to their right on the double quick, noted an anxious Federal captain.[13]

After nearly two months of marching and maneuvering, major elements of Hood's and what had been Sherman's infantry had at last joined in important combat.

In Lowrey's immediate front lay the extreme right portion of Brigadier General Luther P. Bradley's mostly Illinois and Ohio brigade. Having anticipated that his vulnerable western flank might be turned, Bradley had earlier refused his right regiment, the 42d Illinois Infantry, at a forty-five-degree angle from the main brigade line—which fronted generally southeast. The 42d held a position behind a rail fence in an open field, being separated by about 150 yards from the remainder of Bradley's barricaded brigade on the wooded ridge. Only the 64th Ohio Infantry was close by for support, having recently returned from the skirmish line following Bell's earlier attack.[14]

Altogether, Bradley had about 2,000 men, greater numbers than Cleburne's lone brigade then pressing forward in his front. Yet most of his regiments were filled with new recruits who had been little drilled and were experiencing their baptism of fire. In fact, the commander of the 42d said that "having 350 entirely new recruits . . . I did not expect to hold such a line very long."[15]

To aid the Illinois soldiers along their refused front, the ranks of the 64th Ohio quickly rushed up to join in the fray. Through the billowing gunsmoke the re-forming Confederates were seen pushing westward toward the open flank.[16]

Cleburne had been taken at a serious disadvantage due to his en echelon formation. His facility to swing south was the opposite of what was needed to rapidly wheel his brigades north to confront Bradley's line. Hood evidently had failed to observe the entire Federal defensive position southeast of Spring Hill when atop the hill west of the tollgate. As a result, the division's awkward tactical alignment complicated Cleburne's initial response. He was at first able to utilize only Lowrey's regiments in the fighting.[17]

While Lowrey's men were re-forming, their commander sought Cleburne's personal help. Thus far, only the right portion of Bradley's Brigade had been engaged, and from the cheering and waving of hats along the enemy's main line it appeared to Lowrey that they might be preparing to attack. Lowrey excitedly dashed up to Cleburne and told him the enemy was about to charge his flank. Cleburne, the fire of battle in his eyes, jerked his fist upward. With a motion like he was about to whip his horse, the Irish-born general heatedly exclaimed, "I'll charge them!"[18]

Immediately Cleburne dashed off on Red Pepper toward Govan's Brigade, the only troops then available due to the en echelon alignment. Granbury's Brigade, trailing Govan on the left and rear, continued straight ahead, only being aware of firing off to their right beyond the rolling and wooded hills. Within minutes Govan's Arkansas brigade was personally led forward by Cleburne. After wheeling the regiments into a northern alignment, Cleburne directed their march toward Bradley's right flank. With a rush, Govan's men ran directly at Bradley's line. Alongside, Lowrey's re-formed brigade also joined in the charge, rapidly working their way westward around the Union perimeter. Soon they outflanked both the 42d Illinois and the 64th Ohio.[19]

Immediately all became chaos within Bradley's ranks. Lowrey's fire enfiladed the entire Federal line. Amid an intense crossfire the 42d Illinois and 64th Ohio got up and ran. Brigade commander Bradley hastily attempted to lead to the right his old regiment, the 51st Illinois, which was mostly unengaged on the opposite flank. Yet Bradley took a rifle ball in his left arm near the shoulder and was carried off the field.[20]

In ten minutes the fighting was over. Bradley's mostly inexperienced men had fled in disorder. The 42d Illinois' regimental flag was lost when the color guard was shot down or captured. Even the remaining unengaged left flank regiment, the 79th Illinois, had to sprint to safety before being surrounded.[21]

Close on the heels of Bradley's troops ran Govan's and Lowrey's men, yelling, "Halt, you Yankee sons-of-bitches," recalled a fleeing Federal officer later. Some of the frightened Union soldiers were shot in the back. One Federal private was so scared he threw away his knapsack and ran toward Spring Hill for a half mile without stopping despite his wounded knee, which had been struck by a spent musket ball.[22]

Although Cleburne's two full brigades were in hot pursuit, they suddenly came to an abrupt halt. What stopped them was the saving grace of the Federal army—the Fourth Corps artillery that a quick-thinking David S. Stanley had hastily positioned to cover his eastern flank.[23]

Stanley, instead of finding boredom and the ignominious task of guarding wagon trains at Spring Hill, was now in the midst of a hectic and crisis-charged afternoon. Indeed, upon reflection, Stanley would later write, "It was the biggest day's work I ever accomplished for the United States." November 29th's fateful surprise was entirely appropriate, for life had become a series of bizarre twists and turns for the outspoken Stanley. His Fourth Corps had been selected to remain behind in Tennessee by Sherman, so Stanley said, due to "my spat with Sherman over the Jonesboro affair."* While Schofield had been placed under Stanley's orders during the Jonesboro fighting, and even though he was the senior major general, Stanley had found himself politically punished, being made the subordinate during the mid-Tennessee campaign. Ironically, Stanley was now heavily involved in attempting to save Schofield's army, reputation, and perhaps even his career.[24]

At 12:15 P.M. Stanley had received a dispatch from Schofield at Columbia, marked 10:45 A.M., advising him that a considerable enemy force was north of the Duck River. Stanley was told to "select a good position at Spring Hill, covering the approaches, and send out parties to reconnoiter on all roads leading east and southeast."[25]

The timing was most fortuitous. Stanley was just then approaching Spring Hill, and he deployed his three brigades accordingly. Opdycke and Lane were positioned on a perimeter north and east of town to protect the

*Stanley was blamed by Sherman for Hood's escape on September 1, 1864, being "slow to come up." Yet Stanley said he had been ordered by Sherman to thoroughly destroy the railroad before advancing. This led to an exchange of words between them the following day. Wrote Stanley, "He [Sherman] liked to lay his failures on others' shoulders, and, when the scapegoat attempted to explain or argue the case, he was never forgiven."

wagon train. Bradley was sent a half mile southeast of the pike to watch in that direction, per Schofield's message.[26]

Throughout the afternoon Stanley and his staff had hastened to get the trailing wagons and reserve artillery batteries into town. By 4:30 P.M., with the arrival of the 6th Ohio Light Battery, the pike was clear. Yet an enormous quantity of wagons and cannon had been parked west of town, on the commons between the village and the railroad depot. It was these vulnerable military stores that worried Stanley the most.[27]

Through his veteran division commander, George D. Wagner, Stanley ordered the emplacement of a defensive line of artillery along the outskirts of town. Captain Lyman Bridges, Stanley's chief of artillery, soon positioned four batteries of mostly twelve-pounder Napoleons, a total of eighteen guns, on a ridge running diagonally across the turnpike at the south edge of town.[28]

Belatedly, about 5:00 P.M., with Bradley's brigade in danger of being outflanked on their right, Wagner hastened farther south along the turnpike with a section of Battery B, Pennsylvania Light Artillery. Wheeling into battery east of the pike, these two twelve-pounder cannon protected Bradley's flank and began raking Cleburne's line from end to end. Nearby, Wagner's only reserve regiment, the 36th Illinois Infantry, rushed to their support.[29]

Forming under the fire of Confederate skirmishers, the 36th Illinois was soon under an intense fire from Granbury's Brigade, which had advanced straight ahead rather than swing north and attack Bradley. In a few minutes, the 36th was driven back into and through the rapidly firing guns of the Pennsylvania section. Hastily limbering up his two Napoleons, the Federal battery commander barely escaped with his guns ahead of Granbury's charging infantrymen.[30]

Meanwhile, with the disorganized refugees from Bradley's line streaming back past the barricaded line of artillery at the south edge of town, the long line of Federal cannon began to fire percussion shell, spherical case, and even canister into the Confederate ranks. The effect, said Stanley, was amazing. "The ground was planted in corn and was very muddy, and if the Johnnies in gray were not hit with artillery missiles, they were [soon] covered with mud."[31]

Battery A of the 1st Ohio Light Artillery fired 166 rounds, sending the Confederates scurrying for cover. Although their fire seemed too high and the shells often burst well beyond the enemy line, a shell fragment nearly struck Cleburne. Riding behind his front line, Cleburne had briefly halted to talk to his aide, Lieutenant L. H. Mangum, when a shell burst close by. A whizzing fragment struck Red Pepper in the flank, causing the horse to rear and buck in terror. Mangum anxiously asked Cleburne if he had been hurt. "No!" said the general brusquely. "Go on, Mangum, and tell Granbury what I told you!"[32]

Cleburne's anxiety had been heightened by the appearance of another

Federal brigade, seen rapidly shifting from a position east of town to the ridge adjacent to the enemy's blazing line of artillery. Cleburne wanted Granbury's Brigade brought up from the left to help assault this new line before it was fully formed.[33]

Yet there was no further advance. As Lowrey's and Govan's brigades hurriedly re-formed prior to a renewal of the attack, Cleburne was abruptly halted from any further offensive movement. Based on an earlier, routine message from Cleburne to his corps commander about the difficulty initially encountered by Lowrey's Brigade, Cheatham ordered a halt in the attacks. Cheatham, in fact, had already set in motion a ponderous tactical movement that soon would bring an enormous concentration of Southern infantry to confront this stopgap Federal line. By Cheatham's specific order, Cleburne was to halt and await the concentrated attack that might overwhelm Spring Hill's defenders.[34]

In the fading light after sundown, Cheatham began to act with an increasingly narrow, rigidly fixed purpose. From all sectors of the field Cheatham hastily ordered a concentration of troops along the new line occupied by Cleburne, regardless of any unit's present position or circumstances. By Cleburne's order, Granbury's Brigade was soon pulled from within a few hundred yards of the turnpike where they had overwhelmed the 36th Illinois, and his men were sent on the double quick to join their division line, a half mile to the right. Meanwhile, Cheatham sent several couriers to locate Bate and bring his division north to confront the enemy-occupied ridge near Spring Hill. Further, John C. Brown's Division, the last of Cheatham's Corps to cross Rutherford Creek, was hastened forward by Cheatham's order to a position on Cleburne's right.[35]

Like a magnet, the makeshift Federal concentration along the edge of town was drawing large segments of Confederate troops from all directions. Cheatham's objective was one-dimensional: to attack and overwhelm this apparent enemy bastion. All across the picturesque landscape gray infantrymen were seen rapidly forming in the half light of dusk. Cheatham was soon in the process of issuing the necessary orders, and about 5:30 P.M. Brown's Division on the extreme right sent their skirmishers forward.[36]

Combined, there now were two divisions, about 6,800 Rebel infantrymen, poised to make the assault, with perhaps an equal number moving forward or ready to support the attack. It seemed that only a miracle could save David Stanley's vulnerable force.[37]

II

Until the overwhelming assault on Bradley's line, David S. Stanley had considered that he was fighting only Forrest's dismounted cavalry. Bradley's flustered soldiers, however, quickly put Stanley straight. They said the enemy fought too well and with such determination to be anything other than veteran infantry. The incredible truth, that Hood's army was in front and about to overwhelm and rout or capture Stanley's single division, was then little regarded by the old dragoon officer. He was too busy. Stanley, along with his staff, had his hands full trying to rally and re-form Bradley's soldiers behind the artillery. Bradley's men had been driven back about a quarter mile. Beyond their former line, masses of gray troops could be seen in the gathering darkness, forming for another attack.[38]

Wagner, meanwhile, had made a hasty and crucial decision. Confederate cavalry were hovering about north and west of town, threatening to get at the parked trains. Accordingly, he could not send Opdycke's brigade as reinforcements to replace Bradley's shattered unit. There was only one, desperate choice. Lane's Brigade, largely unengaged on the east side of town, would have to plug the gap. Wagner galloped to Lane and directed him to split his command, taking two regiments to the right and form along the line of artillery to support Stanley's guns.[39]

Colonel John Q. Lane, having driven Jackson's Rebel cavalry off the hills in front during the early afternoon, had ordered the construction of a line of fence-rail breastworks east of Spring Hill and south of the Mount Carmel road. Lane's men had just completed these fortifications when Bradley's brigade was attacked to the southwest. Now, following Wagner's peremptory order, the veteran Ohio commander ordered his 2d battalion of regiments to change front to their right rear. Despite materially weakening the only Federal line fronting east, Lane perceived that disaster was imminent to the south.[40]

With a will, the designated contingent rushed south and west to the new line, about a quarter mile distant, where they hastily deployed for battle. Only 1,666 men strong, Lane's six regiments now occupied an L-shaped perimeter, showing a gap-riddled and exposed front to the south. Here the 2d battalion units began throwing up a defensive line with whatever means were available. Odd pieces of lumber, old logs, broken rails, and even mounds of dirt scooped up at bayonet point were hastily fashioned into a breastwork. As the men worked feverishly, through the twilight gloom they observed a ragged enemy line which began moving toward them from the south. Lane already had a line of skirmishers "well out" to delay the Confederates as long as possible.[41]

Suddenly, with keen perception, Lane saw an opportunity. The separated left flank regiments of his brigade, fronting east, were likely to remain unengaged. There appeared to be no enemy threat from that direction. Quickly Lane ordered the 100th Illinois and Company F of the 40th Indiana, a total of about 300 men, to a point forward and east of his 2d battalion line "so as to hit the enemy in flank." These troops soon rushed out beyond the end of Lane's line, crossed the Rally Hill pike, and prepared to fire obliquely into the oncoming enemy's exposed flank.[42]

It was a serious gamble. Lane realized that much of the eastern front which his brigade had formerly defended was now open and exposed to a Rebel attack. Should the lurking line of gray cavalry recently seen beyond the Rally Hill pike come forth, the only Federal troops present to try to stop them were the 100th Illinois and their add-on company. Since their backs were now turned to the east, if this occurred, the detachment might be easily routed or captured.[43]

III

John C. Brown was a man of some accomplishment. A thirty-seven-year-old former attorney from Tennessee, Brown had persevered through captivity following Donelson, a wound at Perryville, and the political infighting of the Bragg tenure to become a Confederate major general following Hood's promotion. As the politically well connected brother of a former governor of Tennessee, Brown had assumed command of Cheatham's old division when Cheatham was promoted. On November 29th his division had been the trailing unit of Cheatham's Corps, having crossed Rutherford Creek about 4:00 P.M., then being sent by staff officers north along the Davis Ford road. While en route, Brown's column was suddenly shifted westward across the Rally Hill pike near the tollgate and was put into line by Cheatham's order adjacent to Cleburne's Division.[44]

Cheatham was present with Cleburne and Brown at about 5:00 P.M. when the planned assault was organized. Cheatham had just come from Hood's headquarters and evidently had briefed the army commander about his pending attack. Since Hood had not been at the front, he did not know of or then question Cheatham about his intended objective, only being aware that fighting was in progress and Cheatham was trying to obtain all available troops.[45]

Cheatham's instructions to Brown were peremptory: "to take" Spring Hill. Brown, with his relatively fresh troops, was to form his battle line in two ranks and lead the assault against the ridge on the outskirts of town. In fact, since it was nearly dark and the rolling, wooded terrain obscured a view of the Confederate line, the sound of Brown's small arms would be the signal for Cleburne and the other troops to attack in their sectors. Forrest's cavalrymen would support Brown's advance on their right flank, from across the Rally Hill pike.[46]

After giving his final orders, Cheatham said that since Bate had not yet come up, he would personally go to the left and bring forward that division. Cheatham trotted off, mentioning only that Hood had just told him Stewart's Corps was close by and would be ordered north to block the turnpike beyond Spring Hill. Meanwhile, Cleburne had ridden back to his division to await the sound of Brown's guns prior to launching his long-delayed attack.[47]

The minutes passed. Cleburne became impatient. One of his brigade commanders, Daniel C. Govan, who with his staff had just rescued a family from a burning house set afire by Federal artillery shells, was also puzzled. Even Cheatham, riding toward Bate's position, remarked to his staff, "Why don't we hear Brown's guns?"[48]

Brown's line of skirmishers had barely begun to advance when up galloped Brigadier General Otto F. Strahl, a veteran brigade commander who had extensive combat experience and was known as a fighter. Strahl had important information for Brown. As commander of the brigade positioned on the division's extreme right, the former Tennessee lawyer said his line was outflanked to the east by a line of Federal infantry on a wooded knoll. If his men continued ahead, said Strahl, he would be taken by a crossfire from both flank and front. Brown went with Strahl and saw the Union troops in position. His 2,730-man division was considerably understrength since States Rights Gist's Brigade, his largest unit, was not yet present. Further, where was the support of Forrest's cavalrymen, which, as Brown had been told, would protect his right flank? Earlier, as his division had marched onto the battlefield, Brown had noticed the cavalrymen of Jackson's division, Forrest's command, on the higher ground east of Spring Hill. Now they were nowhere in sight. Brown conferred with several of his brigade commanders and abruptly made his decision. He would not advance until he had consulted with Cheatham. Since the corps commander had ridden off to bring up Bate, Brown sent two staff officers to find him. Other members of his staff were sent to suspend the division's advance. Until Cheatham arrived, Brown would simply halt in position.[49]

Darkness was already closing about the waiting and poised line of gray infantrymen, and instead of imminent success, the prospect of a major victory now lay in the hands of Cheatham, whenever he might be found.

Benjamin Franklin Cheatham never had been called upon to conduct a battle. At age forty-four the newest corps commander in the Army of Tennessee was being relied on as Hood's principal front-line tactician, a role he did not particularly relish. Cheatham's methods mirrored his long-established credo as a rough-and-tumble fighter. Described by one observer as a curious cross between a well-to-do Southern farmer and a Prussian field marshal, Cheatham had a reputation as a hard drinker that rivaled his ardent fighting spirit. From the Mexican War forth, Cheatham had practiced the obvious: if the enemy was present, the best way to whip him was to fight him. This commitment to the concept of attacking and overwhelming already had been demonstrated on the field at Spring Hill.[50]

Cheatham had gone to the left after leaving Brown, looking for Bate's Division where he presumed it would be, in the vicinity of Cleburne's left flank, near the turnpike. As the daylight faded, Cheatham impatiently kept asking his staff why they failed to hear the sound of Brown's attack. After a half hour his anxiety became too great. "Let us go and see what is the matter," he told his staff.[51]

En route back to the eastern flank, Cheatham met one of John C. Brown's staff officers, bringing the news about the suspended attack. After hastening to find Brown in the growing darkness, Cheatham closely questioned him about his situation. It would be "inevitable disaster," said Brown, if he had to make the attack without any protection on his right flank. Since the enemy had thrown out a seemingly strong line beyond his path, Brown had thought it best to suspend the attack until Cheatham arrived.[52]

Cheatham hesitated in thought. It was now about 6:15 P.M., with total darkness at hand. There was little means to verify the strength of the enemy's position beyond Brown's right flank. If Brown blundered into another bloody Atlanta-type repulse following this frontal assault, the repercussions on Cheatham's career might be disastrous. As a major general temporarily assigned to command of a corps, Cheatham was not anxious to assume undue risks. He was confronting an unknown entity in front. Brown said his men were tired and worn out from marching through woods and fields rather than along the roadway, due to Hood's fear of an attack en route. Also, Forrest's men had mysteriously pulled out and marched away to an unknown location. There were too many questions and not enough answers.[53]

Cheatham blinked in the face of destiny. According to Brown, Cheatham told him that he "fully approved" of his action in calling off the attack. Cheatham then rode off to Hood's headquarters. He would let John Bell Hood decide what to do.[54]

Hood seemed to be a man at ease that afternoon, noted his guide, John Gregory. Sitting on a log by Absalom Thompson's fish pond, Hood appeared to be quite composed and collected. About 4:00 P.M. everything appeared to be going well, and Hood sent off a dispatch to Stephen D. Lee at Columbia, saying that apparently the enemy was ignorant of their movement. At the sound of the initial fighting Hood had little cause for concern. He presumed that Cheatham, as frontline commander, was attacking the enemy to get control of the turnpike. Cheatham's hasty visit to headquarters before 5:00 P.M. only reaffirmed that a renewed attack was in preparation following Cleburne's stalled advance and would soon begin. Hood at the time had ordered up Stewart, then waiting at Rutherford Creek, intending to send his corps north beyond Spring Hill to cut off the enemy's imminent retreat.[55]

Yet as the sun went down, Hood had listened in vain for the sound of Cheatham's guns. Puzzled by the relative silence as the daylight faded to darkness, Hood said he became somewhat uneasy. At first he considered that Cheatham had taken possession of Spring Hill "without encountering material opposition," or else had blocked off the pike. Finally, nothing further being heard, Hood sent a staff officer to learn what had happened.[56]

By the time of full darkness, 6:17 P.M., Hood was found by Stewart beside a small fire along the roadside near Hood's headquarters at the Thompson house. He was complaining bitterly that his orders had not been obeyed, said

Stewart. Hood had just learned from the staff officer that no action had been taken following the original attack. Hood told Stewart to move with his command north along the Davis Ford road and take position beyond Spring Hill, his right across the turnpike, with his left "extending down this way." Stewart promptly departed, taking a local guide to lead the way.[57]

Soon thereafter, Cheatham appeared at Hood's headquarters. According to Hood, Cheatham was greeted with a resounding query, full of pent-up emotion. "Why in the name of God have you not attacked the enemy and taken possession of that pike?" Hood demanded. Cheatham replied that he had been confronted by an enemy force that outflanked his exposed right and he needed Stewart's help. Hood immediately sent a staff officer after Stewart, redirecting his march to the left, to join with Cheatham's right flank.[58]

There is little doubt that Hood, although perhaps angry with Cheatham for his failure to achieve outright success that day, was not then unduly alarmed by these unlooked-for developments. Throughout the remainder of the day Hood's attitude continued to be firm in the belief that these events were not of great significance; in the morning the Confederate army would bag Schofield's trapped columns with relative ease.[59]

Being greatly fatigued by the long, tiresome horseback ride, and having been up since 3:00 A.M., Hood planned to retire early. Following a sumptuous "big feast" dinner at the Thompson residence that featured considerable "toasting" of drinks, said Hood's guide, Hood went to a guest's bedroom which he would share with several staff officers. By about 9:00 P.M. Hood had unstrapped his artificial leg, perhaps swallowed some laudanum (a tincture of opium), and was soon in bed and asleep.[60]

Ironically, the Columbia-to-Franklin turnpike, Hood's especial fixation early that afternoon, was in the process of being cut off to Federal passage as darkness fell on November 29th. William Bate and his 2,100-man division had at last approached their primary objective. Bate's men had often halted and changed direction as they pressed gradually forward across more than a mile of rolling countryside south of Spring Hill. There had been confusion almost from the start. Cleburne's division had advanced and disappeared from sight before Bate was ready to move. Then only belatedly Bate learned that Cleburne "had changed front" after hearing firing away to the right. If not actually lost at this point, Bate was uncertain of his proper position. Following another delay to obtain a guide, Bate learned of the actual location of the turnpike, causing him to shift farther to the right.[61]

Finally, at about 5:30 P.M., his division swept forward across the Nathaniel Cheairs farm, just north of its handsome residence. In their front a battalion of Georgia sharpshooters, armed with deadly Whitworth and Kerr rifles, moved forward to within a hundred yards of the turnpike. Here they discovered the 26th Ohio Infantry regiment, detached from John Q. Lane's brigade to guard a crossroad leading west toward the Nashville & Decatur Railroad. As Bate realigned his brigade for a push forward across the pike, a brief firefight broke out between the sharpshooters and the Ohioans.[62]

It was the noise of this skirmish that probably attracted the attention of Cheatham's staff officers, who had been sent to find Bate's missing division. The sharpshooters were having little difficulty with the small Ohio unit, rapidly driving these Federals back down the crossroad, when suddenly they were ordered to halt. One of Cheatham's staff officers delivered to the sharpshooter commander, Lieutenant A. Buck Schell, an urgent order for Bate's entire division to move up on Cheatham's left flank. Schell promptly went to Bate and reported the order. Bate's main battle line was then within 200 yards of the pike. The Ohioans already had disappeared westward along the crossroad.[63]

Bate was reluctant to yield the wide-open pike, now that he had gained his objective as defined by Hood's 4:00 P.M. instructions. Although it was dark, there were signs of enemy activity along the roadway toward Columbia. Yet Bate soon received another similar message from Cheatham. Evidently this was delivered by the second staff officer sent to find him. Bate reluctantly decided to obey Cheatham's order. With difficulty he pulled his division back in the darkness and belatedly found Cleburne's flank, where he went into bivouac about 10:00 P.M.[64]

Throughout the entire episode Bate was so puzzled by these conflicting orders that as soon as his troops were repositioned near Cleburne he determined to go personally to Hood's headquarters and report the matter.[65]

Bate was not alone in his uneasy concern. There were others equally perplexed by what had occurred, and the path to Absalom Thompson's fine residence would be busy throughout that star-canopied night.

Alexander P. Stewart, like Bate, had been instructed by Hood to cut off the turnpike. After leaving Hood by the roadside about nightfall, Stewart had advanced northward at the head of his corps until he reached a fork in the Davis Ford road. The young guide he was using directed him to the right, past the Caldwell house along an indistinct path known locally as the old Settlers' Road. It was Stewart's intention to go about a mile north of Spring Hill and strike the turnpike. Yet, as Stewart passed the Caldwell residence, he learned that this was Forrest's headquarters.[66]

Stewart promptly dismounted and went to see Forrest, hoping to better learn of the army's positions. Forrest at the time was preoccupied with reports from his scouts that the enemy had left the main turnpike and was moving north to bypass Spring Hill along a more westerly road, the Carter Creek pike. Already Forrest was preparing to go and see Hood on the matter, although now so circumstanced as to be able to do little about it.[67]

Earlier, following the arrival of Cleburne's infantry, Forrest, about 4:30 P.M., had ordered his exhausted troopers to pull back. With few exceptions, Forrest's cavalrymen had expended nearly all of their ammunition, and following their daylight-to-dusk ordeal of marching and fighting needed rest.[68]

Accordingly, Jackson's Division, which held the high ground near John C. Brown's flank, had withdrawn after Cleburne overran Bradley's brigade. Their sudden departure, just at the time when Brown had looked for their support, and when the crucial eastern flank had been left exposed by John Q. Lane's redeployment to outflank Brown, unknowingly had become the flaw that had altered the complexion of the battle. Once Jackson's men had rested, Forrest sent the entire division north toward Thompson's Station, about three miles north of Spring Hill, to "intercept" the enemy. By about midnight Jackson was en route for the turnpike north of town, having rested perhaps six or seven hours. Since Chalmers's Division also had been relieved, there were few cavalrymen now remaining on the field at Spring Hill.[69]

Meanwhile, Stewart, about to mount his horse after talking with Forrest, found his column inexplicably halted. One of Cheatham's staff officers had come up and directed in Hood's name that the corps move to the aid of Brown's Division.[70]

Stewart was astounded. It seemed strange that Hood, having just sent him north to cut the turnpike, would suddenly change these instructions. Furthermore, this engineer officer was not a member of Hood's staff. Stewart questioned him closely. The man insisted that he had just come from Hood's headquarters. Stewart hesitated. Then, remembering Forrest's comment that the enemy was reported attempting to escape via the Carter's Creek pike, Stewart considered that Hood had perhaps changed his mind.[71]

With his 8,000-man corps jamming the roadway, and in total darkness, Stewart was not anxious to redirect his march without first checking on the position he was to occupy. Ordering that his men wait in the road, Stewart went forward with Cheatham's staff officer to find Cheatham or one of his commanders.[72]

Ahead along the Rally Hill pike, Brown's men were found positioned across the roadway, fronting north. Stewart was personally asked by Brown to bring his corps up and form an extension to his line.[73]

Stewart was perplexed. A prolongation of Brown's line would extend east, away from the position across the turnpike that Hood earlier had designated. Feeling that there had been a serious mistake, Stewart told his staff officers to issue orders allowing the men to bivouac while he went to find Hood.[74]

Between 10:00 and 11:00 P.M., said one of Stewart's division commanders, his weary men were at last allowed to bivouac along the side of the road. Including the time spent in line of battle south of Rutherford Creek, most of Stewart's men had been standing in ranks, momentarily awaiting orders, for about six hours.[75]

From Bate on the southern flank, to Stewart, who had been sent northward, the unwitting pullback from the turnpike was now complete. In the rush to bring a decisive force to bear on the tenuous Federal line along the southern outskirts of Spring Hill, Cheatham's one-dimensional concept had led to one of the greatest overreactions in the history of the Army of Tennessee. With the arrival on the battlefield about 10:00 P.M. of Edward Johnson's Division from Stephen D. Lee's Corps, fully 19,000 Confederate infantrymen were arrayed in close proximity to Stanley's single division of about 6,000 Federal troops.[76]

The fortunes of war thus dangled by a slender thread. A host of frustrated and thoroughly confused Confederate generals were in the process of descending upon Hood's headquarters, seeking answers for their many questions. But at Absalom Thompson's fine farmhouse Hood had gone to bed.

CHAPTER XV

A Hand Stronger
than Armies

NOVEMBER 29th had become a succession of unforeseen and recurring crises for John M. Schofield. A dispatch received shortly after 8:00 A.M. from Thomas suggested that he hold the Duck River line until A. J. Smith's men could come forward. Schofield's inclination was to withdraw due to the threat of his flank being turned. With Wilson having been driven off by Forrest's cavalry, Schofield was in the dark, having little ready means to determine what to do. At 8:20 A.M. he had wired to Thomas that he would await the result of an infantry reconnaissance patrol sent "to learn the fact[s]," before retreating beyond the Harpeth River, if necessary.[1]

Thus, by far the most significant event of that morning was the brigade-sized reconnaissance patrol Schofield had ordered about 8:15 A.M. to march east and look for the enemy's infantry. Under the command of Colonel P. Sidney Post of the 59th Illinois Infantry, five regiments, about 1,600 men, were sent from Thomas J. Wood's division to attempt to discover where the Confederates were going, if found across the river. Should they be observed moving westward behind the Union army, Post was told to contest the ground stubbornly. Schofield's fear that Hood might attempt such a move had resulted in the order for Stanley's trailing division, under Kimball, to halt at Rutherford Creek in order to protect the army's rear.[2]

The importance of this patrol was underscored by Schofield's presence, the Federal commander riding along for perhaps several miles before returning to his headquarters. Also present with Post that morning was Captain William J. Twining, Schofield's aide and chief engineer. By about 10:00 A.M. Post had moved eastward toward the Davis Ford road and was in the vicinity of Bear Creek, about six miles from Columbia. Soon thereafter, at Cooper's

Mineral Well, Post's skirmish line advanced toward the Davis Ford road. Suddenly a line of gray soldiers rose to their feet behind a fence between the skirmishers and the road. There was a flurry of shots, and Twining became convinced of the presence of Confederate infantry. At 10:45 A.M. he sent a hasty dispatch to Schofield, warning that a column of infantry was moving north. Yet, since they had subsequently disappeared behind an obstructing hill, Twining did not know "whether they intend to advance or merely hold us in check."[3]

This resulted in more uncertainty. Schofield soon sent a dispatch to Stanley telling him that, at least, there was a considerable enemy force across the Duck River. Accordingly, he would try to hold the enemy in check, then withdraw that night after dark. Later, as the morning progressed, there was no sign of the enemy turning westward along Rutherford Creek toward the Federal rear. As a result, Schofield merely issued orders for Ruger's division and some of Wood's troops to march eastward as a support for Post. Meanwhile, the desultory artillery firing and sharpshooting continued in front of Columbia.[4]

Stephen D. Lee's Corps was putting up a good front. About twenty cannon under the direction of Colonel R. F. Beckham were firing at intervals, dueling with the Federal artillery across the river. When one of the Federal shells exploded near Beckham, a fragment struck him in the head, fracturing his skull. From the beginning it was perceived that the wound was mortal, and a staff officer wrote, "It is hard enough to be killed at all, but to be killed in such an insignificant affair makes it doubly bad."[5]

For Schofield the affair was anything but insignificant. Having belatedly determined to withdraw, due to the continuing enemy pressure at Columbia he decided to disengage only after darkness. Detailed orders were issued for a successive retreat, beginning with Cox's division at dusk. Meanwhile, further difficulties were pressuring the Federal commander. Since he lacked adequate transportation, Schofield had destroyed his heavy wooden pontoon boats following his withdrawal across the Duck River on the night of November 27th. He now had no means of rapidly crossing the Harpeth River. At 1:00 P.M. he urgently telegraphed to Thomas at Nashville asking for pontoons to be put down across the Harpeth River at Franklin.[6]

About 3:00 P.M., however, the crowning touch occurred. Post's brigade had returned to camp bringing word of the heavy movement of Confederate troops toward Spring Hill. To add further emphasis to Post's reports, between the sporadic roar of the guns at Columbia, the distant rumble of artillery fire could be heard in the direction of Spring Hill.[7]

Schofield began to fret. Was it possible that he had been duped by the enemy force at Columbia? "About 3:00 P.M. I became satisfied the enemy would not attack my position on [the] Duck River, but was pushing two corps direct for Spring Hill," he later wrote. Schofield had been operating on a false premise: that if the Confederates did make a flanking march, they would swing west along the Rutherford Creek line to attack in his immediate rear. Spurred into action by the threat of disaster at the more distant Spring Hill, Schofield decided to go personally to that site. About 3:30 P.M. he led two of Brigadier General Thomas Ruger's brigades toward Spring Hill. The remainder of his troops at Columbia would withdraw at dark, as ordered earlier.[8]

Ironically, no sooner was Schofield en route to Spring Hill than Stephen D. Lee's men began to attack at Columbia. Lee had been told to occupy the Federals along the Duck River until Hood reached their rear, then to force a crossing and attack as the enemy attempted to withdraw. Observing the departure of Ruger's troops, sent to the support of Post about midday, Lee thought it was an entire corps pulling out. He then summoned the pontoons to come up, and ordered a crossing at the downtown ford.[9]

Before Lee's preparations were complete, however, it was midafternoon. Several Federal infantry regiments were in rifle pits within a woods about 300 yards from the ford and added to the fire from the emplaced Union artillery. They "annoyed us excessively," said Lee. When the mules brought up to haul the heavy pontoon boats were terrified by the bursting Federal shells, Stephen D. Lee had the animals of one wagon removed from their harnesses. Then, attaching a long rope to the pontoon wagon, he sent a large number of men to the high riverbank to hold the rope and control the rate of descent. With about forty other men pushing on the wagon, a rush was made to the riverbank under the cover of snipers firing from the bluff behind tombstones in Greenwood Cemetery. The wagon and boat skidded and slid for about 250 yards under a gauntlet of Federal fire, but the craft was launched at the ford, and several boatloads of troops hurriedly paddled across. Only one man was wounded, and three regiments of Edmund W. Pettus's Brigade were ferried to the north bank. About 4:00 P.M. these troops charged the two Kentucky regiments occupying the woods, driving them back to the main battle line about 600 yards distant. More Confederate troops were soon crossed, a firm bridgehead established, and by dusk the engineers were busily emplacing the pontoon bridge. When Hood's dispatch arrived that the enemy was cut off, Lee anticipated that a great battle would soon begin at Spring Hill. Thereafter, it seemed that the enemy must be crushed between the jaws of Hood's and Lee's forces.[10]

It was well into the night before Lee was ready to advance with his two divisions, laboriously crossed on the newly emplaced pontoons. Meanwhile, the Federal commander remaining behind at Columbia, Brigadier General Jacob D. Cox, alertly utilized this opportunity to begin the withdrawal ordered by Schofield. Due to the darkness Cox was willing to take somewhat of a gamble. In the wake of his departing divisions he left only the two previously deployed Kentucky regiments and a few skirmishers to hold the extensive length of breastworks along the main line.[11]

The first troops to pull out were those of Brigadier General James Reilly.

They were on the march between 7:00 and 8:00 P.M., with Wood's division of the Fourth Corps following about 10:00 P.M. Despite what appeared to be a clear night, there was no moon, and the darkness seemed almost impenetrable. The march appeared to be exasperatingly slow to the men, who knew something important was in the air. At Rutherford Creek, due to a narrow, flimsy bridge, the column's progress nearly came to a halt. Finally, about midnight, Kimball's trailing division, which had remained at Rutherford Creek most of the day, crossed over the bridge.[12]

The men in the long column stumbled on with increasing effort, frequently stopping and starting with abrupt jolts and lurches. Weariness became fatigue, and fatigue exhaustion. Mile after mile the men shuffled onward in silent agony, the blackness of night concealing their sullen faces. Many of the men in Reilly's division hadn't slept in three nights. As incredible as it seems, wrote a captain of the 112th Illinois, some of his men went to sleep while walking. They were observed to suddenly collapse in the road, where the fall would jar them awake. Then, with pained groans, they would get up and stagger onward.[13]

At last the men could see the glow of campfires close by the road ahead. Some foresaw that these must be the camps of the army in advance. Thereafter, the column stepped briskly forward, eager for the chance to rest or sleep. Said one weary private, he intended to lie down by a blazing fire whether his regiment halted or not.[14]

In the 86th Indiana Infantry, marching at the head of Wood's division, the column suddenly came to a halt. One of Wood's staff officers, Captain M. P. Bostow, slowly rode through the ranks. Quietly he spoke the incredible news: "Boys, this is a Rebel camp lying near the road, and we must march by it as quickly as possible. Arrange everything so there will be no noise." Said one of the 86th's startled men, every soldier who heard immediately knew that they had marched into "a most desperate situation." For a long time thereafter there would be little thought of sleep.[15]

Ahead in Spring Hill, matters had gone from bad to worse for John M. Schofield. His approach to the village just after dark at the head of Ruger's troops had resulted in quite a scare. Ruger's skirmishers were occasionally involved in scattered firing, and as the column moved within two miles of Spring Hill, Ruger halted and put Silas Strickland's leading brigade in line of battle across the road. Proceeding slowly at the head of his men, Colonel Strickland was halted in a meadow near some haystacks by a picket's challenge. Strickland rode ahead, calling to the sentry, "It's all right, my boy, I want to put my brigade in position here." Only then was he warned by one of his men that the sentry "was a damned Rebel." Strickland dashed off, just ahead of a rifle shot from the picket.[16]

As the Confederates seemed to be in control of the pike ahead, Ruger formed his second brigade in line of battle. Now Schofield came dashing along the line, "his beard flying in the wind." He said, "Boys, there's nothing but cavalry [ahead]; just put your bayonets on and go right through them." Ruger's men noted how Schofield kept nervously pulling at his long beard, and wondered if this was so. While probing cautiously forward, the flankers of the 23d Michigan Infantry suddenly found a lone individual in their midst and surrounded him. Their prisoner was Captain R. T. English, one of General Granbury's staff officers. English had crept forward to learn what troops were passing, thinking they were perhaps Bate's men—then believed to be closing up on Cleburne's flank. Soon thereafter, a Federal picket on duty at the bridge a half mile south of the village found an anxious general in his presence. It was Schofield, who eagerly asked what had happened at Spring Hill. Schofield said he had feared everyone there had been captured.[17]

Although Ruger's men, aided by the darkness and a sound-muffling wind, were able to pass into Spring Hill without further difficulty, it was apparent that they had been lucky not to be ambushed. Granbury's men evidently had mistaken the marching column for Bate's troops.[18]

By the time Schofield entered Spring Hill, about 7:00 P.M., he was thoroughly convinced of his army's great peril. Long lines of enemy campfires had sprung up in the vicinity, accentuating reports of extreme danger, which David Stanley grimly confirmed.[19]

William McKissack's brick residence on Main Street in downtown Spring Hill was appropriated for the Federal headquarters that night. After conferring with Stanley and interrogating the captured staff officer, Schofield seemed to better understand his dire predicament. An observer noticed Schofield's state of great agitation in "walking the floor and wringing his hands." About two-thirds of the Union army was only then preparing to evacuate the works north of Columbia and march to Spring Hill.[20]

Not only was Schofield's army divided and strung out over a ten-mile expanse, but the presence of at least two fully deployed Rebel infantry corps had been disclosed by the captured enemy captain. Of immense worry was the Union army's wagon train containing ammunition, baggage, and artillery. There were about 800 wagons, and these slow-moving vehicles and the ponderous ordnance would not allow for rapid movement. Should Hood cut off their retreat to Nashville via Franklin, Stanley felt that it would demoralize the army. Even if they had to flee in another direction, all of the vital stores and some artillery would have to be abandoned. Should they be compelled to battle their way out of Spring Hill, Stanley feared the men might not fight well, knowing they were being attacked from the rear with their retreat cut off. In such circumstances, Stanley envisioned many might be expected to "surrender their way out."[21]

With the sudden arrival of even more disheartening news the situation seemed truly desperate. From Thompson's Station, only a few miles north along the Franklin pike, came reports that the Rebels had cut off the turnpike and were in possession of that site. Before dusk that evening Forrest's cavalrymen from Ross's Brigade, having pursued Wilson as he withdrew toward Franklin, had swung abruptly westward to strike the turnpike at Thompson's Station. A few wagons were moving along the pike and Ross sent his Texans sweeping down on them as they raced for a blockhouse guarding the nearby railroad bridge. A few wagons were taken, and while the Confederates swarmed over the depot at the railroad, a southbound train had appeared.[22]

The train's engineer, when suddenly attacked by mounted Confederates, cut the engine loose and sped off toward Spring Hill. Although the railroad cars, which began rolling backward due to a retrograde, coasted back under the cover of the blockhouse and were saved, Ross's men soon fired the Thompson's Station railroad bridge and depot.[23]

The arrival of the frightened engineer with his engine at Spring Hill had sent shivers down the spines of Stanley and Schofield. With an unknown quantity of Rebels blocking the Federals' line of retreat at Thompson's Station it was imperative that the route be cleared. Schofield determined to make the attempt and about 9:00 P.M. marched with Ruger's full division for that site. Already there was talk of having to destroy the entire wagon train, lest it fall into the enemy's hands. In fact, the prospect of an outright surrender stared Schofield in the face. According to a local account, Mrs. McKissack was told her house might be used "unpleasantly" that night. When she expressed fear that her house might be burned as a military necessity, the Federal general replied, "No, madam, we will not burn the house, but here we will have to surrender this army to the Rebels."[24]

Due to the many difficulties, including bringing up the remainder of the army, the danger was so great "it was like treading upon the thin crust covering a smoldering volcano," wrote Stanley. At any moment the gray ranks surrounding Spring Hill might advance a few hundred yards to the turnpike and pour destruction into the retreating Federal column. Survival of the army was at stake, and Stanley's chief of staff penned in his journal that evening, "Take it all together, we are in a very bad situation."[25]

II

Within the perimeter of the Confederate army that evening there was much speculation about why no attack was in progress against what was obviously a confused and makeshift Union battle line. One South Carolina colonel rode forward in the darkness with several staff officers and heard the sound of fences being pulled down, planks being ripped from outhouses, and barricades hastily being erected. The Yankee line was obviously in turmoil, urgent commands were heard, and the rumble of wagon wheels was distinct in the distance. In frustration, as he turned to ride away the colonel drew his revolver and emptied it in the direction of the enemy. It was inexplicable, he later said, that the enemy was being allowed to stay there without being attacked.[26]

The lack of aggressive action was equally puzzling to many of the Confederate generals. Their men had been poised at dusk to make the attack being organized by Cheatham, at which time it was expected Spring Hill would be easily overrun. Cleburne had waited long and in vain for the sound of guns from Brown's Division, the signal to begin his attack. Having been prevented by Cheatham's order from attacking until Brown's, Bate's, and other troops could be brought up, Cleburne had grown angry with the delay. Already there were so many troops formed for the attack that Granbury's Brigade was sent back to their original position adjacent to the turnpike. No one seemed to know when or if an attack would be made. Cheatham was unavailable, having gone to see Hood at nightfall.[27]

John C. Brown, who was to initiate the attack, claimed he had "no orders," pending Cheatham's referral of the "outflanked" matter to Hood. Although S. R. Gist's missing brigade, which had been deployed as the trailing flankers on the march to Spring Hill, had at last come up and was now in position on Brown's critical right flank, Brown remained adamant in his refusal to move. The curious lack of activity already had caused one of Forrest's generals, James Chalmers, to ride among the infantry to see what was happening. Encountering Brown, Chalmers asked him why an attack wasn't being made. Brown curtly replied, because "I have no orders." The tone in his voice somewhat irritated Chalmers, who remarked before he rode off, "General, when I was circumstanced as you are at Shiloh, I attacked without orders."[28]

Several staff officers, provoked by the long delay with the men in line of battle, found General Brown and again posed the obvious question. Brown's stock reply was that he was without orders. Although they pressed him further, suggesting he might win a new feather in his cap by attacking, he laughed and said, "No, I must wait for orders." When yet another staff officer persisted, Brown said the responsibility of attacking without orders was great, and he didn't care to assume the risk—considering that he was outflanked on the right. Captain John Ingram, a staff officer who allegedly had been drinking, then spoke up and rather scoffingly said if he could take Brown's escort company he would drive away any offending Federal unit beyond the Confederate flank. Brown, flushed with sudden anger, told Ingram he was under arrest.[29]

Since Cheatham soon returned with Hood's order suspending the attack, the word quickly spread among the field commanders that there would be no advance that night. To many, this passiveness was foolish. Where was the logic in allowing a vulnerable enemy to remain under the very muzzles of their poised guns? After the men were ordered to bivouac in line, an exasperated cluster of general officers began to make their way to Hood's headquarters.[30]

*   *   *

The first to awaken John Bell Hood that night was Alexander Stewart. About 11:00 P.M. Stewart awkwardly explained that he didn't understand why he had been redirected into a position adjacent to Brown's right flank. Hood replied that it was not his intention to change the original premise of cutting off the pike north of the village, but Cheatham had arrived following Stewart's departure and said somebody was needed on Brown's right flank. Hood had no idea that Brown was facing north, rather than west, and thus didn't realize the implication of this change. Instead of his line extending from Brown's right northward across the pike, said Stewart, it would, if deployed according to orders, extend eastward, away from the turnpike.[31]

Hood thought for a moment. Stewart's men were already bivouacked. His mind clouded by fatigue and perhaps laudanum, he merely told Stewart that it was not of importance; let the men rest and they would find the Yankees in the morning.[32]

The next commander to see Hood that night was Forrest. The cavalry general's son, Willie, had taken a flesh wound in the leg during the day, and Forrest evidently was in a surly mood. After telling Hood that the enemy was reported moving along the Carter's Creek pike to escape being attacked on the Franklin road, Forrest received permission to send Chalmers's Division south to intercept and check or pursue the enemy's column. Further, since Stewart obviously had not cut the pike north of Spring Hill, Forrest was permitted to send Jackson's Division north toward Thompson's Station to block the pike and attack any traffic along the road. As for Hood's own plans, he'd "find the Yankees in the morning," said Hood cussing.[33]

Awaiting the conclusion of the Forrest-Hood conference was William Bate, still anxious about Cheatham's changing of Hood's original instructions to strike south and cut off the turnpike. Following a lengthy wait, Bate saw Hood and told him how he had been diverted from his original objective. Apparently Hood already knew that the Columbia-to-Franklin pike was not yet effectively blocked. This information came from Major John B. Pirtle, of Bate's staff, who had found Hood in conference with Cheatham at about 6:30 P.M. Pirtle reported his commander's reluctance to move from his position controlling the turnpike. At this point Cheatham had abruptly spoken up in Hood's presence, saying that Bate was to move north and connect with Cleburne, or else report under arrest. Thereafter, to accomplish the anticipated blocking of the pike south of Cleburne's position, Cheatham had been given Edward Johnson's Division, the last major unit in Hood's column of march. They were the troops with which Bate would be replaced.[34]

Six hours later, Bate found Hood very indifferent. Sleepily, Hood told Bate that it made little difference, Forrest had just been sent to block the pike north of Spring Hill, and "in the morning we will have a surrender without a fight." Hood said reassuringly, "We can sleep quiet tonight," and went back to bed. Bate, feeling much better about the matter, returned to his camp.[35]

Well after midnight, Hood was again awakened, by, of all people, a private. The man had wandered within the enemy lines in the darkness and found the Federal troops in great confusion. The turnpike was filled with traffic of all kinds, he reported, and thinking something should be done about it, he had come to Hood's headquarters. Hood's acting aide, Governor Isham G. Harris, his chief of staff, Major A. P. Mason, and Major James D. Porter, one of Cheatham's staff officers, were sleeping in the same room with Hood. Harris heard Hood tell Mason to send a note to Cheatham asking that he move to the road, if not already done, and attack the enemy. Hood remained in bed, as did the others, and was soon asleep. Mason was so sleepy that on the following day he didn't even remember sending the note to Cheatham.[36]

Cheatham, who said he received Mason's note in the middle of the night, had only recently directed the placement of Edward Johnson's Division south of Bate's location. It was now intended that Johnson's division would be the primary "blocking" force to cut off use of the turnpike to the enemy.[37]

Johnson had waited in line of battle with Stewart's Corps south of Rutherford Creek until summoned about 9:00 P.M. to advance and take position as directed by Cheatham's order. At about 10:00 P.M., thought one of Johnson's Mississippi colonels, they had moved up amid the twinkling camp-fires of the Confederate army and had belatedly gone into bivouac south of Cheatham's deployed lines. After seeing to his men, the colonel wrapped himself in his horse blanket and was nearly asleep. Suddenly he was aroused by a staff officer who had orders for the colonel to form his men. The entire division, it was thought, would move to the turnpike and sweep south along the road. After awakening the troops and forming a battle line, guns were loaded, and Johnson's Division drowsily awaited the order to advance.[38]

Minutes passed, and there was no word from headquarters. Some of the men began to sink to the ground and fall asleep. More time elapsed. Where were the orders to move?

Earlier, Cheatham personally had given directions to Major Joseph Bostick of his staff to place Johnson's Division on the extreme left of his corps. About midnight Bostick returned to headquarters and reported Johnson's men in position. Yet Bostick said that there were noises coming from the turnpike, suggesting that the enemy was moving along that road. Thereafter, Cheatham received Mason's hasty note about firing on any Union troops found along the pike. Cheatham then directed that Bostick return to Johnson and have him take care of this matter.[39]

When found by Bostick, General Johnson seemed much perturbed. Not only was it the middle of the night, but Johnson began bitterly complaining about having been "loaned out" to another corps. He even asked why Cheatham hadn't ordered one of his own divisions to do what appeared to be rather routine work.[40]

While his division was aroused, Johnson and Bostick had ridden ahead to scout the turnpike. They found the road empty and everything quiet. It was now about 2:00 A.M., and Johnson saw no reason to advance his lines beyond Cheatham's flank, where they might be isolated and unduly exposed in taking an unfamiliar position in total darkness. "If he [Ed Johnson] went to moving about in the dark, he would be liable to run into some of our own troops, and they would fire into each other," said Johnson. Accordingly, he rode back with Bostick to Cheatham's headquarters and reported what they had observed. Cheatham evidently was satisfied that Johnson's men could not be advanced "intellegintly or safely," and let the matter rest. By this hour nearly everyone in Johnson's ranks had sunk to the ground and was asleep, lying in line of battle within a few hundred yards of the pike.[41]

The approach to Spring Hill, wrote a Federal officer of Cox's division, was fraught with extraordinary danger. As an aide to General Cox passed the long line of campfires, only about a quarter of a mile east of the turnpike, he could easily discern Confederates walking about the fires. In one of Wood's bri-gades, despite the repeated entreaties of their officers for no noise, a new regiment temporarily attached to the brigade was so nervous that it was discovered by the enemy. This regiment, the 40th Missouri Infantry, had previously served on garrison duty at Murfreesboro. The clatter of frying pans, cooking utensils, and all manner of equipment frequently carried by green levies made such a racket as had scarcely been heard in the army, said an Illinois veteran. The 40th Missouri was abruptly fired upon by Confederate skirmishers, sending the Federal ranks scurrying for cover. They were soon piled five deep in the roadway, noted a disgusted officer. When these men hesitated to get up and move on as the fire quieted, the commander of the 13th Ohio Infantry, a veteran unit immediately in their rear, ordered his men to march over the prostrate Missourians. Amid much under-the-breath swearing, the Ohioans walked on and over the green levies, causing them to soon gather their courage and resume the march. Thereafter, the unfortu-nate Missourians were dubbed "the Fortieth Misery" by Wood's veterans.[42]

Beginning about 11:00 P.M. with the arrival of Cox and some of his division, Spring Hill began filling up with bone-weary Federal troops. While the new arrivals were put to work erecting barricades, Stanley awaited word from Schofield about the situation at Thompson's Station. About 11:30 P.M. Schofield returned to Spring Hill with unexpectedly good news. The Rebel cavalry had disappeared upon his approach, leaving their campfires burning. Ruger's division had been left to occupy the site, and thus the road north of the village seemed to be clear all the way to the Harpeth River. Ten minutes later orders were issued for Cox, followed by the entire army, to march to Franklin. Yet most of the Federal troops at Spring Hill were so tired that one of Cox's officers said the men would have chosen to fight a battle there rather than resume the march.[43]

While Cox's men were prodded forward about midnight, an urgent discussion took place between Schofield and Stanley about what to do with the army's huge wagon train. Schofield was fearful that an attempt to save these cumbersome vehicles might occasion a general battle in the morning. According to Stanley, he was urged to burn the train. A narrow bridge constricted passage at a creek north of the village, and Schofield thought it doubtful that the 800 wagons, artillery, and ambulances could clear Spring Hill by daylight. Should the army be attacked while in column of march at daylight, they both anticipated a disaster. Yet the vital importance of these stores and equipment was also obvious. Stanley decided to at least "make an effort to save the train." Orders were issued to get the wagons rolling, and about 1:00 A.M. the rumble of heavy wheels sounded in Spring Hill.[44]

Meanwhile, there was the ongoing difficulty of getting all of Schofield's troops into the village before the enemy blocked the turnpike or advanced from Columbia. So many Confederate stragglers and skirmishers were now active along the turnpike south of Spring Hill that Stanley said it was difficult for individual staff officers or couriers to get through unless moving with a large column. Even the new arrivals at Spring Hill, put to work erecting barricades, found the enemy pressing closely about them. The 96th Illinois was busily building a fence-rail barricade in a cornfield after midnight when they discovered the enemy taking rails from the same fencerow. By the time the trailing division of Nathan Kimball tramped into Spring Hill it was about 1:30 A.M.—just before Ed Johnson and Bostick had gone to the turnpike and found the roadway unoccupied. The only remaining Federal troops in the direction of Columbia at this point were the two Kentucky regiments and the other pickets, left to retard Lee's Corps in their pursuit.[45]

Fortunately for these rear-guard units, their retreat, which began about midnight from near Columbia, was generally uncontested. Leaving their campfires burning brightly to deceive the enemy, the rear-guard detachment stole away silently, even switching their canteens to the side opposite their bayonets to avoid noise on the march. Stephen D. Lee's troops, after crossing the Duck River about dark, had entrenched rather than attack an unknown force in strong earthworks. Although some skirmishers from one of Lee's brigades attacked the line as the last of the Kentuckians withdrew, they captured only a few prisoners. No further initiative was taken that night. Lee waited until daylight to advance with his two divisions, although evidently advised by 2:30 A.M. of the Federal departure. About 4:00 A.M. the Kentucky units under a lieutenant colonel arrived at Spring Hill, and the last of Schofield's troops were present. Miraculously, the army had passed unscathed under the very muzzles of the enemy's weapons.[46]

At that hour Stanley was still busily moving the wagon train out of Spring Hill. In another sixty minutes the task would be completed. Suddenly from the vicinity of Thompson's Station Stanley had word of a disaster. The Confederates had attacked the head of the wagon train, and the entire column was halted. Immediately, the Federals were thrown into despair, said Stanley, who again had to deal with a potentially catastrophic situation.[47]

III

It was perhaps ironic that the Confederates who spread the most panic among the Federals that night were among those who had initiated the fighting at Spring Hill—Forrest's cavalrymen. Lawrence Ross's well-used cavalry brigade from William H. Jackson's Division had withdrawn from the vicinity of Thompson's Station following their midafternoon burning of the railroad bridge. His men had accomplished all that seemed possible then, said Ross, who later withdrew toward Spring Hill to obtain further orders from Jackson.[48]

After midnight Ross was ordered to return to the vicinity of Thompson's Station and again strike the turnpike. Gathering his nearly 700 troopers, Ross approached the pike north of Thompson's Station about 2:00 A.M., just as the head of the Federal wagon train was passing. Dismounting three of his regiments, Ross moved to within a hundred yards of the roadway. Suddenly his men fired a concentrated volley into the column of wagons and animals moving in front. At the sound of the carbines, there was a full stampede on the roadway. Ross's men ran forward yelling, and amid the chaos they captured thirty-nine wagons and many teamsters. While the debris was being sorted through, Ross's men remained posted across the vital turnpike, blocking further passage.[49]

About a half hour had elapsed, wrote Ross, and a number of wagons were set ablaze. Suddenly from both north and south several bodies of infantry were observed approaching. The column advancing from the south proved to be only about thirty-five infantrymen from the 24th Illinois, Stanley's headquarters guard. In the darkness, Ross's men, outlined by the glow from the burning wagons, were unable to observe their minimal strength. Ross and his men pulled out, remounting their horses and abandoning the pike to the oncoming enemy. Thereafter, Ross remained at a distance on the hills overlooking the pike, watching carefully for another opportunity to strike. Yet Stanley had wisely ordered two infantry divisions, Kimball's and Wood's, to escort the main segments of the wagon train, and they were soon observed marching protectively alongside the slow-moving wagons. Further, these infantry columns were doubled up, one on each side of the road, thus shortening by half what one observer estimated would have been a fourteen-mile-long procession. With the heavy columns of infantry moving along the roadway, it was difficult for Ross to get at the long column of wagons, despite the pike remaining choked with hundreds of vehicles.[50]

Finally, at one point where a large stand of timber abutted the pike, Ross's cavalry attempted to approach what appeared to be an unguarded cluster of wagons. It was about daylight, and a nearby Michigan cavalry company observed the enemy stealthily moving toward the exposed wagons. "We were preparing to gallop forward," said a Michigan cavalry officer, but just at that moment a section of artillery unlimbered their Parrott rifles and fired a few shells at the gray horsemen. As Company M of the 2d Michigan Cavalry trotted forward, they found Forrest's riders had taken to their heels. They left in such a cloud of dust, said a nearby Union soldier, that the "boys instinctively ceased firing and commenced laughing." The only evidence they found of the enemy's approach was "a score or more" of campaign hats littering the ground, lost by the Confederates in their hasty flight. It was the final chapter in the saga of Spring Hill.[51]

The last of the Federal troops were on the road and beyond Spring Hill at daylight, including the two Kentucky rear-guard regiments. At 5:00 A.M., said Stanley, he had pushed forward the last wagon across the narrow village bridge. Emerson Opdycke's brigade from Wagner's division was designated as the new rear guard, and Schofield's Federal army slowly stole away from the small mid-Tennessee village without molestation. The miracle of Spring Hill was fully accomplished. Already the Federal soldiers were congratulating themselves on their marvelous escape. Later, an Illinois infantryman wrote with relief, "To say that night was one of terrible suspense was putting it mildly." Wrote another of Schofield's thankful men, "Hood nearly gobbled us up." Perhaps nearly all could agree with the assessment of Brigadier General Luther Bradley, badly wounded in Cleburne's attack at Spring Hill. A few days later he wrote: "It was the most critical time I have ever seen. If only the enemy had shown his usual boldness, I think he would have beaten us disastrously." Indeed, that the Union army had escaped intact soon came to be considered the decree of Providence.[52]

The failure of the Confederate high command at Spring Hill has endured even to this day as one of the greatest missed opportunities of the entire war. Despite the enormous controversy that resulted, actually there is very little mystery about why the Confederates fell victim to their own inertia at Spring Hill. The failure was multilateral, largely being the result of lackluster personal performance and horrendous communications.

The initial flaw was Hood's outdated and inaccurate map, which led to delay and uncertainty of position. This was soon accentuated by his sudden fear about being attacked while en route. The direct result was that Hood lost the essential daylight needed for proper combat operations. Without any cavalry to screen or scout for his column, Hood had been surprised by the appearance of Post's Federal infantry on his flank about midmorning. Unaware that it was merely a reconnaissance sent by Schofield to discover what the Confederates were doing, Hood had greatly overreacted in redeploying his marching columns as if threatened by an attack.

Thereafter, even Hood's attitude seemed to change—from that of an aggressive strike force commander into that of a cautious skeptic. His defensive placement of A. P. Stewart's entire corps in line of battle at Rutherford Creek became a major element of despair when these troops, about half of Hood's column, were unable to arrive on the field before darkness fell.

Hood was convinced from the beginning that Schofield would retreat rather than be trapped in position at Columbia. Although his movement succeeded as planned, Hood had difficulty believing it. Based on Post's infantry being sighted on his flank, he anticipated Schofield's imminent arrival at Spring Hill, hence his order to Bate and others to strike the turnpike and sweep south to block off the junction of the divided enemy forces.

Yet Hood's impromptu decision making and the lack of cohesive, prior planning in defining tactical objectives were at the heart of the difficulty. Hood had been so naive as to regard the tactical elements—to attack and overwhelm—as too obvious to need prior clarification. Accordingly, he all but ignored the considerable staff work, unit coordination, and flexibility of maneuver so necessary for complex offensive operations. His failure to communicate with Cheatham once he had altered his primary objective from attacking the enemy's position at Spring Hill to striking for and moving south along the turnpike was inexcusable. Hood's rapid departure from the front line, trusting to subordinates to manage the tactical aspects in the manner of Stonewall Jackson with Robert E. Lee, was a critical element in the overall failure. By his prolonged presence in the rear, Hood remained unfamiliar with crucial, fast-developing battlefield circumstances. In the narrow time frame of two hours of daylight (4:00 to 6:00 P.M.) available to outmaneuver the enemy at Spring Hill, his relative unavailability resulted in no one making a much-needed decision. Indeed, under these circumstances Hood's generals had proved sadly lacking.

There is little doubt that a major accomplice in the sorry episode at Spring Hill was Cheatham. This corps commander's performance was absolutely woeful. His one-dimensional perspective in massing for an attack on the Federal positions at Spring Hill resulted in thwarting the Confederate army's essential objective. The indispensable element was not to overwhelm Spring Hill's defenders; the key to an enormous victory lay in perpetuating the division of Schofield's forces. Cheatham, instead of grasping that which should have been obvious based on a variety of reports, pulled back crucial troops from vital positions. Instead of inhibiting or preventing an enemy concentration and enormously complicating their retreat, Cheatham's orders resulted in the worst possible result—inaction. Furthermore, once he had sacrificed all other tactical considerations to stage an assault on the position at Spring Hill, that he allowed that attack to be called off over a whim was unpardonable.

Cheatham, relied on by Hood as the tactical battlefield commander, had proved severely lacking. His narrow perspectives, lack of good judgment, and, when pressed, a want of aggressiveness had proved decisive. In contrast to the man who should have had Cheatham's command responsibility—Cleburne—the difference was fatal.

There were others also to blame for the disaster. John C. Brown's adamant refusal to attack when confronted beyond his flank by a single regiment and two companies, about 300 men in total, was the tactical cornerstone of the Confederate fiasco. His miscalculation, and a lack of aggressiveness in the face of often-expressed doubts about the wisdom of his views, perhaps can be traced to the army's "fear of attacking breastworks" syndrome—which Hood had intensified by his futile bloodbath frontal assaults during the Atlanta Campaign.

Also, Ed Johnson, when directed to cut off the turnpike during the early morning hours, showed a lack of reasoned judgment. Although by that hour nearly all of Schofield's troops had passed, the importance of blocking the enemy's major lines of communication and transportation was too obvious to be ignored, even in the middle of the night.

Even Nathan B. Forrest, the brilliant cavalry commander, had failed to realize the implication of pulling back Jackson's division from the crucial eastern zone when there were no other troops to support Brown's exposed flank just prior to dark. At the very least, Forrest should have conferred with Cheatham or another frontline general before ordering the division to pull back.

Although the technicalities of the Spring Hill fiasco were varied, its genesis was a general command breakdown that would remain a classic and outrageous failure throughout the annals of American military history. Like a suddenly unraveling ball of string, once the momentum had been established, the result was inevitable. In the Confederate army's hierarchy there were too few commanders capable of reversing the day's snarled fortunes.

It was "a criminal affair of somebody's" that resulted in the enemy's escape, later wrote an embittered Confederate officer. Corps commander Stephen D. Lee commented a few days thereafter that the entire affair was "one of the most disgraceful and lamentable occurrences of the war, one which in my opinion is unpardonable." In Lee's eyes the primary fault lay with Cheatham. "His excuse being that he was outflanked on the right and did not wish to bring on a night attack," was unacceptable, said Lee. Thus, "the opportunity was lost, never to be got again. Such another chance will not be presented again during the war." Even Hood in later years was fond of assessing Spring Hill as the greatest lost opportunity "to utterly rout and destroy the Federal army." Several weeks afterward he wrote to Secretary of War Seddon that the missed chance at Spring Hill was "one of the best offered us during the war." It was "the best move in my career as a soldier," he later asserted, and it came "to naught." Although Hood blamed Cheatham for "this grave misfortune," he also had strong criticism of Cheatham's division commanders, including John C. Brown and Pat Cleburne.[53]

In all, the commander of the Army of Tennessee refused to accept the obvious. First and foremost, Spring Hill had been a failure of the mind. It was Hood's mismanagement and his assorted careless errors that led to such disastrous consequences. Indeed, despite the failure of others the primary fault was Hood's. His careless attitude can perhaps be explained only in terms of the fatigue and possibly the opium derivative which clouded his mind. The responsibility for the conduct of operations was Hood's, and yet he had acted with gross carelessness. By failing to adequately communicate with his chief subordinates, he had created a fatal leadership malaise.

Above all else, it seems clear that during the night of November 29th Hood firmly believed that Schofield's army was trapped and at his mercy. He thought that Schofield would never be able to march his army through Spring Hill past the arrayed Confederate ranks in the middle of the night. Repeatedly, he expressed his firm conviction that the enemy would be easily beaten on the following morning. He presumed they would be found divided, confused, and in a poor defensive position. In full confirmation of this estimate he had Thomas's captured dispatch of November 29th, wherein Schofield was told to hold Spring Hill until Franklin could be made secure.[54]

Hood's lack of good judgment had betrayed his bold maneuver. Yet, in the final analysis, so many mistakes had been made of improbable cause and effect that many considered the result to be the edict of God. "It seemed then, as it seems now," wrote a graying Confederate veteran many years later, "that a hand stronger than armies had decreed our overthrow."[55]

Corps commander Alexander P. Stewart, writing with profound emotion, explained in his own mind the mystery of what had occurred in the face of almost certain success at Spring Hill: "There is a Divinity that shapes our ends, rough hew them how we may. If in the next life we are permitted an insight into the events of this life and their causes, we shall be surprised to find how much Providence, and how very little human agency and planning have to do with all really noble and grand achievements. And how little credit is due to many who pass among us as great."[56]

CHAPTER XVI

Do You Think the Lord
Will Be with Us Today?

H E IS AS WRATHY as a rattlesnake this morning, striking at everything," wrote a Confederate staff officer of John Bell Hood on the morning of November 30, 1864. When he learned that the entire Federal army had marched past in the middle of the night, Hood was absolutely dumbfounded. While his army prepared to pursue the enemy, Hood called for a conference of his senior generals at the Nathaniel Cheairs house on the Columbia-to-Franklin pike. At a breakfast, famous by local reputation for the names of generals allegedly scratched on several parlor windowpanes, Hood made his anger known, especially to Frank Cheatham. While reliable reports of the gathering are lacking, from circumstantial evidence it appears Cheatham excused his inaction by placing much of the blame for not attacking on Generals Brown and Cleburne, neither of whom were present at the breakfast. Cheatham's explanation for his division commanders' failure to attack centered on their circumstances—due to the enemy outflanking Brown's line on the right, and not wanting to bring on a night attack with uncertain troop positions, according to Stephen D. Lee's version. Yet the Confederate commanding general would not excuse Cheatham's earlier role in the "feeble and partial attack" at Spring Hill.[1]

Stephen D. Lee, whose troops began arriving at Spring Hill about 9:00 A.M., talked extensively with Hood at the time. According to Lee, Hood was so morose about the whole affair that he returned Ed Johnson's division, saying that he did not think the enemy would halt short of Nashville. "If he does," said Hood, "I can whip him with what I have." Lee was told to halt the two divisions which had just made a forced march from Columbia, and when they were well closed up and rested, to move forward with his entire corps in the wake of the army. "He never hurried me once," later wrote Lee, "and instead of keeping my detached division [Johnson's] with his other two corps when he moved from Spring Hill, he returned it to me [and] told me to take my time owing to the distance most of my corps had already marched."[2]

Throughout the morning Hood continued to chafe at and bitterly denounce his generals. While en route to Franklin he "censured" Cheatham "in severe terms," said Governor Isham G. Harris. Finding Major General John C. Brown along the road, Hood rode up and warned him in blunt language:

> I wish you to bear in mind this military principle: that when a pursuing army comes up with the retreating enemy he must be immediately attacked. If you have a brigade in front as advance guard, order its commander to attack as soon as he comes up with him. If you have a regiment in advance and it comes up with the enemy, give the colonel orders to attack him; if there is but a company in advance, and if it overtakes the entire Yankee army, order the captain to attack forthwith; and if anything blocks the road in front of you today, don't stop a minute, but turn out into the fields or woods and move on to the front.[3]

Hood's lingering anger already was the talk among his principal subordinates. Pat Cleburne evidently received word of Hood's displeasure with his conduct at Spring Hill from Cheatham, following that morning's breakfast. After beginning the pursuit from Spring Hill, Cleburne sent word to Brown, who was ahead, to wait for him. Upon Cleburne's arrival, Brown and the Irish general rode together off to the side of the road. Cleburne was visibly distressed and said he had heard from a reliable source that the commanding general was blaming him for allowing the enemy to pass Spring Hill unmolested. He would not allow this falsehood to go unrefuted, said Cleburne with anger, and when the army was free from the enemy's presence he would call for an investigation. When Brown asked who in his view was responsible for the enemy's escape, Cleburne replied that the ultimate responsibility was Hood's—he was present on the field and had been informed of the enemy's movements. Although their conversation was abruptly terminated by the arrival of a courier with orders, Brown could see that Cleburne remained deeply resentful of Hood's accusation.[4]

Hood's despairing opinion—that Schofield's army would not halt short of Nashville—was evidently strengthened by the profuse quantity of debris littering the turnpike as he rode toward Franklin. Clearly, the enemy seemed to be disorganized and in great distress, having thrown away all manner of personal and camp equipment in their hasty flight. Yet, remembering the captured dispatches taken at Spring Hill, Hood by late morning began to reconsider the Yankees' apparent escape. Reports from Forrest's cavalry revealed the prolonged presence of the enemy in and about Franklin. Many of their troops were still en route to that village. Hood began to seriously regard the captured instructions of Thomas for Schofield to hold Spring Hill until the position at Franklin could be made secure. This, said Hood, seemed to indicate the "intention of Thomas to hold Franklin." Was it possible he might catch Schofield at Franklin with the Harpeth River at his rear? With each passing mile the irate Hood's anxiety mounted.[5]

It was several hours after sunup when their ranks were ordered to fall in on the morning of November 30th, said a member of Brown's Division. "Fall in, fall in, quick, make haste . . . promptly, men . . . by the right flank, quick time march; keep promptly closed up," came their orders. "Everything indicated an immediate attack," said the man, and yet, "wonder of wonders!" when they got to the turnpike near Spring Hill they discovered "the bird had flown." The whole Yankee army had passed by during the night. "This state of affairs was, and still is inexplicable to me, and gave us a great disappointment," wrote one of Cheatham's regimental commanders a few weeks later. "I have never seen more intense rage and profound disgust than was expressed by the weary . . . Confederate soldiers when they discovered that their officers had allowed their prey to escape," said a Mississippian.[6]

At daybreak scattered firing between Confederate cavalry skirmishers and the Federal rear guard began through a light ground fog. By sunrise, about 6:50 A.M., the pursuit by Forrest's cavalry had begun along the Columbia-to-Franklin turnpike. Following a "considerable delay," said one of Cleburne's staff officers, the infantry then took up the march north. Alexander P. Stewart's Corps was given the advance, followed by Cheatham's Corps, then the wagons and the few artillery batteries present with Hood on the 29th. Lee's Corps was allowed to rest and later bring up the rear with the bulk of the artillery and baggage.[7]

The quaint if strife-torn village of Franklin was twelve miles distant from Spring Hill, about a half day's march by normal army standards. At Thompson's Station, only a few miles north, lay the smoldering wreckage of burned Yankee wagons. The men were amazed at the quantity of debris scattered along the roadway. Occasionally a Federal straggler would be found, having been too tired or discouraged to continue. The route of march carried Hood's troops among abruptly rolling hills, rising like giant mounds in a landscape of autumn amber hues. Though the trees were barren of leaves, the bright sunshine of an Indian summer day flooded the countryside in mellow warmth, and the spirits of the men were soon rekindled.[8]

Well in advance that morning were Forrest's saddle-sore cavalrymen, sent forward on three fronts between daylight and sunrise. Chalmers, told by Forrest to intercept a column of enemy infantry said to be escaping west of Spring Hill via the Carter's Creek pike, was shocked to find the Federals gone. "When I crossed the Columbia pike I learned to my great astonishment the enemy's whole column had passed up that [Columbia] pike," later wrote Chalmers. There was no sign of the enemy having passed along the Carter's

Creek pike, and Chalmers and his division continued northward toward Franklin. On Hood's opposite flank, Forrest sent Crossland's Kentucky Brigade of Buford's Division to sweep forward along the Lewisburg pike. Meanwhile, gathering the balance of Buford's men, Forrest led them in direct pursuit along the Columbia-to-Franklin pike. About six miles north of Spring Hill, Forrest came up with Jackson's Division, still harrying the flanks of the enemy's rear guard following their late-night attack on Thompson's Station.[9]

With Forrest on the scene about 8:00 A.M., sharp skirmishing intensified between the Federal rear-guard units and Bell's Brigade of Buford's Division. The Federals had an entire infantry brigade, Emerson Opdycke's, deployed in a two-regiment front, withdrawing alternately in two lines of battle, with skirmishers posted well beyond. A section of Battery M, 4th U.S. Artillery under Lieutenant J. M. Stephenson had reported to Opdycke at 6:30 A.M., when the rear guard's withdrawal from Spring Hill had begun. Opdycke's men began rotating their rear battle line, alternately taking position, then withdrawing through the ranks of the line re-forming in their rear. Throughout the morning they repeated the maneuver, in effect keeping a constant battle front to oppose Forrest's advance. Brisk firing occasionally broke out, but it amounted to little. Forrest's men would dismount and deploy for an attack when Opdycke halted, only to have the Yankees retreat at the last moment. Aided by the two field guns, Opdycke's men kept the cavalry's pursuit at bay, despite frequent attempts to outflank and cut off their retreat. About 11:00 A.M., as Opdycke's brigade approached the high hills two miles south of Franklin, there was an abrupt change. The harried Ohio officer was suddenly ordered to halt and make a stand on the high ground.[10]

II

John M. Schofield, exhausted and bleary-eyed from his all-night ordeal, had ridden into the village of Franklin, Tennessee, before daylight on Wednesday, November 30, 1864. The anxiety he had expressed earlier that night seemed only a prelude to the intensifying difficulty that continued to plague him. At Franklin the situation was far worse than he had expected. The means of his army's escape, the pontoons he had asked Thomas to send to Franklin on the morning of the 28th, were nowhere to be found. The Harpeth River was still swollen but fordable at various scattered locations. Because the wagon bridge at the turnpike had been twice destroyed during the last two years, only the railroad bridge remained. Yet this narrow bridge was constructed for locomotives and was unsuitable for wagon or mounted traffic. Schofield made a hard decision. He would reconstruct the wagon bridge and replank the railroad bridge, parking the vast wagon train at Franklin until the construction was completed. Meanwhile, much of the artillery and Wood's division of the Fourth Corps would be sent across the Harpeth to the north shore. The artillery would ford the river, and the infantrymen might cross on the railroad bridge as soon as the engineers planked it.[11]

Due to the considerable amount of time required to prepare both bridges and cross the wagons, the partially obliterated 1863-constructed line of parapets at the south edge of the village would be expanded and improved upon to keep Hood at bay.[12]

Meanwhile, Schofield devoted his personal efforts to several pressing matters: supervising the bridge construction and communicating with Thomas at Nashville. Since the posts of the old wagon bridge were still standing in the river, the engineers sawed them off at the waterline. Then, after emplacing new crossbeams and stringers, they began planking the structure. At the railroad bridge, siding torn from several nearby buildings was used to plank over the rails. The ford presented a further problem. When the riverbanks were found to be too steep to allow passage of the artillery, the ground had to be scarped. By noon much of the construction was completed, and vehicle traffic began to slowly cross to the north shore. Yet it was fully evident that due to the tangled mass of about 800 wagons jamming downtown Franklin it would be nightfall before all of these vehicles were across the river, even by utilizing both bridges.[13]

While the engineers worked with urgency that morning, Schofield had opened telegraphic communication with Thomas at Nashville. Unaware of Thomas's captured dispatch of 3:30 A.M. November 29th, instructing him to fall back and take position at Franklin, Schofield was at first in the dark about Thomas's expectations. Upon his arrival at Franklin, Schofield found various messages from Thomas, few of which were encouraging.[14]

On the evening of the 29th Thomas had wired that A. J. Smith's troops were expected to arrive at Nashville that evening. Yet, eight hours later, another Thomas telegram advised that although A. J. Smith had arrived with nearly all of his command, they were still on their boats. Thus, it would be "impossible for them to reach Franklin today." When at Thompson's Station at 11:00 P.M. on the 29th, Schofield had sent his aide-de-camp, Captain William J. Twining, ahead to Franklin to wire Thomas about the army's situation and press for the forwarding of A. J. Smith's troops. General Schofield "regards his situation as extremely perilous," said Twining in his 1:00 A.M. telegram on November 30th. "[He] fears that he may be forced into a general battle tomorrow [November 30th] or lose his wagon train." Thomas's 4:00 A.M. reply greeted Schofield upon his arrival at Franklin. Said Thomas, Schofield was to make strong efforts to cover his wagon train and get into position at Franklin. This seemed to conflict with Thomas's earlier telegram of 11:00 P.M., in which he told Schofield that if the enemy attempted to outflank his line of march he had better cross the Harpeth at Franklin and retire to Nashville.[15]

Schofield pondered what to do. At first he attempted to again prod Thomas into hastening A. J. Smith's troops forward, telegraphing at 5:00 A.M., "I think he [Smith] had better march for Franklin at once." A half hour later he sent another wire to Thomas, saying that he would attempt to get his troops and material safely across the Harpeth River during the morning.[16]

While he awaited Thomas's response, Schofield conferred with Brigadier General Jacob D. Cox, his informal commander along the defensive line, about the critical situation they faced. Cox said that Schofield, "pale and jaded," talked of the urgency in getting the army across the river and the need to hold Hood back at all hazards until the trains were safely on the north bank. "In all my intimate acquaintance with him, I never saw him so manifestly disturbed by the situation as he was in the glimmering dawn of that morning," wrote Cox. So anxious was Schofield to expedite the withdrawal that he ordered the Twenty-third Corps artillery to cross immediately at the ford, saying their defensive positions might be taken by the trailing Fourth Corps artillery as they came up.[17]

By midmorning Schofield's outlook began to improve. Following an hour and a half nap at Dr. Daniel Cliffe's residence, at 9:50 A.M. he telegraphed to Nashville that his trains were coming in "all right," half the troops were at Franklin, and the other half were within five miles. "I will have all across the river this evening," Schofield announced. Then, reminding Thomas that he could not prevent Hood from crossing the Harpeth River "whenever he may attempt it," the beleaguered Federal general queried Thomas, "Do you desire me to hold on here until compelled to fall back?"[18]

When Thomas answered that if he could prevent Hood from turning his position at Franklin, it should be held, Schofield was clearly upset. Picking up on a comment by Thomas in his last dispatch—"I do not wish you to risk too much"—Schofield replied at noon: "I am satisfied that I have heretofore run too much risk in trying to hold Hood in check. The slightest mistake on my part, or failure of a subordinate, during the last three days might have proved disastrous. I don't want to get into so tight a place again." Clearly, Schofield was making his conservative views evident, while still promising to "cheerfully act in accordance with your views of expediency if you think it important to hold Hood back as long as possible."[19]

Thomas, intent on prodding Schofield into greater effort, wired back, "General [A. J.] Smith reported to me this morning that one division of his troops is still behind. We must therefore try to hold Hood where he now is until those troops can get up. . . . Do you think you can hold Hood at Franklin for three days longer?"[20]

Schofield again was astounded. Delay Hood for three days? Following his narrow escape of yesterday, Schofield was in no mood to mince words. At 3:00 P.M. he sent his grim reply: "I do not believe I can." To hold Hood one day would hazard something, he warned. Hood was even then threatening to cross the river both above and below Franklin, and Schofield felt powerless to stop him. "A worse position than this for an inferior force could hardly be found," Schofield announced. His further request, "It appears to me that I ought to take position at Brentwood [near Nashville] at once," was based on news that had just arrived of Forrest's cavalry crossing the Harpeth three miles upriver. "I will have lively times with my trains again," he fretted. Already, before noon, Schofield had issued orders for the remainder of his army to withdraw to the north bank after dark that night. Without waiting for further communications from Thomas, Schofield went to dinner at the Franklin residence of Dr. Daniel Cliffe. The orders stood. Schofield's remaining troops would pull back across the river under the cover of darkness, which would occur shortly after 6:00 P.M.[21]

Riding with a staff officer early that morning on the march from Spring Hill to Franklin, Union General Thomas J. Wood had asked, "Do you think the Lord will be with us today?" The fact that their army was intact and en route to safety at Nashville was a favorite topic among nearly all the Federal troops that morning. "Good bye Andersonville [prison]," remarked some of the men of the 72d Illinois as they had departed Spring Hill before daylight. "Strategy, Oh, Strategy," joked others in derision of their generals' hasty march past the entire Confederate army.[22]

By midmorning the excitement had worn off, and for many there was only the numbing fatigue of a forced march under arduous conditions. "I think our division would have preferred meeting Hood's whole army . . . right there than to have continued the march on to Franklin, so worn out and discouraged were they," wrote one of Cox's officers. To add to the troops' misery, so many wagons and ambulances choked the road that many of the men marched through the fields to avoid the congestion. The night had been cold, and during the frequent halts along the way the men stood shivering in line. Everyone's nerves were on edge from the want of sleep. So many stragglers from newly organized regiments filled the fence corners along the road that the veterans kept taunting them: "Fresh fish!" and "There lies $1000 [bounty] and a cow."[23]

Many of these new conscripts were loaded like pack mules, observed a veteran. "Pocket bibles, book marks, pots of jam, whiskbrooms, euchre decks, poker chips, love letters, night shirts," and virtually anything else mothers, wives, and sweethearts had given them littered the road in profusion. Opdycke's rear-guard detachment found that they had to prod many of the stragglers along at the points of their bayonets. Some began cutting off their large knapsacks with a knife in order to inspire them to continue on.[24]

Like a giant, unwinding serpent the ranks of Schofield's small army, led by the Twenty-third Corps, had wearily trudged down the long decline from Winstead Hill several miles south of Franklin. Before them the entire village spread out in a vast panorama. Visible in the distance was the U-shaped arc of the Harpeth River, sweeping past an open belt of farm fields and gardens. Interspersed among the quaint brick and plank houses of Franklin were clusters of buildings and church spires. It was a most welcome sight.[25]

Typically, the men of the 72d Illinois were far too tired to then pay much attention to their surroundings. "We arrived about eight in the morning, hungry and tired out, half dead with a want of sleep," wrote an officer. "We drew rations, made coffee, and were given an allowance of whisky," he continued, noting that the liquor ration was an "ominous sign."[26]

Once at Franklin, there proved to be little rest for the men. Further work had to be done despite their loud grumbling. From long and bitter experience, whenever a halt was ordered in the enemy's presence the men were told to build defensive breastworks. At Franklin the dull thud of the pickaxe and shovel soon blended with the rumble of wagon wheels and the tramp of marching men. As units of the Fourth Corps continued to pass within the lines, the Twenty-third Corps began to expand and improve the deteriorated year-old entrenchments along the southern outskirts of town.[27]

East of the main Columbia-to-Franklin turnpike a line of works was soon constructed along a continuous front from the Harpeth River across to the roadway. Curving in an arc for more than a third of a mile, these entrenchments were fashioned of earth and logs, with a ditch in front and rear. Lacking timber due to the cleared fields which spread for nearly two miles south to Winstead Hill, the men of the Twenty-third Corps seized upon the Fountain B. Carter cotton gin which stood less than a hundred yards east of the Columbia pike, stripping it of planks, joist timbers, and even the levers from the screw press. These boards and timbers were used in fashioning a framework barricade of rails. Earth dug from what became trenches on either side of the breastwork was piled on both sides and on top of this structure. Then a heavy head log was laid on top, between which and the underlying earthwork a narrow space was cleared for infantrymen to fire through. In many areas these earthen parapets were five feet high and perhaps four feet or more thick, with wide ditches two to three feet deep on either side. Also, several artillery embrasures were constructed in the breastworks.[28]

Because of the strategic position of the Carter cotton gin along the natural line of defense, a salient was constructed in the breastworks at this point. From the parapets which passed a few yards south of the cotton gin, the line swung sharply northwest for a depth of about forty yards to reach the Columbia pike. The boys worked like badgers, said a soldier, and before noon this line of reinforced earthworks was completed.[29]

In order to make the approach to their line more difficult, the troops in the area between the river and the Lewisburg pike had utilized a hedge of Osage orange in their front, chopping and moving a portion of the tangled, thorny trees so as to form an abatis on the outside of the parapet. This thorny obstruction proved to be so imposing that other troops soon cut various nearby hedges and dragged them in front of their positions. From the Harpeth River westward, the Federal entrenchments assumed such a grim and forbidding character that they clearly seemed more than sufficient to discourage any hasty enemy assault.[30]

In the center of the wide Union arc at the outskirts of Franklin stood the Fountain B. Carter house, the home of an aged and moderately prosperous migrant Virginian. Set back from the pike about forty-five feet on the west side of the road, the Carter house occupied a prominent hill, which Federal General Jacob D. Cox recognized as the key to his entire defensive line. Whereas Cox's expanse of breastworks were unbroken from the Harpeth to the Columbia pike, at this point, where the road passed over the Carter hill, a gap was left in the line to allow wagons and the balance of the army to pass in. Yet Cox's men covered this gap without formal orders to do so by constructing a second line of breastworks about seventy yards in the rear of the first—along the northern boundary of Carter's garden, where his wooden frame farm office and brick smokehouse stood. This second parapet was actually a less substantial line of fence rails fortified with earth. Although it extended east across the Columbia pike a few yards, forcing wagons to detour around it, this retrenchment was only about a hundred yards long,[31] terminating in a line of rail barricades of slight protection.

Only about ninety yards south of the Carter house, and on the southern edge of Carter's garden, the main Federal line of breastworks continued westward. Here they swept sharply northwest along the side of Carter's hill until they straightened and briefly terminated about three-quarters of a mile distant, at the Carter's Creek pike. The primary feature of this portion of Cox's line was a thicket of locust trees, ranging in thickness from four to six inches. This cluster of locusts stood toward the bottom of Carter's hill along its rather steep southwestern slope, and many had been felled for log headboards by the nearby troops. The grove soon had the appearance of a gigantic cropped cane field, said an observer. What downed trees were not used for constructing the breastworks were left lying with their branches tangled among the tops cut from the logged trees. Together with trees and limbs cut from a nearby apple orchard they formed an almost impenetrable abatis.[32]

West of the Carter's Creek pike, a less substantial line utilizing fence rails, apple trees, and planks stripped from outhouses was constructed nearly to the banks of the Harpeth River. By 2:00 P.M. most of these westernmost parapets were completed.[33]

In its entirety the line of Federal entrenchments stretched nearly a mile and a half over a curved front from the Harpeth River on the east across three turnpikes toward the reverse-angle banks of the Harpeth on the west. Enclosed within this perimeter were about 17,000 Union soldiers, nearly all convinced they were at last secure in their formidable if hastily prepared earthwork fortifications. Indeed, wrote an Ohio soldier at the time, it is the "strongest defensive main line I can recall."[34]

Franklin, Tennessee, always seemed to be a "fighting town," noted David S. Stanley. On each of several occasions when Stanley visited the town he had been involved in a fight. In the early settlement days the whir of Cherokee war arrows and the roar of the long rifle were frequently heard in the vicinity. Williamson County was the site of an ancient Stone Age civilization; in the region there were many primitive mounds with crude weapons and artifacts buried under the earth.[35]

Yet it was largely agriculture and money that had brought notoriety to the quaint village enclosed in the horseshoe-shaped bend of the Harpeth River. Largely settled as a part of the Carolinas land grants following the Revolutionary War, the region's black loam soil had contributed to a thriving cotton-growing business. Many large homes graced the community, including the elegant 1826 vintage Randal McGavock mansion, Carnton, where notables such as Andrew Jackson, James K. Polk, and Sam Houston had gathered.[36]

Franklin, from its first log house in 1797, had grown into a modern, upscale village of about 900 white residents by 1861. The town boasted a new courthouse adjacent to its town square, and flourishing schools such as the Harpeth Academy (1810), Franklin Female Institute (1847), and Tennessee Female College (1857). Aside from its rough-hewn background, the community's moderate growth and rather refined status were reflected by various large churches and a local newspaper, the *Franklin Review and Journal*. Of equal significance, and a key element in Franklin's prosperity, was the region's well-developed means of transportation. A portion of the Tennessee & Alabama Railroad, completed in 1859, enabled travel all the way to the Alabama state line. The important Nashville-to-Franklin turnpike had been extended to Columbia about 1832.[37]

In the secession crisis of 1861 the townspeople of Franklin had been reluctant to separate from the Union. Yet with the firing on Fort Sumter active recruitment of Southern troops had begun in earnest. Franklin's "Williamson Greys" militia company had become Company D of the 1st Tennessee Infantry. Other units were later formed in the area and had joined the swelling ranks of Confederate soldiers.[38]

With the appearance of Union troops in mid-Tennessee in 1862, however, the nature of life had changed for the town's populace. There were various Federal occupations and subsequent evacuations of Franklin, and while the majority of citizens remained loyal to the South, some individuals declared their allegiance to the United States. When a new Union regiment, the 125th Ohio Infantry, marched into Franklin in February 1863 they were surprised to find the stars and stripes flying from the window of a house adjacent to Main Street.[39]

Franklin had been the scene of a heavy skirmish on April 10, 1863, when Major General Earl Van Dorn's 28th Mississippi Cavalry charged down the Lewisburg pike into town. The guns of Fort Granger, on the steep north bank of the Harpeth River at the top of the horseshoe bend, had helped repulse Van Dorn, driving off a Confederate battery placed near the Carter cotton gin. It was this fort, first begun in 1862 on Figuers's Hill, that was such a dominant feature of the surrounding terrain. Fort Granger was of simple earthwork construction, with a large powder magazine, but had fallen into disuse over the past several years. Units such as the 124th Ohio Infantry had helped in the initial construction and maintenance of the fort in 1863. At the time they had grumbled about the constant work details, saying: "What is all this [work] worth? . . . [We are] miles from the enemy and the front." Yet the few artillery pieces routinely posted at Fort Granger had helped drive off units of Forrest's cavalry and other raiders during the occasional skirmishes south of the village. Due to its prominent height, the fort commanded the approach of the railroad line into Franklin, as well as much of the ground south and east of Carter's hill. One of the Twenty-third Corps' batteries, Cockerill's Battery D, 1st Ohio Light Artillery, had been sent to Fort Granger during the morning of November 30, 1864. Here they had unlimbered their three-inch rifles along the all but abandoned earthwork parapet. It was another reason why Schofield's earlier concern had largely diminished by that afternoon.[40]

Jacob Cox had aroused the household of the Carter family in the middle of the night, seeking a portion of the residence to use as his temporary head-quarters. Sixty-seven-year-old Fountain Branch Carter was in little position to argue the matter. His oldest living son, Moscow B. Carter, was a Confederate lieutenant colonel, on parole, having been captured at Mill Springs, Kentucky, January 19, 1862. When conditionally released in 1863, Moscow Carter had returned home and was now present, being subject to the close scrutiny of the Federals. Two of F. B. Carter's other sons had joined the Confederate army: Theodrick "Tod" Carter was now a captain on the staff of Brigadier General Thomas B. Smith in Cheatham's Corps. Due to these circumstances, the elder Carter, who was known as a strong Southern man, invited Cox in, and the front parlor was placed at his disposal. Cox said he and his staff promptly removed their sword belts and, flopping down on the floor, were soon asleep. Thereafter, Cox had been awakened by Schofield about dawn and had been busy ever since supervising construction of the temporary fortifications.[41]

Of routine disposition was the placement of the Federal troops as they arrived from Spring Hill. In advance that morning had been Cox's own division, which included three brigades under Brigadier General James W. Reilly, Colonel John S. Casement, and Colonel Israel N. Stiles. The entire division was present at Franklin before daylight, and Cox placed his troops to fill the perimeter between the Harpeth River and the Columbia pike.[42]

West of the Columbia pike Cox had directed Brigadier General Thomas H. Ruger to position his two brigades covering as much front as possible between the Columbia and Carter's Creek pikes. Although Ruger posted Colonel Silas A. Strickland's brigade on the Carter house hill near the locust grove, Colonel Orlando H. Moore's men were so strung out in a thin line all the way to the Carter's Creek road that there were no reserves. The largest brigade of Ruger's division, Brigadier General Joseph A. Cooper's, was still absent, having been sent to Centerville, Tennessee, during mid-November.[43]

With the appearance of Confederate cavalry along the Carter's Creek pike about noon, Cox had strengthened his relatively weak western flank by utilizing Kimball's division of the Fourth Corps. Kimball was sent west of the Carter's Creek pike to deploy his three brigades, William Grose's, Isaac M. Kirby's, and Walter C. Whitaker's, in an entrenched line. Thereafter, Cox awaited only the rear-guard division, George D. Wagner's of the Fourth Corps, which had been slowly withdrawing toward Franklin. These troops were expected to retire within the main line and soon would be available for duty as reserves. Cox thus had control of virtually all of the army's infantry except for Wood's division of the Fourth Corps, which was already across the river.[44]

Jacob Cox seemed to have the situation well in hand. By noon the last of the wagons and artillery were hastening through the gap in the breastworks at the Carter house hill. Wood's division was reported safely across the Harpeth with the artillery of the Twenty-third Corps. Even the slowly trundling quartermaster's wagons had begun to cross on the bridges. It was thought that the entire train would be across by sunset.[45]

The much-relieved mood of John M. Schofield was suggested by his reaction to the midday arrival via railroad from Nashville of the pontoon boats which he had urgently requested several days earlier. With the reconstructed bridges already in use, Schofield ordered that the pontoon train be sent back to Nashville. Following an early afternoon dinner at the home of Dr. Daniel B. Cliffe and his wife Virginia, Schofield departed after 1:00 P.M. for a new headquarters across the river. Absentmindedly, he left his coat and a sheaf of dispatches behind. Although Dr. Cliffe was a noted Union sympathizer, he had originally served the Confederacy as a surgeon in the 20th Tennessee Infantry until captured in 1862 at Mill Springs, Kentucky. Following his release, Cliffe had taken the oath of allegiance and changed his loyalties. In fact, Cliffe already had decided to flee to Nashville with Schofield's troops upon their withdrawal that night. Later that evening Mrs. Cliffe discovered Schofield's coat and dispatches. Being aware of the imminent Federal evacuation of Franklin, she placed them in the overcoat and, sewing up the pockets, hid the coat.[46]

Schofield, along with Major General David S. Stanley, rode to the residence of Alpheus Truett, about a half mile north of the Harpeth River on the pike to Nashville. Here Schofield's new headquarters was established, and he began to review the final details for the evacuation of Franklin.[47]

Of the many difficulties plaguing Schofield on November 30th, perhaps the most frustrating had been the absence of the eyes and ears of his army, the Union cavalry under James H. Wilson. Following Wilson's bivouac the previous evening at the Matthews house about two and a half miles southwest of Franklin, he had sent a message to Schofield, telling him of the cavalry's position. At last, upon his arrival at Franklin before daylight, Schofield learned of Wilson's current location. Schofield's dissatisfaction with Wilson was reflected by his tense message to Thomas at 5:20 A.M.: "I shall try and get Wilson on my flank this morning." A few minutes later, Schofield was very abrupt with Wilson, writing him that he was to cover the army's immediate flank and rear that day; in other words, not to go wandering off.[48]

Meanwhile, Wilson, aware that he had been deceived by Forrest on the 29th, throughout the morning kept sending Schofield reports about the lack of enemy activity in his front. Wilson had most of two divisions in the vicinity of Franklin. Hatch's division remained with Wilson north of the Harpeth River, but one of Richard Johnson's brigades under Brigadier General John Croxton had been sent south of the Harpeth River to watch the Lewisburg pike near Douglass Church, four miles from town.[49]

John Croxton was sitting on his horse, one leg thrown over the pommel of his saddle, looking serenely about the landscape. In his front along a small stream between the Harpeth River and the Lewisburg pike, two of his cavalry regiments had been skirmishing since 10:00 A.M. with the dismounted gray cavalrymen of Edward Crossland's Kentucky Brigade. Not a Rebel had crossed that creek by 1:00 P.M., despite several attempts, noted an observer. Then, at this hour, a report arrived that a strong enemy force was in the process of turning his right flank. Croxton became concerned. Abruptly he withdrew his command to a thick woods near McGavock's Ford, where his men hastily erected a rail barricade across the Lewisburg pike. Croxton's dispositions reflected his latest instructions from Wilson: to hold off the enemy as long as possible before recrossing the river at McGavock's Ford if pressed too severely.[50]

For perhaps an hour Croxton remained undisturbed in his new position. Everything seemed unusually quiet, said a soldier. Croxton was leisurely riding along the road talking with the commander of the 2d Michigan Cavalry when a single shot rang out. A spurt of dust flew up just in front of Croxton's horse, and the general immediately dashed for cover. In front, skirmishers were seen advancing ahead of a heavy line of Confederate cavalry. Soon they rode forward to the attack, boldly charging up to the rail barricade, but were repulsed by a devastating fire from the 2d Michigan's Spencers.[51]

When the Confederates recoiled, Croxton's 1st Tennessee Cavalry, charging in column, chased the gray riders back into the woods. Yet, once there, the Federal horsemen discovered a reserve line of Confederates which rose to their feet and fired several volleys. The Tennesseeans went scurrying back to their lines.[52]

Croxton was very worried. He heard new reports that the Rebels were crossing to the north bank at Hughes's Ford. The enemy line concealed in the far woods appeared to be infantry. His men seemed shaken by the obvious enemy buildup. The jittery right flank company of the 2d Michigan kept firing into the nearby woods, although no enemy was in sight. Croxton ordered his brigade withdrawn across McGavock's Ford to the north bank.[53]

James H. Wilson already had notified Schofield of this burgeoning enemy threat. The officer commanding an Iowa cavalry regiment stationed at Hughes's Ford had reported Confederate infantry approaching, "apparently with the intention of crossing." Wilson's 1:45 P.M. dispatch alerted Schofield that Wilson would resist "as long as possible any real advance."[54]

When Schofield received this message about 3:00 P.M. it was strong confirmation of what he had suspected all along—that Hood was seeking to outflank the Union army and get across his line of retreat to Nashville. Within minutes Schofield alerted Thomas that the enemy seemed about to cross the Harpeth above and below Franklin. Thereafter, he sent word to Wilson that he would send a brigade of Wood's division to Hughes's Ford in order "to check the crossing of the enemy at that point." Wilson was also told to furnish a cavalry escort for the wagon train at 5:00 A.M. the following morning. Clearly, with just three hours of daylight remaining Schofield was thinking only of delaying an enemy crossing and moving away with his wagon train before Hood could approach in his rear the next day. Forrest's cavalry was regarded as the primary threat, not Hood's slower-moving infantry. If A. J. Smith's troops would march to Brentwood early in the morning, Schofield might avoid further difficulty.[55]

While Brigadier General Samuel Beatty's brigade of Wood's division began issuing rations prior to marching to the cavalry's relief at Hughes's Ford, Schofield remained at his headquarters north of Franklin. It was a time of comparative leisure. His army had completed their defensive lines on the outskirts of Franklin, and in a few more hours they would evacuate the town and begin the march to Nashville. For now there seemed to be little concern. Any difficulty would likely come tomorrow, when the army might be "obliged to fall back [all the way] to Nashville before General Smith can reach us."[56]

Amid the ranks there seemed little to do but eat and rest, and already there was the usual grumbling about having expended much energy in building breastworks for which there would be little use. A few Federal officers began to relax by taking nips from their whiskey flasks, and the warm afternoon sun only exaggerated the first feelings of euphoria Schofield's men had experienced in many days.[57]

CHAPTER XVII

One Whose Temper Is Less Fortunately Governed

GEORGE Day Wagner looked rather frazzled. The thirty-five-year-old Union brigadier general with the drooping beard and disheveled appearance had been the workhorse of the army for the past two days. His division had borne the brunt of the fighting and hard duty, having led the hurried march to Spring Hill and suffered there nearly all of the estimated 350 Federal casualties. Then, the following morning, Wagner's men had been required to conduct the rear-guard action, skirmishing all the way from Spring Hill to Franklin. His men were exhausted, and Wagner was sick and tired of what he regarded as unjust and discriminatory treatment. Other Fourth Corps officers, as well, believed Schofield was managing affairs to the preference of his Twenty-third Corps.[1]

Ironically, at the same time, Wagner, a former Indiana state senator with a gruff manner, was being accused of similar favoritism. On the morning of November 30, 1864, his 1st Brigade commander, Colonel Emerson Opdycke, was upset with Wagner for leaving him constantly deployed in line of battle on rear-guard duty. Wagner's other two brigades had been allowed to march comparatively at ease, in column at the head of the division. There is some evidence that the fiery Opdycke complained directly to his corps commander, David Stanley, about not being relieved over the entire ten-mile distance from Spring Hill to Winstead Hill, which was only two miles from Franklin.[2]

Wagner was told by Stanley, about 11:00 A.M., to halt on the high ground and allow his men to eat breakfast. Opdycke's brigade, however, was kept deployed in line of battle, facing Forrest's cavalrymen along the pike, while the other units cooked breakfast. Opdycke's men didn't even have time to make coffee before Forrest's riders began pressing forward west of the pike.[3]

Wagner's two reserve brigades then were east of the road, on a separate knoll, Breezy Hill, preparing breakfast. Nearby, Walter C. Whitaker's brigade of Kimball's division lolled along the slopes of Winstead Hill eating breakfast. At the sharp crack of small arms fire, Whitaker's men hastily rushed to the summit of Winstead Hill, facing south. Lieutenant J. M. Stephenson's section of Battery M, 4th U.S. Artillery, fired about forty rounds at Confederate skirmishers near a stone wall at the foot of the ridge. As Whitaker's men began fashioning a barricade of rocks and logs, incoming fire from Forrest's cavalrymen struck Sergeant Martin Efinger of Company C, 96th Illinois Infantry, in the shoulder. It was perhaps the first casualty of the Battle of Franklin.[4]

Forrest's cavalry, Bell's Brigade of Buford's Division, and Jackson's Division were unable to make headway against the four brigades of Federal infantry arrayed in their front, and they merely continued to skirmish at long range.[5]

By about noon, as the congestion on the Columbia pike cleared, Whitaker was ordered to withdraw to Franklin. When Whitaker's men pulled out, Winstead Hill, west of the Columbia pike, was largely vacated. Wagner saw Whitaker's troops depart and, about the same time, noticed the distant appearance of a large column of Rebel infantry along the pike from Spring Hill. Being unwilling to further remain in an isolated position, Wagner ordered the withdrawal of his own troops.[6]

Breezy Hill, despite its commanding topography overlooking the Franklin Valley, was evacuated in sequence of brigades beginning about 12:15 P.M. Again Opdycke's men were told to remain in the rear and withdraw from the high ground in the wake of the other two brigades. Since David Stanley had already gone to Franklin, Wagner sent a staff officer ahead to notify him of the pullback.[7]

Within minutes, Wagner's infantrymen were marching for the safety of the Franklin entrenchments. With Conrad's brigade leading the way, Wagner rode at the head of the long blue column, his men striding at a "swinging gait" along the paved stone pike, which glistened white in the midday sunlight.[8]

David Stanley had spent much of the morning following his arrival at Franklin at the residence of Dr. Daniel Cliffe. Although Stanley was greatly fatigued and reportedly ill, he spent much time discussing with Schofield the best way to keep Hood from outflanking their position. Thomas's telegram of 10:25 A.M. that morning, received about an hour later, said he wanted Franklin held if Hood could be contained. This message had drastically affected Schofield's thinking. In order to appease Thomas, Schofield sought to delay as much as possible the enemy's advance, even while remonstrating with Thomas about "risking too much." Due to Thomas's telegram, Schofield told Stanley to attempt to hold Winstead Hill with the rear guard until dark. Stanley promptly wrote a dispatch to George Wagner giving him specific instructions to "hold the heights you now occupy until dark, unless too severely pressed." He further told Wagner to relieve Opdycke with one of his other brigades and, keeping Opdycke in support, to cross to the north bank of the Harpeth after dark with his entire command. About noon a staff officer had ridden off with this soon-to-be-momentous message.[9]

Within a half hour the staff officer found Wagner marching along the road to Franklin, his division strung out for nearly a mile along the Columbia pike. Wagner was not pleased to read Stanley's message. Since he was ordered to hold the high ground until actually forced back, Wagner glumly foresaw that he had to countermarch and return to his former position. Reluctantly, he turned his column about and again started for Winstead Hill.[10]

Yet Wagner's message that he was abandoning Breezy Hill was then en route to Stanley. At 12:15 P.M. Wagner had dispatched a mounted staff officer, who belatedly found Stanley across the river at Schofield's new headquarters. Because Jacob Cox had now assumed command on the south bank, Stanley gave no new instructions. While en route to rejoin Wagner on the heights south of town, the staff officer met, much to his surprise, Wagner with his division, again marching toward Franklin with urgent strides.[11]

Wagner appeared to be highly agitated. Certainly he was having a bad day. He had received no further instructions following Stanley's order to "hold the heights," although an hour and a half had elapsed. Immediately after reoccupying Winstead and Breezy hills there was trouble.[12]

Opdycke's men had been the last to leave the high ground, and thus were the first to reoccupy their former position after a short countermarch. When Opdycke again reached the top of the hill he discovered two columns of Confederates advancing nearby. One long, winding corps of gray infantry stretched as far as he could see along the Lewisburg pike. The other column was seen approaching in front, past the William Harrison house on the Columbia pike.[13]

The sound of the Confederates approaching was like the "wild sweep of a tornado heralded by clouds of darkness and muttering thunders," thought a stunned eyewitness. Opdycke had Lieutenant Milton A. Mitchell of Battery G, 1st Ohio Light Artillery, unlimber his section of three-inch rifle guns. Their roar soon sent reverberations echoing through the range of cedar-laced hills.[14]

Wagner was busily positioning some of Colonel John Q. Lane's troops on Winstead Hill when a courier from Opdycke arrived. It was apparent that the column on the Lewisburg pike would easily outflank the Federal line, and Opdycke was greatly alarmed. Further, the Columbia pike column was deploying in line of battle, their rifle barrels glistening in the sunlight as they shifted from right shoulder arms and dressed their ranks.[15]

Wagner hesitated no longer. Again he ordered a withdrawal from Winstead and Breezy hills. Lane's, Conrad's, and Opdycke's ranks wasted little time in rapidly marching for Franklin, the men being convinced that they knew far more about the present risks and dangers than did their generals in the rear.[16]

As he retreated about 2:00 P.M., Wagner, evidently on the spur of the moment, determined to follow the spirit of Stanley's orders to hold back Hood's advance to the extent possible. Halfway back across the two-mile valley he ordered Lane's brigade to halt and occupy the southern slope of a stone-strewn hill on the west side of the Columbia pike, known locally as Privet Knob.[17]

Privet Knob, with an elevation of about a hundred feet, was the highest ground adjacent to the Columbia pike in the Franklin valley. About a mile north of Winstead Hill, and nearly equidistant south of the outskirts of Franklin, the knoll's prominence was accentuated by the comparatively flat and open adjacent ground. Privet Knob, also known as Merrill's Hill, lay close by the western fringe of the pike, with a moderate quantity of scraggly cedar trees clustered along its eastern slopes. Wagner put Lieutenant Mitchell's section of three-inch rifle guns in position with Lane's men on the knob, then continued north toward Franklin with Conrad's and Opdycke's troops.[18]

A little less than a half mile from Cox's outer line, Wagner halted his leading brigade, Conrad's, and directed that commander to take position along a gentle rise of ground east of the Columbia pike. This ground was entirely cleared, being in the midst of a large cotton field, not then in cultivation. Conrad soon had his brigade in line, with five of his six regiments east of the turnpike, and a single unit, the 15th Missouri Infantry, posted just west of the roadway. Evidently, Wagner intended to utilize this line in the same manner that his rear guard had withdrawn: to retreat if pressed too hard by alternately passing his brigades, one behind the other's deployed front. Since it was not expected by Conrad that they would fight along this line, his men were allowed to rest without entrenching.[19]

Marching directly behind Conrad's rapidly deploying ranks was Emerson Opdycke's weary brigade. It was Wagner's intention to place Opdycke's men on the west side of the road adjacent to Conrad's line in order to present a two-brigade front.[20]

As Opdycke's men approached, marching in column for the first time that day, Wagner rode up to Opdycke and issued him orders to prolong Conrad's line west of the turnpike.[21]

Emerson Opdycke fairly exploded. His men had been on arduous rear-guard duty since before daylight, most of them hadn't slept in forty-eight hours, and they hadn't been given the opportunity to eat or make coffee that day. Furthermore, the position he was told to occupy was untenable, being exposed and without natural cover. Angrily, Opdycke rode on without bothering to halt, even while Wagner trotted beside him, demanding his compliance.[22]

Opdycke, his blue eyes flashing and his lusty voice booming, would have no part of it. He kept telling Wagner that his men needed a respite; they were exhausted beyond the point of further service, and they deserved to eat. All the while, his men kept marching for the line of breastworks. The Ohio colonel refused to halt or listen to Wagner's threatening orders. It was insubordination, pure and simple. Wagner and Opdycke, two irate and exhausted officers past the point of convention, kept arguing as they passed on toward Cox's main line. It obviously was a dangerous and potentially explosive confrontation.[23]

Opdycke, the former colonel of the 125th Ohio Infantry, had the kind of stare to look right through you, noted one of his officers. Unafraid of the enemy or his own superiors, his hot temper had earned him a reputation as one of the bravest of fighters, if headstrong and reckless. Only three weeks earlier he had quarreled with Brigadier General Luther Bradley over some trivial matter. Once he had cooled down, Opdycke had forwarded his apology to Bradley: "I have been hasty; I was angry; I have done you unintentional wrong and have done violence to my own sense of right and of manhood and my heart urges me to make you sincere apology and ask your pardon. A gentleman of so fortunate temperament such as yourself may not readily sympathize with one whose temper is less fortunately governed." Mercurial, abrasive, and yet keenly intelligent, Opdycke was prone to press a point to its ultimate. On this day, exhausted and full of anger over what he regarded as Wagner's unjust treatment in managing the rear guard, there would be little reasoning with him.[24]

But in Wagner, Opdycke had no easy opponent. Wagner's rough exterior had earned him few friends in the army, and he had the reputation of a stern fighter. At Shiloh, Stones River, and Missionary Ridge he had been in the thickest of action and earned high praise for his tenacious fighting. When George Wagner was upset, as he was this day, everyone scrambled to get out of his way. Exasperated by the enemy's frequent threatening appearance, the building confusion amid a lack of orders, and all the countermarching, Wagner was in a foul mood. Earlier his horse had fallen and so injured Wagner's leg that Wagner had picked up a heavy stick to use as a crutch. In pain and anger, Wagner repeatedly demanded that Opdycke halt and do as he was told. It was now evident that the controversy had elevated beyond that of a matter of rank. It had become a war of wills.[25]

With their heated discussion continuing for perhaps fifteen minutes, Opdycke's men began passing through Cox's outer line of entrenchments. Wagner suddenly realized that Opdycke's withdrawal within the lines was an accomplished fact. Wagner angrily told Opdycke to do as he saw fit, that being in reserve he was to fight, if need be, wherever he thought best. Probably Wagner was mindful of Stanley's pointed directive in his 11:30 A.M.

orders to relieve Opdycke and leave his brigade in support. Whatever the rationale, it was the decisive turning point in the careers of the two officers, and a major element in the fate of their army.[26]

Opdycke, finding the area immediately in the rear of the entrenchments so crowded with other troops as to leave no room for his brigade, continued north along the Columbia pike to the first available open space, about 200 yards beyond Fountain B. Carter's brick farmhouse. Here, about 2:30 P.M., his men rapidly stacked arms and began gathering firewood to make coffee and cook their belated breakfasts.[27]

Wagner, meanwhile, rode to the Carter house, where instead of an anticipated rest he was notified to report to and act under the orders of Jacob Cox of the Twenty-third Corps—the informal commander of the main defensive line.[28]

Wagner wearily reported to Cox in person and explained his earlier orders from Stanley. Undoubtedly he mentioned the Confederate en masse advance and his difficulties with Opdycke. Cox thought for a minute. He had just received Schofield's orders to withdraw all troops across the river after nightfall. There seemed to be no reason to change Wagner's instructions or compel Opdycke to march back and join Conrad's line. Thus, Cox merely told the Fourth Corps division commander that he should act according to his earlier orders.[29]

From the evidence, it appears that Cox told Wagner that the appearance of the Confederate infantry was in all probability a sham, a deception to convince the Union army they were about to attack, while actually preparing to bypass Franklin by another flanking march. Since little more than heavy skirmishing was anticipated, Cox only added that Wagner should slowly retire his two brigades within the main line if actually compelled to do so. The tenor of Cox's instructions was unmistakable: to hold off Hood so as to allow the Federal army to get away.[30]

Immediately, Wagner was compelled to make a significant decision. Colonel John Q. Lane had sent word from Privet Knob that the Rebels were advancing beyond Winstead Hill, threatening to envelop his flanks. Lane had advanced his skirmishers beyond the low stone wall where his brigade was deployed, and already they were sniping at long range with the enemy. Wagner sent word to Lane to withdraw and take position on the right of Conrad's line, in the middle of the old cotton field.[31]

Although one of his nervous brigade commanders was greatly alarmed, the exhausted and peevish Wagner failed to question the wisdom of his standing orders despite the vast columns of gray infantry seen sweeping over Winstead Hill. Angrily, he rode south to the advanced position where he had left Conrad's brigade nearly a half mile in front of Cox's line of entrenchments.[32]

Wagner appeared to be in an even uglier mood when he found Conrad casually awaiting orders to withdraw within the main defensive lines. Conrad also had a strong skirmish line well advanced in front, and they had begun reporting about 3:00 P.M. the massed Confederate ranks seen deploying in line of battle. In fact, Conrad had been on the verge of sending a staff officer to find Wagner, just as that general trotted up. Conrad explained the situation, and in view of the obvious vulnerability of their position he asked in rather skeptical tones if Wagner actually intended to hold the present line.[33]

Wagner exploded with wrathful invectives and not only told Conrad to stay put, but to have his sergeants fix their bayonets and forcibly keep the men at their posts. Wagner wanted no repeat of yesterday's mauling and rout of Conrad's (then Luther Bradley's) brigade, which had occurred at Spring Hill. Many of Conrad's regiments were filled with new recruits, and it was obvious Wagner had little confidence in them, even when nothing more than a heavy skirmish was expected.[34]

Already Lane's brigade and Mitchell's section were moving back on the pike to take position adjacent to Conrad's line, where Opdycke would have been. Wagner saw Lane's men begin to deploy in the open field west of the roadway, and sent word to Lane to fight the enemy if they advanced. Lane was told that only if overpowered were they to retreat to the main line of works.[35]

At last returning to the vicinity of the Carter house where he could rest and partake in some refreshments, Wagner evidently was in the mood to rid himself of some of the day's frustrations. Within a short time, later claimed David Stanley, Wagner was in a "vainglorious" condition, "full of whisky, if not drunk."[36]

Out beyond the Carter house line of breastworks, Wagner's men stood in line of battle under the basic orders issued at 11:30 A.M.. Conrad, shaken by the unexpected orders to hold this open-field line, hurriedly directed his men to entrench.[37]

"We hastily began to fortify," later wrote an Ohio captain caught up in the sudden commotion. Yet, being positioned in an old, unused cotton field there were no trees or logs at hand. Various troops having earlier camped on the ground, even fence rails were missing. Fortunately, at least two of Conrad's regiments on the march from Spring Hill that morning had taken spades from an abandoned wagon laden with tools. Each company of the 64th Ohio Infantry had removed two spades from the wagon and carried them to Franklin. They were the only tools available in the 64th's ranks with which to work. Some of Conrad's other regiments had not been as thoughtful, and had to dig with their bayonets. As rapidly as possible, a low, crooked line of earthwork parapets was constructed. As the men worked with desperate energy, said an officer, they could see the heavy masses of Confederate ranks crowding from the distant line of timber. "There was not a particle of doubt in the mind of any man in my vicinity as to what was coming," he later wrote.[38]

Already the men were cursing the folly of staying there, and their indignation swelled almost into a mutiny. The recruits were especially rebellious, wrote a captain, and most began pleading with their officers: "What can our generals be thinking about in keeping us out here! We are only in the way. Why don't they take us back to the breastworks?" One of Conrad's dumbfounded regimental commanders remarked, "Our orders were to have sergeants fix bayonets and hold the men to it, thus we stayed [in place]."[39]

George Wagner at last had found somebody who would obey his orders.

II

The march from Spring Hill toward Franklin had been an eye-opening experience for many of the Confederate infantrymen. Along the Columbia pike a number of residents had gathered to urge on the soldiers. Their shouts of, "Push on, boys; you will capture all of the Yanks soon. They have just passed here on the dead run," were answered by rousing cheers. One Confederate soldier counted thirty-four abandoned Federal wagons en route, with the mules shot dead in their harnesses. The abandoned Union equipment and debris that littered the roadway sent the men's spirits soaring. "All that we want to do now is catch the blue coated rascals, ha! ha!" wrote a 1st Tennessee Infantry private. "We all want to see the[m] surrender."[40]

This merriment had come to a sudden halt about noon, when the leading elements of A. P. Stewart's Corps came up with Forrest's cavalrymen near the William Harrison house. Ahead Wagner's rear-guard infantry division was defiantly deployed with artillery along the slopes of Winstead and Breezy hills.[41]

Hood, following a brief reconnaissance, ordered preparations for an immediate assault, in the spirit of the instructions given John C. Brown that morning. Yet Hood sought to use the topography of the region to his advantage. By sending Stewart's Corps on a flanking march east through the timber, around the base of Breezy Hill to the Lewisburg pike, they might be able to pass beyond the range of hills and cross the open Franklin Valley to cut off the enemy's retreat. Cheatham's trailing corps, meanwhile, would prepare to assault in front.[42]

Hood's decision to use Cheatham's Corps for the assaulting column rather than Stewart's, which was in advance, was a significant tip-off of his thinking that day. Instead of Stewart's men screening the movement of Cheatham's troops, which might be able to march unseen for a longer period as they passed through the heavy timber in the rear, Stewart had to file east from a position in plain view of the Federal skirmishers posted along the southern slopes of Winstead and Breezy hills. Hood was still seething about the failure of Cheatham's men at Spring Hill, and by specific design they were going to be his shock troops this day. Cheatham, Brown, and Cleburne would be thrust in the very storm center of any fighting; Hood would purge their ranks of their apparent reluctance to fight except when behind breast-works.[43]

It immediately became a costly decision. While Stewart's Corps pulled out and moved eastward, Wagner had withdrawn from the high ground, the massive appearance of the gray infantry alone being sufficient to scare off the Federals. Yet, though Winstead and Breezy hills were now unoccupied, there were no Confederates available to move forward and hold these two hills. Forrest's men, by Hood's order, also had been pulled back to go with Stewart on his flanking march. By the time Cheatham's Corps came up, Wagner had returned and reoccupied both hills in compliance with Stanley's midday order. A further delay occurred while Cheatham's men deployed in line of battle. Then, about 2:00 P.M., Wagner again suddenly pulled back without making a fight.[44]

John Bell Hood was among the first of the Confederate high command on Winstead Hill. After the advance units of Cheatham's Corps swept over the ground, Hood rode forward alone down the northern slope to a large linden tree and took out his field glasses. Hood was inspired by the Federal retreat from Winstead Hill. Again the enemy hadn't stood and fought; instead they had run away at the direct approach of the massed gray ranks. It seemed all very plain to the Confederate commander. In the distance he could see Franklin jammed with wagons, their teamsters evidently hastening to get the ponderous train across the river on two rickety bridges. Through his glasses Hood observed a line of entrenchments on the outskirts of town, yet they appeared very temporary and makeshift in nature. It seemed clear that he had at last brought the enemy to bay. Riding back to the top of the hill, Hood turned to an officer, perhaps A. P. Stewart, and said, "We will make the fight."[45]

Major General Patrick Cleburne had arrived in advance of his troops on Winstead Hill and, resting a pair of field glasses on a stump, gazed at the line of enemy entrenchments two miles distant across the valley. The seriousness of his mood was revealed by his remark to a staff officer: "They are very formidable." Then, as he awaited the arrival of his men, Cleburne sat on the stump, making notes in his small memorandum book which he kept in his pocket. When a messenger from Hood arrived summoning him to a confer-ence at the William Harrison house on the Columbia pike, Cleburne was evidently playing checkers with a staff officer. Cleburne had drawn a checker-board in the sand with a stick and was using various colored leaves for the checkers. It was a touch of irony. Soon he would be involved in a deadlier game with the commanding general of the army, and playing by Hood's heavily weighted rules.[46]

The ensuing council of war at the William Harrison house had rapidly become only a ratification meeting. Hood announced his decision to make an immediate frontal attack with the extent of the army then present, and asked for comments. Forrest furiously objected, telling Hood that in his opinion the entrenchments could not be taken by direct assault without great and un-necessary loss of life. Hood replied that the Yankees seemed to be only feigning a stand—making a show of force while attempting to hold off a much-feared vigorous pursuit. Still Forrest persisted: "General Hood, if you will give me one strong division of infantry with my cavalry, I will agree to flank the Federals from their works within two hours' time." Of specific use to Forrest was Holly Tree Gap, a defile in the range of hills through which the Nashville pike passed, only about four and a half miles distant from Hood's present position. Here the Yankees might be cut off from Nashville, urged Forrest, since Hood's army was presently as close to this gap as was Scho-field's at Franklin. Cleburne added his comments, saying that the attack across two miles of open valley against what appeared to be impregnable earthworks was courting disaster. Frank Cheatham remarked that he didn't like the looks of this fight, as the enemy had a good position and was well fortified.[47]

All arguments were to no avail. Hood had made up his mind. The protestations of Cheatham and Cleburne perhaps only accentuated their commander's smoldering resentment over the Spring Hill affair. There is evidence Hood expressed his displeasure over yesterday's fiasco and may have suggested to Cheatham and his officers that he was concerned about their willingness to manfully fight on an open battlefield. Amid all of the distortions, misrepresentations, and outright falsifications of Hood's postwar memoir, *Advance and Retreat*, there was a candid admission of what domi-nated his reasoning at Franklin:

> The discovery that the army, after a forward march of one hundred and eighty miles, was, still, seemingly unwilling to accept battle unless under the protection of breastworks, caused me to experience grave concern. In my inmost heart I questioned whether or not I would ever succeed in eradicating this evil. It seemed to me I had exhausted every means in the power of one man to remove this stumbling block to the Army of Tennes-see.[48]

Cheatham, Cleburne, and Brown, in particular, became the focus of Hood's ire. If not outright punishment for their behavior on November 29th, the assault at Franklin would be a severe corrective lesson in what he would demand in aggressive behavior. It was no accident when he assigned Cheat-ham's Corps to make the frontal assault against the center of the enemy's formidable fortifications. Brown and Cleburne were posted to the front rank and told to attack along the Columbia pike, where the Federal lines were the strongest and the ground entirely open.[49]

Cleburne and the others left suitably chastened. As Cleburne mounted to return to the front after the conference, Hood gave him stern instructions: "Form your division to the right of the pike, letting your left overlap the same. General Brown will form on the left with his right overlapping your left. . . . Give orders to your men not to fire a gun until you run the Yankee skirmish line from behind the first line of works, then press them and shoot them in their backs as they run to their main line; then charge the enemy's works. Franklin is the key to Nashville, and Nashville is the key to independence." A grim smile creased Cleburne's face, noted his division surgeon. He remarked that he would either take the enemy's works or fall in the attempt, and promptly rode off.[50]

To the prideful Pat Cleburne, such pointed, personally directed orders must be obeyed no matter what the cost. Stung by Hood's accusatory demeanor and this outrageous tactical blunder, he well realized that the commanding general's orders were likely to be his own death warrant. When he rode forward to Breezy Hill, where his brigade commanders soon gathered, Brigadier General Daniel C. Govan saw that Cleburne was "greatly depressed." Cleburne spoke up in the presence of all: the enemy's works must be carried at all hazards. Hood's explicit orders were to take the works at the point of the bayonet. These orders were to be conveyed to the field and company officers, he announced. When Govan saluted and turned to leave, he remarked, "Well, general, there will not be many of us that will get back to Arkansas." Cleburne's reply was sad but determined: "Well, Govan, if we are to die, let us die like men."[51]

The ranks of the Confederate army had been largely concealed by the timbered slopes and ridges of the high ground. Yet about 2:45 P.M. the columns swarmed forward along the pike, deploying in line of battle at the northern foot of Breezy and Winstead hills. The sight was as if the ground had suddenly poured forth a torrent of butternut and gray. Soon the stone-white surface of the Columbia pike was blotted out with "a living wall of men and glistening steel," wrote a distant Federal observer. From the advanced positions of Wagner's men it looked like "the appearance of a huge monster closed in folds of flashing steel." In the bright sunlight the gleam of rifle barrels with fixed bayonets sent shimmering light waves flickering in the air.[52]

There were slightly over 20,000 Confederate infantrymen moving into battle formation, and the slopes and ridges blackened with their movements. By Hood's concept the attack would be made from three primary directions, each to follow the general course of a major road leading into Franklin. A. P. Stewart's Corps, following his attempt to outflank Wagner on the east, had already formed along the woodland plateau adjacent to the Harpeth River. They would essentially follow the Lewisburg pike north and strike the Federal lines in the vicinity of the railroad cut.[53]

Cheatham's Corps, with its divisions of Cleburne and Brown, had deployed adjacent to the Columbia pike and would march directly for the center of the Union line at the Carter house. Bate's Division of Cheatham's Corps was to swing west past the Bostick farm along a prominent knoll and strike for the enemy's lines near the Carter's Creek pike. Chalmers's Division of Forrest's cavalry would advance along that pike to support Bate's movement.

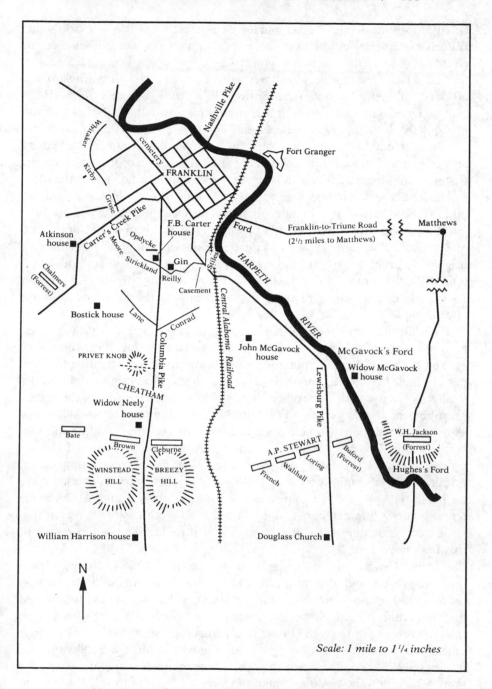

MAP 6   Confrontation at Franklin—November 30

On the opposite flank, the remainder of Forrest's cavalry, Jackson's and Buford's troopers, was ordered to support Stewart's advance, then ford the river and destroy the Federal wagon trains if the attack was successful.[54]

Only two 6-gun artillery batteries were then with the army, most of the artillery still being en route from Spring Hill with S. D. Lee's Corps. Hood thus assigned one battery to each corps, but directed that they be split up into sections to fill the intervals between divisions.[55]

In all, Hood had heavily weighted the assault column against the Federal left. His orders placed four divisions of infantry and two of cavalry on the eastern flank, from the Harpeth River to the Columbia pike. Across the road, on the longer western flank line from the Carter house to the Carter's Creek pike, Hood had only two infantry divisions and a single cavalry division.[56]

So as to provide needed reinforcements at the proper location, each division would advance on a two-brigade front with the third or remaining brigades marching close behind, ready to move forward in support as required. Undetermined were the final movements along the much narrower enemy perimeter, which required a converging as the attacking columns approached.[57]

Within the gray ranks on that balmy Indian summer Wednesday afternoon the sight of the distant Federal works across the open Franklin Valley evoked strong, if mixed, emotions. Many of the men were fighting for Tennessee, their homeland, and their ardor was high. Most were young, under the age of twenty-two. Their officers told them as they formed that the enemy must be beaten at any cost; at Franklin they were fighting for Nashville. The eyes of the Southern women were upon them, and the invading foe was before them. Drive the enemy into the river at all hazards, urged Hood's orders. Some of the men were so excited that they began jesting about Admiral Nelson's famous order at Trafalgar. "England expects every man to do his duty," piped out a soldier in the ranks of the 1st and 4th Missouri (consolidated) Infantry. Since many of the men were Irish, a sergeant hollered to the laughter of all, "It's damned little duty England would get out of this Irish crowd!"[58]

It had required more than an hour for the multitude of troops to pass down the slopes and form properly arrayed with ranks dressed. As the rear units waited to move forward, many of the men had attempted to rest and find something to eat. Some Mississippians of Stewart's Corps feasted on provisions brought from the home of a returning furloughed soldier. Their officers were intent on discussing the coming battle. Most were gloomy and felt they would be killed. Soon the Mississippians were called into line, and there was little time to do anything but prepare for the formidable task at hand.[59]

Charging against veteran, well-entrenched Yankee infantry was no child's play, wrote a grizzled Confederate veteran after the war. It was a fact too well known in Hood's army. Many of the men in William Quarles's

Brigade came to their chaplain bringing watches, letters, and photographs to keep, so he might send them to their families if they were killed. The chaplain turned them away; he would be advancing with the men and exposed to the same danger.[60]

In Stewart's Corps Major General William W. Loring spoke to the assembled ranks. Yet other generals such as Otho F. Strahl wore an expression of great sadness and said little. Cleburne rode ahead to recently vacated Privet Knob, where a battalion of his sharpshooters under Lieutenant A. Buck Schell had just deployed. Cleburne did not have his field glasses, and asked to use a telescope from one of the men's Whitworth sniper rifles. A lieutenant quickly detached the long tubular scope from his rifle and handed it to the general. Cleburne placed it across a stump and closely surveyed the Federal entrenchments. "They have three lines of works," he was heard to remark, adding, "and they are all completed." Cleburne soon returned the telescope and rapidly rode back to his division.[61]

Cleburne's concern about the tiered enemy works was soon translated into an altered combat formation. By his specific request he obtained permission to form his division in column of brigades, wishing to expose as small a front as possible. From this formation he would deploy into line of battle when within small arms range of the enemy's lines. They would then, by Hood's orders, charge with fixed bayonets against the enemy's advanced parapets, reserving their fire until this line was broken.[62]

Across a front from near the Harpeth River on the east to a point close to the Carter's Creek pike on the west, and in a line estimated at more than two miles in length, the Confederate army had deployed in an almost parade ground formation. It was about 4:00 P.M., and some of the troops were lying down; others stood waiting with grim anticipation. A skirmish line already had gone forward 200 yards into the open grass meadows of the valley.[63]

This was something new in the manner of fighting, wrote a dazzled veteran, used to the heavily timbered terrain and close-cover combat that almost always had characterized the Army of Tennessee's battles. For the first time in their three years' experience the veterans could see nearly the entire field of combat. A vast, magnificent panorama lay before them. As far as the eye could see, the ranks of butternut and gray extended across the gently undulating farmland. The men were gaunt—many looked like they had been starved, wrote a soldier—and they stood in tattered ranks with their bayonets already fixed on their imported Enfields, Austrians, and captured Springfield rifle muskets. Their uniforms were threadbare and worn, with many wearing captured Federal clothing. Some had no coats or shoes, and in their haversacks they carried mostly sugar cane and hickory nuts. Nearly all were ragged and dirty. They looked more like a band of robbers than they did soldiers, thought one Federal private who saw some captured prisoners. Another Union soldier noted that "the Rebels rob our dead because they have nothing to wear, especially for our shoes and coats. They still retain their droopy felt hats which gives them a hayseedy look.''[64]

They were all that the Confederacy could muster, what was left of the heart and spirit of the middle South. Yet their ragged appearance belied their ultimate worth. They were the essence of indomitable courage, the best of their generation. A fierce and reckless spirit shone forth, one that seemed to say they could not be overcome, no matter what their fate. Perhaps it was their pride that was most evident. Here were the men who had suffered all, and were about to suffer even more. Their legacy was assured; it could be only that of everlasting glory.

Behind the long gray line, mounted on a brown mare borrowed from one of his escort officers, Cleburne sat and peered pridefully over his beloved division. Cleburne was wearing a new gray uniform coat of the "sack or blouse pattern." His coat was unbuttoned in the warmth of the day, revealing a gray vest and a white linen shirt. Perched on top of his head was a French-style officer's kepi with heavy, looped gold braid, the gift of some ladies. His thoughts perhaps turned to his fiancée, Susan Tarleton. It was close to evening now, and Susan probably would be walking in her garden. The golden rays of the setting sun, bold and red, were cascading through the rim of a dark cloud bank. It was a beautiful and yet ominous sight. Thoughts of unrequited love must have torn at his very being. Pat Cleburne stood trans-fixed at the peak of his destiny.[65]

There was a brief flurry of motion, a rustle of activity on the high hill behind the lines. By prearranged agreement a flag was dropped at Cheatham's order on Winstead Hill. It was the long-awaited signal to advance. A bugle blared within Cleburne's line. Mississippians in A. P. Stewart's Corps sprang to their feet at the command, "Attention." Missourians in Cockrell's Brigade heard the sharp commands: "Shoulder arms! Right shoulder shift arms! Brigade forward! Guide center! Music! Quick time! March!" Bands began playing, Cockrell's eleven-man band tooting "The Bonnie Blue Flag," while Adams's Brigade band struck up "Dixie."[66]

A long, wavering line of brown and gray surged forward. Simultaneously, a burst of bright color fluttered above the line as the regimental, brigade, and divisional battle flags caught in the gentle breeze and flapped softly about their flagstaffs. Conspicuous among the multitude of red St. Andrews cross battle flags were Cleburne's unique colors: faded blue banners with white centers, some emblazoned with crossed cannon battle honors. It was 4:00 P.M. and the ground trembled under the weight of more than 20,000 marching feet. It was a sound, said an eyewitness, like the low, hollow rumble of distant thunder.[67]

CHAPTER XVIII

Tell Them to Fight—
Fight Like Hell!

THE bright, sun-drenched afternoon hours of November 30th were like a summer day, yet misty with the mellow haze of autumn, wrote a Union captain. Nature seemed at rest, which is precisely what many of Schofield's men proceeded to do. A company commander in the 72d Illinois, after sipping a whiskey ration, had pointed out to his men where to dig a line of rifle pits. "The bright sun warmed up the side of a stump," wrote the captain, "[so] I located my headquarters right there and fell asleep at once." Within the ranks of the 104th Ohio, positioned near the cotton gin, the men had gathered bundles of raw cotton and fashioned pillows and mattresses of the white fiber to sleep on.[1]

Many of the men were hungry, and the odor of frying pork, boiling coffee, and steaming flapjacks wafted throughout the bivouac area. In the 50th Ohio most of the men had not waited for the distribution of rations, then lying in bulk on rubber blankets behind the line of works, but had cooked what food they already possessed. One corporal sat on a log and devoured a hearty meal of "slapjacks and molasses, coffee, and bacon." Later he would remember that it was "the last square meal" he ate for more than three months. In other units, particularly among Opdycke's men, rations were short and a detail of twenty men was sent across the river to draw three days' provisions.[2]

By 4:00 P.M., most of the men were lounging about, with some writing letters home and others chatting idly. Many of the men's terms of enlistment had expired in units such as the 57th Indiana and 64th Ohio, and they were merely awaiting their arrival at Nashville to be mustered out. Meanwhile, a familiar pastime, visiting friends in other regiments, was in full vogue.[3]

At the Carter house, Cox's headquarters tents had been struck from the front yard, all baggage packed, and the wagons sent to town prior to crossing the river. At Nathan Kimball's headquarters in the McEwen house, one of his staff officers was flirting with the ladies and asked for some music. One of the women played the piano, and the others sang "Just Before the Battle, Mother."[4]

Even the civilian population of Franklin was caught up in the moment of fleeting commotion within the small Tennessee town. One youth, Hardin Figuers, had shimmied up a tree to get a better look at the goings-on. Also, Colonel Moscow Carter, the paroled prisoner, had taken his father's heavy cedar ladder and climbed on top of the house's roof to see the army's movements. Some of Cox's officers made him come down.[5]

Behind the main line of entrenchments, Lieutenant William O. Mohrmann of the 72d Illinois awoke from a prolonged nap to find his surroundings completely changed. His men had fashioned "little burrows" behind the breastworks and were mostly asleep. Soon the officer of the day summoned Mohrmann and told him to take his twenty-man company on duty as skirmishers, into an old cornfield beyond the cotton field in front. Once there, Mohrmann found a very nervous officer of the 183d Ohio Infantry, Lieutenant Colonel August G. Hatry. Hatry wanted Mohrmann's veterans interspersed among his recruits, who had been assigned skirmish duty for the brigade.[6]

The 183d Ohio was a brand-new regiment, about a thousand strong. Having been enrolled only three weeks earlier, it had received its arms ten days ago and reported for duty on November 28th. Not being familiar with army procedures, the men were ignorant of what to do and stood in the open field without constructing entrenchments. The trouble was, said Mohrmann, there then was too little time for lectures on military science. Off to their left, the men of Colonel John Q. Lane's brigade were seen frantically attempting to fashion some sort of cover from debris and piled earth. Mohrmann looked in front.[7]

With banners flying, drums beating, and their bands playing, here came the entire Confederate army, sweeping onward, straight for the Federal lines, and moving "with the speed of an avalanche." It was the most awesome sight these Illinois veterans had ever beheld. Mohrmann hitched up his sword and dashed for the left flank of his all but stupefied line.[8]

Nearby, Captain John K. Shellenberger of the 64th Ohio Infantry in Conrad's brigade sat on the bank of a shallow ditch, craning his neck to peer over the low earthwork parapet. The day was so warm that Shellenberger had removed his overcoat and was using it as a cushion. Suddenly a nearby sergeant from Company H whose time of enlistment had expired got up swearing and started for the rear. He would not allow his life to be lost by such a stupid tactical blunder, shouted the sergeant. Posting a few men in front of the entire Rebel army was sheer idiocy, he added. Shellenberger, remembering the order to keep the men at their posts with bayonets if need be, jumped to his feet and yelled out, "God damn you, come back here!" The sergeant hesitated, then reluctantly returned.[9]

The sudden appearance of the Confederate army was that of a solid human wave, wrote an eyewitness. The sight was grand, awesome, and terrible, all at once. It was a lifelong impression, forged in an instant. The brown-gray wall of uniforms, the red, tattered flags; a rolling, wavering sweep of movement, dim yet profound in the hazy yellow sunshine; they were images and colors which simply overwhelmed the eye. Growing louder was the sound of marching men, like the distant rumble of mountain boulders.

Ahead of the oncoming gray ranks jackrabbits bounded in wild fright. Coveys of quail exploded into swirling flight, headed toward Franklin, and settled, only to be scattered again, finally whirring over the Federal lines in their search for shelter.[10]

It was the most magnificent sight he had ever seen, the veteran corps commander Benjamin F. Cheatham remembered many years later. An almost unheard-of occurrence, where an entire attacking army could be seen from high ground, the frontal assault at Franklin would be remembered by some as the most imposing martial spectacle of the entire war. "It was worth a year of one's lifetime to witness the marshalling and advance of the Rebel line," thought a Federal eyewitness. "Nothing could be more suggestive of strength, discipline, and resistless power," he added. Even as the gray line swept forward over Privet Knob, a regimental commander in John C. Brown's Division could but marvel at the "magnificent spectacle: "Bands were playing, general and staff officers and gallant couriers were riding in front of and between the lines, 100 battle flags were waving . . . while 20,000 brave men were marching in perfect order against the foe. The sight inspired every man." From the overview on Winstead Hill hundreds of noncombatant onlookers had gathered to watch the assault. The pageantry was splendid, wrote an observer. It was as if the soldiers were marching on dress parade.[11]

Jolting everybody to their senses, Lieutenant Milton A. Mitchell's section of three-inch rifled guns opened with a roar, firing shell a range of about 400 yards directly at Cheatham's line. It was about 4:10 P.M., and thereafter the minutes were as but fleeting instants, each fraught with a thousand events and emotions. Mitchell's section of Battery G, 1st Ohio Light Artillery, having earlier withdrawn from Privet Knob with Lane's brigade, was already taking incoming fire from Confederate sharpshooters posted there. With the deadly Whitworth rifle balls striking down several gunners at their posts, at least one gun changed its fire directly to Privet Knob. One percussion shell struck a few feet from where one of Lieutenant A. Buck Schell's sharpshooters stood, showering rock fragments everywhere. Nearly knocked to the ground by the terrific explosion, the sharpshooter reeled backward, enveloped in smoke, dust, and small bits of gravel. Another sharpshooter yelled to him, asking if he was hurt. "No, not hurt," came the reply, "but scared."[12]

Within the Confederate ranks, Cockrell's brass band changed its tune to "Dixie" as the brigade swept forward on ground west of the Lewisburg pike. Pat Cleburne, frequently conferring with John C. Brown along the Columbia pike, directed his troops' alignment by guiding on the roadway. With a line of skirmishers deployed in front, it appeared to observers that much of the Confederate army was arrayed in multiple lines of battle. Due to the rapidly narrowing range, Mitchell's gunners began calling for grape and canister. "Not yet, not yet," came the reply from an officer; the Confederate lines were still beyond effective small-arms range. The moving wall of gray rolled on in solid ranks, easily closing up the few gaps made by Mitchell's plunging shot and shell. Facing this sudden "stern array" were Conrad's line of skirmishers, who waited no longer, noted an officer, but came scurrying back like a covey of flushed quail dropping into cover.[13]

In watching these movements with nervous apprehension, Captain John K. Shellenberger failed to notice what was occurring beyond Conrad's line, off to the east of his own position. Here the Confederate lines were moving more rapidly, approaching the main Federal line along a shorter plane, and without the obstacles of Privet Knob and Wagner's advanced line in front. Suddenly, with a terrifying roar a shell passed directly over Shellenberger's head and whizzed beyond the main battle line at the Carter house. Unnoticed by nearly everyone, a section of Guibor's Missouri Battery had unlimbered along a wooded knoll and fired the first Confederate artillery shot of the battle. A shell from the second gun struck short, and an agonizing thought raced through Shellenberger's mind—that the third shot would be at precise range and blow "some of us out of that angle."[14]

Already Lieutenant Mitchell's section of guns was limbering up, preparing to withdraw to Cox's main line of earthworks. Their position along the pike was too exposed, the Rebels obviously would soon outflank and engulf this advanced line, and Mitchell determined to withdraw, with or without orders. The section already had taken heavy losses, mostly from the fire of the sharpshooters: two men killed and five wounded. Mitchell's last rounds were canister, shotgunlike blasts of four tiers of forty-eight iron balls packed in sawdust and enclosed in a sheet-iron cylinder. Then Mitchell's gun carriages were hitched by prolonge to their limbers, and guns, caissons, and limbers dashed at full speed for the safety of Cox's line of earthworks. Both Conrad and Lane, watching their artillery support go, were aghast. In an untenable position, with firm orders to stay put, both desperately sent messengers back to find Wagner and tell him the enemy was advancing in heavy force.[15]

Due to the more than one-mile span across the central portion of the field before reaching Wagner's advanced position, it required about fifteen minutes for the Confederate vanguard to approach this line. Cleburne's Division, along the eastern border of the Columbia pike, came to within 400 paces of

Conrad's position, halted, and shifted from brigade column into two lines of battle. Then, with their bayoneted rifle muskets held at "trail," the long gray lines suddenly lurched forward. The order to charge was given, and with a "wild shout," Cleburne's and Brown's men sprinted for Wagner's low line of parapets.[16]

With knotted stomachs and sweating palms, Wagner's men crouched behind the all too meager piles of earth. Amid the crisp, metallic click of cocking gun hammers, there was a flurry of ragged motion as a long, shimmering line of rifle muskets was thrust over the parapet. Sighting down the polished three-foot four-inch barrels with squinting eyes, Wagner's mixture of veterans and recruits nervously tightened their fingers on the taut triggers.

II

George D. Wagner was reclining on the ground behind the main line of earthworks just east of the gap at the Columbia pike. Leaning on one elbow, Wagner was playfully twirling a heavy stick used as a cane following an earlier fall from his horse. Suddenly the roar of Mitchell's artillery sounded in front. Within minutes a screeching shell from Guibor's battery struck the Carter house near the back porch, tearing off a cornice and exploding in the yard. Captain Theodore Cox, the general's younger brother and an aide on his staff, was sitting on the porch steps idly chatting with another staff officer. The shock wave and deafening noise sent the two young officers off at a dead run. Hastily mounting their horses, both officers dashed forward to the gap in the main line at the Columbia pike. Here they found Wagner, standing by the side of the road, in an animated conversation with a courier, who had just arrived from the advanced line.[17]

The courier, T. C. Gregg, was excited, jabbering that the enemy was about to overwhelm both Conrad and Lane, and he didn't think they should remain there any longer. "Go back," said Wagner, "and tell them to fight— fight like hell!" The messenger attempted to argue the point, but Wagner cut him short. "Tell Colonel Conrad that the Second Division [Wagner's] can whip all hell," he roared. Turning to Captain Levi T. Scofield, Wagner then exclaimed, "And that stubbed, curly-headed Dutchman [Conrad] will fight them, too." The courier then galloped back to Conrad's line with the bad news. Immediately thereafter, a second messenger, a staff officer, arrived from in front. Despite his animated plea for a withdrawal, the man was told to have both brigades stand there and fight. "But Hood's entire army is coming," pleaded the amazed officer. In this discussion he was joined by Cox's two staff officers, who reminded Wagner that it was not expected he would fight Hood's whole army.[18]

Wagner, in his wrath, flung his stick at the ground, breaking it in two. Swearing mightily, he again bellowed out, "fight 'em." In an instant the brigade staff officer was gone, fully intimidated by Wagner's irate fury.[19]

Quite possibly, Wagner had been drinking and the whiskey fired his combative ardor. According to Jacob Cox, Wagner had been warned to withdraw his two brigades into the main line if pressed too closely by the enemy. Yet it was a moot point. It already was too late. Once Wagner had given his earlier instructions to Conrad and Lane to stay in position, to the extent of forcing the men to remain at the point of bayonets held by their sergeants, the die was cast.[20]

Just as the various staff officers galloped off, the jolting rumble of artillery wheels on the stone pike heralded the arrival of Mitchell's section. Mitchell had brought his guns in with the horses at a lope. One of Guibor's guns had fired a single shot at the retiring section, but the shell missed, striking the pike behind the fleeing guns before bounding over the earthworks into Franklin. As Mitchell's horses slowed to an easy trot and swung around the interior retrenchment behind the main line, one of the gunners jumped off a caisson. His face was black with powder smoke, remembered Captain Levi Scofield, and he said in a grim voice: "Old Hell is let loose, and coming [in from] out there."[21]

III

Their guns were three-inch ordnance rifles, sleek wrought-iron rifled gun tubes firing a ten-pound elongated projectile with a range of about two miles at maximum elevation. Having earlier taken position on the commanding overlook at Fort Granger, Captain Giles J. Cockerill's Battery D, 1st Ohio Light Artillery, was in position to rake the oncoming Confederate lines, especially along the open ground between the Lewisburg and Columbia pikes. Firing percussion shell, Cockerill's guns opened as the Confederates swept to within about 300 yards of Wagner's advance line. Immediately bursting shells wreathed the air in great circles of smoke, noted an excited South Carolina colonel. An observer in Fort Granger saw that the explosion of the heavy shells severely ripped the enemy's ranks, yet the broken gaps were quickly closed with such obvious spirit and determination that it earned his outright admiration. The whole scene, he remarked, was "most terrifically beautiful and grand."[22]

Within the massed Confederate ranks, rising above the noise of exploding shells and onrushing men, came the terse commands of officers: "Forward, men." Ahead, amid the tensed ranks of Wagner's two brigades under Conrad and Lane there was only a deep and awful silence, wrote a soldier. The cry of "Steady, boys! Reserve your fire!" sounded all too tremulous in tone to one apprehensive rifleman. At a range of about 100 yards a sudden shout rang out: "Fire." Immediately a sheet of flame leapt forth, and the very earth seemed to explode in the faces of the onrushing Confederates. This first volley of Federal musketry was "a rattling fusillade," said an eyewitness. The shock momentarily staggered the Confederate ranks, and their line seemed to come to a halt. Again the cry "Forward, men" rang out, and Cleburne's and Brown's infantrymen surged ahead.[23]

In the swirling smoke and confusion Wagner's men hastily attempted to reload. Yet the massed Confederate lines had not returned the fire, and only a few scattered shots sounded in reply—mostly from skirmishers still in front. Now, bursting forth in all its fury from what seemed like ten thousand throats, came that dreaded, eerie, high-pitched battle cry—the Rebel yell. The sound sent chills through the spine of nearly every man. He saw an age in a moment, wrote a terrified participant.[24]

Captain John Shellenberger looked up. Most of his men in the 64th Ohio had been able to fire only a few shots. The Rebel line was so close that his first impulse was "to throw myself flat on the ground and let them charge over us." Glancing backward, he saw Conrad's ranks give way and break into fragments. Beginning toward the pike, the break ran along the line so fast it reminded Shellenberger of a burning powder train. Already the fighting along most of the line was hand-to-hand, with clubbed muskets and slashing bayonets. Shellenberger jumped to his feet. "I shouted to my company, 'Fall back! Fall back!' and gave an example of how to do it by turning and running for the breastworks."[25]

Just as Conrad's men sprang to the rear, Cleburne's line delivered a staggering volley at point-blank range. "It seemed as if bullets had never before hissed with such diabolical venom," said the veteran Shellenberger. "Every one that passed made a noise seemingly loud enough to tear one in two." The groans of the wounded who went down in this swirling, dust-choked mayhem were pathetic. Their cries, heightened by the fear of being left on the battlefield, were of such despair as Shellenberger "had never heard before."[26]

Due to the unchecked advance of A. P. Stewart's Corps farther to the east, Conrad's line had been easily outflanked. Yet the actual break had occurred from the hard-charging pressure of Hiram Granbury's men near the Columbia pike. Thereafter, the panic had spread like wildfire on both sides of the road. Lane and Conrad combined had less than 4,000 men to face the onset of about 8,000 Confederates in their front.[27]

Lane's men, having had little time and no tools to construct parapets, had watched Conrad's line disintegrate and, with little hesitation, joined in the flight. "Rally behind the works!" someone shouted, and joined by the 183d Ohio and 72d Illinois skirmishers in the adjacent field, Lane's infantrymen ran for their lives. It was simply a race for personal safety as the charging Rebels sprinted close at the Federals' heels, said a bewildered skirmisher. An observer in the main line noticed how many of Lane's and Conrad's men were running bent over nearly to the ground to escape the whizzing bullets, and they kept glancing backward to see if the enemy was gaining on them. It was every man for himself, and the devil be damned, said an officer.[28]

Within minutes of the breakup of Wagner's forward lines there were so many men running in all directions that it was little more than a wild, uncontrolled stampede. An Ohio captain, running at full speed with his head down, ran headlong into another man veering in a different direction. The collision knocked the enlisted man down, just as a Confederate shell exploded overhead. "I caught a glimpse of his upturned face," said the captain, "and in its horrified look, read his belief that it was the shell that had hit him. The idea was so comical that I laughed."[29]

Captain Shellenberger, remembering his new overcoat that had been left behind, suddenly stopped, thinking he would return and get it. One hurried look back, however, again sent the captain running for Cox's main line. The Confederates were pouring over the low embankment like a flock of sheep. Some of their officers stood on the parapet waving their swords, while beside them riflemen were firing into the scattering blue ranks.[30]

With panting lungs and trembling legs, remembered a veteran officer, he strained every nerve to reach the safety of the main Federal line. In the open field there were few obstructions, yet everybody seemed to be crowding toward the gap in the earthworks at the Columbia pike. There was nearly a half mile to traverse, and laden with blankets, knapsacks, haversacks, and all manner of equipment, the men quickly became winded. "We go right after them, yelling like fury, and shooting at them at the same time," wrote one of Cleburne's officers. "The Yanks [were] running for life and we for the fun of it, but the difference in the objects are so great that they out run us, but lose quite a number of their men before they get [away]."[31]

Along the pike the scene was that of mayhem. An observer saw that for perhaps a hundred yards the blue ranks were so densely massed as to impede each other's progress. The fleetest of foot had reached the breastworks and were crossing over and through, but there were so many winded men in the rear that few could move faster than a slow, labored trot. Some were seen doggedly walking, unable to move faster despite the great danger. Already the gray riflemen were among these men, grabbing hold of them or knocking them down with clubbed muskets.[32]

Captain Shellenberger was among those who seemed beyond the limits of endurance. With the safety of the breastwork only a few steps away, "even with life itself at stake, I could go no farther," he exclaimed. "[I] thought my time had come." Then he remembered his mother's parting advice: "Well, if you must go, don't get shot in the back." Shellenberger "faced about to take it in front." Suddenly his attention was riveted to an onrushing Confederate with a poised rifle musket. "I thought I was looking at the man who would shoot me," wrote the terrified Shellenberger. When the man fired into another nearby cluster of escaping Federals, the Ohio captain was so close he heard the bullet strike and the agonizing groan from the victim. With a burst of renewed energy, Shellenberger staggered about and lunged headlong into the nearby ditch at the base of the earthworks.[33]

Behind this tumultuous scene confusion reigned. Pat Cleburne, waving his hat above his head, guided his mount over the low parapet and urged his men forward. The gray ranks were scattered by the pursuit, and some of his men had evidently stopped behind this first barricade. Ahead, most of the division and brigade organization already had been lost. Cleburne's and Brown's men were intermixed with Wagner's fleeing troops in a wedge-shaped mass of humanity, veering haphazardly toward the gap at the pike. Suddenly a cry rang out amid the gray ranks: "Let's go into the works with them!" The shout was quickly taken up, and even General George Gordon vociferously repeated the cry. A lieutenant of the 72d Illinois heard a Rebel officer shout "Right into the works with them, boys!" and he sprinted ahead, squirming through a locust barricade and over the earthwork, convinced that at least 400 of the enemy were beside him.[34]

The entire episode, wrote a chagrined Federal officer, resulted in a disgraceful and unnecessary "butcher's bill" of casualties—due entirely to incompetent generalship. It was a crisis following from a foolish order, and came near losing this decisive battle, later assessed an angered Federal general. What they referred to was not only the unwise positioning and rout of a relatively small, unsupported force in front of the main earthworks, but, even more damagingly, the inability of the main line to fire in their front for fear of hitting their own men. The result seemed to portend a disaster of major proportions.[35]

"We were standing up against the parapet, breathlessly and silently waiting for Lane's and Conrad's men to run in," remembered an officer in Reilly's ranks. With teeth clenched, they stood with poised muskets, unable to fire due to the ragged line of blue still in front. Within the embrasures along the earthwork, gunners of the 1st Battery, Kentucky Light Artillery, stood grim and silent with their four three-inch rifle guns aimed and loaded with canister, but unable to open fire. "Nothing is more helpless than a battery in such circumstances," wrote a nearby officer. For lack of a clear field of fire they awaited what seemed to be their sure defeat, added an infantry captain. As this seething mass came rolling on like a living sea, the yellowish brown Confederate uniforms seemed to be magnified in size. "One could almost imagine them to be phantoms sweeping along in the air," thought a dazed staff officer.[36]

In the ditch outside the parapet by the cotton gin, Captain John Shellenberger was gasping for breath. Raising his head to look about, he was astounded to see the front ranks of Cleburne's men only a few yards away. "They were so tired that they seemed scarcely able to put one foot before the other," he observed. Yet within moments the ditch started to fill with their panting ranks. Then, amid all this tumult of yelling, bewildered men, there was a deafening roar—a blast and shock wave that simply knocked men off their feet as if amid an earthquake. It seemed as if hell itself had exploded in their faces, wrote one dazed Confederate general. Cox's battle line had waited no longer. Beginning with scattered shots from nervous individuals, the densely packed Federal line had fired spontaneously without orders regardless of the mixture of blue and gray in their front. Amid this whirlwind cone of fire the air suddenly was hideous with minie balls. The hailstorm of musketry virtually leveled those in the front ranks. Men of both armies lay writhing on the ground, screaming in agony. The men in the ranks behind were staggered, reeling like a herd of drunken men, said an eyewitness. Flags rose and fell, then a great, gushing cloud of smoke obscured everything.[37]

To Captain Shellenberger the crashing volley of Federal musketry seemed "sweeter than music." Yet his thoughts that the Rebels' turn now had come to take their due medicine were abruptly interrupted by the onset of a second enemy wave. "Transfixed with amazement," he saw them emerge from the smoke and come in all around him, most halting in the ditch to catch their breath. The fixed bayonets on their Enfield rifle muskets made Shellenberger think he suddenly might be pinioned to the ground. This thought was so terrifying, said the captain, that he sprang to the top of the earthwork and, grasping the top log with both hands, attempted to climb over.[38]

The next thing he knew, he was inside the parapet, lying in the ditch, being trampled by dozens of feet. Evidently knocked senseless by a blow from one of Reilly's excited men who was too preoccupied to discern if he was a friend or foe, Shellenberger had fallen across the body of a desperately wounded soldier. The man had been shot through the head, he noted with horror, but was still breathing. Shellenberger's coat was soaked with the man's blood, and the crush of trampling feet was so great he couldn't get up. "In a desperate effort to avoid being trampled to death, [I] managed in some way to crawl out between the legs of the men to the bank of the ditch." Here he lay with burning lungs, still gasping for breath, until a few minutes later he noticed that down the line toward the turnpike all of the Federal troops were gone. Even worse, two of the cannon positioned at the gap on the road were being swung around by men in ragged butternut uniforms. In an instant they were pointed directly down the line of the embankment in his direction. Too exhausted to attempt to get out of the way, Shellenberger saw the Confederates working at the breech of the guns to discharge them. He shut his eyes and set his jaw, momentarily expecting the blasts to tear him to pieces.[39]

IV

The mystery, said an appalled Confederate officer, was "how any man ever reached the [enemy] line." The air seemed literally alive with shrieking rifle bullets, exploding shells, and bursting shrapnel. A hand thrown out might have been caught full of these mad messengers of death, he surmised. The dead and wounded immediately in front of the parapet east of the Columbia pike were thicker than he had ever seen, except perhaps at Kennesaw Mountain, although the fighting had occurred thus far only for a few minutes. There was little cover on the field at Franklin, wrote an observer, and on the rising slope of ground in front of Cox's center there was "not even a stump or bush for shelter." With so many men massed at point-blank range, even the poorest marksman couldn't help but hit a human target, acknowledged one of Cox's officers. It was like the shock of an earthquake, thought a recipient of the scathing Federal fire that poured from the earthworks on Reilly's front. The very elements of heaven and earth seemed to be in one mighty uproar, wrote a Tennessee soldier. Yet in the next amazing instant the Federal line at the center was engulfed with the wreckage of Wagner's men and the overwhelming human wave of Cleburne's and Brown's massed ranks.[40]

More like a wild, howling mob than an organized army, the Confederates poured through the Columbia pike gap and over the adjacent earthworks. Shouts from among Wagner's retreating officers to "rally in the rear" passed among the bewildered throng. Many of the men in Reilly's and Strickland's brigades needed little further incentive. Engulfed by a mad, surging sea of humanity, and hearing the confusing shouts to rally behind the lines, they sprang for the rear amid an ever-expanding tide of chaos and panic.[41]

In the 50th Ohio Infantry, positioned just west of the Columbia pike, the Confederates were rushing past on the pike and pouring over the works on top of them. One of the regiment's lieutenants shouted, "Boys, we have got to get out of here." A corporal glanced up and saw the regimental colors going back. He jumped up to run, only to come face-to-face with "a big Johnnie Reb with a musket pointed at me that look[ed] as large to my eyes as a twelve-pounder cannon." The corporal surrendered, and with his captor soon crouched in the ditch to avoid the incoming storm of lead that seemed to zip through the air from every direction. About sixty of his regiment had been taken when their line was overrun, and they all lay prone to escape the deadly fire. The corporal looked up. Over the parapet jumped a Rebel private, who raised his rifle and fired point-blank at a surrendered sergeant sitting nearby. The bullet sliced across the bridge of the sergeant's nose, and a Confederate officer whirled about, poking his sword in the private's face. If he so much as attempted another cowardly trick like that, said the officer, he would cut him down. The officer then sped off, waving his sword and urging his men forward. Before he had taken several steps, noted the captive corporal, the officer went down. Amid crashes of musketry that exceeded anything he had heard during the Atlanta fighting, the corporal cowered in the ditch. Soon a wounded Rebel fell across his feet, and another tumbled over his shoulder. Their blood, noted the terrified corporal, quickly stained and soaked his uniform to his skin.[42]

East of the Columbia pike the result had been much the same. Here two Ohio regiments, the 100th and 104th, had been posted in support of the 1st Kentucky Battery's four rifled guns. The battery had been unable to fire due to Wagner's retreating men, and already the limbers and caissons had dashed madly away, driven by frightened drivers and terrified horses. Their guns stood loaded and ready, but were quickly abandoned due to the onrushing enemy. Then their supports, the two Ohio regiments, had disintegrated in a swelling sea of fleeing Federals mixed with Cleburne's yelling horde.[43]

In all, a 200-yard front, stretching from near the cotton gin to west of the Columbia pike near the locust grove, had been captured and cleared of Federal troops. Essentially, this section of earthworks was the zone where Wagner's overwhelmed troops had dashed back to safety, preventing a clear field of fire.[44]

As far as the eye could see along the Columbia pike a wild, frightened mob of men and stampeding horses raced to the rear past the Carter house. In their midst, mounted on his horse and facing the horde, was Brigadier General George D. Wagner. Thrusting his broken stick about and swearing loud oaths, Wagner cursed the fleeing men, calling them cowards, and shouted for them to stop. No one seemed to listen, and Wagner and his horse were borne backward by the surging throng. Finally a powder-smeared sergeant stopped by his side and managed to encourage about twenty men to form a line.[45]

In addition to all twelve of Conrad's and Lane's regiments, three of Cox's regiments, plus portions of two others in reserve, had been routed and fragmented. A stream of fugitives darkened the Columbia pike into Franklin, engulfing the streets and overspreading into the yards. An officer sent to obtain ammunition from across the river returned only to confront this panicky throng heading pell-mell for the bridges. "For a few moments it seemed almost impossible to make headway against the tumultuous tide which filled the street from house front to house front," he wrote. "It looked as though our line had been crushed at the center, and nothing could save the little army from destruction."[46]

CHAPTER XIX

The Pandemonium of Hell
Turned Loose

JOHN M. Schofield had spent a rather quiet early afternoon. Comfortably situated at Alpheus Truett's fashionable Georgian-style home a half mile north of Franklin on the Nashville pike, Schofield had dallied over arrangements to position Wood's division north of the river so as to best cover the army's crossing after nightfall. About 3:00 P.M., word had arrived from James H. Wilson that the enemy's infantry was approaching Hughes's Ford, three miles south of Franklin. Schofield had anticipated just such a move by Hood. Less than three hours of daylight remained, and he sensed little danger. Schofield felt his army could march to Brentwood before Hood could force a crossing and complete any full-scale flanking movement. As such, Schofield was confident that his evacuation of Franklin, already in its initial stages, would thwart Hood's apparent movement.[1]

Just before 4:00 P.M., word arrived of the Confederate army forming in battle array at the foot of Winstead Hill, nearly three miles from Schofield's headquarters. Anticipating that Hood was merely making another demonstration in front, as at Columbia, Schofield and his staff were not unduly alarmed. Noisily clambering to the Truetts' upstairs porch with its southern exposure, Schofield and his staff officers peered through their field glasses at the distant enemy throng. Fourteen-year-old Edwin Truett was present, having tagged along with the aggregation as they crowded onto the porch. Now he begged for a chance to look through the field glasses at the gathering ranks of gray. One staff officer gruffly sought to brush him aside, but Schofield spoke up, offering his glasses and telling the boy to look well, for he would never again see such a sight.[2]

Within minutes the harsh rattle of small-arms fire echoed across the valley, and it was apparent that battle had been joined. For the second time in two days, Schofield felt the cold chill of utter helplessness course through his body. Again he had been terribly wrong in his calculations. "For a moment my heart sank within me," he admitted. Only the temporary defensive breastworks erected under Cox's direction—intended to intimidate Hood into not attacking—stood between Schofield's army and possible disaster. Schofield hadn't even bothered to personally inspect these fortifications, so certain was he that the enemy would not attack. His army must fight with their "back[s] to the river," he foresaw. Again Schofield's fate seemed to turn upon the fickle element of luck. His career, the army's destiny—they all rested upon random chance and the unpredictable efforts of others. The "fortune of war" had always seemed to turn in his favor, wrote Schofield of his past inordinate good fortune. The question at Franklin now seemed to be precisely that: Whose good luck would prevail—Schofield's or his old West Point classmate's? Schofield, in remembering how his personal encouragement seemed to keep Hood struggling to pass his exams at West Point, wondered now if perhaps he had made a mistake.[3]

Schofield reacted apprehensively. He sent a message to Wood, the only commander in position to cover a retreat: "Hold your command in readiness to cover the crossing of the river in case the enemy break our lines on the south side of the river." Another dispatch went to the army's chief quartermaster: "Start all your trains, except ammunition, headquarters, and ambulances, to Nashville immediately." Even Samuel Beatty's brigade, recently ordered to the support of Wilson's cavalry at Hughes's Ford, was told to take defensive position adjacent to Fort Granger along the river. Clearly, both Schofield and David S. Stanley had been caught so unawares that their reactions were almost irrelevant. The unexpected battle was in the hands of the soldiers, and the only combat function that remained for the army's senior officers was to encourage the men and respond to developments.[4]

Stanley had been sleeping at the Truett house when the alarm was given. "In view of the strong position we held, and . . . [due to] the former course of the Rebels during this campaign [Columbia], nothing appeared so improbable that they would assault," he admitted. Yet Hood always had been unpredictable. It was now evident he was gambling everything on breaking through and routing the Federal army. That was the one ultimate danger. With the river at the Federals' backs, if Hood's men somehow managed to stampede Cox's men following a breakthrough, the Union army might be virtually destroyed amid an all-consuming panic.[5]

Both Stanley and Schofield mounted their horses and galloped together along the Nashville pike until they reached the wagon bridge. Here Schofield and his staff split away, hastening to Fort Granger along the riverbank road. Stanley, with a single orderly, dashed ahead to the battlefield. En route he met a staff officer from Cox, belatedly bringing word that the enemy was about to attack. As Stanley crossed the river and hastened south on the

Columbia pike, he ran head-on into utter chaos. Wagons, caissons, terrified horses, and bewildered soldiers all were mixed together in a confused tangle. The swelling mass ran past the appalled Stanley and spilled toward the river, oblivious of everything but the safety of the north bank.[6]

The closer Stanley rode toward Carter House Hill, the more pandemonium he witnessed. Soldiers without weapons, unable to run rapidly along the crowded pike, were dashing through the adjacent yards. Some officers from Wagner's division were trying to rally their men, but few seemed to pay any attention. As Stanley galloped forward he noticed a ragged wall of gray spilling over the earthworks ahead, and red, St. Andrew's cross–emblazoned flags emerging through the swirling clouds of smoke. The din was incredible. Cox's soldiers were scattering in fright and confusion. Disaster was in the air. Hood's outrageous gamble—was it possible it might succeed? "The moment was critical beyond any I have known in any battle," wrote an appalled Stanley. Should the enemy even continue to hold that portion of the earthworks, they were already closer to the two vital bridges than both trapped flanks of the Union army, he suddenly realized.[7]

From his brigade's position about 200 yards north of the Carter house, Emerson Opdycke, the fiery Ohio colonel who had defied George Wagner in refusing to post his brigade in the old cotton field, could see the effect that Wagner's routed troops had on Cox's main line as they poured over the earthworks. Instantly a confused, wild-eyed throng began racing pell-mell for the rear. So many of Cox's and Wagner's raw recruits, easily identifiable by their new uniforms, were mixed with the tattered, dark-skinned veterans that it seemed the entire center segment along the turnpike had given way.[8]

Opdycke's six regiments were resting on both sides of the stone pike. In the growing noise and confusion, it was evident orders could not be heard, nor rapidly communicated by messenger. Already the ranks of his brigade were wavering in disorder as they hastily attempted to grab their stacked arms and form in line of battle. Several regiments, having no orders and being uncertain of what to do, lay down as bullets began whistling overhead. Nearly everyone was "struck dumb" by the compelling, if horrifying, scene in front, said a soldier. Tearing down the pike like so many demons came the routed men, rushing toward Opdycke's position in an avalanche of humanity. Mixed among their rear ranks were men in gray uniforms, yelling and firing into the terrified fugitives. "I never felt so bad since the war [began]," wrote one of Opdycke's sergeants. "I thought the day was gone."[9]

Opdycke saw that his men could not stand idle amid the growing turmoil and incoming fire. Impulsively, he sought to move several regiments of his brigade across the road to the east side, "for greater security to the men" and to consolidate their ranks for better maneuverability. In attempting to cross the road amid all the confusion, this movement was misconstrued by some of his troops for an advance.[10]

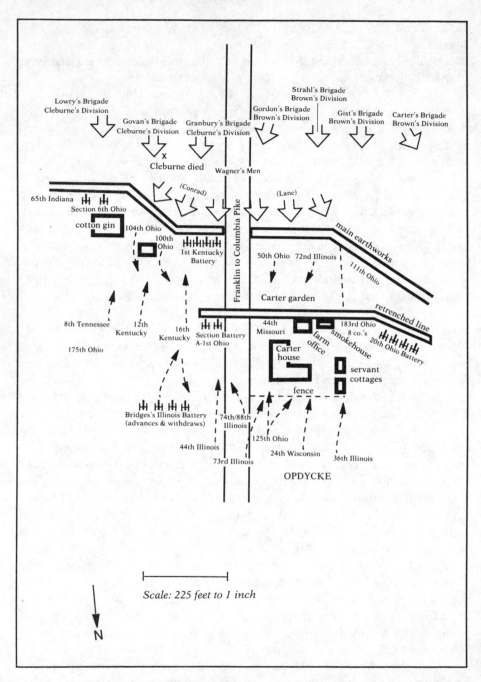

MAP 7   Opdycke's Charge—about 4:45 P.M.
November 30—Franklin

The men had jumped up from their coffee, cursing, remembered a soldier. No one seemed to hear or receive any orders. Because the rows of stacked arms were loaded from the men's earlier rear-guard duty and had fixed bayonets so as to hold the weapons in place, their mostly Enfield rifle muskets were combat ready as Opdycke's men rushed to form. Immediately, said an officer in amazement, everyone seemed to take in the situation. With the 125th Ohio rushing across the road to join the 74th/88th (consolidated) and 44th Illinois, Major Thomas W. Motherspaw of the 73d Illinois, evidently thinking Opdycke had ordered a charge, excitedly shouted, "Go for them, Boys." The order seemed to make sense. No one had to tell the veterans of Atlanta and other hard-fought battles that the safest place when the bullets began zipping about was at the breastworks.[11]

Not everyone in the 73d Illinois heard Motherspaw's orders. Some of the soldiers were confused: "What's the order?" "Who said so?" shouted several men. Yet an impetus had been generated. Most of the men thought that everything happened spontaneously. There was a yell and a bounding rush forward. A sergeant watched as Motherspaw swung into the saddle and again yelled, "Forward, 73d, to the works!" With leveled bayonets, but in irregular order, the 73d swept forward, yelling furiously.[12]

Emerson Opdycke was astounded. Before his very eyes part of his brigade was out of control, rushing without orders amid the confused mob in front. Desperately he sent an aide galloping to Motherspaw to yell, "Stop that regiment, Stop that regiment!" Motherspaw, amid the tumult, yelled to the aide that it was too late—it was impossible to stop the men.[13]

Already Lieutenant Colonel George W. Smith, with his consolidated regiments, the 74th and 88th Illinois, had joined in the rush forward. Mounted and waving his cap, he dashed to the head of his regiments, which by their position at the south end of the brigade now led an expanding, wedge-shaped mass of men into the fray. The rush for the works spontaneously swept through Opdycke's remaining regiments like an electric current. Opdycke looked around. He saw at a glance that it was everyone for himself. The 125th Ohio, in his immediate presence, seemed to hesitate in uncertainty. Opdycke shouted, "First Brigade, forward to the works." Bayonets came down to the charge position, there was a yell, and the 125th Ohio joined in the wild stampede for the front. In the 36th Illinois, the trailing regiment on the west side of the road, shouts of "Forward to the trenches" rang out, and with lowered bayonets they too dashed into the fight.[14]

It was heavy irony. Opdycke, who earlier had refused to obey Wagner's orders to halt with the advanced line, had compelled his division commander to defer to his course of action. Now, when his own brigade failed to obey his orders, Opdycke was forced to conform to their conduct. Drawing his revolver, Opdycke, on horseback, plunged ahead amid the wildly shouting men, his hot temper at the boiling point.[15]

*   *   *

The scene along the stone pike, later remembered an eyewitness, was so remarkable that despite the danger he was "right glad I was there, and would not have been away for $500." He gushed to his brother a few days later, "Oh! what a scene occurred for a few minutes." It was two opposing columns charging at one another, and they "met on the run." The shock was so enormous that it caused him to shudder in remembering the incident more than a week later. The hand-to-hand fighting that instantly erupted was so appalling that he wrote, "I surely do not want to ever witness the like again."[16]

Another observer said it reminded him of two enormous ocean waves crashing together. The horror of that collision on the pike was beyond description, wrote a participant. Everywhere men were running in all directions. The smoke was blinding. The noise was deafening. It was a wild melee where only animal instinct seemed to prevail.[17]

The initial collision had been between Opdycke's massed columns and the Union fugitives fleeing to safety. With the phalanx of glistening, leveled bayonets poised in their faces, most of the fleeing soldiers from the forward lines had scattered right or left, away from Opdycke's onrushing ranks. Those who failed to get out of the way were trampled underfoot.[18]

In the headlong rush for the breastworks, Opdycke's regiments were so crowded together by the fences and obstructions that all had become mixed in a tangled mishmash of regiments, companies, and individuals acting on their own. The lines of the 125th Ohio were immediately broken by two caissons which came thundering through along the pike. Their ranks hastily parted but soon closed up again due to the heavy press of men from behind. Ahead, at the edge of the Carter yard, directly in front of Opdycke's men west of the pike, stood a staked cedar fence. The 73d Illinois, which had crowded forward west of the pike to avoid as much as possible the rush of men in the road, soon encountered this imposing fence. The palings were so thick, said a captain, that they could not be broken with the butt of a gun or kicked down. Even the nails were so large and firmly set that they could not be loosened. The fence was too high to climb over, and the ranks of the 73d and others surged in vain against this unyielding obstacle. So many rifle bullets were striking the fence and felling men that it sounded to one man as if a child were running with a stick along a picket fence and rattling the stakes. "Getting over or through that fence in the face of that fire was one of the most, if not the most, terrible experiences the 73d regiment ever had," thought a veteran officer. Finally, after what seemed to be an age, a breach was made, aided by incoming rifle fire, and the Federal ranks surged through.[19]

Here, in the Carter yard, Opdycke's men ran head-on into the foremost Confederate ranks. These gray-clad soldiers were mostly of John C. Brown's and Pat Cleburne's divisions, yelling at the top of their lungs and sprinting through the smoke in pursuit of the terrified Federal troops. Because of their long, fatiguing chase from the distant ground of Wagner's advanced position, the Confederate ranks were greatly scattered, with clusters of individuals from both commands being mixed among Wagner's and Cox's fleeing men. The collision of the two mobs amid the Carter house and outbuildings became a lifelong memory. The vivid impressions and terrifying scenes witnessed "were so indelibly stamped upon the minds of the participants that even a long life spent in peaceful pursuits will not suffice to erase or even dim them," wrote a Federal veteran many years later. This incredible melee, a "hand to hand contest without parallel," was so vicious it "never [could] be described accurately or portrayed fully," thought a regimental historian. To add to the tangled blue and gray mass of humanity pouring north, hundreds of men from Strickland's reserve regiments at the retrenched line had joined in the stampede. These men, being less fatigued than Wagner's troops, seemed to race past at breakneck speed.[20]

"I well remember what a badly demoralized mob we met just in the yard at the Carter house," wrote one of Opdycke's Illinois privates. "It was a fight, nearly, to get to the front [through the fleeing Federal ranks], they wildly struggling to the rear, and we crowding to the front." Right in among Cox's fugitives were the Confederates. One Illinois infantryman bayoneted a Rebel soldier on the Carter house steps. To an agonized captain of the 73d Illinois, the cursing, yelling men, flailing with clubbed muskets and jabbing with bayonets, were as demons possessed. It was the pandemonium of hell turned loose, he thought. Amid shouts, yells, groans, cries, and the din of gunfire, Opdycke's men by sheer weight of numbers forced their way forward.[21]

Opdycke, now dismounted, was in the midst of the fighting, firing his revolver until it was empty. Quickly reversing the pistol, he grabbed it by the barrel and violently swung with the butt at the heads of the enemy. When the cylinder wedge came out and the barrel fell off, Opdycke grasped an abandoned rifle musket and began bludgeoning the enemy with it. Rebels, Yanks, all manner of men and officers, grappling in the smoke, din, and confusion, were without order or reason. It was a fight where every man was a major general, said a veteran, for everyone was fighting "on their own hook." Due to the smoke and bedlam, it was hard to tell who was who in the deadly strife. A soldier admitted: "We were so badly mixed up with old soldiers going forward, new soldiers going back, and Rebs running both ways . . . I could not tell for several minutes which were prisoners, the Rebs or ourselves— each ordering the other to surrender, and many on each side clubbing their guns and chasing each other around the [Carter] houses."[22]

The wild melee in the Carter yard lasted only a few minutes. Because of the simultaneous charge of Reilly's reserve regiments into the area immediately east of the Columbia pike, there was little room there. A large portion of only one of Opdycke's regiments, the 44th Illinois, remained east of the roadway. The balance of Opdycke's men crowded, bayoneted, and swerved their way around the various Carter buildings, pressing toward the retrenched line west of the pike at the smokehouse and farm office building.

Here they saw the main segments of Brown's and Cleburne's divisions pouring over the low interior breastworks "like sheep in a wheatfield." In an instant the furious hand-to-hand fighting became even more deadly. Everybody seemed to be firing at once, said a participant, and the bullets rattled through the Carters' wooden frame buildings "like hail-stones." Opdycke's men kept going, staggering forward, shooting and reloading, as best they could.[23]

The personal incidents of battle were but fleeting vignettes. One of Opdycke's infantrymen saw a Rebel jump on top of the works and raise the butt of his rifle musket to strike a defender. The Federal quickly drew a bead and fired; the Rebel threw up his hands and fell backward over the parapet. One of the soldiers in the 88th Illinois saw his captain rush into the fray armed with a hatchet in one hand and a Sharps four-barreled pepperbox revolver in the other. An Ohio officer who had been to the rear for supplies jumped off his horse near the Carter barn, hitched his horse to the fence, and ran into the fray unarmed. "I [had earlier] left my sword and revolver on the ground with other headquarters baggage," he explained. Stepping on an abandoned officer's sword as he rushed toward the retrenched line, he grabbed it and sprawled headlong into the ditch. Above him men were fighting bayonet to bayonet, muzzle to muzzle, as they had "never fought before or since." It was "sheet lightning" everywhere he looked. "Smoke enveloped everybody. The curses of the living in their desperate struggle for life mingled with the groans of the dying."[24]

Lieutenant Colonel Porter C. Olson of the 36th Illinois made it to the edge of the breastworks but was shot in the chest, the ball passing entirely through his body. Half dragged, half carried by two of his men to the front of the Carter house, Olson was placed on a shutter ripped from one of the windows, then was borne to the rear amid the turbulent roar of cannon shells and shrieking rifle balls. Feebly, Olson uttered, "Oh, help me Lord!" and was gone. Nearby, the officer who had initiated the incredible charge, Major Thomas Motherspaw, lay bleeding on the ground with a mortal wound. Also, Major Arthur MacArthur, Jr., of the 24th Wisconsin (who would become the father of World War II general Douglas MacArthur), went down with a severe wound.[25]

Taking a heavy pummeling in the rush toward the retrenched parapet was the last of Opdycke's regiments to reach that line, the 36th Illinois. At the front of their ranks the color sergeant fell before getting near the works. The flag was taken from his grasp by another sergeant, who made it to the barricade. Already the flagstaff had been struck three times and severely shattered. The sergeant held on to the top fragment until he was mortally wounded. As usual in the heat of battle, the conspicuous flag was drawing a heavy fire, and the third man who held it aloft noted its folds were nearly in tatters from the scores of missiles that struck it. Suddenly a Confederate soldier reached over the retrenchment and, seizing the splintered staff, attempted to wrest it away. There was a brief struggle, then someone shot the Rebel, and the flag was pulled back. Cutting the remaining fragments from the staff, a man thrust the tattered banner inside his uniform coat and crawled to safety on his hands and knees.[26]

Nearby, a captain of the 36th Illinois huddled near the corner of the Carters' brick smokehouse, attempting to talk with another officer. A bullet struck the captain in the skull, burrowing through the left eye and lodging in his face. Unable to find an ambulance, for they were mostly across the river ready to go to Nashville, the bleeding captain staggered rearward with a crowd of wounded soldiers for two miles before finding help.[27]

Opdycke's men had their hands full in driving the enemy back across the retrenched line. The firing was fury itself, great sheets of flame leaping from thousands of muzzles in a continuous roar. The earth seemed to tremble. "I never see[n] men fight . . . more determined than the Rebs did," said a sergeant of the 44th Illinois. "And I never see[n] enemy men fall so fast. Our boys shot them just like hogs."[28]

So many of Opdycke's men had crowded into the confined area at the smokehouse segment of the retrenched line that the Federal ranks were in some places four and five deep. Many of Wagner's and Cox's men were mixed among Opdycke's ranks, having rallied and returned to the interior line under the urging of their officers. Those in the front ranks kept firing and passing their empty guns to the rear, where they were loaded and repassed to the front. The rapidity of the firing was awesome to hear. The air reverberated with one continuous roar, and the earthworks were all aflame, wrote an eyewitness. "The tempest of lead and iron beat the surface of the earth into dust." No ranks could stand unprotected in front of this scorching, all-consuming firestorm. The Confederates ducked back behind the retrenchment, and many sprinted back to the main line of entrenchments, sixty-five yards north across the Carter garden. Others dropped their guns and, yelling out in surrender, hurriedly leapt across the parapet amid their overwrought antagonists.[29]

Opdycke's men were now firing so rapidly with the pass-back-and-forth system that the guns were becoming fouled with black powder residue.* So many cartridges were being consumed that the bodies of the dead and wounded were searched for ammunition. Shouts of "Give us more ammunition" ran down the line. This sent many of the officers scurrying for cartridges. One sergeant, sent toward the gap at the pike for more ammunition, ran into Emerson Opdycke. In the heat of the fray, the Ohio colonel thought the man was running away and raised his revolver to strike the sergeant.

*Only about twenty to twenty-five rounds could be fired from a muzzle-loading rifle musket under normal conditions before the buildup of powder residue in the barrel prevented ramming home the minie ball. For this reason many battlewise company commanders having .58-caliber Springfield rifle muskets had some .577-caliber Enfield ammunition issued to their men. By having .577 ammunition placed in the lower section of their men's cartridge boxes they could be used in the heat of battle when the guns became so fouled as to be unusuable with standard .58-caliber ammunition.

Barely in time, an officer dashed up and shouted that the man was going for cartridges.[30]

With so many of Opdycke's men occupying the retrenched line, it appeared to the Confederates that strong reinforcements had arrived, and there was a pause in the pressure of their attack. Already many gray infantrymen of the trailing brigades had stopped behind the main line of breastworks. Although Opdycke realized from his earlier occupation duty in Franklin that the Carter House Hill was the key to holding back the enemy attack, he failed to understand that his men had not reoccupied Cox's original line of entrenchments. So much smoke and haze hung above the breastworks that it was difficult to see more than a few yards. Indeed, the men were so mixed, and so much confusion reigned, that about all many of the officers could do was help load the men's guns. Thus far, Opdycke's men had been fighting only about twenty minutes.[31]

Despite the confused nature of the combat, during the countercharge and retaking of the retrenched line by Opdycke's brigade scores of Confederates had been overwhelmed and forced to surrender. A tally of Opdycke's captives at the end of the fighting numbered 394 prisoners, 19 of whom were officers. Among the trophies captured were nine Confederate battle flags and a single Federal flag retaken from its captors. David S. Stanley, who arrived on the scene just as the 44th Illinois began their charge on the left of the pike, saw so many gray uniforms pouring to the rear (as prisoners) that he thought for an instant the enemy had broken through and routed Opdycke's brigade.[32]

Already so much smoke hung in great, rising clouds that Stanley said he could see only about fifty yards. A lone officer on horseback, Stanley was a conspicuous target as he rode forward waving his hat and urging Opdycke's and Wagner's men to charge. He heard someone say, "Come on men, we can go wherever the general can," then his horse was hit and went down. Stanley jumped to his feet, but was immediately struck in the neck. The bullet sliced diagonally through the collar of his uniform coat, inflicting a shallow wound as it ranged across the base of his neck and exited near the spine. Stanley kept going. He met Colonel Joseph Conrad and told him to get every man he could and take them forward toward the cotton gin. Then Stanley was off, hastening behind the front line toward the eastern perimeter, where he soon met Jacob Cox. Cox had one of his aides dismount and give Stanley his horse. After taking a quick look at Stanley's wound, Cox told him he should seek medical attention. Stanley soon trotted away toward Franklin to have the injury treated, while Cox continued toward the critical fire zone at the Carter house.[33]

Jacob Cox already had suffered an extraordinary experience. Following his abrupt realization that the enemy was, in fact, preparing to launch a frontal assault, Cox had watched anxiously from a knoll along the extreme eastern flank of his line. When Wagner's two brigades had been overwhelmed, Cox attempted to gallop back to the Carter house.[34]

Yet, due to the incessant roar of cannon fire from Fort Granger and the bellowing artillery along the Federal works, Cox's horse became terrified. When an enemy shell exploded nearby, stampeding the team of a gun limber, Cox's mount began plunging and rearing. Cox had to dismount and, standing amid the shrieking shells and wild commotion, he calmed the animal by rubbing its nose and ears. By the time Cox approached the vicinity of the Carter house after seeing Stanley, Opdycke's men had pushed the Rebels back across the retrenched line. At one point there had been a shout and cheering when the color bearers rushed to the barricade with the Stars and Stripes, this being evidence to many that the Union lines had been restored.[35]

They were wrong. Repeated assaults from the trailing brigades and regiments of Cheatham's Corps kept the Carter House Hill in the vortex of a firestorm. The converging lines of attack had piled brigades one on top of another along the Columbia pike. Here the Confederates continued to strongly hold the line of main entrenchments on both sides of the pike for a combined distance of about two hundred yards. Advancing gray regiments in the rear echelon, being unimpeded by obstructions or abatis, flowed naturally toward this point in the center, where it was evident from the diminished incoming fire that the attacking columns had met with some success.[36]

Brown's, Cleburne's, and some of A. P. Stewart's troops now held the outside perimeter of the earthworks, firing over and under the head logs at the Federal-held retrenched line. As each new wave of Confederates crowded in from the rear, there would be an attempt to rush the Federal line only yards away. Heavily fought over was the Carter garden, an irregular plot about 65 yards in depth at its widest point and nearly 125 yards long. On the north side at the retrenched line where the Carter smokehouse and farm office building stood, the men of Opdycke's, Conrad's, Lane's, and Strickland's brigades fought from behind the low rail barricade and garden fence. Across the bare garden ground to the south the Confederates returned the fire from the the main earthworks. Where turnips, tomatoes, onions, and watermelons were grown and a pear tree stood occurred some of the most vicious fighting of the entire war.[37]

At least seven of the eighteen Confederate brigades participating in the initial assault fought in this sector. John C. Brown's Division of four brigades was the first present, although staggered in alignment and consequently varied in their time of arrival during the initial surge which overwhelmed Strickland's line. Behind Brown, part of Cockrell's Brigade of French's Division crowded into the same zone. Later, two brigades of Bate's Division came forward here. So many attempts were made to get across the Carter garden that one of Strickland's lieutenant colonels counted thirteen separate, repulsed charges. Due to the converging lines, most Confederate regiments and brigades were randomly mixed together, and no one seemed to be in control. In the blinding smoke, and with the sun setting, few could see what others were doing only yards away. Thus, the many attempts to assault the Federal-held retrenched line, in some places only twenty-five yards distant, became impulsive, uncoordinated, and sporadic.[38]

Each time a portion of the Confederate line leapt over the breastworks and dashed forward, they were met with a hail of fire. "The air was loaded with death-dealing missiles," wrote one of John C. Brown's soldiers. "Never on this earth did men fight against such terrible odds. It seemed that the very elements of heaven and earth were in one mighty uproar." The unbroken blaze of fire from the line in front made it seem like hell itself. "I had made up my mind to die—[but] felt glorious."[39]

Adding immensely to the death and destruction in the Carter garden were six twelve-pounder Napoleon guns being worked mostly by Opdycke's men at the angle in the retrenched line west of the Carter smokehouse. Charles W. Scovill's section of Battery A, 1st Ohio Light Artillery, had been abandoned by all but a single corporal when the men of the 125th Ohio first ran among the guns. Now served by sweating officers and infantrymen, who carried ammunition and loaded the cannon, the section's blasts of canister so cleared the ground between the two entrenchments that it seemed as if an invisible scythe had cut down every visible thing. Also, firing from the left of Scovill's guns were four Napoleons of the 20th Ohio Battery, personally commanded by Lieutenant Scovill, who had hastened to this point due to the battery's lack of experienced officers. These guns soon became one of the focal points of the Confederate fire. The adjutant of the 73d Illinois was shot in the neck and instantly killed while attempting to aim one of the cannon through a log embrasure. At an adjacent piece, one of Opdycke's lieutenants saw every man struck down within minutes. From these guns alone, 169 blasts of canister and shell were fired into the enemy-held parapets at only a few yards distance, sending rails and chunks of earth flying. Some men behind the barricades were decapitated, and others were flung writhing to the ground.[40]

Still, the Confederates attempted to advance. "They charged and fought like perfect fiends," wrote one of Cox's amazed staff officers. Jacob Cox later learned from prisoners that the basis for these repeated attacks was rooted in their commanders' belief that possession of the advanced lines had been at least partially gained. This impression was furthered by men who had earlier gone forward and from whom nothing had been seen of since.[41]

The colors of the 41st Tennessee, one of Brown's regiments, were carried across the main parapet, only to have the arm of the color bearer shot off. The flag remained crumpled on the garden soil until the battle ended. "Why half of us were not killed, yet remains a mystery," wrote a survivor.[42]

The firestorm of leaden missiles caused a Mississippi private to write that as his company dashed forward, "we instinctively pulled our hat brims down as though to protect our faces." The incoming minie balls and canister tossed men about as if they were rag dolls. Groaning men tumbled into the Mississippian as they fell to the ground. Their line wavered badly. The flash of Federal artillery at almost point-blank range was followed by a blast wave and the "rip of canister as it flew past and through us, tearing great gaps in our ranks." Audible was the sound of men's bones cracking like pipe stems, and the "zip, zip, zip" of rifle bullets. It seemed as though a gigantic threshing machine was whirring and clanking in their ears. Ahead, the Federal parapet seemed to be "the fury of hell in [all] its intensity." Glancing backward, the Mississippi rifleman saw that the dead and wounded lay in windrows. Wounded men were staggering to the rear, but fell faster under the hail of bullets than they could move away. On plunged their company line, firing wildly at what were fleeting images in the turgid smoke. A sulfurous odor burned their nostrils. Suddenly the men seemed to hesitate. Instinctively they realized they couldn't carry the Yankee works. As if by silent command, the entire line broke and ran. Stunned and bewildered, the survivors flung themselves over the Yankee's front parapet and lay gasping for breath. The company had been under fire only about ten minutes. One-third of their ranks were missing.[43]

Following the first half hour of fighting, a noticeable decline in the volume of rifle fire seemed to suggest the stabilizing of each side's respective positions. A Federal field officer, believed to be from the 44th Missouri, suddenly jumped on top of the retrenched barricade and shouted for the men to follow him in a charge. An appalled soldier noted the foolishness of such an attempt—to attack with a small segment of the line would be sheer madness—thus the men stayed put. In an instant the officer was shot and fell at the feet of the soldier.[44]

The lull was soon over, and the Carter garden once more became a whirlwind of fire. Again there were no intervals between volleys, said a participant; they sounded as one. So heavy was the incoming fire that men on both sides began holding their rifles up over the parapets and firing blindly with only their arms momentarily exposed.[45]

Amazingly, some of Strickland's men, positioned at the west end of the garden where the extension of the retrenched line joined the main earthworks, still clung to the original breastworks. Their left flank companies had been overrun and largely scattered in the initial Confederate assault through the garden. A captain of the 72d Illinois later told how they had fought while almost surrounded. Rebels seemed to be firing all about them; indeed, some were shooting from behind the Carter outbuildings. Yet Opdycke's charge had driven them back. At this point, the retreating Confederates once more had surged past on their way back to the main earthworks. Again there had been hand-to-hand fighting with bayonets and clubbed muskets. "Every officer was busy with his revolver," said the Illinois captain. "I discharged my own nine times and the most distant man I shot at was not more than twenty feet away." Here he saw a dazed infantryman, bleeding from a severe head wound, rush amid a cluster of gray soldiers and furiously swing with a pickaxe.[46]

Another captain of the 72d ran up to Lieutenant Colonel Joseph Stockton, who due to the obscuring smoke was unaware of the crisis on his left flank. Desperately the captain tried to warn him that the enemy was again ravaging the flank companies. Stockton kept waving his sword, trying to yell something to his men, but was too excited to be understood. Stockton whirled around, bewildered. Again the captain tried to talk to him. "[I] could make no impression on him, so I went among the men . . . and in a few minutes saw him led away wounded in the neck."[47]

Although most of the regiment remained in position, a new danger threatened from the rear. Many of the 183d Ohio's green recruits began firing into the 72d Illinois from the retrenched line, mistaking them for the enemy in the smoke and confusion. Scores of our men were killed or wounded, complained an Illinois officer. "We sent word to them time and time again to cease firing, but without avail." Finally the 72d Illinois, in an untenable position between the two opposing lines, scrambled to safety beyond the west end of the retrenched barricade.[48]

By about 5:00 P.M. the Federal lines had been solidly reestablished across the nineteen-acre Carter house plot of ground, resulting in much optimism within the Federal ranks. Jacob Cox rode up to Emerson Opdycke and told him, "Opdycke, that charge saved the day." Even the abrasive Opdycke displayed rising spirits, reassuring a wounded lieutenant of the 97th Ohio Infantry, and telling him to make his way to Nashville, as "we'll all go there [later] tonight."[49]

As de facto commander of the entire battle line, Cox's main concern was that the Rebels continued to occupy the outside ditch of the main earthworks on both sides of the Columbia pike. Nonetheless, he had noted the diminishing ferocity of their attacks. A new and highly critical factor seemed to be taking its toll among the gray ranks. Because of the southern location of the Carter cotton gin, a salient existed in the main line of earthworks. In order to conform with the natural slope of the Carter House Hill, the main works had been erected on a diagonal line, running away from the apex at the cotton gin. As a result, the Confederates occupying the breastworks in Strickland's front were advanced beyond the cotton gin line—which Cox's men continued to hold. Accordingly, Cheatham's and Brown's troops were exposed to a severe enfilading fire from the east.[50]

At first, in the smoke and turmoil following the initial Confederate success, there had been little warning of this deadly circumstance. Yet, as the fighting continued and the lines were consolidated, the incoming oblique fire became as hell itself.[51]

The right guide of the 41st Tennessee Infantry, S. A. Cunningham, was crouched behind the ditch fifty yards west of the Columbia pike, loading guns for those standing on the parapet. Nearby, Brigadier General Otho F. Strahl was busily handing rifle muskets to those posted on the firing line. Cunningham had passed forward his short Enfield rifle for about the sixth time when the man standing in front of him at the parapet fell dead at Strahl's feet. Strahl summoned Cunningham to take his place.[52]

Because of his short stature, Cunningham had to stand with one foot on the pile of dead bodies in the ditch, and the other on the embankment. With Strahl handing him the guns, Cunningham fired repeatedly, despite the enfilading fire which ravaged their lines from the east. When he next looked around, Cunningham saw only one other nearby man still firing over the works. Behind him there seemed to be hardly enough men to load the guns. So few of them were still alive, said Cunningham, that he asked Strahl what they should do. "Keep firing," came Strahl's reply.[53]

Just then a volley ripped through their position. The man who had been firing next to him fell onto Cunningham with a groan. Also, Strahl had been shot. The general threw up his hands and fell on his face, causing Cunningham to think he was dead. Anxiously asking the wounded rifleman where he had been shot, Cunningham was astounded when Strahl, thinking the question was directed to him, raised his head and answered that he had been struck in the neck. Saying that he must turn over his brigade to the next in command, Lieutenant Colonel Fountain Stafford, Strahl then crawled for about twenty feet over the dead bodies filling the trench to Stafford's position. Stafford was found dead, horribly propped in a semi-standing position by the wedged bodies under and across him. Several nearby staff officers tried to carry Strahl to the rear. Before they had gone fifty feet Strahl was struck twice, the second bullet instantly killing him.[54]

Nearby, a captive Federal officer, held in the outer ditch among the rapidly thinning Confederate ranks, glanced in amazement at the carnage about him. The ditch was filled with dead and wounded. He could hear bullets striking the bodies on both sides of him. Shouts passed up and down the line for a certain ranking officer, but it was reported that officer was dead or wounded. The next in command was sought, but he too was missing. Finally the senior officer present was determined to be a wounded captain, lying by the Federal captive's side. The captain gasped: "Men, this won't do, we must either surrender or run. . . . We are getting all cut to pieces by this terrible cross fire." There was no response—only loud explosions of gunfire and the zip of incoming rifle bullets. Desperately the Confederate captain shouted at the top of his lungs, "We surrender, we surrender, we surrender." No one other than the lone Federal officer heard him. The fighting continued unabated, causing the captive Federal officer to crawl "up against the earthworks as close as possible." Here he wrapped an abandoned blanket about him, as if to hide his exposed body, and cringed despairingly. If only he could pass on this information to Cox's men—that the Confederate ranks were in desperate turmoil—he thought the Federal army might capture the entire assaulting column.[55]

*   *   *

Jacob Cox was uncertain of what to do in the gathering darkness. There had been a lull, then renewed fighting in the vicinity of the Carter house. Smoke hung in a dark covering about the buildings. Cox had heard reports of scattered regiments and fleeing recruits on Strickland's front. He sent to the far left, seeking a reserve regiment, the 112th Illinois of Stiles's brigade. The 112th Illinois, he ordered, should immediately go to Strickland's front and reestablish the forward line. Yet this regiment had about a half mile to cover in reaching unfamiliar and heavily contested ground. Moreover, it was evident that darkness would fall before they could march by the rear to reach Strickland and join in the critical contest for the center.[56]

Captain James A. Sexton unexpectedly found himself in a most extraordinary position. All of the field officers of his regiment had been killed or wounded and he now commanded the remnant of the 72d Illinois. Yet along his sector of the retrenched line, just west of the 20th Ohio Battery's Napoleon guns, there seemed to be between 2,000 and 3,000 disorganized men of mixed commands present. Amazingly, Sexton found himself to be the senior officer there. About 500 of Lane's and Conrad's troops were still present, fighting alongside the remnants of Strickland's brigade. The men in Sexton's line had randomly formed into six to eight ranks, each file rising and firing in separate sequence. Now they began clamoring to charge and retake the front line of earthworks, from which the enemy's fire was noticeably dwindling. Nervously, Sexton agreed to the attempt. Word was swiftly passed along the line to prepare to charge. When Sexton gave the order, the ragged blue line quickly ran forward to the parapet along the western edge of the Carter garden.[57]

Here the sortie abruptly ended. Resistance from the Confederates was light, but from the rear and to the east came a devastating fire that felled many of Sexton's men. In the darkness and smoke Sexton's command had been mistaken for the enemy, and a continuing heavy fire compelled Sexton and his men to crawl back to their former lines.[58]

Once back at their retrenchment barricade, the exasperated Sexton was summoned by an aide to one of the Carter outbuildings. Here he learned that the 112th Illinois was at hand and Jacob Cox wanted the front line reoccupied. Sexton protested. Any storming column would likely be butchered by their own men, as before, he heatedly argued. The aide insisted—saying that the troops along the line would be notified and would not fire upon them. Sexton knew better, but acted to carry out his orders.[59]

The 112th Illinois was brought forward, and the entire line was told to charge. This time only a few men from his mixed command went along, most anticipating what was in store. As expected, once the Illinois regiment had easily sprinted to the forward earthwork, the lines in their rear began firing repeatedly into them. This precipitated a "murderous fire" from everywhere along the earthworks. The lieutenant colonel commanding the 112th Illinois was hit, the men dropped flat, and they soon began backing out of the open garden to the retrenched line.[60]

The profuse swearing and recriminations over the twice-repeated blunder did not atone for the needless loss of life and limb, later judged the historian of the 112th Illinois. Now the men lay gasping behind the safety of the parapet, convinced that all hell couldn't make them go back there again.[61]

Both sides had tried and failed to control the few acres of open ground that had been Fountain B. Carter's private garden. Darkness had fallen over the hideously littered terrain, yet the anguish of this simple plot continued.

Pathetically caught beneath the continuing fire were the wounded of both armies. A Federal officer later told of how bodies were found with thumbs stuck in their mouths, the men having chewed them to shreds "to keep from bleating like calves" under the sustained fire. Many of the bodies lying exposed in the Carter garden were hit so frequently that they were riddled with bullets and nearly ripped to pieces.[62]

The earth was red with blood, wrote a sickened Confederate private. Blood ebbed in pools from the dead and wounded, then ran in little rivulets as it carved its way through the dark garden soil. It was the "hardest, bloodiest, and most wicked fight I was ever in," commented a veteran Illinois soldier. "I never saw the dead lay near[ly] so thick," reflected Emerson Opdycke less than a week later.[63]

It all had been for naught. Stalemate had been reached at the crucial Carter House Hill. The Confederates continued to hold the center segment of the main earthworks, adjacent to the Columbia pike. The Federals occupied in heavy strength the retrenched line west of the pike. It was evident that the impetus for the final result would occur at some other point.[64]

One of the bitter Confederate survivors, reflecting on the tragic carnage and lack of results along the Columbia pike, searched for the proper words to record his frustration. Finally he wrote of the attack simply what he knew in his heart: "Oh, what inconceivable folly! How exasperating! How irretrievable!"[65]

CHAPTER XX

Glorified Suicide at
the Cotton Gin

"**D**OWN IN FRONT," came the cry from the ranks. Some of the men of James W. Reilly's division in Cox's line had been standing on the earthworks near the Carter cotton gin, looking at the vast, unprecedented pageantry of Hood's sweeping advance. Then the dazzling spectacle had been obliterated in a sudden blaze of cannon fire and bursting shells. Hood's men had rolled on, surging like an uneven gray wave over the shallow reef of Wagner's line. When the massed ranks of A. P. Stewart, on the east, and Cheatham, near the Columbia pike, emerged in front, Reilly's men quickly ducked down behind the parapet.[1]

In A. P. Stewart's front there were three Federal brigades defending the earthworks: Thomas J. Henderson's (under Israel Stiles), on the extreme eastern flank near the river and railroad cut; Jack Casement's, in the middle, east of the cotton gin; and Jim Reilly's, between the cotton gin and the Columbia pike.* In total, Reilly's three brigades numbered about 5,000 effectives, arrayed to confront perhaps 10,000 of Stewart's men, 1,300 dismounted cavalry under Abraham Buford, and probably 4,000 of Cheatham's men led by the dashing Pat Cleburne.[2]

Since the attacking Confederates had a more than three-to-one numerical advantage, there was a heavy burden on Reilly's division. The crucial question was thus obvious: Could Hood's frontal assault overwhelm their well-entrenched foe before the punishment became too severe?

The Federal call to arms was sounded by the fiery Colonel Jack Casement of Reilly's line. Jumping on top of the breastworks near the cotton gin,

---

*Reilly retained command of his brigade, as well as assuming temporary control of the division due to Cox's absence as "corps commander."

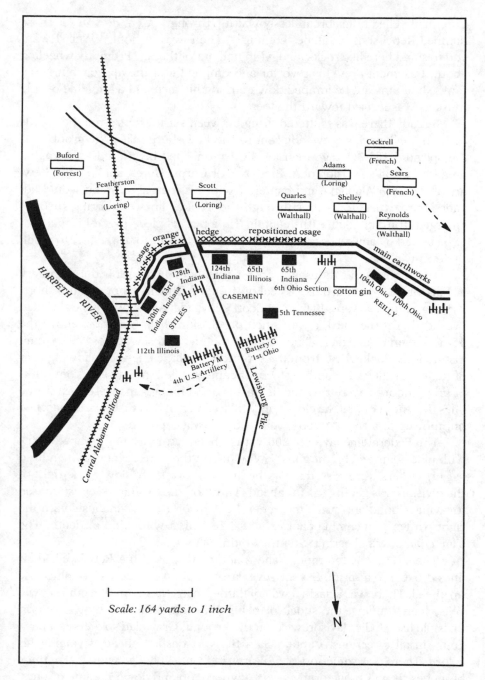

MAP 8   Attack on the Federal Left
November 30—Franklin

Casement yelled to his breathlessly waiting throng, "Men, do you see those damned Rebel sons of bitches coming?" There was a shout. "Well, I want you to stand here like rocks, and whip hell out of them." Promptly wheeling about, Casement drew his revolver and emptied it at the approaching gray ranks. In an instant he jumped down among his men and a long line of rifle muskets was leveled toward the foe.[3]

Already there was scattered firing between skirmishers amid the woods of John McGavock's grove adjacent to the Lewisburg pike. The grounds of the splendid 1825-vintage mansion "Carnton" had been used as a staging area for Loring's Division of A. P. Stewart's Corps. Here Captain Sam Stewart of the 35th Alabama had bantered with his men about who would advance the farthest toward or through the Yankee lines. As Loring's troops emerged from the timber, the captain "in a perfect glee" urged his men not to be bested by any other company in the all-out effort to be the first to reach the enemy's line.[4]

They had about a thousand yards to go when the roar of Federal artillery at Fort Granger sounded like a peal of thunder. The first shot was too short, striking a hundred yards in front of Scott's Brigade. A second missile shrieked overhead. Yet the third, a three-inch percussion shell, burst just above the 35th Alabama. A soldier glanced down the line and saw almost every man instinctively duck. Next, from the ground in front, came the bellowing roar of Reilly's artillery. Instantly a storm of canister filled the air. The front ranks of gray uniforms were ravaged like a sieve. So many gaps were torn in the lines that they couldn't be closed up. Still the men of Scott's Brigade marched on, moving at a rapid, steady walk with bayonets poised.[5]

The Federal line lay only 200 yards ahead, an indistinct parapet "dark with blue coats and bright guns." Why hadn't the Yankee infantrymen fired as yet? Orders were passed along the line to move more slowly, the right of the division was getting too far ahead. Those on the left flank were supposed to swing around and strike the Federal earthworks simultaneously with the right. Now the incoming canister was like hail, a whirlwind of death. The Yankee line was cheering. Still they didn't shoot.[6]

The stress was too much. The Alabamians raised the Rebel yell; their lines broke into a sprint. Seventy-five yards to go. A ragged wall of blue rose up ahead. There was a flash, a wall of flame, then chaos. Smoke, curses, wild yells, men running, the shock of being hit—like a sudden blow from an invisible fist. Bodies lay sprawled on the ground. Gray-clad soldiers ran past, going in all directions. Captain Sam Stewart dashed ahead, swinging his sword. There was some sort of a barrier in front—a hedge with sharp, thick branches. It was osage orange—everywhere, up and down the line of parapets. There was noplace to go. No way to get through.[7]

Captain Stewart began furiously chopping at the hedge with his sword, but he went down, shot four times. Only two men remained of his company. They should fall back and re-form, gasped one. They both disappeared into the smoke, running at full speed. Twenty yards, fifty yards—breathlessly they sprinted onward. A cannonball struck one of them in the right foot, ripping it off. From the ground the dazed man looked up. The same ball had rico- cheted and struck two other fleeing soldiers. There were dead and wounded everywhere, and noplace to hide from the whizzing missiles. The race to get the farthest, he realized, was now being run in the opposite direction.[8]

Forming the eastern flank of Loring's line, a veteran brigade of Mississip- pians commanded by Winfield S. Featherston came at a rush toward the waiting ranks of Henderson's brigade. Unexpectedly, they encountered the same natural osage orange hedge fifty feet in front of the Yankee breast- works.[9]

These osage hedges were a crucial obstruction. For years they had been grown by the residents as a boundary fence to confine grazing livestock. Being fully mature, these thickset, shrublike trees had been chopped off about four feet from the ground by Cox's men. This opened a clear field of fire above, yet presented an almost impassable barrier below. Moreover, the surplus hedge tops had been dragged to other portions of the line. Jack Casement's men had made good use of these hedge tops, and from near the railroad tracks almost to the Columbia pike a thick osage orange abatis lay in front of the assaulting columns. Behind these sharp, thorny hedges, the main earthworks rose defiantly about fifty feet away, with Henderson's men and the twelve-pounder guns of Battery M, 4th U.S. Artillery, deployed there.[10]

Featherston's Brigade approached Reilly's division line with the same intention of smashing straight through it, as had Scott's men. Yet his Missis- sippians also became fragmented by the osage hedge between the railroad and the Lewisburg pike. Featherston's men crept slowly onward, groping their way in the smoke and withering fire toward the flanks of Henderson's line. Along the relatively unobstructed Lewisburg pike the flags of the 3d and 22d Mississippi regiments were planted on the enemy's earthworks—but only momentarily. Both color-bearers were shot, and their flags captured. Of the men who clambered over the parapet here, all were quickly felled in hand-to-hand fighting or forced to surrender.[11]

Farther east, toward the deep railroad cut, the 120th Indiana Infantry stood plugging the narrow gap between the osage hedge and the railroad. Here the Union officers could hear their gray counterparts urging their men to "press to the right" so as to get around the hedge. The 120th Indiana stopped this attempt with repeated volleys of musketry. When the Confeder- ates attempted to use the railroad cut, a section of Battery M, 4th U.S. Artillery, came galloping forward to enfilade the defile. Their blasts of canis- ter soon halted the enemy, now found crawling "on their hands and knees." Added to the storm of projectiles sweeping through the cut was the plunging shell fire from Fort Granger. Within minutes the ground on the eastern portion of the battlefield had became a virtual death zone where not even a rabbit could safely pass, wrote a soldier.[12]

Nearby, Buford's dismounted cavalrymen, working their way forward along the riverbank, met such a devastating blast of artillery fire that they were virtually pinned down. "Our whole line would have been swept away had we not been ordered to throw ourselves on the ground," said one of Buford's men. The entire command lay there, "not daring to raise our heads, nor to crawl forward even a few rods to give succor to the wounded and dying." To another participant, the prospect of charging that osage-fringed Yankee line was little better than "glorified suicide."[13]

Loring's main thrust had been blunted in less than an hour. Featherston's and Scott's brigades were in a shambles. John Adams's Brigade, marching in reserve, had been compelled to detour farther toward the center of the field, away from the snarled congestion in front of the osage hedges. Among the litter bearers in the rear echelon was a chaplain who saw William Loring riding among the retreating ranks of his division. He was commanding, exhorting, entreating, and denouncing, wrote the chaplain, but it was all in vain; his men continued to run. Loring turned his horse to face the enemy's works, raised his glittering sword, and sat perfectly motionless. Suddenly he cried, "Great God! Do I command cowards?" A moment later he was gone, trotting after his departing men, and slowly disappeared into the smoke.[14]

On Loring's west flank marched the well-traveled crack division under Edward Walthall. Walthall had inspired his men with an attitude of beating the enemy at any cost. His Tennessee brigade was led by the veteran Brigadier General William A. Quarles, whose brigade advanced at a full run in Jack Casement's front—right up to the repositioned osage orange hedge tops. Abruptly their ranks came to a halt. Unable to get through the thorny hedge, they desperately tried to pull it away. It was a painful, futile effort; their hands were soon lacerated and torn, and the milling, bewildered men became an easy target for Casement's men. Company A of the 65th Indiana had sixteen-shot Henry repeating rifles, the forerunner of the famous Winchester lever-action firearms. The firestorm that leapt from Casement's earthworks was described by an eyewitness as an incessant, solid plane upon which a man might seemingly walk—"a continuous living fringe of flame." It was "[by] far the most deadly fire of both small arms and artillery that I have ever seen troops subjected to," wrote the astounded Walthall.[15]

"Oh, what a comfort to know that we, who in the [Atlanta] Georgia campaign had to do most of the bucking against fortifications, were on the right side of the works," wrote a veteran Union officer. He noted there was not even a cornstalk to obstruct their fire for a third of a mile. "Our men felt that now was the time for wiping out many an old score." The ghastly heap of dead and wounded that fell in front of Jack Casement's position looked like a rail fence that had been toppled over, the bodies lay so straight in a row. "Never before in the history of war did a command of the [small] approximate strength of Casement's in so short a . . . time kill and wound as many men," wrote a distraught Southern officer. The carnage was appalling, and even to Casement's troops the scene was almost pathetic in its futility. A horse, plunging in terror because of a wound, had run headlong into the staked osage tops, displacing a small segment. Quarles's men attempted to squirm through, but were so riddled in the attempt that piles of dead and wounded soon blocked the gap.[16]

Quarles, a profane man, was swearing mightily when he took a severe wound in the left arm, the muscle of his upper arm being torn away. Again he was struck by a grazing projectile that broke a rib and left a two-inch gash in his side. Most of his men fared little better. Every staff officer with Quarles was shot, and before the fighting ended a captain was the highest-ranking officer in his brigade.[17]

Walthall's Division was being slaughtered before his very eyes. Already he had lost two horses, shot from under him. Walthall asked for another mount from a staff officer. The lieutenant jumped down and gave his steed to the general, who, when about to mount, remembered the army rule of appraising appropriated property. "Has this horse been appraised?" he asked. When the lieutenant answered no, Walthall scrawled out a value on a piece of paper, even as bullets zipped close about him. Then he leapt into the saddle and again galloped into the fight.[18]

After a few minutes the heavy fighting in Casement's front abruptly ended. Terribly torn at every step, Walthall's Division staggered toward the west, away from the osage hedge and in the direction of the Federal salient at the cotton gin. Here Charles M. Shelley's Brigade was struggling to wrest control of this critical sector from Reilly's all but overwhelmed brigade.[19]

The advance of Shelley's Brigade, wrote an Alabama regimental commander, was through a tempest of shot and shell. Not even the grand martial scene of closely marching ranks, great wreaths of smoke, and the thunder of the guns masked the terror of the moment. Shelley's Brigade had been sent from its position as Walthall's reserve forward into the first line after Daniel H. Reynolds's Brigade had swung westward to avoid an interposing thicket. Shelley headed directly for the salient angle in the Federal line, where the top structure of Fountain B. Carter's cotton gin poked above the earthworks.[20]

The Federal position at this point was strong; embrasures for two guns had been cut in the earthworks just at the east corner of the gin, and two twelve-pounder Napoleon guns of the 6th Ohio Light Battery were positioned there under Lieutenant A. P. Baldwin. Baldwin's guns had strong supports: the 65th Indiana in Casement's line, and on the opposite (west) side, the 104th Ohio of Reilly's line. The cotton gin, which had necessitated the placement of a salient angle in the earthworks, was of typical rustic construction, being about thirty-six feet square, with a strong frame built of poplar beams set on stone pillars. Measuring about eight feet from ground level to the sills, the gin house stood two stories high, while a separate cotton press, with its machinery exposed, stood nearby. Run by mules or horses tethered to a yoke, the gin press had a pronounced circular treadway which had been worn into the tightly packed earth. Although originally weatherboarded, this planking had been removed by Cox's soldiers to frame their earthworks, and the gin was now open-sided. Only a few feet remained between the end of the cotton gin and the trench at Reilly's breastworks.[21]

The 104th Ohio of Reilly's line, known as the "Barking Dog Regiment" from their pet bulldog "Old Harvey," had watched almost stupefied as Wagner's two brigades were overwhelmed in front and came streaming back toward their position. A crucial problem involving the 104th Ohio was immediately apparent. Along the right front of the regiment, Wagner's men, mixed with pursuing Rebels, were running at full speed toward the breastworks. From the east, Shelley's Brigade of Walthall's Division was sweeping forward to cut off their retreat. While Baldwin's twelve-pounder guns and the left companies of the 104th Ohio jarred the ground with their thundering fire, the right portion of the line stood with loaded guns, waiting for Wagner's men to get in. It was a desperate moment, realized an Ohio officer. So many of Wagner's men were clambering over the works that the 104th's ranks, and those of the 100th Ohio on their right, became confused and almost panicky in their inability to shoot. Finally, with a few Confederates mixed among the trailing ranks of Wagner's men, firing began all along the line. One of the last to attempt to get in ahead of the onrushing enemy, Captain E. Moons of the 65th Ohio Infantry, was struggling to crawl through the right embrasure at the 6th Ohio Battery. Captain Baldwin saw his plight and, swinging the flat of his sword, whapped him sharply in the buttocks, sending the captain sprawling past the opening.[22]

All the while, Shelley's men surged toward the embrasures at the cotton gin. When only a few paces away, Baldwin's twelve-pounder Napoleons fired with double charges of canister into their massed ranks. Baldwin said he could hear two sounds: the detonation of the charges and the crunching of bones in front of the muzzles. Added to the fire of the riflemen along the parapet, the storm of missiles was so intense that Shelley's men seemed literally blown away as if they were so many leaves in an autumn gust. Yet Shelley's Alabamians would not give up. While some of his men sought shelter in the outside parapet ditch, Shelley and others worked their way west along the line. Here, where Wagner's scattering masses had flung themselves over the works among Reilly's men, there was great confusion and disorder. Shelley and his yelling troops jumped over the parapet. Added to other Confederates already there, they began fighting with a reckless fury.[23]

The four right flank companies of the 104th Ohio were quickly in trouble. Wagner's men, hopelessly mixed with the vanguard of Pat Cleburne's troops, were still struggling among the defenders inside the parapet, all seemingly yelling, fighting, and dodging about in utter chaos. The gunners of the 1st Kentucky Battery at the gap along the pike were gone, having abandoned their unfired guns and sped away when Wagner's men poured through. Also, the 100th Ohio, next in line, was seen streaming to the rear. Their commander—having shouted for Wagner's men to retire and reform—had only helped confuse his own men into doing the same.[24]

Now the right flank companies of the 104th Ohio, including the yelping Old Harvey, joined in the hasty flight to the rear. Into the vacuum created by the milling, bewildered throng at the parapet, more Confederate regiments came pouring over the works. They were the main segments of Pat Cleburne's two frontline brigades, Granbury's and Govan's—part of the hardest-hitting division in the Confederate army. Their unique blue flags with the white center fluttered above the parapets, grim and imposing in the swirling battle smoke. It seemed to a participant that all of Reilly's soldiers, from beyond the angle at the cotton gin across to the Carter grounds west of the Columbia pike, were engulfed in a sea of butternut. The only thing that seemed to keep the men at the cotton gin salient from running was that they were too busy fighting Shelley's men across the parapet to notice the panic on their right.[25]

To add to the desperate plight, the Rebels engulfed the captured Kentucky battery's three-inch Ordnance rifles, and began swinging the deadly cannon about to fire point-blank at the inside of the cotton gin salient.[26]

Lieutenant Colonel John S. White's regiment, the 16th Kentucky Infantry, had been posted as a reserve between the Kentucky battery and the retrenched line following their arrival at Franklin about midday. White's men were overly fatigued and had been the last troops to reach Spring Hill early that morning following their rear-guard action with S. D. Lee's Corps. Instead of rest, White and his men suddenly found themselves amid the vortex of a horrendous battle. White had just moved his regiment to cover behind the retrenched line when he saw a staff officer running toward him. Thinking he had orders, White ran to meet the man. "What is it?" asked White. The wide-eyed staff officer gasped that the Rebels had carried the first line of works. White immediately ordered his Kentuckians forward to the parapet. With a shout heard above the din of battle, the 16th Kentucky sprang over the retrenched line and ran at the enemy.[27]

On their left, the 12th Kentucky, Lawrence Rousseau's men, saw Jacob Cox galloping forward, excitedly waving his sword. Upon his own responsibility, Rousseau ordered his regiment to join with the 16th Kentucky in the charge. By contagious example, the men of the 8th Tennessee Infantry, also in reserve, ran forward. Even a new regiment, the 175th Ohio, unassigned to a brigade but posted with Reilly's reserves, came up on the run.[28]

It became a great, swelling mob of men, engulfing everything in front of it along the nearly sixty-five yards between the retrenched line and main earthworks east of the Columbia pike. Many of the Confederates saw them coming and seemed to hesitate. Two companies of the 12th Kentucky had

Colt revolving rifle muskets, five-shooters, and they began firing repeatedly at Cleburne's winded infantrymen.[29]

Desperately, Cleburne's men at the captured Kentucky battery attempted to fire these guns into the oncoming Federal ranks. It was the focal point of the crisis, a crucial point where momentum tottered precariously and the battle might be won or lost. Yet the captured cannon couldn't be fired without friction primers. The Kentucky gunners, before they had run away, had removed the primers and their lanyards. In the confusion of the moment, none could be found amid the debris. Some of Cleburne's men broke open musket cartridges and poured powder into the vent tubes. By lighting the powder they might fire the cannon by hand. They were moments too late. A surging wall of blue smacked into Cleburne's disordered ranks. It was a collision never to be forgotten.[30]

For five minutes it was a hand-to-hand melee. Bayonets, clubbed muskets, revolvers, broken gunstocks, even bare hands became the weapons of that furious moment. An eyewitness saw a Rebel strike a soldier of the 16th Kentucky, knocking him to the ground with the butt of his rifle. Another Kentuckian clubbed the Confederate, felling him beside his original victim. Before the downed Rebel could recover, the first soldier jumped to his feet and lunged with his bayonet, pinioning him to the ground. A soldier of the 100th Ohio saw three Confederates standing amid the awful din as if dazed. "I raised my gun," he wrote, "but instinctively I felt as if about to commit murder—they were helpless." Turning away for a moment, he glanced back and discovered all three had been shot and lay in a heap. An Ohio officer who had broken his sword picked up a camp hatchet and swung it wildly. The blood and brains of a Confederate soldier struck by a clubbed musket were soon splattered over him. He began grappling hand to hand with an enemy officer. By grasping the pommel of his opponent's sword with one hand and threatening him with his hatchet, the man was made to surrender. Lieutenant Colonel John S. White was shot in the face, but kept fighting; later he would wrap a rag around his wound, and appeared like some old pirate.[31]

"It seemed to me that hell itself had exploded in our faces," wrote Confederate Brigadier General George W. Gordon, who had veered across the Columbia pike with part of his brigade. The air, he found, "was hideous with the shrieks of the messengers of death." Another nearby Confederate brigadier, Hiram Granbury, was on foot urging on his Texan brigade when shot just under the right eye, the bullet passing entirely through his head. Granbury threw both hands to his face and sank to his knees in death.[32]

When White's and Rousseau's countercharge engulfed the zone between the two barricades with what appeared to be overwhelming numbers, the Rebels began throwing down their guns in surrender. At the Kentucky battery, an eyewitness said the cannon seemed to be cleared of their gray captors in an instant. Instead of firing into the Federal ranks and widening the breach, the primerless cannon stood silent, although still loaded. Now a swarming, yelling throng of Union soldiers surged past the battery and filled the inside ditch at the main parapet. Many of Cleburne's men, coming up in the rear, hesitated to go over the barricade in the face of this furious Yankee countercharge. A Union officer, peering under the smoke into the outside ditch, saw that the Rebels were milling about "as thick as sheep in a pen."[33]

Adding to their reluctance to advance, part of Opdycke's brigade, mainly the 44th Illinois and the 74th and 88th Illinois (consolidated) regiments, had joined in the countercharge by Reilly's reserve units. A swollen mass of blue occupied the inner trench of the main earthworks, firing with massed ranks three and four deep into the bewildered gray regiments across the parapet. As quickly as this wildfire crisis had begun, it seemed to be over. Federal flags were waving once more over the parapet.[34]

But only for a moment.

Pat Cleburne was now on foot. Riding a borrowed brown mare belonging to one of his escort officers, Cleburne had plunged on after Wagner's fleeing troops with the trailing elements of Govan's Brigade. Between Wagner's line and the main earthworks the mare had been killed. Cleburne was unhurt, and he called for another horse. Nineteen-year-old James C. Brandon of his escort detachment quickly dismounted and gave his bay to the general. Cleburne was in the act of mounting when this horse was shot. Cleburne now was only about eighty yards from the enemy works. Waving his embroidered kepi above his head, Cleburne dashed forward on foot. Resistance was heaviest in the direction of the cotton gin, and apparently Cleburne wanted to get Lowrey's Brigade forward here from its reserve position. The plan worked. Lowrey, at the head of his brigade, brought his men forward "under the most destructive fire I ever witnessed," said Lowrey. His Mississippians and Alabamians surged forward to the ditch near the salient, despite losing nearly half of their men in the process.[35]

The smoke was so thick, wrote an Alabama rifleman, that he couldn't see the enemy's works until within a few yards of them. "When I reached the ditch it was filled with dead and wounded Confederates, [and] I walked over [the ditch] on dead men." Lowrey made it on horseback to within thirty feet of the works, where his horse was shot. He advanced only a few yards farther than his division commander.[36]

About forty yards from Reilly's works, and nearly in front of the salient at the cotton gin, an ounce of lead, little more than a half inch in diameter and traveling about 1,000 feet per second, found its mark. It was the work of but an instant; a great chasm in Southern history frozen in microseconds. In one shocking moment Pat Cleburne collapsed to the ground, carrying with him perhaps the best hopes of a dying Confederacy's western army. A lone minie ball had struck just below and to the left of his heart, shredding veins and arteries like tissue paper as it ripped through his body. In a few moments he breathed his last. Pat Cleburne lay dead, his battle saber still grasped firmly in his hand, and his lifeblood soaking the white linen shirt and gray uniform vest with a slowly expanding blotch of crimson. After all the glory and the anguish, it had come to this. Perhaps the South's most brilliant major general, the "Stonewall Jackson of the West," his ideas scorned by his president and his competence punished by his commanding general, had been required to lead a suicidal frontal attack like some captain of infantry. Was it God's decreed fate, or simply man's stupidity?[37]

Lowrey's men, jammed into the outer ditch alongside Govan's, Granbury's, Gordon's, and Shelley's, struggled mightily against Reilly's and Opdycke's men. Only a few feet of earth separated the combatants, and the contest became, said Brigadier General Govan, "the most desperate fight I ever witnessed." Of the five or six men near him, one of Lowrey's riflemen discovered that only he had crossed the outer ditch safely. The flag of the 33d Alabama was already across the parapet, and he struggled to climb over the earthwork at the corner of the cotton gin. Laying his rifle musket on the parapet, he reached across to find a handhold, but was instead grabbed by the arm, jerked over the earthwork, and taken prisoner.[38]

One of Shelley's sergeants, acting as an officer and carrying the flag of the 29th Alabama, saw that "to go over the works was certain death, or wounds, or capture." He realized, "To run to the rear, aside from the shame of it, was almost of equal hazard." Thereafter, he rammed the steel-spiked flagstaff into the earth as high upon the parapet as he could reach. Immediately the flag became a prominent target, and the sergeant hugged the parapet for safety.[39]

"I tried to keep a level head, but scarcely knew what to do," wrote another confused Confederate soldier. Panic seized his mind when he saw the hopeless situation they faced." The thought occurred to me that there was more danger in returning, so I continued [ahead] until I fell into the big ditch outside the breastworks. . . . The ditch was . . . full of men, dead, dying, and wounded. If I ever prayed earnestly in my life it was then."[40]

At the cotton gin, the Federal ranks were found to be five or six men deep, with those in the rear loading and passing their rifle muskets to those at the front, who were the ones firing. Behind these men was another rear rank, kneeling with rifles poised at the ready. If a Rebel raised his head over the parapet, he was immediately shot. So vicious was the fire on both sides that the men along the breastworks began firing blindly. Only momentarily exposing their arms above the works, they would raise their weapons and fire at a plunging angle into the opposite ditch. By this manner of fighting, noted a participant, the Federals had a decided advantage. The earthworks were constructed with a nearly perpendicular face on the inside, and a convex profile on the outside—where the dirt had been thrown and tamped as the ditches were dug. Because of the greater arc, those in the outside ditch could not shoot without exposing more of their bodies, and the slaughter there became a "chamber of horrors," observed a Confederate adjutant.[41]

One of Shelley's soldiers, a newly enlisted, beardless, blue-eyed youth of about seventeen, was shot in the neck while crouching in the outside ditch. With an agonizing cry he fell against the man behind him. So crowded was the ditch that there was no space for him to fall. A heavy, turgid flow of blood gushed from his neck and soaked his uniform. No one had a bandage, or even a rag to stop the bleeding. Gasping with shock, he began to panic and flailed desperately with his arms and legs. There was no room to move, and his struggling limbs were pinioned by the press of bodies. An officer watched helplessly as the boy finally sank to the ground. Nothing could be done for him. Before he had ceased to struggle, noted the officer, other soldiers were sitting or kneeling on his prostrate body.[42]

This grisly "carnival of death" already had affected the minds of many. The ravings of the mangled soldiers on both sides of the parapet were frenzied and heart-rending. "Crazed by pain, many knew not what they did or said," wrote a Mississippi soldier. "Some pleadingly cried out, 'Cease firing! Cease firing!' while others in their agony shouted, 'We surrender! We surrender!' " Still the firing and bloodshed continued unabated.[43]

"Help" was then on the way for the Confederates at the cotton gin salient. Moving forward in staggered sequence, the trailing four brigades of A. P. Stewart's Corps had been delayed by several thickets. Although their ranks were generally intact as they approached the flaming earthworks, they experienced a familiar problem. Their attacks were disrupted in alignment and uncoordinated in time and force of impact. Due to the converging lines, many brigades had been displaced from the front line and were compelled to fall behind other units as they spontaneously crowded toward the center of the battlefield. The appearance of multiple gray battle lines resulted in repeated assaults, causing some Federal commanders to assess that they had endured as many as thirteen separate attacks, seemingly by the same troops.[44]

Among A. P. Stewart's displaced units was Brigadier General Francis M. Cockrell's Missouri brigade. Colonel Elijah Gates of the 1st Missouri Cavalry (dismounted) had fretted during the advance, "Boys, look in your front [at the interposing lines of troops]; we won't get a smell." Unfortunately, noted one of his soldiers, he was wrong. With their brass band tooting "Dixie," Cockrell's Brigade first came under artillery fire. The band abruptly stopped playing. Ahead lay the flaming Yankee earthworks. Already refugees from Quarles's and Shelley's brigades were streaming back through Cockrell's battle line, causing their ranks to begin wavering. Into the smoke ran the Missourians. Bullets seemed everywhere. Gates rode up and down the line, cheering his men on. He was shot in one arm. A few minutes later he was hit in the other arm. Helpless and in great pain, he was led away.[45]

Their battle flag had already fallen three times, but the battle-scarred Missourians, part of Major General Samuel G. French's Division, were under orders not to fire until they had gained the top of the enemy's works. Suddenly looming in their faces were the osage orange hedge tops, staked to the ground in front of Casement's brigade. A major from St. Louis, in a vain attempt to create a gap, dashed his horse into the hedge but escaped unscathed. Cockrell's men surged to the west, away from the obstructions and toward the cotton gin salient.[46]

At the parapet it was hell itself. "The air was all red and blue with flames," wrote a Missouri captain. Reilly's men were firing so rapidly that a Confederate officer mistakenly thought that the enemy was using deadly Spencer seven-shot repeating rifles.* In an instant the Missourians were swept away like a whirlwind. The survivors came running back as fast as they had advanced, leaving behind their brigadier, Cockrell, who had been severely wounded in three places. Cockrell's Brigade of 687 men, unsupported and isolated in its attack, had been virtually wiped out. When the ranks were counted after the battle, only 240 men remained, a casualty loss of 65 percent.[47]

Next to continue the series of isolated and uncoordinated Confederate assaults in the vicinity of the cotton gin salient was Brigadier General John Adams's Brigade. Although earlier delayed by a thicket, Adams's troops now made a spectacular assault that was soon the marvel of both armies. As Adams's men approached to within fifty yards of the earthworks, a deadly storm of bullets and projectiles beat the ground into dust, said an observer.[48]

Adams's men were Mississippians—veterans of some of the campaigns of the past three years—and their commander one of the most respected brigadiers in the army. John Adams was a graduate of West Point, Class of 1841, a thirty-nine-year-old former regular-army officer breveted for gallantry during the Mexican War. He seemed to be at his best this day—both in personal leadership and in bearing a charmed existence. As his brigade surged forward in Casement's front, Adams rode back and forth, urging his men onward. Despite his energetic efforts, Adams's Brigade already was in great difficulty. At the osage orange hedge tops his line came to a staggering halt, and the men began milling about, with the earthworks still fifty feet distant.[49]

In the din, smoke, and confusion, Adams couldn't get his men moving forward again. One of his soldiers, a private of the 15th Mississippi who had just returned from leave and had gone into the fight armed only with an axe, was chopping at the hedge tops with little success. Adams wanted his men to skirt the hedges by passing to the west. Yelling orders for his men to follow him, he galloped down the line toward the cotton gin salient. Behind him, a private, already the 15th Mississippi's fourth color-bearer that day, had pried an opening in the osage hedge. Grabbing the colors, he dashed after Adams, yelling, "Come this way, boys!"[50]

*Ironically, there was only one Union infantry regiment armed with the Spencer rifle at Franklin: the 28th Kentucky Volunteers of Lane's brigade, a new regiment who had about 200 Spencers, but had been routed in the initial attack on Wagner's line.

Adams was well in front of his men, riding straight for the colors of the 65th Illinois in Casement's line. Although a conspicuous target, Adams seemed to be immune to the whizzing storm of projectiles. An amazed Federal soldier wrote, "We looked to see him fall every minute, but luck seemed to be with him." Intent on inspiring his men by personal example, Adams spurred his gray mount, "Old Charley," faster and faster toward the blazing earthworks. The colonel of the 65th Illinois, astounded by the rash bravery of this enemy officer, shouted amid the din for his men not to fire on him. It was too late. Adams approached the parapet and urged his galloping steed to jump the ditch and embankment. The horse leapt—and crashed squarely on top of the parapet, dead. Adams was riddled with bullets, some said seven, others nine, and toppled from the saddle. He fell with a thud into the inner ditch just east of the gin house, right at the feet of Jack Casement.[51]

Adams remained conscious, and asked for a drink of water. A canteen was passed forward, and another soldier made a pillow of cotton from bulk taken from the gin house. Calm, but aware of his imminent fate, he thanked the men and gasped, "It is the fate of a soldier to die for his country." Soon thereafter, Adams sought to be sent within the Confederate lines. Casement was too busy to remain at hand, but assured Adams that he would be placed among friends. A few minutes later the Confederate brigadier breathed his last. Above him the head and forelegs of Old Charley remained grotesquely draped over the parapet.[52]

Few of Adams's men had passed the osage tops before being repulsed, and already the men of Casement's line were scrambling for souvenirs and trophies of this extraordinary incident. Adams's saddle was immediately removed and presented to Jack Casement. Adams's watch, ring, and revolver were divided among several of Casement's officers, although the watch and ring were later sent through the lines by a flag of truce to the widow. Even the colors of the 15th Mississippi, carried to the earthworks by the fifth color-bearer, were captured by a private. They were soon confiscated by the colonel of the 104th Ohio, who "in an ecstasy of delight . . .," said one of his soldiers, "mopped the muddy ground [with it] in his excitement, crying out, 'We've whipped 'em, hurrah, we've whipped 'em.' "[53]

As incredible as it seems, the struggle for the salient was far from over. Two more brigades from A. P. Stewart's Corps, Daniel H. Reynolds's (of Walthall's Division), and Claudius W. Sears's (of French's Division), by now were mixed among the multitude surging back and forth in front of Reilly's earthworks. Portions of at least ten Confederate brigades were groping about amid the drifting smoke near the cotton gin. Some of the bolder Southern officers were heard from across the parapet, shouting encouragement to their men and telling them they had the earthworks, "if they only knew it."[54]

The reply from the Federal ranks was a devastating blast of canister from one of the Kentucky battery's three-inch rifles, fired at almost point-blank range directly into the earthwork. Timbers, earth, all manner of equipment, and even bodies were flung about like so much debris. The gun had been fired by a few infantrymen from the 44th Illinois of Opdycke's brigade, who, finding the cannon loaded, had obtained a primer, or ignited musket powder poured into the vent.[55]

Adding to the swarming ranks of Union soldiers now defending what had earlier been the overrun section of Reilly's line were many of that brigade's returning riflemen. The color-bearer of the 100th Ohio, Sergeant Byron C. Baldwin, ran to the parapet and planted his regimental flag upon the works. Another soldier, from the 104th Ohio, crawled under one of the Kentucky Battery's cannon and fired his rifle point-blank into the faces of the enemy as they appeared at the embrasure. By his side a lieutenant stood flinging picks, shovels, axes—anything that came to hand—through the opening as if to obstruct it. "Our line was becoming stronger and stronger every moment by the return of those who at first had abandoned [it]," exulted Lieutenant Colonel Rousseau of the 12th Kentucky.[56]

Within the Confederate ranks all continued to be chaos. The blasts of canister from the two 12-pounder guns at the cotton gin salient piled dead men in front of the embrasures like some grotesque snowdrift in winter. At one point there were so many bodies heaped around these guns, they had to be dragged aside so that the guns could be served. Federal battery commander Lieutenant Aaron P. Baldwin and his mule-team artillery had already achieved a notoriety of sorts. His guns were hauled by mules who had been trained to lie down while the battery was in action. The lead mule, "May-Me," wore an old felt hat with holes cut in it for her ears, which stuck through. Now the mules were gone, but the sweating gunners were fighting with a stubbornness that seemed to typify all the obstinacy of those animals.[57]

Their tenacity, however, was matched by the desperate valor of the Confederates in attempting to squeeze through the narrow openings in the earthworks. Aaron Baldwin described the fighting at the westernmost embrasure as simply unbelievable. In hand-to-hand combat, Baldwin's gunners used sponge staves, axes, and picks to drive back the lunging enemy. One private killed a Rebel soldier in the embrasure with an axe and disabled another with a pick. Through it all, Baldwin kept his guns firing double and triple charges of canister at point-blank range. At one cannon, a Confederate youth, thought to be a drummer boy from a Missouri regiment, jammed a loose timber from the earthwork into the cannon's muzzle, seeking to prevent its use. Unfortunately for the youth, the gun was loaded, and when fired it simply exploded his body like a ripe tomato, showering body parts and splinters in a ghastly rain.[58]

Among the most valiant efforts made to capture these works were those of Claudius W. Sears's Mississippians. Several hundred officers and men spearheaded by the 4th Mississippi rushed forward to the parapet. "Oh! my God from Heaven, it rained fire and brimstone," wrote one of Sears's riflemen. Among the many slain as they frantically struggled to clamber over the parapet was twenty-three-year-old Captain Lee O. Paris, who sank to the ground with five wounds, his Memphis Novelty Works cavalry saber still firmly clenched in his hand. Soon there were so many bodies piled on top of him that his torso was nearly hidden in the bloodsoaked ditch.[59]

Try as they might, the Confederates at the salient could make no headway. "Over this [obstacle] no organized force could go," wrote division commander Ed Walthall. There were too many Yankees, and they had too much firepower. Still, the cruelest ordeal to be endured yet awaited the battered survivors of Hood's failed frontal assault at the cotton gin.[60]

In the mind of a Confederate colonel trapped at the parapet and exposed to the unmerciful harvest of death, the personal terror here was beyond comprehension. The basic tactical problem became that of exposure to multidirectional fire—an engineering accident that placed those Confederates who huddled behind the main parapets at the center of the field under a severe enfilade fire. With the cotton gin salient firmly in Federal hands and a swarm of blue-uniformed soldiers firing obliquely west into the outer ditch, the gray ranks that had pressed in crowds against the parapet along the Franklin-to-Columbia pike were slaughtered like sheep. Brigadier General George W. Gordon even called it a "massacre."[61]

Colonel Virgil S. Murphey of the 17th Alabama Infantry, one of Shelley's officers, huddled miserably against the earthwork, certain that almost every moment would be his last. The blast from the Kentucky battery's cannon, when fired directly into the earthwork, had showered him with dirt, huge fragments of timber, and other debris. Nine men close to his side had been killed by this single blast. Now the deadly enfilade fire from the right zipped through their ranks, striking men down amid anguished groans and cries. "I never saw men put in such a hellish position," wrote an amazed Illinois soldier. "The wonder is that any of them escaped death or capture." Thought Murphey, "To remain in this . . . dangerous position was worse than death." Spontaneously, a cluster of desperate men attempted to rush the Yankees beyond the parapet. Amid shouts of "Forward," Murphey and dozens of others sprang to the top of the earthwork "like infuriated demons."[62]

It was a forlorn effort. Murphey said most were shot on the top of the parapet, before they were able to get across. Others, he noted, were received on the points of the enemy's bayonets. Murphey was lucky. Somehow he made it over the parapet, was captured, and delivered to Lieutenant Colonel Rousseau of the 12th Kentucky, all in a matter of minutes.[63]

Within the remaining Confederate ranks along the outer ditch at the cotton gin the situation seemed beyond endurance. To further add to their plight, many Rebel soldiers had exhausted their ammunition. In order to keep firing, they had to rummage among the dead bodies for cartridges. Their firing noticeably waned, and with a corresponding decrease in the Federal fire, a brief opportunity existed to escape this deadly inferno.[64]

As the clouds of obscuring smoke slowly dissipated, a soldier of the

104th Ohio observed rags, hats, and all manner of apparel stuck on the ends of bayonets, poking above the parapet from the outside ditch. "For God's sake," came the cries from the Confederate ditch, "don't shoot . . . we'll give up and come in." Encouraged to surrender—"Drop your guns and climb over," yelled some of Cox's men—an exhausted, bewildered throng of about 300 Rebels were soon being herded to the rear as prisoners. Among their number was Brigadier General George W. Gordon, who had been psychologically devastated by the fierce enfilade fire.[65]

In the gathering darkness, accentuated by the lingering clouds of gunsmoke, other Confederates sought to escape to the rear. The acting adjutant of the 29th Alabama, R. W. Banks, determined to make a break for safety, taking with him the regiment's flag planted on the earthworks. So riddled was the flagstaff that it broke in three pieces when he attempted to pull it out of the parapet. Hastily furling the flag amid the broken pieces, Banks dashed to the rear, stepping on dead bodies at every stride until he had passed the ditch. By alternately running when the firing was slow, then hugging the ground when it became brisk, Banks safely made it to the rear and presented his riddled flag to General Walthall, found sitting beside a fire.[66]

The severest fighting at the cotton gin had lasted only about forty minutes, thought a Federal lieutenant colonel. The most serious threat having passed, Cox's reserves, including the 112th Illinois, were available to move to other sectors of the field as reinforcements. Although the struggle continued in the vicinity of the cotton gin—the musketry occasionally swelling to a roar, then dissipating to a lull—soon after darkness the firing became sporadic. A Confederate soldier, still at the works, noted how, far away to the east, the firing would rise in intensity, "coming down the line . . . growing gradually louder as it approached and passed, and then die away in the distance as it receded." Like the nature of the fighting over an all but wrecked farm cotton gin, the sound of gunfire had become "irregular, unmethodical, [and] inconsistent," he considered.[67]

Due to the slackening fire and evident pullback of many gray riflemen, several Federal reconnaissances were organized to probe beyond the outer ditch. The grisly carnage that awaited discovery was a horror beyond any description. Indeed, sights indelibly burned in the minds of all who saw the human wreckage in front of that unforgettable salient would last for a lifetime.[68]

On both sides of the parapet the hideous sight of dead and mangled bodies littering the ground was made more appalling by the cotton flax that had been shot from the stored bales into little balls of puff and strewn like snow across the landscape. Now the cries and groans of the wounded became almost unendurable to survivors on both sides. After dark the repeated, plaintive cry of one disabled Confederate was more than a Federal soldier could bear. Saying, "I can't stand that any longer," he scrambled over the parapet and crawled to the side of what turned out to be a badly wounded

Rebel major. "For the love of God help me; roll this horse off me," he pleaded. Somehow, his pinioned leg was freed, and the major gasped that he knew he wouldn't live until morning. He and his men had been greatly deceived, he said, being told that they would be fighting Yankee conscripts, and after running them into the river, they might walk into Nashville. "My God!" exclaimed the dying major. "If Yankee conscripts fight like this, what may we expect from Thomas' veterans [at Nashville]?"[69]

"All war is cruel," Pat Cleburne had once written. At the Carter cotton gin the meaning of this statement had been fully revealed. The Rebel ranks that had fought like "fiends" and "madmen" in their impetuous, brave assaults now lay in death, agony, or cringing in despair beneath the smoldering guns they had sought to take. "If it hadn't been for the mistake your side made [in leaving Wagner's two brigades outside the main entrenchments]," Frank Cheatham later told a Federal officer, the earthworks were so strong that "you would have killed every man in our army." A Confederate private, one of Adams's men, fully agreed, remembering how the enemy's fire was so furious he felt he had been spared only because of the prayers of loved ones at home.[70]

Huddled miserably behind the bullet-riddled timbers of the gin house was Confederate Colonel Virgil S. Murphey, lonely and despondent as a prisoner. "I felt humiliated," wrote Murphey in his diary, as he sat thinly clad and cold in the mud and standing water. Murphey kept thinking about the recent fighting, shuddering at the horror which "human hands had just created." This whole spot, he decided, was "an unholy ground" that exemplified man's inhumanity to man. His captor, an Ohio captain, speaking earnestly and with great respect, began telling him how courageous the Confederate attacks had been against the formidable Federal works.[71]

Murphey suddenly reconsidered. On second thought, somehow it now seemed clear. The fighting at the cotton gin had not been entirely in vain. "The Battle of Franklin will live in history," he seemed to understand. Murphey scrawled in his dairy prophetic words: "It is a monument, as enduring as time[,] to Southern valor."[72]

CHAPTER XXI

Where Is the Glory?

YOUNG AND FOOLISH THING THAT I WAS," later wrote Carrie Snyder, a newly married woman living in Franklin, "I began to fear there would be no fight." She confided, "I wanted to see a battle, or hear one," recalling how with her friend, Mrs. Martha Rainey, she sat on the back porch that afternoon playing backgammon and listening to the distant spatter of rifle fire. They kept on playing backgammon until, late in the afternoon, the firing grew louder, becoming, so it seemed, "a snapping roar." Carrie and Martha got up and walked into the yard. A few bullets whistled overhead, but the women paid little heed. With the brick house between them and the firing, it seemed to be a grand and exhilarating experience. Suddenly there was a swishing roar overhead, then a deafening explosion. A Confederate shell had passed directly over their heads and detonated amid the clustered residences of Franklin.[1]

"Oh—my! I grew short quicker than anything you ever saw. I . . . thought I was hit sure," said a sobered Carrie Snyder. She immediately "got down low" and made a beeline for the cellar, to join the "old folks." Once they were in the cellar, the noise began in earnest. To the three women and one old man huddled in the dark coal bin listening to the fury of the battle, it quickly became an excruciating trauma. "We thought . . . that a shell would come through the walls, explode inside of the house and blow us all into 'Kingdom Come' . . . [any] minute," she wrote. "I hadn't seen anything [of the battle], but I had heard more than I wanted to. I wanted them [the shells] to quit right off, but they wouldn't; they just kept up a roar . . . and screeching that fairly stopped my heart from beating." Within minutes, Carrie Snyder decided she had experienced more than enough of being in a battle. Like trapped animals, Carrie and the others sat in cramped misery for hours, listening to the maddening, incessant roar and the terrified wailings of one of the older women. Military combat, she firmly decided, was an unspeakable horror. "God forgive me," she later wrote, "for ever wishing to see or hear a battle."[2]

Fourteen-year-old Hardin Figuers had climbed a tree to better see the battle. From the treetop to the top of a barn, and then to the roof of a woodshed, Figuers had merrily scooted about, intent on "seeing all that could be seen." Bullets soon began whizzing about, and the thought raced through the youth's mind that he was as liable to get shot as any soldier. Figuers retreated to the cellar of his parents' home, shaken by the sight of a Federal who was struck just across the street. Soon Hardin Figuers was huddled close to a wall in the family cellar, his dog crouched at his feet, whining.[3]

Fountain B. Carter had been reluctant to leave his home site despite the ominous signs of a pending battle, fearing pillage or the outright destruction of his house. Already the Yankees had dismantled his cotton gin and torn down six or seven outhouses west of the pike to use for breastworks. When the battle began, Carter, his son Moscow, four daughters, one daughter-in-law, and nine grandchildren under the age of twelve had used the cellar beneath the house for refuge.[4]

As the adults hastened to gather the children, there were several close calls. One grandson's hat was pierced by a minie ball as he stood in the backyard. Moscow's eleven-year-old daughter, Mary, known as "Lena," couldn't be found when the others raced for the cellar. It was soon found she had run upstairs to get her doll and doll trunk. Finally the Carter family, joined by a neighbor, Albert Lotz, and his family, huddled in the cellar. In all, there were twenty-four persons crammed into the center portion and a small storeroom. Fountain Carter shoved several coils of heavy rope into the windowsills to keep out stray bullets, and the children, terrified by the thunder of the guns, sat crying around their mothers.[5]

Soon Yankee stragglers came running down the cellar stairs, pressing into the south cellar to hide. Several men even crowded into the fireplace to escape the terrible firestorm raging outside. The Carter group retreated into the north storeroom and attempted to secure the door by wedging a plank under it. Yet more frantic soldiers attempted to crowd into the storeroom. This was too much for Moscow Carter. The paroled Confederate lieutenant colonel began shoving the men out, cursing them with such vehemence that they finally left the civilians alone.[6]

At that time, Fountain Carter's tenth of twelve children, Theodrick "Tod" Carter, aged twenty-four, and a captain on the staff of Brigadier General Thomas B. Smith, was then only yards away from his home, preparing to lead a charge against the Federal parapets near the southwest perimeter of the Carter house. As assistant quartermaster he was not required to

234 / Embrace an Angry Wind

fight, yet he told a friend no power on earth could keep him out of the battle—he was literally fighting this day for his own house![7]

Captain Carter was mounted on his big gray, "Rosencrantz," his saber drawn, anxious to begin the charge with a portion of the 20th Tennessee Infantry. A close friend, a sergeant, warned him not to start the men too far away from the works, but Tod Carter could resist no longer. He spurred ahead, his saber thrust at full extension toward the enemy. Amid a fusillade of bullets his horse went down. Carter was flung over the animal's head to the ground and lay desperately wounded in two places. One minie ball had struck him in the head, and he lay helpless, only about 525 feet southwest of his home. Fully conscious but unable to crawl away, he lay waiting for help. For hours Tod Carter hung on, occasionally delirious, calling for help.[8]

II

The locust grove, wrote a local man, was actually a thicket in swampy ground beneath the Carter House Hill with mature trees growing very close together. Although only a portion of the locust trees had been felled for headlogs, the cut branches and snarled treetops had been dragged about to form a crude abatis, protecting a large segment of Ruger's long line. Like Reilly's men on the east side of the Franklin-to-Columbia pike, Ruger's troops, composing the primary infantry of the Federal right flank, had hastily prepared for battle. Some of his men, lacking personalized badges, scratched their names on the inside of their belt buckles so that they might be identified if killed. Others had gathered little wads of cotton from the gin to stuff in their ears and deaden the jolting noise of the guns.[9]

When the battle began, with Wagner's fleeing men overrunning most of Strickland's brigade and threatening Moore's position, chaos had engulfed Ruger's troops. The sound of bullets striking camp kettles and coffeepots made a peculiar ringing noise, thought a soldier, who noted the men doing the shooting must have been properly instructed to fire low. In Strickland's line many riflemen of the 72d Illinois stood bewildered as Wagner's fugitives and the pursuing Confederates overran part of their position. Those who did not join in the flight were so dumfounded by the confusion, noticed an officer, that they failed to open fire. Then the drifting smoke from the east obscured everyone's view. At last there was a puff of breeze and the smoke momentarily lifted. In their front stood a cluster of Rebels, milling about only forty yards away and seemingly puzzled as to where to go. "Open on them, boys!" shouted an officer, and a sheet of flame leapt from the Illinois regiment's rifle muskets.[10]

After being forced back to the retrenched line of rude barricades by the terrific cross-directional fire, including "friendly" fire from Opdycke's charging line, Strickland's men had mixed with Opdycke's right flank regiments and repelled John C. Brown's initial attack. Bridges's Illinois Battery, which

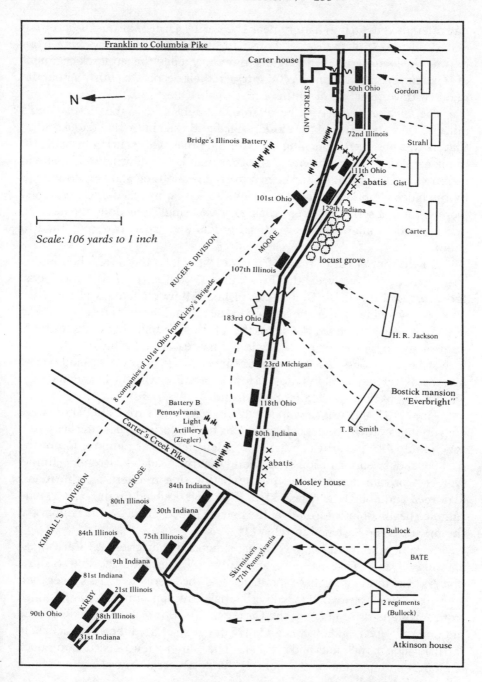

MAP 9   Assault on the Federal Right—November 30 Franklin

(Sources: Cox, 54ff.; C.V. 12-347; O.R. 45-1 (regimental reports); Park Marshall journal, 130; TSL.)

had attempted to go into battery near the Carter garden, instead was repositioned northwest of the Carter house to fire on troops approaching from
beyond the locust grove. These guns materially aided the left flank regiment
of Moore's line, the 111th Ohio Infantry, in their desperate effort to hold the
main earthworks adjacent to the locust thicket.[11]

The very air seemed to be aflame, thought one of the 111th Ohio's
officers. Here the terror of the close-range fighting so intimidated one soldier
that he was observed crouching beneath the breastworks, firing his rifle "in
the general direction of Jupiter." Another man later admitted to his wife in
an emotional letter that he had been completely confused and "confounded"
by the hideous noise and tumult of the attacks. So appalled and frightened
were some that shouts of "Cease firing, cease firing!" ran along the line. No
one seemed to know who gave these orders and most men continued to
shoot.[12]

Due to the retreat of most of the 72d Illinois to the retrenched line, a
large gap existed between the Franklin-to-Columbia pike and the locust
grove. Behind the 111th Ohio, next in line, a few companies of the 183d
Ohio, a raw regiment, were cowering on the ground, hesitant to advance and
cover the critical open flank. One of the 111th's lieutenants ran up to them,
gesturing with his sword and calling in the name of God for the men to move
forward to the works. The lieutenant pointed to the empty ditch and waved
his sword; still they wouldn't move. He was pleading with the frightened men
when he went down with a mortal wound.[13]

The 111th Ohio was now in a tight fix, and with various Rebel brigades
converging on their front, their ability to hold a forward position was very
much in doubt. A nearby captain saw an enemy officer jump on top of the
parapet and, swearing furiously, demand that the Yankees surrender. Immediately a private jammed the muzzle of his rifle musket into the man's
abdomen and pulled the trigger. The explosion doubled up the officer, who
tumbled headfirst into the ditch at the private's feet. "I guess not," remarked
the private as he hastened to reload.[14]

So much ammunition was being expended that cries of "Cartridges,
cartridges" and "Give us more ammunition" ran along the line. Several
officers tried to suppress these shouts for fear the enemy would discover their
shortage. Finally a wagon loaded with small-arms ammunition was obtained
from town and driven behind the Carter house. Boxes were quickly shoved
out and split open, and officers and privates alike carried the vital packets to
the firing line in their hats and blankets. Then, after a few uncertain minutes,
the entire complexion of the fighting along Ruger's crucial eastern flank
quickly changed.[15]

Reinforcements in blue uniforms were now everywhere in sight, moving
up on the run. One of Moore's staff officers, Captain Patrick H. Dowling, had
led forward eight companies of the 101st Ohio from Kimball's division on the
army's far right. Together with a mixture of rallied troops, Dowling's men

advanced to the direct support of the 111th Ohio, enabling a line to be formed at right angles across the gap. Enough reserves were now present to sustain the 111th Ohio at the critical position between the main and retrenched lines. Ruger's partially shattered flank had been firmly reestablished at its weakest point, at the eastern edge of the locust grove.[16]

In front of and west of the locust grove, along Moore's front, S. R. Gist's and John C. Carter's brigades had been the first to attack. Gist's Brigade was the largest of four brigades in John C. Brown's 2,750 man-division. States Rights Gist, a South Carolinian and a graduate of Harvard Law School, was seen riding along the line, waving his hat and urging the men on. When his horse was shot, Gist sprinted for the locust abatis in front. He advanced only a few steps before falling, shot in the heart. His men, South Carolinians and Georgians, raced past their dying commander and charged headlong into the "formidable and fearful" locust abatis. "The entire brigade was arrested by it," wrote Colonel Ellison Capers of the 24th South Carolina Infantry. Yet there had been a noticeable slackening of hostile fire due to the building confusion along the Columbia pike. "We took advantage of it to work our way through [the locust branches]," said Capers. Soon Gist's men were at the earthworks, fighting hand to hand with the remnant of the 72d Illinois and the 111th Ohio. Although the 72d Illinois suddenly gave way, Gist's Brigade now "had only strength enough left to hold its [present] position." When the terrible confusion was sorted out it was found that a major of Gist's staff was the senior remaining officer in the entire brigade.[17]

Although Brown had ordered John C. Carter's Brigade to move up in support of Gist, by the time Carter's men approached, one of Gist's officers saw how the blasts of Federal canister and musketry "tore their line to pieces before it reached the locust abatis." At the time, twenty-six-year-old Brigadier General John C. Carter was recklessly riding in front of his brigade. Only his adjutant was close behind, striving to keep up with the fast-moving general. Carter was convinced that if he kept his mind fixed on his own personal safety he would not be shot. In the urgency and excitement of the moment, "I forgot all danger," Carter later related. Suddenly, when about 150 yards from the blazing Federal breastworks, Carter was shot through the body. As he reeled in the saddle, his aide jumped from his horse and eased him to the ground. Several passing soldiers carried their general to the rear, while Carter's men surged ahead into the tangled locust thicket. "The scene was lit up by fire that seemed like hell itself," thought one of Carter's men. Although some of the 1st Tennessee's riflemen briefly crossed the parapet in their front, Carter's Brigade was so shattered by the blaze of enemy fire that it too was able to do little more than seek shelter beneath the earthworks.[18]

By now the division commander, Major General John C. Brown, had been alerted by one of Carter's messengers that their attack was unsupported on the west. Indeed, Brown had learned that Bate's Division, which was directed to attack there, was nowhere in sight. This was a serious matter. The locust grove effectively blocked any assault in the vicinity of Carter. There were no reserves nearby. Brown had little time to ponder what to do. Suddenly he fell forward on his horse's neck, seriously wounded. After being helped to the ground by his aide, an ambulance was located and the general carried away. Thereafter, little was done to reinitiate the stalled attack.[19]

Among the more remarkable aspects of the fight at Franklin, the scything of Hood's generals and commanders had already reached an unprecedented level. Of twenty-four generals exposed in the fighting before darkness fell, six were killed or mortally wounded, four seriously wounded, and one captured. The army's middle command structure was all but wrecked, with mostly junior officers in command of the shattered units. Even brigades were without senior officers. Before the fighting ended, even more casualties occurred among Hood's hapless commanders, many of whom continued to ride on horseback into the fray.[20]

William B. Bate's Division of three brigades, Jackson's, T. B. Smith's, and Bullock's, had been told to strike the Federal flank along the Carter's Creek pike at the far west end of the battlefield. Hood assumed that due to the shorter Federal line at the point of attack, Bate would support John C. Brown's assault after advancing along the Carter's Creek pike. Delayed by the greater distance traveled—at least an additional three-quarters of a mile considering the nearly thirty-degree divergent angle of advance and the recurved Federal line bending away to the north—Bate had been unable to reach his assigned position until nearly dark. This had resulted in Brown being without Bate's support when John C. Carter's ranks were shattered near the locust thicket. Now, as Bate's troops belatedly advanced west of the still smoldering locust grove, their attack was but another of the isolated and uncoordinated attempts against the Yankee line. Corps commander Frank Cheatham had instructed Bate to use for proper alignment the Widow Rebecca Bostick mansion, "Everbright," which lay just east of the Carter's Creek pike. Yet, once at this point, he saw that the Carter's Creek pike jutted to the north beyond "Everbright," moving away from the desired northeast direction of advance.[21]

Bate lacked sufficient troops to cover the entire Federal front. Thus, the question was what attack route to take—either he must follow the pike to the north, or conform to the alignment of the other divisions by moving northeast toward Franklin.[22]

Curiously, Bate decided to use both routes. By sending his reserve brigade of Floridians under Colonel Robert Bullock to follow the pike, Bate split apart his already understrength division of about 1,600 men. While Bullock advanced near the Atkinson house, even placing two regiments west of the pike, Bate marched with his remaining two brigades toward the shattered locust thicket. "My line [was] now a single one, without support," admitted Bate. One of his men noted that they were not only few in number, but terribly exposed on open ground. Bate's middle brigade, Thomas B. Smith's, passed through the Bostick yard and swung northeast to confront the middle of Federal Colonel Orlando H. Moore's line. On their east, the Georgians of Henry R. Jackson's Brigade were striking for ground just west of the locust grove.[23]

"The Rebels came upon us like tigers," wrote a grim Federal infantryman. Yet, because of their northeast line of advance, Bate's men approached the Union parapets at a diagonal. "This movement gave us a good enfilading fire on the whole mass in our front," said an alert Ohio colonel. Several devastating volleys and shell from Ziegler's Pennsylvania battery sent Bate's men veering toward the shelter of a small elevation about 150 yards from the center of Moore's line. Again their tactics were faulty. As the gray ranks emerged at the top of the knoll in the gathering darkness they were silhouetted against the sky. Bate's line rapidly wasted away under the heavy Federal fire. Suddenly, led by bold if greatly exposed mounted officers such as Captain Tod Carter, Bate's two brigades dashed toward the middle of Moore's brigade front.[24]

To the raw recruits of two companies of the 183d Ohio, earlier sent to plug a gap at the center of Moore's thinly stretched line, the concerted rush of Bate's men seemed irresistible. The Ohioans suddenly broke pell-mell, reported an astounded private of the nearby 23d Michigan Infantry. With four Rebel battle flags waving above the parapet, Bate's men poured across. Instantly the fighting became hand to hand with bayonets and clubbed muskets. Amazingly, Bate's unsupported line seemed to gain headway, and the sharp firing began to wane.[25]

It was the eye of the storm. Lieutenant Colonel Mervin Clark, better known as "Clarkie" among his friends due to his gentle character, was about twenty years old. Having risen from sergeant to captain of his original regiment, Clark had taken a two-rank promotion in the newly formed 183d Ohio. With Bate's men about to overwhelm his position, Clark seized the regiment's colors and rushed back to the parapet, yelling for his men to return to the fight. It seemed to work. Most of his troops came rushing back, but just then Clark was mortally wounded, falling into the arms of the colonel of the 129th Indiana. Again his nervous soldiers broke for the rear.[26]

The brief respite gained just enough time for Ruger's troops. Colonel Orlando H. Moore had sent orders for Ziegler's Pennsylvania battery to pull their twelve-pounder guns from their embrasures and fire obliquely at the Confederate breakthrough. As their shells began bursting amid the enemy with good effect, Moore called for reinforcements from the right of his line. Two companies of the 80th Indiana soon hastened into the fray. As the Rebels began scrambling back across the parapet, the 23d Michigan's colonel sent one of his companies across the earthwork into the unoccupied outer ditch to fire into the flank of the milling crowd. A private of the 23d sat beside his lieutenant, opening packets of rifle musket cartridges and percussion caps.

"We bit them [rifle cartridges—to expose the powder] and handed them to the boys, [who] kept . . . pouring volley after volley [into Bate's men]," said the private. "Oh! such groaning and praying and pleading I never heard before, and God knows that I do not want to again." It was a bitter requiem for many of Bate's men.[27]

Amid the loud groans and cries of the wounded, shouts of surrender were heard from the south ditch. Moore's soldiers called for the Rebels to come in, and many did, quickly climbing over the works and giving themselves up. The random charges of Bate's men had been repulsed "with heavy slaughter to themselves and comparatively small to us," pridefully noted an Indiana colonel.[28]

As the remnant of Bate's two brigades streamed back toward the ravine beneath Everbright to reform, the last hurrah of Bate's Division occurred along the Carter's Creek pike.

The Floridians of Bullock's Brigade never had much of a chance, admitted a Federal colonel in his official report. Due to the presence of the Pennsylvania battery along the Carter's Creek pike, a strong abatis of felled apple trees fronting the pike, and the recurved line of Kimball's division running northwest, there was little opportunity for a small enemy brigade to successfully press an attack.[29]

First fired upon at a range of about 250 yards by Kimball's infantrymen, the Confederates approached no closer than about 100 yards. Although Presstman's Battery had moved up from the Everbright mansion to duel with the Pennsylvania battery, their fire was ineffective. Brigadier General William Grose's brigade, opposing Bullock, lost only a few men on the skirmish line, and within fifteen minutes Bullock withdrew. One of Grose's frontline regiments had fired only three volleys.[30]

Revealingly, Bullock's advance west of the pike had been so tentative as to miss entirely the advance of Chalmers's cavalry division, ordered to cooperate with Bate's attack. Chalmers had waited along the extreme western flank all day for the arrival of the Confederate infantry after marching from Spring Hill along the Carter's Creek pike. Finally, about 5:00 P.M., with distant firing heard in the direction of Carter House Hill, Chalmers had sent his dismounted 2,000-man division forward to attack the right of Kimball's line in front of Brigadier General Walter C. Whitaker's brigade.[31]

The firing was thick and fast for a few minutes, wrote one of Whitaker's men, but the Confederates pressed forward only to within about sixty yards of the parapets before withdrawing to snipe at long range. James R. Chalmers wrote with considerable conviction, "My force was too small to justify an attempt to storm them [Federal breastworks], and I could only hold my position." Having suffered 116 casualties, Chalmers exerted little further pressure on Kimball's division.[32]

Across the nearly mile-long front of the Federal earthworks, from the

Harpeth River on the east to the river's bend on the west, Hood's frontal assaults had been decisively repulsed as total darkness began to cloak the field.[33]

Added to his building disappointment, Hood also learned about 5:30 P.M. of the repulse of Forrest's cavalry north of the Harpeth River. Nathan Bedford Forrest, already irked by Hood's refusal to outflank Schofield's position at Franklin, again had been wholly frustrated by the dividing up of his cavalry command into segments, making them mere adjuncts of the infantry.[34]

Of Forrest's three divisions, Chalmers's had been sent to support Bate's attack along the western flank, and Buford's was assigned to a similar role on A. P. Stewart's eastern flank. Only William H. Jackson's Division of about 2,500 men remained with Forrest for the attempt to pass around Schofield's flank north of the Harpeth River. Furthermore, as Forrest soon learned, most of Wilson's cavalrymen were deployed in concentrated strength to block his progress. Wilson had posted a 2,800-man division under Edward Hatch at the Matthews house, two and a half miles east of Franklin. Also, he had portions of two other brigades within close supporting distance.[35]

Jackson's men, led by the Texans of Ross's Brigade, had crossed the Harpeth about 3:00 P.M. at Hughes's Ford, three miles southeast of Franklin, intending to push Hatch's men back from the high ground. Facing only minimal resistance, Ross's Brigade quickly seized the high hills about a half mile inland, but soon encountered Hatch's advancing cavalry division, armed with the dreaded seven-shot Spencer lever action carbines. When captured during the Atlanta Campaign, some amazed Confederates had marveled at the new breed of Yankee cavalrymen encountered at a river ford. Those Yankees were the "God damnedest fellas they ever see'd," proclaimed the prisoners. As they waded through the river the bluecoats were seen to fire and dive to reload, then fire and dive underwater again. The Michigan cavalrymen had a good laugh—their Spencer carbines worked well using the new metallic cartridges, even if loaded while submersed.[36]

Hatch dismounted his men and sent them forward with their Spencers blazing. Ross ordered the 9th Texas Cavalry to charge, but after routing the enemy skirmishers, the Texans were stopped with a heavy loss in men and horses. When Hatch pursued, Ross had to put in the 3d Texas Cavalry to hold off the swarming pursuit.[37]

Observing that he was outnumbered and outgunned, Ross decided to withdraw to the river and await support. By 5:00 P.M., finding that Hatch's men were again advancing, Ross withdrew to the south bank of the Harpeth River.[38]

Defeated as much by the dispersement of his forces as by Wilson's cavalry, Forrest, instead of seriously threatening the Federal army's line of communications, had been relegated to a minor role in the battle.[39]

Although the issue seemed long since decided by nightfall on November 30th, the deeper agony of the Battle of Franklin then was only beginning. Due and payable were the personal consequences of so many men being trapped under the muzzles of their enemy's guns with few means of escape, front or rear.

III

An appalled Federal lieutenant, hugging the earthworks a few feet across from the outer ditch, heard the terrifying sounds. At first they resembled the plaintive bleating of calves. Yet they were shorter and gasping, like the delirious moans of fevered men. "Water, water," rose the faint cries—an anguished chorus of weakened voices from the darkness. Before, amid the fury of the fighting, there had been groans and curses and random shouts of rage and defiance. In the uneasy aftermath, the sporadic calm had revealed this newly audible, deeply penetrating terror. Over and over again, with maddening impact, came the desperate cries—"Water, water!"[40]

There was nowhere to go for help, no way to escape; the wounded could only cry out in their anguish. To attempt to crawl away seemed certain death. Any sudden noise was likely to bring a volley of shots. Gunfire swelled to a roar at times, then faded away along the line like dissipating thunder—only to soon begin anew with another outburst.[41]

A stray dog joined in the melancholy tumult with long, mournful howls. Behind the parapet a desperately wounded Federal tossed and thrashed about, having been repeatedly hit by incoming fire. "The pain of his wounds had made him crazy, for he would not talk, but kept crawling about on all fours moaning in agony," said a soldier. A rattling of shots continued. The baleful howl of the dog "sounded to me more pathetic than even the cries of our own wounded men," thought a soldier. Finally a lieutenant could stand it no longer. He gathered some canteens, and with the clamor of the wounded ringing in his ears, dashed back along the east side of the Columbia pike, where he had earlier noticed a well. Amazingly, a single provost guard was walking his beat in the open field, to prevent stragglers from leaving the battleground. When confronted by the guard, the lieutenant was allowed to proceed only after he displayed his officer's saber hilt to prove his commissioned rank. Hastily filling his canteens at the well, the lieutenant returned to the wounded. He soon found an old acquaintance, who begged for water. "I poured some into his mouth and he then told me that he was hit in half a dozen places, 'all torn to pieces' he said, and he wanted me to write to his brother."[42]

The situation was so desperate among the survivors of John C. Brown's Division, said Frank Cheatham, that they had fashioned rude breastworks of dead bodies of their own men. The constant enfilade fire had "seemed like hell itself," but still they retained the tenacious Southern fighting spirit. Some of the wounded continued loading small arms and passing them forward to the able-bodied. Once obscured by the gathering darkness, some of Cheatham's troops had made renewed attempts to overwhelm portions of the Union line. Isolated sections of the breastworks were again lighted by gun flashes as brief conflicts erupted. Along the Carter garden perimeter new fighting broke out, with some of Strahl's Tennesseeans firing at the flashes of the enemy's guns. Nearby, a lieutenant of the 24th South Carolina gathered several companies and led a rush over the parapet amid the ranks of the 97th Ohio Infantry. A Federal soldier wrote of the Confederates' pluck, "I never saw men so daring. They came right up to our breastworks, one man grabbing our colors planted at the head of our company." Here a Union soldier whose rifle musket was unloaded lunged with his bayonet at a man atop the works. "With one prod he caught the Rebel," noted the soldier, "and like a man pitching hay he threw him back over his head onto the ground behind us, from which he did not rise." The fighting was short and furious. After a few bloody minutes, the South Carolina lieutenant found his sortie had overwhelmed the Ohioans, yet the incoming fire was so intense he recalled his men and, with forty prisoners and the 97th Ohio's flag, they slipped back across the parapet, having changed little except the casualty lists.[43]

Throughout the early evening these brushfire encounters continued to flare up along much of the line. At times the conflict seemed as ferocious as if wild beasts and not men were engaged, thought a Mississippi veteran. Numbering among the latest casualties were many of Ruger's soldiers, exposed both to the "friendly" enfilade fire coming from the cotton gin salient, and fire from the direction of the Everbright hill.[44]

Bewildered, famished, covered with filth and blood, and exhausted in mind and body, the combatants on both sides seemed to wear down as the night wore on. Eventually, said an Illinois officer, "we intuitively felt the abatement of [the] fierceness [of the Confederate attacks]." Occasionally some noise or imaginary movement caused a squad to fire into the darkness, but as the response was often feeble, by degrees it became quiet.[45]

Out on the battlefield a Federal lieutenant sat in silence, considering the amazing improbability of what had happened. "It is difficult to understand the strategy or the folly of the Confederate commander when he permitted his troops to remain upon that slaughter field for hours under the deadly fire of our guns," he later wrote. "After the first attack it had been demonstrated beyond any possibility of a doubt that the Union lines could not be broken, or our works carried by assault."[46]

The lieutenant would have been shocked had he then foreseen what was about to occur. John Bell Hood had not yet given up the fight. He had, in fact, ordered a night attack against the Federal lines by his only available reserves. The Battle of Franklin had not ended. A splendid 2,700-man division was even then readying itself for the supreme assault that, said Hood, would drive the exhausted Federal army into the Harpeth River.[47]

Now that he had a moment for reflection, a Union officer looked at the grisly scene of dead and mangled men about him and thought about the meaning of it all. "I feel like one who witnesses a bitter wrong, a monstrous injustice," he sadly wrote. "Call it glorious to die a horrible death, surrounded by an awful butchery, a scanty burial by . . . [enemy] hands, and then total oblivion, name blotted out and forever forgotten—where is the glory?"[48]

Only John Bell Hood thought that he knew the answer.

Dashing and almost handsome in his Confederate major general's uniform, John Bell Hood poses here in early to mid-1863, near the zenith of his career. His future seemed assured, and he had just met the beguiling Sally "Buck" Preston. (Eleanor S. Brockenbrough Library, The Museum of the Confederacy, Richmond, Virginia)

The stress of the Atlanta fighting and his political intrigues with the army's high command took their toll and considerably aged "Sam" Hood, as shown in this 1864 photo. His crippled left arm (Gettysburg) and missing right leg (Chickamauga) drained him physically, and he often resorted to the use of laudanum. (Library of Congress)

By 1865 Hood had come to the end of his military odyssey, and he was an angry and tormented man. His body was a wreck, he had lost Buck, and his dreams of glory had faded into oblivion. (The Museum of The Confederacy)

Bilingual, educated in Europe, and always dressed in the most stylish clothes, the beguiling Sally Buchanan "Buck" Preston was the belle of Richmond high society. Yet there was a darker side to Buck that was the talk of the town. Her many lovers seemed to have been afflicted with a deadly spell, and nearly all had been killed. (South Caroliniana Library, University of South Carolina)

Assigned as a theater commander in the crucial western region, General P. G. T. Beauregard found his new administrative position to be merely so much political posturing by Jefferson Davis, designed to relieve pressure from the president and John Bell Hood following the loss of Atlanta. (U.S. Army Military History Institute)

Twenty-four, petite and demure, the witty and captivating Susan Tarleton had swept Major General Patrick Cleburne off his feet at the wedding of his close friend General William J. Hardee. (Hill Junior College Press)

Colonel P. Sidney Post, who led the reconnaissance that uncovered Hood's flanking march to Spring Hill and the frontal charge on Overton Hill at Nashville, where he was severely wounded. (U.S. Army Military History Institute)

Known as the "Stonewall Jackson of the West," Major General Patrick Cleburne was one of the best Confederate commanders of the war. His men worshiped him, and his combat record was the brightest of the Army of Tennessee. (Library of Congress)

Major General John M. Schofield's tentative handling of his command at Spring Hill and excessive caution at Nashville were offset by his good luck at Franklin, assuring him a successful future in the army. (Library of Congress)

Major General David S. Stanley, who played a key role in saving Schofield's command at Spring Hill and became the lone casualty among the Union generals at Franklin. (Library of Congress)

Major General James H. Wilson, a brash twenty-seven-year-old Federal cavalry commander, was badly fooled during the Spring Hill operations by Nathan Bedford Forrest, but his Spencer-armed troopers later, during the Nashville fighting, overran fortified Confederate infantry positions and were crucial to victory. (U.S. Army Military History Institute)

Confederate Major General John C. Brown, a former Tennessee lawyer who had spent more than six months in a Federal prison following the capture of Fort Donelson, was an experienced combat veteran whose hesitation at Spring Hill was the tactical cornerstone of the missed opportunity. (U.S. Army Military History Institute)

Major General Benjamin Franklin "Frank" Cheatham, an ex–Tennessee farmer with a reputation as a rough-and-tumble fighter and a hard drinker, quickly fell into Hood's disfavor because of his shortcomings at Spring Hill, which helped squander one of the best tactical battlefield opportunities of the war. (U.S. Army Military History Institute)

The fiery and outspoken Colonel Emerson Opdycke gained fame as the leader of the countercharge at Franklin that saved Schofield's army. Although at one point he actually attempted to halt this spontaneous charge, his presence amid his men in hand-to-hand combat became one of the most vivid episodes of the furious fighting at the Carter house. (Library of Congress)

Brigadier General George D. Wagner, who had fought with success at Shiloh and Stones River, came under a severe cloud following Franklin because of his positioning of two detached brigades beyond the main breastworks during Hood's frontal assault. (U.S. Army Military History Institute)

Lieutenant General Alexander P. Stewart, known as "Old Straight" to his men, was given command of Leonidas Polk's corps following Polk's death in June 1864. Stewart's competence was never in question, yet only when Hood had been effectively removed from command did Stewart make a critical explanation of what had happened at Spring Hill. (National Archives)

Brigadier General Jacob Cox, who became de facto commander of the frontline Union troops in the fighting at Franklin, later feuded with David Stanley over credit for the victory, but his postwar account of the battle was the best of his contemporaries. (U.S. Army Military History Institute)

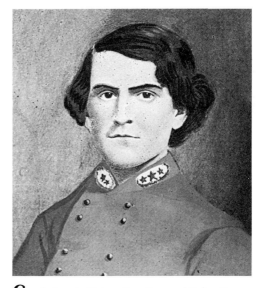

Confederate Brigadier General John Adams, a West Point–educated Irishman with Mexican War experience, led the fatal charge on the Union breastworks near the cotton gin at Franklin, one of the battle's most famous events. (U.S. Army Military History Institute)

Confederate Brigadier General John C. Carter led his brigade at Franklin against the flaming breastworks near the locust grove only to suffer a mortal wound. After lingering at the William Harrison house near Franklin, Carter died only a few days before his twenty-seventh birthday. (Library of Congress)

A mid-1880's view from the north of the then recently reroofed Carter house. Plainly evident below the roof line at the end of the house is the new, lighter-hued brick. Although the original hipped roof was removed, in modern historical refurbishing it has been restored to its Civil War configuration. Evident beyond the southern edge of the house is the picket fence marking the edge of the Carter garden, one of the bloodiest spots of the entire war. (U.S. Army Military History Institute)

This view of Winstead Hill, two miles south of Franklin, circa 1884, was taken from Privet Knob, just west of the Columbia pike. In the foregound is the stone fence behind which the men of Wagner's division formed while withdrawing toward Franklin, even as Hood's columns deployed across the base of Winstead and Breezy hills. The Columbia Pike is visible at the far left, a white line running diagonally below the small white house, then up the saddle between the two hills. (U.S. Army Military History Institute)

This photograph reveals the commanding height of Figures' Hill at Franklin, where Fort Granger loomed over the open countryside. It was taken from the north face of Carter's Hill, east of the Columbia Pike, and shows the exposed terrain across which whizzed the iron hail from Fort Granger. (U.S. Army Military History Institute)

Pictured following the promotion of Emerson Opdycke to brigadier general and the return of the wounded David S. Stanley and Luther P. Bradley to duty, these Fourth Corps generals are: standing left to right, Ferdinand Van Derveer, Washington L. Elliott, Bradley, Opdycke; sitting left to right, Samuel Beatty, Thomas J. Wood, Stanley, and Nathan Kimball. All but Van Derveer participated in the 1864 Tennessee campaign. (U.S. Army Military History Institute)

West Point, Class of 1845, Union Major General Thomas J. Wood was a veteran campaigner whose burning desire was to redeem a reputation tainted by his role in creating the infamous "gap" at Chickamauga. Ambitious and eager to prove himself in corps command, Wood engineered the unsuccessful assault on Overton Hill at Nashville during the second day of fighting. (U.S. Army Military History Institute)

Union Brigadier General John McArthur was one of the most aggressive commanders at Nashville. An intelligent and impulsive Scotsman, McArthur's decision to assault Shy's Hill without specific orders on the afternoon of December 16 was the key element in the most complete Union victory of the war. (Library of Congress)

While the battle of Nashville raged in the distance, an unknown photographer recorded the outer defensive lines on December 15 or 16. As is apparent from their relaxed poses, there wasn't much for the soldiers to do unless at the front. (Library of Congress)

Confederate Brigadier General Thomas B. Smith survived the carnage at Franklin only to be forced to surrender at Nashville during the assault on Shy's Hill. Struck on the head with a sword by an angered Union colonel while being marched to the rear, Smith spent the remaining forty-seven years of his life in the Tennessee State Hospital for the Insane. (Library of Congress)

Confederate Major General William Bate was a capable fighter from rural Tennessee who had suffered multiple wounds in combat, yet the poor performance of his division during the Tennessee campaign at Murfreesboro and, especially, Nashville led to the virtual destruction of Hood's army. (U.S. Army Military History Institute)

The interest of Nashville's largely pro-Southern population was fully evident at the time of the battle as hundreds of citizens lined the high knolls and hills to catch a glimpse of the distant action and hear the thunder of the guns. (U.S. Army Military History Institute)

At age thirty in July 1864, Lieutenant General Stephen D. Lee was the youngest lieutenant general in the Confederate army. Although assigned to command of Hood's largest corps, Lee never played a major role in the decisive fighting. Only following the army's rout at Nashville, when Lee's troops were compelled to save the last remaining line of retreat, were his troops put to a severe test. (Library of Congress)

Confederate Major General Edward C. Walthall, a Mississippi lawyer before the war, by 1864 had earned a reputation as an ardent fighter. After the disaster at Nashville, Walthall was sought by Nathan Bedford Forrest to command the rear-guard infantry. The stout delaying actions of Walthall's troops and Forrest's cavalry virtually saved Hood's battered army from total destruction during their retreat from Columbia. (Library of Congress)

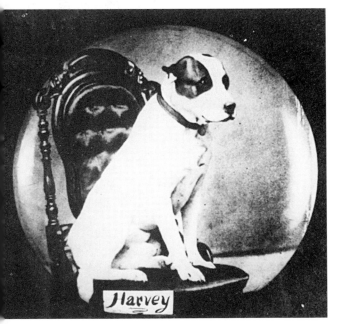

Old Dog Harvey, the beloved bulldog mascot of Company F, 104th Ohio Infantry, wore a leather collar at Franklin with a brass plaque inscribed: "I am Company F's, 104 O.V.I. dog. Who's dog are you?" When the boys sang around the campfire at night, Old Harvey would bark and sway from side to side. "My idea is that the noise hurts his ears, as it does mine," wrote a bemused soldier. (Carter House archives)

CHAPTER XXII

There Is No Hell Left in Them—
Don't You Hear
Them Praying?

HOOD HAD SPENT much of the afternoon in the yard of Green Neeley's modest house along the Franklin-to-Columbia pike. After billowing smoke obscured the battlefield, Hood had ridden here from Winstead Hill and was found sitting on a rock near a campfire, smoking a cigar. Hood was physically drained by the rigors and stress of the past few days, and appeared haggard and ill at ease. About 4:00 P.M., just as the attack of Cheatham's and Stewart's corps was beginning, Stephen D. Lee arrived with the vanguard of his corps from Spring Hill. Following Hood's instructions of that morning, Lee had marched his corps to Franklin at a "leisurely" pace.[1]

Lee was surprised to find a battle in progress, and later insisted that had he known what was intended, his entire corps could have been present from the beginning. Hood seemed largely unconcerned. He merely told Lee to move forward his leading division, Ed Johnson's, and thereafter Clayton's, and be ready to support Cheatham's attack. Following Lee's departure, Hood began receiving reports of "stubborn" enemy resistance. He soon sent word to Lee to ride forward to Cheatham's headquarters on Privet Knob and, if necessary, put Johnson's full division into the fight. Later, when a courier arrived with news of the mauling of Cheatham's Corps, Hood seemed taken aback, muttered something about "an awful day," and told the courier to find Stephen D. Lee and get his troops forward to join Cheatham's men.[2]

Lee was already in the process of moving Johnson's troops into position. Having met Cheatham about dark, Lee was told that his help was needed at once. Despite the darkness, he hastened to organize a night attack without proper guides or a clear understanding of at what point his men were to assault.[3]

Aligned by riflemen carrying flaming torches at each end of the line, four of Ed Johnson's brigades advanced toward the center of the battlefield about 9:00 P.M.. In their left front lay the locust thicket, already shattered and littered with bodies from four hours of vicious fighting. Ahead to their right were the smoldering parapets angling from beneath the cotton gin salient. Only the covering darkness masked the ultimate terror into which Johnson's men were blindly marching.[4]

"We advanced, stumbling over our dead and wounded," wrote an appalled Mississippi private. "The latter shrieked as we trod on their mangled limbs. Powder smoke hung over the field in clouds, reflecting the lurid fire that blazed along the Yankee parapets." The men cringed under a hail of projectiles. "It seemed to me that the air was so full of bullets that I could have caught some by simply grabbing on either side or above me," the private said. An officer had hoped that their approach after nightfall might favor them. Yet when "within thirty paces of the enemy works . . . the darkness was lighted up as if by electric display." The whole Yankee army seemed to be firing in their faces. "Forward to the works," rose the shouts of officers. With a yell, Ed Johnson's troops surged ahead, determined to win a victory at any cost.[5]

In the forefront of the attack was Brigadier General Jacob H. Sharp's command, known as the "High Pressure Brigade" due to their past tenacious fighting. The 41st Mississippi Infantry was among the regiments struggling to crawl, prod, and force their way through the tangled locust branches "that ordinarily a dog could not have gotten through." Up to the Federal breastworks dashed these Mississippians. A color-bearer, shouting for those behind to follow him, clambered over the parapet waving his flag. Immediately he was engaged in a hand-to-hand struggle for the colors. Behind him some soldiers of the 41st tumbled over the works, and a vicious bayonet fight erupted in the dark. Moments later the enemy seemed to vanish in the direction of the retrenched line, leaving several stands of colors behind.*[6]

Yet the Mississippians found that it was a hollow victory—there was noplace to go. An intense storm of incoming rifle fire continued. The men of the 41st dared not rush forward again; that meant certain death or capture. Also, they were unable to withdraw, for other Southern units occupying the reverse side of the parapet were blazing away at the second Yankee line. Amid this tumult and confusion the handful of Mississippians crouched low in the ditch, hoping for a lull. Finally, as the firing briefly waned, they scrambled back across the parapet, feeling lucky to be alive. When the terrible losses were counted, it was discovered a lieutenant commanded their regiment. A survivor heard another Mississippian gasp, "I am glad to get home to you, it was hell itself, boys."[7]

Stephen D. Lee, moved almost to tears by the awful carnage, later

---

*Apparently the flag of the 72d Illinois was lost at this point, the color sergeant having "sneaked away" before eight corporals of the color guard were either shot or captured.

praised three of Ed Johnson's four brigades for their bravery, saying he had never seen greater gallantry than they displayed at Franklin. Only Arthur M. Manigault's Brigade had failed to reach the Federal earthworks after he and his two successors were shot. The terrible frontal blasts of musketry and cannon fire had stopped Johnson's infantrymen at the ditches of the outer earthworks, where they were soon riddled by the horrible enfilade fire from both flanks. Lee wrote a few days later, "My heart was never more moved than when going over the ground where my Mississippians displayed so much valor." His men were literally piled in the ditches and draped over the earthworks. Johnson's Division had suffered 587 casualties in only a few minutes' fighting. A veteran Federal lieutenant concurred in Lee's assessment, later writing, "Not enough praise can be bestowed on the Rebel rank and file and their line officers for their heroic bravery."[8]

As the firing faded along the line, cries of surrender arose from clusters of wounded Confederates trapped in the ditches. An amazed Federal officer heard the shouts and said that "it was the only instance when I heard Johnnies beg for mercy."[9]

The ordeal had reached its zenith; no more were the Confederates able to mount either sustained or sporadic attacks. The remnants of the various mixed commands held their position in pure desperation, admitted a badly wounded Confederate captain lying near the locust thicket. With the blaze of musketry lighting up the area adjacent to the ditch, he saw that "it was certain death to retreat across that plain, and equally bad to remain." His men, often without officers, still continued to fire doggedly across the works amid "the lurid glare of the enemy's artillery, which seemed to sear the eyeballs."[10]

Increasingly, as the night turned gloomy and sharply cold, most of the Confederates used the cover of darkness to abandon the outer ditches and withdraw to the line which Wagner's troops had occupied at the beginning of the battle. Here Stephen D. Lee's reserves were posted under Brigadier General Henry D. Clayton. Clayton admitted his relief when not ordered to follow in the bloody path of Johnson's Division. "Night mercifully interposed to save us from the terrible scourge which our brave companions had suffered," he candidly wrote in his official report.[11]

It was about 10:00 P.M. and the long, terrifying hours of being trapped beneath the enemy's earthworks caused one Southern soldier to believe that the greater part of the battle was fought after dark. Almost any noise brought a flurry of gunshots. Also, some rubbish caught fire along a part of the parapet, revealing in the eerie, flickering light grotesque outlines and shapes. Everything that moved seemed threatening. "Wounded Confederates who moved a leg or an arm were instantly selected as targets and were literally shot to pieces," wrote a stunned observer. Mercifully, due to utter exhaustion, the firing finally died down. By 10:30 P.M. all was quiet in their front except for the wails and moans of the wounded, said one of Opdycke's exhausted officers.[12]

Overhead a bright moon was shining, yet its light was greatly dimmed by the dense pall of smoke and dust that hung above this battlefield of unspeakable horror. "Our spirits were crushed," sadly reflected one of Hood's soldiers. Everywhere he looked there was the grisly carnage of war. It seemed that the quaint village of Franklin had become the very incarnation of the "Valley of Death."[13]

Thomas C. Thoburn, a lieutenant in Strickland's brigade, was thinking about the scriptures, "to watch and fight and pray." He was sure he had done enough of both. Abruptly, someone in the distance began singing, "Rally 'round the flag, boys, we'll rally once again, shouting the battle cry of freedom." The words came faintly at first, then others joined in, until a loud chorus swelled above all other sounds.[14]

II

It already was the talk of the army. The men in the ranks understood it. Officers were excitedly bantering the prospects about. Even Confederate prisoners had confirmed it. Hood's columns had been so thoroughly devastated that the chance for an enormous Union victory, perhaps even the obliteration of the Rebel army, seemed at hand.

Of military significance as well as intense curiosity, the sights and unknown circumstances existing beyond the earthworks had been of compelling allure to the Federal officers and men. As the sound of the guns waned after 11:00 P.M., several organized reconnaissances and various individuals crossed over the parapet to discover the enemy's situation, recover wounded comrades, or gather trophies. Sergeant Elijah Kellogg, of Company C, 74th Illinois, one of Opdycke's men, crawled over the works to find a trophy. Smoke still hung over the ground like a blanket, said Kellogg, yet he couldn't begin to describe the horror he saw in the outer ditch. Among the bodies piled on top of each other "like cord wood," he found a young Confederate officer, almost hidden by the bodies of his men. He was not much older than Kellogg was, and Kellogg saw that the man had five ghastly wounds in his chest, neck, and arm. "He had a fine saber clinched in his hand which I collected." Kellogg also removed a blood-soaked letter in the man's breast pocket. Scrambling back over the parapet with his trophies, Kellogg found that it was a Memphis Novelty Works cavalry saber, and the letter was addressed to "Dear Brother Lee from Your Loving Sister Agnes." Later he learned from prisoners that the officer had been from Sears's Brigade, but he failed to determine his full name.*[15]

*Unable to return the sword and scabbard to the family as he once had hoped to do, Kellogg after the war loaned the historic relic to the Grand Army of the Republic (GAR) post in Rockford, Illinois, where it remained for many years. Only by the research of James C. Harris of Corinth, Mississippi, nearly 120 years later, was the sword identified as that of Captain Lee O. Paris, Company D, 4th Mississippi Infantry.

There were many others who were obsessed with seeing the sights beyond the smoldering breastworks that night. Even Captain John K. Shellenberger had sufficiently recovered from the trauma of Wagner's rout to go beyond the parapet into the outer ditch.

Shellenberger saw in the dim starlight that "the mangled bodies of dead Rebels were piled as high as the mouth of the [artillery] embrasure." Crawling to the side of the ghastly heap, he found the outer ditch entirely filled with a mass of torn humanity. "Heads, arms, and legs were sticking out in almost every conceivable manner." He later wrote, "The air was filled with moans of the wounded; and the pleadings for water and for help of some of those who saw me were heartrending." So thick were the bodies that "a wounded man lying at the bottom [of the ditch] with head and shoulders protruding, begged me for the love of Christ to pull the dead bodies off of him."[16]

Shellenberger soon noticed other Federals scurrying about, some gathering Confederate flags and tossing them over the parapet. The thought crossed his mind that various soldiers inside the works would get undeserved credit, and possibly medals, for their capture. By now, Shellenberger was so thoroughly sick of the sights, sounds, and foul smells that he crawled back within the Federal lines, well convinced that Hood's army had been frightfully slaughtered.[17]

Emerson Opdycke agreed. Twice he went beyond the works at the Columbia pike "to see the effect of such fighting." He reported, "I never saw the dead lay near so thick." A reconnaissance patrol from the 104th Ohio found sights and sounds "enough to shock a heart of stone. . . . The air seemed close and the smell of blood was everywhere." Piles of enemy soldiers carpeted the ground, and the pleas for mercy were pitiful. One man repeatedly gasped in distress "Help me, I am the only son of a widow [masonic plea]." Across a 400-yard front the patrol could hardly move "without stepping on dead and wounded men." Even more ghastly, the ground, they saw, "was in a perfect slop"—pools of blood had turned the earth into slippery red mud. Their reconnaissance discovered no enemy in front except for the fallen, and the patrol promptly returned to report their findings.[18]

From the cotton gin across to the locust grove, perhaps 5,000 dead and wounded were strewn in grotesque "bundles." It was apparent to all who witnessed these horrid scenes that Hood's army, like a surging ocean wave, had been dashed and wrecked upon the earthworks of Franklin.[19]

More significantly to Jacob Cox and his senior commanders, they sensed a prime opportunity to wreak further havoc on Hood's battered survivors. Cox and his officers talked the matter over. It was obvious that Hood had given up the fight, at least for the night. To Cox, the heavy punishment the enemy had taken seemed to guarantee the success of a Federal counterattack in the morning. He soon sent his aide and brother, Captain Theodore Cox, to Schofield's headquarters with this important suggestion. Cox told his brother to tell Schofield he would personally "guarantee our success" and would stake his military career on it.[20]

John M. Schofield had returned to the Truett house by early evening. Although Fort Granger was, according to Schofield, "a much better point from which to exercise intelligent general command over the entire line," the parapet overlooking much of the battlefield was of little advantage once the dense clouds of smoke covered the field. At the Truett house he was apprised by staff officers of "the decisive repulse" of Hood's attacks and the reestablishment of Cox's lines. Although still apprehensive, it was as if an enormous burden suddenly had been lifted from his shoulders. Schofield began to show increasing signs of geniality.[21]

With the arrival of further good news, it appeared to many that the Union army had gained a great victory. From Wilson of the cavalry, word was received about 5:30 P.M. that a division of Forrest's horsemen not only had been badly whipped by Hatch's men north of the Harpeth, but had been driven back across the river. Schofield sent a quick reply to Wilson that "we have whipped them here at every point." News that the army's trains were en route to Nashville, as earlier ordered, was confirmed by 8:00 P.M.[22]

Schofield's newfound optimism was soon evident. Without consulting his principal subordinates, that afternoon, shortly after the heavy fighting began, he had ordered the withdrawal of his army to Brentwood under the cover of darkness. Now, following the favorable news from Franklin, there was the temptation to stay and let Hood completely wreck his army.[23]

The lure did not last long. Schofield's conservative judgment soon prevailed, and he decided not to stay at any risk. By 6:00 P.M. the Federal commander reaffirmed the withdrawal order; at midnight the retreat would begin with his eastern flank troops utilizing the railroad bridge, and the men positioned along the western zone crossing by the footbridge. Wood's division, already in place along the north bank, would cover their retreat. Thereafter, the troops would march by the Nashville pike to Brentwood before halting. "The strictest silence" must be maintained so as not to alert the enemy, and no fires would be permitted despite the cold, read his orders.[24]

Schofield's reasoning was clearly explained in his report, written within thirty days of the battle. Since Wilson had driven back at least one of Forrest's divisions, Schofield considered his immediate eastern flank and rear "secure for the time being." Yet the enemy, he estimated, had "nearly double my force of infantry and quite double my cavalry." Fearing they "could easily turn any position . . . and seriously endanger my rear," Schofield was unwilling to take many chances. "My experience on the 29th had shown how utterly inferior in force my cavalry was . . . and that even my flank and rear were insecure." Ammunition also was a worry—there might not be enough on hand for another battle. "To remain longer at Franklin was to seriously hazard the loss of my army, by giving the enemy another chance to cut me off from reinforcements."[25]

Schofield's admitted good luck—"the fortune of war, was, upon the whole, always in my favor," he confided—would not be completely trusted. Having twice been shockingly surprised by Hood's movements during the past two days, Schofield was a commander seeking only to escape with his army intact, thankful that his men had inflicted upon the enemy "very heavy losses."[26]

In order to provide for his army's withdrawal, Schofield sent a message to Thomas asking for a million rounds of small-arms ammunition and 3,000 artillery shells, to be delivered to Brentwood by tomorrow morning. Also, A. J. Smith's troops should be promptly sent there, he wired.[27]

About 7:00 P.M. David S. Stanley, who had returned to the battlefield following the dressing of his painful neck wound, heard of the pending retreat. Immediately he returned to Schofield's headquarters to question the feasibility of disengaging at midnight.[28]

Stanley's conference with Schofield centered on the ability to withdraw the men while so closely engaged. This difficulty was compounded, Stanley thought, due to the enemy's repeated "feeble" assaults, by which they seemed to be attempting to prevent a Federal retreat. While talking with Stanley, Schofield was joined by Captain Theodore Cox, who delivered his brother's message recommending that Schofield stay and fight Hood in the morning.[29]

Schofield again said no. Just before 7:00 P.M. an important message from Thomas had arrived at Schofield's headquarters, having been delayed due to the transfer of the signal station from town following preparations to evacuate. Thomas's message was a direct answer to Schofield's 3:00 P.M. telegraph which warned that he could not hold Hood back for three days. Said Thomas, "Send back your trains to this place [Nashville] at once, and hold your troops in readiness to march to Brentwood, and thence to this place, as soon as your trains are fairly on their way." Schofield's 7:10 P.M. reply told Thomas of the enemy's failed attack and their loss of 5,000 or 6,000 men. As for Thomas's instructions to march to Brentwood, "I had already given the orders you direct, and am now executing them," he wired.[30]

The issue was settled. Thomas, unaware of the battle in progress or the full circumstances, had provided all the justification Schofield needed. Schofield told Captain Cox: "Go back and tell General Cox he has won a glorious victory . . . [but] my orders from General Thomas are to fall back to Nashville as speedily as possible, and it must be done. Therefore, so soon as the enemy withdraws sufficiently . . . put the whole command in motion and cross the river."[31]

The Federal army had been committed to withdraw in the face of victory. Many years later this matter became a source of controversy, with Schofield claiming that he was merely following Thomas's instructions. Considering the various data, it seems that long before the arrival of Thomas's telegram Schofield was thinking not of wrecking Hood's force so much as saving his own army from a "dangerous situation."[32]

Schofield received further good news as the night wore on. All substantial Confederate attacks had been decisively repulsed and their sorties were growing weaker in intensity and more infrequent, announced the frontline dispatches. Skirmish lines advanced in Reilly's front even found that the enemy had withdrawn from the earthworks. Then, about 10:00 P.M., tangible evidence of the enemy's discomfiture arrived at the Truett house.[33]

Colonel Virgil S. Murphey of the 17th Alabama Infantry had spent a miserable evening following his capture near the cotton gin. Herded through Franklin by a "drunken and boisterous lieutenant colonel," Murphey was cold and despondent as he trudged along the turnpike toward Nashville. After walking a mile, they came to a scene of intensive activity—a house where in the yard "an immense number of staff officers, orderlies, and messengers were chatting, talking, and hurrying to and fro." It was Schofield's headquarters, announced the lieutenant colonel, and Murphey, after being elbowed through the throng by his captor, was unceremoniously ushered into a room full of officers with the announcement, "Rebel Colonel Murphey."

"I was the cynosure of all eyes," suddenly discovered the startled Murphey, who "endeavored to maintain a proud mein and calm composure." "Black, begrimed with powder, my clothes tattered and . . . my hair disheveled, my face pale, and shivering with cold, I was in a bad plight for inspection by critical eyes."[34]

Murphey was offered a chair and closely interrogated by several officers. Nervously, Murphey explained the rationale for the desperate assaults. Hood had told his men that if they could overrun the Federal works and drive the Federals through Franklin, there would be nothing preventing them from marching to the Ohio River. An elderly Federal officer then spoke up, remarking that Hood was a butcher, it being evident only that his men had the courage to respond to his demands so as to create a bloodbath. "You cannot do us a greater favor that to retain him in command," said the man, adding that it had been a mistake to place "a reckless, bold and gallant soldier [who was] without discretion [Hood]" at the head of the army in place of "an able, crafty strategist [Joseph E. Johnston]." Spring Hill was further cited as an example of Hood's folly. "You cannot imagine my relief when the army passed by safe and no attack was made," the Federal officer chided.[35]

Murphey hesitated for a moment. Finally he spoke up, commenting with a touch of humor that it was fortunate Hood's appointment pleased both armies. His butchery always seemed to involve a considerable mixture of the Rebels' enemies, said the spirited Alabama prisoner.[36]

When the Federal officer responded that Hood must have lost 5,000 or 6,000 men at Franklin, Murphey argued the point, saying he thought those figures exaggerated. This Yankee officer "was in buoyant spirits," noted

Murphey, and "his happy conceit" was apparent even though preparations were evident for the retreat to Nashville. Offered a glass of whiskey before being turned over to the provost marshal, Murphey, with a wry smile, "twitted" this senior Federal general by saying that "victors usually held the field, not the vanquished." The man looked at Murphey, chuckled, and said he was merely wooing Hood to his destruction. Only when in the hands of the provost marshal was Murphey told he had been talking to John M. Schofield.[37]

III

The town of Franklin, wrote an observer, was filled with stragglers, who in their desperation to get across the Harpeth River had virtually "taken possession" of the footbridge. Among these men was George D. Wagner, still "very excited and demonstrative," riding among the fugitives, yelling for them to rally and re-form. The men seemed unwilling to listen, but Wagner kept up his harangue, shouting, "Stand by me, boys, and I'll stand by you!"[38]

Within the town, wounded soldiers had overflooded the few hastily improvised medical treatment centers. Many of the army's ambulances, filled with the sick and wounded from Columbia and Spring Hill, had been earlier sent across the river in preparation for the withdrawal to Nashville. By chance, the medical director of Reilly's division, Major Charles S. Frink, had found a train of boxcars loaded with forage standing on the track on the north side of the river, ready to depart for Nashville. Frink raced to get permission to commandeer these cars, and throughout the early afternoon they were emptied and the men from the ambulances placed inside. By about 4:30 P.M. the task was completed, and the train moved off for Nashville, leaving the ambulances empty to receive the wounded from the battle then just beginning.[39]

Prior to the battle, two corps hospitals had been routinely set up in tents just north of the river. When stray shells began to explode in Franklin, the surgeons considered the site too exposed and ordered both hospitals removed nearly three-quarters of a mile north on the Nashville pike. Due to the congestion in Franklin and the jammed bridges, many of the ambulances remained north of the river. Stretcher bearers and the walking wounded had to find their way to the general hospitals as best they could. Then, once at the corps hospitals, the crush of wounded men was so great that generally all that was done was to quickly dress the wounds and start the men to Nashville in the rough, bone-jarring army ambulances. When the plans to withdraw from Franklin were announced after the fighting abated, the medical officers found that not enough ambulances were on hand to evacuate all patients. A large number of wounded at the corps hospitals had to be left behind with a small staff of surgeons.[40]

From the first notice of a retreat, the withdrawal order posed a complex tactical problem for Schofield's battlefield commanders. According to plan, the flanks of the army would be simultaneously withdrawn by the closest of the two bridges, leaving the center elements to follow. A skirmish line would remain in front of the earthworks wherever possible to screen the withdrawal until all units had departed.[41]

Jacob Cox foresaw that one of his greatest difficulties would be in getting the artillery out without alerting the enemy or severely exposing the army. By 8:00 P.M., even before Ed Johnson's night attack, several reserve batteries and those on each flank were pulled out and sent north of the river. During Johnson's attack the guns of the 20th Ohio Battery, positioned along the retrenched line near the Carter smokehouse, had been badly shot up. Lieutenant J. S. Burdick had been mortally wounded, half of his men were shot, and most of the horses had been disabled. In order to withdraw these guns, the help of some of Opdycke's men was needed to wheel the cannon by hand to the pike. The large wooden wheels were wrapped with blankets so as to muffle the noise on the stone pike. Later, as the guns were trundled across the bridges, blankets were spread on the planks to reduce the noise. Bridges's Illinois Battery and the guns of the 1st Kentucky, both positioned near the center, were among the last to withdraw, both going to the rear about midnight.[42]

Cox next concentrated on pulling back the Federal infantry. The men first learned of the intended retreat about 9:30 P.M., when word was whispered along the line that the army would evacuate the earthworks about 11:00 P.M. The regiments were expected to move without orders by the right flank, with each man silently following the man on his right. Because of the position of Wagner's troops, many being "in reserve" behind the front line, and others stragglers in town, it was thought best to initially clear this division to the north riverbank.[43]

Predictably, there was a strong emotional reaction among the ranks during the pullback. In the 64th Ohio Infantry, one of Wagner's units, there was excited talk as the men began re-forming in the rear. A captain noted, "They were all in high spirits over their own escape and over the part they had played in the final repulse of the Rebels, and were talking and laughing over their various adventures in the greatest good humor." In fact, now that the firing had abated, a spirit of elation swept through the officers and men along Cox's line. A lieutenant chatting about the withdrawal with his brigade commander, Israel Stiles, admonished, "We ought to remain here and wipe hell out of 'em." Stiles, mindful of the pained groans, pleas, and prayers coming from the wounded Confederates lying across the parapet, remarked, "There is no hell left in them. Don't you hear them praying?"[44]

There was a sudden hitch in the withdrawal. At 11:00 P.M., just as the flank units began withdrawing, a large blaze flared up in the town of Franklin. "Some villain came very near frustrating . . . [our withdrawal] plan by firing a house in Franklin,'' wrote David Stanley, who feared a large, uncontrolled fire would light up the entire area and make it impossible for his troops to withdraw without being seen. The blaze was found to have occurred in a livery stable, perhaps due to a hay fire. Soon the stable was totally ablaze, and Stanley's staff officers rushed about to locate an old fire engine and fight the rapidly spreading conflagration. Due to the great difficulty in putting out the fire, the flames were not extinguished until about midnight, and eight buildings were totally or partially burned, including an old newspaper building opposite the courthouse.[45]

Because of the blaze, Cox delayed the pullback of many of his regiments. Indeed, as the roof of one building fell in, throwing a great glow of light over the landscape, some of Opdycke's men saw as many as a dozen flags rise along the enemy's line. Thinking the Confederates were preparing to make a rush, the men of the 73d Illinois opened a brisk fire. Soon the flags disappeared and the firing gradually ceased.[46]

With the fire out, darkness again enshrouded the battlefield and most of Cox's men were able to quietly pass to the rear. Only a line of pickets remained in front under an inspector general as the last units of Reilly's division pulled back after midnight.[47]

In town there was considerable congestion, and some ruffled tempers occurred when the men of Kimball's division, who thought they were to be the first across the footbridge, ran into the men of Wagner's division, already blocking passage. By mistake, three divisions had been assigned to cross at the footbridge, while only one was routed via the railroad bridge. During the entire evacuation of Franklin the front line was quiet, wrote Cox's thankful inspector general. This allowed the pickets to abandon the earthworks after 1:00 A.M.[48]

About 2:00 A.M. Schofield's entire army was across, and the bundles of kindling stacked on both bridges were set afire, even as the last of the skirmishers were crossing. With a battery posted to sweep the bridges and their approaches, Wood's division, assigned to rear-guard duty, watched the structures burn until the flaming timbers fell into the river. Then, before 4:00 A.M., the last footsteps of Wood's departing troops sounded on the stone pike to Nashville. A lone company of the 124th Ohio remained to watch the crossings, and they soon sat down with "nothing to do but wait."[49]

IV

John Bell Hood called a council of war at his headquarters for midnight. There the commanders of the three corps, Cheatham, Stewart, and Lee, told a tale of horror about the massacre of their commands. Hood, who had remained brooding over the army's inability to crush Schofield's forces during much of the evening, was unmoved by their plight. After listening to Stewart's and Cheatham's gloomy assessments, Hood turned to Stephen D.

Lee and asked, "Are you, too, going back on me?" Lee answered that although one of his divisions had been badly cut up, he had two others that had not been engaged, and if Hood gave the word, at daylight he would charge the enemy works at bayonet point.[50]

According to another account Hood was almost savage in his fury and rage over the lack of an expected major victory. The conflict at Franklin would be renewed, he announced. At first light in the morning he would call upon all his artillery—a hundred guns, which had just come up from Spring Hill—to shell the Federal earthworks. Then, at 9:00 A.M., the entire army would assault the Yankee lines.[51]

There was no arguing with him. Hood desperately needed a victory, no matter what the cost. An aide left the meeting reflecting on what further agony the morning would bring—"it was a bitter prospect for our poor fellows," he sadly reflected.[52]

Soon the orders went out. Hood would rely on his old tactical concept of attack and overwhelm. He ordered each piece of artillery to fire 100 rounds, beginning at 7:00 A.M. Two hours later the entire army would make a general frontal assault.[53]

After midnight a myriad of staff officers and engineers began emplacing the Confederate artillery on high ground at Winstead and Breezy hills. At least one battery reportedly went forward close to the Federal earthworks, rolling over the bodies of dead and wounded Confederates in their rush to come into battery. The "agonizing shrieks" of the wounded as the heavy twelve-pounder Napoleon carriages and the horses' hooves crushed their bones were appalling, wrote an artilleryman. By about 2:00 A.M. many of the Confederate batteries were in place and the gunners readied their ammunition for the dawn barrage.[54]

Due to the lack of noise within the Yankee lines during the early morning hours, several men crept forward and found no enemy present. Suddenly there was a glow on the horizon from the direction of Franklin. Within minutes a large fire blazed beyond the town, rivaling the earlier conflagration that had been put out about midnight. More Confederate scouts were ordered forward.[55]

At the time of the earlier fire it was felt that the enemy was evacuating the town and burning everything they could not haul away. But then it was discovered from the volleys of rifle fire that Schofield's infantrymen were still present. Now, at 2:00 A.M., the scouts confirmed that the railroad bridge across the Harpeth River was on fire. The enemy had abandoned Franklin![56]

Somehow, due to garbled communications or sketchy reports, it was uncertain whether the enemy had completely evacuated or was still lingering in the vicinity of Franklin. Someone suggested that the Federal army had halted along the north bank and was utilizing Fort Granger to establish a new defensive line. Accordingly, a battery of twelve-pounder Napoleons fired about 150 shots to develop the enemy's new position, directing their fire 200 yards to the right of the blazing railroad bridge. "I thought it [the noise] would take my head off," wrote a surprised Southern officer.[57]

It was a terrible mistake. The Confederate artillerymen were firing at the wrong site. The railroad bridge, which was the first structure to be set afire, had already burned down and fallen into the river by the time the guns opened. The blaze they were using for a target bearing was actually the second bridge set ablaze, the more westerly-located temporary footbridge along the main turnpike to Nashville. Instead of bursting in the vicinity of Fort Granger, the rain of shells fell into the eastern section of the village proper, raking the town between the square and the railroad bridge. Many houses were struck four or five times by the plunging shells. At one homesite the scars of twenty-four separate projectiles were later counted on the walls, some of which were knocked to rubble.[58]

Finally, when the guns stopped, detachments of Confederate infantry entered the smoldering town. It was about 4:00 A.M., and among the first of Hood's generals to enter Franklin was Frank Cheatham. He was hungry and went to a residence to eat—it was the first food he had that day. Out on the battlefield many of his wounded men, roused from an uneasy slumber by the recent jar of artillery, lay moaning in misery. A raw wind was blowing, and it was freezing cold. Now that the firing had stopped, one man painfully made his way out from under a pile of dead and wounded in the ditch by the cotton gin. Though dazed and so stiff he could hardly walk, to him it seemed to be "the happiest time of my life" to escape the gruesome sights of that godforsaken ditch. Soon he could see signs of life on the battlefield. A few lights began to appear, and "here and there" small fires were started. Then a few lanterns began to shine, and there were voices and people who began to move about.[59]

At the Carter homesite the twenty-four civilian occupants had emerged from the cellar and many were standing on the back porch, dazed by their recent ordeal. Brigadier General Thomas Benton Smith rode up, asking for Fountain Carter. He had sad news, he said. Captain Tod Carter was known to have been severely wounded and was then lying nearby on the battlefield. Hurriedly, Fountain Carter, three of his daughters, and a daughter-in-law followed Smith toward the locust grove, lanterns in hand.[60]

The Battle of Franklin had at last ended for the soldiers—but not for their families, or the civilian residents.

CHAPTER XXIII

The Thunder Drum
of War

WIDE-EYED and eager to see the sights of the battlefield, fourteen-year-old Hardin Figuers had scampered from his mother's home at the crack of dawn. He was so fascinated by the military events in his midst that he later wrote, "I lived on excitement for forty-eight hours."[1]

Figuers was barely past the yard gate when he saw a dead Union drummer boy, about his own age, lying pale in the middle of the street with his hands thrown back above his head. The sight shocked the Franklin youth, and thereafter his exuberance was gone; he stalked the streets and fields in a numbed stupor, appalled and sickened by the great carnage all about him.[2]

It was just growing light, and men with lanterns and torches were walking over the field. The terrifying cries and moans of the wounded mixed with the braying of mules, the barking of dogs, and the shouts of search parties, ambulance drivers, and stretcher bearers. Pathetically, so many men were calling out for help, gasping their names and units in hope that some friend might rescue them, that Figuers went home to get a buggy and a mule. He hoped to find a local Franklin soldier, Captain W. E. Cunningham, who reportedly had been shot and was lying on the battlefield. Young Figuers soon returned with the mule and buggy, but the animal became so frightened at the strange sights and sounds that he ran away, dumping Figuers in a ditch and wrecking the buggy.[3]

Figuers wandered east, toward the locust grove. The familiar locust thicket presented an incredible sight. Some of the four- to six-inch-diameter trees had been struck by so many rifle bullets that many had toppled over from their own weight. Virtually all had been stripped of bark from two to twelve feet high, and many stumps were so bullet-riddled as to be shredded.

Splintered branches were everywhere. The whole thicket had the appearance of a field of broken hemp stalks, and the ground in front of the parapets was so bullet-warped it looked as if it had just been harrowed.[4]

In the ditches, randomly strewn across the landscape—everywhere, and in every grotesque position imaginable—lay the human wreckage. There were so many dead and wounded that the appalled Figuers saw he easily could have walked upon bodies and never set foot on the ground. Along the parapets the mangled bodies were piled one upon another three and four deep.[5]

Ahead lay the Carter house and garden. The buildings were so riddled with bullets that it seemed they had been stricken with smallpox. All manner of debris was scattered across the ground amid the slain. Dead men lay everywhere in the yard, and the Carter grandchildren had to step over the bodies as they left the house, nauseated by the awful, pungent "odor of blood and gunpowder." Later, Moscow Carter would count fifty-seven dead Feder- als lying within an area from the smokehouse to about thirty yards north of the house. Figuers saw a Federal soldier leaning against a locust tree in the Carter yard. Yet the man was not moving. At closer glance, Figuers saw that he was dead—he had been shot through the head—but his left shoulder was pinned against the tree. Astonishingly, his body had been propped into a semi-standing pose by his rifle musket, which supported his weight at nearly a forty-five-degree angle.[6]

At the nearby cotton gin nearly all of the Federal dead seemed to have been shot in the forehead, reflecting the intense fighting across the parapet. The heavy headlogs had been shot to pieces, and here Hardin Figuers found a wounded Confederate leaning up against the parapet. He had a hideous wound: his lower jaw had been shot away, and his tongue and upper lip were dangling in a bloody pulp. Figuers leaned down and asked him if he might do anything for him. The man had a pencil and an envelope. Slowly he scrawled, "No, John B. Hood will be in New York before three weeks." Hardin Figuers had seen enough. He went home and helped his mother attend to the wounded.[7]

By early morning a vast mixture of soldiers, civilians, and officers were wandering over the field in astonishment and dismay. During the night, while guarding clusters of Union prisoners gathered about a fire, many of the Confederates in the rear echelon had been exuberant, boasting about their victory and how they would go on to take Nashville. When daylight came and these men observed what lay in front, a Union captive noted that they became downcast. The terrible scenes of the battlefield had quickly put an end to their boasting.[8]

One of Cleburne's infantrymen said he came to a spot where the blood had flowed "in a stream," and "stand[s] in pools." Another stupefied soldier wrote, "I never before or after saw such a frightful battle ground." A rifle- man of the 41st Tennessee found Lieutenant Colonel Fountain Stafford so wedged among the corpses in the outer ditch on Carter House Hill that he was semi-standing even though dead. Nearby, a soldier recovered his short Enfield rifle from the bottom of the ditch. The entire weapon, he noted with horror, was soaked in blood, and the gunstock was a brighter red than if stained by paint and varnish.[9]

The suffering of the wounded during the frigid hours of darkness had seemed almost beyond endurance. Shivering with cold, weakened by loss of blood, and often helplessly pinned by the weight of other bodies, Franklin's victims both in blue and gray lay in physical and mental agony, waiting for help. Thirst was a major difficulty, and so desperate were some of the wounded they drank from several stagnant pools of water at the bottom of the ditches. One of Cleburne's badly injured soldiers said the foul water tasted of blood, causing him to retch with nausea.[10]

At daylight many of the wounded were removed from the battlefield and taken to any available nearby building. The scene at Carnton, John McGavock's fine mansion with the two-story back veranda, was both chaotic and appalling. Within hours of the end of the fighting hundreds of wounded crowded every room except one saved for the family. Yet so many more victims were brought here that they overspilled onto the lawn and into the outbuildings. Though ill-prepared for such an event, Carnton became one vast hospital. Wounded men lay bleeding on the elegant hardwood floors, were strewn thickly across the hall, and even reclined under the stairs. When it was found that not enough bandages were available, Mrs. John McGavock donated her old linen, then her towels and napkins. Ultimately her sheets, tablecloths, John McGavock's shirts, and even her own undergarments were torn up for the use of the wounded. Her patients, such as Colonel Noel L. Nelson of the 12th Louisiana, were suffering terribly. Ripped by multiple canister wounds, Nelson kept moaning, "My poor wife and child." Cold beads of perspiration glistened from his brow, and vainly he pleaded for chloroform to relieve his suffering. Mrs. McGavock scurried about from room to room, dispensing tea and coffee, and doing everything to make the men comfortable. Soon her skirts were stained with blood. The surgeons were kept busy, and piles of amputated limbs were stacked into several wagons to be hauled away. One wounded Confederate captain with a compound fracture of one leg, a lacerated second leg, a shattered arm, and a mangled hand was told by a surgeon that in view of his many wounds amputation was useless. The captain then held up his good arm and with grim humor jested that it was all right, "there is enough left of me to make a first class cavalryman."[11]

At the Carter house similar scenes occurred as the premises filled to overflowing. In the parlor lay Fountain Carter's grievously wounded son, Captain Tod Carter. They had found him where he had fallen near the locust grove. He was delirious, and called out for his friend, Sergeant Cooper. Hurriedly they carried him on an army overcoat past the bullet-riddled farm office building and placed him in the debris-littered family room. Dr. Deering Roberts, the 20th Tennessee's surgeon, probed for the bullet embedded above Carter's eye. Yet his efforts were of little use—the wound was mortal, and within hours Tod Carter must die. Bending above his prostrate form, several of his sisters cleansed the wound. Tears stained their cheeks, and one whispered softly, "Brother's come home at last."[12]

With about 6,000 wounded soldiers lying helpless and without shelter on Franklin's blood-soaked soil, the logistical problems in caring for these men were overwhelming. Eventually there would be forty-four hospitals in town, only three of which were for the Federal wounded. Buildings such as the First Presbyterian Church, the Franklin Female Institute, the Williamson County Courthouse, the Tennessee Female College, and the First Baptist Church were used to shelter the wounded. Food soon became a critical problem, as did clothing, sanitation, and bedding. Most of the citizens helped feed and care for the wounded, and their tender compassion became the marvel of many wounded soldiers on both sides.[13]

By midmorning the burial details had begun their gruesome task, and mostly Cheatham's and A. P. Stewart's troops were utilized in burying the already bloating dead. With an estimated 2,500 corpses strewn over the entire landscape, it was an arduous task to gather the bodies, dig ditches, and cover the remains. Most burial details concentrated on the more numerous Confederate dead; the Yankees were left until last. Procedures were generally to dig a ditch about two feet deep and at least wide enough for several soldiers. Yet often, for expediency, a long trench was dug where many bodies could be placed side by side. A blanket or a piece of oilcloth was spread over the corpses' faces, their hands folded, then the trench filled with dirt. Where possible, those bodies that could be identified were marked by a plank with their names scrawled thereon. Throughout the day the burial details worked with haste. Finally the exhausted, gore-spattered men came to the Federal dead. Most of the bodies were covered with earth by placing them in the parapet ditch and pulling down the earthworks on top of them. Few of the remains were identified.[14]

Impoverished Confederates stripped the desirable clothing and equipment off most of the dead, as well as many of the wounded. Carrie Snyder, who went onto the field to help attend to the wounded, found "a fine looking Union soldier" stripped of all but his shirt and drawers. A burly Confederate soldier spied the shirt and, giving the man a kick, said, "Boys, h'yar's a mighty fine shirt on this 'ere dead Yank." He then proceeded to take his fine flannel shirt. Said Carrie Snyder, "I thought it was bad enough to strip him of hat, coat, pants, boots and socks; they might at least give him a single garment to bury him in."[15]

Emotions were running high on that crisp December 1st morning, and morale had quickly plummeted among the Rebel ranks. The sickening sights of the battlefield were such a grisly spectacle that they haunted and tormented the survivors. John B. Hood, the man who had once told his troops that he was not going to fight like his predecessor did, with picks and shovels, but instead with guns, had well fulfilled this prophecy. Now it was the doubting attitude of the men—their sullen, openly questioning ire following the severest ordeal of their army experience—that Hood must face.[16]

When Hood rode into Franklin that morning, passing the dreadful wreckage of his army, he later remembered indulging in "sad and painful thought" at seeing so many of his men dead. One of his soldiers saw Hood and his staff stop along the pike and look at the vast carnage. "His sturdy visage assumed a melancholy appearance, and for a considerable time he sat on his horse and wept like a child." For the solace of the stricken Army of Tennessee, Hood soon directed that general field orders be published in his name, to be read at the head of each regiment that day. Therein, Hood announced: "The commanding general congratulates the army upon the success achieved yesterday over our enemy by their heroic and determined courage. The enemy have been sent in disorder and confusion to Nashville, and while we lament the fall of many gallant officers and brave men, we have shown to our countrymen that we can carry any position occupied by our enemy."[17]

The largely unbelieving reaction to Hood's proclamation was reflected by a captain serving with Cockrell's Missourians, who wrote: "Our army was a wreck. I can safely say that just two such victories will wipe out any army the power of man can organize."[18]

Stricken by "this great sacrifice of life," Hood again began brooding over the failed opportunity of Spring Hill. More and more, resentment began clouding his mind, until he eventually lashed out against several subordinates. Already Hood's rationale in resorting to a massed frontal assault at Franklin was under bitter debate. It would be regarded as one of the most controversial attack orders in the history of warfare on the American continent. Hood had justified his decision by telling Cheatham and his division commanders during a prebattle conference that the open country around Franklin prevented any attempt to outflank the enemy's position. The Federals would immediately withdraw and escape into Nashville, he said. Saying that there had been only hours for the Federals to fortify at Franklin, while at Nashville they had been erecting defenses for three years, Hood told Cheatham that he preferred "to fight them here."[19]

Such were Hood's excuses. He easily could have outflanked Schofield from Franklin by crossing the Harpeth River at Hughes's Ford or various other sites. The ability of the Federal army to escape with its wagon train intact would have been seriously in doubt, just as Schofield had foreseen. The tactical difficulty of attacking an entrenched enemy was equally apparent once substantial breastworks had been completed, regardless of the length of time for preparation. Yet Hood chose to disregard the ardent opposition of many of his veteran subordinate generals.

Hood's decision to attack at Franklin was essentially an emotional reflex, rooted in his obsession to "prevent the enemy from escaping." Undoubtedly, he misperceived the nature of the Federal retreat, believing that a demoralized enemy was attempting only to get away without risking battle. Yet equally prominent were such factors as Hood's physical disability and a draining exhaustion of his mind and spirit. Hood's frustration following the Spring Hill fiasco caused Stephen D. Lee, the general who seemed closest to Hood, to write after the war, "Franklin was brought about by the great blunder at Spring Hill; there is where the trouble lay and no explanations can evade it." Also, he blamed Hood's physical disability, saying that it was doubtful that any soldier so maimed of body should have had such an important command. This want of "physical faculty," said Lee, "certainly impaired his efficiency as a commander."[20]

Hood on November 30th was angry, overeager, frustrated, and not reasoning well. His resort to tactics of not firing a gun, but to use the bayonet, was a throwback to Gaines' Mill. In Hood's mind failings were often explained in simplistic terms—the want of physical and moral courage. Yet his own failings, and also a vindictive disposition, were masked by his penchant for blaming others.

Worse still, he lacked the competence and ability to learn from his mistakes. The tactical battlefield lessons of the past three years had eluded him. The rifle musket and defensive fortifications had so changed the nature of warfare that to resort to a frontal assault against any sizable number of entrenched enemy troops was little better than mass suicide.

Hood harbored visions of past glory. Disciplined valor had won the day then; a similar attack would ever provide the same result. It was the only way he knew or understood. John Bell Hood was a sad anachronism, a disabled personality prone to miscalculation and misperception. Unfortunately, he was also a fool with a license to kill his own men.

They found him lying on his back as if asleep, his kepi partially covering his face. His new gray uniform coat was unbuttoned and open, as was the lower part of his vest. The white linen shirt was bloodstained on the left side above the abdomen. Missing were his boots, watch, sword belt, and other valuables, taken by some looter during the night. Pat Cleburne lay only about forty yards south of the earthworks at the cotton gin. An ambulance recovering wounded and a few of the dead officers at the breastworks was summoned, just as the body of General John Adams was being loaded. Cleburne was placed by the side of Adams, and the ambulance driven to John MaGavock's Carnton residence. For a few hours the bodies of four generals—Cleburne, Adams, Granbury, and Strahl—lay on the lower veranda, awaiting transportation to Columbia. Some of Cleburne's men, told that their general had fallen, were moved to tears. Word spread through the ranks. "Cleburne is killed!" came the reports, and at first many appeared to doubt it, as if such a calamity could not befall the army. Later, some of the men learned that he was at the McGavock mansion, and came for a last look at their beloved commander. Cleburne's aide, Lieutenant L. H. Mangum, found that someone had placed a finely embroidered handkerchief over his face. It evidently was that of his fiancée, Susan Tarleton, a keepsake which Cleburne had kcpt in his pocket.[21]

By midmorning Mrs. John McGavock took for safekeeping Pat Cleburne's kepi and sword; then the four generals' bodies were loaded in several wagons and taken to Columbia. During the evening of December 1st Pat Cleburne's body lay in the parlor of Dr. William J. Polk's residence. At 3:00 P.M. on December 2d, Chaplain Charles T. Quintard, who had earlier that afternoon officiated at Strahl's funeral, conducted ceremonies in the Polk parlor. Burial occurred at Rose Hill Cemetery, only a few blocks away. Yet Cleburne, Granbury, and Strahl, it was discovered, had been interred in what was known as the "potter's section" of the cemetery, between a row of blacks and Yankee soldiers. Lieutenant Mangum, in particular, was outraged and complained to Lucius J. Polk, who arranged for reburial at Ashwood Cemetery, behind St. John's Church near the Polk family plot. Five new grave sites were dug, and the following day the bodies of Cleburne, Granbury, Strahl, Lieutenant Colonel R. B. Young of the 10th Texas, and Lieutenant John Marsh of Strahl's staff were moved to sites behind the church chosen by Lucius J. Polk.[22]

It was the very spot where one week earlier Pat Cleburne had walked in the rain and spoken of the beauty of St. John's Chapel and its cemetery. "It would not be hard to die if one could be buried in such a beautiful site," he had remarked to his staff.[23]

Lieutenant Walter Whittemore of the 2d Michigan Cavalry had been sent to Franklin at dawn on December 1st to obtain orders for his regiment, then posted on the north riverbank south of Fort Granger. Somehow, the 2d Michigan Cavalry had not been notified of the Federal army's pullback during the night, and the unit remained oblivious of Franklin's occupation by the Confederates. Whittemore crossed at the ford and rode into town, only to suddenly discover that he was surrounded by Confederate soldiers. Amazingly, they took little notice of him. Whittemore hastily withdrew and galloped back to his regiment with the startling news. What had saved him, he later realized, was that so many Confederates were dressed in parts of captured Federal uniforms.[24]

Meanwhile, at the riverbank some of the 2d Michigan's men were found chatting with a few Confederates who had come to the river to wash and make coffee. "Hello, boys!" they had called to the Federals. "What are you doing there? We thought you had skedaddled." The Michiganders replied, "Oh, no, we're guarding this ford." Five minutes later, wrote a Michigan cavalryman, when they found out what had happened, they were galloping for Nashville. It was "some miles" before they came up with their own rear guard. To their considerable relief, the Confederate cavalry, seen hovering in the distance, did not harass their withdrawal. That evening the 2d Michigan Cavalry went into bivouac within a few miles of Nashville, thankful to have escaped without a fight. It was the first day in more than a week that they had not exchanged shots with Forrest's cavalrymen.[25]

When Hardin Figuers had watched John Hood ride through Franklin that morning, he was disappointed by the general's appearance. Instead of a vigorous and vibrant Confederate general there appeared only this rather disheveled man in a long, tawny mustache and whiskers, with a wooden leg sticking out. Later, while he was comfortably seated in Mrs. William Sykes's yard, Hood's mind turned from the suffering of his own army to the escape of Schofield's. Before 11:30 A.M. he sent orders to A. P. Stewart to get his men over the Harpeth River by evening. Forrest's cavalry, followed by Stephen D. Lee's Corps, would lead the pursuit, and the infantrymen were expected to be en route at noon.[26]

Forrest's pursuit had gotten off to a poor start. Following a delay to get his artillery forward, he skirmished briefly with a few of Wilson's cavalrymen near Brentwood. From a few prisoners, Forrest learned that Schofield had already reached Nashville with his trains intact. So frustrated were some of Forrest's men that when several troopers from the 2d Tennessee Cavalry returned from the skirmish line with a Yankee prisoner, one man wanted to "prowl [parole] him" on the spot, evidently to get his boots and equipment. No, insisted another man, he would not be party to cold-blooded murder. Later, the Union captive gave the second man $75 in greenbacks in appreciation for saving his life.[27]

Hood's hoped-for effective pursuit never developed. Stephen D. Lee's Corps, having been directed at 9:00 A.M. to guard Franklin and the captured stores, had to withdraw to camp and prepare for the pursuit. It was about 1:00 P.M. before his leading units crossed the Harpeth River. Cheatham's and Stewart's corps were then in no condition to leave Franklin. Although some of Stewart's troops cleared the battlefield about 3:00 P.M., Cheatham's men remained until December 2d. One of Cleburne's men wrote in explanation: "Our brigade [Granbury's] and the Arkansas brigade [Govan's] are so badly cut up that we can't move. Some officers have no men, and some companies have [no] officers. So we have to reorganize and consolidate; a captain has to command the brigade."[28]

Word of the battle had traveled quickly. The *Detroit Free Press* columns headlined the startling news on December 2d: "Confirmation of Union Victory in Tennessee, General Forrest Reported Killed, Hood's Forces Gathering up Horses, Mules, and Negroes, Federal Forces Have Evacuated Nashville, Are in Line of Battle North of Nashville, A Great Battle Momentarily Expected." Various Northern newspapers thus seemed to give greater coverage to the pending fate of Nashville than to actual accounts of the Franklin fighting.[29]

According to the *Detroit Free Press* the battle had been won when "our generals, rallying their troops, swung around the Rebel flank and got them in the center." The account continued, "The tide was now turned, our men inspired with success gave wild hurrahs, and swung back on the Rebel line like an avalanche, hurling the enemy back in the wildest disorder and confusion. Night was now setting in, yet we followed up our advantage. What once threatened to be a disastrous defeat was turned into a glorious victory." The paper claimed that the Confederate losses were 6,000 men against 300 Federal casualties, and only belatedly reported that General Pat Cleburne had been killed. The news media's inaccurate handling of Franklin became one of the reasons why this extraordinary battle has been among the most unappreciated in American history.[30]

Franklin was "the thunder drum of war," wrote a soldier awed by the battle's terrible fury. Indeed, among the participants many considered that it had been their ultimate test, their severest and most desperate battle ever. A hardened veteran of the Twenty-third Corps felt that it was a much harder fight than Perryville or even Atlanta. The Rebels seemed to have fought with an unusual desperation and "were perfectly reckless of danger." In fact, he believed they were "half drunk." One of Cox's battlewise staff officers confided to his wife on the day following the fight: "I do earnestly believe that it was the hardest fought battle that has taken place during the war. . . . [The enemy] charged and fought like perfect fiends." A. P. Stewart's comment that it was "the most furious and desperate battle of the war in the West" coincided with that of many of his fellow generals. Even Hood, who had been in the thickest of the fighting at Antietam and Gettysburg, acknowledged that Franklin was "one of the fiercest conflicts of the war."[31]

"Franklin was the grave of the Army of Tennessee," considered a still bitter Confederate veteran many years later. "[It was] a desperate fight that shall live in history as one of the bloodiest battles, for the number engaged . . . and the time of actual conflict, that has ever occurred in civilized warfare," thought one of Stanley's officers. Another veteran wrote that the grand charge at Franklin "exceeds in interest and tragic and dramatic results any event in modern war. History will surely place it where it belongs, as the greatest drama in American history."[32]

The tragic loss in perspective from experience to conception was well reflected by a former Federal officer, who many years later admitted that the battle at Franklin, while "unprecedented for desperation, pluck, and determination" by the soldiers of both armies, was "never given the prominence and place in history to which it is entitled."[33]

Although sometimes referred to as the "Gettysburg of the West," Franklin's significance suffered from the beginning due to a variety of circumstances. With the battlefield in Confederate hands, there was no immediate on-site reporting by the Northern press. Despite the shocking tales of severe enemy losses in Northern newspapers, Franklin was accorded only brief publicity amid the ongoing whirlpool of war. With the subsequent drama involving the siege of Nashville, Sherman's march through Georgia, and the building suspense at Petersburg, Franklin was only one episode in what had become a sustained, casualty-filled mode of continuous warfare. Whereas many of the great battles and campaigns of previous years had been isolated and of limited duration, the continual strife in December 1864 was conducive to only brief, fragmentary coverage. In the South, the painful losses of so many men remained largely unpublicized. Much of the news of the enormous carnage came from captured or smuggled Northern papers, and letters from the soldiers. Then, with the ending of the war, the outrageous failure at Franklin was often overshadowed in Southern literature by fonder historical segments—the memory of brilliant leaders and their successful battles. Only in the vividly ingrained memories of the veterans did the true significance remain.

The immediate aftermath of Franklin proved the point that the Confederate army would never again be the same. If no one else, those who were there knew. Devastated, and denied the leadership of some of its best combat generals and officers, the army immediately looked askance upon this fateful fight. Controversy and ill will were soon rife among the senior officers and generals, adding to the further disillusionment of the army.

"[We were] led out in a slaughter pen to be shot down like animals," wrote a disgusted Confederate officer of the fatal frontal assault. "It was an attempt to make good by reckless daring the blunder which incapacity had occasioned the preceding day," he added, concluding that it all had been "a useless sacrifice." Another soldier thought, "To attack intrenched troops, superior in numbers, advancing over an open plain without cover, was a disregard of the rules of war, a waste of precious lives, and a wrecking of an army."[34]

One of Hood's Mississippi privates later wrote about what he had seen and felt as he wandered over the battlefield on the following morning:

> Many of the dead were shot to shreds. And I saw scores of [wounded] men . . . who had put their thumbs into their mouths and had chewed them into shreds to keep from crying, coward-like, as they lay exposed to the merciless fire. . . . Franklin was the only battleground I ever saw where the faces of the majority of the dead expressed supreme fear and terror. . . . Their eyes were wide open and fear staring. Their very attitude as they lay prone upon the ground, with extended, earth clutching fingers, and with their faces partially buried in the soil, told the tale of [the] mental agony they had endured before death released them.[35]

Why had the men been allowed to roam at will over that corpse-strewn field? he asked. Already dispirited by the bloody repulse, from that time on the men seemed to resign themselves to inevitable defeat. The "unwise rambling of our men over the battlefield of Franklin broke their spirit," he sadly wrote.[36]

Thereafter, the specter of Franklin "stalked among us," said this Mississippian. Indeed, the men already knew what Hood didn't—that the army was now but a hollow shell, intact in form only. The substance within, the vital fiber, was gone—drained from the Army of Tennessee's arteries as surely as the torrent of crimson that had forever stained the fertile soil at Franklin.[37]

One of Cleburne's men, brooding over Hood's obvious deception of his own soldiers, became perhaps the best spokesman for the all-suffering ranks when he wrote in his diary: "General Hood has betrayed us. This is not the kind of fighting he promised us at Tuscumbia and Florence, Alabama when we started into Tennessee. This was not a fight with equal numbers and choice of the ground. . . . The wails and cries of widows and orphans made at Franklin, Tennessee, November 30th, 1864 will heat up the fires of the bottomless pit to burn the soul of General J. B. Hood for murdering their husbands and fathers." Hood's actions "can't be called anything else but murder," he asserted. "He sacrificed those men to make the name of Hood famous; when [and] if the history of [Franklin] is ever written it will make him infamous." The men had a right to be told the truth; therefore, "Vengeance is mine sayeth the Lord, and it will surely overtake him."[38]

John Bell Hood, far from acknowledging responsibility, or even that a disaster had occurred, sent his initial dispatch to Richmond three days after the battle, December 3, 1864. Choosing his words carefully, he claimed a victory of sorts, saying: "We attacked the enemy at Franklin and drove them from their center lines of temporary works into their inner lines, which they evacuated during the night, leaving their dead and wounded in our possession, and retired to Nashville, closely pursued by our cavalry. We captured several stand of colors and about 1,000 prisoners." Only in the acknowledgment of "a loss of many gallant officers and brave men," including twelve general officers, was there any hint of misfortune.[39]

Among his own staff, Hood had most believing in his self-righteousness, even deceiving them as to the condition of the army. "Everybody is in the finest humor, and ready for the fight again whenever Gen. John B. gives the word," wrote his admiring aide-de-camp, Captain F. Halsey Wigfall. Young Wigfall even learned from Hood's provost marshal that the morale of the army "was very much improved by the fight [at Franklin], and the men would go into the next with double vim and impetuosity."[40] At the very same time, some of his generals were candidly writing to their wives at home. "My safe deliverance from the peril of that bloody conflict, the bloodiest by far for the time it lasted of all the battles in which [I have been] . . . engaged," seemed to be a miracle, wrote the still suffering Brigadier General Daniel C. Govan. "As usual, General Cleburne's and Cheatham's [John C. Brown's] divisions bore the brunt of the fight and sustained the heaviest loss. It really seems as if it were intended that we should do the fighting of the army—as where the severest opposition is to be encountered then we are surely to be placed. Our division was decimated, losing one half of its officers and men." Solemnly he reflected on the meaning of it all. "That I am left alive to write you I feel is due alone to a 'Special Providence,' whose shield has so often covered me on the day of battle. Just after the fight . . . was over I received one of your affectionate . . . letters. I read it surrounded by the dead and dying, and you can't imagine what exquisite pleasure it afforded me." Even Hood's protégé, Stephen D. Lee, who commanded Hood's old corps, admitted that the army was "a little sad" over the great losses, and that "it really seems . . . as if bad luck follows this army. If we had ordinary luck we would have been in Nashville."[41]

The enormity of what had happened was never revealed. Hood never published the detailed combat losses of his army. His official reports stated that "our entire loss was about 4,500 [men]." Only in the reasonably complete reports from A. P. Stewart's Corps and the Federal army's subsequent accounting of Confederate grave sites, enemy wounded still in hospitals at Franklin, and prisoners taken can a generally accurate estimate be made. Of Hood's approximately 23,000 infantrymen present for the assaults, an estimated 7,000 became casualties, nearly a one-third loss ratio. A. P. Stewart's Corps reported a total loss of 2,108 from eight brigades, numbering perhaps 8,000 men carried into the fight. Cheatham's Corps suffered even greater losses, fighting at the storm center of the battle, and Ed Johnson's Division from Lee's Corps reported a total of 587 casualties. Further to be added were the losses of Forrest's cavalry, a total of 269 men during November, some of which participated in fighting the Federal infantry at Franklin.[42]

When the Federal army reoccupied Franklin in December, they counted 1,750 Confederate grave sites on the field, 3,800 disabled enemy soldiers in Franklin's hospitals, and 702 prisoners who had been taken to Nashville with Schofield's army. In all, this total of 6,252 Confederate casualties should be augmented by the "very large" number of slightly wounded who returned to duty, and other dead and wounded buried and cared for elsewhere. Reflecting the burials at Columbia and the wounded cared for in that area, an assessment of 7,000 Confederate soldiers lost in five hours of fighting seems quite conservative.[43]

In contrast, Schofield's army suffered comparatively small losses. The Fourth Corps lost 1,368 men, nearly all of whom were Wagner's men, and the Twenty-third Corps suffered only 958 casualties, resulting in a combined loss of 2,326 (to this total, however, the cavalry's 287 casualties should be added). Only 189 Federals were listed as killed, but this figure must be increased by a substantial portion of the 1,104 reported missing. Of the approximately 22,000 Federal infantry actually engaged in the battle, only about ten percent became casualties, most having resulted from the tactical mistake involving Wagner's division.[44]

More than 9,000 men suffered injury or capture in close-range combat on the open field at Franklin in merely two hours of daylight and three of darkness. Sixty-five Confederate commanders of divisions, brigades, or regiments were listed as casualties. Thirteen of twenty-eight Rebel generals actually exposed in the fighting had suffered injury or were captured (added to the usual casualty list of twelve generals should be Brigadier General Zachariah C. Deas of Ed Johnson's division, who was "slightly wounded in the leg"). Later, its graying veterans made comparisons with the more publicized battles. At Gettysburg and Franklin the attacking columns of "Pickett's Charge" and "Hood's Assault" (in the central Columbia pike region) were roughly the same, nearly 11,000 infantry. Both assaults occurred over open ground. Yet, as the veterans of Franklin were fond of pointing out, they had approximately two miles to advance, against about one mile for Pickett's men at Gettysburg. There was little artillery support at Franklin, while at Gettysburg a heavy bombardment of nearly two hours had occurred prior to the attack. Further, there were no strong earthworks at Gettysburg to contend with, only a low stone wall and barricades of fence rails. At Gettysburg the attack had been repulsed with an estimated loss of 6,500 total Confederate casualties, about 500 less than had been sustained at Franklin. Unlike the quickly repulsed attack in Pennsylvania, Cleburne's and Brown's men had partially carried their objective and held a portion of the works until the end of the fighting. Thus, some concluded that Franklin was not only a more severe ordeal, but a greater testimonial of the worthy fiber of the Southern fighting man.[45]

Statistics, however, do not tell the whole story. Franklin in many respects had become a dramatic pinnacle of the Civil War. In that magnetic and intensely charged moment of Hood's grand frontal assault, the divergent forces of destiny and human spirit had fatally collided. Magnified by the electrifying emotion of a nation dying, it was for the South one last desperate hurrah. With everything risked on a single, fateful attack, disaster for one army or the other had been certain. For a moment it became eternity in eclipse, the world asunder. No sight was more grand, spectacular, nor became more ghastly.

At Franklin, Tennessee, November 30, 1864, the script somehow evolved into rampant madness. Facing those emplaced batteries, the frowning muzzles of 20,000 poised rifles, the tangled abatis, and the forbidding entrenchments, it seemed the very sacrilege of purposeful combat. "How could a just God look down . . . and witness this horrible tragedy, and not by some hidden hand stop it?" asked a Confederate in retrospect. The cream of Southern blood had been spilled without profit. Only hours following the lost opportunity at Spring Hill, the Confederate Army of Tennessee had been fatally stricken. On Franklin's tragic field lay the wreckage: vital lives and an army's efficacy. Bloody, obscene, godawful, Franklin's carnage represented a mortal scything of the South, in spirit and already too depleted flesh. Infused in the mental torment of an outrageous mistake and a consummate failure was the tantalizing estimate of what might have been. Spring Hill had been the hope, but Franklin became the reality. Stephen D. Lee foresaw one week after Franklin that "such another chance [as Spring Hill] will not be presented again during the war." Triumph, so near, had somehow become tragedy.[46]

Never on a Civil War battlefield, and in few moments in American history, were the elements of contradiction so evident. Franklin witnessed a full embodiment of the Confederacy's power and glory, and the abject disparagement of intelligent reason.

In a larger sense, perhaps for both sides the ultimate meaning of Franklin was reflected in an attitude—showing that there could be solace in the indomitable will of mankind to demonstrate its mettle. As an aged veteran, Frank Cheatham returned to Franklin, where he met a Union veteran who seemed uncertain of being in the company of a former enemy on that terrible field. Cheatham embraced the man and said reassuringly, "Any man who was in the battle of Franklin, no matter which side, is my friend."[47]

CHAPTER XXIV

Forcing the Enemy To
Take the Initiative

IT WAS PERHAPS the most wearisome march of any in their experience, thought one of the Fourth Corps' veteran soldiers. The eighteen-mile night march from Franklin to Nashville, which had begun after midnight, extended through the hours of darkness and well into the midmorning of December 1st. Schofield's dog-tired infantrymen "staggered rather than marched forward" along a roadway crowded with wagons, artillery, and noncombatants, wearily bumping into the men ahead at each abrupt stop. One of Cox's weary officers, while walking and engaged in conversation, kept falling asleep. "Sometimes in the middle of a sentence I would drop off . . . and would stumble and nearly fall, which would wake me," he wrote, noting how "very foolish" he felt at sounding incoherent. David S. Stanley considered that his men "were more exhausted physically than I have ever seen them on any other occasion." Field and staff officers were seen sleeping in their saddles, and even their horses seemed to stagger wearily. Most of the men hadn't slept for two days, and every quarter hour a rest of ten minutes was given. The men would drop at the word *rest* and be asleep when they touched the ground, noticed an officer. It was with great difficulty that the men were aroused to resume the march. In the 96th Illinois, one man continued to sleep even when lifted over a fence. Stragglers and lame soldiers kept falling out along the roadway, and at each fence corner a soldier seemed to be laying there waiting for a wagon to carry him away.[1]

More asleep than awake, the Federal column finally arrived about daylight at Brentwood, nine miles from Nashville. Here the worn-out troops collapsed and began to brew coffee.[2]

*   *   *

John M. Schofield too was utterly exhausted. Upon his arrival at Brentwood he lay on the ground while awaiting the closing up of his army. The removal of Schofield's heavy burden of responsibility and the elimination of many of his anxieties—now that he had finally reached the safe haven designated by Thomas—was an enormous relief. During the night Schofield had received Thomas's guarded reply to the first announcement that Hood's attack at Franklin had been repulsed with heavy losses. "It is glorious news, and I congratulate you and the brave men of your command; but you must look out that the enemy does not still persist." Thomas also reassured Schofield that 5,000 reinforcements under Major General James B. Steedman would be in Nashville by morning, adding, "When he arrives I will start General A. J. Smith's command and General Steedman's troops to your assistance at Brentwood."[3]

But morning found Steedman still on the train to Nashville via railroad from Cowan, Tennessee, and one of A. J. Smith's divisions was only then debarking from their boats. Moreover, Thomas had made another significant decision. Based on information that Schofield was badly outnumbered both in infantry and cavalry, he would not risk another battle until Wilson's cavalry could be reequipped to cope with Forrest. At 3:00 P.M. on the 30th, before the fight at Franklin began, Thomas revealed his concern to a naval officer: "Hood, at present, has a cavalry force so much larger than mine that I have been compelled to fall back and concentrate on Nashville."[4]

Schofield was aroused at Brentwood after daylight on December 1st and told to continue his retreat to Nashville; neither A. J. Smith nor Steedman was coming out to meet him. Schofield was astounded. The more he thought about Thomas's seeming abandonment of his little army, the more he began to resent this "embarrassing" treatment. Schofield had a long list of grievances with Thomas: the preliminary instructions to defend Pulaski, which had been "a false position"; his unwillingness to reinforce him with Steedman's troops while on the Duck River line at Columbia; and the necessity of fighting Hood at Franklin due to Thomas's lack of promptly sending a pontoon bridge. Even more contemptible in Schofield's view had been Thomas's shunting of responsibility by leaving him isolated with two corps to fight off Hood instead of entrusting Nashville to a subordinate and joining the active troops in the field.[5]

Schofield rode ahead to Nashville, where he found Thomas after 8:00 A.M. at his office in the St. Cloud Hotel. Their meeting was icy. According to Schofield, Thomas was "cordial but undemonstrative." Schofield, however, seemed almost abusive in his demeanor. A staff officer noted Schofield's exhaustion, saying he had been so tired and sleepy at Franklin that he seemed unfit to command. By Schofield's account, Thomas remarked that Schofield had done "well," and noticed that he was "tired." Thereafter, the exhausted New York general went to his room in the hotel and slept from noon "until about sunset the next day."[6]

Only minutes before Schofield's arrival, Thomas had learned of Schofield's alleged neglect at Franklin. Lieutenant Colonel William G. LeDuc of Thomas's staff, who had been with Schofield during the battle, advised his commander of "the condition of things and the neglect of Schofield to put the river between his army and Hood's." For a moment Thomas was "dumb with astonishment," said LeDuc, then he seemed "thankful that we had escaped without a disaster." The difficult relationship between the forty-eight-year-old Thomas and Schofield, sixteen years his junior, never had been rectified following Thomas's part in voting a "stern denial of clemency" to Schofield for a minor infraction while a student at West Point. Now, in the days ahead at Nashville, their relationship would become decidedly strained. Schofield began to hold Thomas in increasing disdain for what seemed to be his slow action and faulty leadership.[7]

During the late morning of December 1st there was a proud and emotional entry of Schofield's army within the Nashville lines. Past the onlooking ranks of Thomas's garrison troops marched the veterans of Franklin, their captured battle flags at the head of each regiment. In the 104th Ohio eleven captured banners were vividly displayed. Behind the rows of waving flags marched a sullen column of more than 700 Confederate prisoners, guarded by the 112th Illinois Infantry. "We made the wintry air ring again with our cheers and shouts of triumph," wrote an Ohio veteran. The Southern captives were marched to the penitentiary in Nashville. Prisoners such as Colonel Virgil S. Murphey felt humiliated to endure the curses and taunts of Negro women and children lining the roadway as his column of 113 commissioned officers passed through the suburbs. Soon they were turned over to the provost marshal, paraded for the curious to look at, and then locked up in the large brick penitentiary. Unfed, exhausted, and without blankets, the prisoners thereafter endured what one regarded as "the most miserable [night] of my life." The following day, they were marched to the railroad depot and shipped in locked boxcars to Louisville.[8]

If Schofield's men thought that their triumphant arrival at Nashville would lead to the chance to rest, replenish their needs, and even write letters home, they soon found instead that they were required to return to hard labor. Constructing entrenchments to defend the city would be their lot for the next several days.[9]

Thomas's garrison troops already occupied a defensive network of seven forts and redoubts, some of which had been under construction since 1862, when Nashville was captured after the fall of Fort Donelson. Under the venerable engineer Brigadier General Zealous B. Tower, Nashville's defenses had been rushed toward completion during the fall of 1864. Yet now that heavy numbers of additional troops were present, the Federal lines were pushed outward, well beyond Tower's interior defensive network. Here a series of ridges ran northwest and southeast about a mile and a half beyond

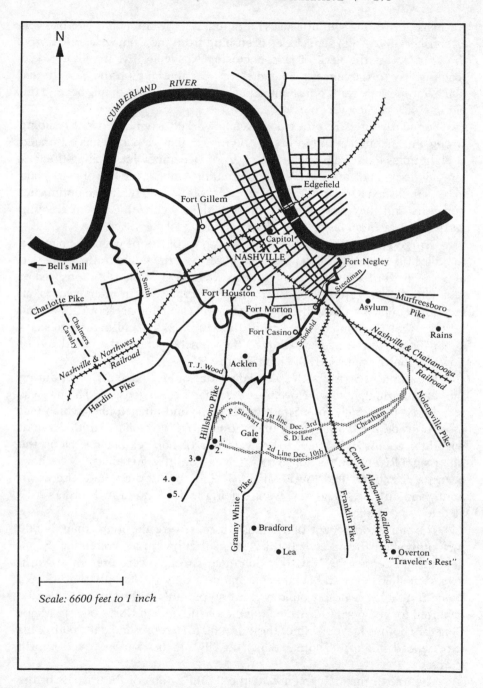

MAP 10   Confrontation at Nashville
December 2–15, 1864

Nashville, providing a natural basis for defense of the city. This outer line was established in a rough semicircle, stretching from the Cumberland River on the west across the neck of land enclosing Nashville. Eventually it would reach nearly to the horseshoe bend of the Cumberland on the east. In distance, it randomly ran from about a half mile to more than a mile beyond the old line of forts and redoubts.[10]

For nearly three days the troops busily worked around the clock building strong entrenchments and fortifying the new defensive perimeter, estimated at eight miles long. Rain fell on the night of December 1st, making the task more difficult, and various houses and buildings outside the line of works had to be demolished to clear a zone of fire. Most of the men remained optimistic, however, and they were mindful of how their wearisome toil in erecting earthworks at Franklin had paid huge dividends.[11]

George H. Thomas had five basic segments of troops which he planned to utilize for Nashville's defense. First there were the 4,000 troops stationed at Nashville during the few days prior to November 30th. Most consisted of garrison soldiers, reserves, and a contingent of the veteran reserve corps, all secondary military elements. So concerned was Thomas about this small number that a volunteer force from the commissary and quartermaster's departments was armed and sent to the trenches under the command of Tower upon the approach of Hood's army.[12]

A. J. Smith's arrival with several divisions of his Sixteenth Corps during the early morning hours of November 30th had been a godsend. Thomas was so relieved he literally took Smith in his arms and hugged him, which was most unusual for the normally undemonstrative Virginian. Smith brought with him about 9,000 men, tough veterans of hard campaigns along the Mississippi River who fashioned themselves "Smith's guerrillas." "We have been to Vicksburg, Red River, Missouri, and about everywhere else down South and out West, and now we are going to Hell, if old A. J. orders us!" asserted one soldier.[13]

The third component of Thomas's forces were the more than 24,000 men of the Fourth and Twenty-third Corps that had just served under Schofield in mid-Tennessee. Now that Schofield's troops were present at Nashville, Schofield reverted back to command of only the Twenty-third Corps. David S. Stanley, whose wound became so painful on December 2d that he departed for the north, turned command of the Fourth Corps over to Major General Thomas J. Wood. Since these 14,000 men represented the bulk of his experienced infantry, Thomas relied heavily on the combat-tested Fourth Corps.[14]

The fourth major segment was the 8,500 troops of the District of the Etowah under Major General James B. Steedman. Steedman had been at Chattanooga, Tennessee, during much of the campaign. Over the past few days Thomas had ordered Steedman to prepare to raid Hood's supply lines at Tuscumbia, Alabama, and destroy his pontoon bridge. Steedman acted accordingly, and was already en route with 5,200 troops at Cowan, Tennessee, on November 30th when Thomas at 5:35 P.M. ordered him to immediately come to Nashville. That night Steedman dutifully reembarked his troops in rail cars. Yet due to the threat of Forrest's cavalry along the railroad, Steedman delayed their departure until daylight. Finally about 7:00 A.M. on December 1st Steedman's trains departed for Nashville, arriving about 5:00 P.M. amid a beehive of activity. Thomas assigned these troops to the extreme Federal left, along the eastern approaches to the city. Many of Steedman's troops were black and, added to Steedman's reputation as a political hack and philanderer, there was considerable gossip about his presence.[15]

Around the last major element of Thomas's command at Nashville, James H. Wilson's Cavalry Corps, there was such an atmosphere of disarray that it precipitated a major crisis. Wilson brought with him about 6,500 badly depleted cavalrymen from the in-field campaign when he rode into Nashville on the morning of December 2d. Wilson's troopers seemed to be in a wretched state, needing clothing, equipment, better arms, and especially horses. Due to Wilson's alarming outcries, Thomas already had made major revisions in his plans. Wilson's assertion that he had only about one-fourth the number of Forrest's cavalrymen caused Thomas to act very cautiously.[16]

Influenced by Schofield's angry assessment of November 30th that "Wilson is entirely unable to cope with him [Forrest]" and Wilson "can do very little," Thomas was convinced that to advance now in a "crippled condition" would be risky and unproductive. Accordingly, he directed that Wilson rest and refit his troops at Edgefield, across the Cumberland River from Nashville, until they were sufficiently equipped and combat-ready.[17]

Due to the navy's presence with various ironclads and gunboats, Thomas estimated that Hood would be unable to cross the Cumberland River. Key towns such as Chattanooga, Bridgeport, Stevenson, and Murfreesboro were strongly garrisoned, and stout blockhouses protected important bridges along the railroads. In Thomas's eyes, he could afford to wait until his consolidated army was in proper condition to fight.[18]

Unfortunately for Thomas, he had made a major political mistake. Having been candid in his conservative views with the Washington authorities, he was unprepared for the storm of controversy that followed. At 9:30 P.M. on December 1st Thomas sent a telegram to Henry Halleck that he would "retire to the fortifications around Nashville until General Wilson can get his cavalry equipped." Thomas's language was explicit: he thought it "best to wait here" until Wilson was ready. "If Hood attacks me here he will be more seriously damaged than he was yesterday. If he remains until Wilson gets equipped, I can whip him and will move against him at once."[19]

Thomas's telegram was brought to Secretary of War Edwin Stanton and was soon shown to Abraham Lincoln. The president was immediately upset by Thomas's intention "to lay in his fortifications for an indefinite period 'until Wilson gets equipments.' '' The president asserted, "This looks like the McClellan and Rosecrans strategy of do nothing and let the Rebels raid the country.'' Lincoln turned the matter over to Stanton with the suggestion that Ulysses S. Grant become involved. Grant, still not on friendly terms with Thomas, promptly fired off two demanding telegrams to Thomas from City Point, Virginia, on December 2d. "If Hood is permitted to remain quietly about Nashville, you will lose all the [rail]road back to Chattanooga, and possibly have to abandon the line of the Tennessee [River]," wrote Grant. He urged Thomas to arm all the noncombatants and leave them in the trenches while he led the army forward to "force the enemy to retire or give fight upon ground of your own choosing. After the repulse of Hood at Franklin, it looks to me that instead of falling back to Nashville, we should have taken the offensive against the enemy where he was," continued the aroused Federal commanding general. "You will now suffer incalculable injury upon your railroads if Hood is not speedily disposed of. Put forth, therefore, every possible exertion to attain this end."[20]

Thomas, somewhat taken aback, advised Grant that evening that following the arrival of A. J. Smith and Steedman he had enough infantry to assume the offensive, and he promised to "take the field . . . as soon as the remainder of General McCook's division of cavalry reaches here, which I hope it will do in two or three days." Thomas also telegraphed to Halleck that he would soon move against the Confederates, "although my cavalry force will not be more than half of that of the enemy."[21]

Thomas was grossly mistaken about Forrest's strength and the overall threat posed by the greatly feared Confederate cavalry leader. Forrest's cavalry numbered less than 6,000 men, was greatly depleted by the hard campaign, and remained deficient in horses and supplies. Moreover, there was a major new development in the offing. Ironically, on the very day Thomas expressed his firm decision to delay his offensive due to the cavalry predicament, John Bell Hood ordered most of Forrest's cavalrymen away from the vicinity of Nashville.[22]

II

The advance of the Confederate army to Nashville had been so uneventful as to become a welcome respite for Hood's soldiers. Forrest's cavalrymen had been the first to arrive near the city, Buford's and Jackson's divisions appearing along the Nolensville pike during the morning of December 2d. Stephen D. Lee's Corps arrived about 2:00 P.M. along the Franklin pike. They were followed on December 3d by A. P. Stewart's Corps and Cheatham's Corps. The appearance of the Confederate infantry along the outlying ridges was cause for the outpouring of intense emotion. As A. P. Stewart's Corps marched past, many ladies were gathered by the roadside, carrying on "in high excitement." The troops were animated, and for some men it was their first glimpse of Nashville and home in many months.[23]

As they swept across the broad range of hills south of Nashville, a vast panorama stretched in full view. "We can see the fine old building of solid granite, looming up on Capitol Hill," wrote one of Cheatham's elated men. It was the Tennessee state capitol, with the Stars and Stripes flying above the large dome. Off in the distance wafted the sounds of Federal bands playing, and the entire scene caused one's pulse to rapidly beat, noted a private. Captain William D. Gale, of A. P. Stewart's staff, said that the spires of the city, appearing so near as to swell their hopes, were as a mecca. "But between us and them there bristles on every hill a fort, and long lines of rifle pits connecting them with the dark blue line of armed men." Visible around the capitol itself were dark earthworks and log stockades mounting frowning siege gun batteries.[24]

About twenty-four hours behind Schofield's army in reaching the vicinity of the Tennessee capital, Hood deployed the Confederate army across nearly a four-mile front. Due to the irregular topography his lines varied from about 500 yards to more than two miles distant from the outer Federal parapets. Stephen D. Lee's relatively unbloodied command, now by far Hood's largest corps, was positioned in the center of the line. A. P. Stewart's Corps connected with Lee on the western flank, stretching toward the Cumberland River below Nashville. Frank Cheatham's soldiers were sent to the far Confederate right, occupying ground opposite Steedman's position.[25]

Already a basic problem was apparent. Hood simply didn't have enough men. Following the bloodbath at Franklin his army had been reduced to about 21,000 effective troops, exclusive of cavalry. All that could be accomplished was to occupy ground from the Hillsboro pike on the left to the Nashville & Chattanooga Railroad on the right. A four-mile gap remained between the Confederate left and the river. On the right flank a void of more than a mile extended to the river above Nashville. Adding to the manpower deficiency, about 2,000 of Cheatham's infantry under William Bate had been detached from the army on December 2d and sent toward Murfreesboro, twenty-eight miles distant.[26]

Other serious problems plagued Hood's "siege." His army was so short on artillery ammunition that he ordered on December 2d, "Not a cartridge of any kind will be burned until further orders, unless the enemy should advance on us." Empty wagons of Lee's Corps were then being rushed to Columbia for ammunition.[27]

Why Hood attempted to besiege Nashville following his devastating loss at Franklin has long been the subject of debate and controversy. In his postwar memoirs, Hood said that his choices were limited: he couldn't advance across the Cumberland River without receiving large reinforcements, and he couldn't turn south and retreat due to the "sinking fortunes of the Confederacy." He thus was left with "the only remaining chance of success"—to advance on Nashville, entrench, and provoke Thomas's attack.[28]

Hood's postwar posturing notwithstanding, he appears to have had no set plan or basic concept when he ordered the pursuit of Schofield to Nashville. Rather, his plans were improvised based on intuition and changing day-to-day circumstances. Immediately after Franklin there were continual changes or revisions in his tactical operations, suggesting a less than structured central plan. Perhaps the best explanation for this is that Hood perceived Nashville much as an evolving dilemma. As long as the political focus was on Hood's northern invasion and siege of a major Federally occupied city, it was positive publicity and salve for Hood's injured ego. Yet the military practicality of the matter was in serious doubt, as Hood knew all too well. Once at Nashville he confronted a vastly superior adversary, being so outnumbered and vulnerable as to face the possibility of utter destruction.[29]

Hood, it appears, had resolved to take all that the enemy gave him in evacuated territory. Yet the Confederate commander could not expect to gain the heavily fortified Tennessee capital unless Thomas made a serious blunder. This, in fact, became the real basis for Hood's actions. The enemy's mistakes were his only hope. John Bell Hood was not thinking of risk so much as the potential reward. Again, he would seek to win by a familiar method—through sheer audacity.[30]

In rationalizing his actions, Hood had ready explanations: Forrest's cavalry would patrol the gaps existing on both flanks, negating an enemy flanking movement. Reinforcements would be summoned from eastern Tennessee and the trans-Mississippi department, enabling the Army of Tennessee to sustain its position. Railroads would be repaired from Alabama through Tennessee, bringing ammunition and critically needed supplies. By building strong entrenchments and heavily fortifying his lines, the enemy would have to attack Hood's army in place to free Nashville from siege. Should the Federals be "handsomely repulsed," the Confederate army might then "follow up our advantage on the spot, and enter the city on the heels of the enemy."[31]

It was an incredible concept. Hood did not seem to know by what exact method he would win—even a highly placed staff officer said a week after their arrival in front of Nashville, "I cannot tell whether we will remain here all winter or not, nor do I think Genl. Hood himself knows." Another close observer, one of Hood's own staff, wrote what might be a fair approximation of Hood's reasoning: "I don't believe myself that the Yankees will allow us to enter winter quarters . . . without a fight. Of course, in order to make a fight they must leave their entrenchments, and if they attack us in ours, or allow us to attack them without works, I feel not the slightest fear of the result."[32]

Hood was gambling his last few assets, attempting to maintain his strategic offensive by means of a defensive ploy. By surrendering the tactical initiative, he hoped to provoke Thomas's attack. No matter that many of his plans seemed conflicting and self-defeating, his maneuvering was intended only to draw the enemy out of their strong fortifications. Despite the enemy's overwhelming strength, Hood intended somehow to improvise victory. For now Hood and his staff rejoiced that the enemy was "cooped up in his works and the fruits of two years hard marching and fighting [was] lost to him [due to the Confederate occupation of much of Tennessee]."[33]

John Bell Hood considered the jumbled disposition of his forces at Nashville. In the face of what he perceived as disorganized and dispirited enemy troops within the city's defenses, early in the siege Hood decided to alter his original plans involving the various isolated Federal garrisons in mid-Tennessee. The town of Murfreesboro, in fact, became an increasingly central element in Hood's calculations, reflecting his growing conviction that it was the key to taking Nashville.

Hood's original concept seems to have been merely to keep the respective enemy forces at Nashville and Murfreesboro separated by destroying the railroad between the two sites. By December 11th, however, Hood had modified his plans to "force the enemy to take the initiative." Regarding the Murfreesboro garrison as vulnerable, and believing his detached troops could prevent the enemy from foraging in the countryside for food, Hood felt he could force a fight with Thomas on favorable terms. By applying continuous pressure on what he understood was Murfreesboro's disheartened 6,000 (actually 8,000) man Federal garrison, Thomas might be forced to march to their relief. "Should this force attempt to leave Murfreesboro, or should the enemy attempt to reinforce it, I hope to be able to defeat them," wrote Hood on December 11th. When Thomas came out of Nashville to relieve Murfreesboro, he must attack the Confederates in their fortifications. Or, if the Murfreesboro garrison attempted to evacuate, there would be an opportunity to cut off that column.[34]

It was Sherman's old strategy of Atlanta recalled. Hood intended to draw Thomas out to his destruction. He was so elated by this new concept that he told Chaplain Quintard the next day that "this campaign will change very greatly the movements of both armies. There will be no more great flanking operations . . . the enemy will have to seek out our armies and fight them. . . . There will be more blood spilled in 1865 than in 1864—but . . . the losses will be on the side of the Federals." Hood thought he plainly saw the key to successful future operations. Thereafter, the Confederate army would cut off and isolate one of the plentiful Federal garrisons throughout the South. Then, once the besieging force fortified, any relieving Yankee army would have to attack heavily prepared lines. Tactical victory would presumably follow.[35]

Hood's reasoning reflected his dire plight. Detached operations by the cavalry and a few infantry units in the vicinity of Murfreesboro would be the key elements of his strategy during the siege of Nashville. The focus of their activity was to threaten this location's 8,000-man Federal garrison. Rather than raid Thomas's vulnerable supply line north of the Cumberland River or disrupt the reorganization and replenishment of Wilson's cavalry, Forrest's command, by Hood's order, was split into fragments. Unknowingly, Hood had expended his only superior military asset on a side bet gambit and seriously weakened the tactical efficacy of the Nashville army that was intended to be his actual basis of victory.[36]

Forrest's cavalrymen already were touting a string of successes that seemed to influence Hood's thinking. On Friday, December 2d, following the arrival in front of Nashville of Stephen D. Lee's Corps, Forrest with Buford's and Jackson's divisions had turned south along the railroad toward Murfreesboro to tear up telegraph lines and destroy various enemy blockhouses guarding key bridges.[37]

Five miles from Nashville at Mill Creek stood Blockhouse No. 2, an oak log structure guarding the railroad trestle bridge. Buford's Kentucky brigade was in the process of surrounding the blockhouse when unexpectedly a train was heard approaching from the south.[38]

Unknown to Buford, it was the last of the northbound trains bringing Steedman's troops to Nashville from Cowan, Tennessee, following a derailment the previous day. Forrest's artillery caught all on board by surprise, and the engine was an easy target, being quickly disabled. In great confusion, 227 men of the 44th and 80 soldiers of the 14th U.S. Colored Troops poured out of the boxcars. They crowded around the blockhouse, only to discover that there was but little room in the small stockade. Hurriedly, the senior officer present, Colonel Lewis Johnson of the 44th U.S.C.T., formed his men and sent them up the hillside near the blockhouse. Here, along the wooded slopes, Johnson's men hastily fashioned crude breastworks of logs and brush.[39]

Forrest, who had been watching from an opposite hill, galloped over to Buford's position, being angry with Buford for not having torn up the track and prevented the reinforcement of the stockade. Take that stockade, ordered Forrest. "How do you expect me to take it, General?" asked Buford. "Stop the portholes with rails and burn it," Forrest replied. As Forrest dashed off, Buford readied his men for an attempt to storm the blockhouse. Yet the fire from Johnson's black infantrymen was too intense. Combined with the fire from the stockade, Buford's Kentuckians and the 2d Tennessee Cavalry were kept at bay until dark.[40]

Having fired nearly all their issued forty rounds per man of small-arms ammunition, Johnson's men were down to an average of four rounds each. Fearful that if he surrendered, "a butchery would follow," Johnson determined to fight his way through the Confederate lines that night. At 3:30 A.M. his men and the stockade garrison pressed silently forward in the rain and darkness. Amazingly, the entire column managed to pass undetected through the line of Confederate pickets and arrived "without much trouble" at the Federal Nashville lines about daylight. Left behind at the abandoned stockade were 12 dead and 46 wounded. Another 2 officers and 113 men were found to be missing. The damaged train also fell into Confederate hands, but for Forrest it was an empty victory—most of the enemy had escaped.[41]

When he arrived in Nashville and reported to Thomas's headquarters, the lieutenant commanding the stockade garrison was surprised to learn that an order for the evacuation of all blockhouses along the railroad from Nashville to Murfreesboro had been issued two days earlier. Yet the courier had failed to deliver the message to many of the half dozen blockhouses, due to the presence of Confederate cavalry. As a result, these small stockades lay vulnerable to Forrest's rampaging horsemen.[42]

Working his way a short distance northward, on December 3d Forrest captured without a fight Blockhouse No. 1, four miles from Nashville. Again riding southward, Forrest lay siege to No. 3. When it surrendered on the 4th after a brief shelling, Forrest ordered the destruction of all captured stockades. Already, Forrest had taken about 150 Federal prisoners.[43]

Next along the railroad line lay Blockhouse No. 4, near La Vergne, Tennessee. The commander of this post had just received Thomas's order to immediately evacuate and was preparing to abandon La Vergne on the morning of the 5th. Without warning, the men of Jackson's Division surrounded his position, and due to the threat of a massacre, the garrison was quickly surrendered. Among the captured property were two field guns, twenty-five horses, and seventy-three men, including the 115th Ohio regiment's band.[44]

Hood was so pleased with his cavalry's operations that he had a circular distributed to the army on December 5th announcing these small victories. Forrest's successes caused Hood to significantly alter the cavalry's basic role and led to several impulsive revisions in his own plans. Earlier, on December 2d, Hood had told William Bate, then en route to Murfreesboro with his infantry division, that "General Forrest will send some of his cavalry to assist you [in destroying the railroad]."[45]

Thus, when Hood ordered Forrest to proceed to Murfreesboro with two entire divisions (Jackson's and Buford's), only 250 cavalrymen were left behind in order to patrol the open ground on the army's right flank. Also, Chalmers's full division would stay at Nashville to watch the army's western flank. Hood's concept then involved the capture of Murfreesboro as part of his newly evolved plan to permanently occupy Tennessee.[46]

On December 7th Forrest suggested that if the enemy were allowed to evacuate Murfreesboro, he could strike their column en route north or northeast. Hood thought "the idea a good one," but a few days later he decided it best to keep the Federal garrison cooped up in Murfreesboro, so as to draw Thomas out of his formidable defenses. Forrest's ever-changing role thus evolved into that of a mere auxiliary. He was to hem in the Murfreesboro garrison and prevent their obtaining supplies or reinforcements, which would compel Thomas to march to their relief.[47]

These changes and modifications so confused Forrest that on December 11th he went to see Hood at his headquarters near Nashville. After meeting Hood at John Overton's fine residence, Forrest stayed the night, sharing a bed with chaplain Charles Quintard due to the crowded conditions at headquarters. An observer noted, "It is the lion and the lamb lying down together." Quintard thought so, too. After listening to Forrest's outspoken manner, he considered the fierce cavalryman a man of remarkably fine personal appearance with a great vigor of thought and expression—"an uncut diamond."[48]

Forrest's detached division under the veteran horseman James R. Chalmers also contributed significantly to Hood's revised program of pressuring Thomas into a rash attack against the Confederate army's fortified lines. Designated to patrol the large area existing between the Southern infantry's flank along the Hillsboro pike and the Cumberland River, Chalmers made a most significant disposition.[49]

On December 3d he sent 300 horsemen and two rifled Parrott guns under Lieutenant Colonel David C. Kelley to a bluff across from Bell's Mill on the Cumberland River, about four miles below Nashville by land, but eighteen by river. Kelley promptly emplaced his section of guns on high ground above the waterway and blockaded the river. Two transports laden with horses and mules soon were compelled to surrender under his guns. A squadron of four Federal "tinclad" gunboats appeared that afternoon and shelled Kelley's artillery, but darkness caused them to break off the fight. On December 4th the gunboats reappeared, and the USS *Moose* and the other boats were able to drive off Kelley's cannon and recapture the transports. Yet Kelley had made away with 56 prisoners and 197 horses and mules. When the gunboats retired he reestablished his artillery, and again blockaded the river. A few days later two more rifled guns were sent to reinforce Kelley's section. When the *Moose* attempted to lead a convoy of transports downriver on December 6th they were driven back under a heavy fire. Again on the 8th a Federal gunboat "came to grief in [an] exchange of iron at Bell's [Mill]," reported a Nashville telegraph operator. Although two days too late to stop A. J. Smith's transports from ascending the Cumberland River to Nashville, Chalmers's artillerists now firmly controlled navigation below the city.[50]

By the 8th, with the water level five feet over the shoals and falling, the Federal naval commander at Nashville, Lieutenant Commander Le Roy Fitch, advised Thomas that even if he ran past the Confederate cannon he could not pass farther down the Cumberland than Ashland. Moreover, the naval commander at Clarksville, Acting Rear Admiral S. P. Lee, warned Thomas that due to low water he could not steam up the Cumberland past Davis's Ripple and the Harpeth River shoals with his powerful ironclad, the *Cincinnati*. As the Confederates occupied the river between the shoals and

Ashland, a seventeen-mile stretch of the Cumberland was inaccessible to the Federal gunboats. In effect, the Cumberland River was blockaded below Nashville with or without Kelley's Parrott rifles. Even worse, with the river expected to remain at low stage for the duration of the winter, there was ample opportunity for the Rebel army to cross the Cumberland to the north shore. Already on the 8th there were reports of enemy cavalry foraging along the north bank, "taking cattle and everything within reach."[51]

On that very day, a fretful U. S. Grant in City Point, Virginia, envisioned "a foot race" between Hood and Thomas to the banks of the Ohio River. Grant urged that the governors of various states be called to send a force into Kentucky if necessary. Thomas's only reply was that he had "requested" the navy to patrol the river and prevent any crossing. To the responsible naval officer, Admiral S. P. Lee, Thomas was more forthright. "I have just received a report . . . that the enemy have crossed the river below [the] Harpeth. I will be much obliged if the *Cincinnati* can get up to the Harpeth Shoals . . . and destroy their pontoon bridge, if they have one laid down." Admiral Lee, however, curtly reminded Thomas that the *Cincinnati* "cannot remain here" due to the falling water, lest it be trapped at Clarksville all winter. Lee, in fact, was then in the process of evacuating Clarksville and steaming down the Cumberland River with all of his deep-draught vessels. Thomas was so upset by this that he requested Admiral Lee to remain and take the risk of wintering with his flotilla at Clarksville. Indeed, three days later, Thomas, in responding to another enemy crossing of the Cumberland, wired Admiral Lee that a Confederate force near Cumberland City had captured two steamers and were using them to cross the river. Lee was asked to "send down the river and recapture the boats and destroy the enemy's force." Thomas urged, "If you can do so, I shall be much indebted to you, as it is very important service."[52]

George Thomas need not have been so worried. Hood was not thinking of crossing the Cumberland River and raiding north. In fact, at the time Hood was busily preparing to attend a wedding.[53]

CHAPTER XXV

Gabriel Will Be Blowing
His Last Horn

JOHN BELL HOOD was in the grandest of moods. Ensconced in his comfortable headquarters, "Traveler's Rest," the home of John Overton, on the Franklin pike six miles from Nashville, Hood was elated with the multitude of captures by Forrest's command and the burgeoning prospects for a victory over Thomas's forces. Thomas seemed to be doing little, while Hood, by means of Forrest's cavalry, was applying severe pressure aimed at drawing the enemy out of their fortifications. Until Thomas responded there was little to do but wait and enjoy what one of his staff officers described as "one of the gardens of the world." Stephen D. Lee confided to his wife on December 6th, "Lily, this is the most beautiful country in the world. I have never seen anything like it. Your Mississippi lands are as rich, but *not* so beautiful. Here everything is rich and luxuriant, even in winter. The country is beautifully rolling with stately and venerable trees—the woods are all lawns—rich lands, fat cattle—hogs, & etc." Lee even thought one other aspect remarkable: "The ladies are all beautiful and assimilated with the general features of this noble country. It is too beautiful to be held by the infernal Yankees and we must hold it."[1]

John B. Hood thought so, too—especially since it involved being in the company of pretty ladies. Several Nashville girls had managed to sneak out of the city and were at Hood's headquarters, among them Bucky Allison, Sally Acklen, and Mary Hadley. Mary Hadley was betrothed to Major William Clare of Hood's staff, and on the spur of the moment they decided to get married. Stephen D. Lee found the two young women who entertained him on the evening of the 6th to be "the most elegantly dressed ladies I have seen since the war. They were Washington belles before the war and [are] perfect ladies of the world," he advised his wife. They "played elegantly on the

harp" and "possessed many accomplishments, particularly in small chat."
Obviously homesick, and enraptured by an uncommon wartime luxury—
female companionship—Lee puffed with obvious delight when told by these
charming ladies "what a great man I was. . . . They told me that the Yankees
said I had written my parole at Vicksburg with blood drawn from my arm.
I informed them I never had been guilty of so foolish an act." Lee then
decided he had better stop writing to his wife about this womanly interlude,
"for fear you may suspect me."[2]

The swirl of social activity must have fondly reminded Hood of Richmond's gala society and his fiancée, Sally "Buck" Preston. Hood wrote to
Buck, nearly six hundred miles away, and presented her with a fascinating
surprise. Excitedly, she came with the news to Mary Chesnut—"Fancy my
raptures," she gushed, "two letters, and he is coming in January to be
married!"[3]

In Mobile, Alabama, Susan Tarleton was working in the garden on the
balmy afternoon of December 5th. It was their "special" garden, where
Patrick Cleburne had proposed to her. Amid a carpet of azalea, and a soft
sprinkle of warm rain that fell in their faces, he had promised his love, and
she hers. It was one of her most cherished moments.

There was a distant commotion of voices out on Claiborne Street. A
newsboy was selling papers. Faintly at first, then more distinctly, she could
hear his youthful cry, "Big Battle near Franklin, Tennessee! General Cleburne killed! Read all about it!" Susan Tarleton fainted.[4]

II

George H. Thomas was exasperated at the task of hastily putting together an
effective army from the scraps and pieces of Sherman's command, and from
widely dissimilar units and inexperienced troops. From only a few thousand
troops—quartermaster's clerks and other noncombatants—the military populace of Nashville had quickly ballooned to about 60,000 by December 10th.
Yet as an agglomeration of diverse personalities and ambitious individuals,
the strain of melding rival factions and disgruntled officers into a serviceable
combat organization weighed heavily on the commander of the Department
of the Cumberland.[5]

Perhaps it was due in part to fatigue, but Schofield's troops were hardly
in their Nashville camps before a variety of internal squabbles began. Emerson Opdycke may have precipitated some of the difficulty on Friday, December 2d, when Thomas reviewed Opdycke's brigade. Thomas addressed each
regiment, thanking the men for their heroic conduct at Franklin, and told
Opdycke, "From what they tell me, Colonel, your brigade saved the day."
Opdycke was moved to write congratulatory orders, praising his men in
bombastic terms: "Your bayonets gleaming in the sunlight assailed the victorious foe, crushed him beneath your mighty energies . . . and saved the army

from disastrous overthrow. . . . Your fame is high; defend it and maintain it, or die gloriously in the effort. It is an honor to belong to the 1st Brigade." Thereafter his soldiers were fond of flaunting their newly acquired nickname, "Opdycke's Tigers."[6]

Yet Opdycke's exuberance contributed to the undercurrent of discord among the officer corps. "What would have become of the Twenty-third Corps, Schofield, Cox, and all, if I had been out with Lane and Conrad, instead of where I was?" asked Opdycke. Thomas closely questioned Opdycke on December 2d, and that very same day took specific action against George D. Wagner, who was held responsible for the near disaster at the center of the line.[7]

George Wagner knew he was in deep trouble. Jacob Cox said Wagner appeared at Cox's headquarters tent early in the afternoon of December 1st and "was most anxious to soften the judgment of his superiors." Wagner told Cox that the trouble with his division had occurred because the enemy's attack at Franklin was so sudden that they were outflanked before the officers involved could withdraw. He said it was overzealous gallantry that had resulted in Conrad's and Lane's men defending their position too long.[8]

Thomas was not fooled. He had heard rumors of Wagner's drinking and already had received a scathing report from Joseph Conrad, who had been the victim of Wagner's stay-in-position order. Conrad had not waited for his subordinates to write their reports, as was customary, but on December 1st submitted a critical account. Cox later wrote that when Conrad stated that he had been ordered to hold his men in place at the point of the bayonet, this not only contradicted Wagner's account, but was an indictment "equivalent to preferring charges" against him.[9]

On December 2d Wagner was relieved from command of the division, reverting back to command of what had been Lane's brigade. Aware that the continuing criticism was likely to lead to an official inquiry, or perhaps even a court-martial, Wagner voluntarily retired from the army. On December 9th orders were published announcing Wagner's relief from further duty at his own request. Four days later Wagner left for Indianapolis.[10]

Factious, irritable, and without patience for slights, real or imagined, many of Thomas's battle-stressed ranking generals continued to create a whirlpool of discord about his Nashville headquarters. Particularly peevish was John M. Schofield, who on December 2d was compelled to reply to Brevet Brigadier General Stephen G. Burbridge's complaint to the secretary of war about being relieved from command in Kentucky. Schofield remained adamant in his position, and his attitude was querulous. Moreover, the Department of the Ohio commander was unimpressed by Thomas's leadership, and he later complained about "the folly of trusting high commands to men without such [professional military] education"—a remark aimed at officers like Wagner, Burbridge, and James B. Steedman. George Thomas attempted to circumvent the political consequences of a disgruntled Schofield. On December 7th he appended an endorsement on Schofield's Franklin report, "recommending the gallantry and skill of Major General Schofield to the commendation of the War Department."[11]

Amid the myriad of personnel controversies and rife misunderstandings that Thomas had to continually deal with at Nashville there was even a brief episode with the navy. Thomas was compelled to soothe Admiral S. P. Lee's ruffled feelings in early December when it appeared he had "ordered" rather than "requested" the independent naval commander to cooperate with the army on November 30th.[12]

The underdeveloped manpower situation was somewhat improved on December 8th when Joseph A. Cooper's brigade from the Twenty-third Corps arrived from Centerville, Tennessee, after a circuitous march of 210 miles. Yet the great difficulty of getting supplies from the north was suggested by Thomas's commitment of a sizable cavalry force to protect his tenuous north bank line of communications with Louisville. Two brigades from Edward M. McCook's division, which Thomas had heavily counted on to provide Wilson with the necessary cavalry to begin an offensive, were instead sent to Bowling Green, Kentucky. There they were to guard the railroad against several thousand Confederates under Hylan B. Lyon, who had crossed the Cumberland below Clarksville and were raiding northward.[13]

Of all Thomas's problems, however, the most vexing was reequipping Wilson's cavalry. Thomas was so intimidated by Forrest, and by Wilson's lack of sufficient cavalry to defeat the bold Confederate "wizard of the saddle," that he risked his entire career on delaying until the Federal cavalry was better prepared to fight. Immediately upon their arrival in the Nashville area Wilson and many of his key brigade commanders had complained of their fatigue and want of equipment. Said John T. Croxton on December 2d, "[my brigade] needs rest and must have it."[14]

Wilson had perhaps 7,000 dismounted men, the result of "a ruinous policy" of sending men to the rear for remounts once their horses had been disabled. Such, said Wilson, put "a premium [on] breaking down horses." Already, 22,000 mounts had been furnished at Louisville, Lexington, and Nashville in little over two months, according to Henry Halleck. With Wilson reporting only 10,000 mounted men, Halleck noted on December 5th, "It may be safely assumed that the cavalry of that army will never be mounted, for the destruction of horses in the last two months has there [Nashville area] alone been equal to the remounts obtained from the entire West." Thomas responded that despite previous losses, Wilson must have mounted men, regardless.[15]

This horse shortage was such a critical matter that even Ulysses S. Grant and Edwin Stanton soon became involved. Grant had asked Stanton's permission on December 2d for Wilson to impress all horses needed to remount the cavalry. Stanton emphatically agreed, and on the evening of the 2d he wired Thomas authority "to seize and impress horses and every other species of property needed for the military service in your command." Receipts were to be given the owners, with a maximum of $160.00 allowed for a first-class horse. Wilson soon had various cavalry detachments roaming the country-side, looking for horses. "Spare nothing which is necessary," urged Wilson, "but have everything done in an orderly manner." Within days search parties expanded their activities into Kentucky and throughout Tennessee, giving vouchers in return for the seized animals. Wrote an optimistic Thomas on December 3d, "I . . . hope to be able to report 10,000 cavalry mounted and equipped in less than a week."[16]

Thomas was badly mistaken. "I found the country all the way to Lebanon cleaned of horses; all run off to the Rebel army [so that] we only obtained eight of any account," wrote one of Wilson's frustrated officers who had sent 400 men "out in all directions pressing." As a result, the various detachments were delayed in returning, which drastically affected Wilson's, and thus Thomas's, estimate of the time required to assume the offensive. The days continued to slide past and there was no prospect of a rapid cavalry concentration. Wilson, on December 8th, warned Thomas that the cavalry wouldn't be ready until at least the afternoon of December 11th. Three thousand of his men were still out searching for horses, he said. When they returned, the new horses would have to be shod.[17]

Interestingly, it was now clear what motivated Thomas in his intense quest for more cavalry; he wanted Wilson fully combat ready for defensive purposes—"to protect my flanks"—rather than to pursue and capture Hood's routed army, as later professed by some. Wilson had to have 4,000 horses in a hurry, since Thomas said he needed at least 6,000 cavalry "to cover my flanks," in opposing Forrest's "at least 12,000." As a result, Wilson ordered the seizure of all carriage, hack, and omnibus horses in Nashville, including all other usable mounts available in the city except Adams Express Company horses. Dan Castello's traveling circus was in town, and every horse was taken, excluding "Mrs. Lake's celebrated trick horse, Czar." Even the matched bay carriage horses of Vice President-Elect Andrew Johnson were seized, much to Johnson's chagrin. Johnson, who had just clashed with Wilson over the disposition of several Tennessee state cavalry regiments, considered the matter a personal affront and later referred to the upstart cavalry commander as a "bumptious puppy."[18]

Ulysses S. Grant at City Point, Virginia, had waited patiently for three days following his peremptory instructions to Thomas of December 2d to take the offensive against Hood. On the evening of the 5th his patience began to wear thin. He wired Thomas that "time strengthens him [Hood], in all probability, as much as it does you." Grant urged an immediate attack. Yet Thomas's rather casual reply the following day merely stated that "as soon as I can get up a respectable force of cavalry I will march against Hood."[19]

Grant had heard enough. The papers were filled with the news of Hood penning Thomas up in Nashville. Sherman had dropped out of sight in Georgia. Stalemate had been reached in the fighting around Petersburg, Virginia. Politically speaking, it was a most uncomfortable situation for the Lincoln administration, and now it was affecting Grant in particular. At 4:00 P.M. December 6th Grant wired Thomas a specific, blunt directive: "Attack Hood at once, and wait no longer for a remount of your cavalry. There is great danger of delay resulting in a campaign back to the Ohio River." Thomas seemed at first willing to comply, and telegraphed in response at 9:00 P.M. on the 6th, "I will make the necessary dispositions and attack Hood at once, agreeably to your order, though I believe it will be hazardous with the small force of cavalry now at my service." Since Wilson was not then ready, and so many of his men were absent searching for horses, Thomas soon decided to wait a few days longer.[20]

On the morning of December 7th Edwin Stanton, secretary of war, wired Grant a strong indication of the administration's growing impatience in the Nashville situation. "Thomas seems unwilling to attack because it is hazardous, as if all war was anything but hazardous," quipped Stanton. "If he waits for Wilson to get ready, Gabriel will be blowing his last horn."[21]

Three hours later Grant, never on friendly terms with Thomas, fully threw his weight behind what he seemed to perceive as the administration's displeasure with that commander. "You probably saw my order to Thomas to attack," he wired Stanton in reply. "If he does not do it promptly, I would recommend superseding him by Schofield, leaving Thomas subordinate." The next day he wired Halleck, "There is no better man to repel an attack than Thomas, but I fear he is too cautious to ever take the initiative." Halleck was somewhat taken aback: "If you wish General Thomas relieved from [command], give the order. No one here will, I think, interfere. The responsibility, however, will be yours, as no one here, so far as I am informed, wishes General Thomas removed."[22]

Grant decided to give Thomas one last chance. Concerned about his official responsibility for the success of the overall war effort, and hence his own reputation, Grant particularly feared that Hood "will get to the Ohio River." Such would be politically damaging and personally embarrassing. Grant wired Halleck an hour after receiving his telegram: "I want General Thomas reminded of the importance of immediate action. I sent him a dispatch this evening which will probably urge him on. I would not say relieve him until I hear further from him."[23]

The dispatch Grant referred to was well disguised in its seemingly candid and mentorlike advice—a document of implied support, when in fact it was intended as a last summons to action:

> It looks to me evident the enemy are trying to cross the Cumberland River and are scattered. Why not attack at once? By all means avoid the contingency of a foot race to see which, you or Hood, can beat to the Ohio. If you think necessary, call on the governors of states to send a force into

Louisville to meet the enemy if he should cross the river. You clearly never should cross except in rear of the enemy. Now is one of the finest opportunities ever presented of destroying one of the three armies of the enemy. If destroyed, he never can replace it. Use the means at your command, and you can do this and cause a rejoicing that will resound from one end of the land to another.[24]

If "Old Pap" Thomas missed the urgency in Grant's tone, he was painfully reminded on December 9th by Henry Halleck's blunt wire. "General Grant expresses much dissatisfaction at your delay in attacking the enemy. If you wait till General Wilson mounts all his cavalry you will wait till doomsday, for the waste equals the supply."[25]

On the afternoon of the 9th Thomas dispatched to Washington and City Point two of the most significant telegrams of his life. In dignified but determined terms he expressed his firm resolve to do as he saw best. To Halleck he stated his regret about Grant's displeasure, but said, "I feel conscious that I have done everything in my power to prepare, and that the troops could not have been gotten ready before this."[26]

With Grant, Thomas used a little psychology. He responded that his preparations were "nearly completed" but having been informed "that you are very much dissatisfied with my delay in attacking," he would "only say I have done all in my power to prepare, and if you should deem it necessary to relieve me I shall submit without a murmur."[27]

Grant's reaction was prompt. At 8:00 P.M. on December 8th a fateful telegram had been sent from Nashville to Grant, reporting the enemy scattered for more than seventy miles down the Cumberland River, and that no attack had been made by Thomas. Sanford Kellogg, one of Thomas's staff officers, later heard that Schofield had wired a dispatch highly critical of Thomas to City Point. Allegedly, Schofield was intriguing with Grant to get Thomas relieved, since he was next in line to command the army. Because the message could not be found in the War Department files after the war, it was stated that Schofield had it destroyed when he became secretary of war.[28]

Because there is no actual record and very meager circumstantial evidence of any such correspondence by Schofield at the time, it appears that Grant probably acted solely upon the news from Captain John C. Van Duzer. Van Duzer's dispatch from Nashville at 8:00 P.M. on December 8th advised Grant that there had been "no change in position" and a large enemy artillery force was positioned below Nashville "between here and the shoals."[29]

At 11:00 A.M. on December 9th Grant wired Halleck to telegraph Thomas "orders relieving him at once and placing Schofield in command." Halleck received the message at 1:45 P.M. Thereafter, the following message was prepared for dispatch to Nashville:

War Dept. Adj. General's Office, Washington, D.C., December 9, 1864. . . . The President orders: I. That Maj. Gen. J. M. Schofield assume command of all troops in the Departments of the Cumberland, the Ohio, and the Tennessee. II. That Maj. Gen. George H. Thomas report to General Schofield for duty and turn over to him all orders and dispatches received by him. . . . By order of the Secretary of War.[30]

III

Murfreesboro, Tennessee, had been the site of a particularly bloody midwinter battle fought December 31, 1862, and January 2, 1863, resulting in more than 23,000 casualties, including 3,000 dead. The Battle of Stones River brought about the crucial loss of Confederate control of mid-Tennessee and was a harbinger of later retrograde movements through Chattanooga and Atlanta.[31]

Yet in December 1864 the village of about 4,000 was little changed, except that Fortress Rosecrans, a large and formidable Federal fort, had been constructed just northwest of town along the Nashville & Chattanooga Railroad. Garrisoned by about 1,800 mostly raw Union soldiers, Murfreesboro had been hastily reinforced by about 3,000 troops sent from northern Alabama on November 24th. Further reinforcements had arrived on December 1st, another 3,000 men who had been guarding the railroad near Tullahoma, Tennessee, under Major General Robert H. Milroy. Also, Major General Lovell H. Rousseau, the successful Alabama railroad raider of the past July, had come from Nashville to take personal command on the 28th.[32]

Rousseau's job, as explained by George Thomas on November 29th, was "to hold Murfreesboro secure." Thereafter, most of the small blockhouse and village garrisons south of that town had been called in. In all, Rousseau had about 8,000 men to "hold Murfreesboro against any force Hood will be likely to send against you until we can get our cavalry ready; in about five days I think," instructed Thomas on November 30th.[33]

Two days later Confederate raiders cut Rousseau's telegraph lines, and for ten days the Federal garrison there was without instructions from Nashville. Although Forrest began operating against the blockhouses near Nashville, the region around Murfreesboro had remained comparatively quiet until December 4th. On that day the 13th Indiana Cavalry was sent to investigate the sound of firing in the direction of Nashville. As he neared the midpoint village of La Vergne, the colonel in charge of the patrol, Gilbert M. L. Johnson, met a detachment of the 5th Tennessee (Union) Cavalry, retiring from the Overall's Creek railroad blockhouse (No. 7), about five miles north of Murfreesboro. The blockhouse was under attack, said the Tennesseans, causing Johnson to proceed there. Once at Overall Creek, Johnson and his men came under cannon fire, and after deploying his men along the creek he sent back to Murfreesboro for orders.[34]

Rousseau promptly sent three infantry regiments and a section of artillery under General Robert H. Milroy to the blockhouse's relief. Milroy was

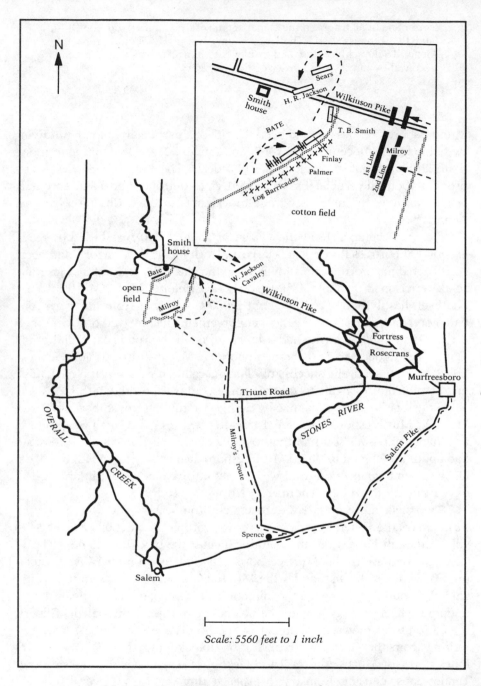

Map 11   Action at Murfreesboro—December 7

still under a cloud, his reputation having been shattered by Richard S. Ewell's troops, who in June 1863 had badly defeated him at Winchester, Virginia, during the preliminary Gettysburg maneuvering. Since Milroy had a price on his head, imposed by Confederates following his antiguerrilla activities in West Virginia, Milroy's transfer west had been timely.[35]

Again spoiling for a fight, Milroy soon found one. On his arrival late in the afternoon, Milroy considered that he was opposing only a portion of Forrest's dismounted cavalry. With more ardor than common sense, Milroy ordered the 13th Indiana Cavalry to make a mounted charge directly at the enemy's three cannon, posted atop a prominent hill. Advancing at dusk, Colonel Johnson's 13th Indiana Cavalry rode into double charges of canister that felled men and horses like tenpins. Being armed with muzzle-loading Enfield rifles, Johnson's men were unable to reload while mounted and under fire. Johnson thus fell back to the creek after losing about forty-two men.[36]

Meanwhile, some of Milroy's infantry had rushed forward beyond Over-all Creek and succeeded in driving back three Florida regiments before with-drawing to the creek under heavy fire. From the estimated twenty Rebel prisoners taken, Milroy learned to his great surprise that the troops he was facing were infantry—Bate's Division of Frank Cheatham's Corps. He wasted little time before ordering a withdrawal. By 1:00 A.M. Milroy and his troops had returned to Fortress Rosecrans.[37]

William Bate had been greatly startled by the encounter. Detached from the army by Hood on the morning of December 2d and told to operate against the Nashville & Chattanooga Railroad—tearing up the track from Murfrees-boro to Nashville—Bate had led his 1,600-man division on what he supposed would be a routine mission. Murfreesboro, he presumed, had been evacu-ated by the Yankees. Instead, on December 4th when Bate arrived at the railroad seven miles north of Murfreesboro, he found that Rousseau, with a 6,000- to 10,000-man garrison, still occupied the fortress and town. Bate was no martyr. His division had taken relatively few casualties at Franklin—only 319 in the less intense fighting along the Carter's Creek pike. Accordingly, he sent a courier to Hood asking for instructions. That night the courier re-turned with Hood's orders to "act according to your judgment," and that some of Forrest's cavalry would soon arrive "to assist you."[38]

Meanwhile, on the 4th Bate had begun operations near the Overall Creek blockhouse, sending Chalaron's battery of three twelve-pounder Napoleons to shell Blockhouse No. 7, while Jackson's Brigade began tearing up the track. Three regiments of Finley's Florida Brigade under Colonel Robert Bullock, and Tyler's Brigade under Brigadier General Thomas B. Smith, were posted in reserve to watch for the enemy. When the fighting began with Milroy's troops, the Florida units had been driven back with the loss of their commander. Once the line was restored, Bate made no effort to attack or pursue the enemy. Indeed, Bate remained on the defensive throughout the fighting on the 4th, being wary of Rousseau. In fact, Bate said the reason he had advanced cross-country from Franklin to the north of Murfreesboro was to avoid being cut off from Hood's army. In all, it was just the sort of nonaggressive attitude that Forrest greatly disdained following his arrival on December 5th.[39]

By Hood's revised instructions delivered to Forrest on December 4th, Forrest and Bate were to operate offensively against Murfreesboro and its fortress in hopes of either capturing these sites or forcing their evacuation. Since Forrest was senior by date of rank, he held command. Forrest thus directed Bate to cease operations on the railroad and march with him to invest Murfreesboro. Bate wanted no part of assaulting the strong fortifications bristling with heavy cannon and said so. Forrest, after closely reconnoitering the fortress, reluctantly agreed that it was too strong to directly attack. Having been reinforced on the evening of the 6th by two small brigades of infantry from the main army (Sears's and Palmer's Brigades), Forrest deployed his combined force of about 6,000 men around Fortress Rosecrans and ordered the construction of earthworks. He wanted to cut off Rousseau's supplies and force the enemy to come out and fight.[40]

Forrest didn't have long to wait. On December 7th Rousseau decided that Forrest's men "were very impudent," coming up to within a mile of the fortress. Noting the presence of Confederate infantry along the Wilkinson pike northwest of town, Rousseau ordered a heavy reconnaissance column to advance on a southwest road, then swing to the right and discover "where the main body of the enemy was." Again the column would move under the command of Robert H. Milroy, but this time he would have seven infantry regiments, one cavalry unit, and a full battery of artillery, a combined total of 3,325 men.[41]

Milroy marched at 10:00 A.M. along the Salem pike for about four miles before learning at a farmhouse that a large force under Forrest was along the Wilkinson pike, three miles northwest of the fortress. Milroy rewarded the farmer for this information by driving off his "60 fine, fat hogs"—to save them from falling into Rebel hands, said the general—then marched cross-country toward the Wilkinson pike.[42]

Forrest had observed the departure of Milroy's column from the fortress, and immediately planned a trap. Wanting to entice Milroy to swing northward and approach his lines from the south, Forrest withdrew his infantry from their position confronting the fortress, and redeployed them on a diagonal southwest of the Wilkinson pike, with their right protected by Overall Creek. Once Milroy advanced to attack this line and was repulsed, he would spring his trap. Jackson's cavalry division was posted in timber north of the Wilkinson pike, ready to swing south and cut off Milroy's line of retreat to the fortress.[43]

From the beginning, Milroy seemed obliging. His infantry approached the Confederate line, which had formed behind improvised barricades across an open field. An artillery duel followed, then Milroy, "finding the enemy would not come across the field to attack me," decided to act with further "prudence." His six-gun battery was out of ammunition and it went back to Murfreesboro to be resupplied. Without artillery, and not knowing in what strength the enemy held the opposite woods, Milroy ordered his troops to fall back through the thick timber. Milroy then began moving to the northeast toward the Wilkinson pike, "not [wanting] to engage them with my infantry without having the fortress in my rear."[44]

Soon Milroy's men emerged from the woods along the Wilkinson pike and formed a line of battle facing west along the road. Within minutes Milroy sent them forward through an old cotton field. Now it was Forrest who was taken unawares. Without cavalry in front to scout Milroy's movements, it was belatedly discovered that Milroy was beyond the Confederate left flank. Forrest hurriedly shifted the entire infantry line to the north. Yet irregular angles with gaps between the various brigades were now evident, and Bate's officers discovered that the two leading brigades had gone too far. Bate went to bring them back.[45]

Meanwhile, Milroy's double lines of infantry had halted in the middle of the field along the Wilkinson pike. Here they began firing repeated volleys at the Confederate line some 200 yards distant. Milroy saw his front line begin to waver, and it seemed that they could not stay there. Milroy was in the act of bringing up his second line when the front line made a spontaneous rush for the enemy's works.[46]

Forrest had just passed among the ranks of the 1st Florida Infantry of Finley's Brigade. "Men, all I ask of you is to hold the enemy back for fifteen minutes, which will give me sufficient time to gain their rear with my cavalry, and I will capture the last one of them," he had shouted. Now Finley's Brigade seemed to be holding their own, despite the 100-yard gap which existed on their left. Suddenly the Floridians jumped up and ran, fleeing from the oncharging Federal infantry in a wild stampede. Evidently, some of the right flank elements of Henry R. Jackson's Brigade, approaching from behind, had fired into the Florida brigade by mistake, instantly sending their ranks scrambling to the rear. Many of Finley's men were wearing Federal coats and jackets, some of which had been recently taken at Franklin. (Before two days passed following the fight, Forrest had field orders published ordering all officers and men "who have blue Yankee clothes and do not have them dyed [gray within ten days] . . . the coats especially will be taken from them. This order is imperative.")[47]

Forrest was infuriated by the unexpected crisis among Finley's men, and then among Palmer's adjacent brigade. He rode among the fleeing men, repeatedly yelling, "Rally, men—for God's sake, rally!" No one paid any attention. The men sprinted away in fright and panic, just ahead of the yelling, rapidly firing Yankees. Amid the swirling smoke a color-bearer ran past, fear etched on his face. Forrest ordered him to halt, but the man kept running. Forrest leveled his revolver and shot him down. Hastily dismounting, he grabbed the flag, remounted, and dashed among the men waving the colors. Again his efforts were futile. "They could not be moved by any entreaty or appeal to their patriotism," later wrote the outraged Forrest. Finally he had to send a staff officer to bring several units of William Jackson's division forward to rescue the remnant of both Finley's and Palmer's brigades.[48]

Milroy's men jubilantly gathered in 207 prisoners, the flags of the 1st and 3d Florida, and two of Chalaron's twelve-pounder Napoleons. When Jackson's division approached on his right flank, Milroy halted pursuit of Bate and withdrew to Murfreesboro.[49]

Forrest complained in his report that the affair on Overall Creek had been "shameful." After withdrawing his beaten infantry to a remote creek, Forrest redeployed his cavalry along the main roads from town in a forlorn effort to keep the enemy from gathering provisions from the countryside.[50]

With his depleted forces, Forrest could but attempt to pen Rousseau's men inside their stronghold. Yet Bate's division was recalled to the main army on December 8th, and on December 9th Hood further tied Forrest's hands by directing him to place his two small brigades of infantry on detached duty at La Vergne, or some midpoint to Nashville. Hood thought this would "prevent the enemy from reenforcing Murfreesboro, and . . . defeat the force at Murfreesboro should they attempt to leave there."[51]

A day later, Hood again revised these plans. Having learned of Wilson's cavalry concentration at Edgefield, and hearing of "talk among the enemy" of Wilson "fitting up for a raid," he now wanted Forrest to guard the country upriver from Nashville. Forrest dutifully sent Buford's Division to the vicinity of Lebanon, to picket the Cumberland River "and prevent any flank movement in that direction." Thereafter, so few troops were available about Murfreesboro that one of Forrest's brigade commanders on December 12th reported his inability to stop a large enemy foraging expedition. "With that [strong enemy] force I could do nothing more than follow them around all day," wrote the exasperated William Jackson. Even Rousseau soon began scoffing at the Confederates' effort to cut off his frequent supply expeditions. "We forage without molestation," he reported on December 12th.[52]

George H. Thomas's dispatch of December 11th to Rousseau announced a firm decision: "You have a good supply of provisions in Murfreesboro, and the major general commanding expects you to hold out against all attacks of the enemy until you are relieved by the forces from this place."[53]

The truth was self-evident. Thomas was not overly concerned about the safety of Rousseau's garrison. Although he was coming out to attack, as Hood had desired, it was with the express objective of destroying Hood's army. Hood had wasted many of his most valuable troops by detaching and scattering them in an attempt to entice Thomas into relieving Murfreesboro.

Moreover, Thomas was ready to attack with an army three times the size of Schofield's former Franklin force, against fewer Rebel troops than were present at Franklin.

Hood had entirely succeeded with his newly developed plan to maneuver the Federal army into attacking—to their prohibitive advantage.

CHAPTER XXVI

The Sunny South Has Caught
a Terrible Cold

THERE IS MUCH EXCITEMENT in Nashville," wrote an alarmed citizen on December 2d. Hood's infantry had just advanced to confront the city's expansive line of defenses, still being constructed by large work details of government employees. The Rebels "are now about 3½ miles from town, and ¾ from our lines," noted one of Stanley's Fourth Corps veterans. "Some people may think that the situation . . . is bad at the best now. [However,] the soldiers can't see it that way."[1]

To Thomas's dogged veterans the prospect of Hood capturing Nashville was beyond belief. "We will defy the whole of Hood's army to get us out of the Rock City," wrote an Illinois soldier. "We are strongly fortified, and all the Rebel hordes could not take the city by assault," boasted a Michigan man. Although skirmishing had broken out and Federal artillery fire was in full play from the forts, the Confederate cannon were generally silent due to a shortage of ammunition. Still, most of the men held an underlying awareness of the decisive fighting that was imminent. A Minnesota lieutenant informed his wife that there would be hot work ahead, and that his men expected some serious fighting soon. Already the bustle of excitement about Nashville gave convincing evidence of the approaching combat. Federal gunboats were busily puffing up and down the Cumberland River looking for signs of the enemy attempting to cross, and all passes to the city were denied pending the expected fight.[2]

By the morning of December 4th most of Thomas's men were in their entrenchments "momentarily expecting an attack." The cannonading of the Federal artillery was almost continuous despite the lack of a Confederate reply, and a portion of the 125th Ohio went outside the works to burn a house between the lines which interfered with the Federal field of fire.[3]

Soon the thoroughly weary men were expressing their anxiety "for the ball to open." Having been posted in their entrenchments night and day for two days, by December 5th they cited renewed skepticism that Hood would attack. "I have no fears of the Rebels taking Nashville but am afraid they will not fight us here," lamented an Ohio gunner.[4]

Although the skirmishing continued, by the end of the first week in December the mood had shifted to that of a semi-relaxed vigilance, and even indifference as to the frequent picket firing among the outposts. The men became so accustomed to this desultory skirmishing that few behind the front lines paid much heed to it, noted a Michigan soldier.[5]

With the fine, unseasonably warm weather that continued from their arrival, many of Schofield's regiments eventually provided passes for their men to visit Nashville. Since many of the guards checking passes couldn't read, according to one of their officers, there was little trouble in going wherever the men wanted. The downtown area, said a member of the 124th Ohio, was a cesspool of evil. No city in the United States had such a bad population, he declared. Thieves, gamblers, prostitutes, and drunken soldiers swarmed the streets. In "Smoky Row," an unsavory locality near the river-front teeming with beer saloons and roughnecks, several murdered soldiers were found. If ever there was a town that should be burned, that city was Nashville, wrote the man.[6]

Yet for the majority of Thomas's soldiers, Nashville was almost as a mecca, filled like the horn of plenty. Large quantities of clothing and food were issued, fresh vegetables were in abundance, and there was the luxury of having access to regimental baggage for the first time in many months. Even camp sutlers had set up their wares in some units by December 4th.[7]

With the occupation of such palatial residences as Belmont, Joseph Acklen's countryside summer retreat, the delight of some of the Fourth Corps' infantrymen was immense. This enormous estate included a private zoo, expansive greenhouses for rare plants, the largest private art gallery in the South, and even a bowling alley. So many marble statues and exotic trees, shrubs, and plants graced the grounds that one soldier thought it looked like a first-class cemetery. Acklen had spent a million and a half dollars on the residence, it was rumored, and the sight of soldiers in muddy boots trampling through the rooms filled with paintings and marble statues seemed outrageous to some.[8]

Since Acklen was a Southern sympathizer and had fled his home, the building was appropriated for corps and division headquarters. Amid the Acklen grounds some of Thomas J. Wood's infantrymen found pleasure in dismantling the "nicely built stone walls" to make chimneys for their tents. The ornamental trees, while not making "first rate fire wood on account of being green," were cut by the dozens and used anyway.[9]

Aside from the regular camp routine of reveille at 4:00 A.M. and details for guard and skirmish duty, there was plenty of time for the grizzled veterans of Franklin to reflect on their recent ordeal. It all seemed like a terrible dream, thought Adam J. Weaver of the 104th Ohio. "Franklin, Tennessee, [is a] name which will haunt me for the rest of my days," he wrote less than twenty-four hours after the battle. Rumors began circulating as early as December 2d that the Rebels had lost 10,000 men at Franklin. David S. Stanley's estimate that 100 wagonloads of ammunition had been expended on November 30th only furthered the understanding that the conflict had been a soldiers' battle. Veteran soldiers marveled in their letters home at the terror of the combat, and boasted with pride about the thirty-three stands of Rebel colors taken at Franklin.[10]

With the muster-out at Nashville of several veteran organizations, such as the 40th Ohio and some of the 57th Indiana, there was a bittersweet send-off for many of these men. The three-year veterans of the 57th were leaving behind on the field of Franklin thirty of their number whose time of enlistment had expired on November 18th. Their sacrifice had been mandated by an emergency order to hold these men until the date occurred that the last company had been mustered in. One indignant Indiana soldier reflected that instead of laying in a lonely grave in Tennessee, "they should have been at home with their friends."[11]

In all, the initial siege interlude was much of a catharsis for Thomas's army. Their pent-up emotions were at last being vented, and many soldiers looked with hard-won reassurance to the remaining task ahead. Despite the desultory fighting along the Nashville skirmish lines during the first week in December, frequent reconnaissance patrols were sent into no-man's-land. Thomas wanted the Rebel lines probed to discover some assailable weak spot, but these patrols only confirmed that Hood's troops were strongly posted.[12]

For most of Thomas's men the end of that first week at Nashville witnessed only the boredom of camp routine and speculation about what move would break the seeming impasse. Yet it didn't take a prophet to foresee what was coming. "We are having great times here," wrote an officer. "No danger or anything of that sort; but Hood pens us in here; and . . . if they don't skedaddle soon, we shall have one of the biggest fights you ever did see."[13]

II

The morning began warm and cloudy, with a southwest wind. Light, desultory skirmishing occurred along the lines and the men continued to construct and improve their fortifications. December 7th seemed to be only another ordinary and uneventful day, observed an Illinois infantryman. At noon there was a sudden change—a squall of wind and rain. Within an hour it was intensely cold, with a piercing north wind. By the morning of December 8th the cold weather had intensified and the ground was frozen hard. A north wind continued to blow, and an officer described to his wife how he was bundled up in his overcoat and hat, sitting in his tent shivering with cold.[14]

It was only the beginning of the rough weather. On Friday, December 9th, a major storm front hit the Nashville area with cruel intensity. A cold and dismal dawn gave way to strong winds and dark, forbidding clouds. At 10:00 A.M. a lieutenant said it was so dark in his tent that he couldn't see the lines on his stationery upon which to write. Then the rain began, but the temperature was so cold that it began freezing as it fell. Soon the rain turned to sleet. By midday snow was falling. This "most terrific storm" was gaining in intensity, and by midnight a local farmer estimated there were two or three inches of snow covering the ice-crusted, frozen ground—and still it was snowing. "The sunny south has caught a terrible cold," observed a cold and grim Michigan officer.[15]

During the 8th the men of the 2d Iowa Cavalry cut a few large gum trees found amid their camp, and all gathered around a big fire to keep from freezing. This so provoked the ire of their officers that on the morning of the 9th an order was published forbidding the cutting of more trees. "Had this order been obeyed," wrote a sergeant, "every soldier in the command must inevitably have frozen to death, except such generals as toasted their toes by warm parlor fires."[16]

December 9th was to be vividly remembered by nearly all who were present on the frozen hills and valleys at Nashville. To those exposed to the icy storm and its frigid blasts, it had suddenly become war with the elements as much as a contest with the enemy. On the 10th a northwest wind continued to blow, and it was so cold that the snow became heavily crusted and frozen. On December 11th, a Sunday, the thermometer dropped to perhaps ten degrees below zero, and an old Tennessee farmer wrote in his diary that "it is the coldest day I think that has been for many years." Noting the strong northwest wind that continued to gust across the frozen fields piled with three inches of frozen sleet and snow, he added that this well may be called "Cold Sunday."[17]

On the 12th, intense cold again prevailed, despite a moderating wind about midnight. It was hard work just to stay warm, complained a soldier, and guards had to be posted over every rail or log in the Federal camps due to the scarcity of firewood. Fortunately, "the boys managed to steal enough [wood] . . . to keep from freezing," reported an Iowa sergeant.[18]

So many trees were being felled from all locations that even a veteran Nashville quartermaster reflected that "if the Rebs coop us up here another fortnight, there won't be a tree left within 5 miles of Nashville." Sadly he noted that "it would take a century" to replace these trees.[19]

One Ohio corporal informed his wife that he managed to keep "passably comfortable" in his tent by building a fire in an old camp kettle and making a vent for the smoke to escape. Even so, he found the smoke "was so bad at times I thought I should need a new pair of eyes." Then, as he looked out over the frozen terrain at the enemy lines, he realized that "the Rebel soldiers . . . are not as well provided for as we are." He noted, "Our scouts reported seeing Rebels frozen to death," and added, "I do not feel like rejoicing at their sufferings—only so far as it tends to prosper our cause—for I do not consider them as personal enemies . . . [only as] the enemies of a government."[20]

"We were without tents, and but one old worn blanket to each man with which to cover at night," wrote a bedraggled Confederate soldier of the 19th Tennessee Infantry. Their camp was on an elevation in an open field, exposed to the full sweep of the wintry winds. Their haggard ranks were thinly clad and most were without overcoats. All slept without cover on the frozen earth, and some had "nothing whatever to keep [on] our sore and bleeding feet." Most could but gaze longingly at the enemy in their comfortable quarters, and view the many cannon frowning from the Federal forts. It was just too much. "Ambition, and even life itself, were almost frozen out of us," admitted the man.[21]

When it began sleeting and snowing on the 9th, a Mississippi rifleman thought that "it was as cold as I ever experienced." There was no firewood in camp, and the nearest trees were a mile away. Most of the men burned cedar fence rails to keep warm. On December 10th the army's supply of fuel became so depleted that Hood was compelled to order the withdrawal of Lee's and Stewart's corps "a short distance" in order to cut wood. Already so many carpets were being taken from houses and cut up into blankets that the entire neighborhood seemed bare-floored.[22]

In the 1st Tennessee regiment a man observed how the ragged soldiers with sunken cheeks and famished bodies looked up into the cold, clear night sky, with twinkling stars and a pale moon that glimmered across the frozen landscape. Their breath seemed to make a thousand scintillations as it froze in the frosty air. In their bivouac on the hard-frozen snow, exposed to the piercing wind, that terrible storm of the second week in December seemed an outrage to humanity. He sadly reflected, "When we walk about, the echo of our footsteps sounds like the echo of a tombstone."[23]

Ensconced in ample tents in a grove by John Overton's large residence, General Hood's staff were finding things "quite pleasant." An acting assistant adjutant general reported, "We had an abundance of good food, beef, mutton, pork, flour, and potatoes. At the door of our tent stood a barrel of Robinson County whisky for the solace . . . of our mess." Another staff officer remarked in a letter home, "so you see we are getting along finely."[24]

As witnessed by the plight of Hood's starving and thinly clad troops, it was evident there was little to be shared with the common soldier. On "Cold Sunday," the most bitter day of the storm, Hood had finished writing his preliminary report of the Tennessee campaign. He said he was going to force the enemy to take the initiative. Yet in the snow and ice few initiatives were possible for either side. Since so many basic difficulties plagued the Confederate army, Hood now turned his attention to logistics, especially the procurement of supplies.[25]

One of the Confederate army's most serious problems was a lack of shoes. There were 3,500 barefoot soldiers in the Army of Tennessee, estimated one of Hood's men. In Bate's Division, marching to Nashville from Murfreesboro on December 10th, the want of shoes was so acute, "every pair of shoes which could be found" was impressed. So desperate were Bate's men that civilians began doling out used shoes. At one brigade headquarters a shoe shop was established, "not to make shoes," but to "take an old worn out pair of shoes and sew moccasins over them of green cow hide with the hair side in." Due to the heat of the body the hide would eventually dry and shrink to a close fit. Some twenty pairs were being turned out each day per brigade, said a staff officer.[26]

Hood had first estimated that the repair of the Central Alabama Railroad, with the use of two captured locomotives and about twenty cars, would materially aid in the subsistence of the army. Yet the railroad was in operation only between Pulaski and Franklin by December 6th, and so few supplies were trickling through that Hood wanted to impress whatever labor and material were necessary to repair the Memphis & Charleston Railroad to Decatur, Alabama. He said this would provide for "the permanent occupation of this country" through an uninterrupted rail supply line. At the time he had exactly three rail cars in working order.[27]

Further concessions in already depleted troop strength had been necessary to get vital flour and grain to the army. On the 7th Hood had to request Forrest to send the 35th Tennessee into three mid-Tennessee counties to break up Federal home guards, gather conscripts and horses, and protect the important mills. Then, with the onset of the ice storm, so many regiments were without blankets and clothing that Hood had to wire for fifty bales of blankets rumored to be at Augusta, Georgia. In all, this makeshift, ramshackle supply system caused the army to rely on the impressment of commissary stores from the local populace.[28]

Despite the mounting concern over supplies and war materiel, undoubtedly it was the morale of his officers and men that troubled Hood the most. Franklin remained a significant millstone around the army's neck, and as Stephen D. Lee wrote, the high command's postbattle assessment was that, had the men gone over even one-half of the main Federal works, "we would have destroyed completely the Yankee army." On December 6th Hood issued general orders which were intended as a subtle critique of the army's performance on November 30th: "Success and safety in battle consists in piercing the enemy's lines as quickly as possible after coming under his fire. No halts should be made, except those temporary ones necessary for partial rectification of alignment." In attempting to inspire his troops to greater effort, Hood directed that the names of those who "passed over the enemy's interior line of works" be forwarded, to be placed on a roll of honor at the War Department. Further, Hood sought to improve morale among his officer corps. Despite the "unfortunate affair" at Franklin, Stephen D. Lee noted that Hood seemed to be in "good heart," and how he had even forgiven Frank Cheatham for the Spring Hill fiasco.[29]

On December 7th Hood had written to Secretary of War James A. Seddon, withdrawing his former recommendation for the promotion of Frank Cheatham, "for reasons which I will [later] write more fully." On the following day he even asked Seddon for a good lieutenant general to command Cheatham's Corps. Later that same day, according to Hood, Cheatham came to his headquarters and "spoke an honest avowal of his error [at Spring Hill] . . . that he was greatly to blame." Accordingly, Hood telegraphed to Seddon again that day, saying Cheatham's "failure" at Spring Hill "will be a lesson to him" and "I think it best he should remain in his position for the present." This appeared to Stephen D. Lee as "misgiven generosity," since Hood, "in the goodness of his heart has passed it over and forgiven it as an error." He added, "I am truly sorry for General Hood, [as] one good brigade would have stampeded the Yankee army."[30]

Such maneuvering appears to have reflected Hood's ulterior motives. By publication of his general orders, blame for the Franklin disaster seemed to be obscured. Was it due to a senseless frontal assault, or to the troops unaccountably stopping at the outer breastworks? Furthermore, the extent of Hood's benevolence involving Cheatham was revealed in his confidential preliminary report to the War Department, written three days after "forgiving" his corps commander. Hood wrote of the affair at Spring Hill:

> Major General Cheatham was ordered at once to attack the enemy vigorously and get possession of this pike, and, although these orders were frequently and earnestly repeated, he made but a feeble and partial attack, failing to reach the point indicated. . . . Thus was lost the opportunity for striking the enemy for which we had labored so long—the best the campaign had offered, and one of the best afforded us during the war. Major General Cheatham has frankly confessed the great error of which he was guilty, and attaches all blame to himself. While his error lost so much to the country, it has been a severe lesson to him . . . and I think that it is best that he should retain for the present the command he now holds.

Hood's purposes seemed to have been well served; he had found both a willing scapegoat for Spring Hill and an excuse for Franklin.[31]

Stephen D. Lee considered the army's recent "bad luck." "We are determined nothing shall stop us in our good work, nor shall we be discouraged because we have not done as much as we should have done," wrote Lee to his wife. "A wise providence will reward us if we push on in so glorious a cause. I always look upon everything as happening for the best, and mark me, the Army of Tennessee will yet be crowned with glorious victory."[32]

At the same time, miles distant across the cold, windswept landscape, Lee's fellow general John C. Carter lay grievously suffering from his Franklin body wound in the William Harrison house. Chaplain Charles T. Quintard was with him and, being aware that the doctors had predicted his days were few, he said prayers with and engaged Carter in a last conversation. Carter's paroxysms of pain were frequent and intense, wrote Quintard. Tactfully the chaplain suggested to him his imminent mortality, but Carter could not be convinced that he was going to die. Quintard replied, "But . . . General, if you should die what do you wish me to say to your wife?"

"Tell her that I have always loved her devotedly and that I respect her more than I can express," came the labored reply. Then Carter, in pain, begged for chloroform, which was freely administered. Chaplain Quintard sat up with him until midnight, but Carter's lucid moments were few. The following day at midnight, nine days before his 27th birthday, John C. Carter expired, the last, but the youngest, of the Confederate generals to die of their Franklin wounds. Chaplain Quintard regretfully wrote to another minister that he would not be able to attend or officiate at the funeral in Columbia, since he had other duties to prepare for.[33]

The following morning, Sunday, December 11th, after a treacherous journey back to the army, Quintard presided at communion services at Hood's headquarters. The next day, Monday, the 12th, the entire headquarters journeyed a short distance to the Methodist Meeting House at Brentwood, where Mary Hadley and Major William Clare of Hood's staff were here united in marriage. Following the ceremony the entire gathering returned to Hood's headquarters at John Overton's home, "where a grand dinner was given." Wrote the well-pleased Quintard, "My empty purse was replenished by a fee of $200.00." That evening he became engrossed in reading an article, "The Beginning of the End" for the South—an account that the success of the Federal armies in 1863 had essentially subdued the Confederacy, and "the rebellion is on its last legs." Noting in his journal "We are at the gates of Nashville, with Tennessee rescued from the grasp of the invaders," the amused chaplain reflected that the author perhaps should revise his prophesy.[34]

Out on the windswept plain in front of Nashville the men of Cheatham's Corps listened to the city clock strike on the hour throughout the long and frigid night. Visible along the picket line in front were the bodies of several Southern soldiers killed in skirmish firing. Their bodies were too exposed to recover and they remained visible for all to see, "froze[n] as hard as a log." From a distance, in the sprawling confines of Nashville, came sounds of marching men and horses. Mused a soldier, time was slowly running out for someone—was it George H. Thomas, or the Confederate Army of Tennessee?[35]

CHAPTER XXVII

Let There Be No
Further Delay

DECEMBER 9, 1864, had all of the makings of an ominous and fateful day. The telegraph wires between Washington, D.C., and Nashville were fairly humming with messages at midday. Then the wires became silent. Just before the arrival of Grant's and Halleck's openly threatening telegrams during the early afternoon, George H. Thomas had dispatched messages to all of his principal subordinates calling off the offensive operations planned for December 10th "owing to the severity of the storm." Any future attack, he announced, would be postponed until the weather cleared. Only minutes thereafter, Thomas had learned from Halleck that his army career was in jeopardy due to his failure to attack Hood. Following Thomas's exculpatory dispatches of 2:00 P.M. to Halleck in Washington, and 1:00 P.M. to Grant at City Point, Virginia, the commander of the Department of the Cumberland glumly awaited a reply. The dark skies and the whistling wind must have mirrored Thomas's despair. He could but look at the swirling snow from his office at the St. Cloud Hotel and wait. The lonely burden of command was never more evident. Thomas was found sitting by the window "for an hour or more," not speaking a word, gazing forlornly off into the distance.[1]

Finally, after a wait of more than ten hours, about 11:30 P.M. the fateful telegram arrived. It was from Grant, written in terse language: "I have as much confidence in your conducting a battle rightly as I have in any other officer; but it seemed to me that you have been slow, and I have had no explanation of affairs to convince me otherwise." Having just heard from Halleck, and then receiving Thomas's direct wire, Grant now knew about the delay due to the storm. Halleck had asked Grant if he still wished to relieve Thomas—as the removal orders were made out. Grant's decision was explained to Thomas in the 11:30 P.M. wire: "Receiving your dispatch of 2:00 P.M. from General Halleck before I did the one to me, I telegraphed to suspend the order relieving you until we should hear further [about your course of action]."

Thomas had a reprieve—of sorts. But Grant added a not too subtle warning: "I hope most sincerely that there will be no necessity of repeating the orders, and that the facts will show that you have been right all the time."[2]

That was the extent of it. There was no encouraging advice; there were no further directives. Grant's tenor was unmistakable. He wanted prompt action and important results, otherwise Thomas would be relieved. Again the impetus for action rested with Thomas. Yet to Thomas, the initiative was strictly dependent on the weather. As such, a serious basis for further misunderstanding remained.[3]

Grant was very much uncertain about leaving Thomas in command. He told Halleck on the evening of the 9th that he had in effect suspended the order relieving Thomas "until it is seen whether he will do anything." Thomas had indicated he would attack on the 7th, Grant reminded Halleck, "but [he] didn't do so, nor has he given a reason for not doing it." Grant did not want to do Thomas an "injustice," and only based on his past "good service" had Grant taken the present wait-and-see course.[4]

Thomas hesitated to communicate with Grant on the 10th, but wrote to Halleck that "the sleet and inclement weather still continue, rendering offensive operations extremely hazardous, if not impossible." Again, on December 11th, "Cold Sunday," Thomas avoided Grant and wired to Halleck the unwelcome news that the Federal army remained inactive at Nashville. "The weather continues very cold and the hills are covered with ice," he reported, adding, "As soon as we have a thaw, I will attack Hood." Thomas further admitted that in response to Lyon's 3,000 Confederate raiders moving north of the Cumberland River he had just sent part of his cavalry force to intercept them.[5]

The news that Confederates were north of the Cumberland River put Grant in a particularly foul mood. At 4:00 P.M. on the 11th he sent a gruff, demanding telegram to let Thomas know just where he stood. "If you delay attack[ing] longer the mortifying spectacle will be witnessed of a Rebel army moving for the Ohio River, and you will be forced to act, accepting such weather as you find. Let there be no further delay. Hood cannot stand even a drawn battle so far from his supplies or ordnance stores. . . . I am in hopes of receiving a dispatch from you today announcing that you have moved. Delay no longer for weather or reinforcements."[6]

Following the arrival of Grant's dispatch during the night of the 11th, Thomas promptly called for an urgent meeting of his corps commanders at his Nashville headquarters the following day. Meanwhile, he seemed to comply with Grant's directive on the night of the 11th, wiring in reply: "I will obey the order as promptly as possible, however much I may regret it, as the attack will have to be made under every disadvantage. The whole country is covered with a perfect sheet of ice and sleet, and it is with difficulty the troops are able to move about on level ground."[7]

With a heavy and troubled heart, Thomas, about 10:00 P.M., ordered his principal commanders to have their units put in readiness during the 12th for offensive operations. The implication was obvious—an attack would be ordered for the 13th. Yet of particular concern was Wilson's cavalry, still across the river at Edgefield. They would have to be brought over the icy bridges on the 12th, despite the wretched weather. By 3:00 P.M., the time set for the council of war on the 12th, Thomas would have a better knowledge about their availability. The urgency of the situation was well reflected in the cavalry's instructions to move to Nashville: "Every man, mounted or dismounted, will cross [the river]," announced Wilson's orders.[8]

On December 12th the day began poorly for Thomas when the cavalry attempted to move at the designated hour of 8:30 A.M. Although the strong north wind had moderated, it was still exceedingly cold. The hard-frozen ground and ice-covered streets and bridges were as slippery as a skating rink. The cavalrymen had to dismount and lead their horses by the bridle. Still they skidded and foundered on the streets and bridges. The horses could not pull the wagons and artillery without slipping or falling. When the early arrivals came to their designated camping ground along the Charlotte pike west of town, the ground was so deeply frozen that the men were unable to erect their tents. The entire day was spent in getting Wilson's 12,500 men, 9,000 horses, and equipment-laden wagons across, and there were many accidents and mishaps.[9]

At 3:00 P.M. the momentous council of war meeting of Thomas's commanders began at his St. Cloud Hotel headquarters. Thomas began by displaying Grant's peremptory order of the 11th to delay no longer for reinforcements or the weather. He then stated "in a tone of lofty dignity and resolution," said one of his generals, that he had replied to Grant based on his own views, but would like to have the opinions of those present.[10]

By tradition it was customary that the junior officer present be the first to speak. All eyes turned to James H. Wilson, a well known Grant protégé. Wilson "hastened to express [his] . . . full approval" of Thomas's earlier actions, adding that until the ground thawed Hood could successfully defend his works "with nothing more dangerous than baskets of brickbats." There was a smile of approval by the other officers, said Wilson. Thomas J. Wood, commander of the Fourth Corps following Stanley's departure, was next, and he added his "hearty concurrence" to Wilson's remarks. Then A. J. Smith and Steedman expressed their agreement. Only John M. Schofield, the senior subordinate, sat silent. This marked silence was noted by all. Although he ostensibly concurred with the others in awaiting more moderate weather based on private conversation, there was an immediate suspicion of his reluctance to openly add his endorsement.[11]

The meeting was short. As the other generals prepared to leave, Thomas asked Wilson to stay for a moment. When the others had gone, "Old Pap" spoke up: "Wilson, the Washington authorities treat me as if I were a boy. They seem to think me incapable of planning a campaign or of fighting a battle but if they will just let me alone until [a thaw] . . . I will show them what we can do."[12]

Wilson, knowing that Thomas was aware of his former closeness to Grant, attempted to soothe the department commander's "wounded feelings." A long conversation over supper followed, and Wilson came away "with a higher opinion of Thomas and his character than I ever had before." Thomas had spoken with emotion and obvious resentment of his mistreatment at the hands of his superiors. Sherman was unopposed on his "holiday excursion" through Georgia—but had taken the cream of the army with him, leaving Thomas with mostly reserves, recruits, and combat-depleted units. Grant, who had been deadlocked in Virginia for seven months, had the temerity to rush him into hasty action only ten days after confronting Hood at Nashville. As the evening wore on, Wilson could see the great resolution in Thomas's mind. The Washington authorities might relieve him from command, he said, but in no case would he fight against his own judgment—that is, until the local conditions were favorable.*[13]

As for Schofield, nothing further was said about his silence. Brigadier General William D. Whipple, Thomas's adjutant general, later raised the question of someone using the telegraph to send misleading information to Washington. According to one source, Major General James B. Steedman learned through one of his aides, Captain Marshall Davis, that Schofield had sent a wire to Grant stating that many officers at Nashville were of the opinion that Thomas was too slow in his movements. Allegedly, Thomas was warned of a "Judas" being in his midst and shown a copy of the offending telegram in Schofield's handwriting from the telegraph office. Following the war, this matter became the basis of bitter allegations by Steedman, who formally published them in the New York Times, June 22, 1881. Yet Schofield, while expressing his reservations about Thomas's ability as a general, vehemently denied that he had communicated with anyone in such a manner at the time. Schofield wrote to Grant in 1881 asking him to refute these "malicious charges," and Grant responded, stating, "I think I can say with great positiveness there was never any dispatch from you to me, or from you to any one in Washington, disparaging General Thomas's movements at Nashville." Since no incriminating evidence was later found in the War Department files, the incident faded into partisan innuendos and was never

*According to Wilson and several others, this meeting occurred December 9th or 10th. These were recollections based on the writing of memoirs many years later. The best evidence of the actual date is in Fourth Corps Chief of Staff Lieutenant Colonel Joseph S. Fullerton's contemporary journal. Also, for Schofield's version of the meeting, see his Forty-Six Years in the Army, 237ff.

resolved. That Thomas remained wary of Schofield while at Nashville, however, is a certainty.[14]

Bolstered by the support of his generals, Thomas proceeded to wire Halleck at 10:30 P.M. on December 12th:

> I have the troops ready to make the attack on the enemy as soon as the sleet which now covers the ground has melted sufficiently to enable the men to march. As the whole country is now covered with a sheet of ice so hard and slippery it is utterly impossible for troops to ascend the slopes, or even move over level ground in anything like order. It has taken the entire day to place my cavalry in position, and it has only been finally effected with imminent risk and many serious accidents, resulting from the number of horses falling with their riders on the roads. Under these circumstances I believe an attack at this time would only result in a useless sacrifice of life.[15]

Thomas was not brazen about it, but he had just firmly and resolutely reversed his earlier telegram of implied compliance with Grant's urgent order to attack immediately. Further, he had not used the council of war as a shield, or even mentioned that his subordinate generals were in full agreement with him. The decision was his alone. He would not shirk the consequences. More significantly, Thomas did not deign to correspond with Grant about his resolve to attack only upon his own judgment, although he knew that Grant would see a copy of the telegram in due time.[16]

U. S. Grant appears to have received a copy of Thomas's latest telegram during the morning of December 13th. At that time he was conferring at City Point with Major General John A. Logan, commander of Sherman's Fifteenth Corps, just returned from a leave of absence in Illinois. Logan, a prominent political general, wanted to be restored to a meaningful active command, but anticipated difficulty with Sherman, who had favored West Point professionals. Logan had journeyed from Louisville on December 4th to see his old friend Grant and seek his favor. Not expecting such an extraordinary break, Logan was undoubtedly shocked when Grant wrote out conditional orders for him to assume command of the Department of the Cumberland, replacing George H. Thomas. The understanding was that Logan would proceed immediately to Nashville. On arrival, if Thomas hadn't moved, Logan would take command.[17]

Grant did not telegraph another word to Thomas. The extent of his anger and impatience was couched only in a cold and stony silence.

Life was more or less dull during the icy interlude of the second week in December, thought a Federal officer. As usual, rumors of all sorts were rife, and in the Fourth Corps word spread of Thomas being replaced by another general. "I do not think the army will take kindly to this if it is true," wrote an apprehensive private. Another rumor spread that Hood was sick with typhoid fever, though this was soon disproved. On the 13th the Confederates were observed moving cannon to their extreme flank. What this meant, no one seemed to know, but since the Federal cavalry had just moved within the outer lines from across the river, it seemed to be the harbinger of new activity. Still, Wilson's troopers appeared to remain idle in camp, apparently unconcerned about any movement. Many of the cavalrymen were found playing cards and writing letters home. It seemed to many of Thomas's listless troops that all the waiting and dreary boredom would never end.[18]

Crash! bang! ding! sounded the noise. A roar erupted from the Confederate lines, and up jumped the Federal infantrymen of the 96th Illinois Volunteers to their breastworks. With rifle muskets poised, they peered uncertainly over their log parapets.

Here came a dog, running at full speed, heading for the Federal lines with a tin pan tied to his tail. The clattering and banging of the tin pan on the frozen ground seemed to frighten the dog into greater speed, and with a bounding leap, the animal scampered over the Federal works and soon disappeared in the direction of Nashville.[19]

As the shouts from the Federal lines died away, perhaps an outburst of laughter was heard within the Confederate lines. An amused Federal soldier might well have remarked that it was about the only way any "fully equipped" Rebel was going to make it into Nashville.

II

John Bell Hood seemed to be puzzled by the events of the past few days. "Reliable" news of the Federal cavalry's recrossing of the Cumberland River to camp on the extreme Union right flank had reached Hood by the following day, December 13th. This appeared to be further evidence that Hood's plan to draw Thomas out to the rescue of Murfreesboro was working and the Federals would soon attack. Yet the menacing presence of Union cavalry along the western sector of his Nashville lines was contrary to Hood's expectations.[20]

Hood's greatest concern was with his eastern flank, which extended well to the south of Nashville and was vital to his plan of sealing off Murfreesboro. On December 9th he had urged A. P. Stewart to "push forward with all possible haste" the construction of fortifications in his rear, so that he might, if called upon, "move with two of your divisions and one other division from another corps . . . to prevent the enemy from reenforcing Murfreesboro, or to capture the force now [there] . . . should it attempt to move off." Hood's preoccupation with this Murfreesboro plan caused him to order about noon on December 10th the transfer of Jacob Biffle's Brigade of cavalry from Chalmers's Division on the far left, across to the opposite, right flank. Hood's orders made it quite apparent that he was willing to weaken his left wing, specifically the segment along the Cumberland River west of Nashville, in order to meet the enemy's anticipated thrust to or from Murfreesboro.[21]

James R. Chalmers was appalled. With only two cavalry brigades he was endeavoring to cover about a four-mile expanse between the Hillsboro pike and the river. Immediately he wrote a letter to Hood complaining that with the minimal strength of his remaining men "it would be impossible" to maintain his position in the event of an attack. Using the inclement weather as an excuse, Chalmers delayed in implementing Hood's order on the 10th. But Hood was insistent. Biffle's men went off on the 12th to the far right, leaving Chalmers with only Edmund W. Rucker's Brigade of about 900 men. The only concession Hood made was to tell A. P. Stewart to send a regiment on picket along the Hardin pike "to support" Chalmers.[22]

Since Forrest's main position was near La Vergne, midway between Murfreesboro and Nashville, his cavalrymen were expected either to strike north against Thomas's forces or south at Rousseau, as the circumstances required. Hood had suspected on the 10th that the Federal cavalry at Edgefield might be preparing for a raid south against Hood's vulnerable supply lines. Accordingly, he had directed Forrest to prepare to meet Wilson "up the [Cumberland] river" with "your main force of cavalry" and drive him back. Thereafter, Forrest sent about half of Buford's Division toward the mouth of the Stones River, some miles above Nashville, while William H. Jackson's Division operated in the vicinity of Murfreesboro.[23]

On the 13th, only a day after Biffle had gone to the right, Hood learned that he had guessed wrong. Wilson had moved from Edgefield, recrossing the Cumberland River, but instead of going upriver he had camped in the vicinity of Hood's weakened western flank. Again Hood sought to juggle the disposition of his troops. He ordered Stewart to send Matthew D. Ector's infantry brigade, commanded by Colonel David Coleman, to the Hardin pike to support Chalmers. On the 14th, Coleman's Texans and North Carolinians moved into position, allowing Chalmers to shift most of his cavalrymen farther north and west, toward the Charlotte pike and the river. At last Hood was beginning to consider his increasingly vulnerable left flank.[24]

Inevitably, Hood had become involved in a vast juggling act, so often redeploying and changing the assignments of his troops that it appeared to his men he had lost all perspective. Bate's infantrymen, nearly one-fourth of whom were still barefoot, upon their return to the army about December 12th had trudged across the ice-crusted ground to bolster the critical right flank under Frank Cheatham. Also, Hood continued to transfer and detach other troops for various purposes. Colonel Charles H. Olmstead's relatively fresh brigade in Cleburne's Division, having just convoyed a supply train to the army from Florence, Alabama—thus missing the bloodbath at Franklin— was sent on December 8th to join Forrest north of Murfreesboro. Francis M. Cockrell's decimated brigade of Missourians was sent on December 10th with an Alabama battery from A. P. Stewart's Corps on a long, difficult march to the mouth of the Duck River near Johnsonville. The purpose was to construct a fort along the Tennessee River to prevent Federal gunboats from operating against Hood's line of supplies. Yet these Rebels never arrived at their intended post. After a harrowing ten days' march through incessant rain and bottomless roads, the detachment was recalled following the Battle of Nashville. These men were thus lost in entirety to Hood's badly depleted army at the most critical time.[25]

Ironically, it was Hood's compelling need for more troops that had prompted many of his more drastic actions, from the very inception of the Nashville siege. On December 5th Hood had sent a proposal for an exchange of prisoners under a flag of truce to Nashville, but Thomas perceived Hood's greater need for more men, and replied that he had already sent all captured Confederates north. The growing plight of the Army of Tennessee, greatly weakened by its Franklin losses, detachments, and desertions, caused Hood on December 11th to plead directly with the War Department for reinforcements. Citing the fact that 15,000 Federals were reported moving from the Mississippi River to reinforce Thomas at Nashville, Hood sought Confederate troops from the trans-Mississippi "in time for the spring campaign, if not sooner." Unknown to Hood, Beauregard, at Montgomery, Alabama, already had learned that A. J. Smith's troops were en route to Nashville, and on December 2d had written to Jefferson Davis, asking that Kirby Smith's troops be sent from the trans-Mississippi to reinforce Hood. Davis had okayed the request on December 4th, but Kirby Smith, when notified of the plan in Louisiana on December 20th, was reluctant to cooperate. Sixteen days later he forwarded a negative reply, saying it was too difficult to cross the enemy-patrolled Mississippi River or advance through devastated country without supplies. Hood could expect no help from the trans-Mississippi region.[26]

Hood then learned on December 13th that his frequently expressed plan to replenish his army with recruits in Tennessee had been an outright failure. The army had gained only 164 recruits since entering Tennessee. Furthermore, of the 296 dismounted cavalrymen who had been assigned to Ed Johnson's Division, all but forty-two had deserted. Hood reacted angrily and resolved "to bring into the army [by conscription] all men liable to military duty." If recruits wouldn't voluntarily flock to his standards, he intended to bring them in at the point of the bayonet. Noting the great resistance among the local men to join the Confederate army, Stephen D. Lee estimated that perhaps 6,000 or 7,000 men had fled the countryside ahead of Hood's army and had gone to Nashville "to get out of the reach of conscription."[27]

With an enemy attack momentarily expected and less than 25,000 troops present, Hood, on December 14th, was so desperate as to direct the brigade protecting his vital supply railroads in northern Alabama to join the army "as soon as possible," leaving only one regiment at Decatur, Alabama.[28]

Hood's plight was so great he even modified his battle orders in order to better protect his rear and flank. On December 10th, when Lee's and Stewart's Corps withdrew their lines for convenience in cutting trees to burn for fuel, Hood considered that this provided for "a better left flank." Specifically, he anticipated being able to more quickly move many of his troops to any threatened point. Hood expected an imminent attack on his fortifications, and his circular to the army of the 10th announced that "it [is] highly probable that we will fight a battle before the close of thc present year."[29]

Basic to Hood's defensive concept were "self supporting detached works"—small enclosed redoubts capable of holding seventy-five to a hundred men, built of logs and earth, with embrasures for artillery. These redoubts were intended to be independent but mutually supporting, allowing a minimum of defenders to hold their ground against greater numbers of attacking troops. Artillery was ordered positioned so as to fire in any direction, and the men were instructed to hold these redoubts "at all hazard, and not to surrender under any circumstances." Generally, these small forts were to be positioned in the rear of each corps' right and left flank, allowing for maximum flexibility in defense. The importance Hood placed on these structures was evident when he directed the corps commanders, in person, to superintend their construction, "not leaving them either to subordinate commanders or engineer officers."[30]

In all, Hood, perhaps the most aggressive, assault-oriented commander in the Confederate army, was putting his reliance upon defensive works in order to beat Thomas. It was quite a psychological about-face for the man who had ordered the all-out frontal assault at Franklin only two weeks earlier.

In Hood's mind the question was not so much would Thomas attack, but where he might strike. With only about 23,000 men positioned across a limited front and surrounded by rolling hills and many valleys, Hood knew he was vulnerable to a flank attack. He thus paid particular attention to reports from his scouts and spies, and to Federal troop movements along his front. Hood probably learned through a spy of the Federal cavalry's recrossing of the Cumberland on December 12th. Yet by the end of the second week in December, Hood could only guess as to where Thomas might strike.[31]

Finally, on December 13th, there was a clue. That afternoon two brigades of Federal troops, Colonel Adam Malloy's and Colonel Charles R. Thompson's, probably 3,000 men combined, marched out the Murfreesboro pike toward the Rains farm. Advancing in line of battle, Malloy's and Thompson's men began a lively skirmish with some of Frank Cheatham's men. Thompson's men were blacks, many of whom were under fire for the first time, yet the Confederate skirmish lines were soon driven back to the main line. The protracted fight continued at a distance until nearly dark, when the Federals withdrew. Malloy suffered only ten casualties, Thompson about a dozen, and the men seemed to consider the whole affair a useless fight. "We should almost have . . . cut steps in the icy covering of the hillside to get to them [enemy]. . . . I should have got along gaily on skates today," wrote an officer of Thompson's command.[32]

This Federal reconnaissance had been of nominal value; it only confirmed that the Confederates remained in force along the Nashville & Chattanooga Railroad. Yet to Hood, looking for evidence of Thomas's intentions, it seemed significant. That day the men of Granbury's Brigade were ordered to build a redoubt on the north side of the railroad cut capable of holding 300 men. Also, Federal pickets observed the Confederates moving artillery into position. A Federal officer considered these developments and wondered about the effect among the enemy's commanders. Was it possible that the series of probes and reconnaissances toward Hood's right flank, which seemed unnecessary and fruitless, actually may have given Hood the impression that this was the point selected for the main assault?[33]

The answer was yes, and decidedly so. This sudden activity along his right flank seemed to convince Hood that an enemy buildup was under way in this sector. If Thomas was going to the rescue of Murfreesboro, as Hood envisioned, inevitably he must attack along the eastern flank.

Of course, Thomas was *not* considering the relief of Murfreesboro. His only objective continued to be the destruction of Hood's army. The essential questions thus were posed: Would Thomas strike where the Confederate army was the most vulnerable? Could Thomas's massive assault avoid a Franklinlike disaster in attacking Hood's defensive fortifications? Would Thomas even be retained in command so as to conduct an attack?

III

On the evening of December 13th, George H. Thomas, trying to sound optimistic, wrote to Chief of Staff Henry Halleck in Washington, "At length there are indications of a favorable change in the weather, and as soon as there is I shall move against the enemy, as everything is ready and [I am] prepared to assume the offensive." That day there had been a shifting of the wind to the east and southeast, bringing more moderate temperatures. Yet the day was still very cold, and the snow in the fields melted very slowly. During the night warmer winds prevailed, so that on the foggy morning of December 14th it seemed actually warm, with a misty rain falling. By 7:00 A.M. the snow and ice had rapidly melted, and again there was only bare ground visible. Under cloudy skies the men tried the footing and found that there now was a new impediment—mud. A Michigan cavalryman discovered that in Nashville "the streets which so lately were covered with ice are today a vast sea of mud."[34]

To George H. Thomas, however, the break in the freezing weather must have seemed like the onset of summer. Despite the thick fog, which as late as 11:00 A.M. prevented the enemy's works from being seen, Thomas was busy on December 14th with his preparations for battle. By midday he sent word to his corps commanders to prepare for operations per previous arrangements. At 3:00 P.M. he conducted a meeting at the St. Cloud Hotel where the final dispositions were made.[35]

By 6:00 P.M. formal orders had been drawn up, it having been decided to attack early the following morning, "if not too foggy." By 8:00 P.M. Thomas sent word to a navy gunboat commander that an attack was imminent, and "if you can drop down the river and engage their batteries on the river bank, it will be excellent cooperation."[36]

Thomas then returned to his correspondence. On hand was a newly arrived, openly threatening telegram from Halleck, dated at 12:30 P.M. that day. Halleck wasted few words. It was seriously feared that while Hood with part of his forces "held you in check near Nashville," other portions of the enemy's force would operate against other vulnerable points, wrote Halleck. Hence, Grant was most upset and anxious, since Federal forces along the Mississippi River had to protect Memphis and Vicksburg, instead of cooperating with William Tecumseh Sherman's march by threatening various Rebel positions. "Every day's delay on your part, therefore, seriously interferes with General Grant's plans," warned the crusty chief of staff.[37]

Thomas, now much relieved about the situation, wired Halleck in reply at 8:00 P.M., "The ice having melted away today, the enemy will be attacked tomorrow morning. Much as I regret the apparent delay in attacking the enemy, it could not have been done before with any reasonable hope of success."[38]

Already word of a pending fight had spread through the army. In the 125th Ohio of Opdycke's brigade, a soldier wrote in his diary, "It is common talk that we are to fight Hood tomorrow." Another private noted that evening how many of the men were writing letters home, knowing that perhaps before the sun set on the morrow they might be dead. In his tent that night James H. Wilson wrote to an officer of Grant's staff, "Everybody else has made his last will and testament, or written to his wife or sweetheart, but, having nothing to dispose of, and neither wife or sweetheart to write to, I give you about four minutes before preparing myself four or five hours of sleep. All arrangements are made for battle in the morning, and much seems in our favor. If we are ordinarily successful, and Hood ordinarily complacent, we shall have but little time for letter writing during the next two weeks."[39]

Another Federal officer, Captain Job Aldrich of the 17th U.S. Colored Troops, had a bad feeling about the coming fight. He seemed convinced that he would die, and gave his money, watch, and personal belongings to his brother-in-law's wife, who was visiting in Nashville at the time. Aldrich then wrote an emotional letter to his wife, "the most affecting I ever read," later said his brother-in-law, Colonel William R. Shafter. Aldrich's letter concluded: "The clock strikes one, good night. At five the dance of death begins around Nashville. Who shall be partners in the dance? God only knows. Echo alone answers who? Farewell."[40]

CHAPTER XXVIII

Matters of Some
Embarrassment

Ulysses s. grant still had reservations. Sending John A. Logan to relieve Thomas at Nashville had been a spur-of-the-moment decision. Logan was not a West Point professional, and Grant didn't want to cause further divisiveness among the Nashville army's generals. On the afternoon of December 14th he suddenly decided to go in person to Nashville. That evening Grant left his headquarters at City Point, Virginia, and journeyed by steamboat to Washington, D.C., where he arrived early the following afternoon. Upon his arrival at the capital Grant found that the telegraph wires to Nashville had been down since about 5:00 P.M. on the 14th and nothing had been heard from Thomas since his "no change" telegram of the 13th.[1]

Grant, on the afternoon of the 15th, met in a tense and climactic conference with Halleck, Stanton, and Lincoln. At one point Major Thomas T. Eckert of the telegraph office was called in, and he confirmed that no new information had been received from Thomas. Although Lincoln and Stanton had misgivings, Grant obtained their reluctant approval for Thomas's removal due to his failure to act. Grant wrote out the formal order and handed it to Major Eckert to transmit once the lines were reopened. He then went back to Willard's Hotel to prepare for his departure to Nashville, while Eckert trudged off to the telegraph office.[2]

II

Thursday, December 15, 1864, dawned warm and cloudy at Nashville. The ground continued to be soft and muddy, but what dominated the attention of all was the vast blanket of dense fog. This misty gray vapor, accentuated by the smoldering campfires of the troops, so obscured the light that every object seemed enveloped in a cloud even at a few feet. Although Thomas's entire army had arisen at 4:00 A.M. to prepare for active operations at 6:00 A.M., the fog so engulfed the camps that it was impossible to see sufficiently to manage the mass movement of troops. The order to move was arbitrarily suspended by some commanders. Full daylight brought little relief. At 7:00 A.M. the fog continued to hover over the ground in a dense blanket. Another half hour passed, and still the fog lingered.[3]

George H. Thomas was observed checking out of the St. Cloud Hotel as if some ordinary traveler. "There was no haughtiness nor ostentatious [show]" in his appearance, noticed a soldier, and he seemed to have an unmistakable "air of business about him." Although Thomas had anticipated a delay, his entire plan was contingent on the timely and coordinated execution of his operational orders. Thomas intended to sweep around Hood's western flank and attack the exposed works defended by A. P. Stewart's Corps. His main tactical maneuver would be the wide wheeling movement by three divisions of Wilson's cavalry along the westernmost roads to envelop Hood's flank. Because much of the cavalry would be mounted, good visibility and sufficient footing were important to their advance. Without the cavalry's help the infantry would remain vulnerable to counterattack beyond their exposed flank. With the weather warm, no rain expected, and all operational planning developed, Thomas decided to simply wait out the fog.[4]

By Thomas's design his primary offensive punch would be supplied by the relatively fresh troops of A. J. Smith. "Smith's Guerrillas," as they liked to fancy themselves, were organized into three divisions of infantry and had been directed to wheel southwest against A. P. Stewart's exposed flank. For supports they would have Wilson's cavalry on their right and Thomas J. Wood's Fourth Corps on their left. Wood's men would stay in close support of Smith's columns, while threatening Montgomery Hill in front and flank. In order to prevent an enemy sortie against Nashville, James B. Steedman, in charge of reserve troops, had been ordered to occupy the interior lines with the post garrison, quartermaster's units, and his own provisional brigades of recruits, furloughed soldiers, and other unassigned volunteers.[5]

All but left out of Thomas's plans had been John M. Schofield, his next ranking subordinate and the former commander of the Franklin forces. Schofield's only assignment was to form his troops for use as a general reserve. In fact, Thomas told Schofield to put most of his men in the trenches to replace a portion of the Fourth Corps, and with the remainder of his troops to "co-operate" with Wood by protecting that general's flank. Schofield took immediate offense. During the night of the 14th he had visited A. J. Smith, and then Wood, suggesting a modification in Thomas's plans. Having obtained Wood's support, Schofield confronted Thomas and "explained to him" that due to the extent of the ground to be covered the 11,000 men of the Twenty-third Corps could better be used on the far Federal right, where the main attack was to occur. Although Thomas approved, Schofield later reflected that "General Thomas did not possess in a high degree the activity of mind necessary to foresee and provide for all the exigencies of military operations, nor the mathematical talent required to estimate 'the relations of time, space, motion, and force.'" Despite the change, Thomas refused to assign Schofield any major operational responsibility in the attack. He decreed that Schofield should advance only as a general reserve to Smith's, rather than Wood's troops.[6]

More significantly, Thomas's subordinates had suggested the modification of operations along the extreme Federal left flank. James B. Steedman, instead of acting as a general reserve, was ordered on the following morning to "divert" the enemy's attention by making "a heavy demonstration" against Hood's right flank. For this effort he would use two brigades of black troops, supported by a demi-brigade of white units.[7]

Due to these last-minute alterations there were a variety of complications on the morning of December 15th. Schofield's men were out of position as supports for A. J. Smith, and they had to pass in the rear of Wood's corps to reach their proper alignment. Most marched back through Nashville's suburbs, traveling by various circuitous roads to the Hardin pike, and lagged behind in forming to support A. J. Smith.[8]

With the fog continuing to obscure everything that morning, the seeds of confusion and delay portended only a burgeoning fiasco. Several of John McArthur's infantry brigades crossed in front of Wilson's cavalrymen when Wilson's units didn't move at 6:00 A.M. in the fog. About 8:00 A.M., when the fog began to lift, there was an immediate uproar from Wilson. As the infantry blocked his way, Wilson could but rant and fume until about 10:00 A.M., when McArthur's troops cleared his front. In the Fourth Corps the heavy fog also caused a delay. The men of the 86th Indiana Infantry at one point were ordered to stack arms, advance to a stone fence 150 yards in front, tear it down, and carry the rocks back to fashion temporary breastworks. Before the work was completed the fog began to lift, and incoming skirmish fire began to strike about them. A soldier said that several rocks were shattered in the grasp of men as they attempted to carry the boulders back to the designated line. Although the 86th Indiana lost about a dozen men, this defensive work continued.[9]

Farther along the line, in front of Jacob Cox's division of Schofield's corps, when skirmish firing followed by several artillery barrages broke out, it was feared that the Rebels might be preparing to advance. This caused Cox to delay in order to find Schofield, thinking it proper to leave behind one brigade.[10]

In all, it was a most frustrating and confusing morning for Thomas's men. An officer grumbled about whether the guide for his regiment "knew just where he was." Other soldiers considered how slowly the offensive movement was developing, and began fretting about the consequences. Overhead, the sun's rays were beginning to burn through the slowly drifting layers of fog, and the men in the Federal lines began to discern a frowning line of enemy works in the distance.[11]

III

James B. Steedman was known as a first-rate character. An orphan at a young age, and a self-made printing entrepreneur with little formal education, Steedman before the war had been active in Democratic politics, leading in 1861 to an appointment as colonel of the 14th Ohio Infantry. A year later he was a brigadier general. Described by David S. Stanley as "the most thorough specimen of a political general I met during the war," Steedman's promotion to major general had been delayed until April 1864, despite his being credited with good service at Chickamauga. Adding significantly to Steedman's controversial status were his personal habits and flamboyant life-style. The Ohio politician-general was heartily disliked by many of his men for his frequent arrogance and abusive manner. During the siege at Nashville, Steedman demanded that his troops work without relief on the construction of a dam during bitter cold weather on December 12th. Steedman rode among the soldiers, ranting and cursing like a madman at their slow work. When Steedman's back was turned, one individual hurled a large clod of dirt, striking the irate general heavily on the back. Blustering that he would send the guilty soldier to hell if he found out who did it, Steedman finally rode away, still fuming.[12]

What made Steedman the talk of the army, however, was his ardent womanizing. According to his superior, David S. Stanley, Steedman, who had commanded the post of Chattanooga for much of 1864, "was living in very high style" with Princess Salm Salm as his frequent guest. "Steedman was dead in love with the woman," later remembered Stanley, "and [he] was such an idiot that I could not get any work out of him. In fact, he was so taken up with making love to the princess, and drinking champagne that it was difficult to see the great potentate of Chattanooga."[13]

According to Thomas's modified battle plans, Steedman was to make a heavy diversionary attack, intended to mislead or confuse Hood as to the real point of assault. Thus, upon Steedman's shoulders rested the initiative of Thomas's attack on the morning of December 15th.[14]

On the night of the 14th, Colonel Thomas J. Morgan of the 14th U.S.C.T. made a personal reconnaissance as far as the picket line, attempting to discern the enemy's position by the line of their campfires. Morgan concluded that "a [log] curtain" culminated by a line of rifle pits had been extended south from the vicinity of the Rains house in order to protect the flank of the enemy's northward-facing earthworks. By marching south along the Murfreesboro pike, then swinging around behind Rains's Hill so as to capture these rifle pits, Morgan thought that "the works near Rains' house would become untenable and the ground east of the Nashville and Chattanooga Railroad be given up to us with little loss."[15]

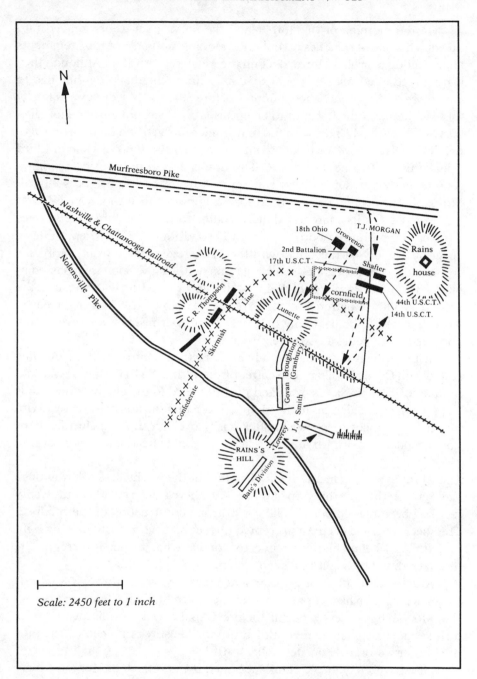

MAP 12 Attack on the Confederate Right
December 15—Nashville

On the morning of the 15th when the provisional troops moved into Steedman's line of trenches at 4:00 A.M., Morgan's brigade of four regiments and a section of artillery formed along the Murfreesboro pike. Although they were poised to advance by about 6:30 A.M., due to the thick fog they had to wait more than an hour. A few minutes before 8:00 A.M. Steedman was finally told by Thomas's chief of staff to begin his attack. Steedman soon launched his two-pronged advance, with the units under Morgan and Lieutenant Colonel Charles H. Grosvenor heading out the Murfreesboro pike, while his third brigade under Colonel Charles R. Thompson moved into position along a railroad culvert to support Morgan's attack from the north. The sound of Morgan's guns would be the signal for Thompson's men to advance.[16]

Morgan's units marched rapidly south, forming in three battle lines parallel to the Murfreesboro pike, well beyond Rains's Hill. Then, under a covering artillery barrage, and with the black regiments in front, Morgan's command began to advance southwest about 10:00 A.M. Soon they passed as planned around the flank of Rains's Hill and moved forward against the secondary line of entrenchments extending southward. These light earthworks seemed to be held only by Confederate skirmishers, and everything appeared to be going as expected.[17]

With Morgan directing the advance, tactical control of the front line rested with Colonel William R. Shafter of the 17th U.S.C.T.* Shafter was told to take the rifle pits in his front and push forward to the enemy's rear, thus trapping the Confederates in the main works along the northern sector. With his three regiments, Colonel Shafter easily overran the light fortifications under moderate skirmish fire, and dashed rapidly ahead into a skirt of timber.[18]

Abruptly they came to a halt. The line of the Nashville & Chattanooga Railroad ran through this strip of timber, and here a deep cut of about twenty feet had been blasted out of solid rock during construction of the roadbed. The sheer sides and deep cut prevented further passage without moving right or left. Yet Shafter had little time to ponder what to do. His troops, he discovered, were caught in a deadly trap.[19]

A devastating blast of canister and musketry swept through Shafter's ranks, felling men like tenpins. On their northern flank the "curtain" of logs that Morgan had observed during the previous day was now discovered to be a rude but strong lunette mounting four guns, hastily fashioned by the men of Granbury's Brigade on December 14th.[20]

Granbury's men had carefully watched the approach of Morgan's force toward their right rear. Realizing that the Federals were unaware of the lunette due to the timbered hillside, they had patiently held their fire until Shafter's troops were trapped beneath their guns. Some of Shafter's men

---

*Later Shafter would be known as "Pecos Bill" following a long and mercurial career in the regular army that included a Medal of Honor and an important command in Cuba during the Spanish-American War.

were as close as thirty yards when Granbury's troops opened fire. Now a battery posted across the railroad track began to fire into Shafter's ranks, spraying canister across their entire front. The resulting crossfire was too much for Shafter's blacks, most of whom were experiencing their baptism of fire. Many jumped into the railroad cut to avoid the devastating fire. Here all became chaos in a matter of moments. Govan's Confederate infantry brigade quickly swung across the mouth of the cut and fired into the milling mass of soldiers. Shafter, on the right of his regiment, was unable to halt the spreading disorder, and his entire line became fragmented and began to fall back in disarray. Indeed, during the next few moments Shafter's command simply vanished. Those able to do so went streaming back across the open terrain, many in panic. The officers and men trapped in the railroad cut were nearly annihilated. In less than ten minutes Shafter lost 110 men and 7 officers from his two principal regiments, including his premonitory brother-in-law, Captain Job Aldrich, who had been shot in the head and instantly killed.[21]

Seeing the disorder among Shafter's men, Colonel Tom Morgan hastened to order up the trailing demi-brigade of white troops under Charles Grosvenor to rush the lunette.[22]

At first Grosvenor's men were fortunate. They had to cross open ground, including a muddy cornfield that mired their shoes and slowed their progress. Moreover, there were two picket fences in their path that had to be knocked down. Yet, due to the attention still being given to Shafter's bewildered troops, Grosvenor's two units were able to approach the smoke-enshrouded lunette. Here they found a ditch in front and heavy logs surmounting a parapet protected by palisades of timber.[23]

Hurriedly, Grosvenor's 18th Ohio Infantry made a rush at the palisade, which was defended by about 300 of Granbury's troops. An Ohio lieutenant yanked at the timbers to create a gap, but was instantly killed. Captain Ebenezer Grosvenor, of the lieutenant colonel's own family, attempted to leap on top of the embankment with his revolver blazing. He tumbled forward, felled by two rifle bullets. Thereafter, the 18th Ohio's soldiers made but little progress, and many stood milling about in the outer ditch, taking heavy casualties.[24]

On their left, Lieutenant Colonel Grosvenor attempted to attack the southern angle of the lunette with his 2d Battalion, Fourteenth Army Corps. These men were "mostly new conscripts, convalescents, and bounty jumpers," and they now "behaved in the most cowardly and disgraceful manner" by running away, Grosvenor reported. Following only a few minutes of fighting, the 2d Battalion's line had been stampeded, leaving the 18th Ohio to stubbornly fight its way back across the open ground following the loss of about 60 men.[25]

Morgan's attack was a complete failure. About noon his men re-formed near the asylum, and Steedman thereafter directed that during the remainder of the day they occupy the Rains outbuildings. These structures were of sturdy brick and were easily "loopholed" [slotted] to provide a safe position for sharpshooters.[26]

During the remainder of the day, Steedman was content to have his men snipe at long range with the enemy's skirmishers. At 2:10 P.M. he wrote to Thomas telling him that he had pressed Hood's right flank "strongly" and had possession of his old works. But all Steedman could think of to say in conclusion was, "[I] hope all will go well."[27]

Good luck did not seem to be following George H. Thomas that morning. Before learning from Steedman about his diversion stalling without applying much pressure against Hood's flank, the Union commander heard of troublesome events along his far right. At first light, the navy's gunboats under Lieutenant Commander Le Roy Fitch had steamed down the Cumberland River to attack the Confederate river battery at Bell's Landing. Due to the fog and the danger of firing into friendly troops, Fitch was unable to accomplish much. After firing a few shells, Fitch withdrew upriver to await more favorable conditions.[28]

Next, the troops designated to operate on the extreme Union right, Brigadier General Richard W. Johnson's 6th Cavalry Division, got off to no start at all. Johnson's men had been in line ready to begin the offensive at 6:00 A.M., but five hours later they still were waiting to advance.[29]

Johnson had 2,100 men in two brigades, 759 of whom were dismounted cavalrymen under Colonel James Biddle. In Johnson's front the only enemy posted along the Charlotte pike—behind Richland Creek—were about 900 Confederate cavalrymen under Colonel Edmund W. Rucker. Rucker's isolated brigade was the sole remnant of James R. Chalmers's Division, assigned to the extreme Confederate western flank following Hood's dispersal of Forrest's cavalry to various widely scattered locations. Ector's Brigade of North Carolina and Texas infantry under Colonel David Coleman was supposed to support Chalmers along the adjacent Hardin pike. Unknown to either Rucker or Chalmers, however, during the initial groping forward of McArthur's infantrymen, Colonel Coleman had been so intimidated as to withdraw his brigade several miles southeast without notifying Chalmers. As a result, Chalmers, in personal command of Rucker's Brigade, remained in position along Richland Creek, unaware that the Hardin pike on his immediate right flank was entirely open to the enemy.[30]

Richard Johnson was an old regular-army officer with a tarnished image following his 1862 defeat and capture at the hands of John Hunt Morgan. Late on the morning of December 15th his division seemed to conduct their advance along the Cumberland River flank much like they were mired in molasses. Unwisely, Johnson had put his dismounted cavalrymen in front, and observing Chalmers's men across Richland Creek, he told Biddle to cross that stream and take the enemy's barricades on the crest of the distant ridge. Many of Biddle's cavalrymen were wearing sabers, and they clanked and clattered their way forward, tripping over the cumbersome scabbards, generally making an absurd spectacle in their attempt to maneuver as infantry. The "shortsightedness" of the regimental commander in allowing his men to bring these awkward and useless sabers along was unpardonable, wrote Johnson, who evidently had not bothered to inspect his men during the morning's long wait. Further, Biddle's men had difficulty in getting across the creek under fire and were unfamiliar with the tactical maneuvers required to preserve their alignment.[31]

Johnson admitted that Biddle's progress was so slow as to soon cause him to order up his larger, mounted brigade under Colonel Thomas J. Harrison. Harrison got his men forward around both flanks of Biddle's floundering troopers, but here the 16th Illinois Cavalry, which charged mounted up a long slope via the right flank, suddenly came to a high stone wall. Their objective was to capture a section of Chalmers's artillery, but the stone wall forced the Illinoisans to dismount and knock portions of the wall down. By the time they were able to get through, the Rebel guns had been limbered up and moved away. Harrison's men captured only a few stragglers as Rucker's Brigade slowly disappeared from sight along the Charlotte pike.[32]

In all, it had been a fruitless and time-consuming encounter. Johnson remained oblivious of the open Hardin pike to his south and only belatedly sought help to outflank Chalmers from his position along Richland Creek. Soon Johnson was made aware of Thomas's and Wilson's growing displeasure with his slow progress.[33]

Gathering up his scattered command, Johnson hastened to push on after Chalmers. Yet four miles west along the Charlotte pike he again encountered Rucker's Brigade strongly posted along a ridge near Bell's Landing. Artillery swept the bridge across a small creek in front, beyond which there were rude barricades of logs and fence rails. Rucker's men were waiting with poised carbines, and a foolish, impulsive attack by a single unsupported Federal regiment resulted in their bloody repulse. Johnson called a halt and sent for help from the navy's gunboats.[34]

By now it was late in the afternoon, and Johnson sat down to wait. Soon the heavy detonations of gunboat shells added to the din in front. But Johnson, having been told by prisoners that Chalmers's entire division was present, wanted Croxton's brigade of cavalry moved up before attacking Rucker.[35]

The sun went down and Johnson was still waiting for Croxton. Chalmers, with all but one regiment of Rucker's Brigade, had already pulled out under the cover of darkness, moving to rejoin Hood's main army along the Hillsboro pike. In Johnson's front only the 7th Alabama Cavalry remained, under orders to withdraw at daylight. Johnson was oblivious of it all. The following morning when his troopers discovered the abandoned enemy barricades Johnson had the effrontery to advise Wilson, "We have driven the enemy from this place and [are] following up."[36]

Johnson, with double the strength of Chalmers and the heavy firepower of the gunboats, had managed to so bungle his assignment as to not only allow the enemy to escape with little loss, but to withdraw from his front without knowing they were gone. Said Johnson in his lengthy after-action report, "I must not neglect to mention that in this day's operations [15th] we captured near fifty horses, so rapidly were our lines advanced."[37]

Thomas was not pleased.

The middle sector of the battlefield had been unusually quiet during the early morning hours. Only the occasional rattle of skirmish fire had broken the tense stillness. At the first opportunity, Thomas had come in person to see the grand and inspiring scene of his bold attack. As far as the eye could see there were blue-uniformed troops stretching across the landscape, poised in line of battle, screened by timber and orchards along the base of the dark and fog-crested hills.[38]

With a roar that shattered the oppressive stillness like a crashing peal of thunder, the Federal artillery in Fort Negley began firing. Negley's heavy siege guns easily arched their thirty-two-pounder shells high above the Confederate lines on Montgomery Hill. Soon other forts, Casino, Morton, Gillem, and Houston, added their guns to the dreadful din. It was pandemonium turned loose, thought a nearby Federal soldier. "The firing was so intense and ceaseless that not an individual gun could be distinguished." The bursting shells filled the air with smoke above the enemy-held hills, and the man wondered if an equal barrage "was ever before witnessed on the American continent, if in the world."[39]

Through all of this din, Wood's Fourth Corps, the largest in Thomas's army, about 13,500 men in line, stood idle. Despite the intense covering fire of artillery and open terrain in front, "nothing further remained for the 4th Corps to do until the cavalry and General [A. J.] Smith had made the long swing [to the east to strike A. P. Stewart's left flank]," wrote the exasperated Thomas J. Wood.[40]

For another two and a half hours, from about 10:00 A.M. until 12:30 P.M., Wood's units waited with growing suspense. Finally the belated movement on the right got under way and Wood ordered forward his entire corps. Across the rolling hills and valleys emerged long battle lines of blue, with banners unfurled, advancing in a "pageant [that] was magnificently grand and imposing," said Wood. There was only light skirmish fire along most of his front, yet when some of Wood's units prepared to rush the enemy works across an open field, the men thought they would surely "catch hell." Indeed, Thomas Wood looked at the imposing sight of Montgomery Hill, a cone-shaped eminence rising about 150 feet above the surrounding terrain, and concluded it would be too costly to directly assault. There were strong entrenchments just below the crest, with an abatis and rows of sharpened stakes set into the steeply sloping ground. Wood was so worried that he halted his advance and about 1:00 P.M. directed a brigade from Samuel

Beatty's division to assault the hill from the left rear, where the slope was more gradual. Colonel P. Sidney Post's brigade was selected for the assignment and, forming along the Granny White pike, they were soon prepared to charge toward the burned-out brick house atop the hill. With fixed bayonets, Post's five regiments sprang forward at the double quick.[41]

They were in for a surprise. On December 12th a Confederate deserter had reported that a new line was being prepared along Hood's front, about a mile in the rear of the visible entrenchments. Here, said the man, the Rebel army would permanently remain. This, of course, was the pulled back line, established on December 10th by Hood for access to timber for fuel. As a result, only a skirmish line occupied the old breastworks that Post's men were now assaulting, although these works once had been part of the main Confederate line.[42]

Despite several reconnaissances by Emerson Opdycke during the past few days, the unsuspecting Wood thought the Confederate line continuous across his front. Now his soldiers could hardly believe their luck. Instead of heavy volleys of musketry and a shower of canister, there were only scattered shots fired at them. The 124th Ohio Infantry sprinted past the burned-out Montgomery residence to a stone wall some 200 yards beyond and looked around. "There was not an armed Rebel in front of us that we could discover," wrote an astonished soldier. In a few spots along the line there was brief firing, and a few prisoners were taken. Yet the division commander joked that it seemed to be a race between the attacking column under Post and their supports, Abel D. Streight's brigade, as to who would reach the summit first. The grand assault was such a farce that Wood at first didn't know what to do once he had taken Montgomery Hill. "All we want is to feel safe, and then we will push ahead," wrote another officer who learned of the success in the center, yet fretted about a movement against the Federal right and rear. Wood had his men dig in and erect breastworks, pending word from Thomas.[43]

At first Wood's attack seemed to be a significant event, particularly with the capture of Montgomery Hill and the occupation of the advanced line of enemy entrenchments. Yet soon Thomas and his generals began to realize that the Union army hadn't even approached the main Confederate line of battle. It was now past 2:00 P.M., and an enormous amount of artillery ammunition had been expended, not to mention the extensive use of manpower in order to capture a mere skirmish line.[44]

When and where would all this embarrassment end?

John Bell Hood had spent most of the morning catching up on his correspondence. Hood had learned through newspapers that the enemy claimed the capture of thirty Rebel flags at Franklin, which, added to the widespread rumors of the appalling bloodbath, caused the Confederate commander much discomfort. That morning he wrote to Secretary of War James A.

Seddon what was intended to be a rebuttal. "We lost thirteen [colors], capturing nearly the same," he asserted. "The men who bore ours were killed on and within the enemy's interior line of works." Hood also wrote that day to Beauregard and others, seeking more troops. Ironically, his chief of staff at that very time was drafting a circular outlining the proper dispositions for defending the redoubts then being constructed on the army's flanks.[45]

About 10:00 A.M. Hood learned via signal flags of a simultaneous Federal advance toward his eastern and western flanks. Yet his corps commanders then anticipated only "a demonstration," several strong reconnaissances having gone out from the Federal lines during the past few days. As the morning progressed and the volume of firing increased, Hood became concerned and left his headquarters at "Traveler's Rest" in order to visit A. P. Stewart's position along the Hillsboro pike. By the time Hood arrived it was apparent that Thomas had more than a demonstration in mind. Heavy columns of troops were observed advancing in multiple lines of battle, and swarms of skirmishers were pushing forward beyond the Confederate flank.[46]

Hood quickly saw that the crucial aspect was to hold back the enemy until he could bring forward reinforcements. It was for this very purpose that he had ordered A. P. Stewart to construct a series of five redoubts protecting the extreme left flank and rear of the army. Hood sent word to Stephen D. Lee along the Franklin pike front to rush help to Stewart. Meanwhile, he went in person to Redoubt No. 4 and told the men to hold the fort at all hazards until reinforcements arrived. Since he was operating on interior lines, the advantage in bringing troops to any threatened point still rested with the Confederate army.[47]

It was a most interesting battle scenario; the impending battle was developing much as the Confederate commander had foreseen, with a threatened attack against his exposed flanks. Accordingly, Hood would rely on traditional defensive tactics: the application of massed firepower to defeat frontal assaults against strong works. Already Hood had learned that Thomas's thrust against the single lunette on his far right flank had been hurled back in a bloody repulse.

All that seemed to be required was for A. P. Stewart's veteran infantrymen, the soldiers who repeatedly had been called upon to rush up against so many Federal breastworks from Atlanta to Franklin, to resolutely hold these forts. John Bell Hood must have relished the thought. It seemed to be the Battle of Franklin reversed.

CHAPTER XXIX

Now, Boys, Is Our Time!

ANDREW J. SMITH, with his austere gaze, long, snowy white hair, and stiff-brimmed army hat, looked the part of a Puritan preacher, thought an Illinois officer. Smith's prim appearance belied his rough-and-tumble background. An old, West Point–trained Dragoon officer with more than twenty years of rugged service in the West, Smith was revered by his soldiers, yet had remained in the background within top army circles despite having beaten Nathan Bedford Forrest at Tupelo, Mississippi, in July 1864. His troops "were a rough looking set" and were fond of boasting that they had been to Vicksburg, Red River, Missouri, and about everywhere else in the South and West, and if old A. J. ordered them to, they would go to hell itself.[1]

From the first days of their arrival at Nashville, Smith's troops had been poised for combat. During the past year most of Smith's troops had been continually on the march, having fought and traveled over more than a thousand miles within the past three months. The result, said an Iowa colonel, was that his men seemed to act with a more aggressive spirit, disdaining the necessity of earthworks, and were more "reckless and daring" in their attitudes about attacking fortifications. George H. Thomas was so impressed with A. J. Smith's troops that he designated them as the primary assault force on December 15th. Accordingly, A. J. Smith's three divisions were among the first troops to deploy early that morning in preparation for the fray.[2]

But the dense fog not only delayed, but quickly complicated the army's anticipated grand left-wheel movement. Smith's men now blocked the path of Wilson's cavalrymen, who were to support Smith's attack and protect their flank. On Smith's right, with McArthur's division delayed by fog, skirmish fire, and a battery of enemy artillery, the cavalry didn't move forward into its assigned position west of the Hardin pike until about 9:00 A.M. Another hour was spent in aligning the infantry and cavalry units, dismounting the cavalry—all but one regiment of each brigade was to advance on foot by Wilson's order—and chasing away the Confederate skirmishers and battery in front.[3]

Finally, just after 10:00 A.M., Smith's infantrymen advanced across the open, stump-littered ground east of the Hardin pike, executing a left-wheel movement with Wood's Fourth Corps as the pivot point. The cavalry also moved across the Hardin pike, placing virtually all of Thomas's primary strike force east of that road. Since Ector's Confederate infantry brigade under Colonel David Coleman had rapidly withdrawn in their front, fourteen wagons containing the division ordnance stores and headquarters papers belonging to James R. Chalmers were now uncovered along the Hardin pike. Although the wagons attempted to escape south along the pike, one of Wilson's brigade commanders ordered in pursuit his only mounted regiment, the 12th Tennessee Cavalry. After a chase of some miles, Chalmers's wagons were brought to bay and captured. Chalmers, who had sent the wagons in rear of the infantry "for greater security," was greatly angered by the irresolute behavior of Coleman's men. Prior to 2:00 P.M. it was the only Federal success along the significant western sector of the battlefield.[4]

A. J. Smith's left-wheel movement had covered about a mile and a half along the outer arc when George H. Thomas discovered that Smith's infantrymen were crowding too closely to the left, leaving a larger than anticipated area along the right for Wilson's cavalrymen to fill. About 1:00 P.M. Thomas directed Schofield to bring up his Twenty-third Corps and form on the right of A. J. Smith's troops. This would allow Wilson to "turn the enemy's left completely," said Thomas, whose attention was now focused on possession of the Hillsboro pike, where A. J. Smith's men had just found the refused extreme left flank of Hood's main line. While Schofield's and other troops moved up from the rear toward the far right, the infantry's forward movement along Wood's pivot flank was suspended. Here Brigadier General Kenner Garrard's division of A. J. Smith's troops halted after arriving in front of A. P. Stewart's strong line of redoubts adjacent to the Hillsboro pike. While Garrard waited for the more westerly units of McArthur's division to come up, he ordered several batteries of artillery to begin shelling the redoubts from any available cover. Meanwhile, for nearly three hours many of A. J. Smith's men remained idle in ravines and other sheltered sites, waiting for McArthur's division and the cavalry to complete their wide-swinging arc.[5]

Wilson's dismounted cavalrymen discovered that moving along the outer arc of the left-wheel movement was hard work. The troopers had to double quick much of the time and were continually pressed to keep up with the infantry, which had a shorter distance to travel. Wilson was using only two divisions, spreading the 5th Division under Brigadier General Edward Hatch across the cavalry's entire front, while Brigadier General Joseph

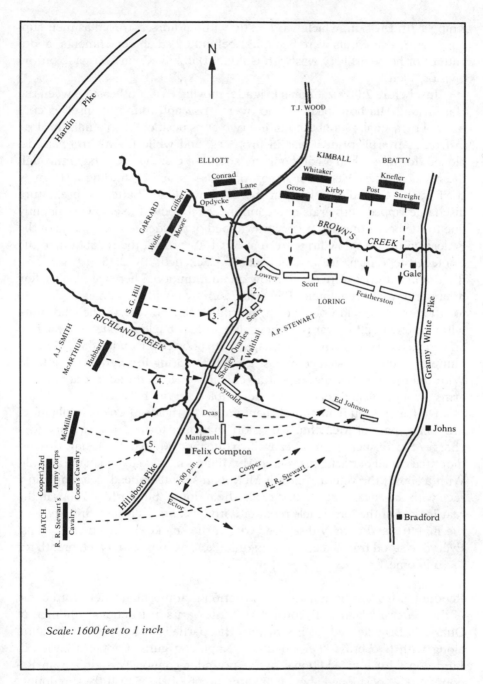

MAP 13 Assault on the Confederate Left
December 15—Nashville

Knipe's 7th Division, which was mostly without horses, trailed as their supports. Hatch's mounts were being led behind by small detachments, and a battery of horse artillery was with Colonel Datus E. Coon's Brigade on the division's left.[6]

Just before 2:00 P.M. Coon's Brigade, moving east-southeast between the Hardin and Hillsboro pikes, came over a rise and found themselves confronted by a small redoubt mounting two guns positioned on a hillside close in front. An artillery duel was in progress, and while Coon's troopers deployed, for more than a half hour the sound of cannon fire echoed through the ravines. There were four Union batteries in action, hurling a storm of shell at the Confederate fort. In the 2d Iowa Light Battery a premature discharge ripped both arms of a cannoneer off above the elbows, evidently due to the bore not being properly swabbed of powder residue. Some of the Federal guns were now firing from about 150 yards of the redoubt, and the Confederate return fire had noticeably slackened. By 2:15 P.M. some of the Union batteries were running low on ammunition. There were only a few hours of daylight remaining. Edward Hatch by now had seen enough. "Go for the fort," he told Coon's men, warning them to reserve their fire until within a few hundred yards of their objective. A bugle sounded the charge, and so eager were the men to escape their poor cover under the redoubt's plunging fire that it seemed almost a relief to spring forward to the attack. With their deadly Spencer repeating carbines held high, almost at present-arms position, Coon's cavalrymen scrambled up the hillside.[7]

On Hatch's left flank the adjacent infantry brigade of Colonel William L. McMillan, part of McArthur's division, had just formed preparatory to a charge. Skirmishers were already in front, and McArthur, seeing the dismounted cavalry attacking, ordered McMillan's brigade to join in the assault. With a shout, the veteran units of McMillan sprinted ahead, seemingly in a race with the cavalrymen to first reach the redoubt. Supporting troops in the rear looked at the formidable redoubt with its cannon flashing fire, and saw the infantry and cavalry disappear within the smoke of the enemy's guns. Everyone stood transfixed, wrote an onlooker, waiting with bated breath for the outcome.[8]

Redoubt No. 5 had been under construction that morning when word came of the Federal advance. Following A. P. Stewart's instructions, 100 men of Quarles's Brigade had been sent into the partially completed fortification along with two brass twelve-pounder Napoleon guns. Captain Charles L. Lumsden with four additional twelve-pounder cannon was already in Redoubt No. 4, positioned about 600 yards north of No. 5. Yet these redoubts were unconnected by regular entrenchments, being isolated works along the upper slopes of several adjacent hills. Their supporting infantry, Major General Edward C. Walthall's division, were so diminished in numbers as to be unable to cover the entire front of the refused line. By A. P. Stewart's order,

Walthall had posted his men along the Hillsboro pike behind the double stone wall that lined this road. Yet Walthall's left flank stretched south only to a point nearly opposite and several hundred yards in the rear of Redoubt No. 4. That left the flank of No. 5 and the ground beyond unprotected—temporarily.[9]

The only help Walthall had obtained that morning was from Ector's Brigade, under Colonel Coleman, which, having retreated from A. J. Smith's front, came up and reported to Walthall after 11:00 A.M. They were soon posted in close proximity to Redoubt No. 5 as an extension of Walthall's left flank. About 1:00 P.M., however, with an artillery duel in progress along the line of the five redoubts, Walthall had learned of a threat farther south beyond his exposed left flank. An enemy force had been sighted moving north along the Hillsboro pike, and it was feared they would soon envelop the refused Confederate line. Walthall quickly consulted with A. P. Stewart, who ordered Ector's infantrymen south along the pike to meet this threat. Just before 2:00 P.M. Colonel Coleman marched away in obedience to these instructions. Again, Walthall's flank along the southernmost sector remained exposed, pending the arrival of reinforcements from Stephen D. Lee's Corps, just ordered up by Hood.[10]

The attack up the hillside was made amid a whirlwind of noise and turmoil. The troopers of the 2d Iowa Cavalry, part of Coon's brigade, seemed to run right into the sheet of flame leaping from the muzzles of the Confederate guns. The gunners had switched from shell to canister, and the small-arms fire was incessant. Yet the redoubt's fire was mostly too high, as Coon's men had discovered. Several cavalrymen, including Lieutenant George W. Budd of the 2d Iowa Cavalry, were the first to reach and climb over the parapet. Immediately in their rear a seemingly endless column of blue uniforms rushed at the stockade walls. McMillan's infantrymen were there too, scrambling over the logs and tumbling into the redoubt, every man yelling and shouting at the top of his lungs.[11]

Within the redoubt all became chaos. There was a brief flurry of flailing gun butts, jabbing bayonets, and pistol fire. Lieutenant Budd, brandishing his saber, thrust it in the face of several Confederate gunners, making them swing one of their Napoleons around to fire at a few of Quarles's men who had been quick enough to escape. Advancing just behind the first assault wave were Hatch, McMillan, and several other ranking Union officers. Hatch was excited, and he yelled to those near him to turn the guns around, even ordering by mistake a captive Rebel officer to help man the cannon. The look of astonishment on the face of the prisoner, said an observer, was ludicrous. Hatch realized his mistake and leapt to the side of the gun himself. Within three minutes, thought one soldier, the redoubt had been secured and the captured guns were firing at the enemy's second fort, visible to the northeast.[12]

It hadn't been much of a contest. With two field guns and perhaps 100 men arrayed against Coon's and McMillan's combined brigades of about 1,500 men, A. P. Stewart's defenders had little chance. Yet the spontaneous shout of triumph from the Union soldiers was short-lived. From the higher hill to the northeast Redoubt No. 4 began pouring a heavy artillery fire into the captured fortification. Captain Charles L. Lumsden had swiftly pulled two of his smooth-bore guns out of their embrasures and faced them south to fire on No. 5. Also, a 100-man detachment of the 29th Alabama Infantry deployed along the side of Lumsden's redoubt, opening a heavy fire of musketry. Hatch immediately saw his plight. "To remain in our captured fort was certain death," said one of the 2d Iowa Cavalry's noncommissioned officers, "to retreat promised little better, while to attempt the capture of this second fort seemed madness." Hatch looked around. His men and the infantry were badly winded by the charge. All were mixed together "like a crowd of schoolboys." Already some of his cavalrymen were chasing after a few Rebel stragglers attempting to escape eastward. Hatch waited no longer; he again ordered the charge sounded. Up and out of the ditch scrambled the cavalry and infantry together. Yet Coon's mostly exhausted men, being unused to attacking on foot, soon slowed to a walk despite the incoming fire. Many men were seen to sink down behind a tree and randomly fire their Spencer carbines. Their division commander, Hatch, again on horseback, began urging the men onward. He told one exhausted trooper to grab hold of his horse's tail; the sturdy mount, he said, would pull him up the sloping hillside.[13]

Important help arrived when John McArthur ordered his 2d Brigade under Colonel Lucius F. Hubbard to support the attack. Hubbard's men were relatively fresh and soon gained ground on the far left, rapidly approaching Redoubt No. 4 despite the heavy brush, fallen timber, and a severe enemy fire. Simultaneously, a four-gun battery assigned to Hubbard's brigade galloped up the slope near the still smoldering Redoubt No. 5 and began firing fuzed shell at the second fort. By chance, one of their guns was still loaded with a one-second shell due to the earlier combat. If the gun was fired at the fort, the shell surely would burst over Coon's and McMillan's men, realized a gunner. Not having the time or tools to unload this gun, he asked the battery commander what to do. The officer pointed toward the Hillsboro pike where only a long stone wall was visible and shouted to let her go over there, and get back to work in front. Just after the cannon's discharge the shell burst directly above the stone wall. To everybody's surprise, up from behind the stone wall jumped what seemed to be a full brigade of Confederate infantry. Within moments they scattered in confusion, remembered an amused cannoneer.[14]

Meanwhile, on the hillside between the two redoubts it seemed to become another race between the infantry and cavalry. Coon yelled to his men "to take those guns before the infantry could get up." Some of his troopers were even crawling on their hands and knees toward the redoubt.

At one point Coon found a sergeant of the 2d Iowa Cavalry halted within twenty yards of the work, heavily panting as if "completely exhausted." "Sergeant," shouted Coon, "can you put those colors upon the works?"

"I can, if supported," gasped the sergeant. Coon again urged the 2d Iowa's troopers forward.[15]

With the Yankees' Spencers emitting a continuous rain of fire, the Confederates were unable to take careful aim in shooting back. Captain Lumsden's gunners kept firing with double charges of canister until the ragged Union line reached the log palisade. Amid hand-to-hand combat the sergeant of the 2d Iowa Cavalry thrust the regiment's flag above the parapet, but was struck in the abdomen. Nearby, a lieutenant of the 9th Illinois Cavalry shot what he thought was the commander of the redoubt, just as the combined ranks of blue infantry and cavalry swarmed over the walls into the redoubt. Some gunners were still at their posts, but at one Napoleon a cannoneer with the needed primers had already fled. "Captain, he's gone with the friction primers," yelled one of Lumsden's desperate men. The captain shouted back, "Take care of yourselves, boys," and all who could get away promptly fled down the opposite hillside.[16]

Within moments resistance ended. Hatch, Coon, and McMillan soon were present to stare at the bewildered prisoners and smoking wreckage. Altogether they had taken six guns and about 150 prisoners. Coon's and McMillan's men seemed so severely depleted that the men virtually collapsed about the captured fort. Meanwhile, Hubbard's brigade, advancing on the north flank, swept past the redoubt and angled eastward toward the Hillsboro pike. They were now moving beyond the flank of yet another Rebel fort, toward a gray line of infantry visible behind the low stone walls at the pike. Hubbard saw that the Rebels were making a strong effort to rally. His own left flank was unsupported and the enemy infantry seemed likely to attack through the void. Hubbard halted his men and changed front, sending several companies of skirmishers forward. Clearly, he would need help. A. J. Smith hurriedly began looking around for additional troops to continue the overwhelming momentum of his successful attack.[17]

The men of John McArthur's 3d Brigade were wild with excitement, wrote an officer. For several hours they had remained in reserve watching the action in front from a sheltered ridge. Now they wanted part of the glory. "Bring us a fort, bring us a fort," they shouted when Major General A. J. Smith rode past. "I'll get a fort for you, [and] you won't have to wait long for it, either," he responded. Smith told Colonel Sylvester G. Hill that the third redoubt in front was threatening McArthur's progress, but to attempt to take the fort with his lone brigade would be a hazardous undertaking. Hill, however, was eager for the fray. "Oh, no," he responded, "our men will go right up there; nothing can stop them; they will go up without a bit of trouble." A. J. Smith remained skeptical. He told Hill to stay where he was until he could go and get Hubbard's Brigade swung around to assist in the attack. Smith rode off, but Hill didn't wait. "Scarcely a minute had elapsed after General Smith rode away, when Colonel Hill ordered his bugler to sound the charge," wrote an amazed Iowa colonel.[18]

Hill's men promptly sprang forward and began climbing the steep hill. There was a blaze of fire from the redoubt, and a hail of iron whizzed overhead, but the yelling of Hill's men seemed to drown out everything. Hill had ordered his brigade to advance without firing, only discharging their single-shot rifle muskets when actually within the fort. Fortunately for Hill and his men, the Confederates again had fired too high. The guns in Redoubt No. 3 couldn't be depressed sufficiently to fire into the oncoming Union ranks. Hastily, the Rebels attempted to withdraw their four-gun battery, just as some of Hill's men opened fire. A fusillade of minie balls scattered many of the cannoneers, and two of the guns were abandoned. By the time Hill's men entered the redoubt nearly all the defenders had fled.[19]

A wave of blue engulfed the hilltop, yet as had earlier happened at the other captured forts, there was a new burst of incoming fire. This time it was from the small Redoubt No. 2, located several hundred yards distant across the Hillsboro pike. As officers attempted to round up their men and re-form the ranks, Colonel Hill impulsively shouted to charge the enemy's second work. No sooner had Hill spoken than a rifle bullet struck him in the forehead, killing him instantly.[20]

Due to the noise and confusion, only about two hundred men responded to Hill's last order. Engulfed in smoke, they dashed forward, led by a Minnesota colonel. Amazingly, before they reached the redoubt nearly all the defenders fled, leaving behind one piece of artillery, a caisson, and various equipment. A Union officer later reported in triumph, "From this point we poured a most galling fire upon the retreating enemy."[21]

A. P. Stewart knew he was in serious trouble. Hood's concept of isolated, self-sustaining forts without strongly entrenched infantry support had proved to be an outright failure in the face of Thomas's overwhelming assault. Not only had Hood initially guessed wrong about the location of the attack, but Ector's Brigade had been detached from the critical extreme southern flank just at the most inopportune time, shortly before Coon's dismounted cavalry assault on Redoubt No. 5. Furthermore, the reinforcements ordered by Hood from Stephen D. Lee's corps were late in arriving despite marching along "interior lines." Redoubts Nos. 4 and 5 had been captured before the arrival of these two brigades from Ed Johnson's Division.[22]

Lee's troops consisted of Arthur M. Manigault's Brigade, followed by Zachariah C. Deas's Brigade, and arriving piecemeal, they were sent toward the stone wall along the Hillsboro pike to plug the gap opposite Redoubt No. 4. Already there was an atmosphere of disaster in the air. Union troops and their six-gun batteries seemed everywhere in front, swarming over the hill-tops and captured redoubts.[23]

Thus far the contest generally had involved Thomas's troops attacking small forts defended by artillery and a few infantry supports. Now the battle was on the verge of involving large-scale infantry units—with the Confederates protected only by what natural cover they might find. No earthworks had been prepared along A. P. Stewart's refused line. Ironically, the men chosen by Stephen D. Lee to go to Stewart's aid had been Ed Johnson's Division, the only portion of his corps to be heavily bloodied at Franklin.

Ed Johnson's two brigades were hardly in place before they were confronted by McArthur's infantrymen, moving east toward the Hillsboro pike. Simultaneously, the 2d Iowa Light Battery opened fire on Johnson's line from behind captured Redoubt No. 5. The result, said the disgusted A. P. Stewart, was that Johnson's men fled after making "but feeble resistance." Indeed, the gunners of the 2d Iowa Battery could hardly believe it. Under their exploding shell fire a confused mass of enemy broke from the stone wall at the Hillsboro pike and scattered across an open field to the east. Incredibly, when the battery commander elevated his guns to play upon the open field, the shot and shell, plowing up the ground and exploding among the terrified soldiers, caused the larger number of them to run back to the wall for safety. Meanwhile, several of McArthur's regiments had dashed up to the opposite stone wall and began firing into Ed Johnson's men. These Rebels "appeared panic stricken and fired badly," noted a Union lieutenant colonel whose regiment suffered only two men wounded in the entire encounter. Two companies of McArthur's skirmishers soon charged with fixed bayonets up the Hillsboro pike, capturing a reported 450 prisoners.[24]

Johnson's remaining men streamed back across the field in disarray. Desperately, Stewart attempted to rally them along a small hill behind his primary east-west battle line. Finally, due to the timely arrival of a battery from Loring's main line at this place, Stewart was able to bring most of them to a halt.[25]

Nearby, Major General Edward C. Walthall was attempting to contend with increasingly crucial difficulty. His entire south flank was exposed and outflanked following the loss of Redoubts Nos. 4 and 5, and Walthall hastened to shore up this threatened sector. He pulled Brigadier General Daniel H. Reynolds's Brigade from his right as supports for Redoubt No. 3 and sent it to the southern flank to keep the Yankees from rolling up the entire refused line. Thereafter, Walthall extended his two remaining brigades farther north to cover Reynolds's former position, but he soon began to perceive that this line was threatened on three of four sides, and too few troops were available at any one point. Moreover, the Union battle lines now extended beyond Reynolds's redeployed flank, causing Walthall to send a staff officer to Stewart saying that unless Reynolds received help all was lost. To Walthall, the crucial question was all too apparent. It was simply a matter of whether

A. P. Stewart's makeshift line could hold back the Federals along all three sides until Frank Cheatham's troops came up and darkness put an end to the conflict.[26]

With Brigadier General Joseph A. Cooper's infantrymen from Schofield's Twenty-third Corps on the left and the dismounted cavalrymen of Colonel Robert R. Stewart on the right, this newly formed most advanced Federal line swept across the Hillsboro pike into an open field to probe for further enemy resistance. Cooper's men were marching in line of battle at quick time, little more than the pace of a brisk walk, when a battery of Confederate artillery suddenly opened from a knoll in front. It was A. P. Stewart's hastily repositioned battery from Loring's line, supported by the re-formed ranks of Ed Johnson's two brigades.[27]

Cooper's and Stewart's men were caught in the open field amid bursting shells and a shower of canister. Immediately Cooper's men raised a cheer and spontaneously ran forward. Several officers tried to stop them, but the men continued running ahead in a ragged, disjoined line, making for the crown of the knoll. There were volleys of musketry and more whizzing canister, but Cooper's troops scrambled up the slippery slopes yelling at the top of their lungs. Ed Johnson's men had had enough. Again they fled, abruptly abandoning the battery they were supporting. Cooper's men quickly overran the crest of the knoll and dashed on after the battery, which was seen hastily attempting to escape eastward through the valley below. Yet these field guns were soon cornered by Stewart's cavalrymen, many of whom had sprinted around the base of the knoll to cut off the enemy's escape. Three of the still smoking cannon were captured and hastily swung into action. With Stewart's cavalrymen serving as gunners, they poured shot after shot into the remnants of Ed Johnson's wildly fleeing men.[28]

A. P. Stewart saw at a glance that the situation was "perilous in the extreme." Although he had hoped to hold on until Cheatham's troops came up, there now was little alternative; he ordered Loring and Walthall to retreat.[29]

Stewart was too late; Walthall had already given the order to fall back. Not only was A. P. Stewart's line broken along the third (south) side, but Walthall's weakened division and many of their supporting troops had been driven back from the stone wall bordering the Hillsboro pike.

Some of Hubbard's regiments from McArthur's division had swung east and north across the pike. Joined by the 6th Tennessee Infantry of Cooper's brigade, they began sweeping north along the Hillsboro pike, taking many prisoners. Also, one of A. J. Smith's reserve brigades, eager for the fray and having found a gap in the lines, ran forward beyond the Hillsboro pike. Here they saw the Confederates fleeing in wild disorder. "It was a splendid scene to see them scatter in confusion through a cornfield that was so muddy that it almost was impossible to travel, and then to see them turn back, as we supposed to stand and fight—but only to surrender. . . . Our regiment took the most of them, and without firing a gun." So excited were the men of the 33d Wisconsin that a corporal said their officers could barely halt them there.[30]

Adding to the overwhelming pressure on A. P. Stewart, the long-idle Fourth Corps under Thomas Wood had begun attacking along Loring's front soon after fighting intitiated by A. J. Smith on the southern and western perimeters had begun. About 4:00 P.M. Wood ordered Brigadier General Washington L. Elliott to attack with his division and capture the main Confederate line anchored by Redoubt No. 1. Yet Elliott delayed in making the assault, "waiting for General [A. J.] Smith to come up and connect with his right." When about a half hour had passed and no movement had occurred, Wood impatiently ordered Nathan Kimball's division forward to attack east of the Hillsboro pike. Kimball's attack was straight across a muddy, 200-yard-wide cornfield at the heavily entrenched line in front, defended by Loring's three brigades. Kimball had two brigades in the front line, Kirby's and Grose's, and they stumbled up the slopes fully laden with knapsacks and equipment. An officer noted how their progress was slowed by the burdensome packs. About seventy paces from the enemy line he halted the line and ordered the knapsacks unslung. Then the Union battle line fairly raced for Loring's works.[31]

Most of Loring's men were gone by the time Kirby's wildly yelling soldiers, followed by Grose's ranks, swept over the entrenchments. At 4:35 P.M. Kirby claimed four captured cannon, hundreds of prisoners, and a wide variety of small arms, trophies, and abandoned equipment that littered the ground.[32]

On their right flank, Elliott's division had belatedly joined in the assault and, spearheaded by Emerson Opdycke's prominent brigade, they rapidly approached Loring's works in the vicinity of Redoubt No. 1. Opdycke's men, with Lane's brigade on their left, arrived at the entrenchments only to find them already in the possession of their skirmish line. A lieutenant of the 36th Illinois, William Hall, with twenty-two skirmishers had crept along the stone wall bordering the west side of the Hillsboro pike until beyond Redoubt No. 1. Observing the advance of Colonel Edward H. Wolfe's Brigade of A. J. Smith's corps along the same front, and the men of their own Fourth Corps attacking Loring's line to the north, Hall perceived an opportunity. Fragments of the Confederate line had begun to pull out, streaming to the rear from the vicinity of the salient angle. Hall yelled to his men: "Now, boys, is our time! I believe we can take that Rebel fort—the Johnnies are more than half whipped. How many of you are ready to go in?"[33]

There was a shout of assent, and Hall and his handful of men bolted across the pike, scaled the wall in the rear of the redoubt, and flung themselves at the astonished defenders. There was little resistance. A few of the Confederate artillerists fought with revolvers, but they were quickly subdued at the point of Hall's bayonets. Just behind Hall's men were the skirmishers of Wolfe's brigade, who rushed through the redoubt and claimed their share in the capture of three artillery pieces and forty prisoners. Both lines of Federal skirmishers now found themselves burdened with trophies and prisoners. A Union corporal grabbed a battle flag, and Lieutenant Hall secured the sword of an Alabama officer. In the span of about ten minutes, A. P. Stewart's last remaining redoubt had been taken, and its guns turned on the fleeing remnant of its infantry supports.[34]

It was a "full stampede," wrote a Confederate soldier. A. P. Stewart's entire corps was now in utter flight, streaming east and south along the adjacent Granny White pike. One of Stewart's staff officers, Captain William D. Gale, saw Mary Bradford run out of her house and shout to the fleeing men to stop and fight. Yet they were so panic-stricken they refused to halt.[35]

Other attempts to re-form the men added to the growing disaster. Brigadier General Claudius W. Sears, who had served with Walthall's line, was wounded in the right leg by a Federal artillery shell that passed completely through his horse and struck him just below the knee. The limb was so badly damaged it was soon amputated. Not more than 150 men remained of his entire brigade when they were finally halted.[36]

Through it all Gale was aghast: "The men seemed utterly lethargic and without interest in the battle. I never witnessed such want of enthusiasm, and began to fear for tomorrow, hoping that Gen'l Hood would retreat during the night."[37]

John Bell Hood had informed Frank Cheatham about 3:00 P.M. that help was urgently needed on the Confederate far left flank. Although Brown's and Bate's divisions were directed to march to A. P. Stewart's relief, by the time Bate was notified he said it was evening. Bate's men soon started, marching in column, but after reaching the Franklin turnpike, a steady stream of horses without riders, stragglers, and large numbers of dispirited soldiers greeted their eyes. It was the sure indication of a defeat, thought Bate, who apprehensively formed his ranks in line of battle and sought specific orders.[38]

The only thing to do under such circumstances, reasoned Brigadier General Randall Lee Gibson, was to stand one's ground and hope that darkness would prevent further embarrassment. Gibson's Brigade was posted along the extreme left flank of Stephen D. Lee's Corps, and Gibson had to put his entire brigade in a makeshift line facing west to stave off threatened disaster.[39]

Drifting to the rear toward the Brentwood hills moved the isolated brigade of Texas infantry commanded by Colonel David Coleman—Ector's Brigade—cut off from A. P. Stewart's flank by the advance of Hatch's cavalrymen earlier that afternoon. Hood and his staff sat watching Coleman's approach from a high hill adjacent to the Granny White pike at twilight. Grimly, Hood rode among Coleman's men, directing them into position along the crest of the hill. "Texans, I want you to hold this hill regardless of what transpires around you," he shouted.

"We will do it, General," they replied, and Hood rode off to face an uncertain conclusion to the day's events.[40]

The sun had set at about 4:33 P.M. and it would be dark by 6:00 P.M., noted a Federal officer. With the breakthrough of Wood's and A. J. Smith's men, George H. Thomas sent word about 5:00 P.M. to rapidly pursue the enemy toward the Franklin pike, two and one-half miles eastward, which was Hood's main line of retreat. Yet Wood's Fourth Corps was in such disorder following their successful assault that it was half an hour before their ranks re-formed. Advancing slowly in line of battle, at 6:00 P.M. Wood's men reached the Granny White pike. Here it was too dark to further maneuver the men and Wood ordered a halt. A. J. Smith's soldiers, meanwhile, were still busily rounding up prisoners and captured cannon, and most remained along the Hillsboro pike as darkness fell. Only elements of Wilson's cavalry and some of John M. Schofield's troops continued to press eastward into the evening gloom on December 15th.[41]

West of the prominent hill adjacent to the Granny White pike the men of John Mehringer's brigade suddenly encountered skirmish fire as they advanced toward the rising ground. Throwing forward his brigade in line of battle to the crest of an intervening ridge, Mehringer's men exchanged rifle fire for about twenty minutes with the Texans of Ector's Brigade under David Coleman. Yet it was so dark that when two brigades from Jacob Cox's line moved up to support Mehringer they simply lay down behind the ridge and waited for the firing to cease. Coleman's men, however, were convinced that they had defeated a desperate effort to drive them from the hill where Hood had posted them. As the fighting sputtered to a halt they dropped to the ground and bivouacked for the night in line of battle.[42]

Luck, it appeared, had not entirely deserted Hood's army. The early winter darkness seemed to have intervened to save the Army of Tennessee from ruin. Night had fallen with Thomas's vast numbers groping for the exposed arteries that would cut off Hood's retreat. A mounted brigade from Wilson's reserve division was then on the verge of completely severing the Granny White pike. Schofield's entire Twenty-third Corps was massed east of the Hillsboro pike, nearly all being fresh troops unexposed to heavy combat on the 15th. Two of A. J. Smith's divisions had been either lightly engaged or had not fought at all during the day's action. Further, Wood's Fourth Corps had been barely tested, having to overcome only an advanced skirmish line and earthworks largely abandoned by their defenders prior to the 4:30 P.M. attack.[43]

On two broad fronts, the northern and western, the Federal columns were again massing to further hammer the Confederate lines, while to the south there was the dire threat of cavalry operations aimed at cutting off

344 / EMBRACE AN ANGRY WIND

Hood's army from its line of retreat. An overwhelming host was poised on Hood's flank, awaiting only daylight to complete the task successfully begun.

Conversely, an entire Confederate corps, A. P. Stewart's, had been wrecked during the day's fighting. Only Stephen D. Lee's corps seemed fully prepared for combat on the 16th. At nightfall, it appeared that the only unclear aspect was the nature of Hood's reaction. Would he retreat, or stay and risk everything?

George H. Thomas was elated. The day's results were rapidly pouring in to his field headquarters; sixteen pieces of Rebel artillery captured, between 800 and 1,000 Confederate prisoners, and the enemy swept back over more than eight miles. To brighten the victory, he had just learned at about 7:00 P.M. that one of his greatest concerns had been without foundation. Prisoners confirmed that Nathan Bedford Forrest with three divisions of cavalry and another infantry division were absent from Hood's army, being detached in the vicinity of Murfreesboro. Wilson of the cavalry had fairly shouted the news. No wonder Hood's vulnerable left flank was so easily approached![44]

Thomas gladly tallied the consequences. As the Union commander rode back to Nashville that evening, he began planning the following day's movements. To a staff officer he remarked with an almost gleeful, wry humor, "So far I think we have done pretty well. Unless Hood decamps tonight, tomorrow Steedman will double up his right, Wood will hold his center, Smith and Schofield will again strike his left, while the cavalry [will] work away at his rear."[45]

Thomas could hardly wait to get to Nashville. His first stop there would be at the telegraph office to send the news east.

CHAPTER XXX

I Shall Go No
Farther

In WASHINGTON, D.C., Major Thomas T. Eckert learned that the telegraph lines had been repaired and a line was open to Nashville. His duty was to transmit Grant's order removing Thomas. Yet Eckert hoped a message from Nashville would soon arrive, announcing that Thomas had attacked and gained a victory, which would materially alter the need for "Old Pap's" removal. Recalling that Lincoln and Stanton had not ardently endorsed Grant's action, Eckert decided to wait for Van Duzer's daily telegram, which he knew must soon be forthcoming.[1]

After an hour's delay, at 11:00 P.M. the wires began to hum. It was a message from Thomas, in cipher. Nervously, Eckert's office manager began to translate: "Nashville, Tenn. Dec. 14, 1864, 8 P.M. . . . the ice having melted away today, the enemy will be attacked tomorrow morning."[2]

More suspense! It was only Thomas's telegram of yesterday, which had been delayed more than twenty-four hours. Immediately afterward, however, came Van Duzer's long-expected telegram reporting on the Nashville situation at nightfall on the 15th. It was only a half hour old, and Eckert anxiously read the slowly transmitted message:

Our line advanced and engaged the Rebel line at 9 this A.M. . . . the results are very fair. The left occupies the same ground as at morning, but [the] right has advanced five miles, driving [the] enemy from [the] river, from his entrenchments, from the range of hills on which his left rested, and forced [him] back upon his right and center. His center [is] pushed back from one to three miles, with [the] loss, in all of 17 guns and about 1,500 prisoners, and his whole line of earthworks, except about a mile on his extreme right, where no serious attempt was made to dislodge him. From our new line General Thomas expects to be able to drive the enemy at daylight east of the road to Franklin. . . . The whole action of today was splendidly successful. . . . I have never seen better work. . . . J. C. Van Duzer.[3]

Eckert was out of the door in a flash. He ran down the stairs with both telegrams in his hand and raced for the waiting ambulance at the curb in front of the War Department. In minutes his vehicle clattered to a halt in front of Stanton's residence on K Street. Stanton heard the racket outside and soon appeared at the second-story window. "Good news," shouted Eckert—Thomas had whipped the Rebels. "Hurrah," shouted Stanton, and soon the secretary was poring over the telegrams. A few minutes later both were on their way to see Lincoln at the White House. Lincoln was roused out of bed and, in his nightshirt with candle in hand, read Van Duzer's dispatch. Lincoln was immediately elated.[4]

On the way to see Lincoln, Eckert had pulled Grant's unsent telegram out of his pocket and handed it to Stanton, saying that he had held it on his own responsibility until he could hear from Nashville. Expressing fear that he might be court-martialed, Eckert looked at Stanton. The secretary put his arm around Eckert's shoulders. "Major, if they court-martial you, they will have to court-martial me. You are my confidential assistant, and in my absence were empowered to act in all telegraph matters as if you were the Secretary of War. The result shows you did right." Stanton explained to Lincoln what had happened, and the president fully approved of Eckert's action.[5]

Following the arrival of Thomas's own dispatch of 9:00 P.M., but received at 11:25 P.M., there was further confirmation of the Federal triumph. Ulysses S. Grant was notified at Willard's Hotel and first shown Van Duzer's telegram. About 11:30 P.M. he wired Thomas, "I was just on my way to Nashville, but receiving [the] dispatch from Van Duzer detailing your splendid success of today, I shall go no farther. Push the enemy now, and give him no rest until he is entirely destroyed. . . . Do not stop for trains or supplies, but take them from the country, as the enemy have done. Much is now expected." Fifteen minutes later, after reading Thomas's dispatch, Grant again wired, "I congratulate you and the army under your command for today's operations, and feel a conviction that tomorrow will add more fruits to your victory."[6]

It had been a fateful few minutes. Thomas's career was saved. Grant wired his chief of staff at his City Point, Virginia, headquarters that he was not going to go to Nashville. Lincoln went back to bed. In the morning he would wire Thomas, "Please accept for yourself, officers, and men, the nation's thanks for your good work of yesterday. You made a magnificent beginning. A grand consummation is within your easy reach. Do not let it slip. A. Lincoln." Stanton also wired his congratulations before retiring, announcing that "we shall give you a hundred guns [salute] in the morning."[7]

Major Thomas Eckert went back to his telegraph office. There must have been a broad smile on his face.

George H. Thomas didn't know how close he came to being removed from command. Not until the following summer, when visiting Washington, did he learn from Stanton of the details involving Eckert, and see a copy of Grant's final removal order. On the night of December 15th, Thomas was excited and happy. He even wired his wife in New York the glad tidings: "We have whipped the enemy, taken many prisoners and considerable artillery."[8]

Yet Thomas's self-gratification was short-lived. He well realized that much work remained to be done, and the night of December 15th was both eventful and busy at his headquarters. The presumption among nearly all of the headquarters staff was that Hood was whipped and would swiftly retreat. Even Thomas seemed convinced Hood's army would retire rather than face the prospect of a complete disaster. According to Schofield, when he visited with Thomas that evening he had to remonstrate with him about the prospect of Hood's remaining to fight. Schofield was worried that the aggressive Hood might suddenly hurl his forces at the exposed Federal western flank, which was somewhat in disorder following the pursuit of A. P. Stewart's troops.[9]

James H. Wilson found Thomas exuberant about the prospects for the morrow, "Old Pap" saying that his only regret was that the attack had been delayed on the 15th, resulting in insufficient daylight to finish the rout of Hood's army. Thomas ordered Thomas J. Wood about 8:00 P.M. to attack the enemy if found in front at first light on the 16th, otherwise to pursue him southward. This reflected the latest intelligence from the cavalry: a recently captured Rebel prisoner had stated that Cheatham's command had moved to the Confederate left flank and that their wagons were retreating on the Franklin pike. Moreover, Wilson reported the enemy "very much demoralized," and that all of Forrest's cavalry were detached from Hood's army except for Chalmers's division.[10]

All but overlooked was the matter of Hood's unpredictable personality. Schofield, the only apprehensive general among the army's commanders, said he was finally able to convince Thomas to have Wilson delay his advance in the morning until it was learned if Hood had withdrawn as anticipated. Otherwise, the combined Federal ranks would push forward rapidly and endeavor "to capture or destroy" the retreating Rebel army.[11]

It was now apparent to John Bell Hood that Thomas's troops would attack at an early hour on the morning of the 16th. Moreover, Hood was convinced that the enemy's objective was to operate against the flanks of his army. By his estimation, the fighting of the 15th had been favorable to the Army of Tennessee until near sundown, when some of A. P. Stewart's "partially completed redoubts" had been lost. Although A. P. Stewart's Corps had been badly mauled, to retreat now would sacrifice any prospect of a successful campaign. Further, the failure to win at Nashville would probably cost Hood his command. He could only lose by withdrawing, but by remaining he might recoup his fallen military fortunes. It was an outright gamble, risking complete disaster. No matter; the alternatives were unacceptable. Hood decided to remain and fight. As early as 8:00 P.M. that night he began directing his troops into a new defensive line.[12]

Believing that perhaps his original line had been overextended, Hood determined to shorten his new defensive front. A series of bold heights, part of the Brentwood hills, ran conveniently across Hood's immediate rear, from west of the Granny White pike to east of the Franklin turnpike. Since this natural line was adjacent to the position where Ector's Brigade defended the rolled-back Confederate left flank at dark, Hood decided to utilize this high ground for his new line of works.[13]

By anchoring the right flank with Stephen D. Lee's strong corps on a high hill known locally as Peach Orchard Hill (Overton Hill), and placing Frank Cheatham's relatively fresh troops on the army's extreme left with Ector's Brigade, Hood anticipated that Thomas's assaults might be decisively repulsed. With A. P. Stewart's battered but still capable corps occupying the strongly fortified center, they could be used as reinforcements if needed on either flank. In all, the new line was about two and a half miles long, yet due to the refused flanks on both high hills, Hood's new battle line actually presented a front of more than three miles.[14]

Hood, at his new headquarters at Judge J. M. Lea's home, "Lealand," spent much of the night in preparation for the morning's fight. An extensive line of entrenchments were ordered prepared, and Hood's weary soldiers, after stumbling through the darkness into their designated positions, began cutting trees and fashioning strongly barricaded lines. The naturally rolling terrain and the artillery emplaced on the commanding hills seemed to assure the advantage of fighting on the defensive. Yet the possibility of defeat caused Hood to take a few precautionary measures. The army's stores and wagons were ordered south to Franklin. Also, early the following morning Hood advised A. P. Stewart that "should any disaster happen to us today," he was to withdraw via the Franklin pike, re-forming in line of battle beyond Brentwood so as to allow the army to pass through.[15]

Ironically, one of the most critical combat dispositions to be made, the recall of Forrest's two cavalry divisions to the army, was held in abeyance. Earlier that evening Forrest had been advised by one of Hood's couriers that a battle was in progress and to hold his mixed command of infantry and cavalry in readiness to move at a moment's notice. When notified, Forrest was east of Murfreesboro, seeking to capture a Federal forage train, and his command was widely scattered throughout the area. Forrest immediately ordered a concentration at Wilkinson's Cross Roads northwest of Murfreesboro. Yet there was no further word from Hood. Forrest was compelled to wait at the crossroads until the night of the 16th before learning what had

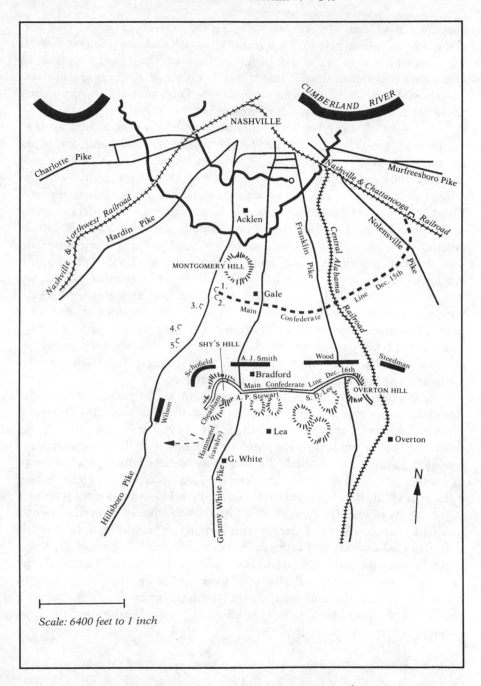

**Map 14 Situation Early Morning, December 16
Battle of Nashville—2nd Day**

happened near Nashville. Although there is little reason to believe that Forrest would have been able to reach Hood's position with anything but a small fragment of his cavalry on the 16th, the fiery cavalry general's presence might have counted for much. Indeed, in the tension-filled hours ahead Hood would need every able individual available to keep alive his rapidly fading hopes for a measure of victory in Tennessee.[16]

The night of December 15th remained warm and very windy. Most of the Federal troops had bivouacked where darkness found them, and amid the maimed and dying on the battlefield they witnessed pathetic scenes of distress. One of McArthur's Iowa colonels, intrigued by a captured redoubt a short distance in the rear, went with several officers to look over the site. En route they made a startling discovery. An unconscious Confederate, grievously wounded in the head, lay on the ground. His wound was obviously mortal, and it seemed miraculous that he was still breathing. Beside the man someone had placed an empty ammunition box with a piece of bacon, a hardtack cracker, and a tin cup half filled with water. Apparently a stretcher bearer, noting the man's plight, had provided the food, straightened his legs, wrapped a chunk of wood in a blanket, and placed it under his head for a pillow. The snack was intended for his comfort in case he regained consciousness. As the Iowa colonel remarked, the pathetic scene was both gruesome and touching. They could do nothing for him, said the colonel, so they turned away and left him there to die alone under the stars.[17]

In Nashville there was little sleep that night for the busy surgeons who found their once nearly empty wards overcrowded with wounded and dying soldiers from both armies. Ambulances had begun rolling in with many serious cases by midafternoon, and before nightfall the hospitals were crowded. In one small hospital 597 cases were admitted during the course of the battle, 57 of whom were Confederates. To a headquarters clerk visiting a surgeon's tent, the many gruesome sights and scenes were a grim reminder of the cruelty of war. On the operating table beside a pile of severed arms and legs he found a lanky Confederate with a sponge of chloroform held to his nose. He was unaware that his right leg was being sawed off below the knee. In ten minutes the severed limb had been cast upon the pile in the corner, the arteries cauterized, flaps of flesh lapped over, and strips of plaster placed on the stump. When the man was revived, he held up his leg, reacting with shock and sorrow, before being carted away to make room for the next patient.[18]

Sunrise on Friday, December 16, 1864, was shrouded in what one observer described as a "Scotch mist." Yet the fog was not as thick as it had been on the 15th, and by about 8:30 A.M. the sun's rays had burned off all but a few lingering patches. At 10:00 A.M. a citizen in Nashville recorded the temperature as sixty-five degrees, and expansive clouds had begun to build in a broken sky. To the troops of Thomas's army the vivid martial scene that spread in full view that morning was breathtaking. Looking out over the rolling landscape from the Federal-held knolls, a long battle line in blue stretched across the valley below, twisting like a giant serpent around the base of an opposite hill. Beyond, the enemy's works were visible across the summit, with a ragged line of earthworks extending southward from the crest. Along the hillside the enemy's skirmish line was marked by wisps of white gunsmoke drifting skyward amid the mottled brush and dark timber.[19]

With banners waving and bayonets glistening in the hazy morning sunlight, two divisions of A. J. Smith's troops began to advance about 8:00 A.M., marching in a half right wheel to close proximity of the Confederate line along the Granny White pike. Artillery firing had begun with the movement of Smith's troops, and the bursting Confederate shells soon wreathed the air with smoke above the slowly moving lines of blue infantry.[20]

To the men in the ranks, the closer they came to the high enemy-held hill in front, the more imposing and steep-sided it seemed. An Iowa officer wrote that it appeared foolhardy to even think of capturing that hill by direct assault. Moreover, the abatis-obstructed slopes and the rugged line of breastworks stretching west to east across the level ground beyond the Granny White pike seemed equally formidable. The Rebels along the main front were even utilizing a heavy stone wall reinforced by rails set outside the wall in the manner of a staked abatis.[21]

A. J. Smith's troops moved up to within 600 yards of the heavily entrenched lines, and by 9:00 A.M. halted along a nearly mile-long front. The intense shell fire had already claimed a number of victims, causing one division commander, McArthur, to throw up rifle pits while his skirmish line went forward to within 100 yards of the enemy's pickets.[22]

During the night, by Schofield's request, A. J. Smith had sent to the right as reinforcements his entire Third Division, under Colonel Jonathan B. Moore. Having only Garrard's and McArthur's divisions remaining, Smith now seemed to lack the strength to successfully assault the heavily entrenched Confederate line in front. Accordingly, he ordered forward all six of his available artillery batteries to shell the enemy's entrenchments while he advanced his men to confront Hood's main line. He then expectantly looked for the troops on his right, Schofield's Twenty-third Corps, to resume the offensive. Smith reasoned that Schofield's troops were in entrenchments close by the base of the high hill in front, and almost at a right angle with Smith's line. Therefore, being beyond the flank of the enemy's main line, and facing a refused position, the initiative for an attack clearly rested with John M. Schofield's infantry and James H. Wilson's cavalrymen.[23]

Schofield was not having a good morning. Instead of planning offensive operations, Schofield was greatly worried about the threat of an attack. Because of the Twenty-third Corps' "much exposed" position astride Hood's flank, Schofield was fearful the enemy "would mass and attack our right." Other units of Thomas's army were generally not in contact with the enemy's

main line at daylight on the 16th, and Schofield believed his troops the most
vulnerable. Already he had urgently requested help on the night of the 15th,
causing Jonathan B. Moore's 1,600 reinforcements to be put in reserve
behind his right flank before daylight.[24]

Due to a brief firefight at dusk on the 15th between Colonel John Mehringer's Brigade, part of Major General Darius N. Couch's division, and Colonel David Coleman's men (Ector's Brigade) along the high knoll later known
as Shy's Hill, Schofield had become concerned about a Confederate offensive. After pushing rapidly up the hill to meet the supposed threat, Mehringer
said he had "repulsed" the enemy attack, losing nineteen men and three
officers. Although the brief encounter had halted at dark, word spread
through channels that Mehringer had "met the enemy, much superior to
him . . . and held him in check." Schofield was convinced it was the enemy's
"evident design of turning our flank and recovering the position just lost." It
was the basis for his apprehension on the night of the 15th, and the reason
he requested Thomas to hold Wilson back on the 16th until Hood's intentions
were known. Only two weeks earlier Schofield had been surprised by Hood's
reckless, attack-against-all-odds manner of fighting. Apparently he was now
fearful of another rash, Franklinlike assault.[25]

This whole episode held out the increasing prospect of Hood's salvation.
During the morning of the 16th Schofield's operations were limited to "preparations for defense and cooperation with the cavalry." With Schofield staying put and Wilson waiting for Thomas's revised instructions, the main thrust
of the Federal offensive had abruptly sputtered to an ignominious halt. What
Schofield didn't know was that he had been intimidated by the presence of
Ector's lone brigade, less than 1,000 men, which at nightfall on the 15th was
merely attempting to defend the high knoll per Hood's direct order. (Later
Schofield sought to save face by saying that he spent the whole forenoon of
the 16th "in impatient anxiety and fruitless efforts to get from General
Thomas some orders or authority that would enable us all [the cavalry and
the two infantry corps] to act together.")[26]

At midmorning Schofield was still so fearful of an attack that he sent
messages to both Thomas and A. J. Smith asking for more reinforcements.
Schofield wanted another division, even though his Twenty-third Corps was
not then engaged. Thomas, mindful of the crucial role assigned to his right
flank, soon obliged, instructing Smith to send Schofield "a good division," as
"the force you have [earlier] sent he reports as inadequate." Smith, however, was so exasperated that he protested to Thomas and refused to send the
men. As late as 1:30 P.M. Schofield continued to sulk, advising Thomas, "I
have not attempted to advance my main line today, and do not think I am
strong enough to do so."[27]

It was absurdity of the highest order. One man's apprehensions had
essentially stifled the Federal army's prospects for a rapid, overwhelming
victory.

The chaotic effect on Thomas's tactical situation was well illustrated by the plight of Major General James H. Wilson and his cavalrymen. At nightfall on December 15th Wilson had anticipated the continued pursuit of his objective, which was "to take the enemy in the rear, if possible." Accordingly, he had bivouacked his command along the Hillsboro pike, intending to advance at daylight south of the Confederates' final position of the 15th. Following the arrival of Thomas's message later that night ordering Wilson to remain in place until Hood's intentions were known, Wilson's only activity on the morning of the 16th was to send some of Brigadier General John H. Hammond's dismounted troopers on a reconnaissance. Hammond was then on the extreme right flank of Thomas's army, having advanced at nightfall close to the Granny White pike.[28]

In the half-light of early morning Hammond pushed forward a single regiment, the 19th Pennsylvania Cavalry, which discovered "heavy masses of infantry" seemingly moving westward. The 19th Pennsylvania took ten prisoners along the Granny White pike, most of whom were from Frank Cheatham's Corps—"all of whom came over from their right last night and this morning." Hammond quickly sent this crucial intelligence to Wilson, who considered it of such importance he forwarded copies to Thomas's and Schofield's headquarters. When some of Chalmers's cavalrymen were encountered that morning farther south along the Hillsboro pike, it seemed possible that Hood was moving troops into position for a flank attack. Wilson ordered Hammond withdrawn to the Hillsboro pike.[29]

Although then poised on one of the only two roads open to Hood for a retreat, Wilson's cavalrymen soon pulled back. Schofield, meanwhile, became even further alarmed by Wilson's dispatch, probably sent before 9:00 A.M. It was the apparent reason why the Twenty-third Corps commander requested additional reinforcements from A. J. Smith. Furthermore, at 10:10 A.M. the dismayed Wilson sent a curious dispatch to Schofield, telling him that the country east of the Hillsboro pike was "too difficult for cavalry operations." Wilson added, "It seems to me if I was on the other flank of the army I might do more to annoy the enemy, unless it is intended that I shall push out as directed last night."[30]

Although Schofield forwarded this dispatch to Thomas, he told Wilson that "until you receive other orders from General Thomas, you had better hold your forces in readiness to support the troops here, in case the enemy make a heavy attack."[31]

Wilson was stymied, and at 11:00 A.M. many of his troops still languished in their bivouac areas. Already the partially sunny skies of the early morning had given way to leaden gray clouds. As if to add further misery to an already dismal situation, Wilson learned that Chalmers's cavalry division had rejoined Hood's main army, having eluded Richard Johnson's cavalrymen along the Cumberland River flank. Wilson rather peevishly told Johnson that if this was true, he had no force of enemy in his front and should return with his command and rejoin the main cavalry corps.[32]

George H. Thomas, intending to investigate the prospect of an imminent enemy attack as suggested by Hammond's report, rode up to Wilson's head-quarters at the six-mile post on the Hillsboro pike about 10:30 A.M. Wilson conveyed his frustration about not being able to advance pending clarification of the enemy's intentions, and again suggested that his men be moved to the eastern flank. Thomas was irritated by the morning's delay and said no. In fact, he told Wilson to resume his movement toward the Granny White pike, which would uncover any threatening movement by Hood. Once Wilson reached that pike, Thomas could begin his general assault on Hood's positions, commencing right to left. Thomas then rode off, evidently to see if Wood was as yet in position on the eastern flank.[33]

For the uneasy Federal soldiers on the idle Wilson–Schofield–A. J. Smith flank, beyond wondering what had happened, the unanticipated wait was exceedingly frustrating. Adding to their growing misery, the events of midday seemed entirely fitting.

It began with a mist. By about noon a light rain was falling. Thicker and faster came the pattering raindrops, and soon a drenching rain was falling. With the rain came a cold front, and the temperatures began dropping. "With our oil cloths wrapped about our shoulders we sat in our trenches, waiting and watching," wrote a disgruntled Federal infantryman.[34]

The minutes and hours slowly passed. Nothing appeared to be happening. No one was giving orders, or seemed to know what was planned. Even Schofield began to fret. At 1:30 P.M. he sent a message to Thomas—"Will you be on this part of the line soon?"[35]

George H. Thomas spent much of the morning visiting various commanders, anxiously waiting for his army to move up and confront Hood's new defensive line. It had taken Thomas J. Wood's Fourth Corps most of the morning to march nearly two miles southward in the face of a heavy enemy skirmish line and come abreast of A. J. Smith's position.[36]

Even more retarded had been the advance of Thomas J. Steedman's troops along the extreme Federal eastern flank. Steedman discovered that the enemy had evacuated their position of the 15th only after advancing his skirmishers in battle formation at daylight. But Steedman advanced so cautiously that it was 12:25 P.M. before a junction was made with Wood's troops east of the Franklin pike. Meanwhile, Thomas, like the rest of his army, had impatiently waited. A headquarters orderly saw him sitting alone on the end of a log, his elbow on his knee, with his hand nervously rubbing his stubby whiskers.[37]

By late morning Thomas was with Thomas J. Wood, reviewing the situation and telling Wood that the general plan of battle for the preceding day, to outflank and turn the Confederate left, was still in force. Thomas wanted Wood to harass the enemy's Franklin pike front, remaining alert for an opportunity to make a decisive attack, but to bide his time for the present. Thomas then rode back toward the critical right flank, leaving Wood to seek out and confer with Steedman about securing their left from a possible enemy turning movement.[38]

Thomas J. Wood had always been ambitious. As a new corps commander following the wounding of David S. Stanley, Wood was on the lookout for an opportunity to solidify his position and gain recognition. Accordingly, when Thomas gave him the discretion of taking the offensive—if he found "any opening for a . . . decisive effort"—Wood began contemplating an attack.[39]

Hood's main battle line was across a large cornfield, with the stalks still standing. Here, halfway up the long, rising slope of 300-foot-high Overton Hill (or Peach Orchard Hill), were downed trees and various obstructions in front of the breastworks. Visible upon the works were a large number of flags, a sure sign, as the veterans well knew, of a heavily defended line. Overton Hill was steep and very imposing. Most of the approaches were across cleared ground. Further, with the rain falling, mud and soft ground were to be found everywhere.[40]

Thomas J. Wood had an inspiration. "A close examination" had satisfied him that if Overton Hill could be carried, the enemy's right would be turned and his line taken in reverse, and Hood's main line of retreat would be cut off. "The capture of half of the Rebel army would almost certainly [follow]." While it was evident the assault would be most difficult and would involve a heavy loss, Wood thought "the prize at stake was worth the hazard."[41]

Among his officers Wood had a colonel most eager to earn a brigadier's star. Colonel Philip Sidney Post of the 59th Illinois Infantry had been at the forefront of the Fourth Corps' successful attack on Montgomery Hill on December 15th. As a former Illinois lawyer who had risen rapidly from second lieutenant of his regiment in 1861, Sidney Post was one of the most aggressive brigade commanders in the army. Indeed, some of his men were leery of him, especially of his ambition, which seemed to put them into every dangerous situation. Most of the day Post had encouraged Wood to charge the enemy; now he volunteered his brigade for the assault on Overton Hill.[42]

About 1:00 P.M. Wood told Post to make a personal reconnaissance in order to determine the feasibility of the attack and the best point to assault. When Post returned forty-five minutes later, he told Wood that the enemy's position on Overton Hill was truly formidable, but he thought he could carry it with his brigade by attacking along the northern face.[43]

Wood agreed, and in order to support Post's attack he ordered up Streight's brigade to advance closely behind. Further, Wood went to see James B. Steedman, whose troops connected with Wood's left flank near the Tennessee & Alabama Railroad and fronted the refused portion of the Overton Hill line. Wood asked for Steedman's cooperation in the attack, to advance supports along Post's exposed left flank.[44]

Although Steedman had no formal orders from Thomas other than to pursue the enemy, he had advanced that morning "without anything but ammunition, not expecting to move more than a mile." Feeling that he could best protect the army's extreme left flank by keeping forward, Steedman continued until he joined with Wood and, eager for glory, quickly agreed to help in taking Overton Hill. In fact, emboldened by the enemy's rout of the preceding day, he would not only cover Post's attack from the flank, but send several of his own brigades to participate in the actual assault, "with a view to carrying whatever might be in its front."[45]

Most of Steedman's 3,000 men were black troops, largely inexperienced in battle, and they would witness their first major combat by staging a frontal assault against heavily entrenched positions defended by the strongest corps in Hood's army. Steedman chose Colonel Charles R. Thompson's brigade of the U.S. Colored Troops for the primary role. They would be supported by Lieutenant Colonel Charles H. Grosvenor and his provisional brigade of white infantry, to which a small regiment of black troops had been added that morning.[46]

As Wood's and Steedman's units organized their ranks for the coming effort, the artillery began bombarding the enemy line on Overton Hill. Logs forming a part of the Rebel earthworks were splintered and knocked down. Smoke from the bursting shells seemed to enshroud the rugged works. Yet, ominously, there was no return fire from the Confederate cannon.[47]

"The practice of the batteries was uncommonly fine," noted Thomas Wood. "The ranges were accurate . . . and the ammunition being unusually good, the firing was consequently most effective. It was really entertaining to witness it." Five of Wood's batteries and one of Steedman's were firing from ranges of less than 1,000 yards, and although some of the gunners cut the fuses too short, causing several shells to burst prematurely, mortally wounding a sergeant in the 96th Illinois, the devastating fire was believed to utterly wreck the Confederate earthworks. Indeed, it seemed impossible that anything could survive that furious shelling.[48]

At 2:45 P.M. Wood gave the order to attack. A long line of men, appearing almost to emerge from the earth in the gloom and drizzle, began moving in solid columns toward the smoldering works on Overton Hill.[49]

CHAPTER XXXI

Mine Eyes Have Seen
the Glory

IT HAD BEEN A GRISLY SIGHT. Early that morning the men of Colonel Thomas J. Morgan's and Lieutenant Colonel Charles H. Grosvenor's brigades had found their dead lying on the battlefield of the 15th, stripped of their clothing and left exposed to the vermin and wildlife. Scattered about the abandoned lunette defended by Granbury's Brigade, and along the gap in the Nashville & Chattanooga railway line, slain blacks and dead white soldiers of the 18th Ohio Infantry had lain for nearly twenty-four hours. Confederate infantrymen needing shoes, clothing, and equipment had randomly rifled the bodies, taking everything of use. Colonel William Shafter found his brother-in-law, Captain Job Aldrich, lying on his face, stripped of "all his clothes—everything." Near Aldrich's body was the corpse of another white officer, Captain Gideon Ayers. A wounded black soldier related how Ayers was still alive when the Confederates had stripped him, with Ayers begging them not to hurt him so much as they roughly removed his belongings. Ironically, according to Shafter, the wounded blacks had been left alone and not bothered by the enemy, even as the corpses about them were being pilfered.[1]

Now, on the afternoon of the 16th, the troops of Steedman's command were ordered to make another effort against a Rebel stronghold—the works along Overton Hill. "It was probably their strongest position," wrote a Federal officer. "The slope of the hill was obstructed by tree tops," and the approach was over a plowed field heavy with mud. Further, the officer noted, "In front of the 12th Colored Regiment of Thompson's brigade was a thicket of trees and underbrush so dense as to be almost impenetrable . . . a kind of wooded island in the midst of a cornfield." Steedman's men girded for what clearly would be a most desperate assault.[2]

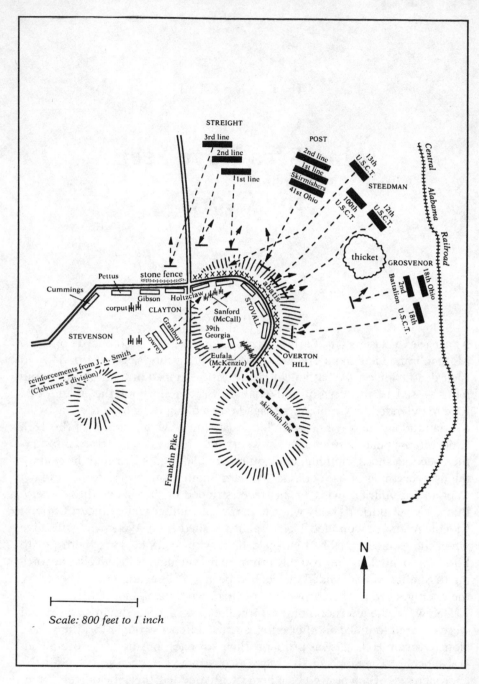

MAP 15 Assault on the Confederate Right
3:30 P.M. December 16—Nashville

(*Sources: O.R. Atlas, 73-1; O.R. 45-1, regimental reports.*)

Steedman selected Colonel Charles R. Thompson's black brigade, largely unbloodied on the 15th, to advance in the front line. Grosvenor's men would march behind in close support, with Morgan's brigade of the U.S. Colored Troops remaining in reserve.

Steedman's two brigades began briskly advancing about 3:00 P.M., keying on Sidney Post's brigade of Wood's corps, which was forty yards ahead and to their right. As supports designated to protect Post's left flank, Thompson's and Grosvenor's men were advancing without a specific objective, intending to adapt to the tactical situation encountered by Post as he attacked the north face of Overton Hill.[3]

Thompson's three regiments hadn't advanced more than fifty feet before being hit with shell fire. Two Rebel batteries firing from Overton Hill filled the air with bursting shells and whizzing shrapnel. A single shell took out an entire file of men in the 12th U.S.C.T., and the angry zip of minie balls added to the terrible din. Men began falling on all sides. "Captain, I'm wounded, what shall I do?" cried a soldier, not wanting to seem as if he was shirking his duty. He was told to lie down, and the ranks pressed steadily onward through the cornfield, advancing in column with flags flying. In the steady drizzle, the successive lines of black soldiers almost seemed to vanish, then abruptly emerge as they passed over several swells. Leaden gray skies cast a pall of gloom over the field. The soft earth stuck to the men's shoes, miring their every footstep.[4]

Directly in front of the 12th U.S.C.T., marching on the left of Thompson's line, loomed the large, imposing thicket. By prior agreement, the regiment was supposed to march around this obstruction, while their brigade commander halted the other units beyond the thicket to allow the 12th to catch up. Yet Thompson's entire line remained under a heavy fire, and as the 12th double quicked to deploy as directed, the other men, seeing them running, thought a charge had been ordered. Many of the 100th U.S.C.T.'s soldiers began dashing forward. Thompson thought that only greater confusion would occur if he attempted to stop them, and he ordered his command to charge. With a yell the ragged line of blacks sprang ahead.[5]

Thompson's men were in two lines, the 12th and 100th regiments in front, followed by a trailing unit, the 13th U.S.C.T. With the 12th still strung out in disarray, Thompson's brigade was badly fragmented before reaching the base of Overton Hill. Even worse, Post's brigade, originally on their right front, had scrambled up the hillside toward the breastworks directly ahead of Thompson's men. This forced both the 12th and 100th to angle to the left to avoid running into Post's troops. The result was a disaster.[6]

Firing from a salient angle in the works on Overton Hill, the Confederates poured volleys of musketry and double charges of canister into Thompson's line, enfilading both regiments. Desperately, the men dashed for the wooded hillside beneath the enemy's earthworks. After clambering over a rail fence, they lunged forward into the timber. Here they ran headlong into a line of felled trees. Beyond the trees there was a sturdy abatis. The interlaced branches of the downed trees seemed almost impassable. Thompson's blacks were soon caught amid the branches like flies in a spider's web, thought one of their officers. The 12th's ranks had crowded together, and every enemy shot seemed to have a devastating effect. Hundreds of men were already down, and still the agony continued. An officer shouted, "By the left flank," and the 12th U.S.C.T. scattered along the hillside. Soon the men flung themselves to the ground along the slopes, not daring to further expose their bodies. Grosvenor's command had been able to reach only the base of the hill, the battalion of conscripts and recruits again having fled. The 12th and 100th regiments had been stopped in their tracks, and now they looked to their right, where the swirling smoke continued to rise from the north face of Overton Hill.[7]

Sidney Post's men were having no better luck. Tactically, Post had hoped to protect his main attack force by throwing out a heavy line of skirmishers to draw the enemy's fire. Accordingly, an entire regiment, the 41st Ohio Infantry, had deployed across Post's front. The 41st was told to go as far as possible ahead of the main line, which proved to be across the valley, up the hillside, and within 100 yards of the Rebel works. Here a fusillade of musketry was added to the bursting shells and shotgunlike blasts of canister. Yet the rifle fire was not intense, as if delivered by a weakened enemy battle line. The skirmishers started on a run for the earthworks. Thirty yards from the entrenchments the 41st Ohio reached a heavy line of abatis. The Ohioans grasped and tugged at the rude barricades, intending to push them aside, yet found these obstructions staked to the ground. A few men continued to pull at the thick timbers and sharpened stakes, but most flung themselves on the ground and began firing at the entrenchments ahead. Behind the stalled skirmishers, Post's main battle line began rushing forward. Most failed to make it to the skirmish line at the abatis.[8]

Stephen D. Lee's troops were behind the breastworks, strung out in a thin line with the men about five feet apart. Only two brigades, Brigadier General Marcellus A. Stovall's and Brigadier General James T. Holtzclaw's, were defending the works east of the Franklin pike, with a single battery, Sanford's Mississippi, playing upon Post's front. During the two hours prior to Post's and Thompson's assault, the heavy artillery bombardment seemed to suggest a pending Federal attack on Lee's front. Hood became concerned and had ordered two brigades from Cleburne's former division, Granbury's and Lowrey's, to move across from the extreme left to the support of Lee. Now the Federals fighting Holtzclaw's men east of the Franklin pike observed two brigades of Confederate reinforcements pour into the entrenchments. Immediately a sharply intensified fire devastated Post's ranks.[9]

Post was on horseback, directing the movements of his two separate lines. When 200 yards from the works, Post ordered the charge sounded, and his lines surged forward—only to run headlong into a "furious" fire. Post and his horse were among the first hit; his horse was killed, and he took a severe wound from a blast of canister, the ball ripping through his right side just above the hip and passing out near the backbone. Obscured by the smoke and mist, his first line attempted to reach the abatis but fell short, most of the men seeking cover along the hillside. Immediately behind came Post's trailing two regiments. They too failed to get very far, leaving a trail of dead and wounded as they staggered toward the abatis. A regimental commander looked behind for Streight's supporting brigade, but they had halted and were merely firing over the heads of Post's men. "Fall back; we are falling back," someone shouted, and Post's second line disintegrated in disorder. A few men attempted to sprint forward and renew the stalled attack, but their efforts were in vain. Three color-bearers of a trailing regiment were shot down in attempting to get their flags forward to the abatis.[10]

Even Streight's supporting brigade failed to accomplish much. When several regiments attempted to rush over some of Post's prone soldiers, they were met with an intense fire that claimed in the 51st Indiana three officers and eighty men within ten minutes. It was a disaster. The lines were badly mixed, men were running wildly to the rear, and many others were clinging to the ground for safety. Post's replacement and Streight called off the attack. Their shattered ranks fell back without waiting for orders, streaming to the rear in disarray.[11]

Like ocean waves crashing in futile sequence against the rocky shore, Post's, then Streight's men had failed in their hastily conceived frontal assaults, suffering fearful losses in the process. It had been close to a slaughter. More than a thousand Federal casualties occurred during the Overton Hill attack, representing about one-third of Thomas's entire loss during the two days of battle. Even the Confederate commanders were shocked and sickened by the frightful carnage. Wrote an appalled Holtzclaw, "I have seen most of the battlefields of the West, but never saw dead men thicker than in front of my two right regiments."[12]

Incredibly, the attack did not end with the repulse of Post, Streight, Grosvenor, and Thompson's two regiments. In fact, one of the most remarkable aspects of the battle occurred only after their lines had been shot to pieces. Colonel Thompson's trailing regiment from his second line, the 13th U.S. Colored Troops, had belatedly arrived in front of the works defended by Stovall's Brigade near the salient on Overton Hill.[13]

The 13th was a regiment generally inexperienced in combat, having served for about a year on railroad guard duty in Tennessee. Numbering only 556 men and 20 officers, the 13th had entered the fray in considerable apprehension; for the first time they were about to face a fire "such as veterans dread." Already many troops of other units in their front had begun to sulk and lie down. This, observed the 13th's commander, would not inspire courage in men who had never before taken such fire. Yet the 13th had been fortunate. Thompson's front ranks had taken most of the small-arms fire, and while a few shells exploded in their midst, the regiment had passed intact across the open ground and through the light timber. Advancing between Post's Brigade and Thompson's front line, the 13th U.S.C.T. managed to push their way through the downed trees and other obstructions while the enemy's attention was largely directed toward Post's regiments. Having re-formed in brush beneath the salient, the 13th suddenly burst forth, rushing at the Rebel works with a loud yell.[14]

It was a charge into hell itself. With the firing nearly ended on other sections of the line, Stephen D. Lee's defenders were able to concentrate their fire on the lone regiment of colored infantry, which was attacking head-on without supports or even a covering artillery bombardment. Many Federal infantrymen trapped on the slopes beneath the works watched in amazement as the 13th made straight for the line of blazing breastworks. He never saw such a sight, wrote an astonished Ohio veteran. These men were recently slaves, and yet they kept going although being slaughtered by the hundreds. Right up to the works they ran, their bayonets dripping with mist and rain. Several sergeants had the colors, and one man jumped on top of the parapet and furiously shook his flag in the Rebels' faces. He was instantly riddled with bullets. Both color-bearers were killed, their flags fallen to the ground, but still the 13th's men fought on. General Holtzclaw could hardly believe it. Five separate color-bearers, one after the other, seized a fallen flag and attempted to plant it over his works. Each was shot down. Urged on by their white officers, these black soldiers repeatedly surged against the breastworks. "They came only to die," wrote the amazed Holtzclaw. In fact, this Confederate commander was so impressed by the valor of these black soldiers that he formally cited their bravery in his battle report, almost an unheard-of circumstance involving a Southern general. Holtzclaw even highly praised the 13th's officers, saying that after the attackers had fallen back, "their brave officers" again attempted to lead their men "to certain death. . . . I noticed as many as three mounted [officers] who fell far in advance . . . urging them forward."[15]

The heavy bloodshed had been in vain. In a matter of minutes the fighting was over. The 13th's commander wrote that despite his soldiers' bravery, with their small numbers and no support it was useless to continue the struggle. An officer rescued the regiment's national flag, just as the 13th streamed to the rear "in wild disorder." Holtzclaw's men wanted to pursue, and some of his men sprang over the works, but their commander feared that a counterattack might overrun his position. With great difficulty Holtzclaw was able to restrain his men, but an Alabama lieutenant ran over to the 13th's regimental flag and brought it in as a trophy. It was inscribed, "Thirteenth Regiment U.S. Colored Infantry, Presented by the colored ladies of Murfreesboro."* The ladies might well have been proud of their regiment. "I never

*In the official report of Holtzclaw's division commander, Major General Henry D. Clayton, this flag appears to have been mistakenly identified as that of the 18th U.S.C.T., which was with Grosvenor's line of supports, and not described as having approached the Rebel works.

saw more heroic conduct shown on the field of battle than was exhibited by this body of men so recently slaves," observed a veteran Ohio officer. When a badly wounded black soldier was brought to the field hospital, an assistant surgeon noted the man's three wounds and remarked, "They went for you didn't they?"

"Yas," came the reply. "I jes shouted, rally 'roun de flag boys, an dey heard me."

The surgeon later rode over the battlefield where the fallen blacks were found closest to the works, their faces toward the foe. "Don't tell me negroes won't fight!" wrote the surgeon in a letter home. "I know better." It was perhaps a fitting tribute to the 220 officers and men (nearly 40 percent of combat strength) lost by the 13th U.S. Colored Infantry in their maiden battle.[16]

The last of the drifting banks of smoke rose silently skyward, dissipating in the murky clouds that continued to shower rain on the stricken land. Thomas J. Wood had gambled and lost—including perhaps his chance for promotion. Sidney Post had dared fate, and it had cost him his leg. Their men, however, had too often paid with their lives for another grim lesson in the futility of frontal assaults against well-defended entrenchments.

To George H. Thomas it must have seemed as if the bright promise of yesterday's victory had suddenly vanished in the aftermath of his subordinates' bad decisions. The well-defined plan of operations had required a maximum effort on the western flank. Instead, his commanders in that sector were bogged down and confused, wallowing in their excessive apprehensions. Yet on the eastern flank, when told to proceed cautiously, his generals had rushed into an overly aggressive posture that resulted in a failed frontal assault. How could this logically have happened? It was just the opposite of what Thomas had planned. Was fate deserting the Federal commander at the most inopportune moment? What could all this be leading to? Thomas went to his right flank to seek the answers.

James H. Wilson was finally proceeding with the forward movement ordered by Thomas. About noon the youthful cavalry commander's dismounted troopers had advanced eastward in skirmish order through the rugged ground toward the Granny White pike, from which Hammond's men had withdrawn earlier that morning. Between the Hillsboro and Granny White pikes, heavy underbrush and thick timber covered the many small knolls and prominent hills over the expanse of about a mile and a half. Even Jacob Cox of the Twenty-third Corps had recognized the importance of seizing these unoccupied hills, if only to prevent the enemy from outflanking his infantry's position opposite Shy's Hill.[17]

With five regiments abreast, Coon's men had cautiously pushed eastward from the Hillsboro pike through this difficult terrain beginning about noon. Their primary objective, in view of Thomas's instructions, was to move abreast of the infantry's position near the Granny White pike. Schofield reported at 1:30 P.M. that Wilson was "trying to push in toward the Granny White pike, about a mile south of my right." Yet tactically Coon's men were having great difficulty. Some of the hills were 200 feet high, and it was almost impossible for his dismounted men to advance in an unbroken line of battle. Coon finally resorted to breaking up his line, and sent two or three regiments progressively forward from hill to hill. In this manner Coon was able to advance for about a mile before encountering enemy resistance. In front of Coon's men were James R. Chalmers's bedraggled cavalrymen, who before daylight had been ordered by Hood to guard the Confederate left rear. When Chalmers discovered the Union cavalry crossing to the east toward the Granny White pike, he had hastened with many of his men along a back-woods road to head them off. Here he had barricaded a hill near the pike with his escort and the 26th Tennessee Battalion, just before Coon's men approached.[18]

Finally, after about an hour of skirmishing, the cautious Coon attacked with a single regiment, the 7th Illinois Cavalry. Rapidly firing their breech-loading Spencers, they charged straight up the hill and soon put Chalmers's men to flight, capturing seventy-five prisoners. Yet Coon had hesitated too long. Help was then close at hand for Chalmers's thin line.[19]

When first confronted by Coon's brigade, Chalmers had sent to Hood for reinforcements, saying he was fighting the enemy with only a single regiment. Promptly Ector's Brigade, then lying in reserve behind Walthall's line on Shy's Hill, had been double quicked south to help Chalmers. Finding only what seemed to be a skirmish line from the 7th Illinois Cavalry in possession of the disputed hill, Ector's Brigade, led by David Coleman, now charged up the steep slopes, severely mauling the blue troopers. Many of the Confederate prisoners were recaptured, and Coleman's and Chalmers's men reoccupied the hill. Soon a desultory, long-range skirmish fire developed, and Coon pondered his next move.[20]

When Brigadier General Edward Hatch arrived, he ordered artillery moved up to the top of a hill. Using ropes and tugging at the wheels, the men brought two guns up the side of an adjacent hill. Even Hatch personally helped wheel the cannon up the slopes. Finally, about 3:00 P.M., the cannon were in place, and they began pummeling the lower elevation hilltop. About fifty shots had been fired when Coon ordered his entire brigade to begin firing at the Rebel lines, some 500 yards distant.[21]

Chalmers and Coleman, aware of their pending defeat, began evacuating the hill and were seen trampling off toward Brentwood along an old country road. When Coon's Brigade advanced in pursuit, there was virtually no resistance. Over the hill dashed Wilson's cavalrymen, angling toward the Granny White pike. At last, Hood's entire rear and flank had been uncovered. For the want of Forrest's cavalry divisions there were no troops available to defend the Army of Tennessee's vulnerable rear. Even worse, the army's line of retreat was threatened, with one of its two available escape routes on the verge of being severed.[22]

There was heavy irony here. At 3:15 P.M., while Chalmers and Coleman were preparing to withdraw, Hood had sent an urgent message via courier to Chalmers: "You must hold that pike [Granny White]; put in your escort and every available man you can find." When the message was received about 4:30 P.M. Chalmers had already retreated "in front of Brentwood" along the Franklin pike. Hood's good luck had run out.[23]

John McArthur was no ordinary man. A. J. Smith's fiery, thirty-eight-year-old 1st Division commander was a native Scotsman, an immigrant iron-worker who had risen to civilian prominence in Chicago as owner of the Excelsior Iron Works. McArthur had exceptional talent and boasted many military accomplishments. From Fort Donelson and Shiloh to Vicksburg and the Missouri Campaign with A. J. Smith, McArthur had a most distinguished service record. Yet after more than two years in rank he was still a brigadier general. The outspoken McArthur had run afoul of army politics. Firm in his convictions, and a man willing to make hard decisions, McArthur, despite his disappointments, continued to exhibit not only courage, but common sense and energy.[24]

When McArthur replaced the popular division commander Joseph A. Mower in the Sixteenth Corps, many of the men had been crestfallen. Within a few months, however, they realized he was every bit as good a soldier as Mower, and many of his men proudly considered themselves the elite of the army.[25]

On December 16, 1864, John McArthur was about to alter the entire complexion of the battle. Some of his men later thought that his presence was, in fact, divine providence.[26]

McArthur had chafed and fretted all morning about the inaction along his division's front. From his initial position along the Granny White pike fronting the main east-west Confederate defenses, McArthur had moved his three brigades forward to within 600 yards of the enemy's breastworks.[27]

At a glance, McArthur saw that the prominent hill on his right front, anchoring the enemy's western flank, was "the key point to his works." If it could be captured and held, Hood's entire line would become untenable. During the morning McArthur observed that the enemy lines were not heavily defended here, and that the enemy gunners could not sufficiently depress the muzzles of their cannon to use them effectively against attacking infantry. Due to the steep angle of the slopes, Confederate defenders would have to expose themselves in order to fire down the hillside. Furthermore, the Rebel earthworks were constructed too far back, along the actual crown of the hill, rather than on the forward slopes (which was the proper military crest).[28]

McArthur rode over to talk to Major General Darius N. Couch of Schofield's Twenty-third Corps, who was positioned directly in front of this enemy-held hill. Yet Couch was uncooperative. Apparently he was influenced by Schofield's apprehensions of a pending enemy assault and would make no commitment to attack the hill in front. A disgruntled John McArthur returned to his division and ordered his men to begin constructing rifle pits for protection from enemy snipers. Then, while the corps artillery continued to aimlessly shell the enemy's lines, McArthur glumly sat on a log behind an Iowa battery, awaiting orders.[29]

Hours later McArthur was still chafing under what seemed to be outright timidity in the face of a fleeting opportunity. About 2:00 P.M. he again went to the right to see Couch. Couch reported that Thomas's chief of staff had asked him before noon to find out what the enemy was doing and to determine if an attack was feasible. Couch had later replied there were too many hills and woods in front to make the observations as directed, and although he "might" be able to attack the hill, he was "not certain" that he could hold it. Clearly, Couch was unwilling to take many risks.[30]

McArthur had had his fill of procrastination and indecision. If no one would assume the responsibility for making a crucial decision, he would do so. He told Couch that he was going to attack the hill in front before the opportunity was lost due to approaching darkness. Couch repeated he had no orders to advance, and promised only limited support; he would send a brigade to move into McArthur's vacated trenches—to provide a rallying point in the event of a repulse.[31]

About 2:30 P.M. a flushed McArthur rode up to his 1st Brigade commander, Colonel William L. McMillan, and told him to "take that hill." McMillan was amazed. His men were still building defensive rifle pits, "in case of an [enemy] assault, preparations for which . . . I thought could be seen."[32]

Promptly, McMillan pulled back his skirmishers, withdrew his regiments, and marched about 500 yards to the right, halting in front of Couch's position, where he formed his brigade in two lines of battle. Specific instructions were given to the men. They would advance in silent ranks, with fixed bayonets, under the cover of an artillery barrage. A heavy skirmish line would draw the enemy's fire, and the main battle line would press forward to within close range of the breastworks "without a cheer, or firing a shot," until they reached the actual works.[33]

By McArthur's plan, the division's other two brigades would advance to McMillan's support in delayed sequence along the Granny White pike. To McMillan's men, however, it was evident that upon their efforts would rest success or failure. The men tightened their belts, adjusted their cartridge boxes, and gazed at the steep hill looming before them. It seemed to a rawboned Minnesota youth who would be in the front line that it would take a miracle to reach the top.[34]

At the last moment, Cogswell's Independent Battery of Light Artillery, McMillan's lone supporting battery, was discovered to be nearly out of ammunition. An attempt to replenish their supply from rear ordnance wagons bogged down in mixed communications. The pause became a delay. The off-again, on-again rain and drizzle saturated the waiting men. Their grumbling was growing louder. Suspense continued to build. Forty-five minutes passed, and there was no further word. The daylight was growing dim; it was approaching 4:00 P.M. and even McArthur was getting nervous.[35]

An hour earlier John McArthur had sent a dispatch to his corps commander, A. J. Smith, saying that he was making preparations for an attack on the key enemy-held hill, and unless he received orders to the contrary he would promptly order the charge.[36]

When McArthur's message was received by Smith, by chance he was talking with George H. Thomas, who had reacted immediately. "Don't let him start yet," said Thomas. "Hold him where he is until I can ride over and see Schofield. I will have him charge at the same time." A staff officer then galloped off to find McArthur, but unknowingly was involved in a critical race.[37]

After a hasty search, the lieutenant commanding Cogswell's battery obtained from a nearby battery enough ammunition to fire ten shells from each cannon. Within a few minutes McMillan was alerted and he ordered Cogswell's battery to open fire. A crescendo of flame leapt from Cogswell's guns, the sudden roar nearly knocking the startled infantrymen senseless. Bursting shells wreathed the crown of the distant hill, and at his prompt order, McMillan's men strode grimly forward.[38]

James H. Wilson was excited. Coon's men had driven back the Rebel defenders and were beyond the enemy's flank, virtually advancing unopposed across their rear. Despite the lack of enemy resistance, one lone brigade could not be expected to trap Hood's army. Wilson's reserve brigades were out of position, and due to the extensive delay in getting them forward through the rough terrain, the obvious answer was to advance Schofield's infantry. Wilson sent three staff officers, one after the other, urging Schofield on. As he received no reply, an increasingly peevish Wilson rode toward the left to find Thomas.[39]

"Between three and four o'clock" he found him talking with Schofield behind the reverse side of a small hill. Wilson rode up, and with "ill concealed impatience" urged Thomas to order the infantry forward without further delay. His cavalry were in full pursuit of the enemy and could be seen pressing forward toward the rear of the high, enemy-held hill, said the aroused Wilson.[40]

Thomas seemed unmoved. Schofield and Thomas had just been discussing the prospect of attacking Shy's Hill, and Schofield was reluctant to participate in McArthur's pending assault due to the loss inherent in a frontal attack against such a strong position.[41]

Thomas "lifted his field glasses and coolly scanned what I had clearly showed him," later wrote Wilson—who thought the Federal commander was acting with unnecessary deliberation. Finally Thomas turned to Schofield and "as calmly as if on parade" said, "General, will you please advance your whole line." Well realizing that the crisis was at hand, Wilson quickly dashed back to his cavalry on his gray steed, "Sheridan."[42]

CHAPTER XXXII

Where the Grapes of Wrath
Are Stored

To a confederate staff officer, December 16th was just the kind of day the Army of Tennessee had hoped for: "everything was going well" as the afternoon waned. Amazingly, there had been few crises, and the dispatch of minimal reinforcements had easily handled each enemy threat. About 3:00 P.M., when Hood received Chalmers's dispatch about being threatened by Wilson's cavalry along the Granny White pike, it seemed to be simply another easily remedied tactical situation. Although Ector's Brigade had been sent earlier, Hood ordered A. P. Stewart to give Chalmers added help. Stewart pulled Brigadier General Daniel H. Reynolds's Brigade from the front line on Shy's Hill "under cover of the mist" and sent them southward along the Granny White pike to cut off what was presumed to be a small Federal force.[1]

Unknowingly, Hood had created an enormous crisis in his army. Within a few minutes the bright prospects of a defensive victory—a Confederate reversal of Franklin—seemed to turn on a bizarre and unexpected event.

Not more than fifteen minutes after Reynolds's departure, the entire northern face of Shy's Hill seemed to vanish amid bursting enemy shells. Although Hood had considered this sector one of his strongest, it was soon evident the enemy were preparing to assault along the steep northern face. This was a shocking development. Being aware of the great strength of this imposing height, Hood had repeatedly weakened the defenses along his left flank to reinforce other sections that appeared more vulnerable. While the natural strength of Shy's Hill seemed sufficient to compensate for the reduced number of troops present—at least in Hood's mind—a nagging precedent remained. In the past, the final issue too often had turned against Hood due to some critical and unforeseen element, referred to by many of his officers as their army's peculiar "bad luck." Yet Hood thought it "impossible" for the enemy to break this line. His men were in well-established entrenchments on a commanding height, fighting a defensive action with a clear zone of fire in front. All that was required was for his men to fight with valor and determination to win the redeeming victory John Bell Hood so desperately needed.[2]

Hood, remarkably, at first failed to react to the unfolding crisis in the Shy's Hill sector. As the artillery bombardment continued, he remained in the rear on the Lea property, talking with A. P. Stewart about the situation along his front.[3]

In their positions along the crest of Shy's Hill, the ill-equipped infantrymen of William Bate's division had been repeatedly stretched into a more attenuated line. First, Ector's Brigade was pulled out of the front line after noon to support Chalmers, causing Bate's left brigade, Brigadier General Thomas B. Smith's, to extend to the left. When Cheatham's two brigades departed to reinforce Stephen D. Lee in the midafternoon, the line to the south had been further weakened. Now, with the departure of Reynolds's Brigade, Sears's and Shelley's remaining brigades had to spread out to cover the vacated ground on the eastern slopes. Hood had pulled four brigades out of the vital western flank perimeter in little more than three hours. As a result, William Bate was left with severely depleted ranks to defend the northern and western faces of Shy's Hill.[4]

Bate's soldiers were still suffering from their ordeal at Murfreesboro and were largely without shoes and adequate clothing. They had arrived on Shy's Hill after midnight as the leading elements of Cheatham's corps, and the past twenty-four hours for them had been a sleepless nightmare of shifting positions, constructing entrenchments, and enduring intense shell fire from the enemy's batteries. Their assigned position was of importance, being an extension of Ector's original line from the apex of the hill northeast down the slopes toward the Bradford residence, where the battle line of A. P. Stewart's Corps lay. Due to the intense darkness, a fire had been kindled by Frank Cheatham's order behind Mrs. Bradford's house to mark the proper direction to extend Bate's line.[5]

Getting his men into a proper alignment that night had been exasperating. The cultivated ground adjacent to the turnpike was so soft that wheeled vehicles and artillery could not pass. After great difficulty, Bate finally connected with Ector's Brigade at the crown of the hill, but found he didn't have enough men to join with Stewart, as planned. When he complained to Frank Cheatham about this awkward position, Cheatham merely replied that he had no authority to change the lines. Bate then ordered his men to dig in with the few available tools. During the remainder of the night they had worked laboriously to construct breastworks along their new line.[6]

In the light of morning, Bate discovered that a serious mistake had been made. A. P. Stewart's Corps, instead of extending near the Bradford house,

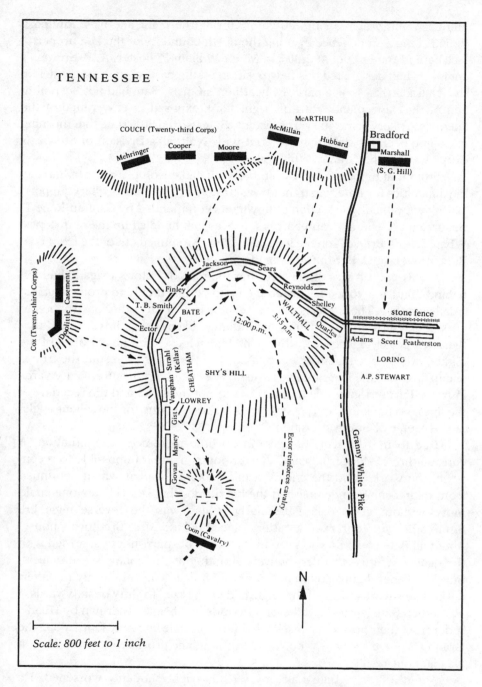

MAP 16 Assault on the Confederate Left
4:30 P.M., December 16—Nashville

had been withdrawn about 200 yards during the night and was now positioned along a stone fence fronting the north boundary of the Lea property, well behind Bate's line. At 2:00 A.M. Major William F. Foster, A. P. Stewart's engineer, had designated this new position on the basis of its stronger defensive characteristics. As a part of Cheatham's Corps, Bate had not been notified of this movement. With his right flank exposed in easy range of the enemy's artillery some 400 yards distant, Bate wasted little time that morning in pulling back his right flank to abut with Walthall's Division of Stewart's Corps west of the Granny White pike.[7]

From that point onward December 16th had become a series of harrowing difficulties for Bate. First, there was trouble in obtaining artillery support. With great difficulty, a section of howitzers commanded by Captain Rene T. Beauregard (General Beauregard's son) was manhandled up the rear slopes. When Ector's Brigade, on the immediate left, was pulled out of the front line, Bate sent Thomas B. Smith's Brigade to occupy their works.[8]

At this point it was discovered that the men of Ector's Brigade had left behind "flimsy" works, hastily erected and designed only to protect against small-arms fire. There was no abatis, felled trees, or any other obstruction to impede the movements of attacking infantry. Even worse, it was found that these temporary barricades, which "had been located in the darkness of the night," were placed along the actual crest of the hill. As a result, the troops occupying this line were unable to see more than from five to twenty yards in front. Furthermore, due to the curvature of the slope and the receding of the lines, no flank fire was possible on attackers making for the salient angle, at the center of Smith's position.[9]

Due to the daylight, Bate could do little to remedy the situation. A constant fire of skirmishers and sharpshooters made it impossible to reconstruct the works, and the enemy artillery bombardment which continued from midmorning so demolished the barricades that scarcely anyone could move without great risk. Particularly galling was the reverse-angle fire Smith's Brigade took from a battery placed behind Mrs. Bradford's house. About all Bate could do was keep his battalion of sharpshooters, armed with the deadly Whitworth rifles, actively shooting at the enemy's cannoneers. Still, the Federal guns continued to fire with deadly accuracy. By midafternoon Bate's works south of the angle had been razed for fifty or sixty yards.[10]

When Bate learned that Ector's Brigade had been withdrawn by Hood's order from their position in reserve behind the angle and sent south along the Granny White pike, he was outraged. Although he protested to Cheatham, it was without result.[11]

About 3:30 P.M. Bate's already serious plight suddenly worsened. He discovered two lines of Federal infantry massing in his front and swarms of skirmishers forming beneath the angle. Bate quickly sent a staff officer to warn Cheatham and obtain reinforcements. Yet his corps commander had no men to spare and would not send help. Moreover, Bate was told to extend his already depleted ranks farther to his left. Word had just arrived of the Federal cavalry's menacing presence in the rear, and Cheatham needed more troops at the southern end of his line to stop them.[12]

Bate looked to the rear. Govan's Brigade, on the extreme left of Cheatham's line, was fleeing in disorder through the field beneath Shy's Hill. Long lines of blue-clad troops with repeating carbines were closely pursuing. Bullets began to zip into Bate's lines, striking men down from behind.[13]

Bate looked to the front. Here came McArthur's men, swarming up the steep face of Shy's Hill directly at Thomas B. Smith's Brigade, their poised bayonets glistening in the drizzle. Bate was in a nutcracker, with his weakened line entirely unsupported. Hood, a few hours earlier, had taken away his only reserves.[14]

It was "terrible beyond description," climbing that damned hill, wrote an excited private of McMillan's brigade. "A perfect storm of musket balls rained continuously upon [us]," but still the men "pressed bravely forward." Up the steep, slippery northwest slope of Shy's Hill scrambled the men of McMillan's brigade, about 1,500 strong. Attacking along the greatest curvature of the hill, most of the men found to their surprise that they were little exposed to the enemy's frontal fire. Only the 10th Minnesota, on McMillan's left, seemed to take heavy losses on its exposed western flank. Although eight of twenty-three officers in its ranks were hit, McMillan's other units could hardly believe their luck. There was scarcely any incoming fire. Ahead, the crest of the hill was shrouded with gunsmoke, and McMillan's men kept climbing. At last, as they neared the crown of the hill, the deflecting angle of the ground ended and they suddenly saw their opponents. They were within only a few feet of the enemy's parapet, wrote McMillan, when a heavy volley was poured in their faces. It went right over their heads. There was a yell, and McMillan's regiments "cleared the enemy's works with a bound." Although Lieutenant Colonel Samuel P. Jennison of the 10th Minnesota was mortally wounded, a color-bearer scrambled over the barricade and began vigorously waving his flag.[15]

Right on top of Smith's men poured McMillan's ranks. The fighting was hand-to-hand, and vicious. Bate saw that within moments most of Smith's men had been overwhelmed. Lieutenant Colonel William M. Shy, commanding six consolidated Tennessee regiments, refused to surrender although engulfed by McMillan's yelling men. Shy was furiously fighting amid the ranks, Enfield rifle musket in hand, when he was shot through the head at point-blank range. The big .58-caliber minie ball ripped into his skull above his right eye, knocking a large chunk out of the posterior lobe as it exited from his brain. Shy thus gave his name to Felix Compton's prominent wooded hill which had witnessed the end of his life. Much later, after a bizarre sequence of events that carried well into the twentieth century, Shy would receive a new notoriety of sorts, including a second funeral.*[16]

By Bate's account, just prior to McMillan's attack the incoming fire had intensified from three directions: front, left flank, and rear. Bullets were crisscrossing in the air, whizzing, and thudding into men at the breastworks. The pressure was enormous. Although most of Bate's men were putting up a stout fight, apparently some units did not. Finley's Florida Brigade, the men who had broken little more than a week ago at Murfreesboro, were posted in the middle of the division. Seeing the breech in Smith's lines, the Floridians suddenly fled in confusion. Ector's Brigade had once been posted at this very angle, but now Bate was without reserves to restore the line.[17]

Instantly Bate's entire line seemed to disintegrate. Before his eyes his entire division panicked. Men threw down their weapons and ran for their lives. Although pockets of resistance formed, only a few companies, squads, and individuals continued to fight. Within minutes Bate's entire division had either fled or thrown down their arms to surrender. McMillan's men were virtually inundated with prisoners; later they counted 1,533 enlisted men; 85 field, staff, and line officers, including Brigadier General Thomas B. Smith; 4 captured battle flags; and 8 trophy cannon.[18]

It was a stunning, seemingly improbable victory. Once McMillan's men realized what had happened, they ran about "shouting, yelling, and acting like maniacs for a while," wrote one of his Illinois soldiers. Evidently Brigadier General Smith was so exasperated he became belligerent. While being marched to the rear, he reportedly exchanged words with Colonel William McMillan. The Federal colonel was excited, with the adrenaline still flowing from his charge up the hill. Whatever the cause, McMillan allegedly struck Smith three vicious blows to the head with his sword, inflicting serious damage to the brain. After the war, Smith, who was twenty-six years old when injured, was committed to the Tennessee State Hospital for the Insane, located only a few miles from the Nashville battlefield. Here he remained for forty-seven years until his death in 1923.[19]

On Bate's right flank, Hubbard's and Marshall's brigades had attacked the lower elevations and were in clear view of the Confederate lines on Shy's Hill. Their advance seemed at first to involve a slaughter. An appalled Iowa gunner watched in horror as the two brigades struggled to cross a muddy, 400-yard open field, only to be riddled from the east by repeated blasts of canister. A six-gun Confederate battery hidden in underbrush along A. P. Stewart's line seemed to butcher these men at every step. The brown field was literally covered with blue-clad bodies in the wake of their advance. Still, the men bent low, plunging onward without firing a shot until hidden by the smoke billowing from the Rebel breastworks.[20]

Directly in front of Hubbard's brigade loomed the parapets defended by Henry R. Jackson's men, and three weakened brigades under Edward Wal-

*See p. 442.

thall. The intense fire streaming from the Rebel works was "the most terrific and withering fire of musketry and artillery it has ever been my fortune to behold or encounter," wrote a veteran Minnesota lieutenant colonel. Three times the colors of the 11th Missouri Infantry went down, each time being picked up by another man. The last soldier who carried the flag had to hold the shivered flagstaff together, it having been "shot into three pieces." Hubbard's men were in such disorder that Walthall thought they had been repulsed. Indeed, Hubbard's men suffered the worst of any of McArthur's brigades, losing nearly 300 officers and men from the 1,421 men who entered the fight.[21]

Yet Jackson and Walthall hadn't counted on the precipitate break to their left, in Finley's Brigade. A wild "hurrah" was their first warning, as McMillan's men poured through the line vacated by Bate's center brigade. Henry Jackson saw at a glance that his line was taken in flank, with the enemy on higher ground and able to enfilade his line at will. Jackson hurriedly ordered his staff to move the men out by the right flank. Soon, with the fleeing men of Finley's Brigade streaming through their ranks, all became chaos and confusion. Just at this point, Hubbard's men charged in their front. Jackson's Brigade promptly went to pieces and joined the wild rush to safety. Walthall's men, next in line, also were caught up in the stampede. It was everything he could do just "to save any part of my command," said the horrified Walthall. Chaos had already engulfed much of the main Confederate east-west line, running from the apex of Shy's Hill to and beyond the Granny White pike. Here, A. P. Stewart's Corps, badly mauled on the 15th, stood looking on with astonishment.[22]

For A. P. Stewart's men there had been little warning of a frontal attack. William Marshall had received no orders from McArthur to advance but, believing Hubbard "ought to be supported," had sent his men against Stewart's line east of the pike. Marshall's men had taken relatively little fire until they had reached the far end of the cornfield. With no obstructions in their front, his men could easily see the enemy works ahead. There was no weak spot apparent, and it seemed that "it would be impossible for us to take it," wrote their anxious colonel. At this point Marshall's men discovered their salvation. In front of these breastworks the Rebels had posted "an unusually large force of skirmishers." Evidently these men had only belatedly discovered Marshall's advance, due, so it was thought, to having intently watched McMillan's and then Hubbard's attacks on Shy's Hill. At the last moment the Confederate skirmishers jumped up and broke for their earthworks. "The Lord was on our side that day," said a much-relieved Federal officer. These skirmishers "served as a blanket to shield us from the fire of the main enemy line." Just as Cleburne's and Brown's men had done at Franklin, McArthur's 3d Brigade, "with a wild shout," sprinted in close pursuit after these Rebel skirmishers. Already the Confederates in A. P. Stewart's main line had begun to flee.[23]

A howling, excited mob of Federals dashed up to the old stone wall, which was heavily obstructed with timbers and sharpened stakes. Since the afternoon-long Union artillery bombardment had knocked numerous holes in these otherwise imposing breastworks, Marshall's men easily poured through. "In less time than it takes to tell it, we had captured guns, caissons, colors, and prisoners galore," wrote a jubilant regimental commander. "Had the enemy made a determined stand they might have inflicted very serious injury on us . . . but their line having been broken on the left . . . they were thrown into a panic, and fled from their works in confusion," reported another.[24]

Henry R. Jackson, a forty-four-year-old, Yale-educated Georgia brigadier general, was having difficulty getting back to where his horse was tied. Hurrying as fast as he could over the soft ground, Jackson was laboring to walk at a brisk pace. Bullets were zinging past, and there were shouts of "Surrender," but Jackson made it to his horse, only to have the animal slip as it attempted to jump the stone fence at the pike. Jackson was thrown into the ditch, and an officer ran to him. Because the general's boots were so caked with mud that he could hardly walk, the officer helped pull them off. Jackson had removed only one boot when from across the fence came a shout, "Surrender, damn you!" Jackson and the officer looked up into the muzzles of four leveled rifles, and they promptly raised their hands. When the three privates and a corporal discovered they had taken a Confederate general, the corporal let out a yell, hollering, "Captured a general, by God. I'll carry you to Nashville myself." The men were from the 5th Minnesota Infantry of Hubbard's brigade, and Jackson was later hauled in front of Major General A. J. Smith. Begrudgingly, the mud-spattered Jackson admitted that powder and lead weren't adequate to stop McArthur's charge.[25]

All along the Shy's Hill–Overton Hill front the sudden panic had spread like wildfire. Captures were so frequent and easy that regiments such as the 5th Minnesota found that their prisoners outnumbered their own ranks. Entirely vulnerable were the generally immobile Confederate cannon positioned in support of the front line. Nearly all of the horses earlier had been taken to the rear to avoid exposure to Federal artillery fire. Knowing it was impossible to get the horses, hitch up the guns, and escape across the soft ground before the Yankees were upon them, most of the cannoneers had abandoned their guns where they stood. McMillan said his men took 8 cannon, Hubbard claimed 7, and Marshall was credited with 2. Ultimately, 2 brigadier generals, 4,273 prisoners of war, 24 cannon, and an estimated 4,500 small arms were claimed as captured by McArthur's division during the two days of battle at Nashville (the great majority of which were taken on the 16th).[26]

While the fleeing ranks of men in gray scattered in wild disorder toward the Franklin pike, mop-up operations began along the Shy's Hill front. Squads of blue-clad infantrymen ran at will over the captured ground, round-

ing up prisoners and attending to the wounded. One of William Loring's
Mississippi riflemen, lying wounded and helpless on the ground, looked up.
A soldier with a poised bayonet was about to run him through. Just at the last
instant an officer shoved the man from behind and the soldier ran off. The
Mississippi private was soon in the hands of two Illinois soldiers, who saw
that he was placed in an ambulance and carried to Nashville. Another captive, an officer, when told by a guard that if he tried to run away his head
would be shot off, replied that the man needn't worry, he had run about as
far as he could.[27]

It was the most shocking sight he ever remembered seeing. Colonel Andrew
J. Kellar, the commander of Strahl's Brigade, led the next unit in line south
of Bate's position on Shy's Hill. Kellar had been stunned when the crown of
the hill had been "given up to the enemy without a struggle." One of his
officers had shouted, "Look there at the United States flag on the hill!" Then
the men of his brigade had jumped up and scattered without even attempting
to make a stand. Kellar was embarrassed, and two days later he indignantly
wrote a formal apology, saying, "It was not by fighting, nor the force of arms,
nor even numbers, which drove us from the field."[28]

Kellar was correct. Hood's army had given way to fear. Yet it was not
the fear of fighting, but only a fear of wasting their lives, of too long being
abused in the field and sacrificed to no sensible purpose. Hood's soldiers had
suffered, until further suffering just didn't make sense anymore. Since Franklin the army had become essentially a disaster waiting to happen.

The feeling was contagious by example. So many men were fleeing that
it put old fears into the hearts of those yet to be engaged. They fled almost
by reflex. It was an army running away—from its enemy, from its commanders, from itself. No longer were the men confident and proud. At that moment their perspectives had shifted from that of military duty to one's self and
personal survival. Running away simply had become the most practical solution for many individuals no longer willing to trust their leaders.

For many of Frank Cheatham's soldiers caught in the Shy's Hill pincers
between Wilson's and McArthur's troops, even the option of running away
no longer existed. South of Bate's line, disaster was imminent when McMillan's soldiers burst through Bate's ranks about 4:30 P.M.[29]

Cheatham had been too busy with the disaster threatening his southern
flank to worry much about Bate's and Kellar's situation. Cheatham had sent
Brigadier General Daniel C. Govan's Arkansas brigade to the elevation below
Shy's Hill, refusing its position so that Govan's line faced generally south.
Here Govan's brigade had taken such a pummeling from concentrated artillery fire that their line rapidly began to give way. Cheatham then had called
on Mark Lowrey, commanding what had been John C. Brown's division, for
additional troops. Promptly, George Maney's (formerly John C. Carter's) and
Gist's brigades were sent to reestablish the line just vacated by Govan.[30]

Yet these reinforcements already were in an anxious state. "Everything seemed confused," wrote a private. "It seemed to be somewhat like a flock of wild geese when they have lost their leader. We were willing to go anywhere . . . [but] I have never seen an army so confused and demoralized. The whole thing seemed to be tottering and trembling [on disaster]." Ordered at a run to the hill south of their former line, the 1st Tennessee Infantry of Maney's Brigade was suddenly brought to a halt. With the enemy's shells bursting amid the field in front, the regiment's adjutant proceeded to read an announcement just received from Hood's headquarters. "Soldiers—The commanding general takes pleasure in announcing to his troops that victory and success are now within their grasp . . . in every attack and assault the enemy have been repulsed; and the commanding general [says] . . . be of good cheer—all is well. [signed] General John B. Hood."[31]

The soldiers looked at one another in puzzlement. In front of them, across the wide sweep of countryside, they could see a host of Yankee cavalry, infantry, and artillery cutting across their line of retreat. "Oh, shucks; that's all shenanigan," thought a soldier. Most seemed to agree, and this order caused the greatest mistrust in the minds of the men, said a private.[32]

Maney's and Gist's brigades had no sooner scrambled up the steep southern hill, slick with wet, dead grass, when Federal artillery opened fire on them. Some of the men began dodging the incoming shells, causing their colonel to yell at them to stand there without flinching. Behind their backs, from the direction they had just left, there was the sound of heavy firing. Then a soldier shouted out, "Colonel, look yonder!" and pointed at a long line of dismounted cavalrymen surging through a field close beyond their left flank. The colonel, observed a soldier, "never thought any more about dodging shells." He shouted, "Boys, [it's] every fellow for himself." Away they went, said the man, and Maney's and Gist's brigades fled northward—in the direction of Shy's Hill.[33]

Frank Cheatham was talking with a staff officer by a big white oak along the southern slopes of Shy's Hill. Suddenly a bullet zipped between them, coming from behind. Cheatham and the staff officer looked about. The army's entire southern flank had broken ranks and was streaming back in flight. Cheatham looked to the right, toward the top of the hill. Federal flags were flying above the crest. Many of Mark Lowrey's men were seen running away, and heavy firing was heard all along the slopes.[34]

Much upon his own judgment, Colonel Charles C. Doolittle had ordered his brigade to attack about 4:30 P.M. Doolittle had been authorized by Jacob Cox, his division commander, to advance as soon as the crown of Shy's Hill had been carried by McArthur's troops. Doolittle thus was the only unit of Schofield's entire corps to participate in the final assault on Cheatham's line. Since his brigade was within 500 yards of Mark Lowrey's breastworks, Doolittle's infantrymen rapidly advanced in the wake of McMillan's successful assault.[35]

The side of the hill was steep and rocky, wrote an officer, but in advance was the 12th Kentucky Infantry, which had fought so well at Franklin. Their assault required only a few minutes. Lowrey's men fired "several very severe volleys," said the 12th's commander, but due to the deflected angle they had aimed too high. With Rebel bullets whizzing over their heads, the Kentuckians lunged for Lowrey's works, only to discover that most of the enemy already had fled.[36]

On their left the 8th Tennessee and 100th Ohio regiments climbed over the enemy parapet just as several cannon were being loaded. The cannoneers abandoned their pieces with the charges still in the muzzles, and Doolittle's men engulfed the line. Eight cannon and about 300 prisoners were their spoils. The resistance had been very light, almost feeble, thought several regimental commanders. Indeed, during their charge Doolittle's brigade had suffered only nine casualties, with none killed.[37]

South of Shy's Hill a Confederate general noticed that with thousands of Federal soldiers pouring across his front, flank, and rear, the only way out was across the heel of what seemed to be an iron horseshoe. "At first I saw no chance for myself or any considerable portion of my division to escape capture," wrote a dismayed Mark Lowrey. Yet his aide-de-camp was able to rally a few men and hold off pursuit for a few precious minutes. Lowrey's favorite war horse, "Rebel," was killed, but the general made it safely through the heel of the horseshoe and was soon caught up in "the inglorious retreat."[38]

For most of the trapped Confederates there was little opportunity to escape through the overwhelming Federal ranks. One Mississippi rifleman got up to run but was pulled back several times by his lieutenant. They begged him to surrender, later wrote the man, but he told them he was going to run despite everything. He was the only man of his company to get away, surviving with bullet holes in his clothes and "my gun shot into splinters."[39]

The entire western and center segments of Hood's army were gone. Bate's division, French's two brigades, Walthall's and Loring's divisions, now the remnant of Frank Cheatham's Corps, all had been routed within a few minutes. Only one intact corps yet remained in Hood's entire army—Stephen D. Lee's, still posted along the Overton Hill front. Although only an hour earlier Hood had confidently expected news of a great victory, upon Lee's shoulders now rested the very survival of the Army of Tennessee.[40]

Along the opposite ridge, across the valley from misty and smoke-shrouded Shy's Hill, A. J. Smith sat on his horse, intently watching the distant fighting. Suddenly, in haste, up to his side rode George H. Thomas. Excitedly, he blurted out, "General, what is the matter, are your men being captured [up] there?'' Smith glanced at the swarm of gray uniforms streaming down the far hillside. "Not by a damn sight," he replied. "My men are capturing them, [and] those are Rebel prisoners you see." George H. Thomas let out a hearty laugh. It was the only time A. J. Smith could ever remember seeing General Thomas laugh out loud.[41]

CHAPTER XXXIII

Crying Like His Heart
Would Break

IT'S IMPOSSIBLE to give you any idea of an army frightened and routed," a still suffering staff officer wrote to his wife more than a month later. During the afternoon of December 16th the sudden break in the Confederate lines was like a "wide awake nightmare," thought one of Cheatham's men. The woods were full of running men. Officers were shouting amid the tumult, "Halt! halt!" but to no avail. Everywhere one looked there were gray-clad soldiers fleeing in terror. Past a panting Confederate private dashed a limbered field gun, its horses straining at their harnesses. Suddenly the gun was halted and unlimbered on the road. Quickly the gunners sprang to their posts and began firing the piece down the roadway—into the ranks of the fleeing Confederates. It was a Yankee cannon, realized the man with a shudder, and he began running a little faster.[1]

Nearby, Reynolds's Brigade, which had been pulled from Walthall's line before McArthur's attack, was marching south to help fend off Wilson's encircling cavalrymen. Observing the disintegration of Cheatham's and Stewart's corps, a staff officer hastened to post Reynolds's men across "the path of the flying mass." Soon they were engulfed by a mob of terror-stricken fugitives. Despite the shouts and curses of officers pleading with them to halt, "not a man would stop," said the staff officer.[2]

The commander of the 1st Tennessee Infantry, Lieutenant Colonel John L. House, was the only person observed to rally at Reynolds's line. When it was apparent that none of his men would stop, House too wandered off. Soon fragments of Reynolds's units began leaving. The enemy was closing in. Reynolds's men, the staff officer, and his clerks went streaming to the rear in disorder.[3]

Along the Granny White pike wagons, abandoned cannon, caissons, limbers, horses, mules, and bewildered soldiers were all intermixed in a frantic mass. Jaded mules refused to pull, despite the lashings of panicky wagon drivers, whose eyes looked like they might pop out of their skulls with fright. Several wagons, their wheels interlocked, clogged the road. Demoralized officers rode past in apparent indifference. At one spot a youthful officer, thought to be from A. P. Stewart's staff, endeavored to block the road, yelling at the top of his lungs, "Halt here, men, halt, form [a] line here." Back and forth across the road he rode, excitedly shouting and gesturing. He accosted one old veteran, powder-grimed and covered with mud. Pointing down the road toward the enemy, he yelled at the soldier, "Halt. Where are you going? There is no danger down there." The old veteran hardly hesitated. Angrily he spat out as he stalked off, "You go to hell, I've been there."[4]

It was like trying to stop the current of the Duck River with a fish net, observed one of Frank Cheatham's Tennesseeans. For the many trapped Confederates along the original Granny White perimeter, their attempt to escape southward became a race with the closing jaws of Wilson's cavalry on the south and Doolittle's and McArthur's troops on the west and north.[5]

John Bell Hood had been talking with A. P. Stewart near his headquarters on the Lea property when word of the disaster on Cheatham's flank was brought to him by a staff officer. According to Hood, he was on horseback, contemplating plans for the next day's operations. Hood said he wanted to withdraw his entire army, march around Thomas's right flank, and "attack the exposed flank in rear." Hood later remembered, "I did not . . . anticipate a break at that time." Yet within minutes the stunned Confederate commander was amid the routed, fleeing troops, where he soon "discovered that all hope to rally the troops was in vain." Hood was later found by one of Bate's officers along the Franklin pike, trying without success to rally the men. His staff officers were with him, and it seemed to be a shameful, inexplicable rout. The panic that gripped the army was found to be beyond remedy. No matter what any of the officers did or said, the men would not stand and fight. "It was sad to see men disgrace themselves so," bitterly wrote one of the general's aides three days later. To Hood and his senior officers it appeared as if the whole army had been routed, with each man terror-stricken and stupefied.[6]

They were wrong. Stephen D. Lee's Corps was still in line along the Overton Hill front. Unknowingly, and without warning, Lee suddenly found himself charged with the responsibility of saving the army.[7]

Lee was east of the Franklin pike, talking with one of his mounted escorts about 4:30 P.M., when a commotion was noticed west of the road. Although very little firing had been heard in that direction, "suddenly all eyes were turned to the center of our line of battle. . . . Our men were flying to the rear in the wildest confusion." Immediately Lee dashed for the pike, leaping his horse over both stone fences, and rode among the men of Stevenson's Division. Ed Johnson's Division, on Lee's extreme left, already appeared to have broken up in flight, and its men were racing for the Franklin pike along the rear of Stevenson's line. Lee and several of his staff rode among them, shouting, "Rally, men, rally! For God's sake, rally!" A few men gathered in small clusters, but most continued to run away. Lee grabbed a flag and began waving it, and his staff did likewise.[8]

Just behind the fleeing troops a blue line was discovered approaching from the west, with banners waving and shouts of triumph rising from their ranks. Firing broke out on the flank, and then on the front. Here the opposite line of battle, Wood's Fourth Corps, was making a spontaneous attack in the wake of McArthur's successful penetration of A. P. Stewart's line. Lee was in the midst of a rapidly closing pincers, and although "he looked like a very god of war" to at least one bewildered soldier, Ed Johnson's men kept running.[9]

Portly Ed Johnson was found huffing and puffing in his attempt to get away. "Being very corpulent and unaccustomed to running, he was soon far behind," noted a soldier. Johnson's orderly was well ahead, leading the general's horse away as fast as he could run across the muddy ground. One of Johnson's men caught up with him, but the orderly refused to take the horse back or release the animal to anyone else. Johnson kept falling farther and farther behind. He had just been released from a Federal prison, he gasped to an officer running past, and said that he was too tired to go farther. Soon Johnson was surrounded by three privates from Kenner Garrard's division and taken prisoner. He then joined many of his men who had surrendered without attempting to run away. In minutes, Johnson's Division had virtually ceased to exist. Many of its men had been captured, and the remnant became a fleeing mob. Already, Cummings's Brigade of Stevenson's Division had joined in the flight.[10]

Edmund W. Pettus's Brigade, on Stevenson's right flank, stood next in line. Although the brigade's officers kept urging the men to remain and wait for orders, chaos ran down Pettus's line from the left like an electric shock. The men began running to the rear faster than their officers could rally them. When the 20th Alabama got up to leave, Pettus sprang among them, yelling and gesturing for the men to stay. He kept shoving them back, and to an Alabama officer it looked for a moment like they might hold. Yet in their front, Wood's entire corps had closed to within short range and was about to overrun their line. Pettus's line fragmented, many of the men streaming to the rear as others crouched in their entrenchments, waving handkerchiefs and hats as signs of surrender. A captain ran down the line, shouting for the men to follow him out, but most refused to go. They had had enough fighting under dire circumstances. Now they only wanted to be survivors.[11]

Stephen D. Lee's Corps was rapidly crumbling away. Only Major General Henry D. Clayton's Division, posted on Lee's right flank, remained mostly intact. Lee hastily sent a staff officer to tell Clayton to withdraw.[12]

From Clayton's position on Overton Hill in the mist and gathering darkness, it was impossible to observe what was happening west of the Franklin pike. Clayton ordered his artillery to withdraw; then suddenly he saw the throng of wild-eyed men racing in disorder along the Franklin pike. Within minutes Clayton learned that the whole army, except his division, "was then in complete rout." Clayton discovered that Steedman's skirmish line was advancing near the top of the hill. He had time only to alert part of Holtzclaw's Brigade, which was in a split position on both sides of the Franklin pike. Holtzclaw said he was unable to give any order before the flying mass from the left swept through his ranks. Yet he was able to get most of his regiments out intact, thanks to a brief stand by his reserves, the 39th Georgia Infantry, earlier sent to support Clayton's line during Steedman's attack. Beyond Holtzclaw, the last remaining Confederate brigade, that of Brigadier General Marcellus A. Stovall, scrambled to escape from Overton Hill. Despite orders to remain in position and await instructions, Stovall finally "took the responsibility of moving off." With what seemed to be the entire Federal army closing in about him, Stovall hurriedly marched his men south in column.[13]

The last remnant of the Confederate army was in flight. From the vicinity of Shy's Hill across to the still smoldering breastworks on Overton Hill, scores of Union flags were waving in triumph. In the ranks of the 57th Indiana Infantry of Wood's corps, the rush to join in the victory had been spontaneous. From their positions in the opposite timber, Wood's men had seen the panic and disorder run down the Confederate line like an ocean wave. At first the men were ordered to remain where they were. Yet many individuals began running forward. "All in vain were the efforts of the officers who attempted to keep the men in line," said a soldier. The 57th bolted toward the Confederate lines with a rousing yell. In the 86th Indiana regiment the men were working to strengthen their entrenchments when "the wave of action" ran along Wood's front. "Forward," shouted their colonel, and they too joined in the impromptu charge. There was no time to fall in and form a line, wrote a private. All that could be done was grab one's gun and rush forward.[14]

With loud shouts Wood's corps streamed across an open cornfield. Bullets from a few Confederate skirmishers sliced through the cornstalks like the sound of hail, and the ground was so muddy the charging Union infantry often sank to their ankles. Enemy resistance was lighter than expected—most of the skirmishers surrendered rather than run—but a few Rebels continued firing from their main parapet. Several gunners at a four-gun battery discharged their cannon in the faces of Wood's veterans. The blasts of canister splintered a rail fence in front and sent boughs of cedars cascading through the Federal ranks. Some men went down, but through the abatis and over the breastworks poured Wood's troops. "With rare exceptions the enemy threw down their guns and ran to the rear," observed an Illinois infantryman.[15]

There was so much confusion here, with the milling, bewildered Rebel prisoners continuing to wave their hats and handkerchiefs as tokens of surrender, that some late-arriving new recruits mistook the enemy's waving as taunts and opened fire on clusters of prisoners. Officers soon stopped the firing, but the emotional stress of that last assault was plainly evident. The confusion was compounded when a Federal battery in the rear continued to fire on the works despite the waving of Union flags above the parapets. Their shells came whizzing down amid some of Wood's men, causing them to curse and dodge about.[16]

On Wood's left flank the troops of Steedman's command had belatedly joined in the irregular wave of assault. Since most of Stephen D. Lee's Corps were already in confusion, there was little opposition as Steedman's troops, both black and white, surged up the bloody slopes of Overton Hill. It seemed to be "a second Missionary Ridge," wrote a veteran who had participated in that famous 1863 Federal assault. Among the stragglers and trapped men found in Lee's trenches were several officers who considered it a disgrace to be captured by black troops. One Rebel captain, when being marched to the rear, impulsively grabbed his guard's rifle musket and shot down "the smoked Yankee." In turn, the Rebel captain was viciously stabbed with the sword of a white officer.[17]

Despite various incidents, the rounding up of Hood's men all across the Shy's Hill–Overton Hill front seemed almost too easy. "The Rebels shook their hats and handkerchiefs from behind every log and tree," noticed one elated Illinois soldier. Placed in heavy columns, the Confederate prisoners were soon herded to the rear, many laughing and joking about going into Nashville, noted a Federal lieutenant. "They were all ragged and dirty, and so filthy that we could smell them as plainly as if it had been a flock of sheep on a hot June day." Further, he was shocked to notice that about one-third of them were without shoes.

Inevitably, the uncoordinated attacks along Hood's eastern flank produced widespread disorganization among Wood's and Steedman's troops. Due to the confusion and approaching darkness, many of Wood's units re-formed their ranks before leisurely continuing southward. Steedman's troops had encamped after moving into the captured lines, and he wrote to Thomas "to know your wishes," since he was without everything except ammunition, and not prepared to go forward.[18]

Across the rolling terrain, where the initial break had occurred, James H. Wilson was reorganizing for the mounted pursuit of Hood's fleeing ranks. Yet the heavily wooded and hilled terrain which had caused Wilson's men to fight dismounted served to further delay their progress. Due to the considerable distance from which their horses had to be led forward and the prevailing disorder at the front, it was nearly dark before two of Hatch's brigades moved in pursuit along the Granny White pike.[19]

While Wilson gathered his cavalrymen, John M. Schofield's Twenty-third Corps had been ordered to pursue Hood's army in the wake of McArthur's success. Thus far the extent of Schofield's contribution had been the attack of Doolittle's lone brigade on Cheatham's front. In pursuit Schofield was equally slow. Couch's division failed to advance until nearly nightfall. Jacob Cox's men, including Doolittle's troops, were halted before reaching the Granny White pike when A. J. Smith's men were observed advancing along that roadway. Thereafter, Schofield arrived and ordered Cox to bivouac for the night, "as the roads were occupied by other columns moving in pursuit." Later, Schofield reported his order "to advance in conjunction with the cavalry . . . was not executed with the promptness or energy which I had expected."

Thomas was less than pleased. Thereafter, Schofield was ordered to bring up the army's rear as an escort to the wagon train. Since McArthur's fatigued troops had gone forward only a short distance before being recalled, pursuit of Hood's army along the Granny White pike now was entirely in the hands of the cavalry. Farther east, along the Franklin pike, Wood's troops had become the Confederate army's only pursuers.[20]

The Confederate army was not only beaten and routed, estimated a Federal general, but its spirit seemed to be gone. The interrogation of captured Confederate officers that evening convinced Schofield that "Hood's army is more thoroughly beaten than any troops I have ever seen." In view of the disorderly mass of fleeing men streaming over the hills and along the Franklin pike at dusk that day, this conclusion seemed well justified. So many frightened refugees were pouring past Hood, Stewart, and Cheatham that these leaders reluctantly gave up in their attempts to stop them. The exasperated Cheatham at one point had positioned his horse sideways across the Franklin pike to block the path. Most merely walked around horse and rider, but one man, undaunted, simply ducked under Cheatham's horse and continued on his way. In the rain and mud, with wagons, cannon, thousands of guns, accoutrements, and all manner of thrown-away equipment littering the ground, the Army of Tennessee had never witnessed such a sad, pathetic scene.[21]

Amid the demoralized men streaming south along the pike, a captain of the 46th Alabama Infantry kept thinking about the disgrace of it all, how "it was the only rout of which I was ever a participant." Looking back over his shoulder from a knoll, the captain saw that the pursuing Federals seemed little organized, merely "straggling along," firing into the backs of the fleeing Confederates. He asked the handful of men near him to halt and give the enemy a few shots. Enough turned and fired that soon perhaps a dozen riflemen stood along the side of the road shooting at the approaching Yankees. The firing seemed to check the enemy's progress for a few minutes; then, with the blue infantrymen getting "uncomfortably close," someone cried out, "It's no use, boys, let's give it up or we will be captured." All then fell back in confusion.[22]

Ahead in the road, the captain of the 46th Alabama saw a line of about 200 men drawn up across the pike, behind which a number of flags were flying. It was the remnant of Henry Clayton's division. Stephen D. Lee was there, and this stand was his idea, having earlier unsuccessfully posted fragments of Randall Gibson's Brigade along the road about a half mile north. Gibson had scarcely delayed the enemy, and to the soldiers streaming down the Franklin pike there seemed to be many flags here, but few men. There were two field guns of the Efuaula Light Artillery posted along the road, with most of the 39th Georgia standing beside them. Sweeping down the pike in the gathering darkness appeared the advanced units of the pursuing Federals. Already Clayton's men were in an uproar, and their officers were heard swearing mightily, trying to keep the men in line. Nervously, a little drummer boy stood beside the wheel of a field gun, beating the long roll.[23]

To the most advanced men of the pursuing 86th Indiana Infantry this stopgap Confederate line was like a sudden apparition. Only a handful of their regiment was as yet present, many men having dropped behind from sheer exhaustion, and the thought occurred to one man that if the enemy had the nerve, they might charge and capture the entire lot of them. Yet, from the curses and shouts coming from the Confederate ranks, the 86th discovered it was all the enemy officers could do to keep their men from running away. Every few minutes some of the Rebel ranks were seen breaking for the rear. The 86th Indiana had halted across a small swale from Clayton's battle line, only about fifty yards distant. When Clayton's two cannon opened with a roar, their shots went wild. More men began fleeing from the Rebel line. The two cannon were limbered up and pulled out, then the ranks of infantry followed. "One by one they went [back], until their officers saw it was the sheerest folly to try to hold them, when they all scampered," said an amazed Indiana rifleman.[24]

The entire 86th regiment was then ready to go forward; more of Wood's men were coming up. Yet with darkness at hand and an unknown situation ahead, a halt was ordered and the men told to bivouac at the edge of the swale. Fires were soon lighted and the men began to cook and talk over the day's events. "The boys almost hugged one another in the excess of their joyous good humor." Officers and men happily caroused about the campsite, being "free and easy" in their chatter. The Rebels had been chased from their breastworks "like the wild deer of the forest," they joked. Hood had been more badly beaten than Bragg at Missionary Ridge. Every Rebel unit had been routed and its men demoralized, thought Wood's soldiers. There seemed to be no end to the enemy's despair. Amazingly, the cost to the Union army had been minimal. All agreed it was a grand, unprecedented victory.[25]

*   *   *

Stephen D. Lee considered himself rather lucky. With his last few troops in disorder, he thought it "a fortunate circumstance that the enemy was too much crippled to pursue us on the Franklin pike." Lee was with the rear guard, marching southward through the near darkness, when he learned that this good fortune was suddenly in doubt. One of Hood's aides rode up and alerted Lee that it was necessary to get beyond Brentwood at once. The enemy was on the Granny White pike, moving toward Hollow Tree Gap where the two pikes merged, warned the aide. If Chalmers's cavalry was forced back beyond that point, Lee and all troops north of that point would be cut off. Immediately Lee hastened everyone to the rear. Again the survival of the main remnant of the Confederate army seemed to totter in uncertainty.[26]

James R. Chalmers had deployed at Brentwood on the Franklin pike, preparing to protect the army's wagons and ambulances collected there. Yet about 4:30 P.M. he had received Hood's 3:15 P.M. dispatch to hold the Granny White pike—"put in your escort and every available man you can find," Hood had urgently decreed. Chalmers quickly ordered the brigade of Colonel Edmund W. Rucker to return to the Granny White pike and defend that roadway.[27]

In responding to this emergency order, Chalmers and Rucker were unaware that the survival of Lee's rear guard largely depended on them. Hood's intent at 3:15 P.M. had been to protect the immediate rear of his army from the then imminent attack of Wilson's troopers. Chalmers at the time had been retreating to Brentwood, and when Hood's order was finally delivered, Chalmers did not know that the entire army had been routed.[28]

Edmund W. Rucker was known as an ardent fighter, but his men had been rather fortunate on December 16th, being only lightly engaged due to their position on the extreme left flank along the Hillsboro pike. Here Rucker had skirmished with Richard W. Johnson's cavalry division until ordered to pull back and concentrate at Brentwood. By Hood's order, Rucker went about barricading the Granny White pike north of the Little Harpeth River, about eight miles from Nashville. With darkness at hand, Rucker had just posted one of his regiments and was returning to the main barricade across the pike when he encountered a body of mounted troops. Thinking they might be his own men, Rucker, saber in hand, rode up to an officer giving commands. "Who are you?" he demanded. The unknown horseman replied that he was an officer of the 12th Tennessee Cavalry. Immediately Rucker knew he was in the presence of Yankees. Quickly swinging his saber, he struck the rider across the forehead with a glancing blow and then again lashed out with his blade. Yet his horse reared, and Rucker, thrown off balance, dropped his saber as he lunged to regain the saddle. His adversary, Captain Joseph C. Boyer of the 12th Tennessee (Union) Cavalry, by now had recovered sufficiently to draw his sword and grapple with Rucker. Rucker soon grasped the saber and wrenched it from Boyer's hand. During the melee, Rucker noted some of the enemy's troopers closing in. He struck spurs to his mount and the big white bolted for the line of barricades. Boyer shouted for his men to shoot the man on the white horse, and a volley of shots zipped past. One pistol ball struck Rucker in the left elbow, shattering the bone, and his mount leapt wildly, throwing him to the ground, where Rucker was soon made a prisoner.*[29]

Meanwhile, a mad, confused melee had erupted between two advancing Federal regiments (the 9th Illinois Cavalry and the 12th Tennessee Cavalry) and Rucker's Brigade. Amid the rain and darkness, frequent hand-to-hand encounters occurred. A private of the 12th Tennessee Cavalry shot a Confederate color-bearer and was in the process of gathering in the flag when a Rebel officer rode up to him and said, "Stick to your colors, boys!" Sarcastically replying, "I'll do it," the Federal private made off with the flag in the darkness. Due to the gloom "it was impossible to reform the men, or indeed to distinguish between friend and foe, so closely were they mingled together," said Chalmers. Amid scattered firing, Rucker's Brigade was finally compelled to retreat to the Franklin pike.[30]

It had been one of the most vicious, if brief, encounters of the war, thought James H. Wilson. Sheets of flame had leapt from the Spencer carbines of his men, lighting up the darkness like Fourth of July fireworks. Now, with nightfall at hand and the enemy gone, Wilson was faced with a decision about further pursuit. Edmund Rucker was brought in before 6:30 P.M., Hood's urgent dispatch having been found in his pocket. Wilson promptly understood that "the safety of his [Hood's] army depends upon the ability of Chalmers to keep us off; time is all he wants." Moreover, he was convinced "the Rebels are badly beaten and in full retreat." Rucker, however, told his captors that "Forrest has just arrived with all the cavalry, and will give you hell tonight." Although this was presumed to be a ruse, Wilson made a curious decision. "The night was so dark and wet, and the men and horses so jaded," said the Federal cavalry commander, that "the pursuit was necessarily discontinued." Wilson would "move at daylight, or if practicable, by 4:00 A.M.," intending to rapidly gallop toward Franklin. Meanwhile, Hood's army would be allowed to proceed unhampered in their retreat.[31]

By 10:00 P.M. a raging storm had set in across the already saturated Tennessee countryside. The Federal soldiers lying on the muddy ground in the cold rain soon found themselves wallowing in pools of water. Drowsily the men shuffled to stumps, logs, tree limbs, or even rocks to escape the water. Amid the ranks of McArthur's units a gill of whiskey, issued in celebration of their victory, helped ward off the damp chill.[32]

*   *   *

*Traditional accounts of Rucker's hand-to-hand encounter state that he fought with Colonel George Spalding of the 12th Tennessee. From a close examination of contemporary reports it is evident that he fought with Captain Boyer. Part of the confusion may have occurred from the fact that Spalding obtained Rucker's sword as a trophy and ultimately returned it twenty-five years later amid considerable publicity.

James H. Wilson heard the sound of galloping horses along the macadamized pike in his rear. Through the rain and darkness he recognized the bulky form of George H. Thomas, coming to check on the cavalry's progress. Approaching Wilson, Thomas blurted out, "Dang it to hell, Wilson, didn't I tell you we could lick 'em, didn't I tell you we could lick 'em?" In a few minutes "Old Slow Trot" was gone again, galloping back to his headquarters to send a victory dispatch to Washington. Wilson was stunned. Thomas never used profane language. His "Dang it to hell, Wilson" had been spoken with all the vehemence of an old dragoon. It was the closest thing to profanity the Federal cavalry commander had ever heard Thomas utter. The mood seemed to fit. "This has been a splendid day," concluded Wilson. "The day is glorious!"[33]

Out on the debris-strewn battlefield that night there was little cause for celebration for the victims in blue and gray. Among the wounded soldiers both North and South there now seemed to be no enmity, noted an assistant surgeon. Throughout the night ambulance drivers, medical orderlies, and stretcher bearers searched through the pouring rain for unattended wounded. Later found on the battlefield was a Nashville civilian, severely wounded in the hips. A soldier had caught him robbing the dead and shot him, leaving him there to suffer in agony. An outraged soldier who later saw the civilian in the hospital wrote, "When I [last] saw him he was in a fair way to go to hell."[34]

Despite the miserable weather, that night each man of Thomas's army seemed to collapse wherever circumstances found him. One of Cox's staff officers found his general in the drenching rain, stretched out in the mud beside several other officers, each having two fence rails for a bed. Edmund Rucker, after having his shattered left arm amputated, was taken to Mr. Tucker's farmhouse, near the site of his fight with Hatch's cavalry. Here he shared a room with James H. Wilson and Edward Hatch. Wilson, who came in late, sat up in bed all night, cross-legged like a tailor, writing orders. "I don't think that either General Wilson or I slept a wink," later remembered the fever-tortured Rucker. Hatch laid down on the floor and frequently went to get water for the wounded Confederate colonel. The following morning, when Rucker was taken to Nashville, Hatch provided him with "a small flask of good whisky."[35]

Rucker's kind treatment mirrored that of the Confederate generals captured on December 16th, Ed Johnson, Henry R. Jackson, and, belatedly so, Thomas B. Smith. All were taken to Thomas's field headquarters at the Hale residence and feted to officers' mess. When proffered some cigars and a flask of spirits by one of Thomas's staff officers, a Confederate brigadier (probably Henry R. Jackson) related how the Yankees had marched up to and over his works as "cool as fate." Remarked the general, "It was astonishing, sir, such fighting . . . it was really splendid."[36]

Their comfortable circumstances as prisoners seemed to greatly contrast with those of another Confederate general, one who had escaped and was then contemplating the day's events at Mrs. Maney's residence near Franklin. John Bell Hood had suffered the ultimate consequences of his management of the Army of Tennessee. Beaten, disconsolate, his army scattered along the Franklin pike from Brentwood to Franklin, with many survivors already having deserted for home, Hood was at the end of his wits. There seemed to be no hope. For tomorrow, forever, his military career appeared to be ruined. How would he ever be able to explain to Jefferson Davis, or even to Buck?[37]

A weary, begrimed private, wounded in the foot, his uniform soaked with blood, called at Hood's headquarters for a pass and a wounded furlough. While there, he saw that Hood, the bold commander who had once promised his men victory in Tennessee, was now the picture of despair. "He was much agitated and affected," noted the private, "pulling his hair with his one [good] hand, and crying like his heart would break."[38]

CHAPTER XXXIV

A Retreat from the
Lion's Mouth

THE BATTLE OF NASHVILLE, thought a Federal participant, surely would be the end of the Confederate army. A Wisconsin corporal exuberantly wrote to his wife, saying "our brilliant and easy victory" was so thorough that all of Hood's forces had been completely routed. Another soldier, one of McArthur's men, happily speculated that Hood's "whole army will be captured before he can cross the Tennessee River."[1]

Within hours of the final volleys on December 16th, the usually taciturn George H. Thomas dispatched a lengthy telegram to Washington, declaring that "the greatest enthusiasm prevails" over what was obviously an enormous victory. So many prisoners and cannon had been captured that they were still being counted, announced Thomas, and they would "greatly exceed" those taken on the 15th. "The woods, fields, and entrenchments are strewn with the enemy's small arms, abandoned in their retreat." Later, "with pride and pleasure," Thomas published Lincoln's, Stanton's, and Grant's congratulatory telegrams about the victory of the 15th and announced, "a few more examples of devotion and courage like this, and the Rebel army of the West, which you have been fighting for three years, will be no more, and you may reasonably expect an early and honorable peace."[2]

The army was wild with excitement despite the rainy weather on the morning of the 17th, wrote an officer, and everyone was anxious to have a hand in the destruction of the remnant of Hood's forces. Wilson had reveille sounded shortly after 3:00 A.M. "Go for him [Hood] with all possible celerity," urged the cavalry commander.[3]

Wilson's plan called for the cavalry, which was in advance on the Granny White pike, to strike boldly on the roads west of Hood's only line of retreat, the Franklin pike, so as to reach the village ahead of most of the enemy's straggling ranks. Richard W. Johnson's division would utilize the Hillsboro pike, Hammond's brigade following, while Wilson would go with Hatch's and Knipe's troopers down the Granny White pike. Wilson intended to be on the march by 4:00 A.M., if practicable. Thus, he notified Thomas's headquarters at 6:30 P.M. on the 16th that if there were to be any other plans, "please send [them] at once."[4]

Thomas, in fact, did have other plans for Wilson. At 9:15 P.M., without consultation, he ordered the cavalry commander to "leave Johnson's division . . . on the Hillsboro pike to observe the enemy and protect our right and rear, and move with the balance of your command over to the Franklin pike, to operate on that road and the road running east of the same."[5]

Wilson received this most significant order about 3:00 A.M., and was immediately upset. Clearly, Thomas was not being as aggressive as the circumstances seemed to warrant. To shift his cavalrymen to the opposite flank would require considerable time. Moreover, an extension of the Granny White pike merged with the Franklin pike several miles below Brentwood. Wilson quickly protested, of sorts, saying some of his men would be compelled to continue on the Granny White pike as far as Brentwood. "It seems to me that I shall be able to do the enemy more damage by crowding him now by the shortest routes, instead of losing any time to get to the other flank," he replied. Yet, so as to comply with Thomas's directive, Wilson felt compelled to send Knipe's division and Croxton's brigade across to the Franklin pike.[6]

Citing the "time is all we want" dispatch captured with Rucker, Wilson again urged Thomas to reconsider. The infantry should press Hood's forces along the Franklin pike, while the more mobile cavalry swept around his western flank to cut him off before Forrest's cavalrymen came up from Murfreesboro. Yet, with operations set to begin shortly, it was already too late to alter the dispositions ordered by Thomas. Wilson's order of 3:30 A.M. directed that various units cross to the Franklin pike, which stripped his primary command of significant strength.[7]

Because the infantry along the Franklin pike was delayed by the rain and darkness until about 8:00 A.M., it was soon apparent that the cavalry must initiate the pursuit. Since both Rebel infantry and cavalry were known to be on the Franklin pike, it was expected that Wilson would face some opposition. Only Richard W. Johnson's division would remain largely unopposed in its advance along the Hillsboro pike.[8]

To the men in the vanguard of Thomas's pursuit, there was little pondering of the tactical maneuvering then under way. They only knew and seemed to care that they were going after a beaten and routed enemy. Thomas J. Wood said that his whole corps was burning with impatience to get forward. By the time they were half dressed, noted a Federal artillerist, they were on the road in pursuit of Hood's army. As they wallowed through the slush and mud, the men, in buoyant spirits, began to sing:

> Hoe your cake and scratch your gravel,
> In Dixie's land I'm bound to travel.
> Look away, look away, look away down south in Dixie.[9]

II

The march south had begun before daylight. Many of the men were somewhat amazed. There had been no pursuit by Thomas's troops during the night, so that the rear guard under Stephen D. Lee had been able to camp about seven miles north of Franklin at 10:00 P.M. By early morning so many of the previously scattered Confederates had come together that the sullen columns began to look more like an army again, thought an Alabama captain. If Hood's ragged and sadly depleted ranks had endured an ultimate defeat, they at least had survived. Reasoned one Tennessean, "Thomas could, and ought to have captured us that night." Yet the men were still there, wearily plodding south toward Franklin. Where there was existence, there was at least life.[10]

It wasn't much of a fighting force; many of the men had thrown away their rifle muskets, and everything else that would impede their progress. The roadside was littered with all manner of equipment, even blankets. It was a retreat from the lion's mouth, said a lieutenant colonel, and the object was to escape before the jaws came crashing closed. In the half-light of dawn some of Chalmers's cavalrymen came riding past, going north along the Franklin pike. They twitted the soldiers about running away, said one of Stephen D. Lee's officers. "They were going back to show us how to whip Yankees, so we need not be afraid any more," the horseman jested.[11]

Stephen D. Lee's men continued south. Being the last of the semi-organized troops on the Franklin pike, at full daylight their ranks were halted at Hollow Tree Gap, about five miles north of Franklin and near the point where the road extending the Granny White pike joined with the Franklin pike. Most of Pettus's and Stovall's brigades were there, under Henry Clayton's command, with a battery of artillery posted on the pike. About an hour after Lee's rear guard deployed, there was firing in the distance—in the direction the cavalry had gone. Within minutes the clatter of hooves sounded on the pike. Soon the road ahead was filled with horsemen in blue coats as far back as one could see. The trouble was, said an officer, with so many of the Confederate cavalrymen wearing captured Yankee overcoats, there was no way to tell whose side they were on. Belatedly, it was discovered they were Chalmers's men—the same cavalrymen "who were going to show us how to fight Yankees," noted a captain. Mixed in among their ranks were the most advanced of Wilson's troopers, sabering and shooting without seeming to notice Lee's ranks drawn up in front. Some of Wilson's men had already passed within Lee's lines when a ragged volley was fired from the line in gray, abruptly halting the oncoming Federal horsemen. After a few minutes the shooting stopped. The Yankees in front soon fled, and a few surprised enemy troopers who had passed within the Confederate lines surrendered. Although Chalmers was aghast over the "shameful" rout of his cavalrymen, little damage had been done.[12]

About 9:00 A.M. two mounted Federal regiments again attempted a frontal charge on Clayton's line, but were repulsed with the loss of twenty-two killed and wounded and sixty-three captured. About 10:00 A.M. Lee's rearguard detachment withdrew, following reports that the Federal cavalry was advancing along roads on both sides of the Franklin pike. Lee was forced to hurry his men toward Franklin to escape the encircling Yankee horsemen.[13]

James H. Wilson's pursuit had gotten off to a poor start. While Hammond's brigade under Joseph F. Knipe's personal command had suffered severe losses and several bloody repulses along the Franklin pike, Hatch's division, which had the shorter route to travel, had been so delayed by a rutted country road that it belatedly came up in the rear of Knipe's men. Even troops sent east to outflank Stephen D. Lee's line at Hollow Tree Gap had halted, waiting for reinforcements. Thus, Lee had escaped, losing only about a hundred prisoners from Randall Gibson's trailing brigade. Finally, as Wilson's troopers approached Franklin about 10:30 A.M., he saw his chance.[14]

The last of the wagons carrying Rebel wounded and munitions were passing over the bridges into Franklin, and already the temporary pontoon bridge was being disassembled. Posted in an earthwork near the Harpeth River in Wilson's front was Randall Gibson's Brigade of Louisiana infantry, less than 500 strong. Gibson also had two field guns and a portion of Buford's cavalry, just arrived from the vicinity of Murfreesboro. With an estimated 3,000 Federal cavalry charging in front, Buford's cavalrymen were overwhelmed and driven "in confusion into the river." Gibson was surrounded and had to fight his way back, suffering forty casualties. The artillery was barely able to escape, and there was so much panic among the men fleeing across the temporary bridge that when one man slipped and fell, no one stopped to help him. He clung precariously to the side of the bridge, begging for help. "The last I saw of him," wrote an officer, "he was still wallowing in the mud and the men were running over him."[15]

What saved many of Gibson's men, and some of Hood's refugees still loitering in Franklin, was the section of Bledsoe's Battery posted along Front Street. Their shells began exploding above the heads of Wilson's cavalrymen, briefly causing them to draw back.[16]

With sniper fire continuing along the riverbank, Stephen Lee's pioneers hastened to sink the temporary bridge and pontoons and destroy the railroad trestle bridge near Fort Granger. By herculean effort, a detachment of pioneers under an engineer officer was able to topple the trestle bridge into the rising waters of the Harpeth. With both bridges gone and a slow rain continuing to fall, Wilson realized that he would have to act quickly to get his men across at the fords before the rising waters prevented passage.[17]

Meanwhile, aware that the respite from pursuit would be brief, and in order to avoid the shelling of Franklin due to the large number of wounded there, Lee had ordered the immediate evacuation of the village. Just how timely this order was, few seemed to understand.[18]

Richard W. Johnson had departed from his bivouac, about nine miles from Franklin, at 4:00 A.M. Following the Hillsboro pike to its crossing of the Harpeth River a few miles west of Franklin, Johnson had encountered only a few enemy pickets barricaded on ridges in front. Despite having made a preliminary reconnaissance the night before, and being aware that the way was open, Johnson was so cautious as to use about six and a half hours to advance nine miles on horseback. Finally, after fording the river, Johnson approached the village from the west about 10:30 A.M.[19]

Already, the last of the Confederates were scrambling to evacuate Franklin, rushing down the Columbia turnpike south of town. At the last minute, Lee's men set fire to the freight house in town, a building containing seven wagonloads of ammunition. As the last of Lee's soldiers ran from the village, a citizen dashed with a ladder to the burning building and threw buckets of water on the blazing roof. Although cinders and charred shingles fell through onto the parked wagons, an explosion was avoided and the building saved.[20]

Just as Johnson's men dashed through the village capturing about fifty prisoners, Knipe's men forded the Harpeth near the ruined railroad bridge and entered the downtown area. Knipe had already captured a seventy-five-man detachment of Rebel infantry from Holtzclaw's Brigade, which had been cut off when the bridges were destroyed. James H. Wilson was caught up in the emotion of the moment. "The Rebels are on a great skedaddle," he proclaimed. "The prisoners report the Rebel army in a complete rout, and all the Tennesseans are deserting." The Rebel army seemed to be down on Hood, Wilson added, and he forwarded information from one of the Federal surgeons left behind in Franklin, who said "he never saw a worse rabble; they are completely demoralized."[21]

One look around the war-ravaged village seemed to confirm Wilson's estimate. With about 2,000 Confederate wounded in town, and perhaps 200 Federal victims of the Franklin battle, there had been no time to evacuate these men. Every building seemed crammed with wounded, and as Johnson's men entered the village there were cries and shouts of joy from the Union soldiers able to hobble or crawl to the windows.[22]

William A. Quarles, the wounded Confederate brigadier, was at Carnton, the McGavock residence, unable to move due to his severe injuries. Aware that Franklin was being evacuated, Quarles ordered several attendants to make their escape. They dashed for an ambulance and, raising a yellow (hospital) flag, trotted past the oncoming ranks of Wilson's cavalry-men without being stopped.[23]

Just south of Franklin, behind the deadly breastworks that had proved so formidable on November 30th, Hood's rear-guard elements, some of Holtzclaw's men, had formed under the personal supervision of Stephen D. Lee. When some of Wilson's cavalrymen galloped toward them, three or four volleys caused them to fall back. Yet about 1:00 P.M., as the Confederate line of battle slowly withdrew toward the gap at Winstead Hill, fragments from a bursting Federal shell ripped into Stephen D. Lee's boot. The spur was torn off and fragments sliced into his heel, breaking several small bones. Despite the severe wound, Lee insisted on remaining in command of the rear guard. Lee estimated he had already gained four or five hours for the main segment of Hood's army, now nearing Spring Hill, and as he withdrew southward he ordered the remnant of Carter L. Stevenson's Division to relieve Clayton's men. Stevenson soon put Chalmers's cavalry on both flanks, and his men trudged steadily down the Columbia pike amid intermittent rain showers, thankful that the enemy was not heavily pressing them.[24]

James H. Wilson by 1:30 P.M. had reorganized his pursuit to encompass the elements of his cavalry actually present. Johnson's men were to march down the Carter's Creek pike on the west, Hatch and Knipe would pursue directly down the Columbia pike, and Croxton's brigade would advance eastward along the Lewisburg pike. By pushing his flanking columns rapidly ahead, Wilson anticipated that he would soon pass beyond Lee's rear guard and bring them to bay from behind. Since Wood's leading infantry corps was stalled on the north bank, having found the rapidly rising Harpeth River "much too swollen" to ford following their arrival opposite Franklin about 1:20 P.M., Wilson knew he would have no infantry support.[25]

Wilson's flanking plan worked nearly to perfection. By midafternoon Hatch's and Knipe's men were skirmishing with Stevenson's rear-guard units along the Columbia pike, compelling them to maintain a line of battle as they retreated slowly in the direction of Spring Hill. About 4:00 P.M., with the rain falling and a gloomy darkness descending over the muddy landscape, Stevenson's troops were found drawn up in a solid line in open country a mile north of the West Harpeth River. Although an artillery battery supported them, Wilson didn't hesitate. After sending Hammond's and Coon's brigades to swing around the enemy's flank, he turned to his personal escort detachment commanded by Lieutenant Joseph Hedges and ordered a frontal saber charge directly south along the Columbia pike. Hedges commanded about 200 men of the 4th U.S. Cavalry, regulars whose experience included hard fighting from Fort Donelson to Atlanta. With drawn sabers, Hedges's men trotted forward in a column of fours, aiming at the center of Stevenson's line, about 300 yards distant. On both flanks Hammond's and Coon's men gal-loped onward, presenting a formidable line that seemed to extend nearly a mile and a half.[26]

Although it was apparent that the Yankee line would easily envelop both flanks, due to some confusion in the gathering darkness about whose troops were approaching—Federal and Confederate cavalrymen too often wore the same apparel, it seemed—Stevenson's men were slow in withdrawing.[27]

"They swooped down on us with pistols, carbines, and sabers, hewing, whacking, and shooting" almost before the Rebels could react, said a Confederate officer. Stevenson had a total of about 700 infantrymen posted on both sides of the road. Hedges's 4th regulars crashed into the Rebel line with the impact of a plunging mountain boulder. Men scattered in every direction, trying to avoid the galloping horses. It was a melee to end all others, thought a participant. The 4th Cavalry were fighting like demons. Sabers versus bayonets. Gunsmoke, gloom, rain, curses, groans, the swirl of men and horses—they were but brief, frantic vignettes. Yet in an instant the fighting suddenly abated. Too many of Stevenson's men had stayed to fight. Hedges's cavalrymen took to their heels, leaving their commander trapped behind the Rebel line. Thinking fast, Hedges waved his hat and shouted, "The Yankees are coming, run for your lives." The ruse worked. A gap opened, and Hedges spurred his mount to safety.[28]

Stevenson, however, was still in trouble. On both flanks Chalmers's cavalry had "retired in disorder, leaving my small command to their fate," wrote the furious Stevenson. Already his supporting artillery had limbered up and was dashing to the rear. "This was a critical moment," wrote the exasperated rear-guard commander. His only solution was to deploy his men along three sides of a hollow square and withdraw. With his grim ranks formed in a ragged line to the front, rear, and side, Stevenson began to pull back, the angular bayonets of his men jutting outward in a threatening perimeter of steel.[29]

The 2d Iowa Cavalry of Hatch's division had just rammed headlong into Abraham Buford's Rebel cavalrymen. Although Buford remained behind, fighting hand to hand with the Iowans, most of his troopers had put up only a momentary fight. One Federal trooper aimed a saber blow at Buford's head, but this was deflected at the last moment by a Rebel trooper's empty carbine. The general then reached out and grabbed the startled Yankee, jerking him from his horse and squeezing him so tightly that the man later said he had been "hugged by a bear." Buford soon escaped in the direction of Spring Hill, leaving only Stevenson with his makeshift phalanx to face Hatch's swarming cavalrymen. They came at the Rebel hollow square with a rush.[30]

Stevenson crossed the West Harpeth, fighting every step of the way. Finally, with near darkness at hand, he briefly halted to reorganize his lines, only to be struck again by Hatch's advancing horsemen. Due to the darkness, both sides at first were uncertain who was present. Hatch's men were almost on top of the Rebel rear guard before heavy firing erupted. Once more it was cavalry against infantry. Only this time there were far more Federals than

Confederates—and they were armed with seven-shot Spencer repeating carbines.[31]

This melee in the dark "for fierceness exceeded any the regiment ever engaged in," wrote a veteran sergeant of the 2d Iowa Cavalry. Many of Stevenson's men were posted behind a roadside fence, and so many were dressed in captured Federal overcoats, "it was with great difficulty we discovered friend from foe," said a participant. Most of the fighting was hand-to-hand, with clubbed muskets and side arms. In one brutal encounter, a Yankee private leveled his carbine at an opponent and ordered him to surrender. Instead, the man fired at the private but missed. Just as the private was about to shoot him, the Rebel pleaded for mercy. The private's response was a shot from his Spencer—but it too missed its target. Now the Rebel leapt at the private, drawing a revolver from his belt and shouting, "Damn you, I'll teach you to shoot at me after I have surrendered." With one blurred motion, the private felled the onrushing enemy with the butt of his carbine, then, levering another cartridge into the chamber, shot the man dead.[32]

Alongside the 2d Iowa, Hatch's other units began pressing forward. Farther down the road appeared Knipe's troopers, having at last forced their way across the West Harpeth River. The pressure was too great. Stevenson's men streamed back along the Columbia pike. Abandoned in their haste to get away were three 12-pounder guns of Douglas's Battery. General Hatch, having lost his revolver and wielding only a riding crop, reportedly led the rush of nine men that overtook these guns.[33]

Down the mud-coated pike ran Stevenson's troops. A short distance ahead, they unexpectedly found help. Hearing the firing in his rear, Henry Clayton, who previously had been on rear-guard duty, had formed his division across the road. His men were nervous, and amid the chaos of Stevenson's men running past, one of his brigades discovered a heavy column of cavalry approaching from the west. They were Hammond's troopers, and when Clayton's men opened fire virtually in their faces, they fell back in disorder, leaving behind a stand of colors.[34]

Although Holtzclaw's Brigade went forward to help the remnants of Stevenson's command withdraw, they ran head-on into the 9th Illinois Cavalry of Hatch's division. The Rebel infantrymen were soon driven back by repeated volleys of Spencer carbine fire which lit up the night sky. Holtzclaw's men were only too anxious to retreat to the vicinity of Thompson's Station and bivouac with the rest of Lee's exhausted troops. As a bone-weary Alabama officer noted, three days had passed with but little sleep, rest, or food. The fighting, mental torment, and muddy soil had taken its toil. At last Lee's beleaguered rear guard flopped down in the mud and slept soundly.[35]

James H. Wilson's exuberance with the day's results was well reflected in his 6:00 and 7:15 P.M. dispatches to Thomas's chief of staff. "We have 'bust up' Stevenson's Division of infantry," he proclaimed. Three captured guns were the booty of "several beautiful charges" by the 4th Cavalry and Hatch's men. "Hatch is a brick!" he declared. "If it had only been light we would certainly have destroyed their entire rear guard; as it was, they were severely punished."[36]

For George H. Thomas, now near Franklin, December 17th, instead of witnessing the destruction of Hood's scattered forces, had revealed a particularly embarrassing mistake. In fact, a miscue at Thomas's headquarters was responsible for a vexing problem now threatening his attempt to overtake Hood's fleeing army. On the night of the 16th instructions had been issued for the pontoon train to march from Nashville and join the army in the field. Major James B. Willett, in charge of the pontoons, was told to "move the pontoon train at as early an hour as possible, on the Murfreesboro pike, being prepared to report with it to the commanding general at any point between Brentwood and Columbia." When Thomas's adjutant, Captain Robert H. Ramsey, wrote the order, he said Thomas had just awakened from a deep sleep, and evidently the Federal commander was still drowsy.[37]

By mistake, Thomas had said "Murfreesboro pike" when he meant "Franklin pike." The error was compounded when Willett failed to perceive that the Murfreesboro pike would take him away from "any point between Brentwood and Columbia," where he was to be ready to report. Willett, as a result, on the 17th had marched about fifteen miles toward Murfreesboro before the mistake was discovered and he was ordered to move over to the Franklin pike. Willett then attempted to travel by a soft country road across the twenty miles necessary to reach Franklin. The mud-choked road turned out to be impassable, and Willett's 500 horses and mules became hopelessly mired. As a result, on the 18th, despite Thomas's expectation that the pontoons would be up that day, Willett was forced to haul his heavy wagons out of the mud and backtrack to Nashville. Finally, on December 19th, he was able to proceed down the Franklin pike. Due to this critical mistake, the pontoons failed to arrive at the front of the army until December 21st, five days late.[38]

Thomas was so embarrassed over this matter that he apparently attempted to cover up his involvement in the episode, saying only in his official report that the "pontoon bridge, hastily constructed at Nashville" was delayed by bad roads and the "incompleteness of the train." Wrote Thomas, in what was obviously less than the whole truth, "The splendid pontoon train properly belonging to my command, with its trained corps of pontoniers, was absent with General Sherman."[39]

It was a major blow. The absence of the pontoons became a critical matter when the weather began to further deteriorate. Despite relatively mild temperatures, the lingering rain showers so flooded the Harpeth River that the vanguard of the infantry, Thomas J. Wood's corps, was prevented from crossing for more than eighteen hours following their arrival opposite Franklin. Finally, after working all night through intermittent rain and battling the rising waters which once washed out the makeshift bridge, the colonel of the

9th Indiana was able to report a temporary bridge open at 7:30 A.M. on December 18th.[40]

Wood's troops had no sooner begun to cross when dark storm clouds again burst forth in rain, sending a steady downpour which lasted until about 3:00 P.M. Meanwhile, Wilson's cavalrymen, having resumed their advance at daylight, about 11:00 A.M. chased the last of Hood's stragglers out of Spring Hill. Despite constant skirmishing, during the remainder of the 18th Wilson's troopers were unable to bring the rear guard to bay. In the rain and mud, travel off the turnpike was exceedingly difficult and slow. By 2:00 P.M. Wilson was thoroughly wearied, his men were without rations and forage, and he went into camp several miles south of Spring Hill after learning that Hood had two pontoon bridges across the Duck River at Columbia.[41]

Thereafter, the Fourth Corps infantry began arriving at Spring Hill and, although "very much jaded," were ordered forward by Wood. About 4:15 P.M. they passed the camped cavalrymen and actually took the lead in Thomas's pursuit. Finally, with darkness closing about them, Wood went into camp about three and a half miles from Rutherford Creek and seven miles from Columbia.[42]

Although the enemy was still being described by deserters and prisoners as demoralized, at nightfall on the 18th Wilson and Wood had a new worry— the expected presence of Forrest's missing cavalrymen. A prisoner taken that day reported Forrest was en route to Columbia with Jackson's division. Wilson estimated that the Confederate "wizard of the saddle" would soon be found in front, protecting the rear of Hood's army. Moreover, the Federal cavalry commander's other troubles continued to mount. By 6:00 A.M. on the 19th he was still without rations and nearly out of ammunition. There were so many wagons belonging to the infantry on the Columbia pike that his wagons couldn't get through. Wilson wrote despairingly, "I [have] started Hatch after the enemy on the Columbia road, but the balance of the command will have to remain here until the [wagon] train overtakes them." Three days after the rout of Hood's army at Nashville, Thomas's army was beginning to founder in their pursuit.[43]

Despite maintaining an optimistic outlook, Thomas already had begun to consider alternate plans to entrap the remnant of Hood's army. On the evening of the 17th Thomas had asked Admiral S. P. Lee to proceed up the Tennessee River with ironclads and gunboats in order to destroy Hood's pontoon bridge near Florence, Alabama. Thomas wanted Lee's boats at Florence by December 24th, which he estimated would coincide with Hood's arrival. Admiral Lee was soon reported en route with five or six gunboats.[44]

Thomas's other contingency plan involved James B. Steedman's provisional corps. With so many troops stranded on the north bank of the Harpeth during the 17th, Thomas realized all would not be needed to chase Hood. Accordingly, Steedman was directed to march to Murfreesboro, procure trains, and proceed via Stevenson to Decatur, Alabama. From that point,

Steedman would sail down the Tennessee River on transports and destroy any Confederate bridges in the vicinity of Tuscumbia. Thomas hoped by this two-pronged run around both flanks of Hood's army to cut off their escape and damage the enemy's railroad communications.[45]

The great battle between Thomas's army and those of the Rebel Hood had "resulted in a great and decisive victory for the Union arms," proclaimed Edwin Stanton in his December 17th dispatch to fifteen governors, two mayors, and seven generals. "This great victory" had been won and the Confederate army broken thanks to the Almighty and Thomas's skill, he proclaimed. Immediately, the praise and accolades came pouring in. George G. Meade, at Army of the Potomac Headquarters, ordered a 100-gun salute at sunrise on the 18th, "in honor of this brilliant triumph." Phil Sheridan, with the Army of the Shenandoah, joined in the celebrating with "200 guns [salute] and much cheering." Even U. S. Grant, still at Washington, D.C., telegraphed his congratulations on the 18th, mentioning the 200-gun salute "in honor of your great victory." When Thomas later recounted the details of the two-day battle, saying he had taken 53 pieces of artillery, 3,034 small arms, and more than 8,500 prisoners, there was added rejoicing.[46]

Added to the news from Sherman's army that Fort McAllister, the key to Savannah, Georgia, had been captured, Thomas's Nashville victory created a wave of joy that swept throughout the North. The Confederacy seemed to be in military bankruptcy. At no time in the war had an army of either side been so completely routed as at Nashville, said knowledgeable military men.[47]

Edwin Stanton was so pleased by the good news he began to consider a possible future reduction in the draft due to the changing military situation. One of the most surprising circumstances of the Nashville battle had involved the small loss suffered by Federal troops, said Stanton.* This reflected the "admirable skill and caution of General Thomas in his disposition of the battle," wrote Stanton, and he promptly began championing the Virginian for promotion to major general in the regular army.[48]

George H. Thomas found it difficult to bask in the glory of his unprecedented victory. On the night of December 17th he was surrounded by a grim reminder of the heavy price his army had paid in making "any sacrifice" to strike a blow aimed at ending the rebellion.[49]

The town and battlefield at Franklin, Tennessee, presented a sobering and timeless memorial to the agony of human conflict. "Thousands of wounded . . . crowded the hospitals and residences," observed an appalled veteran of the Franklin fighting. Their sufferings and the often unsanitary conditions they were subjected to reflected their terrible ordeal. Even worse, the surrounding scenes were morally devastating. Many of Schofield's for-

*By mistake, an error in transmission caused the total Federal loss to initially read 300, rather than the 3,000 as originally telegraphed by Thomas in his dispatch of 6:00 P.M. December 16th.

mer soldiers took the opportunity of visiting the battlefield of November 30th. "I could not resist the temptation to go over the scene of our night struggle," wrote an Illinois officer, who later admitted, "I never want to see another battlefield like that." Here, across a vast cemeterylike landscape, were found the graves of former comrades and opponents alike. "The enemy had thrown our dead into the ditch [beneath the earthworks]," observed an Ohio captain. "The rails which formed the revetment of the bank had been dumped in, on top of the bodies, and enough earth was then shovelled in to nearly fill the trench." Yet with the rain of the past week, much of the dirt had washed away, leaving a horrendous sight of jumbled, decaying bodies, and various arms and legs sticking out in grotesque array. "The bodies had been stripped of hats, coats, shoes, and sometimes even of their pants and shirts, and had been dumped into the pit like so many logs in a corduroy road," discovered a sickened Ohio youth. "In most cases the heads and feet had been uncovered by the rain, and . . . many lay entirely uncovered in all their ghastly nakedness."[50]

Volunteer fatigue parties soon cleaned out the rotting remains, reburying many in graves upon the hill behind the Carter house. Although it was noted that the Confederate dead had been buried with more care, in extended trenches, the great quantity of grave sites appalled the Federal onlookers. "For the first time we began to realize the extent of the damage inflicted upon the enemy," wrote an Illinois soldier. "We were told that some of the trenches contained the remains of nearly whole regiments."[51]

It was all very demoralizing; amid this melancholy setting so many individual hopes and aspirations common to all men had been blotted out forever. Perhaps it was best that the hideous scars of Franklin were hidden forever, thought a soldier—"hidden in the bosom of our common mother, Earth."[52]

CHAPTER XXXV

The Cards Were Damn
Badly Shuffled

JOHN BELL HOOD had spent the night of December 17th at the fateful village of Spring Hill. Wearily, he had prepared a dispatch to Secretary of War James A. Seddon in Richmond. His army, he announced, had fought at Nashville for two days. Everything had been going well until late in the afternoon of the 16th, "when a portion of our line to the left of the center suddenly gave way, causing, in a few minutes, our line to give way at all points, our troops retreating rapidly down the Franklin pike." Aside from the loss of fifty pieces of artillery, his casualties had been "very small," said the Confederate commander. "I still have artillery enough with the army, and am moving to the south of [the] Duck River." That was it. He made no admission of a failed campaign, the rout of his army, or his plight in safely reaching the south bank of the Duck River.[1]

By the evening of the 18th, his friend Chaplain Charles Quintard found Hood at the Vaught residence in Columbia, much recovered from the recent disaster, and bearing up "with wonderful faith." Hood showed Quintard a personal letter from Colonel Andrew J. Kellar, who was commanding Strahl's Brigade of Cheatham's Corps. Kellar had apologized for the panic on the 16th, saying his troops had fled after seeing the enemy break Bate's line. "It was not fighting" that had caused his men to flee, said Kellar, it was fear. "For the first time in this war we lost our cannon. Give us a chance and we will retake them." This explained the disaster, thought Quintard. It was uncontrolled panic, traceable to the division of William B. Bate. Already the senior staff officers were blaming Bate for the rout. Colonel Ed Harvie, Hood's inspector general, "expressed both indignation and disgust at the conduct of our troops," said Quintard. "Bate's lines gave way and the whole army seems to have fled like a pack of whipped hounds." Captain F. Halsey Wigfall, Hood's aide-de-camp, indignantly wrote to his wife that Bate's men had broken when the enemy was 150 or 200 yards from their line. "It was utterly inexcusable," he added. Even Henry R. Jackson, one of Bate's brigade commanders, was so disgusted with the behavior of Tyler's and Finley's (Florida) brigades that before Nashville he wrote a "private and confidential" letter to Frank Cheatham, virtually demanding a transfer from the division. Too, Quintard was shown a dispatch from Forrest about the poor performance of Bate's men at Murfreesboro on December 7th. The affair involving Bate's men had been most disgraceful, asserted Forrest, who added, "I do not think [they] can be relied on to charge the enemy's works." While Chaplain Quintard considered Bate "a most gallant man," he thought his division's conduct had been "shameful."[2]

Hood began to feel better. Much sympathy was being expressed for him, and only the unfortunate incident with Bate seemed to have prevented a Confederate victory, so it was implied. Following prayers, Hood sat down to chat about future movements with Quintard and a staff officer. With bolstered confidence, Hood talked at length about the prospects. His army was moving to safety behind the Duck River at Columbia. Forrest, with a large portion of his cavalry, was due from Murfreesboro at any moment. Should the Army of Tennessee stay in mid-Tennessee? he asked.[3]

Both Quintard and the staff officer urged Hood to remain. To fall back across the Tennessee River would dispirit the men and cause desertions, they said. By holding the Duck River line, the machinery of a Confederate state government could be put in place; thus, "the campaign, even with our reverses, will be a splendid success." As for the defeat of the 15th and 16th, it was expressed that "while God is on our side, so manifestly that no man can question it, it is very apparent that our people have not yet passed through all their disappointments and sufferings."[4]

Hood remained undecided. The remark about God being on the Southern side was just, he agreed. Yet at Spring Hill, "where the enemy was completely in our grasp," there had been a failure. Also, at Nashville, "after the day's fighting was well nigh over . . . the enemy made a last feeble effort to recover the fortunes of [the] day, [and] when all had gone successfully until evening, our troops had broke in confusion and fled." The following morning Hood met with Nathan Bedford Forrest at headquarters before daylight. Forrest had been near Murfreesboro on the evening of December 16th when alerted by one of Hood's staff officers of the enormous defeat. After ordering Buford's division to move cross-country from the vicinity of the Cumberland River and link up with the retreating army, Forrest attempted to fall back in the direction of Pulaski with his infantry contingent, Jackson's scattered division, and his wagon train with the sick and wounded. Forrest had reached the Duck River at Lillard's Mills on the 17th, but after only part of his command had forded the river the rising waters prevented further passage. The irate Confederate cavalry commander had to travel miles downstream, finally crossing on the army's pontoons at Columbia during the night of the 18th.[5]

Greatly fatigued, soaked with rain, and upset over the failed campaign, Forrest evidently was in no mood to mince words with Hood about remaining in Tennessee. According to Quintard, Forrest told Hood that if he was unable to hold Tennessee with certainty, the state should at once be evacuated. Hood, perhaps remembering Forrest's unheeded council about outflanking rather than attacking Schofield at Franklin, decided to order the withdrawal of his troops south of the Tennessee River, due to "the condition of the army." Although many of Hood's associates and officers were disappointed, even Governor Harris agreed that "it is the best we can do."[6]

The once proud Army of Tennessee had "degenerated to a mob," wrote a veteran private. "Citizens seemed to shirk and hide from us as we approached them." So depleted and ragged were Hood's soldiers that a Columbia resident said "they are the worst broke down set I ever saw."[7]

The turnpike, rutted and broken from the wear of supplying two armies, had been converted into "a terrible mixture of mud and sharp stones, very destructive of foot leather." Subjected to the muddy grime and water-soaked conditions, the shoes of the men had been so shredded that about a third of the army remained barefoot. With the loss of many food stores at Nashville and Franklin, there was not enough subsistence for the men. "We were pinched by hunger and cold," said a famished soldier. In Columbia a farmer recorded in his diary how the Rebel soldiers were "taking what little corn is in the country." In fact, they were "trying to take everything," he added. "We are badly treated by them. . . . They drove off our cattle, cows, and calves yesterday, but we got them back. It is hard work to keep anything."[8]

To add to the shroud of misery engulfing the Confederates at Columbia, the weather began to turn violent and cold. On the 19th the southeast wind which had brought mild temperatures turned to the north, adding a chill to the intermittent rain. By the 20th an ice-cold rain was pelting down, causing an agonized citizen to write in his journal, "The very heavens are shedding tears for the sufferers in this deadly strife." That night there was sleet, and by the morning of the 21st snow.[9]

Hood well realized that he had to act rapidly to save the remnant of his army. Once the decision had been made to retreat to Alabama, his wagon trains were immediately ordered to leave. Beginning on the 19th, and continuing to the 21st, the army's transportation and artillery were wheeled south as rapidly as possible. Yet the more difficult circumstances involved the withdrawal of his remaining troops. If the army was to escape across the Tennessee River, Thomas's pursuing cavalry and infantry would have to be kept at bay. Also, there was great danger in attempting to recross the Tennessee River, especially if due to the high water the Federal navy was able to proceed close to the shoals and destroy Hood's pontoon bridge.[10]

Hood knew that he had expended most of his best remaining troops, Stephen D. Lee's, during the disorderly retreat from Nashville to Columbia. Stevenson's division had been badly mauled on the 17th, so that Frank Cheatham's sadly depleted corps had to take over rear-guard duty on the 18th. Moreover, following his wounding on the 17th, Lee had departed from the army that night.[11]

Hood conferred with Forrest, who of necessity would command in the army's rear. If he could have in addition to his cavalry the pick of a beefed-up division of infantry—troops of his own choice—said Forrest, he would attempt to protect the army's rear until Hood's main columns escaped across the Tennessee River. Hood agreed, and a total of 1,900 infantry in eight separate brigades was designated to join Forrest's command of about 3,000 cavalrymen. Four brigades were selected from A. P. Stewart's Corps (Quarles's, Reynolds's, Ector's, Featherston's), three from Cheatham's (Maney's, James A. Smith's, Strahl's), and one from Stephen D. Lee's (Joseph B. Palmer's). Many of these troops had been absent from Franklin or Nashville or had seen limited fighting, and thus remained in better condition and spirits. Yet when it was found that about 400 of the designated infantry were without shoes, they were told to go with the wagon train, thus reducing the effective infantry to 1,601 men.[12]

Forrest had selected Major General Edward Walthall as the commander of these infantrymen. On the morning of December 20th Hood sent for Walthall and told him, "I have resolved to reorganize a rear guard. Forrest says he can't keep the enemy off of us any longer without a strong infantry support, but says he can do it with the help of three thousand infantry with you to command them. . . . It is a post of great honor, but one of such great peril that I will not impose it on you unless you are willing to take it. . . . The army must be saved, come what may, and if necessary your command must be sacrificed to accomplish it."

Walthall's reply was brief and to the point: "General, I have never asked a hard place for glory nor a soft place for comfort, but take my chances as they come. Give me the order for the troops, and I will do my best."

When Forrest learned that Walthall had agreed, he remarked, "Now we will keep them back."[13]

On the 19th, with a steady rain falling, Forrest's cavalrymen moved up to support Frank Cheatham's troops, then on rear-guard duty at Rutherford Creek. A high line of hills on the south bank had been occupied and fortified by Cheatham's men, who had emplaced artillery and destroyed all bridges across the creek. Due to high water and the harassing fire of sharpshooters and artillery, Forrest saw that the Federals would make little progress in crossing Rutherford Creek that day.[14]

Although several divisions of Wood's corps were later discovered felling trees in an attempt to bridge the creek, the trees were not large enough to reach across, and those cut were swept away by the rapid current. With the creek running fifteen feet deep in most places and rising, Wood's and Wilson's troops now seemed to await darkness to cover another attempt to obtain a foothold on the south bank.[15]

Meanwhile, about 3:00 P.M. Forrest received Hood's orders to fall back across the Duck River into Columbia. By 4:00 P.M. Cheatham's and Forrest's troops had pulled back, abandoning the Rutherford Creek line. Despite an altercation between Cheatham and Forrest after reaching the Duck River pontoons over who had the right to cross first, Hood's entire army was safely across by midnight on the 19th. Thereafter, the pontoon bridge was dismantled, and again a major, water-swollen barrier had been interposed between Hood's and Thomas's armies.[16]

Despite the misery it produced among the troops, the bad weather had become an increasingly important ally of Hood's. With the Federal army stalled in front of the heavily swollen creeks and rivers, the evacuation of Columbia was completed on the 20th. Although Chaplain Quintard found it "a day of darkness and thick gloominess to me," the high command's departure from Columbia that day was without incident. As some of Cheatham's men marched from Columbia on the Pulaski pike, Hood rode among them, seemingly unaffected by his misfortunes. Being asked by some privates when he would give them a furlough, he remarked, "After we cross the Tennessee," and added, "Boys, the cards were fairly dealt at Nashville, and Thomas beat the game." Promptly, a private close to Hood looked him in the face and wryly said, "Yes, General, but the cards were damned badly shuffled!" Hood rode away to the yells and guffaws of his hooting men. Said an observer in bitter reflection, "I feel in bidding farewell to Columbia that I am parting with my dearest and most cherished hopes. . . . I remember our march into Tennessee, so full of delightful intercourse . . . and [now] I turn away . . . with a very bitter spirit."[17]

According to Hood's instructions, the initial march to Pulaski would cover "not less than 15 miles" each day. Lee's Corps, now commanded by Carter L. Stevenson, led the way from Columbia, followed by Cheatham's and A. P. Stewart's troops. Since many of the wagons and artillery already were en route to Pulaski, about thirty miles distant, the turnpike was presumed to be clear for the infantry's march.[18]

The rains of the past few days had finally halted about midnight on December 19th, and on the 20th the weather was cold but clear. By late afternoon Stevenson's leading units had moved so rapidly as to be within a few miles of Pulaski.[19]

Ahead in Pulaski, the town was filled with all manner of wagons, equipment, straggling troops, and the wounded. The railroad was in operation only from Columbia to Pulaski, and the cars were jammed with munitions, ordnance, and wounded soldiers. Yet beyond Pulaski there was no railroad or turnpike to facilitate the army's journey south.[20]

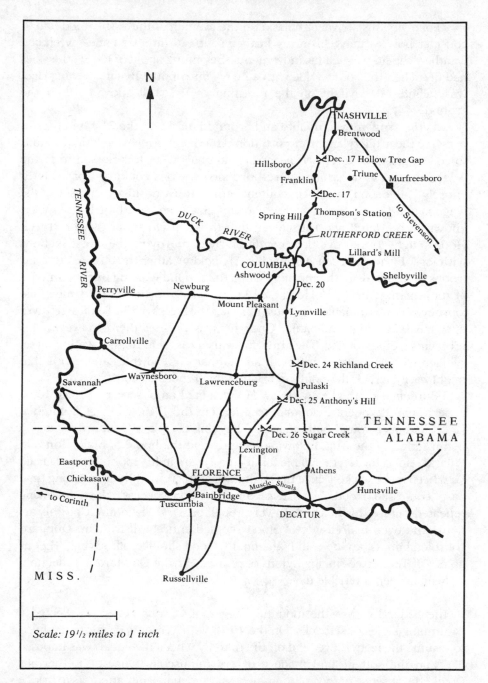

MAP 17   Retreat from Tennessee—December 16–28

(*Sources: O.R. Atlas, pl. 302; 149; O.R. 45-1-966*)

Following his arrival at Pulaski on the evening of the 20th, Hood had to consider how to move his army farther south. A familiar bane—wretched weather—again plagued his movements. Beginning about 3:30 P.M., the skies had drenched the countryside with a heavy downpour. By late evening sleet was falling. At daylight on the morning of the 21st snow covered the ground.[21]

As the army moved up into and around Pulaski on the 21st, in order to preserve the artillery and transportation, Hood sent out strong fatigue details to collect grass for forage. If necessary, animals were to be taken from the wagons to draw the artillery. Overburdened wagons could be "partially or entirely" unloaded and their contents thrown away, just to preserve the wagons and teams. Since the red clay country roads south of Pulaski were known to be mired and rut-scarred due to extensive supply-wagon travel, Hood sought to improve their condition by corduroying the worst sections with logs. Further, because of the bitterly cold weather, he directed that his troops march early in the morning while the ground was still frozen, for ease of movement. Ahead, as Hood well knew, was a torturous forty-nine-mile journey over abominable roads just to reach the banks of the Tennessee River opposite Bainbridge, Alabama. Once he was present there, however, his problems would not end. The army still must cross that mighty watercourse, swollen with rains and adrift with all manner of dead trees and debris that might easily wreck the pontoon bridge which must be constructed.[22]

Burdened by the heavy stress, Hood, noted an observer, seemed to be experiencing frequent emotional trauma. On the 19th, while at Columbia, Hood had been found quite maudlin, begging Chaplain Quintard to have a hymn sung. By the 21st, following a baptism at the home of Major Jones in Pulaski, Hood invited the whole family to prayers in his room. He was afraid he'd been more wicked since the beginning of the retreat than for a long time past, confessed Hood. He had set his heart on success. Now, following repeated failure, his heart was "very rebellious." Questioning God, his actions, and even his self-worth, Hood seemed entirely distraught. Quintard consoled him as best he could, and finally Hood shuffled off, saying, "Let us go out of Tennessee singing hymns of praise." Wrote Quintard in reflection, "This has been a terrible day."[23]

In the Federal camps the mounting anger of various generals reflected a continuing series of setbacks. On the 19th, with Wilson's cavalry scheduled to resume the lead, movement off the road by wheeled vehicles was impossible, and the soft ground made progress minuscule. Once at Rutherford Creek, the absence of the pontoons necessitated makeshift attempts to bridge the overflooded and deep creek. These attempts had ended in failure and even embarrassment. After probing down the creek for an unguarded and crossable site, the piers of an old railroad bridge were found. Throughout the afternoon the cavalrymen of Hatch's division worked laboriously amid the pouring rain, piecing together logs and timbers from barns and outhouses and felling trees. Once across their makeshift bridge, they discovered to their chagrin that they had crossed Carter's Creek and were still on the wrong side of Rutherford Creek. That night several men who attempted to cross on a raft were drowned. To complete the day's frustrations, it was learned about midnight that all these efforts had been unnecessary. At 8:30 A.M. that morning General Thomas had called off the day's operations due to inclement weather. Although the troops were supposed to remain in camp and issue provisions, somehow Wilson and Wood failed to get the word. Wood considered it "one of the most dreary, uncomfortable, and inclement days I remember to have passed in the course of 19 ½ years of active field service."[24]

Finally, at midmorning on the 20th, the enemy having retreated, two "clumsily built" footbridges were fashioned by Wood's and Hatch's units (one at the wrecked railroad bridge), and all began crossing. Hatch's cavalry again took the lead, and in the early afternoon they arrived opposite Columbia. The town seemed nearly deserted, with the bridges over the Duck River destroyed. Yet Hatch began shelling Columbia from the north bank with several Parrott rifles. Nathan Bedford Forrest soon appeared with a flag of truce on the ruined abutment of the turnpike bridge. The town had been evacuated, he shouted across the river, and continued shelling would only injure noncombatants, as well as the sick and wounded. General Hatch, from the opposite abutment, agreed to cease fire, but would not exchange prisoners as requested by Forrest.[25]

Thereafter, Wood said that with a raging river in front and no way to cross except by pontoon bridge, the army was stuck. "It is much to be regretted that we have no pontoon train here," he chided, especially since Columbia had been evacuated, except by Forrest's cavalry, and the enemy were even then escaping southward with their burdensome trains. In reply, Thomas, now at Rutherford Creek, said that A. J. Smith would assist in getting the pontoon train forward—at 6:00 P.M. that day it was passing through Spring Hill—and the Duck River could be bridged in the morning. Thomas wanted the entire army over the Duck River before nightfall on the 21st, and estimated that "the greater part of Hood's army may be captured, as he cannot possibly get his trains and troops across the Tennessee River before we can overtake him."[26]

Within a day George H. Thomas had begun to change his mind. Quartermasters were having difficulty getting forage and subsistence to feed the pontoon train's 500 horses, due to downed bridges in the rear. Thomas had to order the Fourth Corps to gather sufficient local forage. Further supply difficulties were evident when Wood requested 15,000 pairs of shoes and socks. The wet weather and rough turnpike had chewed up so many shoes that Wood said many of his troops would be disabled "in a very few days." Wilson, of the cavalry, was still grumbling about a lack of supplies and had just sent two dismounted brigades back to Louisville for remounting. Even the railroad, counted on to bring supplies and forage forward, was inoperable south of Franklin due to delays in reconstructing the railroad bridge there.[27]

When another heavy rainstorm moved in late on the afternoon of the 20th, the pontoon train's progress was again retarded. The following morning's cold snap turned the soft roads into a rutted moonscape crusted with ice. Although a portion of the train arrived at Rutherford Creek about 1:00 P.M. on the 21st, it was dismantled there to bridge the stream so that the remainder of the heavy pontoon wagons might proceed. A thousand troops were sent from the Twenty-third Corps to help with the bridge. Here the men had to work in the falling snow, with ropes that stiffened and froze, and a treacherous footing due to the buildup of ice on the boats and planking.[28]

Thomas discovered on the evening of the 21st that due to the horrendous weather the pontoon bridge would not be completed over Rutherford Creek before nightfall. As a result, work on laying the Duck River bridge could not begin before daylight on the 22d. Even more disconcerting, on that fateful December 21st Thomas learned that the administration in Washington, D.C., was not pleased with the speed of his pursuit. A dispatch from Henry Halleck demanded, "Every possible sacrifice should be made, and . . . submit to any hardship and privation to accomplish the [anticipated] great result." The capture or destruction of Hood's army was imperative, said Halleck, since Sherman was about to begin a new campaign to "entirely crush out the Rebel military force in all the Southern States. . . . A vigorous pursuit on your part is therefore of vital importance to Sherman's plans. No sacrifice must be spared to attain so important an object."[29]

The implication was plainly evident. Thomas was too slow. Hood was being allowed to escape through a less than "vigorous pursuit." Thomas's prompt, indignant reply was soon lying on the desks of Halleck, Stanton, and Grant. "General Hood's army is being pursued as rapidly and as vigorously as it is possible for one army to pursue another," telegraphed the aroused Thomas. "We cannot control the elements . . . and nothwithstanding the inclemency of the weather and the partial equipment, [we] have been enabled to drive the enemy beyond Duck River, crossing two streams . . . without the aid of pontoons. . . . Pursuing an enemy through an exhausted country, over mud roads, completely sogged with heavy rains, is no child's play, and cannot be accomplished as quickly as thought of." Reminding Washington that Sherman had taken with him the best transportation and equipment, Thomas decreed, "Although my progress may appear slow, I feel assured that Hood's army can be driven from Tennessee, and eventually driven to the wall, by the force under my command."[30]

The next day, Stanton reassured Thomas of his "most unbounded confidence in your skill, vigor, and determination . . . to pursue and destroy the enemy." The War Department was thankful for "the great deeds you have already performed." Even Grant wired that Thomas had the congratulations of the public "for the energy with which you are pushing Hood." Yet Grant subtly made his feelings known, saying, "You now have a high opportunity, which I know you are availing yourself of. Let us push and do all we can before the enemy can [recover]." If Thomas destroyed Hood's army, "there will be but one army left to the so-called Confederacy capable of doing us harm. I will take care of that," he added.[31]

Thomas's estimate of his superior's begrudging appreciation was exactly on the mark. When queried about a promotion for Thomas in the regular army on December 20th, Grant said, "I think Thomas has won the major-generalcy, but I would wait a few days before giving it, to see the extent of the damages done."[32]

On December 22, 1864, work began at 5:00 A.M. on the pontoon bridge across the Duck River at Columbia. Yet at 7:00 A.M. Forrest's cavalrymen on the opposite shore began firing on the construction party. With considerable difficulty, the infantry was able to push across a single regiment, the 51st Indiana, in canvas pontoon boats to occupy a bridgehead on the south bank. Then it was learned that there were only three pontoniers with the entire train. The infantrymen who were directed to lay the bridge knew nothing of its construction. Accordingly, it required all day to fashion a rickety, poorly secured bridge. Two or three times the partially completed bridge broke apart, and in the fifteen-degree temperatures the exposure of the men was both painful and debilitating. The work finally was completed at 6:30 P.M., well after dark, and Wood's Fourth Corps began crossing because the cavalry had already gone into bivouac. Throughout the night, Wood's infantrymen struggled to get men and equipment across, since everything had to be over to the south side by 5:00 A.M., the time designated for the cavalry to cross.[33]

On the morning of the 23d, however, with frigid temperatures again prevailing, the cavalry found the bridge in such bad condition and the approaches on both sides so slippery with a kneaded muck that it required nearly the entire day for them to cross. Accordingly, Wood, tired of waiting for the cavalry, ordered his leading brigade to begin the march south at 2:30 P.M. An hour and a half later, on the Pulaski pike five miles from Columbia, Wood's infantrymen came up with a few Confederates deployed in a gorge between two high hills. A few shells from a rifle battery chased these Rebel cavalrymen away, and a halt was ordered for the night.[34]

By 7:00 A.M. on December 24th Wilson's cavalrymen began trotting past, again assuming the lead in the pursuit of Hood's rear guard. Finally, after six days and a total of about eight miles traversed, Thomas's army was again in full pursuit of Hood's fleeing army.[35]

On the afternoon of December 22d Hood learned from Forrest that Thomas's advanced units were across the Duck River. There was no more time for delay. Already Stevenson's leading troops were en route from Pulaski along the Lamb's Ferry Road for the Tennessee River. Hood ordered his entire army to follow rapidly.[36]

December 21st had been cold and snowy, with blustery winds that cut to the marrow. Yet December 22d dawned as a cruel new experience, an ultimate misery for Hood's haggard men. The winds were out of the north, whistling like a zephyr across the frozen landscape. The temperature hovered in the teens, and the ground glistened white with snow. With their bare feet, many of Hood's infantrymen shuffled as best they could across the frozen ruts and ice-covered chuckholes. Those with improvised green-hide moccasins fared little better. The hide formed hard wrinkles on the soles as it dried, which chafed and blistered the men's feet. Most threw them away. Along the way men were observed limping with frostbitten feet so swollen they left blood with every footstep. Others had legs discolored blue by the frigid wind.[37]

The men did not bother to march in unit formations. Brigade, regimental, and even company formations were forsaken. They moved in squads of from six to twenty men, each halting or marching at their own discretion. Few had little more than parched corn in their pockets. Many had thrown away their rifle muskets, so that only a few guns were available to shoot stray cattle or game found along the road. Along the roadside for miles south of Pulaski virtually everything from abandoned wagons to castaway accoutrements littered the ground. Dead horses and mules with blankly staring eyes lay frozen by the roadside. Overturned and looted wagons, broken pontoons, abandoned limbers, cast-aside rifles and boxes of ammunition—the debris of defeat was strewn everywhere in profusion. No one seemed to care. The agony of the march was the men's only consideration. No one but those who were there would ever know the full extent of the suffering, perceived a soldier. An admiring veteran later reflected on their sad ordeal and wrote, "Never was an army made of better stuff."[38]

Six miles was all they could do that day. At nightfall they stumbled to the side of the road and built campfires that singed their frayed pants legs. Mostly there was nothing to eat. Houses in the area were few, but an army of stragglers visited every nearby log cabin or farm that night, begging, borrowing, or stealing what they could. That night, ensconced in the Jones's gracious residence at Pulaski, John B. Hood dined on oyster soup.[39]

Nathan Bedford Forrest had been at Columbia on the frigid morning of December 22d when he learned that about 200 Federal infantry had forced a crossing of the Duck River about two miles above town. Forrest hadn't looked for a crossing at this site; quickly he sent a youth, J. P. Young, back to Columbia to bring up Armstrong's Brigade. Young rode six miles, buffeted by a piercing northwest wind. When he reached Armstrong's headquarters he was so nearly frozen he couldn't dismount. As they carried him into the house, he managed to whisper, "Boots and saddles," and soon Armstrong's

Mississippians hastened forward to support Forrest. Yet by the time they arrived, Forrest already had decided to withdraw. Pausing only to drop off a note at the home of William Galloway, on Ninth Street, Forrest led his cavalrymen and Walthall's infantrymen toward Pulaski on the battered and frozen pike. Hastily scribbled in the note was a somber message to Laura Galloway: "My compliments to Miss Laura, hoping she may never have to mourn over another defeat of the Confederate army, N. B. Forrest, Maj. Genl."[40]

December 23d had passed largely without incident among Forrest's rear guard. The Yankees were nowhere to be found until late in the afternoon, and that night Forrest and Walthall had retreated to near Lynnville. By the morning of the 24th, however, Forrest decided to put a little distance between Wilson's cavalrymen and his wagon train, encumbered by livestock. Instead of retreating that day, he would send his men back toward Columbia and "check" the enemy. It was well that he did, since Hood's main column was again encountering difficulty.[41]

At daylight on December 23d their ordeal had begun anew. On approaching a steep hill in Giles County some of Frank Cheatham's ordnance and quartermaster's wagons were having difficulty moving up the ice-glazed hillside. Cheatham told his adjutant general to pick out a hundred well-shod men and detail them to help push the wagons forward. As the adjutant walked among the ranks, the men would laugh and stick up their feet. Some had "a pretty good shoe on one foot, and on the other a piece of rawhide," or a part of a shoe tied up with strips of rawhide. Others displayed old shoe tops with the bottoms of their feet sticking out. The adjutant found only about twenty-five men with good shoes from the entire corps, but somehow they manhandled the wagons up the hill.[42]

That night much of Hood's army reached the proximity of Lexington, about two-thirds of the way from Pulaski to the river. Due to the terrible condition of the roads, Hood had ordered many wagons loaded with ordnance stores left behind at the first day's encampment in order to utilize double teams for the heavy pontoon train. Also, at a point six and a half miles below Pulaski, the Lamb's Ferry Road had divided into roughly parallel tracks. Each of these roads proved to be quagmires of mud and ice, rutted and worn, and often overflooded at the creeks and streams. Some of the chuckholes were so large that a mule could get lost in them, swore the cursing teamsters. Due to the horrible conditions, many men chose to travel on either side of the road, walking on brush and leaves on the edge of the woods.[43]

With the pontoon train in advance, hastening to reach its destination on the night of December 24th, everything seemed to depend on the rapid construction of a temporary pontoon bridge. Yet so many broken-down pontoon wagons were found abandoned along the road to Bainbridge that a staff officer began counting them. After reaching fifteen, he reported, "every mind was haunted by the apprehension that we did not have boats enough, or barely enough to make [the] bridge." Hood became so alarmed at seeing these abandoned pontoons by the side of the road that he ordered a special detail of 200 men to go back and retrieve the "broken" boats.[44]

As early as December 10th Hood had attempted to improve his means of transit across the Tennessee River. On that day he had sent a special detail to Decatur, Alabama, to repair the pontoon bridge there. Decatur had been occupied by units of Brigadier General Philip D. Roddey's cavalry command following its evacuation by Federals under Brigadier General Robert S. Granger on November 25th. Among the abandoned Federal equipment the Confederates had found fifteen pontoon boats. Following the threatening of the city on December 12th by Federal gunboats, and the subsequent retreat from Nashville by Hood's army, Roddey, who had been planning to join Hood's command, was instead compelled to prepare for the evacuation of Decatur.[45]

With Hood desperately in need of a safe crossing site after the decision had been made to withdraw from Tennessee on the 19th, Roddey was directed to float his fifteen pontoon boats down the Tennessee to Bainbridge, Alabama, six miles above Florence at the foot of Muscle Shoals. Following the loss of so many pontoon wagons en route to the river, it was now critical to obtain Roddey's pontoons before the pursuing Federals caught up.[46]

John T. Croxton's brigade led the Federal advance on December 24th. Encountering Confederate skirmishers near Lynnville, Croxton's men rapidly pushed ahead, driving the enemy through open country "without much fighting." By about 4:00 P.M., however, Forrest's entire cavalry command was found drawn up in front of Richland Creek, about seven miles north of Pulaski. Here the ground was broken and densely timbered, and Forrest had six field guns emplaced along the pike. As the Federal artillery moved up to duel with the Rebel guns, Croxton's dismounted men began working their way forward.[47]

Wilson saw that the key to breaking Forrest's line was to turn his flank, and he sent Hatch eastward, intending to bypass the Rebels' position. Meanwhile, Croxton's men pressed onward, skirmishing heavily with Buford's and Chalmers's men. At one point, a corporal from the 1st Tennessee Cavalry of Croxton's command dashed among the Rebel line and seized Chalmers's headquarters flag, for which he was later awarded the Medal of Honor. In the brief fighting, Buford took a flesh wound in the leg from one of the 7th Illinois Cavalry's Spencer carbine bullets. Although Hatch's flanking attempt was stopped by unfordable Richland Creek, Forrest soon ordered a retreat. Forrest reported only one man killed and six wounded, but Wilson referred to the encounter as a "short stand" and said his cavalrymen had pushed the enemy so rapidly that they were unable to burn the pike bridge over Richland Creek.[48]

That night Forrest's and Walthall's men occupied Pulaski, burning wagons of abandoned ammunition and destroying a locomotive and five cars which could not run farther south due to downed bridges. From Pulaski, Forrest knew he would be traveling over rutted dirt roads, heavy with mud and water. They had more than forty miles to travel to the Tennessee River at Bainbridge, and Wilson's increasingly aggressive cavalrymen had to be stopped. Forrest talked with Walthall. Both agreed that on December 25th they would plan a special Christmas present for the Federal cavalry.[49]

Christmas Day 1864 began for James H. Wilson with a bold rush through the outskirts of Pulaski. The enemy had set fire to a covered bridge over swollen Richland Creek, yet the vanguard of his cavalry was able to extinguish the flames, and only a portion of the covered roof was damaged. It was an important incident, reasoned Wilson. The creek was unfordable, and considerable time was saved in the pursuit of Forrest by saving the bridge. His 9:10 A.M. dispatch to Thomas announced that the Rebels had been driven through Pulaski "on the keen jump." Forrest was scarcely out of sight, "literally running away, making no defense whatever," said Wilson.[50]

Thomas, who was journeying toward Pulaski that day, was duly encouraged. "I have my troops well in hand . . . well provided with provisions and ammunition, and close upon the heels of the enemy," he telegraphed Washington that night. "[I] shall continue to press him as long as there is a chance of doing anything."[51]

Wilson, who had reported as early as December 20th that Hood would make no stand north of the Tennessee River, was now convinced that the enemy's two-day lead had been reduced to practically nothing. Further, nearly half the Rebel army seemed unarmed, having thrown their rifle muskets away. Two scouts reported on the 23d that Forrest's cavalry numbered not more than 1,500 mounted men. Many of his dismounted troopers were without shoes and would give themselves up if pushed, the scouts said.[52]

Wilson hastened onward in the falling rain during the 25th, noting the abundance of abandoned wagons loaded with munitions, and a vast amount of debris littering the road. By Wilson's original instructions the cavalry was supposed to advance along the road until the enemy was encountered, then swing wide "to operate on the [enemy's] flanks and rear." The nearby infantry would then move up and "make all direct attacks."[53]

This arrangement had lasted for less than one day. Wilson's men had found it "impossible to move off the turnpike" due to the mired ground, and the terrain along the Lamb's Ferry–Florence road was even worse. Accordingly, about 3:00 P.M. on the 25th, with Harrison's brigade of cavalry in advance, Wilson's skirmishers approached a gorge leading to the top of Anthony's Hill, about seven miles south of Pulaski. Here the timber was so thick along the slopes that it was hard to see more than a few feet ahead. The

Federals found Rebel skirmishers in their front, and due to strong resistance Harrison dismounted three regiments and ordered an attack. They pushed rapidly forward to within a few yards of a strong rail barricade when suddenly a sheet of flame exploded in their faces. Forrest had masked three field guns in the timber and posted two brigades of Walthall's infantry behind the barricades. Also, a brigade of cavalry was posted on each flank. No sooner had these Confederates delivered a devastating fire from ambush than the infantry and cavalry sprang forward over the barricade at Harrison's men.[54]

Stunned by the sudden onslaught, Harrison's regiments fled in disorder. Wildly they dashed back through and stampeded the advanced units of Hammond's brigade, just deploying in support of Harrison. Within minutes the fleeing troopers of both brigades raced down the hill into a narrow valley, where a single gun of Battery I, 4th U.S. Artillery, had been unlimbered. The onset of Walthall's and Forrest's pursuing men was so rapid that this gun and its limber was engulfed and captured. Many of the cavalry's mounts were abandoned and lost, and for a half mile Harrison's and Hammond's men scattered in flight.[55]

Ahead in the narrow valley lay the third command in Wilson's line, Edward Hatch's division. Hatch had been feeding his horses on corn and fodder, and their bridles were off. Just ahead of Harrison's routed men, Wilson came dashing up, thoroughly surprised to find Hatch seemingly at leisure. As Hatch hastily formed his men, Wilson appeared excited and nervous. Forrest's men by now had halted and were attempting to wheel the captured field gun back up Anthony's Hill. "There they are, hurry up!" shouted Wilson. Hatch's troopers dashed forward, their Spencers blazing. It was too late to recover the lost cannon, but Forrest's men soon retreated to the rail barricades. Hatch's men moved up to within seventy-five yards of the rude breastworks but were unable to force their way past on the flank due to heavy timber.[56]

Wilson soon sent a hasty note to Wood's infantry, some five miles back. "We have met a slight check," announced Wilson. "There are eight brigades of infantry in our front, with rail entrenchments. Please hurry up as rapidly as possible." It took an hour for the infantry to come forward, and by then Forrest and Walthall had already withdrawn in the gathering darkness.[57]

It was all very humbling. Wilson spent Christmas evening writing a rather embarrassing dispatch about the loss of one of his guns, and saying he would push on in the morning "in hopes of getting back the lost gun and one or two besides." Instead of meeting feeble resistance, Wilson had found a hard fight and a tactical defeat. Only twenty-four hours earlier he had derisively commented that the Federals' slower than anticipated progress was due more to "the difficult nature of the country than to the resistance of the enemy." Now he could only anticipate another difficult fight on the 26th.[58]

*   *   *

Nathan Bedford Forrest had retreated during the night of the 25th to the vicinity of Sugar Creek, fourteen miles south of Anthony's Hill on the road to Florence. The roads had been as bad as ever before encountered; the men and horses had to wallow through mud and slush often belly-deep on their mounts. Many of Walthall's infantrymen were entirely barefoot, but after wading ice-cold Sugar Creek about 1:00 A.M. the men had halted and, washing the mire from their feet, built blazing fires in order to dry out. Forrest learned that night that many of Hood's wagons were nearby, having been stripped of mules to add to the teams hauling the heavy pontoons. If these wagons were to be saved, Forrest would have to hold Wilson off until the mules could be returned.[59]

By the early morning of December 26th a thick fog enshrouded the area, and at 8:30 A.M. the sound of cavalry fording the pebble-bottomed waters of Sugar Creek echoed through the mist. Once on the south side of the creek, the cavalrymen were heard to dismount. Slowly their skirmishers inched forward through the drifting vapor, every eye straining to see through the veil of gray. Dimly they saw a narrow ravine ahead, about two hundred yards south of the creek. There were lurking shadows along the ground only thirty paces ahead. It was . . . a barricade. A trap. They began to raise their carbines. Too late. The wall of gray lighted up in their faces. Flame and a devastating roar erupted on every side. Men went reeling to the soft clay. There was a yell; running men with bayoneted muskets loomed in front. The cavalrymen of John H. Hammond's brigade ran for their lives.[60]

Forrest had done it again! With two of Walthall's brigades posted across the road, and the cavalry on both flanks, Forrest's men had ambushed Wilson's advance, again throwing it into disorder. Across waist-high Sugar Creek and beyond waded the Rebel infantry in pursuit. On both flanks Ross's and Armstrong's horsemen swam the creek and galloped into the defile on the north side. Hammond's men kept fleeing, for three hundred yards, said Hammond; for more than a half mile, reported the Confederates. At last Forrest called off the pursuit, having taken at least twelve prisoners and inflicted an estimated 150 casualties. After returning to his barricades and waiting without incident for about two hours, Forrest ordered a retreat. Later, the Federals brought up artillery to shell the remaining skirmishers out of their fog-enshrouded barricades. By now it was about 4:00 P.M., and Wilson's rapid pursuit again had been thwarted.[61]

James H. Wilson had seen enough. On the evening of December 26th he virtually gave up the main pursuit. His cavalry were low on ammunition and out of rations. The infantry were wallowing far behind; only the Fourth Corps had marched beyond Pulaski, and they were so short on provisions that Wood's men lay idly in camp six miles south of the village awaiting a supply train. Before the supply wagons arrived that afternoon, Wood's famished troops scoured an already harvested cornfield for every stray ear or kernel.

These could be washed of mud and grime, reasoned a soldier, and made "clean enough" for a hungry private.[62]

Wilson was so disgusted with the broken and poor countryside and its abominable roads and scarce food supply that he described it as a desolate wilderness, the "worst [country] we had seen." The roads, either churned and rutted quagmires or frozen, ice-laden paths filled with enormous chuckholes, had so debilitated his horses that he later estimated 5,000 animals were lost by his troops during the march from Nashville to the Tennessee River. Each night the rain-softened roads would freeze, so that ice from half an inch to an inch thick would form. In the morning the ice would break under the horses' weight, ripping their legs and covering them with mud, which soon froze. "In all my experience I have never seen so much suffering," said the distraught cavalry commander. Even Wilson's own mount, "The Waif," was disabled.[63]

On December 26th his men seemed in wretched condition, being utterly exhausted and filthy. Most hadn't changed clothes in weeks. Wilson now despaired of bringing Forrest to bay. On the following morning he ordered an extended halt at Sugar Creek and wrote, "I must get out of this region in three or four days, or we shall leave our horses." About all he could do that morning was send 500 men under Colonel George Spalding of the 12th Tennessee Cavalry to strike for the Tennessee River. Wilson thereafter would "see what could be done."[64]

The Confederate Army of Tennessee was in a shambles, ripe for total destruction, if only Thomas's men could get at its battered ranks. Yet Forrest, Walthall, the mud, and the terrible weather kept getting in the way. Thomas wired Halleck on the evening of the 25th that he would continue to press on "as long as there is a chance of doing anything." By the 27th, however, with Wilson stalled at Sugar Creek, Thomas looked to his only remaining hope: the destruction of Hood's pontoons by either Steedman's expeditionary force or Admiral Lee's gunboats. Should that fail, he was thinking of forming a depot on the Tennessee River "to recruit and organize for an early spring campaign."[65]

Christmas day 1864 found Hood's chief engineer, Lieutenant Colonel Stephen W. Presstman, busily at work laying pontoons on the river as rapidly as the slowly trundling wagons arrived. The weather was cold, drizzly, and gloomy, but Hood had his Christmas present. Roddey's pontoons were on hand, having passed beyond the shoals without difficulty due to the flooded conditions. Working throughout the day and into the night, Presstman's men battled what one man jokingly referred to as a fifty-mile-per-hour current. Meanwhile, the trailing elements of the army continued to cross Shoal Creek, two miles from the river, and began constructing earthworks "to protect the bridge in case the enemy should move on us from below."[66]

Just how precarious and uncertain a successful recrossing of the river had become was revealed by the events a few miles distant at Florence. Admiral S. P. Lee had arrived at Chickasaw, Alabama, with a flotilla of about four or five Union gunboats on December 24th. Steaming up the river to Florence, these vessels on the 24th and 25th had randomly shelled the vacant earthworks there. From a few stragglers picked up along the river, Lee learned that he was "in good time to meet" Hood's attempt to recross the Tennessee. Of equal importance, he learned that the pontoon site was about six miles above Florence, at the foot of Muscle Shoals. Although Lee's pilot "thought the water too swift" in the area of Bainbridge to emplace pontoons, on the 26th Lee sailed past Florence with two lighter draft gunboats. After steaming about two miles upriver, Lee's vessels encountered along the north bank a Rebel battery protected by earthworks. Two Parrott rifles from Hood's artillery fired in unison at Lee's boats, and a lively exchange of shots followed.[67]

The morning of December 26th had found Presstman's exhausted engineer detachment just completing the pontoon bridge following their night-long labors. About sunrise the first wagons began to cross, personally supervised by Frank Cheatham. At 8:00 A.M. some wounded troops crossed, followed by artillery and more wagons. Suddenly the sound of heavy detonations—naval artillery fire—echoed from several miles downriver. Everybody knew its significance. Anxious looks downriver confirmed the crisis. Drifting banks of smoke began to rise against the horizon. Yet within minutes a steamboat whistle blew, and the firing soon ceased. The Federal gunboats had withdrawn. Later, Admiral Lee sent a report citing "foggy weather and a rapidly falling river" as the reason for not proceeding farther. Although Lee's gunboats again cruised upriver to Florence on the 27th, it was apparent that Lee would not take many risks to reach the pontoon bridge. An angry James H. Wilson wrote a few days later, "The gunboats were within a mile of the Rebel bridge at Bainbridge, and the [local] people say [Lee's vessels] could have reached it without trouble." Hood again had avoided a fatal coup de grace.[68]

On the 26th most of Lee's and Cheatham's men crossed, followed on the 27th by Stewart's troops. Once the majority of the army had reached the south shore, the march was continued to and past Tuscumbia. After nightfall on the 27th Forrest with his haggard cavalrymen trotted across the rickety pontoon bridge of about eighty boats. By the morning of the 28th only the rear-guard infantry under Walthall remained. At 3:00 A.M. December 28th Walthall issued his orders: before dawn their movement would begin so as to reach the bridge at daylight. One brigade would depart at a time. Ector's Brigade under David Coleman would be the last to cross before the engineers dismantled the bridge.[69]

By the late morning of December 28th the Army of Tennessee's withdrawal was an accomplished fact. Walthall had crossed without incident, the 39th North Carolina Infantry being the last unit across. Walthall left a 200-

man detachment to help remove the pontoons, and by midafternoon only the rushing waters of the muddy, debris-strewn Tennessee River remained in view.[70]

After an unprecedented odyssey, a thirty-eight-day campaign heavy with destiny, Hood had escaped into northern Alabama with a fragment of his army. The stark reality of what had occurred was now beginning to register. Along the muddy, rutted road to Bainbridge there had been a spot where Hood and his staff were passing and some of the men had to move out of the way. As Hood went by he heard the men singing a familiar tune, "The Yellow Rose of Texas." Only the words seemed somewhat strange. He listened closely:

> So now I'm marching southward;
> My heart is full of woe.
> I'm going back to Georgia
> To see my Uncle Joe.
> You may talk about your Beauregard
> And sing of General Lee,
> But the gallant Hood of Texas
> Played Hell in Tennessee.[71]

George H. Thomas had received what was intended to be a fence-mending Christmas present on December 25th from Edwin M. Stanton, secretary of war. Stanton wired: "With great pleasure I inform you that for your skill, courage, and conduct in the recent brilliant military operations . . . the President has directed your nomination . . . as a major general in the U.S. Army. . . . No commander has more justly earned promotion by devoted, disinterested, and valuable service to his country."[72]

According to one of his staff officers, Thomas glanced at the message and cast it aside, merely remarking, "I earned that a year ago at Chattanooga."[73]

CHAPTER XXXVI

The Darkest of All
Decembers

ON DECEMBER 28TH George H. Thomas had been at Pulaski, Tennessee, when he learned that William Tecumseh Sherman had taken Savannah, Georgia, on December 21st, offering the capture of that city as a Christmas present to the president. In honor of the victory, Thomas ordered a 100-gun salute fired at Nashville on the 28th. That day Thomas's entire army was halted on the march and a circular announcing Sherman's great victory was read. In the greatest of humor, a staff officer told James H. Wilson, who was at Pinhook, Tennessee, a hamlet of two or three log houses, that they should present Pinhook, Tennessee, to Lincoln as a New Year's gift. Added to word of the wounded Rebel General Claudius Sears's capture near Pulaski that day, the news of Sherman's conquest gave cause for much celebrating.[1]

A day later the news turned sour. On the 28th, with Thomas still holding out hope of capturing Hood's entire army, James H. Wilson had learned from Colonel Spalding's cavalry detachment, sent ahead to scout at the Tennessee River, that Hood's rear guard had crossed over and taken up the pontoons that morning. Thomas received this news on the afternoon of the 29th, which coincided with a dispatch from Admiral Lee that he hadn't been able to get at the enemy's crossing site. Since Steedman had already wired that he had experienced much difficulty in taking Decatur—it was finally reoccupied on the 27th—Thomas knew that Hood's escape was an accomplished fact.[2]

Somewhat crestfallen, Thomas telegraphed to Halleck that night that due to the bad weather, exhausted country, and overly fatigued troops and animals, he was going to halt, refit, and reorganize for a renewal of the campaign, provided Hood remained at Corinth. Otherwise, if Hood retreated farther south, as expected, Thomas would rest until early spring. Thomas had already ordered Wilson to withdraw most of his command to Pulaski. Wood with the Fourth Corps infantry was at Lexington, Tennessee, and said he would go no farther without new instructions.[3]

That evening Thomas's chief of staff announced the final troop movements and directed "that the pursuit cease," as the army would go into winter quarters in Alabama and Georgia.[4]

Two days later, on December 31st, there was a major change. Halleck wired Thomas in Grant's name, telling him to collect all his men on the Tennessee River at Eastport or Tuscumbia, to be "ready for such movements as may be ordered." Grant "does not intend that your army shall go into winter quarters; it must be ready for active operations in the field," announced Halleck.[5]

Thomas, while proceeding to carry out these orders, argued that "to continue the campaign without any rest, I fear, will cost us very heavy losses from disease and exhaustion. . . . I do believe that it is much the best policy to get well prepared before starting on an important campaign." To Halleck, however, this was further evidence of Thomas's plodding, deliberate ways. Grant, agreeing with Halleck's assessment, wrote on January 18th that Thomas is "too ponderous in his preparations and equipment to move through a country rapidly enough to live off of it." He confided to Sherman that Thomas's pursuit of Hood indicated "a sluggishness" not conducive to making a rapid strike against the enemy. "He is possessed of excellent judgment, great coolness, and honesty, but he is not good on a pursuit," said Grant. Thereafter, Thomas's army was broken up and dispersed into fragments, leaving Thomas in command of two departments, but with very few active combat duties for the remainder of the war.[6]

Although Thomas was awarded in March 1865 the Thanks of Congress for his victory at Nashville, he was not again allowed to play a major part in the war. Indeed, with Thomas stuck in Nashville, most of his remaining primary combat forces were soon removed from his direct control. James H. Wilson took his 13,500 reequipped and heavily Spencer-armed cavalrymen on an extensive raid through Alabama and Georgia in late March. The capture of Selma, Alabama, by Wilson's strike force within a few weeks forewarned of the total devastation of the Confederacy's vulnerable interior. Wilson's raid not only paved the way for the end of the war, but some of his cavalrymen succeeded in capturing Jefferson Davis with his entourage on May 10, 1865, near Irwinville, Georgia.[7]

While others were fighting the closing actions of the war, Thomas was reduced to writing to Washington, D.C., listing the captures and trophies from his late campaign. Although the public euphoria over his campaign was soon overshadowed by the dramatic events occurring at the end of the war, Thomas's formal report, written on January 20th, 1865, well documented the magnitude of the Franklin and Nashville victories. Over the span of little more than a month Hood's army had been wrecked. Although a preliminary count of the captures resulting from the Battle of Nashville included 53 pieces of artillery, 3,034 small arms, and 4,462 Rebel prisoners, a few weeks later the total for the entire campaign had been tabulated. Seventy-two pieces of Confederate artillery, 13,189 prisoners of war, including 8 generals, and more than 2,000 deserters were in Federal hands, taken by Thomas's troops during the period between September 7, 1864, and January 20, 1865. Considering the estimated 6,300 Confederates killed and wounded at Franklin (plus 700 prisoners), and an educated guess of about 2,300 similarly struck at Nashville (10 percent of the Army of Tennessee's approximate combat strength), Hood had suffered during the campaign perhaps 23,500 casualties from a total strength of about 38,000 men. This appalling loss of nearly two-thirds of a major American army as the result of actual fighting was unprecedented. Never had there been such an overwhelming victory during the Civil War—indeed, never in American military history. Remarkably, Thomas's own losses during the campaign had numbered less than 6,000 men.[8]

Despite the enormously successful campaign, Thomas's status was declining among the military hierarchy. George H. Thomas had been the man of the hour; but that hour had slipped past. Although offered promotion to lieutenant general in command of the U.S. Army by President Andrew Johnson in February 1868, Thomas with characteristic humility declined the appointment. He had done nothing since the Civil War to merit the appointment, he said, and it was too long after the war to be honored for anything that he had accomplished then. If cast aside by the rush of events, Thomas's mettle would not be forgotten. Great men are distinguished not only by their deeds, but equally so by what is in their hearts. There perhaps never beat a heart more worthy and true than that of the outcast Virginian who had triumphed over mind and matter at Nashville, George H. Thomas.[9]

Weary and sadly depleted, the remnant of Hood's army stumbled from Tuscumbia to Iuka, then to Burnsville. For most there was little rest, it was on to Rienzi or Corinth, with most arriving during the first few days of the new year 1865. "We expected to draw clothing at Corinth," wrote a haggard Confederate soldier, "but there was none for us." Brigadier General Benjamin H. Grierson, with 3,500 Federal cavalry raiders, had just torn up large sections of the Mobile & Ohio Railroad between Corinth and Tupelo during the last few days in December. Hood, with a broken railroad at his rear, was unable to procure needed supplies. Beginning on January 3d he ordered a further retreat to Tupelo, Mississippi, about fifty miles south of Corinth.[10]

With the rain pelting down during much of their continued, painful trek, Cheatham's Corps was the last to arrive in camp at Tupelo on January 12th. Once at Tupelo there was such a shortage of food and supplies that Hood devised a system of furloughs to lessen the logistical burden. Although the furloughs were supposedly for only a few days, few men ever returned to the army again, later acknowledged a veteran. En route from Corinth to Tupelo, Hood's bedraggled men had marched past the vast network of crumbling breastworks and ditches constructed during the campaigns of 1862. Everywhere the men looked amid these old ruins stood gravesites, marked by crude, weathered headboards with carved names and regiments. The entire countryside was a vast cemetery, observed an officer, but the names on the markers were nearly all Southern boys. It was a reminder of war as they had never perceived it before; previously there had been mostly the enemy's dead to contemplate. The vast majority of the Army of Tennessee was now mustered in a graveyard. The message hit home.[11]

On January 8th, when the men of Walthall's command were counted, the entire division numbered less than one of its brigades of only eight months earlier. In fact, an inspecting officer on January 10th said the entire army "cannot muster 5,000 effective men. Great numbers are going home every day, many never more to return. . . . Nine-tenths of the men and line officers are barefooted and naked." In toto, Hood's army is believed to have numbered not more than 15,000 officers and men present for duty.[12]

In supplementing his first formal report of February 15th, Hood listed 25,053 officers and men present as of January 20th, following furloughs (excluding Forrest's cavalry). Yet Hood was attempting to prove his losses during the entire campaign did not exceed 10,000 men, and that the army was "in better spirits and with more confidence in itself than it had at the opening of the campaign." Hood cited 8,317 present in Lee's Corps (his largest) on January 20th, but Beauregard, who was then present with the army, one day earlier reported the corps "about 5,000 strong." Also, a formal return from Beauregard's papers dated January 20th shows an effective total of 15,304 infantry, and a combined effective total present of all forces of 19,973. Aside from garrison troops picked up at Corinth and other locations following the evacuation of northern Alabama and Mississippi, Hood continued to lose more men than he gained with each passing day. Even the pursuing Federal cavalry judged that Hood had escaped across the Tennessee River with only 12,000 infantry and 35 pieces of artillery. From the number of prisoners lost (13,189), deserters (more than 2,000 taken in by Federal authorities alone), and men killed or wounded (estimated at 8,600), the combined total of casualties for the campaign has been set at 23,789. This figure, subtracted from the army's gross estimated strength (including reinforcements added after Franklin) of about 38,000 men, suggest only 14,211 Confederate survivors present from Hood's campaign at Tupelo, Mississippi, in mid-January 1865. Since this number closely coincides with General Beauregard's report, made January 13th, that Hood's command "does not number 15,000 infantry," it is probably more accurate than the figures Hood utilized.[13]

Whatever the actual numbers, the entire army was on the verge of collapse. The cavalry was in such bad shape that James R. Chalmers wrote on January 8th that his men were deserting, a great many horses were giving out, and there was so little food some of his animals hadn't eaten a grain of corn for two days. "We whip ourselves faster than the enemy could possibly do it, for every day we remain . . . without forage we will be losing strength faster than if engaged in battle," Chalmers complained on January 3d.[14]

Nathan Bedford Forrest was so appalled at the condition of the army and his men he wrote in a bitter letter to Lieutenant General Richard Taylor on January 2d, "The Army of Tennessee was badly defeated and is greatly demoralized, and to save it during the retreat from Nashville I was compelled almost to sacrifice my command." Many of his men who were sent to the rear with unserviceable horses "are now scattered through the country or have gone to their homes," warned Forrest, and he had neither enough horses, mules, nor forage for his remaining batteries. So desperate was his plight, with a complete reorganization of his command necessary, that Forrest asked permission to visit Richmond to confer with officials.[15]

Astoundingly, P. G. T. Beauregard's first inkling of Hood's defeat came in a telegram from Stephen D. Lee, on wounded furlough, about December 25th. Lee's telegram stated that he wished to confer with Beauregard on the "recent events in Tennessee." Beauregard, who was in Charleston, South Carolina, wrote on the 27th, "[I] do not understand General Lee's telegram. I am apprehensive some reverse may have occurred." There had been rumors and accounts from enemy sources that Hood had sustained a serious reverse and, anticipating the worst, Beauregard had telegraphed to Jefferson Davis on Christmas Day recommending the appointment of Lieutenant General Richard Taylor to Hood's post, "should circumstances require another commander."[16]

A few days later Richard Taylor, at Meridian, Mississippi, wired Beauregard that he had heard reports that Hood had met "a serious reverse and is retreating from Tennessee." Thus he asked Beauregard to promptly return to Alabama. Beauregard, still without word from Hood, became more alarmed. Again he telegraphed to Jefferson Davis, asking if upon reaching the Army of Tennessee he was authorized to appoint Taylor, "should I find its condition such as to require a change of commander." Davis, already having heard rumors of a disaster, reluctantly forwarded his approval.[17]

An aroused Beauregard left Charleston on January 2d, en route to the Army of Tennessee. Not having received any explanation or notice of the existing circumstances from Hood, Beauregard was both frustrated and upset. His demand for a report was forwarded to Hood on January 1st, saying, "We have no dispatches since yours of the 15th of December."[18]

Finally, on January 3d, nearly a week after recrossing the Tennessee River, Hood replied to Beauregard from Corinth, saying his preliminary report of December 17th had been forwarded from Spring Hill. Hood now said only that he had "thought it best" to withdraw from Tennessee, and that "to make the army effective for operations, some rest is absolutely necessary, and [also] a good supply of clothing and shoes.'' He added, ''It is important that you should visit this army.''[19]

On January 7th, Beauregard, now at Macon, Georgia, read what seemed to be a long-delayed dispatch from Hood about the Nashville battle, this being the Spring Hill report Hood had recently referred to. Immediately Beauregard telegraphed the contents to Richmond, noting Hood's claim in an accompanying dispatch dated January 3d that his army had safely recrossed the Tennessee River ''without material loss since the battle of Franklin.'' Beauregard was less than satisfied, however, and ordered Hood to make a more thorough report of the full campaign.[20]

It was only after reaching Montgomery, Alabama, on January 9th that Beauregard learned Hood's report was highly misleading. Furthermore, Hood had circumvented proper channels and again was forwarding his communications directly to Richmond. Beauregard was furious. On the 9th he endorsed Hood's December 11th preliminary report of Franklin: ''This report should have been addressed to these headquarters, to be forwarded thence to the War Department. General Hood does not seem to understand that he is responsible directly to these headquarters, and *not* to the War Department.'' When Beauregard learned from Richard Taylor that Hood's assessments were distorted and unreliable, the Creole general fairly bristled with anger. Several rather bluntly worded telegrams were forwarded to Hood that day, and Beauregard advised the harried army commander he was coming to Tupelo.[21]

Hood understood all too well the great difficulty he was facing. His friend Chaplain Charles Quintard reported how the troops at Tupelo were longing for the restoration of Joe Johnston to command. Time was rapidly running out. Already he had sent Lieutenant Colonel J. P. Johnson of his staff to Richmond about December 25th, in order to ''explain'' to Jefferson Davis ''the campaign in Tennessee.'' His telegrams to the authorities in Richmond had been without admission of defeat; indeed, they had minimized the army's losses. Even Isham G. Harris, the deposed Tennessee governor, forwarded a letter by Lieutenant Colonel Johnson on Hood's behalf, praising Hood and blaming the performance of others for the ''disastrous'' campaign.[22]

Hood knew that he would need much help to restore his army, and he began petitioning Jefferson Davis, Beauregard, Richard Taylor, and others for assistance. He asked Taylor on January 3d to visit the army for a conference, but that general's arrival at Tupelo about January 6th foreshadowed a political disaster.[23]

Richard Taylor, already alerted by numerous reports of Hood's severe defeat, was appalled at what he saw at Tupelo. The army was a complete disaster. Taylor soon telegraphed to Jefferson Davis that ''if moved in its present condition it will prove utterly worthless; this applies to both infantry and cavalry.'' After journeying back to Meridian, on January 9th Taylor wired to Richmond his recommendation for the Army of Tennessee's "rest, consolidation, and reorganization."[24]

On January 13th Beauregard wired Hood from Meridian that he would leave the next morning for Tupelo. Since Taylor had conferred with Beauregard, Hood anticipated the worst. Hood began to fret. Perhaps Beauregard was coming to remove him from command.[25]

In an apparent fit of melancholia, Hood wired Secretary of War Seddon that day a one-sentence message of ominous portent: "I respectfully request to be relieved from the command of this army." Later he said in his official report that the reason for this was an awareness of "so much dissatisfaction throughout the country as in my judgment to greatly impair, if not destroy my usefulness." Yet Hood seemed to be mostly posturing. He would now be able to say he was not removed, he had voluntarily "requested" such. If circumstances warranted and Beauregard was amenable to his staying on as commander, he might simply say to the government he had changed his mind.[26]

The following day Hood appeared to employ this exact strategy, telegraphing to Seddon, "General Beauregard will arrive here tomorrow. I will then communicate more fully in regard to my request [to be relieved] contained in [my] cipher telegram of yesterday morning. I have only [the] interest of my country at stake." Hood seemed to be keeping his options open by creating doubt as to his exact intentions.[27]

That Beauregard would have the best impression possible, Hood, in a flurry of activity, directed on January 14th that a thorough inspection be made, and ordered a quick crackdown on deserters. Arms were to be kept constantly stacked on the color lines and company rolls called frequently during the day to discourage absenteeism from camp.[28]

Hood's strategy seemed to work. Upon his arrival January 15th, Beauregard acted far more moderately than the circumstances might have warranted. There was no question that Hood's army was in horrible condition. "If not in the strict sense of the word, a disorganized mob, it was no longer an army," later wrote one of Beauregard's staff officers. Another observer reported at the time, "It is a shattered debris of an army and needs careful yet vigorous handling to hold it together." Yet when Beauregard sat down to confer with Hood on the 16th, Hood revealed he had asked to be relieved from command, and appeared "so humiliated, so utterly crushed" in appearance that Beauregard, according to a staff officer, "had not the heart virtually to disgrace him by ordering his immediate removal."[29]

Apparently Hood convinced Beauregard that he would have won a great victory at Spring Hill if it were not for the failings of Cheatham, John C. Brown, and others. Undoubtedly, he displayed the December 8th dispatch about Cheatham's "failure." And by showing Beauregard a copy of his telegram asking to be relieved, Hood removed the urgency of an immediate change in commanders. Beauregard saw that no onus would fall upon him if he merely waited for the government to respond. As a result, he endorsed Hood's plan to reorganize his troops, and wired to Jefferson Davis for authority to remove "all inefficient and supernumerary officers." Moreover, Hood convinced Beauregard that in order "to prevent disorder and desertion" a "judicious system" of furlough was necessary—despite the Creole general having only a few days earlier fully agreed with the government's position that it was "dangerous" and perhaps even "fatal" to now furlough troops.[30]

An even more astounding reversal of position was Beauregard's siding with Hood on not sending reinforcements east. For nearly a month Beauregard had been urged, and in turn had been pressuring Hood, to send all available troops to Hardee in the Carolinas to fight Sherman. Jefferson Davis was most insistent on this, telegraphing to Beauregard on January 7th, "Hardee needs aid. If Hood has not complied . . . please give the matter prompt attention."[31]

Yet Beauregard wired the president on January 17th, "To divide this small army at this juncture to reinforce General Hardee would expose to capture Mobile, Demopolis, Selma, Montgomery, and all the rich valley of the Alabama River. Shall that risk be now incurred?"[32]

Hood must have been overjoyed. Instead of censure and blame for a disaster, and perhaps even removal from command, he had managed by a familiar tactic—blaming others—to prevent the worst from occurring. On the 16th Hood showed his true intent involving the request three days earlier to be relieved from command, telegraphing to Jefferson Davis: "If I am allowed to remain in command of this army, I hope you will grant me authority to reorganize it and relieve all incompetent officers. If thought best to relieve me, I am ready to command a corps or division, or do anything that may be considered best for my country." As was now quite apparent, Hood had wanted all along to remain in command of the army. His request appears to have been little more than an attempt to avoid public disgrace. With Beauregard's tacit approval, and based on his long-standing popularity with the administration, Hood expressed renewed hope that he might keep his job. Beauregard seemed to be cooperating with this program by requesting on January 17th the cooperation of "friends in Congress to support actively the plan I have today recommended by telegraph to the President relative to this army."[33]

About 8:00 P.M. on the night of January 17th, John Bell Hood's plans, career, and life suddenly came crashing down about him. Secretary of War James A. Seddon on January 15th had wired a three-sentence message to Hood that was finally received on the evening of the 17th. "Your request is complied with. General Beauregard is instructed to relieve you. On being relieved, you will report to the War Department in Richmond."[34]

Jefferson Davis, pressured by friends, opponents, and all manner of individuals for the removal of Hood following the recent disasters, had deferred to the politics of the situation. Even Congress on January 9th had passed a resolution urging the reappointment of Joe Johnston to command the Army of Tennessee. At the moment of decision, Hood had been his own worst enemy.[35]

Since Beauregard not only had received a companion telegram directing him to remove Hood and install Taylor, but had been ordered to return to Georgia and South Carolina with "such troops as may be spared" from the Army of Tennessee, the matter was irrevocably decided. Beauregard immediately notified Taylor (the former brother-in-law of Jefferson Davis, and the son of Zachary Taylor) and issued orders the following day for Hood to prepare Lee's Corps, the army's largest and best conditioned, for movement to Augusta, Georgia, beginning on the 19th. On the following day Beauregard directed that Cheatham's Corps prepare to follow, based on Jefferson Davis's instructions issued January 12th to leave only "Polk's old corps" with Taylor. Due to the wretched logistical situation that had the army "almost out of provisions," according to Hood's Inspector General on January 14th, this was probably welcome news for most of the men. By the 19th Lee's troops, "about 5,000 strong," began moving from their Tupelo camps. On the 20th Cheatham's Corps began to follow.[36]

Hood was so upset and depressed by it all that when serenaded by Gibson's Louisiana brigade band and called upon for a speech, he hobbled outside and launched into a bitter tirade against his critics. Citing the many difficulties with which he had to contend, Hood said he had not originally sought command of the army, but since that time he had not received the army's support because he had been attacked by "the croakers and scribblers in the rear," an apparent reference to newspaper criticism of Joe Johnston's removal and Hood's appointment. After rambling on about new uniforms and equipment, Hood said that he hoped the army might be supplied with more bayonets—because "it was the bayonet which gave a soldier confidence in himself, and enabled him to strike terror [in]to the enemy." Then, saying that he hoped the men would support Richard Taylor and avenge their recent losses, he bade the men good night and shuffled inside "without making any allusion to the campaign in Tennessee."[37]

It was the same old Hood: stubborn, outmoded in tactical concepts, and unwilling to admit his mistakes. One of his officers wrote in bitter reflection that, after having "butchered 10,000 [men]" around Atlanta and "as many more in Tennessee," Hood had "betrayed his whole army. . . . He might command a brigade, and even a division, but to command the army, he is not the man. General Joe Johnston has more military sense in one day than Hood ever did or ever will have. . . . [To] call him a general is a disgrace to those generals . . . who are worthy to be so called."[38]

On January 18th Hood was sufficiently recovered in spirit to telegraph to Jefferson Davis his newly revised program: "General Taylor will arrive tomorrow, and I will leave soon after for Richmond. Please consider the propriety of my going west of the Mississippi River. I would like it; I think I can be of more service there than east of the river." If his old friend and sponsor Jefferson Davis would agree, Hood might cross the Mississippi and "bring to your aid 25,000 troops." Hood pleaded a few days later, "I know this can be accomplished, and earnestly desire this chance to do you so much good service."[39]

By the 22nd, Hood learned of the final disaster to befall troops under his command. After being disassembled at Bainbridge, Hood's large pontoon train had been loaded on wagons and ordered to Columbus, Mississippi, along with many of the army's supply wagons. On the evening of December 31st, Colonel William J. Palmer of the 15th Pennsylvania Cavalry, operating from the direction of Decatur with a strong detachment, swooped down on Hood's pontoons and captured the entire train. Palmer's cavalrymen had scattered Roddey's troopers and, learning that the pontoon train was only a few miles beyond Russellville, Alabama, rode clear through the ponderous wagon train, meeting virtually no resistance. The train extended for five miles, wrote the amazed Federal colonel, and consisted of 78 pontoons and about 200 wagons. All of the mules and oxen, except what the teamsters were able to cut loose and ride off, "were standing hitched to the wagons." Beauregard acknowledged a loss of 83 boats, 150 wagons, and 400 mules— caused by Roddey's poor performance, said Beauregard—and the Federals promptly burned the well-appointed train, which had been "built at Atlanta last winter."[40]

For the deposed commander of the Army of Tennessee it was a fitting finale. On Monday morning, January 23, 1864, John Bell Hood journeyed to the Tupelo train depot for the trip east, a bitter and disconsolate man. The published orders issued that day announced the formal change in command. In parting, Hood had left behind sort of a memoir, a farewell address to the soldiers of the Army of Tennessee. It read in part: "Soldiers: At my request I have this day been relieved from the command of this army. In taking leave of you accept my thanks for the patience with which you have endured your many hardships during the recent campaign. I am alone responsible for its conception and strived hard to do my duty in its execution." Sadly, Hood left unmentioned the windrows of dead and maimed whose graves and shattered bodies bore mute testimony to the "conception" of his generalship.[41]

Hood boarded the train. If less than a hero and defamed as a general, he was going back to Virginia, away from this land of dismal promise. En route he would hasten to Columbia, South Carolina, to see Buck. Despite all the crushing defeats and the lost fame and fortune, at least he had Buck. He would bury his pain in her caresses.

The train gathered speed. Hood looked out the window for the last time on the few remaining soldiers of the Army of Tennessee. There was no joy on their faces. No one seemed to know or care John Bell Hood was leaving. Outside there was snow on the ground, with cold temperatures that chilled to the very marrow. The wind was blowing from the north, swirling the overcast skies past in a rapid, squally flow. They were angry winds, with the bite of winter, and a low, eerie howl, like the faraway moan of dying men.[42]

It was perhaps a fitting send-off for Hood, the six months' commander of the Army of Tennessee whose tenure had witnessed an anguish and tragedy unprecedented in more than three years of deadly warfare.

CHAPTER XXXVII

Epilogue:
The Twilight's
Last Gleaming

H<small>E HAD SAID</small> he was coming in January to be married, and Sally Preston was all aglow. In early February, when he arrived, Buck was taken aback. "He can stand well enough without his crutch, but he does very slow walking," noticed Buck's friend Mary Chesnut. Yet it was Hood's war-worn countenance that was so eerily shocking. There was a continual agony in his face, his features were gaunt, and the fire in his eyes had been transposed into an austere sadness. Instead of returning as a war hero, or at least a celebrity and a feted, honored man, he had limped back in disgrace, his body wrecked and his future clouded.[1]

Although staying at the Prestons with Buck's brother Jack, Hood soon found that among much of the family he was an outcast. Mrs. Preston remained strongly opposed to the match. Even Buck's brother-in-law, John Darby, Hood's former physician, and the man who had gone to Europe for Hood's artificial leg—indeed, the very person who had introduced him to Buck—had turned against Hood and was inveigling to break the engagement. Mary Darby, Buck's sister, joined her husband in bitterly condemning him.[2]

Hood was no longer the great lion among its pride. "He blushes like a girl," noted Mary Chesnut. "After all, he is a queer compound . . . the simplest, most transparent soul I have met." Hood was found dejectedly staring into space. When a friend tried to tell a funny story to cheer him up, he did not listen. Hood had not heard a word of the story, remarked Jack Preston. He seemed to have forgotten them all. "Did you notice how he stared in[to] the fire? And the livid spots which came out on his face, and the huge drops of perspiration that stood out on his forehead." He seemed to be going over some bitter hour. He had seen Willie Preston with his heart shot away at Atlanta. Perhaps he remembered Nashville and its shame. "I can't keep him out of those absent fits," remarked Jack Preston. "[He] seems [to be] going through in his own mind the torture of the damned."[3]

Buck, too, was distressed, and seemed to be waning in her enthusiasm for their engagement. When Hood left for Richmond on February 7th, she showed little sadness at his going. He wanted to be at the capital by the 8th—his "good luck day"—the anniversary of his engagement. Within a few weeks Mary Chesnut heard that "the Hood melodrama" was over, "though the curtain has not fallen on the last scene." Mary confided, "Hood's stock is going down." Buck's enthusiasm was definitely at low ebb. Perhaps it was like the snuffing out of a candle—one moment here, then gone forever, Mary surmised.[4]

In Richmond, John Bell Hood had to face a storm of criticism and account for what obviously was a serious military disaster. Already, when en route to South Carolina, he had passed through Augusta and probably met with a distant relative, Gustavus Woodson Smith, the crusty old army engineer who was Hood's good friend. Hood apparently poured out his bitterness to Smith, who then may have published the long, rambling article that appeared in the Augusta, Georgia, *Daily Constitutionalist* on February 5, 1865. Under the byline initials "G.W.Y." (later corrected to "G.W.S." by the paper) the article strongly condemned William Hardee, in particular, for not obeying orders at Atlanta, and termed Franklin a "decisive victory" where the Army of Tennessee had been restored to "its old fighting spirit." Nashville had been lost only when a division had "unaccountably" given way, spreading panic through the army. It was asserted in the article that the failures of others were to blame for the disastrous campaign. As for Hood's performance, the article said he had the "characteristics of a great general . . . fully equal to [Robert E.] Lee himself."[5]

Such self-serving propaganda soon was to get Hood into considerable difficulty in Richmond. Called upon to tender his official report, he produced a document so highly critical of Joe Johnston and others that Johnston indicated he would prefer charges. Jefferson Davis's role in influencing the report was questioned. P. G. T. Beauregard was outraged that Hood had ignored him, as his superior officer, and had submitted the report directly to the War Department. Moreover, there were "several errors and inaccuracies in the report," fumed Beauregard. William Hardee inquired into the authorship of the distorted *Daily Constitutionalist* article, and an increasingly rancorous correspondence ensued. When Hood's official report was published, a storm of criticism resulted. Hood had blamed everyone but himself for the failures in the west. It was in marked contrast to what he had despondently told the Prestons and others upon his arrival in South Carolina. "He said he had nobody to blame but himself," wrote Mary Chesnut.[6]

With Hood having conferred with Jefferson Davis and filed his report, the question remained, what next? Although there was some talk of Hood receiving a command in West Virginia, Robert E. Lee felt that due to the controversy with Joe Johnston it was best that he go to Texas. Accordingly, Hood was ordered to proceed to the trans-Mississippi region to investigate the procurement of reinforcements. Hood left Richmond about April 1st, writing a note to Jefferson Davis before his departure in which he reasserted his righteousness: "I am more content and satisfied with my . . . work whilst in command of the Army of Tennessee than all my military career."[7]

"It is all over. The game is up," wrote Senator Louis T. Wigfall, an ardent Davis and Hood detractor. Wigfall asserted that he would go to Texas so that "when the hanging begins" he might flee to Mexico. The basis for this despair was the fall of Richmond, Virginia, on April 3d. With a vast fire raging out of control, government employees, soldiers, and civilians fleeing in every direction, the chaos and confusion existing in the Confederate capital on the night of April 2d well reflected the disarray in the hearts of Southerners everywhere. For Hood the news came as a hard enough blow, yet about the same time he learned that Joe Johnston would prefer charges against him for false allegations in his Atlanta report. Hood, at Chester, South Carolina, on April 4th requested a formal court of inquiry, saying he would delay his departure for Texas accordingly. The government, however, was then in flight from Richmond, and no opportunity existed to investigate the case. Telegraphing from Danville, Virginia, on April 4th, Adjutant General Samuel Cooper told Hood to proceed to Texas as ordered.[8]

Hood had wanted to resolve his engagement with Buck prior to leaving for Texas. Yet time was running out. His frequent and lengthy letters to Buck had been received with indifference and reserve. Apparently Hood even sent an aide or a friend to reason with her. "Princess Bright Eyes is kept busy writing explanatory letters," noted Mary Chesnut. "She can't say yes and she will not say no." Would-be suitors were constantly buzzing about her, "becoming troublesome." Hood was getting angry, yet Buck remained serene.[9]

Now, nearly two months after their parting, Hood again stopped at Chester, evidently to enlist the aid of Mary Chesnut in an attempt to rekindle the romance. Hood wanted Mary to go with him to Yorkville, South Carolina, where Buck had fled following the occupation of Columbia by Sherman's army. As Mary Chesnut recorded in her journal diary, matters already had reached the critical stage. Buck had written from Yorkville early that month, "Keep Sam in Chester." To Hood she had written, "I leave it to your discretion." As Mary Chesnut wryly noted, the discretion was that of a man "madly in love." He would go, she affirmed. When a visitor asked if his engagement was broken, Hood had replied, "Is my neck broken, did you ask?" Though Mary chose not to go, Hood was soon prepared to wend his way to Yorkville, where the "Hampton and Preston ladies [were] drawn up in battle array!"[10]

About April 10th Hood made the fateful journey. A week later he was back, with Buck and Mary Darby in tow. Hood "was awfully proud of that feat," observed Mary Chesnut. "He had never dreamed they would come back with him."[11]

But Hood had lost. Their presence was only to say good-bye. Hood, desperate for love, had gambled again—with tragic results. "I think it began with those beautiful silk stockings that fit so nicely," confided Buck to Mary Chesnut. Buck had been warming her feet on the fender by the fireplace. Hood had always raved about her slender feet and ankles. They were alone. She'd had no warning. He came up behind her, apparently unnoticed due to the crackling fire. Suddenly "he seized me around the waist and kissed my throat," gasped Buck. The horror on her face stopped him short. Always he had been so respectful—kissing only her hand, and telling her she was his queen and how lucky he was that she cared for him. Now the awkward silence was broken by his stammering apologies. Her throat was so soft and white, he could not help it, he sputtered. Buck flew into a rage. She drew back, and said she would go away. Hood tried to save the situation. He grabbed her strongly about the waist. "He said I should stay until I forgave his rash presumption, and he held me fast," said Buck in shock. After all, Buck had promised to marry him, Hood insisted, and that made a difference. Buck could not see it. "I never mean to be treated so outrageously again," she ranted.[12]

About April 15th Hood had departed for good. Mary Chesnut and Buck watched him go. He held his hat off while he was in sight of the house. "Why did he remain uncovered so long?" asked Mary. "In honor of my being here," said Buck quietly.[13]

Although Sally Preston later claimed she would have married him if he had been persistent and not given in to the wishes of her parents, Hood never knew it. Their "love" affair was over, and within weeks Mary Chesnut heard that the engagement formally had been broken off. Days after Hood's departure, Buck was riding with dashing young Captain Rawlins Lowndes. Following a sojourn in Europe with her family, Buck Preston returned to South Carolina and the arms of Rawly Lowndes. By coincidence, Lowndes in March 1864 had gone to his tailor in Richmond, Virginia, to buy cloth for a new uniform. Having selected a fine bolt, he was told no: "You can't have that. It is laid aside. General [Hood] asked us to keep that and our best stars for his wedding clothes." On March 10, 1868, Rawly Lowndes was married to Sally Preston.*[14]

*   *   *

*They would share twelve years together and produce three children before Buck died in December 1880.

The legacy of the Army of Tennessee was both the ardent pride and enduring passion of its soldiers. Under some of the worst combat commanders to serve in the war, the army had fought and suffered as had few others. Despite the final crushing defeats, its efficacy had been measured not in battles won or lost, but in its intense fighting qualities. Citing the "heroic fortitude and valor" of the Confederate Army of Tennessee, an admiring Union veteran wrote, "The whole North was filled with fearful evidence of its persistent courage and daring."[15]

In the waning years of their lives the old veterans would gather at reunions to debate the war and reflect upon their service in the lost cause. They remembered the frightful carnage of Franklin and the cruel ice storms at Nashville. Always there were memories of the tortured agony of Hood's retreat from Tennessee, and the bloodstained, snow-encrusted footprints of his shoeless men. In defeat there existed a certain camaraderie, a feeling that only they knew the meaning of having seen and endured so much. Finally there was often a mellowing of perspectives. Instead of dwelling on what might have been, often the men found cause for reflection and pride at having met both the best and worst of life and survived.

"Blue-black is our horizon," wrote Mary Chesnut in contemplation of the South's loss of the war. The world seemed turned upside down once more. The Confederacy's military bankruptcy had translated into shattered lives and fortunes. Many ex-Confederate officials fled the country to escape perhaps a hangman's noose, so they thought. John Smith Preston took his family to Europe at the end of the war, secure in the knowledge he had ample funds abroad. For others, there was an attempt to carry on in the cause by traveling west of the Mississippi River, or else settling in Mexico.[16]

John Bell Hood was among the many who avoided surrendering until at last there was little choice. Hood spent much of May 1865 vainly seeking a crossing of the flooded Mississippi River. On May 31st Hood finally gave himself up at Natchez, Mississippi, and was paroled. Eventually settling in New Orleans, Hood's postwar career was marked by varied swings in fortune. In 1866 Hood entered the cotton factoring and commission merchant business, often petitioning former army colleagues such as Stephen D. Lee to place their cotton business through his firm. By 1870 Hood was selling life insurance, but with only moderate success. His real passion involved the defense of his career as a Southern general.[17]

After long contemplating writing an account of the Atlanta and Nashville disasters, Hood seemed to bog down in the preliminary effort. In 1874, however, Joe Johnston's memoirs were published and Hood felt compelled to respond. His *Advance and Retreat: Personal Experiences in the United States and Confederate States Armies* was published posthumously in 1880. Unfortunately, it is merely a bitter, misleading, and highly distorted treatise of a self-serving nature, more of an awkward apologia than a meaningful book.[18]

Nearly three years to the day from when he had lost Buck—indeed, little more than a month after Rawly Lowndes had married Buck—Sam Hood claimed his own bride. On April 13, 1868, he married an attractive European-educated woman, Anna Marie Hennen, six years his junior, the daughter of a prosperous Louisiana lawyer. As if to refute any inference that he might be a "lame" lover due to his crippled body, Hood fathered eleven children in eleven years, including three sets of twins. The eight girls and three boys were often referred to as "Hood's Brigade," and when his family was traveling Hood reportedly sent ahead for a large supply of milk in order to feed his brood.[19]

Yet Hood remained a tragic figure. After enduring the terrible carnage of Antietam, Gettysburg, and Chickamauga, what finally sent Hood to his final resting place was a tiny insect—an *Aedes aegypti* mosquito. In the summer of 1879, amid an outbreak of yellow fever, much of Hood's family was stricken. His wife died August 24th, two days after becoming sick and only a few weeks following the birth of her daughter Anna. Hood's eldest child, Lydia, was next, dying at age ten, a few days after her mother. On August 27th Hood was stricken with a high fever. On the 30th his labored breathing and moans foretold of his fate. At 3:30 A.M. he shuddered convulsively and died. Yellow fever had completed the tragedy that had plagued much of his life.[20]

Often described as an excellent soldier but a poor general, John Bell Hood perhaps was best assessed by one of his contemporaries who had witnessed the carnage at Franklin: "General Hood expected more of his men than any general ever did." Another observer, one of James Longstreet's staff officers, wrote just after the defeat at Nashville, "Hood [is] a tolerable division commander, and a very poor corps commander." Yet the root of Hood's misfortunes, the officer continued to say, lay with the false assessments and conniving of others. Somebody should be hung for what had occurred, he declared. There were three principals to blame for the late Confederate disaster: one was Jefferson Davis, for his prejudice in appointing Hood; the second was Bragg, for misrepresentation and lies that led to the vacancy in the command; and the third was Hood, for his insidious actions, having "wireworked" his way into a position he was totally unsuited for.[21]

John Bell Hood was always a man to harken to a fight, and he displayed unquestioned physical courage on the battlefield. To this day there are many who extol his virtues, and cite his performance in various actions such as Gaines' Mill and Antietam as a basis for their support. Yet no segment of a man's life stands alone; it must be put in the context of the whole. Hood, ultimately, was a tragic failure, a sad, pathetic soldier whose ambitions totally outstripped his abilities. Essentially, he was an anachronism: an advocate of outmoded concepts, and a general unable to adapt to new methods or technology. Always prone to blame others, and unable to admit his mistakes, to the bitter end Hood never understood his failings. "They charge me with having made Franklin a slaughter pen," he admonished a group of aging veterans, "but, as I understand it, war means fight, and fight means kill." Perhaps Hood's own words, written in anticipation of defending his military career, should serve as his epitaph: "To conquer self is the greatest battle of life." Unfortunately for many of his men, that had never occurred.[22]

Of the many lives John Bell Hood had touched, few were more pathetic than the widows and sweethearts of his soldiers. Susan Tarleton may never have recovered from Pat Cleburne's death. In October 1867 she married Captain Hugh L. Cole, a lawyer in Mobile, Alabama. Less than a year later she suddenly died.[23]

Writing to the newly widowed wife of one of his soldiers shortly after returning from the Tennessee Campaign, Lieutenant Colonel C. P. Neilson, the commander of the 33d Mississippi, described how the widow's husband had died in the bloody charge at Franklin:

> [We found him] lying on his back, and he appeared to be peacefully sleeping. A smile was on his countenance and everything indicated that he had passed away without a struggle. . . . One ball struck him directly in the front, just below the breast bone, passing through. Another struck him on the right side, passing through. Another in the right cheek, and another in the left hand. . . . I found his testament lying on his breast and thinking of his widow far away I put it in my pocket for you. . . . It would certainly be a consolation to you to have received some last message from your loved one, but the unexpectedness of the battle and the circumstances of his death prevented [it]. . . . Your loss is great . . . but you "mourn not as one without hope."[24]

These words, and many others like them, brought anguished tears to many a home throughout the South that winter. Hope was often a hard aspect to comprehend; it never provided food on the table, or a loving caress. For a grieving young widow, it was only a shallow grave in Tennessee that endured.

The great tragedy at Franklin and its many painful memories caused Frank Cheatham to avoid the site for many years. Finally in the early 1880s he returned to tramp over the fields with a newspaper reporter. The great charge at Franklin was "the grandest sight I ever saw," he said. Yet for him it had been the "bloodiest battle of the war," where he had seen his men make crude breastworks of their comrades' bodies for protection from the terrible incoming fire. Such thoughts soon caused him to turn away, unable to speak further of so many tortured memories.[25]

Within the ranks of the Northern veterans the brightest of Federal victories on the battlefield, ironically, produced a divisive postwar bickering that far exceeded the controversies among the vanquished Southerners. Among the most prominent disputes were outright feuds involving such ardent personalities as David S. Stanley, Jacob Cox, and John M. Schofield. Cox argued long and vehemently that he had commanded the line at Franklin, to the great discomfort of Stanley, who as senior officer present felt that it tarnished his role. Stanley eventually became so bitter following a series of newspaper articles and private correspondence as to call Cox "a reckless inventor of lies" and "a very false knave." Said Stanley, "All his writings are full of the spirit of falsehood." Bitter in his reflections, an aging Stanley feuded with Emerson Opdycke, and even Thomas J. Wood. As for John M. Schofield, Stanley dismissed the Twenty-third Corps commander's memoirs, in which he seemed to claim "grand superiority and wisdom" during the Spring Hill and Franklin maneuvering, as "the merest bosh." According to Stanley, Schoefield escaped disaster in both encounters purely by accident and a "run of luck."[26]

For Schofield, who published his memoirs, *Forty-Six Years in the Army*, in 1897, the war's aftermath found him embroiled in an extended controversy over the supposed telegram he had sent to Grant from Nashville, seeking Thomas's removal and his own appointment. Schofield accused James B. Steedman of this "vile slander," and he went to great lengths to refute the charges. When Schofield's critical appraisal of Thomas's generalship was featured in his memoirs, a renewed controversy began. Since the corpulent Thomas had died at age fifty-three in San Francisco on March 28, 1870, his former associates and staff officers took up the challenge, one regarding Schofield's presence as a pallbearer at Thomas's funeral as an outrage. Remarked a former Union general present for the ceremony, "If Thomas only knew it, he would turn in his coffin."[27]

For many of the principal Union personalities involved in the high drama at Spring Hill, Franklin, and Nashville, shades of glory and gloom had followed. Emerson Opdycke, after obtaining a brigadier's star in July 1865, petitioned the secretary of war in September 1866 to be breveted as major general of volunteers. "I have felt deeply hurt that my service at Franklin did not attract some official recognition from the Government, and I make this direct appeal to your honor in the hope of receiving your favorable action," wrote the unhappy Opdycke. Opdyke got his brevet, worked as a dry goods merchant in New York City, and was accidentally mortally wounded by a pistol shot while cleaning his revolver in April 1884.[28]

After the war, Jacob Cox briefly became governor of Ohio, served as secretary of the Interior in the Grant administration, and later practiced law. His prolific writings on Franklin reflected his fervent interest in that battle. John McArthur, whose troops had led the rush up Shy's Hill at Nashville, returned to various enterprises in Chicago, but suffered numerous financial and political setbacks. John M. Schofield became commanding general of the army in 1888, having previously served as secretary of war and superintendent at West Point. Some of the Federal army's subordinate officers, such as Captain John Shellenberger of the 64th Ohio, spent years analyzing, studying, and writing about the fight at Franklin. Other Union veterans returned to the site of their most furious combat for more romantic reasons. One Federal colonel, wounded and left at Franklin in the care of a good Southern family, returned after the war and married the "little dark eyed Rebel" who had helped nurse him back to health.[29]

For most of the men who valiantly had fought and suffered in mid-Tennessee during 1864, over the years the significance of the campaign became increasingly obscured by the ongoing, daily episodes of life. Then, long after the last of the aged veterans was gone, as if some specter from the troubled past, a body appeared to remind all of the tragic reality of Hood's invasion.

Lieutenant Colonel William M. Shy had died almost instantly atop the hill that now bears his name at Nashville. Yet in death he was to receive a prominence more than a hundred years later that few could have imagined. On Christmas Eve 1977 a headless body was discovered lying on top of a dug-up casket behind the antebellum mansion that had been Lieutenant Colonel Shy's residence. Police officials feared someone had been murdered, and that the murderer, in an attempt to hide the body, had dug up Shy's grave, only to be scared off before completing the work. A medical examiner estimated that the victim, dressed in what appeared to be a tuxedo, had been dead six to twelve months. The corpse was estimated to be a white male, approximately five feet eleven inches, 175 pounds, and about twenty-six years old. When the head and other body parts were found nearby, the examiners learned the victim had died from a blow to the head. "It looks like we have a homicide on our hands," said a chief deputy. A few weeks later, based on further laboratory evaluation, the mystery about the body was solved. The corpse had turned out to be that of Lieutenant Colonel Shy, so perfectly embalmed (evidently by Dr. Daniel Cliffe) that 113 years later some of the flesh was still pink. In the rush to provide answers to a curious public and press, no one had considered that a body in such an excellent state of preservation could be that of a long-dead Civil War officer. The cast-iron coffin had been dug from the grave and his body pulled out in an apparent attempt to locate valuable artifacts. Within a few weeks Lieutenant Colonel Shy's body was reburied in a brief ceremony. Today the damaged iron coffin originally used to bury Shy in 1864 can be seen at the Carter House Museum in Franklin. Said the examining physician of the incident, "I got the age, sex, race, height, and weight right, but I was off on the time of death by 113 years." If a tragicomic episode, it was perhaps a fitting reminder of history's often hidden reality.[30]

Today a visitor to the battlefield at Franklin will find little evidence of some of the American Civil War's most bloody and hallowed ground. Civilization has persisted in devouring the land. At the site of the old cotton gin, once strewn with ghastly human carnage, a quiet, modest neighborhood exists, filled with romping dogs and playing children. Where the locust grove stood to entrap the struggling men of John C. Brown's division, there is now only a ramshackle warehouse and the litter of old coffee cans and abandoned tires. The spot where Pat Cleburne likely died is blacktopped—part of a pizza establishment's parking lot. A small frame house stands dominant on the site of the Carter house garden and its bullet-tilled soil. Forlornly surrounded and nearly choked from view by its urban setting, only the Carter house and its bullet-riddled outbuildings yet remain to serve as grim reminders of a far different scene.

In a certain sense the desecration of this important and historic site is an outrage. From another perspective, however, it may be all too fitting. That one of the ugliest episodes of the most tragic of American wars should be overwhelmed by a greater monument—civilization—is a reminder that war is but a cruel and unacceptable aberration in man's existence. The ultimate consequence of the Battle of Franklin and a thousand other conflicts—peace in a civilized world—perhaps may be a greater memorial, after all.

ORDER OF BATTLE
CONFEDERATE ARMY OF TENNESSEE
General John Bell Hood

INFANTRY

Lee's Corps: Lieut. Gen. Stephen D. Lee (wounded Dec. 17th at Franklin)
   Johnson's Division: Maj. Gen. Edward Johnson (captured at Nashville Dec. 16th)
      Deas's Brigade: Brig. Gen. Zachariah C. Deas (wounded at Franklin)
         19th, 22d, 25th, 38th, 50th Alabama
      Manigault's Brigade: Brig. Gen. Arthur M. Manigault (Franklin; wounded
         at Franklin); Lt. Col. William L. Butler (Nashville)
         24th, 28th, 34th Alabama; 10th, 19th South Carolina
      Sharp's Brigade: Brig. Gen. Jacob H. Sharp
         7th, 9th, 10th, 41st, 44th Mississippi; 9th Battalion Mississippi Sharp-
         shooters
      Brantley's Brigade: Brig. Gen. William F. Brantley
         24th, 27th, 29th, 30th, 34th Mississippi; Dismounted Cavalry Company
   Stevenson's Division: Maj. Gen. Carter L. Stevenson
      Cummings's Brigade: Col. Elihu P. Watkins
         24th, 36th, 39th, 56th Georgia
      Pettus's Brigade: Brig. Gen. Edmund W. Pettus
         20th, 23d, 30th, 31st, 46th Alabama
   Clayton's Division: Maj. Gen. Henry D. Clayton
      Stovall's Brigade: Brig. Gen. Marcellus A. Stovall
         40th, 41st, 42d, 43d, 52d Georgia
      Gibson's Brigade: Brig. Gen. Randall L. Gibson
         1st, 4th, 13th, 16th, 19th, 20th, 25th, 30th Louisiana; 4th Lousiana
         Battalion; 14th Louisiana Battalion Sharpshooters
      Holtzclaw's Brigade: Brig. Gen. James Holtzclaw
         18th, 32d, 36th, 38th, 58th Alabama

Stewart's Corps: Lt. Gen. Alexander P. Stewart
   Loring's Division: Maj. Gen. William W. Loring
      Featherston's Brigade: Brig. Gen. Winfield S. Featherston
         1st, 3d, 22d, 31st, 33d, 40th Mississippi; 1st Mississippi Battalion

Adams's Brigade: Brig. Gen. John Adams (Franklin; killed at Franklin); Col. Robert Lowry (Nashville)

6th, 14th, 15th, 20th, 23d, 43d Mississippi

Scott's Brigade: Brig. Gen. Thomas M. Scott (Franklin; wounded at Franklin); Col. John Snodgrass (Nashville)

27th, 35th, 49th, 55th, 57th Alabama; 12th Louisiana

French's Division: Maj. Gen. Samuel G. French (Franklin; absent at Nashville due to severe eye infection); Brig. Gen. Claudius Sears (Nashville; wounded at Nashville Dec. 15th, captured Dec. 27th)

Ector's Brigade: Col. David Coleman

29th, 30th North Carolina, 9th Texas; 10th, 14th, 32d Texas Cavalry (dismounted)

Cockrell's Brigade: Brig. Gen. F. M. Cockrell (wounded at Franklin), brigade detached prior to Nashville under Col. Peter C. Flournoy

1st, 2nd, 3d, 4th, 5th, 6th Missouri; 1st Missouri Cavalry (dismounted); 3d Missouri Cavalry Battalion (dismounted)

Sears's Brigade: Brig. Gen. Claudius Sears (wounded at Nashville Dec. 15th, captured Dec. 27th) Lt. Col. Reuben H. Shotwell (Nashville)

4th, 35th, 36th, 39th, 46th Mississippi; 7th Mississippi Battalion

Walthall's Division: Maj. Gen. Edward C. Walthall

Quarles's Brigade: Brig. Gen. William A. Quarles (wounded at Franklin, captured Dec. 17th); Brig. Gen. George D. Johnson (Nashville)

1st Alabama; 42d, 46th, 48th, 49th, 53d, 55th Tennessee

Cantley's Brigade: Brig. Gen. Charles M. Shelley

17th, 26th, 29th Alabama; 37th Mississippi

Reynold's Brigade: Brig. Gen. Daniel H. Reynolds

4th, 9th, 25th Arkansas; 1st, 2d Arkansas Mounted Rifles (dismounted)

Cheatham's Corps: Major General Benjamin F. Cheatham

Cleburne's Division: Maj. Gen. Patrick Cleburne (killed at Franklin); Brig. Gen. James A. Smith (Nashville)

Lowrey's Brigade: Brig. Gen. Mark P. Lowrey (Franklin)

16th, 33d, 45th Alabama; 5th, 8th, 32d Mississippi; 3d Mississippi Battalion

Govan's Brigade: Brig. Gen. Daniel C. Govan

1st, 2d, 5th, 6th, 7th, 8th, 13th, 15th, 19th, 24th Arkansas

Granbury's Brigade:) Brig. Gen. Hiram B. Granbury (killed at Franklin); Capt. E. T. Broughton

5th Confederate; 35th Tennessee; 6th, 7th, 10th, 15th Texas; 17th, 18th, 24th, 25th Texas Cavalry (dismounted); Nutt's Louisiana Cavalry (dismounted)

Smith's Brigade: on detached duty before Nashville—Brig. Gen. James A. Smith; Col. Charles H. Olmstead (Nashville)

54th, 57th, 63d Georgia; 1st Georgia Volunteers

Brown's (Cheatham's Old) Division: Maj. Gen. John C. Brown (Franklin; wounded at Franklin); Brig. Gen. Mark P. Lowrey (Nashville)

Gist's Brigade: Brig. Gen. States Rights Gist (killed at Franklin); Lt. Col. Zachariah L. Watters (Nashville)

46th, 65th Georgia; 2d Battalion Georgia Sharpshooters; 16th, 24th South Carolina

Maney's Brigade: Brig. Gen. John C. Carter (mortally wounded at Franklin); Col. Hume R. Field (Nashville)

1st, 4th (provisional), 6th, 8th, 9th, 16th, 27th, 28th, 50th Tennessee

Strahl's Brigade: Brig. Gen. Otho F. Strahl (killed at Franklin); Col. Andrew J. Kellar (Nashville)

4th, 5th, 19th, 24th, 31st, 33d, 38th, 41st Tennessee
Vaughan's Brigade: Brig. Gen. George W. Gordon (captured at Franklin);
Col. William M. Watkins (Nashville)
11th, 12th, 13th, 29th, 47th, 51st, 52nd, 154th Tennessee
Bate's Division: Maj. Gen. William B. Bate
Tyler's Brigade: Brig. Gen. Thomas B. Smith (wounded and captured at
Nashville)
37th Georgia; 4th Battalion Georgia Sharpshooters;
2d, 10th, 20th, 37th Tennessee
Finley's Brigade: Col. Robert Bullock; Maj. Jacob A. Lash
1st, 3d, 4th, 6th, 7th Florida, 1st Florida Cavalry (dismounted)
Jackson's Brigade: Brig. Gen. Henry R. Jackson (captured at Nashville
December 16th)
25th, 29th, 30th Georgia; 1st Georgia Confederate; 1st Battalion
Georgia Sharpshooters

ARTILLERY

Lee's Corps: 1) Col. Robert F. Beckham (mortally wounded at Columbia Nov. 29th)
2) Maj. John W. Johnston
Courtney's Battalion: Capt. James P. Douglas
Dent's Alabama Battery; Douglas's Texas Battery; Garrity's Alabama
Battery
Eldridge's Battalion: Capt. Charles E. Fenner
Eufaula Alabama Battery; Fenner's Louisiana Battery; Stanford's Mississippi Battery
Johnson's Battalion: Capt. John B. Rowan
Corput's Georgia Battery; Marshall's Tennessee Battery; Stephens's
Light Artillery

Stewart's Corps: Lt. Col. Samuel C. Williams
Truehart's Battalion:
Lumsden's Alabama Battery; Selden's Alabama Battery
Myrick's Battalion:
Bouanchaud's Louisiana Battery; Cowan's Mississippi Battery,
Darden's Mississippi Battery
Storrs' Battalion:
Guiborps Missouri Battery; Hoskin's Mississippi Battery; Kolb's Alabama Battery

Cheatham's Corps: Col. Melancthon Smith
Hoxton's Battalion:
Perry's Florida Battery; Phelan's Alabama Battery; Turner's Mississippi
Battery
Hotchkiss's Battalion:
Bledsoe's Missouri Battery; Goldtwaite's Alabama Battery; Key's Arkansas Battery
Cobb's Battalion:
Ferguson's South Carolina Battery; Phillip's [Mwebane's] Tennessee
Battery; Slocumb's Louisiana Battery

CAVALRY
Maj. Gen. Nathan B. Forrest

Chalmers's Division: Brig. Gen. James R. Chalmers
> *Rucker's Brigade:* Col. Edmund W. Rucker (wounded and captured at Nashville Dec. 16th)
>> 7th Alabama Cavalry; 5th Mississippi Cavalry; 7th, 12th, 14th, 15th Tennessee Cavalry; Forrest's Regiment Tennessee Cavalry
>
> *Biffle's Brigade:* Col. Jacob B. Biffle 10th Tennessee Cavalry

Buford's Division: Brig. Gen. Abraham Buford (wounded at Richland Creek Dec. 24th)
> *Bell's Brigade:* Col. Tyree H. Bell
>> 2d, 19th, 20th, 21st Tennessee Cavalry; Nixon's Tennessee Cavalry Regiment
>
> *Crossland's Brigade:* Col. Edward Crossland
>> 3d, 7th, 8th, 12th Kentucky Mounted Infantry; 12th Kentucky Cavalry; Huey's Kentucky Battalion

Jackson's Division: Brig. Gen. William H. Jackson
> *Armstrong's Brigade:* Brig. Gen. Frank C. Armstrong
>> 1st, 2d, 28th Mississippi Cavalry; Ballentine's Mississippi Regiment
>
> *Ross's Brigade:* Brig. Gen. Lawrence S. Ross
>> 5th, 6th, 9th Texas Cavalry; 1st Texas Legion

Artillery: Morton's Tennessee Battery

ORDER OF BATTLE
FEDERAL ARMY

Major General John M. Schofield (Franklin)
Major General George H. Thomas (Nashville)

FOURTH ARMY CORPS MAJ. GEN. DAVID S. STANLEY (WOUNDED AT FRANKLIN; BRIG. GEN. THOMAS J. WOOD (NASHVILLE)

First Division: Brig. Gen. Nathan Kimball
 1st Brigade: Col. Isaac M. Kirby
  21st, 38th Illinois; 31st, 81st Indiana; 90th Ohio
 2d Brigade: Brig. Gen. Walter C. Whittaker
  96th, 115th Illinois; 35th Indiana; 21st, 23d Kentucky, 45th, 51st Ohio
 3d Brigade: Brig. Gen. William Grose
  75th, 80th, 84th Illinois; 9th, 30th, 36th, 84th Indiana; 77th Pennsylvania

Second Division: Brig. Gen. George D. Wagner (Franklin); Brig. Gen. Washington L. Elliott (Nashville)
 1st Brigade: Col. Emerson Opdycke
  36th, 44th, 73d, 74th, 88th Illinois; 125th Ohio; 24th Wisconson
 2d Brigade: Col. John Q. Lane
  100th Illinois; 40th, 57th Indiana; 28th Kentucky, 26th, 97th Ohio
 3d Brigade: Col. Joseph Conrad
  42d, 51st, 79th Illinois; 15th Missouri; 64th, 65th Ohio

Third Division: Brig. Gen. Thomas J. Wood (Franklin); Brig. Gen. Samuel Beatty (Nashville)
 1st Brigade: Col. Abel D. Streight
  89th Illinois; 51st Indiana; 8th Kansas; 15th, 49th Ohio
 2d Brigade: Col. P. Sidney Post (wounded at Nashville)
  59th Illinois; 41st, 71st, 93d, 124th Ohio
 3d Brigade: Col. Frederick Knefler
  79th, 86th Indiana; 13th, 19th Ohio

Artillery: Maj. Wilbur F. Goodspeed
 Light Batteries: 25th Battery Indiana (Sturm); 1st Battery Kentucky (Thomasson); 1st Michigan Battery (De Vries); 1st Ohio Battery G (Marshall); 6th Ohio

Battery (Baldwin); Battery B Pennsylvania Light Artillery (Ziegler); Battery M, 4th U.S. (Canby)

TWENTY-THIRD ARMY CORPS:
BRIG. GEN. JACOB D. COX
(FRANKLIN); MAJ. GEN. JOHN M.
SCHOFIELD (NASHVILLE)

Second Division: Brig. Gen. Thomas H. Ruger (Franklin); Maj. Gen. Darius N. Couch (Nashville)

1st Brigade: (Nashville only) Brig. Gen. Joseph A. Cooper
130th Indiana; 26th Kentucky; 25th Michigan; 99th Ohio; 3rd, 6th Tennessee
2d Brigade: Col. Orlando H. Moore
107th Illinois; 80th, 129th Indiana; 23d Michigan; 111th, 118th Ohio
3d Brigade: Col. Silas Strickland (Franklin); Col. John Mehringer (Nashville)
91st, 123d Indiana; 50th, 183d Ohio

Artillery:
Light Batteries: 13th Battery Indiana (Harvey); 19th Battery Ohio (Wilson)

Third Division: Brig. Gen. James A. Reilly (Franklin); Brig. Gen. Jacob D. Cox (Nashville)

1st Brigade: Brig. Gen. James A. Reilly (Franklin); Col. Charles C. Doolittle (Nashville)
12th, 16th Kentucky; 100th, 104th Ohio; 8th Tennessee
2d Brigade: Col. John S. Casement
65th Illinois; 65th, 124th Indiana; 103d Ohio; 5th Tennessee
3d Brigade: Col. Israel N. Stiles
112th Illinois; 63d, 120th, 128th Indiana

Artillery:
Light Batteries: 23d Indiana Battery (Wilber); Battery D, 1st Ohio (Cockerill)

DETACHMENT ARMY OF THE
TENNESSEE MAJ. GEN. ANDREW J.
SMITH

First Division: Brig. Gen. John McArthur

1st Brigade: Col. William L. McMillan
114th Illinois; 93d Indiana; 10th Minnesota;
72d, 95th Ohio; Cogswell's Battery Illinois Light Artillery (McClaury)
2d Brigade: Col. Lucius F. Hubbard
5th, 9th Minnesota; 11th Missouri; 8th Wisconsin; 2d Battery Iowa Light Artillery (Reed)
3d Brigade: Col. Sylvester G. Hill (killed at Nashville Dec. 15th); Col. William R. Marshall
12th, 35th Iowa; 7th Minnesota; 33d Missouri; Battery I 2d Missouri Light Artillery (Julian)

Second Division: Brig. Gen. Kenner Garrard

1st Brigade: Col. David Moore
119th, 122d Illinois; 89th Indiana; 21st Missouri; 9th Battery Indiana Light Artillery (Calfee)
2d Brigade: Col. James L. Gilbert

58th Illinois; 27th, 32d Iowa; 10th Kansas; 3d Battery Indiana Light Artillery (Ginn)
3d Brigade: Col. Edward H. Wolfe
49th, 117th Illinois; 52d Indiana; 178th New York; Battery G 2d Illinois Light Artillery (Lowell)

Third Division: Col. Jonathan B. Moore
1st Brigade: Col. Lyman M. Ward
72d Illinois; 40th Missouri; 14th, 33d Wisconsin
2d Brigade: Col. Leander Blanden
81st, 95th Illinois; 44th Missouri

Artillery:
11th Battery Indiana Light Artillery (Morse); Battery A 2d Missouri Light Artillery (Zepp)

PROVISIONAL DETACHMENT—DISTRICT OF THE ETOWAH MAJ. GEN. JAMES B. STEEDMAN

Provisional Division: Brig. Gen. Charles Cruft
1st Colored Brigade: Col. Thomas J. Morgan
14th, 16th, 17th, 18th, 44th U.S. Colored Troops
2d Colored Brigade: Col. Charles R. Thompson
12th, 13th, 100th U.S. Colored Troops; 1st Battery Kansas Light Artillery (Tennessee)
1st Brigade: Col. Benjamin Harrison
three battalions from 20th Army Corps (detached)
2d Brigade: Col. John G. Mitchell
composed of men on detached duty from the Army of the Tennessee
3d Brigade: Lt. Col. Charles H. Grosvenor
68th Indiana; 18th, 121st Ohio; 2d Battalion 14th Army Corps

Artillery:
20th Battery Indiana Light Artillery (Osborne); 18th Battery Ohio Light Artillery (Aleshire)

POST OF NASHVILLE BRIG. GEN. JOHN F. MILLER

Brigade: (20th Army Corps, 4th Division, 2d Brigade) Col. Edwin C. Mason
142d Indiana; 45th New York; 176th, 179th, 182d Ohio
Unattached: 3d Kentucky; 28th Michigan; 173d Ohio; 78th Pennsylvania; Veteran Reserve Corps; 44th, 45th Wisconsin
Garrison Artillery: Light Batteries: Bridges's Illinois (White); 2d (Whicher), 4th (Johnson), 12th (White), 21st (Andrew), 22d (Nicholson), 24th (Allen) Indiana Batteries; Battery F, 1st Michigan (Paddock); Batteries A (Scovill), E (Reckard) 1st Ohio; 20th Ohio Battery (Backus); Batteries C (Grisby), D (Leinert), 1st Tennessee; Battery A, 2d U.S. Colored (Meigs)

QUARTERMASTER'S DIVISION BVT. BRIG. GEN. JAMES L. DONALDSON

Composed of quartermaster's employees, used to man trenches

CAVALRY CORPS MAJ. GEN. JAMES
H. WILSON

First Division: Brig. Gen. Edward M. McCook
1st Brigade: Brig. Gen. John T. Croxton
8th Iowa Cavalry; 4th Kentucky Mounted Infantry; 2d Michigan Cavalry; 1st Tennessee Cavalry; Board of Trade Battery, Illinois Light Artillery (Robinson)
2d Brigade: Col. Oscar H. La Grange
Detached in pursuit of Lyon's raid into Western Kentucky
3d Brigade: Bvt. Brig. Gen. Louis D. Watkins
Detached in pursuit of Lyon's raid into Western Kentucky

Fifth Division: Brig. Gen. Edward Hatch
1st Brigade: Col. Robert R. Stewart
3d Illinois Cavalry; 11th Indiana Cavalry; 12th Missouri Cavalry; 10th Tennessee Cavalry
2d Brigade: Col. Datus E. Coon
6th, 7th, 9th Illinois Cavalry; 2d Iowa Cavalry; 12th Tennessee Cavalry; Battery I, 1st Illinois Light Artillery (McCartney)

Sixth Division: Brig. Gen. Richard W. Johnson
1st Brigade: Col. Thomas J. Harrison
16th Illinois Cavalry; 5th Iowa Cavalry; 7th Ohio Cavalry
2nd Brigade: Col. James Biddle
14th Illinois Cavalry; 6th Indiana Cavalry; 8th Michigan Cavalry; 3d Tennessee Cavalry
Artillery: Battery I 4th U.S. (Frank G. Smith)

Seventh Division: Brig. Gen. Joseph F. Knipe
1st Brigade: Bvt. Brig. Gen. John H. Hammond
9th, 10th Indiana Cavalry; 19th Pennsylvania Cavalry; 2d, 4th Tennessee Cavalry
2nd Brigade: Col. Gilbert M. L. Johnson (dismounted)
12th, 13th Indiana Cavalry; 8th Tennessee Cavalry
Artillery: 14th Battery Ohio Light Artillery (Myers)

REFERENCE NOTES

ABBREVIATIONS

BHL—Bentley Historical Library, University of Michigan, Ann Arbor, MI.

CHA—Carter House Archives, Franklin, TN.

CL—Clements Library, University of Michigan, Ann Arbor, MI.

CV—*Confederate Veteran*. Cited with volume and page number following. For example, CV 5-123.

DPL—Du Pont Library, University of the South, Sewanee, TN.

LOC—Library of Congress, Washington, DC.

MCCW—C. Vann Woodward, *Mary Chesnut's Civil War* (New Haven, CT, 1981).

MOLLUS—Military Order of the Loyal Legion of the United States.

OR—*War of the Rebellion: Official Records of the Union and Confederate Armies*, Series I, Washington, D.C.—cited with volume, part, and page numbers following. For example, OR 45-2-345.

SHC—Southern Historical Collection, University of North Carolina Library, Chapel Hill, NC.

THSL—Tennessee Historical Society Library, Nashville, TN.

TSL—Tennessee State Library, Nashville, TN.

USAMHI—United States Army Military History Institute, Carlisle Barracks, Pennsylvania.

WRHS—Western Reserve Historical Society Library, Cleveland, OH.

73rd Illinois—*A History of the Seventy-Third Regiment of Illinois Infantry Volunteers* (Springfield, Il, 1890).

86th Indiana—*The Eighty-Sixth Regiment Indiana Volunteer Infantry: A Narrative of its Services in the Civil War of 1861–1865* (Crawfordsville, IN, 1895).

CHAPTER 1

1. Charles Todd Quintard, diary, November 21, 1864 (DPL).
Bender, Jacob, letter, November 21, 1864, The Bender Family Papers (USAMHI).
Norman D. Brown, ed., *One of Cleburne's Command: The Civil War Letters and Diary of Capt. Samuel T. Foster, Granbury's Texas Brigade, C.S.A.* (Austin, TX, 1980), 145.

2. Ibid., 145. diary, November 22.

3. Quintard, (DPL).

4. F. Halsey Wigfall, letter, December 5, 1864, Wigfall Family Papers (LOC).

5. William C. Buchanan, diary, Miscellaneous Collections (USAMHI), 24.

Luther P. Bradley, letters, November 3 and 15, 1864, Bradley Papers (USAMHI).

6. Patricia L. Faust, ed., *Historical Times Illustrated Encyclopedia of the Civil War* (New York, 1986), 187, 335–336.

7. Thomas L. Livermore, *Numbers and Losses in the Civil War in America, 1861–65* (Bloomington, IN: 1957), 47, 63.

8. Faust, 383–382.

Dunbar Rowland, ed., *Jefferson Davis, Constitutionalist: His Letters, Papers and Speeches* (Jackson, MS, 1923), 2:357.

9. Rowland, 2:352–357.

10. Ibid., 343–359.

11. Ibid., 344–347, 355, 358.

12. Ibid., 358.

13. William T. Sherman, *Memoirs of General William T. Sherman* (New York, 1875), 2:226, 227.

14. Ibid., 111, 126.

15. Ibid., 170.

16. Ibid., 178, 179.

17. Ibid., 127.

CHAPTER 2

1. MCCW, 441.

John P. Dyer, *The Gallant Hood* (Indianapolis, IN, 1950), 23.

2. Dyer, 23.

3. MCCW, 511.

Richard M. McMurry, *John Bell Hood and the War for Southern Independence* (Lexington, KY, 1982), 33.

4. Faust, 368–369.

Dyer, 26.

5. McMurry, 9.

Dyer, 25.

6. Ibid., 41–44.

John Bell Hood, *Advance and Retreat: Personal Experience in the United States and Confederate States Armies* (Bloomington, IN, 1959), 12.

7. McMurry, 21, 24, 25.

Dyer, 48ff.

8. McMurry, 26.

9. Ibid., 28, 35.

10. Ibid., 34, 35.

11. Ibid., 46–49.

Dyer, 88–93.

Hood, 26–29.

12. OR 11-2-446.

McMurry, 49.

Dyer, 95.

MCCW, 441.

13. Dyer, 88, 144.

McMurry, 58–59.

Hood, 45, 46.

14. McMurry, 61.

Dyer, 158, 175–178.

15. Ibid., 190–199.

OR 27-2-362.

16. Dyer, 198.

Hood, 60, 61.

McMurry, 75.

17. Dyer, 165, 166.

18. MCCW, 430–431, 442–443.

Virginia G. Meynard, *The Venturers—The Hampton, Harrison, and Earle Families of Virginia, South Carolina and Texas* (1981), 503.

19. MCCW, 873.

20. Dyer, 167, 178.

MCCW, 442–443.

21. Dyer, 199.

Thomas L. Connelly, *Autumn of Glory: The Army of Tennessee, 1862–1865* (Baton Rouge, 1971), 149–151.

MCCW, 516.

22. Ibid. 804.

23. Ibid., pp. 430, 431, 516.

McMurry, 29, 48.

24. Ibid., 77.

Hood, 64, 65.

Mrs. D. Girard [Louise Wigfall] Wright, *A Southern Girl in '61* (New York, 1905), 149.

25. MCCW, 502.

26. Ibid., 516.

27. Ibid., 551, 554.

28. Ibid., 554, 561–562.

29. Ibid., 551–562.

CHAPTER 3

1. Howell Purdue & Elizabeth Purdue, *Pat Cleburne: Confederate General* (Hillsboro, TX, 1973), 205, 269ff.

2. Ibid., 269ff.

3. Ibid., 270.

4. Ibid., 5, 7, 9, 21, 23.

5. Ibid., 31, 204.

Charles Edward Nash, *Biographical Sketches of Gen. Pat Cleburne and Gen. T. C. Hindman* (Dayton, OH, 1977), 39.

6. Nash, 39.

Purdue & Purdue, 31, 37, 38, 44, 49, 52.

7. Ibid., 52.

8. Ibid., 67–74.

9. Ibid., 63–79.

10. Ibid., 67, 75.

11. Irving A. Buck, *Cleburne and His Command* (Wilmington, NC, 1987), 78ff.

OR 10-1-580, 581.

12. OR 10-1-570.

13. OR 16-1-934; OR 20-2-508, 509.

Purdue & Purdue, 163–164.

14. Ibid., 163, 164, 438.

15. Ibid., 50–52, 69, 75.

16. Ibid., 137–139, 149.

Nash, 202.

17. Purdue & Purdue, 182, 183, 238, 240ff, 263, 279.
18. Ibid., 188–189.
19. Ibid., 454ff.
20. Ibid., 271–273.
21. Ibid., 269–270.
22. Ibid., 238, 267, 290.
23. Ibid., 285.
24. Clement Easton, *Jefferson Davis* (New York, 1977), x, xi, 269ff.
25. Ibid., 13ff.
26. Ibid., 161.
Faust, 75.
Connelly, 70ff., 277, 278.
27. Ibid., 278.
Rowland, 2:503.
28. Buck, 360.
29. Rowland, 2:159, 160.
30. Connelly, 313.
31. Ibid., 319.
32. Ibid., 321–322.

CHAPTER 4

1. Ibid., 321.
MCCW, 555.
2. McMurry, 85–88.
MCCW, 565.
3. Ibid., 552, 559, 567.
4. Eaton, 140, 182.
Connelly, 281–283.
McMurry, 88–89.
5. Connelly, 323, 390.
6. Ibid., 413.
OR 30-2-35.
7. Connelly, 322–323.
8. Ibid., 323.
9. MCCW, 551.
10. Connelly, 321.
11. Ibid., 322–323.
John Bell Hood, letters, March 10, April 3, April 13, 1864, Braxton Bragg Papers (WRHS).
12. Hood, letter, April 13, 1864, Braxton Bragg Papers (WRHS), 323–324.
13. Faust, 28–30.
14. Ibid.
15. *Civil War Times Illustrated, Special Atlanta Edition*, (Harrisburg, PA, 1964), 38.
16. Ibid.
Faust, 28–30.
17. Connelly, 391.
James N. Beatty, diary, 1864, private collection (Seattle, WA), 57.
18. Connelly, 390.
MCCW, 635.
19. Connelly, 371, 387, 388.
MCCW, 635, 636.
20. Connelly, 411–413.
21. Ibid., 411–416.

22. Ibid., 415–419.
OR 38-5-881.
23. Connelly, 416–420.
OR 39-2-712–714.
24. OR 39-2-712–714.
Connelly, 416–420.
25. OR 38-5-885.

CHAPTER 5

1. MCCW, 579, 608, 622.
2. Ibid., 622.
3. Ibid., 635, 636.
4. Ibid., 622.
5. OR 38-5-885, 888.
6. Isham G. Harris, letter, September 16, 1864, Braxton Bragg Papers (WRHS).
OR 38-5-988.
7. John Bell Hood, letter, April 13, 1864, Braxton Bragg Papers (WRHS).
OR 38-5-879, 880.
8. OR 38-5-885–888; OR 39-2-714; OR 52-2-692.
McMurry, 122–123.
Connelly, 418ff.
9. Brown, 107.
James C. Nisbet, *Four Years on the Firing Line* (Chattanooga, TN, 1914), 305.
10. Sherman, 2:72–75
OR 38-5-183.
11. Oliver O. Howard, letter, July 23, 1864 (Brunswick, ME, Bowdoin College Library).
12. Connelly, 419–423.
OR 38-5-888.
Isham G. Harris, letter, September 16, 1864, Braxton Bragg Papers (WRHS).
13. Connelly, 424, 439ff.
14. Ibid., 446ff.
15. Ibid., 454ff.
16. OR 38-5-940.
17. Connelly, 458ff.
18. Ibid., 459ff.
19. Ibid., 460ff.
20. Sherman, 2:75ff.
21. Ibid.
Connelly, 453–468.

CHAPTER 6

1. MCCW, 646–647.
2. Ibid.
3. Ibid., 653.
4. Connelly, 468ff.
McMurry, 157.
5. OR 38-5-1016, 1018.
6. OR 38-5-946.
7. OR 38-5-908.
8. MCCW, 646.
Jefferson Davis, *The Rise and Fall of the Confederate Government* (New York, 1881), 2:565.

9. Dyer, 274–276.
Connelly, 470ff.
10. MCCW, 646.
11. Nash, 15, 38–39.
Purdue & Purdue, 69.
12. Ibid., 284, 285.
13. Ibid., 285.
14. Ibid., 285, 286, 298.
15. Ibid., 293.
16. Ibid., 294–295.
17. Ibid., 295, 339.
18. Ibid., 293, 339, 340.
19. Ibid., 272.
20. Ibid., 272–273.
21. Ibid., 273.
22. Ibid., 274.
Thomas Robson Hay, *Pat Cleburne: Stonewall Jackson of the West* (Wilmington, NC. 1987), 52.
23. Purdue & Purdue, 270.
24. Ibid., 387.

CHAPTER 7

1. Connelly, 432–433.
2. Eugene McWayne, letters, June 22, July 17, 1864, private collection, (Birmingham, MI).
3. Gerald F. Linderman, *Embattled Courage: The Experience of Combat in the American Civil War* (New York: 1987), 61–62.
4. Claud E. Fuller, *The Rifled Musket* (Harrisburg, PA, 1958), 3, 4, 53.
Wiley Sword, *Firepower From Abroad: The Confederate Enfield and the LeMat Revolver 1861–1863* (Lincoln, RI, 1986), 68.
Dean S. Thomas, *Ready, Aim, Fire! Small Arms Ammunition in the Battle of Gettysburg* (Biglersville, PA, 1981), 1–5.
5. Linderman, 135–139.
6. Eugene McWayne, letter, August 8, 1864, private collection, (Birmingham, MI).
OR 38-5-792.
7. OR 38-5-909.
Connelly, 470.
8. Eugene McWayne, letter August 1, 1864, private collection, (Birmingham, MI).
9. OR 38-5-792.
10. OR 39-2-893.
McMurry, 154, 155.
Rowland, 2:335.
11. Connelly, 470ff.
Hood, *Advance and Retreat*, 243–253.
See also Robert Underwood Johnson & Clarence Clough Buel, *Battles and Leaders of the Civil War* (New York, 1936), 4:336–344.
12. OR 38-5-972, 1021; OR 39-2-832.
Hood, *Advance and Retreat*, 249.
13. OR 38-5-1023, 1024.
Hood, *Advance and Retreat*, 245ff.

14. John B. Hood, letters, March 10, April 3, April 13, 1864, Braxton Bragg Papers (WRHS).
15. MCCW, 519.
Eaton, 2:272–273.
16. Connelly, 476–479.
17. Ibid., 479, 492.
18. Davis, 2:565.
19. Hood, *Advance and Retreat*, 254, 255.
20. Ibid., 255.
OR 39-2-880.
21. OR 39-2-879.
22. OR 39-2-880.
Rowland, 6:353.
23. Davis, 2:565.
Rowland, 6:353.
OR 39-2-880; OR 39-3-782, 870, 874.
Hood, *Advance and Retreat*, 258.
24. Connelly, 472ff.
MCCW, 652.
25. Connelly, 472ff.
D. W. Adams, letter to Braxton Bragg, September 16, 1864, Braxton Bragg papers (WRHS).
OR 39-3-782.
26. Alfred Roman, *The Military Operations of General Beauregard in the War Between the States 1861 to 1865* (New York, 1883), 2:277ff.
27. Connelly, 476ff.
28. Ibid., 481ff.
Roman, 2:281ff.
OR 39-3-795, 812.
29. Roman, 2:290ff.
Connelly, 486ff.
30. OR 39-3-870, 891.
31. OR 39-3-825, 826, 870, 874.
Connelly, 472–476.
32. MCCW, 658.

CHAPTER 8

1. MCCW, 650–652.
Rowland, 6:349–356.
2. MCCW, 650, 651.
3. Ibid.
4. Ibid.
5. Ibid., 652.
6. Sherman, 2:141, 142.
7. Purdue & Purdue, 382, 387.
8. Ibid., 388.
9. Brown, 140.
10. Ibid., 137, 138.
OR 39-1-806.
11. OR 39-1-802, 806, 807.
12. OR 39-1-802, 816–818.
13. OR 39-1-588.
Brown, 138.
14. OR 39-1-802; OR 39-3-804.
Hood, *Advance and Retreat*, 258, 259.

15. OR 39-1-753, 796, 802, 807; OR 39-3-812.
16. OR 39-1-718–720.
17. OR 39-1-720–723.
18. OR 39-1-802.
Brown, 140, 141.
19. OR 39-1-802; OR 39-3-831.
20. MCCW, 441, 648, 649.
Wright, 161.
21. MCCW, 620–625, 709.
Wright, 183.
22. OR 39-2-413, 464, 532, 540.
23. OR 39-3-3.
24. OR 39-3-202, 222.
25. OR 39-1-581; OR 39-2-502–504, 518, 540.
Sherman, 2:144.
26. OR 39-1-581, 760–782.
Sherman, 2:147.
27. OR 39-1-581ff.
Sherman, 2:151.
28. Sherman, 2:113, 152.
OR 39-2-412.
29. OR 39-3-202ff.
30. OR 39-3-202.
31. OR 39-1-582ff; OR 39-3-202.
32. Sherman, 2:152, 153.
33. OR 39-1-601, 731, 752ff, 791.
Sherman, 2:154.
34. Sherman, 2:154, 157.
OR 39-1-601, 602, 754, 791.
35. OR 39-3-203.
36. OR 39-1-604.
37. Sherman, 2:158, 159.
38. OR 39-2-480; OR 39-3-222.
39. Eugene McWayne, letter, October 23, 1864, private collection, (Birmingham, MI).
Andrew McCornack, letter, November 8, 1864, (Birmingham, MI).
40. OR 39-1-588; OR 39-3-467.
41. OR 39-3-406.

CHAPTER 9

1. Roman, 2:286ff.
2. Ibid., 2:288.
Hood, *Advance and Retreat*, 269.
OR 45-1-647.
3. Ibid.
4. Ibid.
5. Ibid.
6. OR 39-3-841.
Roman, 2:291.
7. Ibid., 2:293.
OR 39-1-695, 696.
8. OR 45-1-648.
Roman, 2:292.
Hood, *Advance and Retreat*, 259.
9. OR 39-1-696, 697; OR 39-3-613, 858, 865, 866, 870.

10. Roman, 2:292, 295.
Brown, 142.
J. M. Miller, *Recollections of a Pine Knot in the Lost Cause* (Greenwood, MS, 1900), 29.
11. OR 39-3-613, 746, 858.
Marshall P. Thatcher, *A Hundred Battles in the West—St. Louis to Atlanta, 1861–1865—The Second Michigan Cavalry* (Detroit, 1884), 350ff.
12. OR 39-3-867, 870.
13. OR 39-1-808, 811; OR 39-3-746.
Roman, 2:296.
14. OR 39-3-874, 890.
15. OR 39-1-799; OR 39-3-879, 880.
Roman, 2:298.
16. OR 39-3-843.
17. OR 39-1-869, 870; OR 39-3-853, 863, 913.
Nathan B. Forrest, letter, November 3, 1864, to J. B. Hood, Schoff Collection (Ann Arbor, MI: William L. Clements Library, University of Michigan).
18. Ibid.
OR 39-1-868, 869.
19. OR 39-1-871; OR 45-1-752.
20. OR 39-1-808; OR 39-3-879, 880, 913; OR 45-1-752.
Roman, 2:297.
21. OR 39-3-613, 845, 846, 856, 868, 871, 881.
Hood, *Advance and Retreat*, 271.
Brown, p. 142.
Mary A. H. Gay, *Life in Dixie During the War*, (Atlanta, 1979), 248.
22. OR 39-1-808; OR 39-3-881, 900, 904; OR 45-1-669.
23. Edward Whitesides, diary entries, October, November 1864, Civil War Times Illustrated Collection. (USAMHI).
Wayne E. Morris, letter, October 23, 1864 (BHL).
OR 39-3-880.
24. Thatcher, 350.
OR 39-1-808; OR 39-3-904.
25. Hood, *Advance and Retreat*, 271.
Roman, 2:608.
OR 45-1-1208, 1210, 1215, 1219.
26. Roman, 2:299ff.
27. Ibid., 2:606.
OR 39-3-913.
28. OR 39-3-914.
29. Roman, 2:607.
30. OR 45-1-1209, 1213.
31. OR 39-3-891, 913.
32. OR 39-3-896.
33. OR 39-3-913.
34. OR 39-1-808; OR 39-3-903, 904, 911, 914.
35. OR 45-1-669.

C. T. Quintard, diary entries, November 1864 (DPL).

Edward Whitesides, diary entries, November 1864 (USAMHI).

36. OR 45-1-1211.

Brown, 145.

37. OR 39-3-747.

38. OR 39-3-871; OR 45-1-669.

39. OR 45-1-1210–1216.

40. OR 39-1-803; OR 45-1-649, 650, 1215, 1218–1225.

Roman, 2:303–306.

41. OR 45-1-1210.

42. C. T. Quintard, diary entries, November 1864 (DPL).

OR 45-1-1219, 1221, 1228.

43. OR 45-1-1215, 1227.

44. OR 45-1-1220, 1226.

45. OR 45-1-1215–1220.

46. OR 45-1-1225, 1237, 1251, 1254, 1257.

47. OR 45-1-1220, 1221.

48. OR 45-1-1227.

49. MCCW, 657, 669.

CHAPTER 10

1. Freeman Cleaves, *Rock of Chickamauga: The Life of General George H. Thomas* (Norman, OK, 1948), 3–5, 44.

2. Ibid., 28, 178, 179.

3. Ibid., 54, 55.

Francis McKinney, *Education in Violence: The Life of George H. Thomas* (Detroit, 1961), 65.

4. Cleaves, p. 76.

McKinney, p. 93

5. Cleaves, 78.

6. Ibid., 186, 187.

McKinney, 138.

7. Cleaves, 108, 112, 118.

8. Ibid., 185, 187, 191ff.

9. Ibid., 192, 208.

10. Ibid., 220.

OR 38-5-793.

11. OR 38-5-150, 594; OR 39-2-501, 502, 517; OR 39-3-202.

12. OR 39-1-588, 594.

13. OR 39-1-588ff, 858ff.

14. Cleaves, 179, 186.

15. Ibid., 9.

James F. Rusling, *Men and Things I Saw in Civil War Days*, (Cincinnati, 1899), 80.

McKinney, 300, 301.

16. Cleaves, 20.

McKinney, 304–305.

17. McKinney, 52, 479.

Cleaves, 49.

18. OR 39-3-202, 449, 746; OR 45-1-920, 923, 933.

19. OR 45-1-572.

20. Ezra J. Warner, *Generals in Blue* (Baton Rouge, LA, 1964), 104.

OR 39-3-435.

21. Thatcher, 193.

OR 45-1-572.

22. OR 45-1-572.

Records of the Chief of Ordnance, 1864, Summary Statements of Ordnance in the Hands of the Troops, Records Group 156, National Archives, Washington, DC.

23. OR 39-3-607.

24. OR 45-1-575, 581.

25. OR 39-3-547; OR 45-1-577, 936, 937.

26. OR 39-3-540–547.

27. OR 39-3-646.

28. OR 45-1-888.

29. OR 45-1-887, 898.

30. OR 45-1-896, 910.

31. OR 45-1-942, 943.

32. Ibid.

33. OR 45-1-945, 954, 956.

34. OR 45-1-955.

35. OR 45-1-955.

36. OR 45-1-970.

37. OR 45-1-970, 983, 989.

38. E. L. Humphreys, letter, November 20, 1864, *Civil War Miscellaneous Collection*, (USAMHI).

E. G. Whitesides, diary, November, 1864, *Civil War Times Illustrated Collection* (USAMHI).

L. P. Bradley, letters, October 12, November 15, 1864, *Bradley Papers* (USAMHI).

39. Jacob Cox, diary, November 21, 1864, (Marietta, GA: Kennesaw Mountain National Military Park).

OR 45-1-357.

40. OR 45-1-970–974.

41. OR 45-1-974.

42. OR 45-1-970.

43. Bill Coleman & Sue Coleman, eds., "The Civil War Letters of William Troyer, 112th Illinois Volunteers," *The Kepi* (August–September 1985), p. 37.

44. OR 45-1-895, 1034.

45. OR 10-1-1034; OR 39-3-615; OR 45-1-557, 560, 1034.

Edward G. Longacre, *From Union Stars to Top Hat: A Biography of the Extraordinary General James Harrison Wilson* (Harrisburg, PA, 1972), 166, 179.

46. OR 45-1-919, 920, 970, 1024, 1034.

47. OR 39-1-370; OR 39-3-537.

48. OR 39-2-250.

49. OR 39-3-509, 537.

50. OR 39-3-595, 746.

51. OR 45-1-894.

52. OR 45-1-995, 1032,

53. OR 45-1-1056.

54. OR 45-1-53, 953, 954, 969, 1014.
55. Coleman & Coleman, 37.

CHAPTER 11

1. OR 39-1-805; OR 45-1-730.
Brown, 144.
2. George Peddy Cuttino, ed., *Saddle Bag and Spinning Wheel, Being the Civil War letters of George W. Peddy, M.D. and his wife Kate Featherston Peddy* (Macon, GA, 1981), 296.
OR 39-1-808.
Wright, 174.
3. Cuttino, 174.
Stephen D. Lee, letter, November 12, 1902, Capers Papers (SHC).
McMurry, 83, 99.
Wright, 161, 173.
MCCW, 576, 709.
4. OR 45-1-1227, 1236.
5. Brown, 145.
6. Quintard, diary, November 22, 1864 (DPL).
7. OR 45-1-657, 669, 670, 730, 752.
8. OR 45-1-657, 719, 736.
9. OR 45-1-669, 730.
10. OR 45-1-730, 736.
Brown, 146.
11. OR 45-1-597, 752, 763, 1005.
12. John A. Wyeth, *Life of Nathan Bedford Forrest* (Dayton, OH, 1968), 536, 537.
Thomas Jordan & J. P. Pryor, *The Campaigns of Lieut. Gen. N. B. Forrest and of Forrest's Cavalry* (Dayton, OH, 1988), 615.
OR 45-1-752, 763.
13. OR 45-1-657, 670, 1243.
14. OR 45-1-1243.
15. OR 45-1-768.
16. OR 45-1-357, 768.
Henry M. Hempstead, journal, 1864 (BHL), 169.
Brown, 146.
17. OR 45-1-400, 999, 1005, 1020.
18. OR 45-1-357, 400, 428, 1021.
Coleman & Coleman, 37.
19. OR 45-1-357, 400, 401, 763.
20. OR 45-1-357, 378, 401.
21. Quintard, diary, November 25, 1864 (DPL).
OR 45-1-1245.
22. Brown, 146.
F. Halsey Wigfall, letter, December 5, 1864 (LOC).
23. Purdue & Purdue, 392.
Author's field notes, Columbia, TN, May 1989.
Frank H. Smith, *History of Maury County, Tenn.,* book 1, (Columbia, TN, 1959), 27.
Buck, 280.

Irving A. Buck, *Cleburne and His Command* (Wilmington, NC, 1987).
Brown, 146.
24. Quintard, diary, November 26, 1864 (DPL).
OR 45-1-670.
25. OR 45-1-670, 752, 769.
26. OR 45-1-670.
Quintard, diary, November 27, 1864 (DPL).
27. OR 45-1-730.
Smith, 255.
28. Quintard, diary, November 27, 1864 (DPL).
29. OR 45-1-687, 731.
Smith, 254.
Quintard, diary, November 28, 1864 (DPL).
30. OR 45-1-1243, 1254.
Quintard, diary, November 28, 1864 (DPL).
31. OR 45-1-657.
Quintard, diary, November 28, 1864 (DPL).
32. Sam R. Watkins, *"Co. Aytch," Maury Grays First Tenn. Regiment, Or a Side Show of the Big Show* (Wilmington, NC, 1987), 216, 217.
Smith, 51.
Brown, 146.
33. OR 45-1-693, 731, 1255.
Smith, 26.
34. Ibid., p. 76.
Quintard, diary, December 15, 1864 (DPL).
OR 45-1-693.
35. OR 45-1-604, 752, 753.
Jordan & Pryor, 619.
Confederate Veteran, 16:25.
36. OR 45-1-604, 769.
CV 16:25.
37. Smith, 250, 254.
OR 45-1-721, 742.
38. Smith, 33, 250.
OR 45-1-742.
39. Quintard, diary, November 28, 1864 (DPL).
40. Hood, *Advance and Retreat*, 283.

CHAPTER 12

1. James Lee McDonough, *Schofield, Union General in the Civil War and Reconstruction* (Tallahassee, 1972).
James Lee McDonough & Thomas L. Connelly, *Five Tragic Hours: The Battle of Franklin* (Knoxville, TN, 1983), 24–27.
2. Ibid.
3. OR 38-5-792, 793; OR 39-2-540; OR 39-3-64, 685; OR 45-1-959.
4. OR 45-1-340, 650, 955, 956.
5. OR 45-1-972, 1020.
6. OR 45-1-357, 973, 974, 998, 1017.
7. OR 45-1-113, 144, 357, 1016, 1017, 1039.

8. OR 45-1-1016, 1018.
9. Faust, 161.
Smith, 25.
Hempstead, journal, 1864, (BHL), 169.
10. Quintard, diary, November 26, 1864 (DPL).
OR 45-1-1252.
Smith, 26, 244.
11. Smith, 3, 4, 26.
Coleman, 36.
12. OR 45-1-113, 146.
David S. Stanley, *Personal Memoirs of Major General David Sloane Stanley, U.S.A.* (Cambridge, MA, 1917), 194.
13. OR 45-1-1039, 1040.
14. OR 45-1-145, 1035, 1036, 1056, 1061.
15. OR 45-1-1065, 1068, 1085–1087, 1089, 1093.
16. OR 45-1-1085.
17. OR 45-1-1085, 1087, 1090.
18. Quintard, diary, November 27, 1864 (DPL).
OR 45-1-1087, 1088.
19. OR 45-1-1106.
20. Ibid.
21. OR 45-1-402, 1059, 1088, 1116, 1160.
22. OR 45-1-147, 1107.
23. OR 45-1-1111, 1122, 1123.
24. OR 45-1-588, 1112.
25. Jordan & Pryor, 619.
OR 45-1-769.
26. OR 45-1-604, 1123, 1124.
27. OR 45-1-558, 1112, 1113, 1143, 1149.
28. OR 45-1-1143.
Jacob D. Cox, *The Battle of Franklin, Tennessee November 30, 1864* (Dayton, OH, 1983), 26.
29. OR 45-1-147, 1144.
30. OR 45-1-112, 1107, 1108.
Smith, 33, 250.
31. OR 45-1-147, 1115.
32. OR 45-1-1112.
33. OR 45-1-1108, 1111–1115.
34. OR 45-1-147, 1107, 1115.
35. OR 45-1-147, 1107, 1115.
36. Faust, 841, 842.
OR 45-1-147, 1114, 1115.
37. OR 45-1-113, 147.
38. OR 45-1-1113.
39. OR 45-1-1141–1144.
John M. Schofield, *Forty-Six Years in the Army* (New York, 1897), 210.
40. Schofield, 212.
Cox, 27, 28.
OR 45-1-147, 1108.
41. OR 45-1-1108.
Cox, 27, 28.
42. Schofield, 210, 213.
Cox, 27.

43. Schofield, 210.
OR 45-1-1137, 1139, 1141.
44. OR 45-1-1137, 1141, 1142.
45. OR 45-1-996, 1015, 1036, 1108.

CHAPTER 13

1. Longacre, 66, 67, 93.
2. Ibid., 75, 153, 155.
3. Ibid., 95–104, 110.
4. Ibid., 30, 53, 133–144, 153–155.
5. Ibid., 160.
OR 39-2-442.
6. Faust, 832, 833.
7. Longacre, 153.
OR 45-1-1112.
8. OR 45-1-53, 54, 558, 559, 588.
9. OR 45-1-559, 680, 753.
W. R. Carter, *History of the First Regiment of Tennessee Volunteer Cavalry in the Great War of the Rebellion* (Knoxville, TN, 1902), 209.
10. OR 45-1-753.
11. Carter, 208.
OR 45-1-559.
12. Summary Statement of Ordnance Returns, RG 156, Vol. 8, National Archives, Washington, DC.
Granville C. West, *Personal Recollections of Hood in Tennessee* Washington, D.C., (1906), 7.
13. OR 45-1-588.
West, 8.
14. Ibid.
15. OR 45-1-1144.
16. Ibid.
17. OR 45-1-559.
18. OR 45-1-559, 1144, 1146.
19. OR 45-1-588, 1144–1146.
20. OR 45-1-1144, 1145, 1146, 1151.
21. OR 45-1-1145, 1177.
22. Quintard, diary, November 29, 1864 (DPL).
23. Memoir, Joseph B. Cummings Papers (SHC), 72.
24. OR 45-1-687, 731.
Cox, 27.
25. OR 45-1-742, 1137.
Smith, 237, 254.
Hood, *Advance and Retreat*, 254.
W. O. Dodd, "Reminiscences of Hood's Tennessee Campaign," *Southern Historical Society Papers* 9:528.
26. CV 16-26.
Dodd, 9:520, 528.
Smith, 237, 254.
OR 45-1-1137.
Purdue & Purdue, 393.
27. Smith, 127, 237, 238, 250, 254.
Purdue & Purdue, 393.

28. Smith, 237, 238, 250.
29. Ibid., 238, 250, 254.
30. Ibid., 238.
Dodd, 9:537.
31. Watkins, 217.
32. Smith, 238.
33. Smith, 254.
34. Dodd, 9:524.
45-1-712.
35. OR 45-1-753, 769.
West, 8.
36. CV 16-26.
OR 45-1-753, 763, 1146.
37. OR 45-1-1070, 1152.
38. OR 45-1-248, 331.
Hempstead, journal, 1864 (BHL), 172.
Cox, 31.
39. OR 45-1-1152.
40. OR 45-1-1125, 1149–1151.
41. OR 45-1-88, 559, 576, 753, 1111–1113.
42. Hempstead, journal, 1864 (BHL), 172.
OR 45-1-88, 559, 753.
43. Hempstead, journal, 1864 (BHL), 172.
44. Ibid.
45. OR 45-1-753.
Summary Statement of Ordnance Reports, RG 156, Vol. 8, National Archives, Washington, DC.
46. OR 45-1-753.
Hempstead, journal, 1864 (BHL), 172.
47. OR 45-1-753.
48. Hempstead, journal, 1864 (BHL), 172.
OR 45-1-248, 331.
49. OR 45-1-753.
50. OR 45-1-122, 148, 174, 229.
51. OR 45-1-114, 147, 148, 1141, 1142.
Stanley, 315.
52. OR 45-1-113, 148.
Cox, 27.
53. Stanley, 315.
OR 45-1-113, 148, 1152.
54. OR 45-1-122, 148, 229, 239, 250, 255.
55. OR 45-1-230, 255.
CV 16-30.
56. OR 45-1-113, 230, 268, 275, 277, 331.
Hempstead, journal, 1864 (BHL), 172.
John K. Shellenberger, "The Battle of Spring Hill, Tennessee" (MOLLUS, Missouri Commandery, 1907), 8, 9.
57. OR 45-1-753.
David E. Roth, "The Mysteries of Spring Hill, Tennessee," *Blue and Gray Magazine* 2(2):23.
58. Shellenberger, 8–10.
OR 45-1-268, 319, 320, 322, 330, 331.
Roth, 23.
59. OR 45-1-753.
60. OR 45-1-653, 1137.
Bromfield L. Ridley, *Battles and Sketches of the Army of Tennessee* (Dayton, OH, 1978), 416.
61. CV 12-338.

CHAPTER 14

1. Dodd, 9:524.
OR 45-1-712.
B. F. Cheatham, "The Lost Opportunity at Spring Hill," *Southern Historical Society Papers* v.9 p. 535.
2. Ibid., 524.
Purdue & Purdue, 396.
CV 12-342.
3. Hood, *Advance and Retreat*, 284, 285.
Cheatham, 9:534.
OR 45-1-113, 657, 753.
4. OR 45-1-753.
5. Purdue & Purdue, 395.
Dodd, 9:520
6. CV 16-31.
Thomas R. Hay, *Hood's Tennessee Campaign* (New York, 1929), 232.
OR 45-1-753.
7. OR 45-1-753.
8. CV 12-342; 16-31.
OR 45-1-742, 753.
9. OR 45-1-742.
CV 12-342; 16-31.
10. OR 45-1-670.
Roth, 37.
Smith, 238.
CV 16-38.
11. OR 45-1-230, 753.
Purdue & Purdue, 398, 399.
CV 16-31.
Buck, 272.
12. OR 45-1-113, 268, 275.
13. Cheatham, 9:536.
Shellenberger, 13.
14. OR 45-1-268, 275, 286.
CV 16-30.
Shellenberger, 12, 13.
15. OR 45-1-275.
16. OR 45-1-275.
17. CV 16-31.
18. Cheatham, 9:536.
OR 45-1-268, 277, 279.
Purdue & Purdue, 397.
19. Buck, 272.
Purdue & Purdue, 397.
Cheatham, 9:536.
OR 45-1-275.
20. OR 45-1-230, 275, 277.
21. OR 45-1-269, 275, 279.
Shellenberger, 13.
22. Ibid.
Shedd, letter, November 28, 1864, CWTI Collection (USAMHI).

23. Shellenberger, 14.
Stanley, 202.
24. Stanley, 181–183, 189, 193, 195.
25. OR 45-1-113, 1141.
26. OR 45-1-113, 148.
27. OR 45-1-63, 148, 230, 334.
CV 16-30.
OR 45-1-114.
28. OR 45-1-322.
Stanley, 201.
29. OR 45-1-230, 245, 336.
30. OR 45-1-245, 336.
31. OR 45-1-330.
Shellenberger, 14.
Stanley, 202.
32. OR 45-1-330.
Shellenberger, 14.
CV 16-32.
33. CV 16-32.
34. Ibid.
Cheatham, 9:525, 526.
35. Ibid., 537, 538.
OR 45-1-742.
36. OR 45-1-148.
37. CV 16-32.
OR 45-1-148.
38. OR 45-1-113, 114, 148, 268, 269.
39. OR 45-1-114, 230.
40. OR 45-1-255, 265.
41. Ibid.
Shellenberger, 13.
42. OR 45-1-255.
43. Ibid.
44. Faust, 83.
CV 16-33, 36.
Cheatham, 9:525, 526, 537, 538.
45. CV 16-33.
Cheatham, 9:525, 526.
46. CV 16-33, 35.
Cheatham, 9:538.
47. CV 16-33.
Cheatham, 9:526.
48. Buck, 272, 273.
CV 16-33.
49. CV 12-343; 16-33–35.
Cheatham, 9:525, 526, 538.
50. Faust, 135.
Levi T. Scofield, "The Retreat from Pulaski to Nashville," Sketches of War History (MOLLUS, Ohio Commandery), 2:137.
Connelly, 84–85.
51. CV 16-33, 34.
52. Cheatham, 9:525, 538.
53. Ibid.
Purdue & Purdue, 399.
Watkins, 217.
54. Cheatham, 9:538.
55. Smith, 238, 239.
OR 45-1-657, 712, 1258.
56. Hood, Advance and Retreat, 285.

57. Ibid., 285, 286.
Purdue & Purdue, 399.
CV 16-39.
Cheatham, 9:535.
OR 45-1-712.
58. Hood, Advance and Retreat, 286.
Cheatham, 9:526.
CV 16-34, 36, 39.
OR 45-1-712.
59. OR 45-1-712.
Cheatham, 9:541.
60. Smith, 238.
61. OR 45-1-742.
CV 16-32.
62. OR 45-1-230, 742, 751.
Smith, 219.
63. Shellenberger, 18.
Smith, 219.
OR 45-1-742.
64. Cheatham, 9:541.
65. Ibid.
66. OR 45-1-712.
CV 16-39.
Roth, 38.
67. CV 16-39.
OR 45-1-742, 753, 764.
68. OR 45-1-753, 763.
69. OR 45-1-753, 763.
CV 16-36, 40.
70. OR 45-1-712.
CV 16-39.
71. OR 45-1-712, 713.
CV 16-39.
72. CV 16-32, 39.
OR 45-1-712, 720.
73. CV 16-39.
OR 45-1-713.
74. Ibid.
75. OR 45-1-720.
76. OR 45-1-742, 1133.
CV 16-26, 37, 38.

CHAPTER 15

1. OR 45-1-1108, 1137, 1142.
2. OR 45-1-122, 148, 1139, 1141.
3. OR 45-1-1139.
Smith, 98.
Robert L. Kimberly & Ephraim S. Holloway, The Forty-First Ohio Veteran Volunteer Infantry in the War of the Rebellion (Cleveland, OH, 1897), 98.
4. OR 45-1-1141.
86th Indiana, 472.
5. Stephen D. Lee, letter, December 6, 1864, James Thomas Harrison Papers (SHC).
OR 45-1-687.
F. Halsey Wigfall, letter, December 5, 1864, (LOC).
6. OR 45-1-1138, 1140.

David C. Bradley, letter, January 7, 1865, Miscellaneous Collection (USAMHI).
Whitesides, diary, November 27, 1864 (USAMHI).
Kimberly & Holloway, 98.
Arnold Gates, ed., *The Rough Side of War: The Civil War Journal of Chesley A. Mosman, 1st Lieutenant Company D, 59th Illinois Volunteer Infantry Regiment* (Garden City, NY, 1987), 312.
7. OR 45-1-122, 428.
8. OR 45-1-342, 1140.
9. OR 45-1-687, 693.
S. D. Lee, letter, December 6, 1864 (SHC).
10. Ibid.
Smith, 255.
CV 16-26.
OR 45-1-403, 694.
11. OR 45-1-404.
12. OR 45-1-123, 176.
86th Indiana, 473.
13. 86th Indiana, 473, 474.
B. F. Thompson, *History of the One Hundred Twelfth Regiment of Illinois Infantry in the Great War of the Rebellion 1862–1865* (Toulon, IL, 1885), 260.
14. 86th Indiana, 474.
15. Ibid.
16. OR 45-1-279, 379, 384, 393, 396.
Erastus Winters, *In the 50th Ohio Serving Uncle Sam,* (Cincinnati, n.d.), 116.
17. Thomas C. Thorburn, *My Experiences During the Civil War* (Cleveland, OH, privately printed, 1963), 143 (copy in CHA).
OR 45-1-148, 379.
CV 16-37.
Shellenberger, 19.
18. OR 45-1-148, 379.
19. OR 45-1-114, 148, 342.
20. Shellenberger, 21.
Smith, 255.
Roth, 34, 35.
OR 45-1-114.
21. OR 45-1-114, 148.
Stanley, 204.
22. OR 45-1-148, 769, 770.
23. Ibid.
24. OR 45-1-114, 148, 342, 770.
Henry M. Field, *Bright Skies and Dark Shadows* (Freeport, NY, 1970), 225.
CV 16-40.
Smith, 255.
25. Stanley, 204.
OR 45-1-148.
26. CV 16-35.
OR 45-1-736.
27. CV 16-32.
28. CV 16-34.
OR 45-1-736.
29. CV 16-35.

30. Cheatham, 9:541.
31. S. D. Lee, letter, June 12, 1878 (SHC).
OR 45-1-713.
CV 16-39.
32. OR 45-1-713.
33. Smith, 238, 239.
OR 45-1-770, 764.
34. Cheatham, 9:541.
Purdue & Purdue, 401.
35. Cheatham, 9:541.
36. Ibid., 532.
Hood, *Advance and Retreat*, 257.
CV 12-343.
Ridley, 436, 437.
37. CV 16-38.
38. CV 16-32, 38.
39. Ibid.
40. Ibid.
41. Field, 218, 219.
CV 16-38.
42. Charles A. Partridge, *History of the Ninety-Sixth Regiment Illinois Volunteer Infantry* (Chicago, 1887), 421.
Thompson, 261.
CV 16-38.
OR 45-1-114, 123, 148, 1057, 1085.
David C. Bradley, letter, January 7, 1865 (USAMHI). 86th Indiana, 475.
I. G. Bennett & William M. Haigh, *History of the Thirty-Sixth Regiment Illinois Volunteers during the War of the Rebellion* (Aurora, IL, 1876), 639.
43. OR 45-1-114, 148, 149, 342.
Partridge, 421.
David C. Bradley, letter, January 7, 1865 (USAMHI).
44. Cox, 34.
OR 45-1-114, 1138.
45. OR 45-1-114, 177.
Partridge, 421.
46. Cox, 33–35.
OR 45-1-416, 684, 687, 704.
S. D. Lee, letter, December 6, 1864 (SHC).
47. OR 45-1-115.
Stanley, 205.
48. OR 45-1-770.
49. OR 45-1-769, 770.
50. OR 45-1-115, 770.
Stanley, 205.
Field, 226.
51. Hempstead, journal, 1864 (BHL), 174.
OR 45-1-338.
W. S. Thurston, *History of the One Hundred and Eleventh Regiment O.V.I.* (Toledo, OH, 1894), 76.
52. OR 45-1-115.
Shellenberger, 18.
73rd Illinois, 457.
Wayne E. Morris, letter, December 6, 1864 (BHL).

L. P. Bradley, letter, December 20, 1864 Bradley Papers (USAMHI).
53. S. D. Lee, letters, December 6, 1864; May 17, 1878 (SHC).
Dodd, 9:521, 522.
Cheatham, 9:538, 539.
Hood, *Advance and Retreat*, 287–290, 356.
OR 45-1-653, 657.
CV 16-36.
54. OR 45-1-653, 1137.
55. Dodd, 9:522.
56. Alexander P. Stewart, letter, February 16, 1886, Lionel Baxter Collection, CWTI archives (USAMHI).

CHAPTER 16

1. CV 16-32.
Author's interviews with Laurie Kay and Jill Garrett, May 1989.
Cheatham, 9:532.
OR 45-1-657.
S.D. Lee, letter, December 6, 1864 (SHC).
2. Ibid.
3. Cheatham, 9:532.
CV 16-36.
4. J. B. Hood, letter, April 14, 1879, to S. D. Lee, Lee Papers (SHC).
Cheatham, 9:538.
5. R. R. Hancock, *Hancock's Diary: Or A History of the Second Tennessee Confederate Cavalry* (Nashville, TN, 1887), 520.
S. D. Lee, letter, December 6, 1864 (SHC).
Ridley, 409.
OR 45-1-239, 653.
Charles T. Clark, *Opdycke's Tigers, 125th O.V.I., A History of the Regiment and of the Campaigns and Battles of the Army of the Cumberland* (Columbus, OH, 1895), 332.
6. Watkins, 217.
OR 45-1-736.
73rd Illinois, 475.
7. Kimberly & Holloway, 101.
Partridge, 421.
OR 45-1-653, 731.
Thomas A. Head, *Campaigns and Battles of the Sixteenth Regiment Tennessee Volunteers in the War Between the States* (Nashville, TN, 1885), 375.
8. Cox, 35.
Watkins, 217.
Thompson, 265.
Hardin Perkins Figuers, "A Boy's Impression of the Battle of Franklin," Figuers Papers (TSL), 2.
Carter, 216.
9. Hancock, 519, 520.
OR 45-1-753, 754.
10. Hancock, 519.
73rd Illinois, 458

Clark, 332.
OR 45-1-239, 338.
11. OR 45-1-1168.
Cox, 24, 38, 39.
G. W. Lewis, *The Campaigns of the One Hundred Twenty Fourth Regiment Ohio Volunteer Infantry* (Akron, OH, 1894), 194.
Park Marshall, journal, *Williamson County* (TSL).
Thompson, 262.
Clark, 327, 328.
12. Bennett & Haigh, 648.
Cox, 39.
13. Schofield, 176, 177.
Thompson, 262.
Clark, 327, 328.
Partridge, 422.
OR 45-1-342.
14. OR 45-1-1137, 1139, 1146, 1168.
Schofield, 217, 218.
15. OR 45-1-1138, 1139, 1146, 1168.
Cox, 37, 38.
16. OR 45-1-1168, 1169.
17. Cox, 39.
18. OR 45-1-1169.
Field, 229.
19. OR 45-1-1169, 1170.
20. OR 45-1-1170.
21. OR 45-1-352, 1170.
Cox, 67.
Shellenberger, letter, October 2, 1913, Shellenberger Papers, Collection No. 845 (LOC).
Clark, 333.
Henry Stone, letter, March 19, 1889, Shellenberger Papers, Collection No. 845 (LOC).
22. Cox, 332.
Adam Weaver, letters, November 1864 (CHA).
William O. Mohrmann, journal, 1864 (CHA).
23. David C. Bradley, journal, 1864 (USAMHI).
Mohrmann, journal, 1864 (CHA), 91.
Hempstead, journal, 1864 (BHL), 173.
Lewis, 192.
Bennett & Haigh, 644.
24. David C. Bradley, journal, 1864 (USAMHI).
OR 45-1-239.
25. Cox, (Franklin), pp. 44, 45.
26. Morhmann, journal, 1864 (CHA), 91.
27. Bennett & Haigh, 648.
Miscellaneous notes (CHA).
28. Ridley, 418.
Smith, 202.
Miscellaneous notes (CHA).
N. A. Pinney, *History of the One Hundred Fourth Regiment Ohio Volunteer Infantry from 1862 to 1865* (Akron, OH, 1886), 60.
John Johnston, memoir (Nashville, TN: Tennessee Historical Society Library), 41.

29. Cox, 53.
Bennett & Haigh, 648.
30. OR 45-1-351.
Cox, 53.
31. Cox, 43, 44, 48, 55–57, 236.
32. Ibid., 53–55.
Figuers, 4.
33. Cox, 60.
Figuers, 4.
34. OR 45-1-53, 54.
35. Stanley, 205.
Anon., *History of Tennessee* (Nashville, 1886), 788.
36. *History of Tennessee*, 788–807.
37. Ibid.
73rd Illinois, 459.
38. *History of Tennessee*, 798ff.
39. Clark, 37, 42.
40. Ibid., 55.
Charles Marshall, "Battle of Franklin" (CHA).
Cox, 45, 48, 59.
Lewis, 193.
OR 45-1-432.
41. Cox, 39, 43.
Miscellaneous notes, (CHA).
Rosalie Carter, *Captain Tod Carter—Confederate States Army* (Franklin, TN, 1978), 8, 9, 34.
42. Cox, 52–55.
OR 45-1-350ff.
43. Cox, 52–55.
44. Ibid., 59–61.
OR 45-1-351.
45. Cox, 62.
46. Ibid., 50n, 280n.
Henry Stone, letter, March 19, 1889, Shellenberger Papers (LOC).
Quintard, diary, December 14, 1864 (DPL).
Shellenberger, letter, October 2, 1913, Shellenberger Papers (LOC).
Rosalie Carter, 10.
47. Cox, 280n.
48. OR 45-1-342, 343, 559, 1169, 1177.
49. OR 45-1-559, 560, 1177.
50. Thatcher, 202, 203, 306.
Summary Statement of Ordnance Reports, RG 156, National Archives, Washington, DC.
W. R. Carter, 214.
Hempstead, journal, 1864 (BHL), 174.
OR 45-1-573.
51. Thatcher, 203, 204, 305.
Hempstead, journal, 1864 (BHL), 174.
52. Thatcher, 204.
OR 45-1-573.
Hempstead, journal, 1864 (BHL), 174.
53. Ibid.
OR 45-1-573.
54. OR 45-1-1178.
55. OR 45-1-1170, 1171, 1178.

56. OR 45-1-150, 1174.
Cox, 280n.
57. Thompson, 267.

CHAPTER 17

1. Faust, 785.
OR 45-1-115, 123, 231, 269.
Cox, 221, 222.
A. P. Baldwin, letter, December 12, 1890, Shellenberger Papers (LOC).
2. Faust, 785.
OR 45-1-231.
3. OR 45-1-231, 239, 240.
Clark, 332.
4. OR 45-1-195, 338.
Partridge, 423.
5. Hancock, 720.
6. Partridge, 423.
OR 45-1-195, 231.
7. OR 45-1-231, 240.
Whitesides, diary, November 30, 1864 (USAMHI).
8. Partridge, 423.
9. Cox, 280n.
OR 45-1-349, 1169, 1174.
10. OR 45-1-231, 1174.
11. OR 45-1-149, 256, 352.
Whitesides, diary, November 30, 1864 (USAMHI).
Cox, 69, 70.
12. OR 45-1-231.
13. OR 45-1-240.
14. OR 45-1-331.
Bennett & Haigh, 644.
15. OR 45-1-231.
73rd Illinois, 452.
16. John K. Shellenberger, *The Battle of Franklin, Tennessee November 30, 1864* (Cleveland, OH, 1916), 16.
OR 45-1-231.
73rd Illinois, 436, 461.
17. 73rd Illinois, 436.
OR 45-1-231, 256.
Cox, 46, 73.
18. OR Atlas plate 73-4.
Cox, 46, 73, 75.
OR 45-1-231.
19. OR 45-1-231, 270.
Shellenberger, *Battle of Franklin*, 14.
Cox, 74.
20. Whitesides, letter, October 27, 1890, Shellenberger Papers (LOC).
73rd Illinois, 466, 467.
21. 73rd Illinois, 451.
Whitesides, letter, October 27, 1890, Shellenberger Papers (LOC).
22. 73rd Illinois, 466, 467.
Whitesides, letter, October 27, 1890, Shellenberger Papers (LOC).

23. Ibid.
Clark, 2, 3.
24. Clark, 2.
Stanley, 213.
Emerson Opdycke, letter to L. P. Bradley, November 8, 1864, Bradley Papers (USAMHI).
25. Cox, 223.
Faust, 795.
Scofield, 130.
26. Whitesides, letter, October 27, 1890, Shellenberger Papers (LOC).
Emerson Opdycke, letter, September 9, 1866, West-Stanley-Wright Papers (USAMHI).
David S. Stanley, memoir, West-Stanley-Wright Papers (USAMHI), 4.
OR 45-1-240, 1174.
27. Whitesides, letter, October 27, 1890, Shellenberger Papers (LOC).
73rd Illinois, 402, 433, 459.
OR 45-1-240.
28. OR 45-1-352.
29. OR 45-1-352, 1174.
Cox, 68.
30. Cox, 91.
OR 45-1-352.
31. OR 45-1-231, 256; OR Atlas plate 73-4.
32. OR 45-1-270.
33. OR 45-1-270.
34. OR 45-1-270, 284.
Shellenberger, *Battle of Franklin*, 19.
35. OR 45-1-256.
J. C. Lane, letter, May 10, 1889, Shellenberger Papers (LOC).
36. Thatcher, 208, 249.
37. OR 45-1-1174.
38. Shellenberger, *Battle of Franklin*, 14–17.
OR 45-1-280.
39. Shellenberger, *Battle of Franklin*, 17.
OR 45-1-280.
40. CV 12-338; 24-102.
Watkins, 217.
41. OR 45-1-231.
42. OR 45-1-653, 658.
CV 16-36.
OR 45-1-708.
43. Hood, *Advance and Retreat*, 290.
44. OR 45-1-231, 708, 736.
45. CV 1-16; 12-339; 18-19, 20.
Wyeth, 544.
S. D. Lee, letter, December 6, 1864 (SHC).
Field, 230.
46. Buck, 280, 281.
Virginia McDaniel Bowman, *Historic Williamson County Old Homes and Sites* (Franklin, TN, 1971), 157.
47. Head, 375.
Buck, 280.
Indianapolis Journal, March 12, 1883.
Wyeth, 544.

Hancock, 720.
Park Marshall, journal, 1864 (TSL), 135.
48. S. D. Lee, letter, June 4, 1879, Claiborne Papers (SHC).
Hood, *Advance and Retreat*, 290.
49. OR 45-1-731.
Buck, 280.
50. Head, 375.
51. Purdue & Purdue, 420.
Buck, 290, 291.
52. Cox, 46, 80, 280.
James A. Sexton, "The Observations and Experiences of a Captain of Infantry at the Battle of Franklin, November 30, 1864" (MOLLUS, Ohio Commandery), 2:473, 474.
Bennett & Haigh, 650.
53. OR 45-1-653, 678, 679, 708, 736, 737.
Hay, 130.
Cox, 86ff.
54. Ibid.
OR 45-1-653.
55. Cox, 87.
OR 45-1-708.
56. Cox, 87.
57. Ibid.
58. Ridley, 410.
CV 12-389; 24-102.
OR 45-1-720.
Thatcher, 315.
Buck, 290.
Hood, *Advance and Retreat*, 293.
Robert S. Bevier, *History of the First and Second Missouri Confederate Brigades, 1861–1865* (St. Louis, 1879), 251.
59. R. W. Banks, *The Battle of Franklin, November 30, 1864* (New York, 1908), 60–62.
Cox, 78, 80.
60. CV 24-102; 26-117, 118.
61. CV 12-339; 15-125, 126.
Ridley, 423.
62. Buck, 281.
Head, 375.
63. Purdue & Purdue, 421.
Brown, 147.
Indianapolis Journal, March 12, 1883.
64. William Houghton, letter, November 22, 1864 (BHL).
Adam Weaver, letters, November 30, 1864 (CHA).
65. Buck, 30, 289, 292.
Purdue & Purdue, 214.
CV 24-102.
66. *Indianapolis Journal*, March 12, 1883.
Miller, 27.
CV 24-102, 103.
W. D. Mintz, memoir: n, d. (CHA).
67. Scofield, 133.
Bennett, 650.

CHAPTER 18

1. Sexton, 473.
Thurston, 77.
Mohrmann, journal (CHA), 91.
Pinney, 77.
2. Clark, 332.
Winters, 118.
73rd Illinois, 439, 440, 442.
3. Morris, letter, November 30, 1864
(BHL).
Whitesides, diary, November 30, 1864
(USAMHI).
William C. Buchanan, diary, 1864, Civil War
Miscellaneous Collection (USAMHI).
Shellenberger, *Battle of Franklin*, 17.
Asbury L. Kerwood, *Annals of the Fifty-Seventh Regiment Indiana Volunteers* (Dayton,
OH, 1868), 298.
4. Cox, 53.
W. W. Gist, "The Battle of Franklin," *Tennessee Historical Magazine* 6(3):224.
5. Figuers, 1.
Smith, 202.
6. Morhmann, journal, CHA 92.
7. Sexton, 471.
8. Mohrmann, journal, 92.
9. Shellenberger, *Battle of Franklin*,
(BHL), 17, 19.
10. Hempstead, journal (BHL), 171.
CV 24-14.
Scofield, 132.
11. *Indianapolis Journal*, March 12, 1883.
Cox, 33.
W. R. Carter, 216.
John N. Beach, *History of the Fortieth Ohio
Volunteer Infantry* (London, OH, 1884), 97.
CV 12-339.
Morris C. Hutchins, "The Battle of Franklin,
Tennessee," (MOLLUS, Ohio Commandery),
5:279.
12. OR 45-1-322, 737.
Cox, 94.
A. J. Moon, letter, December 4, 1864, Leigh
Collection (USAMHI).
Adam Weaver, letters, November 30, 1864
(CHA).
CV 15-125.
13. CV 14-261, 262; 24-102, 346.
Brown, 147.
Mohrmann, journal, 1864 (CHA), 92.
Winters, 119.
Daniel C. Govan, letter, December 4, 1864,
Govan Papers (SHC).
Shellenberger, *Battle of Franklin*, 18.
14. Ibid.,19.
15. OR 45-1-331.
Faust, 321.
Scofield, 132.
Cox, 104, 107, 108, 337.
16. Purdue & Purdue, 422.

17. Scofield, 131, 132.
Cox, 336.
18. Ibid., 104–108, 337.
Scofield, 332.
19. Ibid.
20. Thatcher, 208, 249.
Cox (Franklin), 68, 71, 72.
21. Scofield, 133.
Winters, 119.
22. Cox, 94, 95.
The Civil War Collector's Encyclopedia, 27,
29.
Francis A. Lord,: Harrisburg, Pa.; 1963.
CV 12-339; 14-261.
OR 45-1-737.
23. Watkins, 219.
Kerwood, 296.
David C. Bradley, memoir, 1865 (USAMHI).
OR 45-1-270, 271.
Shellenberger, *Battle of Franklin*, 20.
24. Brown, 147.
Shellenberger, *Battle of Franklin*, 20.
Sexton, 475.
Buck, 276.
25. Shellenberger, *Battle of Franklin*, 21,
22.
26. Ibid.
27. J. C. Lane, letter, May 10, 1889, Shellenberger Papers (LOC).
OR 45-1-1133.
28. Gist, 276.
Kerwood, 297.
OR 45-1-256.
Mohrmann, journal, 1864 (CHA), 92.
Scofield, 133.
29. Shellenberger, *Battle of Franklin*, 21,
22.
30. Ibid., 22–25.
31. Ibid.
Mohrmann, journal, 1864 (CHA), 92.
Brown, 147.
32. Shellenberger, *Battle of Franklin*, 22–
25.
33. Ibid.
34. Mintz, memoir (CHA).
CV 9-117.
Winters, 120.
Buck, 286.
George W. Gordon, memoir of Franklin (n.d.)
(CHA).
Mohrmann, journal, 1864 (CHA) 92.
35. Shellenberger, *Battle of Franklin*, 35.
Winters, 120.
Stanley, 207.
36. Thomas Speed, "The Battle of Franklin" (MOLLUS, Ohio Commandery), 3:77.
Sexton, 475.
OR 45-1-322, 326, 419.
Cox, 108.
Scofield, 133, 134.

37. Shellenberger, *Battle of Franklin*, 24, 25.
Purdue & Purdue, 422.
Adam Weaver, letters, November 30, 1864, (CHA).
38. Shellenberger, *Battle of Franklin*, 24–26.
39. Ibid.
40. Gordon, memoir (CHA).
OR 45-1-232.
Potter, letter, January 15, 1865 (BHL).
Adam Weaver, letters, November 30, 1864 (CHA).
Pinney, 61.
Watkins, 219.
41. Buck, 286.
OR 45-1-421.
D. C. Bradley, memoir (USAMHI).
Pinney, 61.
42. Winters, 121, 122.
43. Cox, 52, 108.
OR 45-1-326.
44. Smith, 202.
45. Scofield, 134.
46. Thurston, 82.

CHAPTER 19

1. Cox, 67, 280n.
Bowman, 112.
OR 45-1-175, 1174, 1178.
2. OR 45-1-150.
Cox, 281n.
Bowman, 112.
3. Schofield, 138, 178, 180, 187, 233, 234.
4. Ibid., 233.
OR 45-1-150, 1173, 1174.
5. OR 45-1-115.
Stanley, 207.
6. Ibid.
OR 45-1-116.
Cox, 281n.
7. Thurston, 82.
Stanley, 207.
OR 45-1-116.
8. Clark, 333.
Cox, 95.
OR 45-1-240.
73rd Illinois, 444, 641.
9. 73rd Illinois, 402, 439, 440, 452.
Bennett & Haigh, 651, 652.
Clark, 338.
Israel P. Covey, letter, December 22, 1864 (BHL).
10. Bennett & Haigh, 651.
OR 45-1-240.
73rd Illinois, 444.
11. 73rd Illinois, 434, 437, 444, 461.
Summary Statements of Ordnance Reports, RG 156, National Archives, Washington, DC.
Clark, 338.

12. 73rd Illinois, 433, 434, 444.
13. Ibid.
14. Ibid., 434.
OR 45-1-240.
Sexton, 476.
Cox, 117.
Bennett & Haigh, 651, 652.
15. Emerson Opdycke, letter, September 9, 1866, Stanley Papers (USAMHI).
16. Morris, letters, December 2, 6, 1864 (BHL).
17. Scofield, 134.
73rd Illinois, 403, 462, 463.
18. Clark, 339.
73rd Illinois, 402, 440.
OR 45-1-251.
19. Clark, 339.
73rd Illinois, 440, 452, 462.
20. 73rd Illinois, 403, 433, 449, 462, 642.
21. Ibid., 440, 461, 462, 642.
22. Ibid., 444, 463.
Opdycke, eg. letter, September 9, 1866 (USAMHI).
23. 73rd Illinois, 403, 437, 442, 449, 463.
Clark, 339, 340.
Cox, 99.
24. 73rd Illinois, 440.
CV 15-563.
Thurston, 82, 83.
25. Bennett & Haigh, 653, 654.
26. Ibid., 656, 657.
73rd Illinois, 643.
Clark, 338.
OR 45-1-253.
27. Bennett & Haigh, 655.
28. 73rd Illinois, 404.
Covey, letter, December 22, 1864 (BHL).
29. 73rd Illinois, 404.
Clark, 341.
Joseph Conrad, letter, May 24, 1889, Shellenberger Papers (LOC).
Thurston, 83.
Cox, 42.
Smith, 202.
30. Thurston, 83.
Samuel G. Smith, "Military Small Arms" (MOLLUS, Ohio Commandery), 1:179.
Clark, 341.
31. Scofield, 136.
Brown, 148.
OR 45-1-240, 354.
Cox, 234.
Stanley, 207, 208.
Sexton, 417.
Gist, 244.
73rd Illinois, 461–463.
32. OR 45-1-241.
Stanley, 208.
33. Stanley, 208.
OR 45-1-116.

Cox, 99, 100.
J. Conrad, letter, May 24, 1889, Shellenberger Papers (LOC).
34. Cox, 91, 96.
35. Ibid.
73rd Illinois, 423.
36. Cox, 91, 96.
Smith, 202.
37. Smith, 202.
38. Cox, 149–153.
OR 45-1-354, 395.
39. Watkins, 219.
40. 73rd Illinois, 452, 464.
OR 45-1-321, 335, 336, 340, 251, 330.
Winters, 122.
41. D. C. Bradley, letter, December 1, 1864 (USAMHI).
Mohrmann, journal, 1864 (CHA), 93.
OR 45-1-354.
42. CV 12-334.
43. 73rd Illinois, 477, 478.
44. Ibid, 405.
CV 24-14.
45. 73rd Illinois, 404.
Brown, 149.
46. Sexton, 478.
Mohrmann, journal, 1864 (CHA), 93.
47. Ibid.
48. Sexton, 478.
49. Miscellaneous notes (CHA).
73rd Illinois, 467.
William D. Thompson, letter, February 24, 1890, Stanley Collection, West-Stanley-Wright Papers (USAMHI).
50. Cox, 47ff.
51. W. J. Worsham, *The Old Nineteenth Tennessee Regiment, C.S.A., June, 1861— April, 1865* (Knoxville, TN, 1902), 143.
52. CV 12-340.
53. Ibid.
54. Ibid.
55. Winters, 123.
56. Cox, 146, 147.
OR 45-1-354.
Thompson, 270.
57. Sexton, 479–481.
58. Ibid.
59. Ibid.
60. Ibid.
61. Thompson, 271.
62. Shellenberger, *Battle of Franklin*, 21, 22.
Mintz, memoir (CHA).
63. Watkins, 219.
73rd Illinois, 449, 450.
OR 45-1-241.
64. Smith, 202.
65. John Johnston, memoir (Nashville, TN: Tennessee Historical Library).

CHAPTER 20
1. Thompson, 269.
2. Cox, 52.
OR 45-1-53, 678–680.
C.S. Archives, Inspector's Report of Cleburne's Division, Records Group 109, Microcopy No. 935, Roll 5, National Archives, Washington, DC.
Jordan & Pryor, 611.
3. Scofield, 140.
4. Ibid., 130, 131.
David R. Logsdon, ed., *Eyewitnesses at the Battle of Franklin* (Nashville: 1988), 25, 26; quoting Joseph Nicholas Thompson, in *Williamson County Historical Journal* 15 (Spring 1984).
5. Ibid.
6. Ibid.
7. Ibid.
8. Ibid.
9. Banks, 55.
10. Carter family notes (CHA).
Scofield, 138.
OR 45-1-430.
11. Thompson, 269.
Banks, 56.
OR 45-1-430.
C. P. Neilson, letter, January 11, 1865 (CHA).
12. Thompson, 269.
Cox, 125.
OR 45-1-331, 430.
13. Field, 242.
Banks, 55.
14. Cox, 128.
Logsdon, 27.
CV 26-117.
15. Faust, 607.
OR 45-1-353, 720, 721.
Scofield, 138.
CV 11-166.
Thomas H. Williams, letter, December 7, 1864 (BHL).
Speed, 77.
16. Scofield, 131, 138, 140.
Thompson, 277.
17. Smith, 51, 115.
OR 45-1-721.
18. Banks, 52.
19. OR 45-1-720.
20. Virgil S. Murphey, diary, 1864 (SHC).
OR 45-1-720.
21. Cox, 42, 52–58.
Shellenberger, *Battle of Franklin*, 33.
Smith, 202.
73rd Illinois, 443.
22. Pinney, 61.
OR 45-1-720.
A. P. Baldwin, letter, February 12, 1890, Shellenberger Papers (LOC).
23. Scofield, 139.

Murphey, diary, 1864 (SHC), 3.
OR 45-1-720.
  24. Pinney, 61.
OR 45-1-216, 419, 421.
  25. OR 45-1-421.
Shellenberger, *Battle of Franklin*, 26, 27.
  26. Ibid., 26.
OR 45-1-326.
  27. OR 45-1-415, 418.
Hutchins, 281.
  28. Speed, 79.
Cox, 100, 103, 109, 113–115.
OR 45-1-411, 412, 415.
Scofield, 141,142.
  29. Smith, 202.
Cox, 111.
Speed, 80.
  30. Shellenberger, *Battle of Franklin*, 26.
  31. Hutchins, 281.
CV 15-563.
Thatcher, 207, 209.
Speed, 81.
  32. Purdue & Purdue, 422.
George W. Gordon, memoir, (CHA).
Brown, 148.
Head, 377.
  33. OR 45-1-412.
Shellenberger, *Battle of Franklin*, 26, 27.
Cox, 98n, 109–111.
Brown, 148.
  34. OR 45-1-246, 412.
  35. Buck, 289–291.
Purdue & Purdue, 414, 424–425.
  36. CV 18-426.
Purdue & Purdue, 424, 425.
  37. Buck, 289–292.
Purdue & Purdue, 423.
John P. Dyer & John Trotwood Moore, compilers, *The Tennessee Civil War Veterans Questionnaires*, Vol. 2 (Easley, SC: 1985), 489, 490.
  38. Purdue & Purdue, 424, 425.
Govan, letter, December 4, 1864 (SHC).
CV 18-426.
  39. Banks, 75, 77.
  40. CV 30-289.
  41. Shellenberger, *Battle of Franklin*, 29, 30.
Banks, 75, 76.
  42. Banks, 77–79.
  43. Ibid, 76.
Murphey, diary, (SHC), 7.
  44. Cox, 149.
Banks, 283.
OR 45-1-395.
  45. CV 19-32; 24-102, 103.
Logsdon, 21.
  46. CV 19-32; 24-102, 103.
  47. CV 21-582; 24-103, 551; 15-563.
Bevier, 252, 253.

Report of Chief of Ordnance, Records Group 156, Summary Statements, National Archives, Washington, DC.
  48. Thurston, 83.
  49. Faust, 2.
Field, 252.
CV 11-166, 167.
  50. Banks, 58, 59.
Logsdon, 27.
  51. CV 10-155; 11-166, 167.
Ridley, 417–420.
Miller, 21.
  52. Ridley, 417.
Field, 252, 253.
  53. Ridley, 417–420.
Pinney, 62.
OR 45-1-276.
  54. Cox, 152.
Speed, 94.
OR 45-416.
  55. Murphey, diary (SHC), 9.
OR 45-1-286.
  56. OR 45-1-416, 419.
Pinney, 62.
  57. Scofield, 139.
Thomas H. Williams, letter, December 7, 1864 (BHL).
Weaver, letters, November 30, 1864 (CHA).
  58. OR 45-1-334.
Scofield, 143.
  59. J. G. Harris, "A Souvenir of Franklin," *North-South Trader* (July-August 1982), 15ff.
  60. OR 45-1-720.
  61. Murphey, diary (SHC), 6, 7.
OR 45-1-421, 422.
Gordon, memoir (CHA).
  62. Murphey, diary, (SHC), 9.
Purdue & Purdue, 423.
  63. Murphey, diary (SHC) 8.
  64. Ibid.
Sexton, 477.
  65. Pinney, 62.
Gist, 229.
OR 45-1-422.
Gordon, memoir, (CHA).
  66. Banks, 79–83.
  67. Ibid, 79.
OR 45-1-418.
Thompson, 270, 271.
Sexton, 477.
  68. Shellenberger, *Battle of Franklin*, 33, 34.
Pinney, 63.
  69. Thatcher, 311, 315.
  70. Nash, 205.
D. C. Bradley, memoir (USAMHI).
Scofield, 138.
Milton A. Ryan, Civil War memoirs (CHA).
  71. Murphey, diary, (SHC), 10–12, 15–18.
  72. Ibid.

CHAPTER 21

1. Thatcher, 309.
2. Ibid.
3. Figuers, 3.
4. Partridge, 429.
CV 3-72, 73.
Rosalie Carter, 37–39.
Smith, 202.
5. Rosalie Carter, 38–40.
Logsdon, 3–5.
6. Rosalie Carter, 40, 41.
Field, 244.
7. Rosalie Carter, 34, 43.
8. Ibid.
James L. Cooper, "Diary of Captain James L. Cooper," *Tennessee Historical Quarterly* (June 1956), 165–167.
9. Figuers, p. 4.
Scofield, 143.
Cox, 245.
Thurston, 87.
Weaver, letters, November 30, 1864 (CHA).
10. Winters, 125.
Mohrmann, journal, 1864 (CHA), 93.
11. Sexton, 477.
Thurston, 82.
Cox, 108.
12. Thurston, 83, 85.
Mohrmann, journal, 1864 (CHA), 94.
Bradley Thompson, letter, December 7, 1864, Leigh Collection (USAMHI).
Gist, 228.
Bennett & Haigh, 654, 655.
73rd Illinois, 405, 454.
13. Thurston, 89.
14. Sexton, 479.
15. Mohrmann, journal, 1864 (CHA), 94.
Thurston, 83.
Sexton, 477.
16. Cox, 131.
OR 45-1-380, 387.
17. CV 12-343, 347.
OR 45-1-387, 680, 737.
Faust, 312.
18. CV 12-347.
OR 45-1-737.
J. Harvey Mathes, *The Old Guard in Gray* (n.d.), 170.
Logsdon, 42.
Quintard, diary, December 3, 1864 (DPL).
Watkins, 219.
19. CV 12-347.
Field, 239.
20. OR 45-1-684.
21. OR 45-1-743.
Park Marshall, journal, (TSL) 135.
Cox, 132, 133.
22. OR 45-1-743.
Park Marshall, journal, (TSL) 137, 139, 142–145.

23. OR 45-1-680, 743.
Cooper, 166, 167.
24. Covey, letter, December 22, 1864 (BHL).
OR 45-1-365, 388.
25. Morris, letters December 2, 6, 1864 (BHL).
OR 45-1-380, 383, 386.
26. Scofield, 145, 146.
Morris, letters, December 2, 6, 1864 (BHL).
27. OR 45-1-380, 384, 386.
Morris, letters, December 2, 6, 1864 (BHL).
28. Ibid.
OR 45-1-384, 385.
29. OR 45-1-208, 365.
30. OR 45-1-214, 743.
Cox, 138.
31. OR 45-1-743, 764.
Cox, 136–140.
32. Partridge, 429.
OR 45-1-764.
33. Cox, 147n.
34. OR 45-1-1179.
Park Marshall, journal, 133 (TSL).
35. Cox, 172, 174.
OR 45-1-678, 1181.
36. OR 45-1-576, 754, 770.
Cox, 176.
H. A. Potter, letter, July 19, 1864 (BHL).
37. OR 45-1-576, 770.
38. OR 45-1-576, 770, 1179.
39. OR 45-1-342, 344.
40. Mohrmann, journal, 1864 (CHA), 94.
41. Ibid.
42. Ibid., 94, 95.
Shellenberger, *Battle of Franklin*, 32, 33.
43. *Indianapolis Journal*, March 12, 1883.
CV 12-340.
Watkins, 219.
OR 45-1-737.
J. W. Kimmel, memoir, (CHA), 51.
44. Banks, 65.
Thurston, 83.
Cox, 81, 81n.
45. Mohrmann, journal, 1864 (CHA), 94, 95.
46. Sexton, 478.
47. OR 45-1-678, 679.
48. Sexton, 483.

CHAPTER 22

1. OR 45-1-669, 687.
Cox, 89.
Field, 240, 250.
John Johnston, memoir, 141.
Brown, 160n.
S. D. Lee, letter, November 12, 1902, Capers Papers (SHC).
2. OR 45-1-687.

J. B. Hood, letter, April 28, 1879, S. D. Lee Papers (SHC).
Field, 241.
Indianapolis Journal, March 12, 1883.
3. OR 45-1-687.
4. Mohrmann, journal, 1864 (CHA), 94.
S. D. Lee, letter, December 6, 1864, J. T. Harrison Papers (SHC).
5. 73rd Illinois, 478, 479.
CV 10-501.
6. Ibid.
Banks, 44–47.
7. Sexton, 479, 481.
Mohrmann, journal, 1864 (CHA), 96.
OR 45-1-393.
Banks, 44–47.
8. OR 45-1-688.
Thurston, 86.
S. D. Lee, letter, December 6, 1864 (SHC).
Mohrmann, journal, 1864 (CHA), 94.
9. Shellenberger, *Battle of Franklin*, 30.
Mohrmann, journal, 1864 (CHA), 94.
10. Cox, 164.
11. 73rd Illinois, 465.
Cox, 163, 164.
OR 45-1-354, 697.
12. 73rd Illinois, 454, 465, 478.
CV 12-341.
13. CV 12-341.
14. Thoburn, 149.
15. J. C. Harris, "A Souvenir of Franklin," *North South Trader* (July–August, 1982: 15ff.
16. Shellenberger, *Battle of Franklin*, 33, 34.
17. Ibid.
18. OR 45-1-240.
Pinney, 63.
Moon, letters, December 4, 24, 1864, Leigh Collection (USAMHI).
19. Hutchins, 280.
Mohrmann, journal, 1864 (CHA), 95
20. Cox, 169, 338.
21. Ibid, 287n.
John M. Schofield, letter to Jacob Cox, July 19, 1888, Stanley Papers (USAMHI).
Cox, 167, 169.
OR 45-1-1179.
Murphey, diary (SHC), 18–24.
22. OR 45-1-150, 1179.
23. OR 45-1-175, 1179.
24. OR 45-1-150, 1123, 1172.
Cox, 169.
25. OR 45-1-343, 344.
26. Schofield, 234.
OR 45-1-334.
27. OR 45-1-1171.
28. Cox, 169, 170.
OR 45-1-150.
Joseph S. Fullerton, letter to David Stanley, May 14, 1889, Stanley Papers (USAMHI).

29. Fullerton, letter, May 14, 1889 (USAMHI).
Cox, 338.
30. OR 45-1-1171.
Schofield, 224.
31. Cox, 338.
32. Shellenberger, *Battle of Franklin*, 41.
Schofield, 233.
33. OR 45-1-150.
34. Murphey, diary (SHC), 18–24.
35. Ibid.
OR 45-1-151.
36. Murphey, diary (SHC), 18–24.
37. Ibid.
38. Cox, 339.
39. Ibid., 180–185.
C. S. Fink, "The Organization of the Surgical Department in the Field and Experience of its Officers in the Battle of Franklin" (MOLLUS, Ohio Commandery), 4:428.
40. Fink, 428.
Cox, 180–185.
41. Ibid.
Cox, 186–193.
42. Ibid., 187.
OR 45-1-321.
Bennett & Haigh, 660.
Lewis, 198.
43. Sexton, 482.
Thurston, 84.
Bennett & Haigh, 660.
OR 45-1-117.
Cox, 188, 189.
44. Shellenberger, *Battle of Franklin*, 31.
Thomas E. Milchrist, "Reflections of a Subaltern on the Hood-Thomas Campaign in Tennessee," (MOLLUS, Illinois Commandery), 4:461.
45. OR 45-1-117, 151.
Thatcher, 310.
Park Marshall, journal, (TSL) 141.
46. 73rd Illinois, 405.
47. 86th Indiana, 479.
Thompson, 271.
Cox, 188, 192.
Mohrmann, journal, 1864 (CHA), 96.
48. Cox, 188–192.
49. Lewis, 198.
OR 45-1-126.
Partridge, 430.
Pinney, 63.
86th Indiana, 479.
Lewis, 198, 199.
50. Ridley, 411.
Field, 250.
Scofield, 147.
51. Field, 147.
OR 45-1-658, 694, 721.
52. Ridley, 411.
53. OR 45-1-721.

54. Thatcher, 211, 316.
Ridley, 411.
55. Ridley, 411.
56. CV 10-501.
Park Marshall, diary, (TSL) 140, 141.
57. Ibid.
Brown, 150.
Field, 250.
58. Park Marshall, diary, (TSL) 140, 141.
59. CV 3-72, 73; 30-288.
Indianapolis Journal, March 12, 1883.
Mintz, memoir (CHA).
60. Logsdon, 43.
Rosalie Carter, 44.

CHAPTER 23

1. Figuers, 3.
2. Ibid.
3. Ibid., 5, 6.
4. Ibid., 4.
CV 11-273; 31-423.
Scofield, 143.
Johnston, memoir (THSL).
5. Ryan, memoirs (CHA).
6. Scofield, 143.
Logsdon, 40.
Smith, 203.
Figuers, 4.
7. Thatcher, 311.
CV 31-425.
Figuers, 4.
8. Cooper, 166, 167.
Winters, 127.
9. Brown, 150.
73rd Illinois, 479.
CV 1-16; 18-19, 20.
10. Ryan, memoirs (CHA).
CV 2-186, 282; 21-345.
Mintz, memoir (CHA).
11. Ridley, 411.
CV 5-600.
Thatcher, 312.
12. CV 3-72, 73.
Cooper, 166, 167.
Logsdon, 43.
Rosalie Carter, 44, 45.
13. OR 45-1-35, 47.
Logsdon, 51, 52.
Bowman, 114, 115, 130, 133, 137.
S. D. Lee, letter, December 6, 1864 (SHC).
Figuers, 4.
Ryan, memoir (CHA).
Cooper, 166, 167.
Watkins, 220.
Banks, 86, 87.
Watkins, 220.
CV 19-32; 34-301.
14. Cox, 211–215.
Ryan, memoir (CHA).
Figuers, 4.

15. Thatcher, 311, 312.
Hood, *Advance and Retreat*, 295, 296.
16. Buck, 287.
CV 12-346.
Hancock, 521.
Govan, letter, December 4, 1864 (SHC).
17. OR 45-1-628.
18. CV 3-103.
19. CV 12-346.
Buck, 280.
Indianapolis Journal, March 12, 1883.
20. OR 45-1-653.
S. D. Lee, letters, June 12, 1878; June 4, 1879,
Clairborne Papers (SHC).
Buck, 290.
21. Ibid., 292, 293.
CV 3-103.
Purdue & Purdue, 430–432.
22. Ibid.
Head, 378, 379.
Quintard, diary, December 2–4, 1864 (DPL).
Smith, 27.
23. Head, 378, 379.
24. Hempstead, journal, 1864 (BHL), 176,
177.
25. Thatcher, 314.
26. Figuers, 4.
CV 3-72, 73.
Logsdon, 40.
27. OR 45-1-658, 705, 731, 754; OR 45-2-5,
6.
Hancock, 522n.
28. OR 45-1-721, 731.
Brown, 150.
29. *Detroit Free Press*, December 2, 1864.
30. Ibid., December 2, 3, 1864.
31. Thurston, 87.
Govan, letter, December 4, 1864 (SHC).
Rieger, Paul E., ed., *Through One Man's
Eyes; The Civil War Experiences of a Belmont
County Volunteer* (Mount Vernon, OH;
1974), 192.
D. C. Bradley, letter, December 1, 1864
(USAMHI).
Hancock, 521.
Hood, *Advance and Retreat*, 295.
32. Irving Buck, letter, December 21, 1906,
Buck Papers (SHC).
73rd Illinois, 434.
Buck, *Cleburne and His Command*, 286.
33. Hutchins, 283.
34. Buck, *Cleburne and His Command*,
2871.
CV 3-103; 12-346.
Dyer & Moore, 5:1831.
Worsham, 379.
35. 73rd Illinois, 479.
36. Ibid.
37. Ibid.
38. Brown, 151.

39. OR 45-2-643, 644.

40. Wigfall, letter, December 5, 1864, Wigfall Papers (LOC).

41. Govan, letter, December 4, 1864 (SHC).

S. D. Lee, letter, December 6, 1864 (SHC).

42. OR 45-1-654, 658, 691, 715, 716, 724, 760, 761.

43. OR 45-1-344, 356, 650.

44. OR 45-1-46, 343, 347.

45. OR 45-1-684, 686.

Zachary, Deas, telegram, December 1, 1864, Polk Family Papers, (SHC).

Buck, *Cleburne and His Command*, 285.

George R. Stewart, *Pickett's Charge* (New York; 1959), 127, 185, 263.

46. Worsham, 339.

S. D. Lee, letter, December 6, 1864 (SHC).

47. Scofield, 137.

Govan, letter, December 4, 1864 (SHC).

CHAPTER 24

1. Beach, 98.

OR 45-1-117, 397.

Partridge, 430, 431.

Gist, 232.

Mohrmann, journal, 1864 (CHA), 97.

2. Partridge, 431.

3. William G. Le Duc, letter, September 26, 1903, Shellenberger Papers (LOC).

Schofield, 226.

OR 45-1-1171.

4. Schofield, 226.

OR 45-1-35, 453, 503, 1146, 1167; OR 45-2-3, 17, 18.

5. Schofield, 175, 182, 195, 196, 199, 202, 216, 226, 281, 284.

6. Ibid., 226, 227.

Sanford Kellogg, letter, January 12, 1881, Stanley Collection, West-Stanley-Wright Family Papers (USAMHI).

William G. Le Duc, letter, September 26, 1903, Shellenberger Papers (LOC).

7. William G. Le Duc, letter, September 26, 1903 (LOC).

Schofield, 241, 242.

8. Pinney, 66, 68.

Whitesides, diary, December 1, 1864 (USAMHI).

Partridge, 431.

Clark, 354.

OR 45-1-422.

Murphey, diary, (SHC), 32–54.

9. Partridge, 431.

OR 45-1-153, 153.

10. OR 45-1-151, 152, 1015, 1168.

OR Atlas plate 72, 112.

Stanley F. Horn, *The Decisive Battle of Nashville* (Knoxville, TN, 1957), 28.

11. Partridge, 431.

Henry A. McConnell, letter, December 5, 1864 (USAMHI). 86th Indiana, 480, 481.

Clark, 356.

Glenn Sunderland, *Five Days to Glory* (New York, 1970), 197.

12. OR 45-1-52; OR 45-2-7.

Rusling, 85.

13. OR 45-1-34, 53, 55.

Rusling, 87, 88.

14. OR 45-1-52-57, 152.

15. OR 45-1-53, 503, 510, 1050, 1100, 1126, 1159, 1190.

Faust, 715.

Stanley, 190ff.

16. OR 45-1-54, 560; OR 45-2-3, 24, 26.

17. OR 45-1-1169, 1170; OR 45-2-3, 17, 18.

18. OR 45-2-3.

19. OR 45-2-3.

20. OR 45-2-15-17.

21. OR 45-2-17, 18.

22. OR 45-1-679, 754.

Jordan & Pryor, 611.

23. OR 45-1-688, 754.

Hancock, 523.

William D. Gale, letter, January 19, 1865 (SHC).

24. Watkins, 221.

W. D. Gale, letters, December 3, 9, 1864 (SHC).

25. OR 45-2-640, 641; OR Atlas plate 72.

26. OR 45-1-663, 680, 688, 744.

Horn, 35.

27. OR 45-2-630, 641.

28. Hood, *Advance and Retreat*, 299, 300.

29. Ibid.

30. Ibid.

31. Ibid.

Horn, 36.

OR 45-1-654, 658, 671; OR 45-2-648, 653, 656.

32. W. D. Gale, letter, December 9, 1864 (SHC).

F. H. Wigfall, letter, December 5, 1864 (LOC).

33. Ibid.

34. OR 45-1-658; OR 45-2-669.

35. Quintard, diary, December 12, 1864 (DPL).

36. OR 45-1-36, 58, 658.

37. OR 45-1-705, 754.

38. OR 45-1-540, 541, 631.

Hancock, 523, 524.

39. OR 45-1-535, 540, 631.

Hancock, 523–525.

40. Hancock, 523, 524.

41. OR 45-1-538, 541, 631, 632, 754.

42. OR 45-1-632.

43. OR 45-1-632, 754, 755.

44. OR 45-1-632, 755.

45. OR 45-1-744, 755; OR 45-2-651.
46. OR 45-1-652, 654, 745; OR 45-2-657.
47. OR 45-1-658, 660.
48. J. P. Strange, letter to William H. Jackson, December 11, 1864, Nutt Papers (SHC). Quintard, diary, December 11, 1864 (DPL).
49. OR 45-1-764.
50. OR 45-1-764; OR 45-2-44, 45, 85, 87, 105.
Jordan & Pryor, 636, 637, 657.
51. *Detroit Free Press*, December 9, 1864, p. 3, col. 1.
OR 45-2-100, 101.
52. OR 45-2-97–99, 144.
53. Quintard, diary, December 12, 1864 (DPL).

CHAPTER 25

1. CV 17-17.
OR 45-1-671.
F. H. Wigfall, letter, December 5, 1864 (LOC).
W. D. Gale, letter, December 9, 1864 (SHC).
S. D. Lee, letter, December 6, 1864, Harrison Papers (SHC).
2. F. H. Wigfall, letter, December 5, 1864 (LOC).
W. D. Gale, letter December 9, 1864 (SHC).
Quintard, diary, December 10, 1864 (DPL).
S. D. Lee, letter, December 6, 1864 (SHC).
3. MCCW, 683.
4. Purdue & Purdue, 433.
5. OR 45-1-46, 55ff.
6. Clark, 356.
73rd Illinois, 452, 483.
OR 45-1-409.
7. 73rd Illinois, 467.
OR 45-2-21.
8. Cox, 222.
9. Ibid., 79n, 229.
OR 45-1-269, 270.
10. OR 45-2-21, 117, 146.
Cox, 224.
Edward Whitesides, diary, December 12, 1864 (USAMHI).
11. Henry M. Cist, letter, November 30, 1889, Stanley Collection, West-Stanley-Wright Papers (USAMHI).
OR 45-1-1109; OR 45-2-22, 59, 72, 73, 88.
Schofield, 181, 182.
Henry Stone, letter, March 19, 1889, Shellenberger Papers (LOC).
12. OR 45-2-18, 19, 30; OR 45-1-1107.
13. OR 45-1-36; OR 45-2-18, 36, 102, 149, 150.
14. OR 45-2-6, 24, 26.
15. OR 45-1-560, 1118; OR 45-2-55, 71, 1062.
16. OR 45-2-16–18, 34, 35, 75.
17. OR 45-2-63, 91, 106.

18. OR 45-2-106.
Lewis, 203.
James Harrison Wilson, *Under the Old Flag*, 2 volumes (Westport, CT, 1971) 33, 34.
Longacre, 181.
19. OR 45-2-55, 70.
20. OR 45-2-70, 106.
21. OR 45-2-84.
22. OR 45-2-84, 96.
23. OR 45-2-96.
24. OR 45-2-97.
25. OR 45-2-114, 115.
26. OR 45-2-114.
27. OR 45-2-115.
28. OR 45-2-115, 116.
Sanford Kellogg, letter, January 12, 1881, Stanley Papers (USAMHI).
Horn, 54.
29. OR 45-2-97, 98, 195.
30. OR 45-2-114, 115.
31. Faust, 722, 723.
James L. McDonough, "Cold Days in Hell; The Battle of Stones River Tennessee," *Civil War Times Illustrated* (June 1986), 19, 48.
32. OR 45-1-924, 1004, 1036, 1127, 1188; OR 45-2-12, 13, 164.
Faust, 645.
33. OR 45-1-36, 1154, 1186, 1188; OR 45-2-614.
34. OR 45-1-630; OR 45-2-50.
35. OR 45-1-615.
Faust, 486.
36. OR 45-1-615, 616, 630, 745.
37. OR 45-1-616, 630, 631, 745.
38. OR 45-1-743, 744.
39. OR 45-1-744, 745, 755.
40. OR 45-1-745, 755.
Jordan & Pryor, 632.
General Orders, Forrest's Cavalry, December 8, 1864, Nutt Papers (SHC).
41. OR 45-1-613, 617.
42. OR 45-1-617.
43. Wyeth, 550, 551.
OR 45-1-755.
44. OR 45-1-617, 619, 627.
45. OR 45-1-746.
46. OR 45-1-618, 619.
47. Wyeth, 551.
OR 45-1-746.
W. J. McMurray, *History of the Twentieth Tennessee Regiment Volunteer Infantry, C.S.A.* (Nashville, TN: 1904), 345. General Orders No. 3, Forrest's Cavalry, December 9, 1864, Nutt Papers (SHC).
48. Wyeth, 532.
OR 45-1-755.
49. OR 45-1-614, 618, 620, 747.
50. OR 45-1-614, 615, 755, 756.
51. OR 45-1-756, 670; OR 45-2-666.
52. OR 45-1-615, 756; OR 45-2-673.

William Jackson, letter, December 12, 1864, Nutt Papers (SHC).
53. J. P. Strange, letter, December 11, 1864, Nutt Papers (SHC).
Quintard, diary, December 11, 1864 (DPL).
OR 45-1-756; OR 45-2-152.

CHAPTER 26

1. John B. Lindsley, diary, December 2, 1864 (TSL).
Sunderland, 198.
2. Sunderland, 198.
W. E. Morris, letter, December 6, 1864 (BHL).
Simeon McCord, letter, November 30, 1864, Hess Collection (USAMHI).
Rusling, 339.
Lewis, 202, 203.
William C. Buchanan, diary, December 3, 1864 (USAMHI).
Andrew S. Parsons, letter, December 3, 1864 (CL).
E. L. Humphries, letter, November 30, 1864 (USAMHI).
3. W. D. Gale, letter, December 4, 1864 (SHC).
OR 45-1-152, 510; OR Atlas plate 73-1.
Henry A. McConnell, letter, December 5, 1864 (USAMHI).
Lewis, 356.
4. Henry A. McConnell, letters, December 5, 8, 1864 (USAMHI).
Simeon McCord, letter, December 4, 1864 (USAMHI).
OR 45-1-152, 671.
5. Hempstead, journal, 1864 (BHL), 177.
86th Indiana, 482.
6. Partridge, 435.
Hempstead, journal, 1864 (BHL), 177.
Lewis, 205.
W. E. Morris, letter, December 10, 1864 (BHL).
7. Lewis, 204.
Clark, 356, 357.
8. Lewis, 204.
James A. Hoobler, *Cities Under the Gun: Images of Occupied Nashville and Chattanooga* (Nashville, TN, 1986), 17, 71.
9. Lewis, 204.
10. Sunderland, 198.
OR 45-1-35, 116; OR 45-2-50.
73rd Illinois, 460.
Thurston, 85.
Sexton, 480, 483.
L. P. Bradley, letter, December 7, 1864, Bradley Papers (USAMHI).
Clark, 352.
11. Partridge, 435.
Kerwood, 288, 298, 299.
12. OR 45-1-153, 503, 535.

13. Rusling, 339, 340.
14. Nimrod Porter, diary, December 7, 1864 (SHC).
W. C. Buchanan, diary, December 7, 1864 (USAMHI).
OR 45-1-153.
Hempstead, journal, 1864 (BHL), 177.
Clark, 357.
McConnell, Henry A., letter, December 8, 1864 (USAMHI).
15. Hempstead, journal, 1864 (BHL), 177, 178.
86th Indiana, 482.
Nimrod Porter, diary, December 9, 1864 (SHC).
Clark, 358.
16. Lyman B. Pierce, *History of the Second Iowa Cavalry* (Burlington, IA, 1865), 140.
17. W. R. Carter, 223.
Nimrod Porter, diary, December 10, 11, 1864 (SHC).
W. C. Buchanan, diary, December 10, 1864 (USAMHI).
Pierce, 140.
18. Porter, Nimrod, diary Dec. 12, 1864 (SHC).
W. C. Buchanan, diary, December 11, 1864 (USAMHI).
Pierce, 140, 141.
19. Rusling, 340.
20. Simeon McCord, letter, December 13, 1864 (USAMHI).
21. Worsham, 152.
22. Miller, 21.
Brown, 153.
OR 45-1-672.
Detroit Free Press, December 13, 1864, p. 1, col. 7.
23. Watkins, 221.
24. Miller, 21.
OR 45-1-747.
Brown, 153.
F. H. Wigfall, letter, December 5, 1864 (LOC).
25. Nimrod Porter, diary, December 11, 1864 (SHC).
OR 45-1-657, 658.
26. Brown, 153.
F. H. Wigfall, letter, December 5, 1864 (LOC).
27. OR 45-2-653, 656, 657.
F. H. Wigfall, letter, December 5, 1864 (LOC).
Isiah Cain, letter, December 19, 1864 (CHA).
28. OR 45-1-658; OR 45-2-660, 685.
29. OR 45-2-653, 654.
Watkins, 221, 222.
S. D. Lee, letter, December 6, 1864 (SHC).
30. Ibid.
OR 45-2-659, 665.
Hood, *Advance and Retreat*, 289.
31. OR 45-1-658.

32. OR 45-1-658, 702, 705.
S. D. Lee, letter, December 6, 1864 (SHC).
33. Quintard, diary, December 6–12, 1864 (DPL).
34. Ibid., December 12, 1864.
35. Brown, 152, 153.
Clyde C. Walton, *Private Smith's Journal: Recollections of the Late War* (Chicago, IL, 1963), 190, 191.

CHAPTER 27

1. OR 45-1-114, 115, 118; OR 45-2-122.
Johnson and Buel, 4:455.
2. OR 45-2-115, 116.
3. OR 45-1-115.
4. OR 45-2-116.
5. OR 45-2-130, 143.
6. OR 45-2-143.
7. OR 45-2-143, 146, 147.
8. OR 45-2-147, 149.
9. OR 45-2-149, 155.
Nimrod Porter, diary, December 12, 1864 (SHC).
Hempstead, journal, 1864 (BHL), 178.
W. R. Carter, 225.
OR 45-1-551, 576.
10. OR 45-1-154.
Wilson, 2:100.
11. Ibid., 100–106.
12. Ibid., 101, 102.
13. Ibid., 102–106.
OR 45-1-154.
14. Cleaves, 304.
Schofield, 293–295.
15. OR 45-2-155.
16. Wilson, 2:104–106.
17. Ibid., 93, 94.
OR 45-2-46, 171.
18. Mohrmann, journal, 1864 (CHA), 98.
Simeon McCord, letter, December 13, 1864 (USAMHI).
86th Indiana, 482, 484.
William Lewis, letter, December 11, 1864 (BHL).
Scofield, 149.
Walton, 190.
Detroit Free Press, December 10, 1864, p. 1, col. 4.; Dec. 15, 1864, p. 1, col. 7; Dec. 17, p. 4, col. 1.
Henry A. McConnell, letter, December 8, 1864 (USAMHI).
OR 45-1-154.
Hempstead, journal, 1864 (BHL), 178.
19. Partridge, 437.
20. OR 45-2-686.
21. OR 45-2-669, 673, 755.
22. OR 45-1-676, 677, 764, 765.
23. J. P. Strange, letter, December 13, 1864, to William H. Jackson, *Nutt Papers* (SHC).

OR 45-1-756; OR 45-2-673.
Hancock, 519.
24. OR 45-1-765; OR 45-2-686.
25. Watkins, 222, 223.
OR 45-1-731, 739, 740, 747; OR 45-2-669.
Bevier, 256.
26. OR 45-1-658; OR 45-2-56, 636, 639, 640, 766.
Detroit Free Press, December 8, 1864, p. 3, col. 1.
27. OR 45-1-658; OR 45-2-685.
S. D. Lee, letter, December 6, 1864 (SHC).
28. OR 45-1-679, 774; OR 45-2-680, 685, 687, 698.
Hood, *Advance and Retreat*, 299.
29. OR 45-2-672, 676.
30. OR 45-2-672, 690, 691.
31. Hood, *Advance and Retreat*, 299.
Detroit Free Press, December 8, 1864, p. 3, col. 1.
OR 45-2-686.
32. OR 45-1-503, 511, 533, 542, 548.
Henry V. Freeman, "A Colored Brigade in the Campaign and Battle of Nashville" (MOLLUS, Illinois Commandery), 2:408, 409.
33. OR 45-1-739.
86th Indiana, 486.
Freeman, 408, 409.
34. OR 45-1-154; OR 45-2-168.
Nimrod Porter, diary, December 13, 14, 1864 (SHC).
W. J. Watson, diary, December 14, 1864 (SHC).
Hempstead, journal, 1864 (BHL), 178.
35. OR 45-1-154.
36. OR 45-1-154; OR 45-2-182.
37. OR 45-2-180.
38. OR 45-2-160, 192.
39. Clark, 359.
Walton, 191.
Wilson, 2:109.
40. William Shafter, letter, December 19, 1864, private collection, (Birmingham, MI).
Mrs. William Shafter, letter, December 20, 1864, Shafter Papers, Collection No. 845 (LOC).

CHAPTER 28

1. Wilson, 2:94ff.
Horace Porter, *Campaigning With Grant* (New York, 1897), 348.
David Homer Bates, *Lincoln in the Telegraph Office* (New York, 1907), 314.
2. Ibid., 315.
3. Nimrod Porter, diary, December 15, 1864 (SHC).
OR 45-1-128; OR 45-2-185.
John H. Stibbs, "McArthur's Division at Nashville as Seen by a Regimental Commander" (MOLLUS, Illinois Commandery), 4:491.

4. Thatcher, 222.
OR 45-1-37, 38.
　5. Rusling, 88.
OR 45-1-38.
　6. OR 45-1-38, 84, 184, 185, 344, 345.
Schofield, 242ff.
　7. OR 45-1-38, 504.
　8. OR 45-1-344, 345.
　9. Wilson, 2:107, 109.
Stibbs, 490.
Kerwood, 299.
OR 45-1-128, 437, 562; OR 45-2-205.
73rd Illinois, 485.
86th Indiana, 488.
　10. OR 45-1-405.
　11. Stibbs, 490.
Thompson, 285.
OR 45-1-155.
　12. Faust, 714, 715.
Stanley, 191.
Lyman Potter Spencer, diary, December 12, 1864 (LOC).
　13. Stanley, 191.
　14. OR 45-1-38, 504, 535.
　15. OR 45-1-535.
　16. OR 45-1-504, 536, 542.
Freeman, 410.
　17. OR 45-1-536.
　18. OR 45-1-536, 539.
　19. Mrs. William Shafter, letter, December 20, 1864 (LOC).
　20. Ibid.
OR 45-1-536, 739.
　21. CV 17-12, 18.
OR 45-1-539.
Mrs. William Shafter, letter, December 19, 1864 (LOC).
William Shafter, letter, December 20, 1864, private collection, (Birmingham, MI).
　22. OR 45-1-527, 536.
　23. OR 45-1-527, 536.
　24. OR 45-1-527, 739.
CV 17-18.
　25. OR 45-1-507, 527.
　26. OR 45-1-504, 528.
　27. OR 45-1-503, 542; OR 45-2-199.
　28. OR 45-1-765; OR 45-2-197.
　29. OR 45-1-599.
　30. OR 45-1-599, 765.
CV 12-348.
　31. Warner, 253, 254.
OR 45-1-599.
　32. OR 45-1-599, 600; OR 45-2-206.
　33. OR 45-2-205, 206.
　34. OR 45-1-600, 606.
　35. OR 45-1-600; OR 45-2-206.
　36. OR 45-1-765; OR 45-2-220.
　37. OR 45-1-601.
　38. Hempstead, journal, 1864 (BHL), 179.
　39. Lewis, 207, 208.

　40. OR 45-1-55, 128.
　41. Clark, 362.
OR 45-1-128, 155, 289.
　42. OR 45-1-359, 672.
CV 17-17.
　43. OR 45-1-128, 289, 295, 304; OR 45-2-184, 206.
Lewis, 207.
　44. OR 45-1-155; OR 45-2-198, 201.
　45. OR 45-2-690, 691.
　46. OR 45-1-209; OR 45-2-691, 692.
W. D. Gale, letter, January 29, 1864 [1865] (SHC).
　47. OR 45-1-722.
Pierce, 144.
E. A. Davenport, *History of the Ninth Regiment Illinois Cavalry Volunteers* (Chicago, IL, 1888), 158, 159.

CHAPTER 29

　1. Mohrmann, journal, 1864 (CHA), 98.
Faust, 694.
Warner, 454, 455.
Rusling, 87, 88.
　2. E. L. Humphries, letter, November 30, 1864 (USAMHI).
H. A. McConnell, letter, December 12, 1864 (USAMHI).
Stibbs, 487.
OR 45-1-38, 437.
　3. OR 45-1-433, 437, 562, 576, 589.
Pierce, 142.
　4. Davenport, 157.
OR 45-1-589, 765; OR 45-2-200.
CV 12-348.
　5. OR 45-1-38, 155, 201, 345, 433, 472, 473; OR 45-2-201, 692.
　6. OR 45-1-551, 552, 589.
　7. OR 45-1-155, 434, 441, 577, 589, 590.
Pierce, 142, 143.
Lewis F. Phillips, memoirs, 1864, Civil War Miscellaneous Collection (USAMHI).
Davenport, 157.
　8. OR 45-1-441, 438.
Stibbs, 491.
　9. OR 45-1-590, 709, 722; OR 45-2-691; OR Atlas plate 73, fig. 1, 2.
　10. OR 45-1-722.
CV 12-348.
　11. Davenport, 157.
Pierce, 143.
OR 45-1-438, 441, 577, 590.
　12. OR 45-1-590.
Davenport, 158.
Pierce, 143.
　13. OR 45-1-55, 577, 590, 709, 722.
Pierce, 143.
Horn, 95, 96.
Pierce, 143, 144.

14. OR 45-1-438, 445, 450.
Phillips, memoir, 1864 (USAMHI).
15. Pierce, 144.
OR 45-1-590, 591.
16. Pierce, 144.
OR 45-1-590, 722.
Horn, 96.
17. Pierce, 145.
OR 45-1-445, 446, 450.
18. Stibbs, 491, 492.
19. Ibid., 491–493.
OR 45-1-460, 463, 465.
20. OR 45-1-434.
21. OR 45-1-460, 463, 467.
22. OR 45-1-709, 722.
23. OR 45-1-709, 722.
24. OR 45-1-446, 459, 469, 709.
Mohrmann, journal, 1864 (CHA), 99.
25. OR 45-1-709; OR 45-2-693.
26. OR 45-1-722.
27. OR 45-1-369, 371, 376, 577, 709.
28. OR 45-1-371, 373, 376, 577, 709.
29. OR 45-1-709.
30. OR 45-1-378, 453, 457, 710, 723.
Andrew S. Parsons, letter, December 23, 1864
(CL).
31. OR 45-1-155, 180, 187, 221.
32. OR 45-2-198.
OR 45-1-185, 211, 221, 254.
33. OR 45-1-246, 254, 258, 490, 491.
Bennett & Haigh, 677–679.
34. OR 45-1-190, 243, 490, 491.
35. W. J. Watson, diary, December 15,
1864 (SHC).
W. D. Gale, letter, January 29, 1864 [1865]
(SHC).
36. Ibid.
Horn, 104.
OR 45-1-723.
37. W. D. Gale, letter, January 29, 1864
[1865] (SHC).
38. OR 45-1-743; OR 45-2-693.
39. OR 45-1-702.
40. CV 12-348.
41. *Sunrise and Sunset Tables for Key Cities and Western Stations of the United States*
(No. 1274) (Detroit, MI: 1977).
OR 45-1-155, 441, 446, 466.
42. OR 45-1-392, 397, 406, 417.
CV 12-348.
43. OR 45-1-552.
44. OR 45-2-38, 194, 202.
45. Rusling, 96.

CHAPTER 30

1. Bates, 314–316.
2. Ibid., 316.
OR 42-2-180.
3. OR 45-2-196.

4. Bates, 316–318.
5. Ibid., 317, 318.
6. Ibid., 318, 319.
OR 45-2-194, 195.
7. OR 45-2-195, 210.
8. Bates, 321.
OR 45-2-195.
9. Rusling, 96.
Schofield, 244, 245.
OR 45-2-215, 216, 345, 346.
10. Wilson, 2:213.
OR 45-1-156, 198.
OR 45-2-201, 202, 207.
11. Schofield, 244, 245.
OR 45-1-345.
OR 45-2-202.
12. OR 45-1-654, 660, 710, 747.
OR 45-2-699.
13. OR 45-1-132, 654.
14. OR 45-2-686.
Horn, 108–112.
15. W. D. Gale, letter, January 29, 1864
[1865] (SHC).
CV 12-345.
OR 45-1-696
Bennett & Haigh, 684.
16. OR 45-1-740, 756; OR 45-2-693.
17. Nimrod Porter, diary, December 16,
1864 (SHC).
Davenport, 159.
Mohrmann, journal, 1864 (CHA), 99.
Stibbs, MOLLUS, p. 495.
18. Stephen C. Ayres, "The Battle of Nashville, with Personal Recollections of a Field Hospital" (MOLLUS, Ohio Commandery),
5:293, 294.
Walton, 193.
19. Ayres, 292.
Mohrmann, journal, 1864 (CHA), 99.
20. Stibbs, 496, 497.
OR 45-1-435.
21. Ayres, 292.
Mohrmann, journal, 1864 (CHA), 99.
Stibbs, 496.
22. OR 45-1-438, 441.
23. OR 45-1-435, 438, 442.
Stibbs, 496, 497.
24. OR 45-1-345, 346, 392, 435.
25. OR 45-1-345, 370, 392, 397, 435.
CV 12-348.
26. OR 45-2-217.
27. OR 45-1-346, 435; OR 45-2-202, 214–217.
Schofield, 245.
28. OR 45-1-552, 563, 607; OR 45-2-223, 224.
29. OR 45-1-607; OR 45-2-223, 224.
30. OR 45-1-591, 607; OR 45-2-215–217.
31. OR 45-2-216.
32. OR 45-1-591, 695; OR 45-2-220.

33. Thomas B. Van Horne, *The Life of Major General George H. Thomas* (New York, 1882), 330–332.
OR 45-1-131.
34. Kerwood, 303.
Partridge, 443, 444.
35. OR 45-2-215.
36. OR 45-1-39, 130, 131, 155, 156; OR Atlas plate 73-1.
37. OR 45-1-156, 505, 543.
Walton, 194.
38. OR 45-1-131.
39. OR 45-1-131, 132.
40. Partridge, 443.
Bennett & Haigh, 687.
OR 45-1-132.
41. Ibid.
42. Ibid.
Mark Mayo Boatner, *The Civil War Dictionary* (New York, 1959), 664.
Lewis, 209.
43. OR 45-1-132, 156.
44. OR 45-1-132.
45. OR 45-1-132, 133, 505.
46. OR 45-1-505, 528, 543.
OR 45-2-218.
47. Kimberly & Holloway, 104.
48. OR 45-1-131, 323, 327, 332, 335, 507, 531, 692.
Partridge, 443.
49. OR 45-1-133, 156.
Bennett & Haigh, 687, 688.

CHAPTER 31

1. OR 45-1-528.
William Shafter, letter, December 19, 1864, private collection (Birmingham, MI).
2. Freeman, 415.
3. OR 45-1-312, 505, 528, 543.
4. Freeman, 416, 417.
OR 45-1-689.
5. Freeman, 4-5-417.
OR 45-1-543.
6. Ibid.
OR 45-1-528, 543.
7. Freeman, 416–418.
OR 45-528, 689.
8. OR 45-1-301, 305, 308, 688.
Kimberly & Holloway, 104.
9. OR 45-1-290, 305, 308, 312, 688, 689, 698, 740.
CV 12-350.
Kimberly & Holloway, 104.
10. OR 45-1-133, 135, 153, 305, 307, 308, 310, 312.
Lewis, 210.
OR 45-2-697.
Gates, 322.
Kimberly & Holloway, 104.

11. OR 45-1-296, 299, 305, 312.
12. OR 45-1-98, 102, 103, 105, 296, 698, 702, 705.
13. OR 45-1-543, 548.
Freeman, 418.
14. OR 45-1-5543, 548, 549.
15. Lewis, 209, 210.
OR 45-1-549, 705, 706.
16. OR 45-1-548, 549, 698, 705.
Lewis, 209, 210.
Joseph B. Griswold, letter, December 28, 1864 (BHL).
17. OR 45-1-406, 407, 577, 591, 607; OR Atlas plate 73-1.
18. OR 45-1-591; OR 45-2-215.
19. OR 45-1-591, 595, 723.
Pierce, 147.
20. Ibid.
CV 12-348.
OR 45-2-697.
21. OR 45-1-577, 591.
Pierce, 147.
Davenport, 160.
22. OR 45-1-591, 765.
CV 12-348.
23. OR 45-1-765, 766; OR 45-2-697.
24. Faust, 455.
Warner, 288.
25. Stibbs, 488.
26. Ibid., 487.
27. OR 45-1-435, 447.
28. OR 45-1-438, 439, 442, 749; OR 45-2-217.
Stibbs, 497.
29. OR 45-1-408, 438.
Lewis T. Phillips, memoirs, December 16, 1864 (USAMHI).
30. OR 45-1-438; OR 45-2-216, 217.
31. OR 45-1-439; OR 45-2-217.
32. OR 45-1-442.
33. OR 45-1-439, 442, 444.
34. OR 45-1-439, 442, 447.
McConnell, letter, December 18, 1864 (USAMHI).
35. OR 45-1-440, 442, 444.
36. Stibbs, 498.
OR 45-1-435.
37. OR 45-1-435.
Stibbs, 498.
38. OR 45-1-442, 447, 451.
Stibbs, 499.
McConnell, letter, December 18, 1864 (USAMHI).
39. Wilson, 2:115-117.
40. Ibid.
41. Van Horne, 330–332.
42. Wilson, 2:115-117.
Scofield, 151.

CHAPTER 32

1. F. H. Wigfall, letter, December 19, 1864 (LOC).
OR 45-1-697, 723, 749; OR 45-2-696.
2. OR 45-1-459, 655.
Hood, *Advance and Retreat*, 303
S. D. Lee, letter, December 6, 1864 (SHC).
3. OR 45-1-711.
4. OR 45-1-747, 749.
5. OR 45-1-747–749.
6. Ibid.
7. Ibid., 710, 723, 747–749.
8. OR 45-1-747–749.
9. Ibid.
10. Ibid.
11. Ibid., 479.
12. Ibid.
13. Ibid.
14. Ibid.
15. McConnell, letter, December 18, 1864 (USAMHI).
OR 45-1-442, 444, 448.
16. OR 45-1-749.
McMurray, 398, 399.
David E. Roth, "Profile—Lt. Col. William Shy, C.S.A.," *Blue and Gray Magazine* 2(1):16.
17. OR 45-1-748, 749, 750.
Watkins, 224.
CV 17-12, 13.
18. OR 45-1-442, 749.
19. Mohrmann, journal, 1864 (CHA), 100.
McMurray, 397.
Faust, 698.
20. OR 45-1-447, 464, 749.
Phillips, memoirs (USAMHI), 76.
21. OR 45-1-448, 449, 454, 451, 464, 467, 723.
22. CV 17-13, 13.
OR 45-1-723.
23. OR 45-1-461.
Stibbs, 499, 500.
24. Ibid.
OR 45-1-464.
25. Faust, 389, 390.
CV 17-12, 13.
OR 45-1-436, 448, 451.
26. OR 45-1-436, 440, 442, 448, 451, 461, 462, 695.
27. Milton A. Ryan, memoirs (CHA).
CV 17-13.
28. OR 45-2-707.
CV 15-405.
29. OR 45-1-407, 414.
30. CV 17-19.
Mark Lowrey, autobiography, Civil War Miscellaneous Collection (USAMHI).
31. Watkins, 222.
32. Ibid.
33. Ibid., 223.
CV 13-68.

34. CV 15-405; 17-19.
35. OR 45-1-407, 414, 431.
36. OR 45-1-407, 414, 417
37. OR 45-1-407, 414–419, 423.
38. Mark Lowrey, autobiography (USAMHI).
39. Abner J. Wilkes, manuscript (CHA), 15.
40. OR 45-1-675, 680, 698.
41. Stibbs, 500, 501.

CHAPTER 33

1. William D. Gale, letter, January 29, 1864 [1865] (SHC).
Worsham, 155.
Watkins, 224.
2. William D. Gale, letter, January 29, 1864 [1865] (SHC).
3. Ibid.
OR 45-1-667.
4. Watkins, 224.
McMurray, 349, 350.
5. Watkins, 224.
6. OR 45-1-711.
Hood, *Advance and Retreat*, 303.
CV 17-13.
F. H. Wigfall, letter, December 19, 1864 (LOC).
7. OR 45-1-689.
CV 12-351.
8. CV 12-350.
OR 45-1-689.
9. CV 12-350.
10. CV 7-154, 311.
OR 45-1-476.
11. CV 18-327.
12. OR 45-1-698, 702, 703.
13. OR 45-1-698, 701, 706.
14. Partridge, 444.
73rd Illinois, 489.
Kerwood, 303.
86th Indiana, 406.
15. Partridge, 444–446.
J. W. Kimmel, memoir (CHA).
86th Indiana, 497.
16. Partridge, 445–446.
OR 45-1-199.
17. OR 45-1-505.
Clark, 367.
Walton, 196.
86th Indiana, 495.
18. Partridge, 446.
OR 45-1-197, 201, 218.
19. OR 45-1-564.
Wilson, 2:117.
20. OR 45-1-346, 347, 360, 372, 375, 407, 451, 455.
21. Schofield, 246.
OR 45-215.
CV 17-13.

22. CV 7-154; 18-327.
23. CV 12-350, 351; 18-327
OR 45-1-698, 699, 703, 706.
86th Indiana, 497, 498.
24. 86th Indiana, 497–499.
25. Ibid., 499–505.
26. OR 45-1-689.
27. OR 45-1-765, 786.
28. OR 45-1-765, 766.
29. OR 45-2-220, 221; OR 45-1-578, 591, 592, 595, 601.
Wyeth, 556–559.
Wilson, 2:122, 123.
30. OR 45-1-592, 595, 765, 766.
Davenport, 160, 161.
31. Wilson, 2:122, 123.
Davenport, 160, 161.
OR 45-1-552, 564; OR 45-2-218, 221, 222.
Wyeth, 559.
32. 86th Indiana, 506.
Lewis F. Phillips, memoirs (USAMHI).
33. Wilson, 2:126, 127.
34. Ayers, 294.
Bennett & Haigh, 693.
Thomas H. Williams, letter, December 30, 1864 (BHL).
35. Scofield, 152.
OR 45-2-318.
Wyeth, 559.
Wilson, 2:127.
36. Rusling, 100, 101.
37. OR 45-1-673.
38. Watkins, 225.

CHAPTER 34

1. Andrew S. Parsons, letter, December 23, 1864 (CL).
H. A. McConnell, letter, December 20, 1864 (USAMHI).
2. OR 45-1-50; OR 45-2-20, 215.
3. Partridge, 450.
OR 45-1-135; OR 45-2-237.
4. OR 45-2-222, 218, 223.
5. OR 45-2-218, 219.
6. OR 45-2-237.
7. OR 45-2-237, 239.
8. OR 45-1-134.
9. OR 45-1-135.
L. P. Phillips, memoirs, (USAMHI), 77.
10. CV 18-327.
OR 45-1-689.
Worsham, 155.
11. OR 45-1-135.
CV 15-407; 18-327.
12. CV 18-327.
OR 45-1-689, 699.
13. OR 45-1-607, 689, 699; OR 45-2-237.
14. OR 45-1-607, 699, 703; OR 45-2-237.
15. OR 45-1-699, 703, 706.
CV 7-311; 18-327.

16. OR 45-2-706.
Park Marshall, journal (TSL), 145.
17. OR 45-1-690; OR 45-2-297.
CV 18-328.
Nimrod Porter, diary, December 17, 1864 (SHC).
18. OR 45-1-690.
19. OR 45-1-565, 601; OR 45-2-222, 237.
20. CV 18-327.
Park Marshall, journal (TSL), 145, 146.
21. OR 45-1-553, 601, 706; OR 45-2-237, 238.
22. OR 45-1-565.
Logsdon, 52.
23. Smith, 51.
24. OR 45-1-690, 696, 699, 706.
Herman Hattaway, *General Stephen D. Lee* (Jackson, MS, 1976), 146.
25. OR 45-1-135, 157; OR 45-2-238, 565.
26. OR 45-1-553, 565, 566, 690.
Pierce, 149.
27. Ibid.
28. CV 18-328.
OR 45-1-566, 592, 696.
29. Hancock, 534.
OR 45-1-696.
30. Pierce, 147–153.
OR 45-1-592.
Hancock, 534n.
31. OR 45-1-696.
32. Pierce, 147–153.
33. OR 45-1-553, 566.
CV 15-401.
Pierce, 152.
34. OR 45-1-566, 607, 696, 699, 700, 703.
CV 18-328.
35. OR 45-1-699.
Davenport, 163.
CV 18-328.
36. OR 45-2-238.
37. OR 45-1-157, 161; OR 45-2-214, 228.
38. OR 45-1-161; OR 45-2-158, 214, 253, 285.
Arthur L. Conger, diary, December 17, 18, 1864, Civil War Miscellaneous Collection (USAMHI).
39. OR 45-1-40.
40. OR 45-1-151, 158; OR 45-2-233, 254.
41. OR 45-1-158, 566; OR 45-2-253, 256.
42. OR 45-1-158; OR 45-2-253, 254.
43. OR 45-1-158; OR 45-2-256, 275.
44. OR 45-1-43; OR 45-2-229, 231, 263, 357, 371.
45. OR 45-1-43; OR 45-2-260.
46. OR 45-2-227, 228, 230, 248, 370, 405.
47. OR 45-2-228, 230.
Thurston, 104.
Partridge, 448.
48. OR 45-2-211, 228, 265.
49. OR 45-2-231, 250, 296.

50. Bennett & Haigh, 696.
Mohrmann, journal, 1864 (CHA), 100.
Thurston, 105.
Pinney, 70.
51. Thurston, 105.
Bennett & Haigh, 697.
52. Ibid.

CHAPTER 35

1. OR 45-1-673; OR 45-2-699.
H. R. Jackson, letter, December 10, 1864, B. F. Cheatham Papers (TSL).
2. Quintard, diary, December 18, 1864 (DPL).
OR 45-2-707.
F. H. Wigfall, letter, December 19, 1864 (LOC).
3. Quintard, diary, December 18, 1864 (DPL).
4. Ibid.
5. Ibid, December 19, 1864.
OR 45-1-756, 771.
6. Quintard, diary, December 19, 1864 (DPL).
OR 45-1-661.
7. CV 15-401.
Watkins, 225.
Nimrod Porter, diary, December 18, 1864 (SHC).
8. Mohrmann, journal, 1864 (CHA), 101.
McMurray, 351.
Watkins, 225.
Nimrod Porter, diary, December 18–20, 1864 (SHC).
9. Ibid., December 18–21.
Jacob Cox, diary, December 18–20, 1864 (Marietta, GA: Kennesaw Mountain National Park).
OR 45-1-159, 160.
10. Nimrod Porter, diary, December 19, 20, 1864 (SHC).
Brown, 156.
OR 45-1-661; OR 45-2-710.
CV 15-401.
11. OR 45-2-706.
12. Hancock, 535.
OR 45-1-724, 726, 757; CV 15-401, 406.
13. CV 15-401.
14. Jacob Cox, diary, December 19, 1864 (Marietta, GA: Kennesaw Mountain National Park).
OR 45-1-159, 731, 756, 766.
15. OR 45-1-135, 159.
16. OR 45-1-724, 756.
Smith, 29.
Quintard, diary, December 22, 1864 (DPL).
Worsham, 157.
17. Quintard, diary, December 20, 1864 (DPL).

OR 45-1-673.
CV 15-406.
Worsham, 158.
18. OR 45-1-673; OR 45-2-423, 710.
Quintard, December 22, 1864 (DPL).
19. OR 45-1-159, 160, 673.
Brown, 157.
Quintard, diary, December 20, 1864 (DPL).
20. OR 45-1-758.
Brown, 157.
21. OR 45-1-160, 673.
Quintard, diary, December 20, 1864 (DPL).
22. OR 45-2-719, 721.
Hancock, 538.
23. Quintard, diary, December 19, 21, 1864 (DPL).
24. OR 45-1-135, 159, 160, 578; OR 45-2-272, 287, 291.
Smith, 28, 29.
Bennett & Haigh, 700.
25. Ibid.
OR 45-1-578, 593; OR 45-2-287, 293, 294.
CV 15-402.
Quintard, diary, December 22, 1864 (DPL).
Davenport, 166.
26. OR 45-2-287.
27. OR 45-2-275, 285–288, 295, 296, 299, 300.
28. OR 45-1-160, 161, 299, 361; OR 45-2-285, 299.
29. OR 45-1-161; OR 45-2-295.
30. OR 45-2-295, 296.
31. OR 45-2-307.
32. OR 45-2-283.
33. Brown, 157.
Nimrod Porter, diary, December 22, 1864 (SHC).
John B. Lindsley, diary, December 22, 1864 (TSL).
OR 45-1-161, 162.
Smith, 29.
34. OR 45-1-162, 163.
35. OR 45-2-163.
36. Quintard, diary, Dec. 22, 1864.
OR 45-1-673.
37. Quintard, diary, December 21, 1864 (DPL).
OR 45-1-161.
Nimrod Porter, diary, December 22, 1864 (SHC).
Lindsley, diary, December 22, 1864 (TSL).
Brown, 157.
CV 18-329.
Worsham, 158.
38. OR 45-1-164; OR 45-2-423.
Watkins, 225.
W. D. Gale, letter, January 29, 1864 [1865] (SHC).
CV 18-328.
39. OR 45-1-673.

CV 18-329.
Worsham, 163, 164.
Quintard, diary, December 22, 1864 (DPL).
40. OR 45-2-727, 757.
CV 15-406.
Smith, 30.
41. OR 45-1-757.
42. Brown, 157.
Nimrod Porter, diary, December 23, 1864 (SHC).
CV 17-20.
43. OR 45-1-673; OR 45-2-351, 721.
Quintard, diary, December 23, 1864 (DPL).
CV 17-20.
86th Indiana, 512.
73rd Illinois, 497, 498.
44. Nimrod Porter, diary, December 24, 1864 (SHC).
W. D. Gale, January 29, 1864 [1865] (SHC).
OR 45-1-673; OR 45-2-729.
45. OR 45-1-727, 774, 1028, 1046, 1248, 1251; OR 45-2-655, 687, 726.
Isiah Cain, letter, December 19, 1864 (CHA).
46. Ibid., January 29, 1864.
47. W. R. Carter, 240, 241.
CV 15-403.
OR 45-1-757.
Mohrmann, journal, 1864 (CHA), 101.
48. OR 45-1-567, 593, 603, 757; OR 45-2-334.
49. OR 45-1-603, 726, 757.
Hancock, 538.
50. Quintard, diary, December 25, 1865 (DPL).
Nimrod Porter, diary, December 25, 1864 (SHC).
OR 45-1-163, 164, 567.
Pierce, 153.
51. OR 45-2-342.
52. OR 45-291, 307, 308; OR 45-2-324.
53. OR 45-1-164, 603; OR 45-2-325, 331.
Partridge, 453.
54. OR 45-1-567, 578, 603, 727, 757; OR 45-2-331.
55. OR 45-1-603, 607, 727.
56. Davenport, 164, 165.
OR 45-1-758, 772.
57. OR 45-1-165; OR 45-2-348.
58. OR 45-2-334, 352.
59. Hancock, 540, 541.
60. OR 45-1-758, 772.
61. OR 45-1-608, 758, 772.
62. OR 45-1-164, 165; OR 45-2-348, 352, 365.
Partridge, 453.
63. OR 45-2-352, 369.
Wilson, 2:141, 143.
73rd Illinois, 497, 498.
86th Illinois, 512, 513.

64. Simeon McCord, letter, December 26, 1864 (USAMHI).
OR 45-1-567; OR 45-2-369, 381.
65. OR 45-2-329, 342, 356, 362, 388.
66. OR 45-1-674, 732; OR 45-2-731.
Quintard, diary, December 25, 1864 (DPL).
Brown, 158.
W. D. Gale, letter, January 29, 1864 [1865] (SHC).
Worsham, 162.
67. OR 45-1-674; OR 45-2-357, 371, 507.
73rd Illinois, 499.
Miller, 22.
68. OR 45-1-674, 732; OR 45-2-371, 507.
Brown, 157.
69. OR 45-1-674; OR 45-2-744, 804.
70. OR 45-2-728, 732.
McMurray, 352.
71. Ibid.
Horn, 418.
72. OR 45-2-328, 329.
73. Rusling, 104.

CHAPTER 36

1. OR 45-2-369, 335, 377, 381, 382, 386.
73rd Illinois, 498.
Wilson, 2:161.
2. OR 45-2-384, 388, 389, 397, 400, 402.
3. OR 45-2-394, 397, 402, 403.
4. OR 45-2-396, 408, 409.
5. OR 45-2-419, 420, 441.
6. OR 45-2-101, 377, 420, 421, 441, 442, 528, 540, 593, 594, 609, 621, 628.
7. OR 47-1-343–345, 350ff.
Faust, 834.
8. OR 45-1-40, 46, 47, 49, 344, 356, 715, 716; OR 45-2-345, 370, 650.
Partridge, 448.
9. Bates, 321.
10. McMurray, 353.
Worsham, 163, 166.
OR 45-1-644, 674, 844–846; OR 45-2-306, 482.
11. OR 45-1-764; OR 45-2-620, 757.
Worsham, 166.
Brown, 160.
12. OR 45-1-724, 775, 780.
13. OR 45-1-46–48, 644, 663, 664; OR 45-2-780, 795.
Roman, Alfred, *The Military Operations of General Beauregard in the War Between the States 1861 to 1865*, vol. 2 (New York, 1883), 633.
14. OR 45-2-758, 770.
15. OR 45-2-756.
16. OR 45-2-731, 738, 741, 749, 759.
Roman, 2:328.
17. OR 45-1-749; OR 45-2-739, 741, 749, 753.
18. OR 45-2-751, 756.

19. OR 45-2-758.
20. OR 45-2-768, 769.
21. OR 45-2-772.
Roman, 2:614, 631.
22. Quintard, diary, January 20, 1865 (DPL).
OR 45-2-732, 757.
23. OR 45-2-759.
24. OR 45-2-741, 756, 772.
25. OR 45-2-772, 780, 781.
26. OR 45-1-656; OR 45-2-781.
27. OR 45-2-782.
28. OR 45-2-782, 783.
29. OR 45-2-785, 808.
Roman, 2:332.
30. OR 45-2-665, 772, 786, 789.
31. OR 45-2-726, 768, 772.
32. OR 45-2-789.
33. OR 45-2-786, 789.
34. OR 45-2-781, 785.
35. OR 45-2-771.
36. OR 45-2-778, 779, 782, 784, 785, 791–796, 800.
Faust, 743, 744.
37. McMurry, 183.
38. Brown, 158, 159.
39. OR 45-2-792, 804.
40. OR 45-1-642, 643, 655; OR 45-2-804, 894.
41. Roman, 2:639.
OR 45-2-804, 805.
42. Quintard, diary, January 23, 1865 (DPL).
Nimrod Porter, diary, January 23, 1865 (SHC).

CHAPTER 37

1. MCCW, 683, 708, 709.
2. Ibid., 554, 556, 570, 658, 708, 710, 818.
3. Ibid., 658, 708, 709.
4. Ibid., 709, 710, 769.
5. McMurry, 183–185.
Faust, 695, 696.
6. OR 38-3-628–638; OR 45-1-646, 652ff.
McMurry, 186–188.
MCCW, 708.
7. MCCW, 779.
McMurry, 188.
8. MCCW, 771.
Faust, 630, 631.
OR 38-3-637, 638; OR 47-1-1203.

9. MCCW, 712–714, 773.
10. MCCW, 779, 780, 782.
11. MCCW, 783.
12. MCCW, 804, 805.
13. MCCW, 785.
14. MCCW, 588, 798, 804, 805, 807, 825.
Meynard, 503.
John Frederick Dorman, The Prestons of Smithfield and Greenfield in Virginia (Louisville, KY, 1982), 213.
15. Richard M. McMurry, Two Great Rebel Armies (Chapel Hill, NC, 1989).
Bennett & Haigh, 694.
16. MCCW, 782.
Thurston, 104.
Dyer, 309, 362n.
17. McMurry, John Bell Hood, 189, 193, 194.
John B. Hood, letter to Stephen D. Lee, February 9, 1866, S. D. Lee Papers (SHC).
18. McMurry, John Bell Hood, 196, 197.
19. Ibid., 195.
Richard O'Connor, Hood: Cavalier General (New York, 1949), 267.
20. McMurry, John Bell Hood, 202, 203.
21. Ibid., 191.
Robert Selph Henry, As They Saw Forrest: Some Recollections and Comments of Contemporaries (Jackson, TN, 1956), 283.
Langston James Goree, V, ed., The Thomas Jewett Goree Letters, vol. 1 (Bryan, TX, 1981), ltr. of Dec. 18, 1864.
22. McMurry, John Bell Hood, 196, 211.
John B. Hood, letter, January 9, 1866, S. D. Lee Papers (SHC).
23. Purdue & Purdue, 433, 434.
24. C. P. Neilson, letter, January 11, 1865 (CHA).
25. The [Louisville, Ky.] Courier Journal, December 4, 1881.
26. Cox, 258ff.
Stanley, 210–214.
27. Schofield, 293–296.
Sanford Kellogg, letter, January 12, 1881, Stanley Papers (USAMHI).
28. Emerson Opdycke, letter, September 9, 1866, Stanley Papers (USAMHI).
Faust, 546, 547.
29. Faust, 188, 455, 661, 754.
Pinney, 70.
30. John T. Dowd, The Pillaged Grave of a Civil War Hero (Nashville, TN, 1985), 9, 12, 13, 16, 17.

BIBLIOGRAPHY

ABBREVIATIONS

BHL—Bentley Historical Library, University of Michigan, Ann Arbor, MI.
CHA—Carter House Archives, Franklin, TN.
CL—Clements Library, University of Michigan, Ann Arbor, MI.
CV—*Confederate Veteran*. Cited with volume and page number following. For example, CV 5-123.
DPL—Du Pont Library, University of the South, Sewanee, TN.
LOC—Library of Congress, Washington, DC.
MCCW—C. Vann Woodward, *Mary Chesnut's Civil War* (New Haven, CT, 1981).
MOLLUS—Military Order of the Loyal Legion of the United States.
OR—*War of the Rebellion: Official Records of the Union and Confederate Armies*, Series I, Washington, D.C.—cited with volume, part, and page numbers following. For example, OR 45-2-345.
SHC—Southern Historical Collection, University of North Carolina Library, Chapel Hill, NC.
THSL—Tennessee Historical Society Library, Nashville, TN.
TSL—Tennessee State Library, Nashville, TN.
USAMHI—United States Army Military History Institute, Carlisle Barracks, Pennsylvania.
WRHS—Western Reserve Historical Society Library, Cleveland, OH.
73rd Illinois—*A History of the Seventy-Third Regiment of Illinois Infantry Volunteers* (Springfield, Il, 1890).
86th Indiana—*The Eighty-Sixth Regiment Indiana Volunteer Infantry: A Narrative of its Services in the Civil War of 1861–1865* (Crawfordsville, IN, 1895).

SOURCES

With the exception of background material utilized primarily in Chapters 2 through 7, the vast bulk of the information for this project was obtained from primary sources. Much emphasis was placed on obtaining materials comtemporary to the events depicted, and, where possible, cross references were utilized in resolving particularly contradictory or unclear testimony. Due to the nature of the events, and considerable controversy among the principals as to responsibility for certain failures and successes, much care was taken to investigate with objectivity each incident as a separate situation. Since interpretation, logic, and common sense are a part of not only depicting the events, but deciding what to include or leave out, the author is solely responsible for the degree of veracity which he has strived to maintain. With regard to individual characters, including John Bell Hood, every effort was made to assess decisions and motives based on the actual evidence at hand.

One additional matter requiring explanation is the writer's normalizing of spelling and punctuation. In certain quotations from original sources spelling and punctuation have been corrected. Care has been taken to maintain the veracity of all quotations, and it is simply my opinion that normalization is appropriate for the sake of clarity and to eliminate reader distractions.

MANUSCRIPT MATERIALS

Bailey, L. M. Letter, June 13, 1929. CHA.

Beatty, James N. (Company I, 81st Ohio Volunteer Infantry). Diary, 1864. Possession of Steve Beatty, Seattle, WA.

Beauregard, P.G.T.. Correspondence, 1864–65. William Palmer Confederate Collection. WRHS.

Bender, Jacob (24th Wisconsin Infantry). Letters, December 1864; January 5, 1865. The Bender Family Papers. USAMHI.

Bradley, David C. (65th Illinois—A.D.C.). Letters, 1864; memoir, 1865. Civil War Miscellaneous Collections. USAMHI.

Bradley, Luther P. Letters, October 12, 18; November 3, 15; December 7, 20, 1864. Luther P. Bradley Papers. USAMHI.

Buchanan, William C. (36th Illinois Infantry). Diary, 1864. Civil War Miscellaneous Collections. USAMHI.

Buck, Irving A. Correspondence, 1864–1906. Irving A. Buck Papers. SHC.

Cain, Isiah (7th Mississippi Infantry). Letter, December 19, 1864. CHA.

Carter, Fountain B., miscellaneous Carter family notes. CHA.

Cheatham, Benjamin F. Papers. TSL.

Conger, Arthur L. (115th Ohio Infantry). Diary, 1864. Civil War Miscellaneous Collection. USAMHI.

Covey, Israel P. (44th Illinois Infantry). Letter, December 22, 1864. BHL.

Cox, Jacob. Diary, 1864, 1865. Kennesaw Mountain National Military Park, Marietta, Georgia.

Cummings, Joseph B. Memoir. Joseph B. Cummings Papers. SHC.

Deas, Zachary C. Telegram, December 1, 1864. Polk Family Papers. DPL.

Erwin, George P. Correspondence, 1864. Erwin Papers. SHC.

Figuers, Hardin Perkins. "A Boy's Impression of the Battle of Franklin." Figures Family Papers. TSL.

Forrest, Nathan Bedford. Letter to J. B. Hood, November 3, 1864. Schoff Collection. CL.

Fullerton, Joseph S. Letter to David S. Stanley, May 14, 1889. Stanley Collection. West-Stanley-Wright Papers. USAMHI.

Gale, William D. Letters, 1864–1865. Gale and Polk Papers. SHC.

Gale, William D. Correspondence, 1864–1865. Polk Family Papers. DPL.

Gordon, George W. Memoir of Franklin (n.d.). CHA.

Govan, Daniel C. Letter, December 4, 1864. Govan Papers. SHC.

Griswold, Joseph B. (assistant surgeon). Letter, December 28, 1864. BHL.

Halleck, Henry. Letter, May 1, 1862. AC 6582. LOC.

Harris, Isham G. Letter, September 16, 1864. Braxton Bragg Papers. WRHS.

Hempstead, Henry M. (2nd Michigan Cavalry). Journal, 1864. Michigan Historical Collections. BHL.

Hood, John Bell. Letters, March 10; April 3, 13; July 14, 1864. Braxton Bragg Papers.

Hood, John Bell. Miscellaneous papers, 1864–1879. The Henry E. Huntington Library, San Marino, CA.

Hood, John Bell. Correspondence, 1865–1879. S. D. Lee Papers. SHC.

Hooper, John A. Letter, November 19, 1864. SHC.
Houghton, William. Letter, November 22, 1864. BHL.
Howard, Oliver Otis. Letter, July 23, 1864. Bowdoin College Library, Brunswick, ME.
Humphries, E. L. (12th Indiana Cavalry). Letter, November 20, 1864. Civil War Miscellaneous Collections. USAMHI.
Johnston, John, (7th Tennessee Cavalry). Memoir, ca. 1900. THSL.
Kellogg, Sanford. Correspondence, 1881. David S. Stanley Papers on Franklin, West-Stanley-Wright Family Papers. USAMHI.
Kimmel, J. W. (50th Ohio Infantry). Memoir, ca. 1905. CHA.
Latture, Joseph. Letter, November 28, 1864. Lewis Leigh Collection. USAMHI.
Lee, Stephen D. Letter, November 12, 1902. Capers Papers. SHC.
Lee, Stephen D. Letter, December 6, 1864. James Thomas Harrison Papers. SHC.
Lee, Stephen D. Correspondence, 1878–80. Claiborne Papers. SHC.
Lewis, William A. (23rd Michigan Infantry). Letters, 1864. BHL.
Lindsley, John B. Diary, 1864. TSL.
Lowrey, Mark P. Autobiography. Civil War Miscellaneous Collections. USAMHI.
McConnell, Henry A. (10th Minnesota Infantry). Letters, November 30 to December 27, 1864. Civil War Times Illustrated Collection. USAMHI.
McCord, Simeon (14th Ohio Light Battery). Letters. "Camp and Campaign Life of a Union Artilleryman." Earl M. Hess Collection. USAMHI.
McCornack, Andrew (127th Illinois Infantry). Letters, 1864. Collection of Wiley Sword (Birmingham, MI).
McCumsey, Thomas (23rd Michigan Infantry). Diary, 1864. BHL.
McWayne, Eugene (127th Illinois Infantry). Letters, 1864. Collection of Wiley Sword (Birmingham, MI).
Marshall, Charles. "Battle of Franklin." CHA.
Marshall, Park. Williamson County (journal). TSL.
Mintz, W. D. Memoir. CHA.
Mohrmann, William O. (72nd Illinois Infantry). Journal, 1864. Possession of George L. Thurston, III, copy in CHA.
Moon, A. J. (104th Ohio Infantry). Letters, December 4, 24, 1864. L. Leigh Collection. USAMHI.
Morris, Wayne E. (23rd Michigan Infantry). Letters, October–December, 1864. BLH.
Murphey, Virgil S. (17th Alabama Infantry). Diary, 1864. SHC.
Neilson, C. P. (33rd Mississippi Infantry). Letter, January 11, 1865. CHA.
Opdycke, Emerson. Letter, November 8, 1864. Luther P. Bradley Papers. USAMHI.
Opdycke, Emerson. Letter, September 9, 1866. Stanley Papers, West-Stanley-Wright Papers. USAMHI.
Parsons, Andrew S. (33 Wisconsin Infantry). Letters, November 30; December 3, 23, 28, 1864. Schoff Collection. CL.
Phillips, Lewis F. (4th Iowa Light Artillery). Memoirs, 1861–1865. Nashville, TN, 1909. Civil War Miscellaneous Collections. USAMHI.
Polk, William. Letters, September 27; October 17; December 3, 1864. Polk Family Papers. DPL.
Porter, Nimrod. Diary at Columbia, TN, 1864, 1865. SHC.
Potter, Henry A. (4th Michigan Cavalry). Letters, July 10–December 20, 1864; January 15, 1865. BHL.
Quintard, Charles Todd (chaplain/bishop). Diary, 1864, 1865. DPL.
Ryan, Milton A. (15th Mississippi Infantry). Memoirs. CHA.
Schofield, John M. Letter to Jacob Cox, July 19, 1888. Stanley Collection, West-Stanley-Wright Papers. USAMHI.
Shafter, William R. Letter, December 19, 1864. Collection of Wiley Sword (Birmingham, MI).
Shafter, Mrs. William R. Letter, December 20, 1864. Collection No. 838. LOC.
Shedd, Henry G. (97th Ohio Infantry). Letters, June 27, November 26, 1864. Civil War Times Illustrated Collection. USAMHI.
Shellenberger, John K. Correspondence, 1864–1913. Collection No. 845. LOC.
Spencer, Lyman Potter. Diary, 1864. LOC.
Stanley, David S. Miscellaneous correspondence, 1881–1898. West-Stanley-Wright Family Papers. USAMHI.
Stewart, Alexander P. Letter, February 16, 1886. Lionel Baxter Collection, Civil War Times Illustrated Archives. USAMHI.
Strange, J. P. Correspondence, orders, 1864 (N.B. Forrest's Cavalry). Nutt Papers. SHC.

Thompson, Bradley (112th Illinois Infantry). Letters, December 3, 7, 1864. Lewis Leigh Collection. USAMHI.
Thompson, Joseph Nichols (35th Alabama Infantry). "Battle of Franklin Nov. 30, 1864." CHA.
Thompson, William D. Letter, February 1–24, 1890. Stanley Collection, West-Stanley-Wright Papers. USAMHI.
Trowbridge, George N. Letter, July 22, 1864. Schoff Collection. CL.
Watson, W. J. (53rd Tennessee Infantry). Diary, 1864. SHC.
Weaver, Adam (104th Ohio Infantry). Letters, 1864; journal, 1864. CHA.
Whitesides, Edward (125th Ohio Infantry). Diary, 1864. Civil War Times Illustrated Collection. USAMHI.
Wigfall, F. Halsey. Letters, December 5, 19, 1864. Wigfall Family Papers. LOC.
Wilkes, Abner James (46th Mississippi Infantry). Privately owned manuscript, Prentiss, MS; courtesy CHA.
Williams, Thomas H. (103rd Ohio Infantry). Letters, December 7, 30, 1864. BHL.

NEWSPAPERS, WAR PAPERS, AND PERIODICALS

Ayers, Stephen C. "The Battle of Nashville with Personal Recollections of a Field Hospital." *Sketches of War History 1861–1865, Papers Prepared for the Commandery of the State of Ohio* (MOLLUS, Ohio Commandery, Cincinnati, OH) 5 (1903): 284ff.
Boyce, Joseph. "Missourians in Battle of Franklin." *Confederate Veteran* 24:101–103.
Brewer, George E. "Incidents of the Retreat from Nashville." *Confederate Veteran* 18:327–329.
Carter, T. M. "Written While Hood was Before Nashville." *Confederate Veteran* 18:507.
Cheatham, Benjamin F. "The Lost Opportunity at Spring Hill." *Southern Historical Society Papers* 9(1881):524–541.
Cheatham, Benjamin F. "The Battle of Franklin." *The Indianapolis Journal* (March 12, 1883).
Cheatham, Benjamin F. "Hood's Defeat." *The Louisville [Ky.] Courier Journal* (December 4, 1881).
Civil War Times Illustrated, Special Atlanta Edition (Harrisburg, PA, 1964).
Cooper, James L. "Diary of Captain James L. Cooper." *Tennessee Historical Quarterly* (June 1956): 166ff.
Coleman, Bill and Sue, eds., "The Civil War Letters of William Troyer, 112th Illinois Volunteers." *The Kepi* (August–September 1985): 15ff.
Crownover, Sims. "The Battle of Franklin." *Tennessee Historical Quarterly* 14, no. 4 (December 1955). Reprint.
Cunningham, S. A. "Disastrous Campaign in Tennessee." *Confederate Veteran* 12:338–341.
The Detroit Free Press. Issues November 4, 1864, to January 15, 1865.
Dodd, W. O. "Reminiscences of Hood's Tennessee Campaign." *Southern Historical Society Papers* 9(1881):518–524, Richmond, VA 1881.
Fink, C. S. "The Organization of the Surgical Dept. in the Field and Experience of its Officers in the Battle of Franklin." *Sketches of War History '61–'65* (MOLLUS, Ohio Commandery, Cincinnati, OH) 4 (1896): 418–428.
Finlay, Luke W. "Another Report on Hood's Campaign." *Confederate Veteran* 15: 404–407.
Freeman, Henry V. "A Colored Brigade in the Campaign and Battle of Nashville." *Military Essays and Recollections, Papers Read Before the Commandery of the State of Illinois* (MOLLUS, Illinois Commandery, Chicago, IL) 2 (1894): 399–421.
Garrard, Louis F. "Gen. S. D. Lee's Part in Checking the Rout." *Confederate Veteran* 12: 350–353.
Garrett, G. W. "The First Day's Battle at Nashville." *Confederate Veteran* 18: 470–471.
Gist, W. W. "The Battle of Franklin." *Tennessee Historical Magazine* 6, no. 3 (October 1920): 213–265.
Gist, W. W. *Confederate Veteran* 24: 13–15.
Harris, James C. "Souvenir of Franklin." *North South Trader* (July—August 1982): 15–34.
Hickey, J. M. "Battle of Franklin." *Confederate Veteran* 17:14.
Hutchins, Morris C. "The Battle of Franklin, Tennessee." *Sketches of War History 1861–1865, Papers Prepared for the Commandery of the State of Ohio* (MOLLUS) 5 (1903): 275–283.
Indianapolis Journal, March 12, 1883.
Kearney, W. H. "Concerning the Battle of Nashville." *Confederate Veteran* 13:68. "Last Shots in the Battle of Nashville." *Confederate Veteran* 7:154.

Leavell, George W. *Confederate Veteran* 10:500–502.
Lindsay, R. H. "Retreat from Nashville." *Confederate Veteran* 7:311. *The Courier Journal*, (Louisville, KY), Sunday, December 4, 1881.
McDonough, James L. "John McAllister Schofield." *Civil War Times Illustrated* 13, no. 5 (August 1974): 10ff.
McDonough, James L. "Cold Days In Hell: The Battle of Stones River, Tenn." *Civil War Times Illustrated* (June 1986): 12ff.
Maften, Charles B. "Jackson's Brigade in Battle of Nashville." *Confederate Veteran* 17:11–13.
Merrifield, J. K. "Opdycke's Brigade at Franklin." *Confederate Veteran* 13:563–564.
Milchrist, Thomas E. "Reflections of a Subaltern on the Hood-Thomas Campaign in Tennessee." *Military Essays and Recollections, Papers Read Before the Commandery of the State of Illinois* (MOLLUS, Illinois Commandery, Chicago, IL) 4 (1907): 461ff.
Morton, M. B. "Battle of Nashville." *Confederate Veteran* 17:21.
Porter, James D. "Spring Hill and Battle of Franklin." *Confederate Veteran* 12:341–349.
Roth, David E. "Profile—Lt. Col. William Shy, C.S.A." *Blue and Gray Magazine* 2, no. 1 (1984): 12ff.
Roth, David E. "The Mysteries of Spring Hill, Tennessee." Blue and Gray Magazine 2, no. 2 (1984).
Sanders, D. W. "Hood's Tennessee Campaign." *Confederate Veteran* 15:401–404.
Scofield, Levi T. "The Retreat from Pulaski to Nashville." *Sketches of War History* (MOLLUS, Ohio Commandery, Cincinnati, OH) 2 (1888); 121–152.
Sexton, James Andrew. "The Observations and Experiences of a Captain of Infantry at the Battle of Franklin, November 30, 1864." *Military Essays* (MOLLUS, Illinois Commandery, Chicago, IL) 4 (1907): 466–481.
Sharp, Arthur. "The Spirit of Christian Warfare? Greek Fire." *Civil War Times Illustrated* (September, 1984): 32ff.
Shellenberger, John K. "The Battle of Spring Hill, Tennessee." (MOLLUS, Missouri Commandery, St. Louis, MO, 1907).
Smith, Samuel G. "Military Small Arms." *Sketches of War History 1861–1865.* (MOLLUS, Ohio Commandery, Cincinnati, OH) 1(1888): 176.
Speed, Thomas, "The Battle of Franklin." *Sketches of War History 1861–1865*, vol. 3 (MOLLUS, Ohio Commandery), 44–99.
Stibbs, John H. "McArthur's Division at Nashville As Seen by a Regimental Commander." *Military Essays and Recollections* (MOLLUS, Illinois Commandery, Chicago, IL) 4(1907): 485ff.
Vought, John E. "An Incident in the Last Nashville Campaign." *War Papers* (MOLLUS, Indiana Commandery, Indianapolis, IN (1898): 382ff.,
Walford, S. C. "From the Other Side at Franklin." *Confederate Veteran* 17:15–16.
Young, J. P. "Hood's Failure at Spring Hill." *Confederate Veteran* 16:25–41.

BOOKS

Atlas to Accompany the Official Records of the Union and Confederate Armies. Washington, DC.; 1891–1895.
Banks, R. W. *The Battle of Franklin, November 30, 1864.* New York, 1908.
Bates, David Homer. *Lincoln in the Telegraph Office.* New York, 1907.
Beach, John N. *History of the Fortieth Ohio Volunteer Infantry.* London, OH, 1884.
Bevier, Robert S. *History of the First and Second Missouri Confederate Brigades, 1861–1865.* St. Louis, MO. 1879.
Bennett, I. G., & Haigh, William M. *History of the Thirty-Sixth Regiment Illinois Volunteers during the War of the Rebellion.* Aurora, IL. 1876.
Boatner, Mark Mayo, III. *The Civil War Dictionary.* New York, 1959.
Bowman, Virginia McDaniel. *Historic Williamson County Old Homes and Sites.* Franklin, TN, 1971.
Brown, Norman D., ed. *One of Cleburne's Command: The Civil War Reminiscences and Diary of Capt. Samuel T. Foster, Granbury's Texas Brigade, C.S.A.* Austin, TX, 1980.
Buck, Irving A. *Cleburne and His Command.* Wilmington, NC, 1987 (reprint of 1908 edition).
Burr, Frank A., & Williams, Talcott. *The Battle of Franklin.* Philadelphia, 1883.
Carter, Rosalie. *Captain Tod Carter—Confederate States Army.* Franklin, TN, 1978.

Carter, W. R. *History of the First Regiment of Tennessee Volunteer Cavalry in the Great War of the Rebellion.* Knoxville, TN, 1902.

Clark, Charles T. *Opdycke's Tigers, 125th O.V.I., A History of the Regiment and of the Campaigns and Battles of the Army of the Cumberland.* Columbus, OH, 1895.

Cleaves, Freeman. *Rock of Chickamauga: The Life of General George H. Thomas.* Norman, OK, 1948.

Connelly, Thomas Lawrence. *Autumn of Glory: The Army of Tennessee, 1862–1865.* Baton Rouge, LA, 1971.

Cox, Jacob D. *The Battle of Franklin, Tennessee November 30, 1864.* Dayton, OH, 1983 (reprint of 1897 edition).

————. *The March to the Sea: Franklin and Nashville.* New York, 1882.

Cuttino, George Peddy, ed. *Saddle Bag and Spinning Wheel, Being the Civil War letters of George W. Peddy, M.D. and his Wife Kate Featherston Peddy.* Macon, GA, 1981.

Davenport, E. A. *History of the Ninth Regiment Illinois Cavalry Volunteers.* Chicago, 1888.

Davis, Burke. *The Long Surrender.* New York, 1985.

Davis, Jefferson. *The Rise and Fall of the Confederate Government* (2 volumes). New York, 1881.

Dorman, John Frederick. *The Prestons of Smithfield and Greenfield in Virginia.* Louisville, KY, 1982.

Dowd, John T. *The Pillaged Grave of a Civil War Hero.* Nashville, TN, 1985.

Dyer, Gustavius W., & Moore, John Trotwood, compilers. *The Tennessee Civil War Veterans Questionnaires* (vols. 1–5). Easley, SC, 1985.

Dyer, John P. *The Gallant Hood.* Indianapolis, IN, 1950.

Eaton, Clement. *Jefferson Davis.* New York, 1977.

The Eighty-Sixth Regiment Indiana Volunteer Infantry: A Narrative of its Services in the Civil War of 1861–1865. Crawfordsville, IN, 1895.

Faust, Patricia L., ed. *Historical Times Illustrated Enclyclopedia of the Civil War.* New York, 1986.

Field, Henry M. *Bright Skies and Dark Shadows.* Freeport, NY, 1970 (reprint of 1890 edition).

Fuller, Claud E. *The Rifled Musket.* Harrisburg, PA, 1958.

Gates, Arnold, ed. *The Rough Side of War: The Civil War Journal of Chesley A. Mosman, 1st Lieutenant Company D, 59th Illinois Volunteer Infantry Regiment.* Garden City, NY, 1987.

Gay, Mary A. H. *Life in Dixie During the War.* Atlanta, 1979 (reprint of 1897 edition).

Goree, Langston James, V, ed. *The Thomas Jewett Goree Letters* (vol. 1). Bryan, TX, 1981. (Copy in Charleston, Historical Society Collections, Charleston, SC.)

Hancock, R. R. *Hancock's Diary: Or A History of the Second Tennessee Confederate Cavalry.* Nashville, TN, 1887.

Hattaway, Herman. *General Stephen D. Lee.* Jackson, MS, 1976.

Hay, Thomas Robson. *Pat Cleburne: Stonewall Jackson of the West.* Wilmington, NC, 1987.

————. *Hood's Tennessee Campaign.* New York, 1929.

Head, Thomas A. *Campaigns and Battles of the Sixteenth Regiment Tennessee Volunteers in the War Between the States.* Nashville, TN, 1885.

Henry, Robert Selph. *As They Saw Forrest: Some Recollections and Comments of Contemporaries.* Jackson, TN, 1956.

A History of the Seventy-Third Regiment of Illinois Infantry Volunteers. Springfield, IL, 1890.

History of Tennessee. Nashville, TN, 1886.

Hoobler, James A. *Cities Under the Gun: Images of Occupied Nashville and Chattanooga.* Nashville, TN, 1986.

Hood, John Bell. *Advance and Retreat: Personal Experience in the United States and Confederate States Armies.* Bloomington, IN, 1959 (reprint of 1880 edition).

Horn, Stanley F. *The Decisive Battle of Nashville.* Knoxville, TN, 1957.

————, ed. *Tennessee's War, 1861–1865, Described by Participants.* Nashville, TN, 1965.

Johnson, Robert Underwood, & Buel, Clarence Clough, eds. *Battles and Leaders of the Civil War* (4 volumes). New York, 1936 (reprint of 1887 edition).

Jordan, Thomas, & Pryor, J. P. *The Campaigns of Lieut. Gen. N. B. Forrest and of Forrest's Cavalry.* Dayton, OH, 1988 (reprint of 1868 edition).

Kerwood, Asbury L. *Annals of the Fifty-Seventh Regiment Indiana Volunteers.* Dayton, OH, 1868.

Kimberly, Robert L., & Holloway, Ephraim S. *The Forty-First Ohio Veteran Volunteer Infantry in the War of the Rebellion, 1861–1865.* Cleveland, OH, 1897.

Leeper, Wesley Thurman. *Rebels Valiant, Second Arkansas Mounted Rifles (Dismounted).* Little Rock, AR, 1964.

Lewis, G. W. *The Campaigns of the One Hundred Twenty Fourth Regiment Ohio Volunteer Infantry.* Akron, OH, 1894.

Linderman, Gerald F. *Embattled Courage: The Experience of Combat in the American Civil War.* New York, 1987.

Livermore, Thomas L. *Numbers and Losses in the Civil War in America: 1861–65.* Bloomington, IN, 1957 (reprint of 1900 edition).

Logsdon, David R., ed. *Eyewitnesses at the Battle of Franklin.* Nashville, TN, 1988.

Longacre, Edward G. *From Union Stars to Top Hat: A Biography of the Extraordinary General James Harrison Wilson.* Harrisburg, PA, 1972.

Lord, Francis A. *Civil War Collector's Encyclopedia.* Harrisburg, PA, 1963.

Losson, Christopher. *Tennessee's Forgotten Warriors, Frank Cheatham and His Confederate Division.* Knoxville, TN, 1989.

McCaffrey, James M. *This Band of Heroes Granbury's Texas Brigade, C.S.A.* Austin, TX, 1985.

McDonough, James Lee, & Connelly, Thomas L. *Five Tragic Hours: The Battle of Franklin.* Knoxville, TN, 1983.

McDonough, James Lee. *Schofield: Union General in the Civil War and Reconstruction.* Tallahassee, FL, 1972.

McKinney, Francis. *Education in Violence: The Life of George H. Thomas.* Detroit, MI, 1961.

McMurray, W. J. *History of the Twentieth Tennessee Regiment Volunteer Infantry, C.S.A.* Nashville, TN, 1904.

McMurry, Richard M. *John Bell Hood and the War for Southern Independence.* Lexington, KY, 1982.

———. *Two Great Rebel Armies.* Chapel Hill, NC, 1989.

Mathes, J. Harvey. *The Old Guard in Gray.* n.d.

Meynard, Virginia G. *The Venturers—The Hampton, Harrison, and Earle Families of Virginia, South Carolina and Texas.* 1981.

Miller, J. M. *Recollections of a Pine Knot in the Lost Cause.* Greenwood, MS, 1900.

Nash, Charles Edward. *Biographical Sketches of Gen. Pat Cleburne and Gen. T. C. Hindman.* Dayton, OH, 1977 (reprint of 1888 edition).

Ness, George T., Jr. *The Army on the Eve of the Civil War* (vols. 1 & 2). Manhattan, KS, 1983.

Nisbet, James C. *Four Years on the Firing Line.* Chattanooga, TN, 1914.

O'Connor, Richard. *Hood: Cavalier General.* New York, 1949.

Partridge, Charles A. *History of the Ninety-Sixth Regiment Illinois Volunteer Infantry.* Chicago, 1887.

Pierce, Lyman B. *History of the Second Iowa Cavalry.* Burlington, IA, 1865.

Pinney, N. A. *History of the One Hundred Fourth Regiment Ohio Volunteer Infantry from 1862 to 1865.* Akron, OH, 1886.

Porter, Horace. *Campaigning With Grant.* New York, 1897.

Purdue, Howell, & Purdue, Elizabeth. *Pat Cleburne: Confederate General.* Hillsboro, TX, 1973.

Ridley, Bromfield, L. *Battles and Sketches of the Army of Tennessee.* Dayton, OH, 1978 (reprint of 1906 edition).

Rieger, Paul E., ed. *Through One Man's Eyes: The Civil War Experiences of a Belmont County Volunteer.* Mount Vernon, OH, 1974.

Roman, Alfred. *The Military Operations of General Beauregard in the War Between the States 1861 to 1865* (2 volumes). New York, 1883.

Rowland, Dunbar, ed. *Jefferson Davis, Constitutionalist: His Letters, Papers and Speeches* (6 volumes). Jackson, MS, 1923.

Rusling, James F. *Men and Things I Saw in Civil War Days.* Cincinnati, OH, 1899.

Schofield, John M. *Forty-Six Years in the Army.* New York, 1897.

The Seventy-Seventh Pennsylvania at Shiloh. Harrisburg, PA, 1908.

Shellenberger, John K. *The Battle of Franklin, Tennessee November 30, 1864.* Cleveland, OH, 1916.

Sherman, William T. *Memoirs of General William T. Sherman* (2 volumes). New York, 1875.

Smith, Frank H. *History of Maury County, Tennessee* (book 1). Columbia, TN, 1959.

Stanley, David S. *Personal Memoirs of Major General David Sloane Stanley, U.S.A.* Cambridge, MA, 1917.

Stewart, George R. *Pickett's Charge*. New York, 1959.

Stockton, Joseph. *War Diary (1862–1865) of Brevet Brigadier General Joseph Stockton*. Chicago, 1910.

Sunderland, Glenn. *Five Days to Glory*. New York, 1970.

Sword, Wiley. *Firepower From Abroad: The Confederate Enfield and the LeMat Revolver 1861–1863*. Lincoln, RI, 1986.

Thatcher, Marshall P. *A Hundred Battles in the West—St. Louis to Atlanta, 1861—1865—The Second Michigan Cavalry*. Detroit, 1884.

Thoburn, Thomas C. *My Experiences During the Civil War*. Cleveland, OH, 1963.

Thomas, Dean S. *Ready, Aim, Fire! Small Arms Ammunition in the Battle of Gettysburg*. Biglersville, PA, 1981.

Thompson, B. F. *History of the One Hundred Twelfth Regiment of Illinois in the Great War of the Rebellion 1862–1865*. Toulon, IL, 1885.

Thurston, W. S. *History One Hundred and Eleventh Regiment O.V.I.* Toledo, OH, 1894.

Van Horne, Thomas B. *The Life of Major General George H. Thomas*. New York, 1882.

The War of the Rebellion: A Compiliation of the Official Records of the Union and Confederate Armies (Series 1, 73 volumes) Washington, DC, 1880–1902.

Walton, Clyde C. *Private Smith's Journal: Recollections of the Late War*. Chicago, 1963.

Warner, Ezra J. *Generals in Blue*. Baton Rouge, LA, 1964.

———. *Generals in Gray: Lives of the Confederate Commanders*. Baton Rouge, LA, 1959.

Watkins, Sam R. *"Co. Aytch," Maury Grays First Tennessee Regiment, Or, a Side Show of the Big Show*. Wilmington, NC, 1987 (reprint).

West, Granville C. *Personal Recollections of Hood in Tennessee*. Washington, DC, 1906.

Wilson, James Harrison. *Under the Old Flag* (2 volumes). Westport, CT, 1971 (reprint of 1912 edition).

Winters, Erastus. *In the 50th Ohio Serving Uncle Sam*. Cincinnati, OH, n.d.

Woodward, C. Vann, ed. *Mary Chesnut's Civil War*. New Haven, CT, 1981.

Woodward, C. Vann, & Muhlenfeld, Elisabeth. *The Private Mary Chesnut*. New York, 1984.

Worsham, W. J. *The Old Nineteenth Tennessee Regiment, C.S.A., June, 1861–April, 1865*. Knoxville, TN, 1902.

Wright, [Louise Wigfall] Mrs. D. Girard. *A Southern Girl in '61*. New York, 1905.

Wyeth, John Allan. *Life of Nathan Bedford Forrest*. Dayton, OH, 1988 (reprint of 1901 edition).

INDEX

Military units are entered under the commanding officer's name.

Acklen, Joseph, summer home, 301
Acklen, Sally, 286
Acworth, Georgia, 54
Adams, John, 184, 218, 226–27, 263
Advance and Retreat: Personal Experiences in the United States and Confederate States Armies, Hood, 179, 438–39
Aldrich, Job, 318, 325, 357
Allatoona, Georgia, 54–56, 59
Allison, Bucky, 286
Anderson, Robert, 76
Anthony's Hill, 417–18
Armstrong, Frank C., 117, 121, 414–15
Army politics, Confederate, 21–22, 24–26, 48–50; Bragg and, 28–29; Cleburne and, 17–19, 40; Hood and, 27, 32, 33, 306, 430–31
Army politics, Federal, 290–93, 308–12, 319; McArthur and, 365; Schofield and, 99; Stanley and, 129; Thomas and, 76, 78, 277–78, 423
Army of Tennessee, xi, 24–25, 27–28, 53–57, 95, 305–6, 425–27, 438, 444–47; Atlanta Campaign, 37, 42; bands, 87; Bragg and, 20–21, 29; Franklin battle, 187–88, 190–96, 269; Hood and, 22, 31–32, 47; Nashville battle, 334–35, 355, 365, 377–78, 381–91, 406; Nashville siege, 278–85; retreat, 393–403, 406–22; Spring Hill battle, 138–39
Artillery: Confederate, 198–99, 284–85, 316, 394, 395, 399, 402, 425; Federal, 159–60, 161, 166, 254; Franklin battle, 172–73, 182, 187, 188, 190, 193, 195–96, 208–9, 216,

220–22, 227–29, 236, 239, 256–57; Nashville battle, 328, 334–36, 351, 364, 366–67, 372, 376, 379; Spring Hill battle, 130–31, 141
Ashwood Hall (Polk residence), 95
Athens, Alabama, 77, 81
Atlanta, Georgia, 24, 26, 27–29, 33–37, 42–44, 72
Atlanta & Chattanooga Railroad, 54
Atlanta & West Point Railroad, 34
Augusta *Daily Constitutionalist,* 435
Ayers, Gideon, 357

Bainbridge, Alabama, 65, 80, 416
Baldwin, Aaron P., 219–220, 228
Baldwin, Byron C., 228
Bands, Confederate, 87, 95, 184, 188
Banks, R. W., 230
Barking Dog Regiment, 220–21
Bate, William B., 57, 114, 115, 124, 126, 131, 136–37, 279, 283, 295–98, 305, 314, 446; Franklin battle, 180, 207, 237–40; Nashville battle, 342, 370–74, 379, 404–5; Spring Hill battle, 147
Battlefields: Franklin, 402–3; Nashville, 357
Bear Creek, Tennessee, 115, 117, 140
Beatty, Samuel B., 169, 198, 329
Beauregard, Pierre Gustave Toutant, 20, 24, 37, 48–50, 56, 96, 315, 426; Davis and, 52; and Hood, 63–70, 73–74, 427–32, 435; and Sherman's march, 72–73
Beauregard, Rene T., 372
Beckham, R. F., 141

Bell, Tyree H., 120, 121–22, 126–28, 159, 171, 447
Bell's Landing, Tennessee, 326, 327
Bell's Mill, Tennessee, 284
Belmont (Acklen residence), 301
Biddle, James, 326–27
Biffle, Jacob B., 97, 313–14, 447
Big Shanty, Georgia, 54, 59
Bigby Creek, Tennessee, 93–94
Black soldiers, 56–57, 282–83, 316; Cleburne's proposal, 14–15, 18–22, 39–40; Davis and, 21–22; Nashville battle, 321, 324–25, 356, 357–63, 385
Blacks, refugees in Tennessee, 101
Bleak House plantation, 38–39
Bledsoe's Battery, 395
Blockhouses: Forrest and, 283; No. 2, 282; No. 7, 293–98
Blue Pond, Alabama, 63
Bostick, Joseph, 148–50
Bostick, Rebecca, mansion of, 238
Bostow, M. P., 143
Boyer, Joseph C., 388–89
Bradford, Mary, 342
Bradford house, Nashville battle, 372
Bradley, Luther P., 83, 121, 127–30, 132; Opdycke and, 174; Spring Hill battle, 152
Bragg, Braxton, 18–21, 64, 77, 439; and Cleburne, 17, 40; and Hardee, 32; and Hood, 24–26, 32, 37; and Johnston, 28–29
Brandon, James C., 223
Bravery. *See* Courage
Breastworks, Franklin, Tennessee, 163–64
Breezy Hill, 171–73, 177–78, 180
Brentwood, Tennessee, 207, 251, 265, 272–73, 388
Brewster, Henry P., 28, 30

Bridges, Lyman, 130, 234–36, 254
Brown, Joe, 49
Brown, John C., 115, 131, 133–35, 156; Franklin battle, 180, 188–89, 191, 193, 202, 204, 207–8, 210, 234, 237–38, 242; Hood and, 154, 177, 179–80, 429; Spring Hill battle, 138, 146, 153–54, 156–57
Budd, George W., 335
Buell, Don Carlos, 76
Buford, Abraham, 89, 92, 97–98, 105, 119–20, 121, 159, 171, 278, 282–83, 298, 314, 405, 447; Franklin battle, 182, 214, 218; retreat, 395, 398, 416
Bullock, Robert, 238, 240, 295
Burbridge, Stephen G., 288
Burdick, J. S., 254
Burial of dead, 261; Confederate generals, 264

Caldwell residence, Spring Hill, 137
Calhoun, William Ransom, 11
Campbellsville, Tennessee, 92
Capers, Ellison, 237
Capron, Horace, 81, 91–93, 97–98, 103, 105, 112, 113
Carnton (McGavock mansion), 165, 263–64, 216, 260, 396
Carr's Mill, Tennessee, 97
Carter, Fountain Branch, 166, 233, 257; cotton gin, 163, 214–31; house, 164, 189, 202–13, 259, 443
Carter, John C., 237–38, 307
Carter, Mary "Lena," 233
Carter, Moscow B., 166, 186, 233, 259
Carter, Theodrick "Tod," 166, 233–34, 239, 257, 260–61
Carter family, 166, 232–33, 257
Carter House Hill, 199, 207, 210, 213
Carter's Creek, 411
Carter's Creek pike, 137, 158–59, 164, 167, 180, 397; Franklin battle, 238, 240
Casement, John S. "Jack," 166, 214–19, 227
Castello, Dan, circus of, 290
Casualties, x, 33, 34, 54, 78, 425, 426; Franklin, 171, 226, 238, 242–43, 247–49, 259–60, 269–70, 307; Murfreesboro, 293; Nashville, 325, 361, 375, 379
Cavalry, 84; Confederate, 34, 67, 89–93, 97–98, 103, 117, 447; Federal, 102, 111, 241, 289–90, 313
Cave Spring, Georgia, 49, 56
Cedartown, Georgia, 56
Central Alabama Railroad, 305
Chalaron's battery, 295
Chalmers, James R., 89, 91, 92–93, 97, 112, 122, 158–59, 284, 426–27, 447; Franklin battle, 180, 240, 241; headquarters papers, 332; and Hood's strategy, 313, 314; Nashville battle, 326–27, 353, 364–65, 369, 370, 388–89; retreat, 394, 416; Spring Hill battle, 138, 146, 147
Chattahoochee River, 27, 54

Chattanooga, Tennessee, 20, 76–78
Chattooga Valley, 57, 60–61
Cheairs, Nathaniel, farm of, 136, 156
Cheatham, Benjamin Franklin, 34, 40, 71, 82, 89, 95, 115, 158, 257, 271, 278–79, 314, 425, 431, 445–46; burial of dead, 261; Franklin battle, 177–80, 187, 207, 210, 214, 231, 238, 242–43, 245, 255–56, 269, 440; Hood and, 177, 179–80, 306, 429; Nashville battle, 342, 348, 353, 370–73, 377–79, 386; retreat, 407–8, 415, 421; Spring Hill battle, 124–27, 131, 133–37, 146, 147–49, 153, 154, 156–57; Tennessee River crossing, 69, 81, 87
Cherokee Station, Alabama, 68, 69
Chesnut, James, 38, 51
Chesnut, Mary Boykin, 11, 74, 287, 438; and Darby wedding, 58; and Hood's defeat at Atlanta, 36; and Hood-Preston romance, 436–37; view of Davis, 51–52; views of Hood, 6, 12–13, 23, 45, 50, 88, 434–35; views of Sally Preston, 10, 30
Chickamauga, battle of, 11, 20, 23, 75, 76; Bragg and, 18
Chickasaw, Alabama, 421
Cincinnati (gunboat), 284–85
Civil War, ix–x, 43; Cleburne and, 16
Clare, William, 286, 307
Clark, Mervin, 239
Clarksville, Tennessee, 285
Clayton, Henry D., 247, 362n, 383–84, 387, 394–95, 399
Cleburne, Joseph, 16
Cleburne, Patrick Ronayne, 14–18, 38–41, 53, 94–95, 114, 115, 231, 314; black soldier proposal, 18–22, 39–40; Cheatham and, 156; Franklin battle, 178–79, 180, 183–84, 188–89, 191, 192–93, 202, 204, 207, 214, 221–24, 263–64; Hood and, 154, 177, 179–80; Spring Hill battle, 126–31, 133, 146, 157
Cleburne, Robert, 16
Cliffe, Daniel B., 167, 442; residence of, 161, 162, 171
Cliffe, Virginia, 167
Cockerill, Giles J., 166, 190
Cockrell, Francis M., 184, 188, 207, 225–26, 314
Cogswell's Independent Battery, 366–67
Colbert Shoals, 65, 77
Cole, Hugh L., 440
Coleman, David, 314, 421; Nashville battle, 326, 332, 335, 342, 343, 352, 364–65
Columbia, South Carolina, 4, 51–52
Columbia, Tennessee, 83, 91–92, 93–97, 100–109, 142, 150, 406, 408, 411
Columbia pike, 136–37, 147, 158–59, 172–75, 179, 180; Confederate retreat, 397, 399; Federal fortifications, 163–64;

Franklin battle, 188–89, 192–96, 199, 202, 207, 213
Colyar, A. S., 39–40
Communications: Confederate, 153, 256; Federal, 85, 102, 160–61, 172, 251, 345
Compton, Felix, 373
Comrades of the Southern Cross, 14
Confederate army, 3, 66n; casualties, 33, 34; cavalry, 84; morale, 44, 56. See also Army of Tennessee
Confederate flag, 18
Confederate states, xi, 2–3
Conrad, Joseph, 171–73, 175–77, 188, 190, 191, 206, 207, 288
Conscription of troops, Hood and, 315
Coon, Datus E., 112, 334, 335–37, 363–64, 367, 397
Cooper, Joseph A., 166, 289, 340
Cooper, Samuel, 436
Cooper's Mineral Well, 115, 140–41
Coosa River, 56
Corinth, Mississippi, 67–70, 87, 425
Corse, John M., 59
Cotton gin, Franklin, 163–64, 210, 214–31, 259
Couch, Darius N., 352, 365–66, 386
Courage, 42–43; of Cleburne, 17; of Confederate soldiers, 242–43, 247, 270, 438; of Hood, 7, 9
Cowan, Tennessee, 277
Cox, Jacob D., 83, 93–94, 100, 103, 142, 149, 164, 172, 186, 288, 390, 440–41, 449; Franklin battle, 166–67, 193–95, 206–8, 210, 212, 221, 249–50, 254, 255; Nashville battle, 321, 343, 363, 378, 386; and Schofield, 161; and Wagner, 175, 190
Cox, Theodore, 189, 249–50, 251
Crossland, Edward, 117, 159, 168, 447
Croxton, John T., 66, 69, 80–81, 103, 105, 111–13, 168–69, 289, 327, 393, 397, 416
Cumberland River, 276, 284–85, 298, 300, 326
Cumming's Brigade, 383
Cunningham, S. A., 210–11
Cunningham, W. E., 258
Custer, George, 110; and Wilson, 111

Dallas, Georgia, 27, 59
Dalton, Georgia, 15, 56, 61
Darby, John T., 10, 58, 88, 434
Darby, Mary Preston, 58, 434, 437
Davies, Henry E., 110
Davis, Jefferson, 3–4, 19–20, 36–38, 44, 46–48, 51–52, 64, 71–72, 75; and Beauregard, 48–50, 66–67; and Bragg, 18; capture of, 424; and Cleburne, 17, 19, 40; and Hood, 8, 23–25, 37–38, 45–47, 71, 315, 427, 428, 430–32, 435–36, 439; and Johnston, 24–25, 28; personnel decisions, 20–22, 24–25, 29, 31–32, 33, 40, 47–48

Davis, Marshall, 311
Davis Ford road, 136, 137, 141
Davis's Ford, Tennessee, 98, 114
Day of prayer, proclaimed by
Davis, 71–72
Deas, Zachariah C., 270, 338
Deaths, in Civil War, x. *See also*
Casualties
Decatur, Alabama, 64–65, 79,
401, 416
Deceptive reports: by Bragg,
28–29, 37; by Hood, 25–28,
45–46, 268–69, 404, 426,
427–28, 435
Democratic party, and war, 26
Deserters, Confederate, 426–27
Destruction, by Federal troops,
101
Detroit Free Press, account of
Franklin battle, 265–66
Doolittle, Charles C. 378–79, 386
Douglass Church, Tennessee,
168
Dowling, Patrick H., 236
Duck River, Tennessee, 91, 95,
97–98, 101–6, 114, 142,
314–15, 405–6, 408, 411–13

Eckert, Thomas T., 319, 345–47
Ector, Matthew D., 314; Nashville
battle, 326, 332, 335, 338, 342,
343, 348, 352, 364, 369, 370,
372, 374; retreat, 407, 421
Edgefield, Tennessee, 298, 314
8th Tennessee Infantry (Federal),
221, 379
18th Ohio Infantry, 325, 357
80th Indiana Infantry, 239–40
86th Indiana Infantry, 143, 321,
384, 387
88th Illinois Infantry, 204
11th Indiana Cavalry, 118
11th Missouri Infantry, 375
Elk River trestle, 77
Elliott, Washington L., 341
Enfield rifle muskets, 43
Enfinger, Martin, 171
English, R. T., 144
Etowah River, 27
Eufaula Light Artillery, 387
Everbright (Bostick mansion),
238–40
Ewell, Richard S., 295
Ezra Church, Georgia, battle of,
34, 43

Featherston, Winfield S., 217,
218, 407
Federal army, 3, 26, 34–35,
42–44, 66n, 83–86, 254–55,
448–51; casualties, 33, 34,
269–70, 425; cavalry, 84;
dissension in, 287–89, 440–41;
Franklin battle, 185–86, 199,
201, 204–5, 272; Grant and, 27;
Nashville defense, 276–78
5th Iowa Cavalry, 105
5th Minnesota Infantry, 376
5th Tennessee Cavalry (Union),
293
15th Arkansas Infantry, 16
15th Mississippi Infantry, 226–27
15th Missouri Infantry, 173
15th Pennsylvania Cavalry, 432
15th Tennessee Cavalry
(Confederate), 93
50th Ohio Infantry, 185, 195
51st Illinois Infantry, 129

51st Indiana Infantry, 107, 185,
361, 384, 413
59th Illinois Infantry, 140
Figuers, Hardin, 186, 233,
258–59, 265
Finley's Florida Brigade, 295,
297–98, 374–75
1st Arkansas Infantry, 16
1st Florida Infantry, 297
1st Kentucky Artillery (Federal),
195–96, 220–21, 254
1st Missouri Cavalry, 225
1st Ohio Light Artillery, 130, 166,
172, 187, 190, 208
1st Tennessee Cavalry (Federal),
168, 416
1st Tennessee Infantry
(Confederate), 97, 98, 165, 177,
378, 381
Fitch, Le Roy, 284, 326
Flags, Confederate, 18
Florence, Alabama, 1, 65–66, 69,
71, 80, 81, 87, 401, 421
Forrest, Nathan Bedford, 59,
66–68, 82, 84, 87, 95–97, 101,
117, 278, 282–83, 289, 314,
331, 427, 447; Duck River
crossing, 97–98, 105; and
Franklin battle, 171, 177–82,
241, 269, 278; Hood and, 114;
and Murfreesboro, 283–84,
293; and Nashville battle, 344,
348–50, 405–6; Overall Creek
battle, 296–98; pursuit of
Federal army, 158–59, 265; and
retreat, 401, 407–8, 411,
413–19, 421; and Spring Hill
battle, 119–22, 127, 134, 137,
144–45, 147, 154; and
Tennessee invasion, 74, 77–78,
89, 91–92; and Wilson, 111–13
Forrest, Willie, 147
Fort Casino, 328
Fort Gillem, 328
Fort Granger, 165–66, 190, 198,
216, 217, 250
Fort Houston, 328
Fort McAllister, 402
Fort Mizner, 97
Fort Morton, 328
Fort Negley, 328
Fortifications: Franklin, 163–64;
Nashville, 274–76
Fortress Rosecrans, 293–96
40th Indiana Infantry, 132
40th Missouri Infantry, 149
41st Mississippi Infantry, 246
41st Ohio Infantry, 360
41st Tennessee Infantry, 208,
210, 259
42nd Illinois Infantry, 127–29
44th Illinois Infantry, 201, 203,
205, 206, 228
44th Missouri Infantry, 209
44th U.S. Colored Infantry,
56–57, 282–83
45th Tennessee Infantry
(Confederate), 97
46th Alabama Infantry, 386–87
Forty-Six Years in the Army,
Schofield, 441
Foster, William F., 372
Fouche Springs, Tennessee, 91
Fourth Corps, U.S. Army, 60, 83,
101, 122, 129, 143, 159, 161,
163, 167, 170, 269, 272, 276;
and Confederate retreat, 401,
411, 413, 419, 424; Nashville

battle, 321, 328, 332, 341, 343,
354–55, 383
4th Mississippi Infantry, 228–29
4th New Jersey Regiment, 8–9
4th Texas Infantry, 7–8
4th U.S. Artillery, 159, 171, 217,
418
4th U.S. Cavalry, 397
Fourteenth Corps, U.S. Army, 59,
83, 325
14th Illinois Cavalry, 93
14th Tennessee Cavalry
(Confederate), 117
Franklin, Tennessee, 108, 122,
157–59, 162–67, 253, 396,
402–3, 442–43; battle of, x–xi,
171–257, 266–71, 306, 307, 425
Franklin pike, 348, 386, 393, 394;
Nashville battle, 343, 354–55,
382–84, 388
Franklin Review and Journal,
165
Fredericksburg, battle of, 9
French, Samuel G., 54–56, 207,
225, 227, 379, 445
Frink, Charles S., 253
Fullerton, Joseph S., 311n

Gadsden, Alabama, 57, 61, 63
Gaines' Mill, battle of, 8
Gale, William D., 279, 342
Galloway, Laura, 415
Galloway, William, 415
Garrard, Kenner, 332, 351, 383
Gates, Elijah, 225
Gaylesville, Alabama, 61
Generals, Confederate, 20, 153,
156–57, 178–79; casualties,
238, 263–64, 270, 307;
prisoners, 376, 390–91, 425
Generals, Federal, 288–89,
310–11
Georgia, Sherman and, 5, 27–28,
60–62, 72, 96
Gettysburg, battle of, 270; Hood
and, 9–10
Gibson, Claud, 11
Gibson, Randall Lee, 66, 80, 342,
387, 394, 444; brigade band,
431
Giles County, Tennessee, 415
Gist, States Rights, 134, 146, 237,
377–78
Goldwaithe, Henry, 39
Gordon, George W., 193, 222,
224, 228, 230
Gordon, Wash, 98
Govan, Daniel C., 126–29, 131,
133–34, 180, 221, 223–24, 265,
268–69, 325, 373, 377
Granbury, Hiram B., 31, 117,
126, 128, 130–31, 144, 146,
191, 221, 222, 224, 263, 265,
317, 324–25, 357, 360
Granger, Robert S., 81, 416
Granny White pike, 329, 348,
382, 386, 393, 394; Nashville
battle, 342–43, 351, 353,
363–66, 369, 375, 388
Grant, Hector M., 17
Grant, Ulysses S., 27, 59, 60, 61,
107, 285, 290–92; and Nashville
battle, 346, 402; Tennessee
invasion, 108; and Thomas,
76–77, 84, 86, 278, 290–93,
308–9, 311–12, 318, 319,
412–13, 424; and Wilson, 110,
111, 289

Gregg, T. C., 189
Gregory, John, 114–15, 135
Grierson, Benjamin H., 425
Grose, William, 167, 240, 341
Grosvenor, Charles H., 324, 325, 356–61
Grosvenor, Ebenezer, 325
Guibor's Missouri Battery, 188, 189–90
Gunboats, Federal, 64, 284–85, 300, 326, 327, 421
Guntersville, Alabama, 57, 63

Hadley, Mary, 286, 307
Hall, William, 341–42
Halleck, Henry, 43, 61, 77, 289, 412; and Schofield, 99–100; and Thomas, 277–78, 291–93, 308–9, 312, 318, 319, 424
Hamilton Place (Polk home), 94
Hammond, John H., 118, 353, 399; and Confederate retreat, 395, 397, 418, 419
Hampton, Sally, 50
Hardee, William J., 7, 16, 17, 19, 21, 24, 27, 32–35, 37–40, 45, 47, 430, 435
Hardin pike, 326, 332
Hardison's Mill, Tennessee, 97, 103, 105
Harpeth River, 141, 159–62, 165, 167, 241, 255, 395–96, 400–401
Harris, Isham G., 2, 37, 148, 157, 405, 428
Harris, James C., 248n
Harrison, Thomas J., 327, 417–18
Harrison, William, residence of, 177, 178
Harvie, Ed, 404
Hatch, Edward, 80–82, 92, 100, 103, 105, 112, 168, 334–37, 390; and Confederate retreat, 395, 397–400, 410–11, 416, 418; Franklin battle, 241; Nashville battle, 332, 342, 364, 386
Hatry, August G., 186
Hedges, Joseph, 397–98
Helena, Arkansas, 15, 17
Henderson, Thomas J., 101, 214, 216, 217
Hennen, Anna Marie, 439
"High Pressure Brigade" (Sharp's), 246
Hill, Benjamin, 29
Hill, Daniel H., 19, 21
Hill, Sylvester G., 337–38
Hillsboro pike, 327, 332, 335, 336, 338–41, 343, 353–54, 363, 393
Hindman, Thomas C., 17, 21
Hoefling, Charles C., 118–19
Holland's Ford, Tennessee, 97
Hollow Tree Gap, 388, 394–95
Holly Tree Gap, 179
Holtzclaw, James T., 360–62, 384, 396–97, 399
Hood, John Bell "Sam," 6–12, 20, 22, 27, 31–38, 45, 53, 68–74, 87–88, 100–103, 265, 404–6, 432–33, 435, 438, 439; army politics, 25–26, 329–30; and Beauregard, 49–50, 63–70, 73–74, 429–31; and Davis, 23–25, 46–47; deceptions by, 27–29, 45–46, 268–69, 426, 427–28, 435; and Forrest, 278, 283–84, 298; and Franklin

battle, 177–82, 241, 243–44, 255–56, 262–63; and Nashville battle, 330, 342–44, 347–50, 360, 364–65, 369–70, 373, 377–78, 382, 386, 391; Nashville campaign, 278–86, 296, 304–6, 313–17; retreat from Tennessee, 407–10, 413–16; romance with Sally Preston, 10–13, 30, 36, 436–37; and Spring Hill battle, 133, 135–39, 146–48, 152–57; strategies, 44–45, 56–58, 60, 63–66, 71–74, 91–92, 96–98, 113–17, 124–27, 298–99, 338–39; Tennessee invasion, 94–96; and Thomas, 79; views of, 52, 252–53, 268, 431, 439–40
Hospitals, 253, 261, 350
House, John L., 381
Howard, Oliver O., 33, 34
Hubbard, Lucius F., 336–38, 340, 374–76
Huey's Mill, Tennessee, 103
Hughes's Ford, 168–69, 197, 241
Hurt's Crossroads, Tennessee, 103, 105, 111

Infantry: Confederate, 114, 131, 139, 180–84, 278–79; Federal, 254
Information, Federal, of Confederates, 80–83, 100, 102, 105–9, 111, 140–41, 167–69
Ingram, John, 146
Irwinville, Georgia, 424

Jackson, Henry R., 238, 239, 295, 297, 374–76, 390, 405
Jackson, Thomas J. "Stonewall," and Hood, 9
Jackson, William H., 74, 89, 92, 97, 111–12, 121, 159, 282, 283, 298, 447; Franklin battle, 171, 182, 241; Nashville campaign, 278, 314; Spring Hill battle, 138, 147, 151
Jacksonville, Alabama, 63
James, Joseph H., 101
Jameson, T. E., 115
Jennison, Samuel P., 373
Johnson, Andrew, 290, 425
Johnson, Edward, 139, 147–50, 154, 156, 245–47, 254, 269, 339–40, 383, 390
Johnson, Gilbert M. L., 293–95
Johnson, J. P., 428
Johnson, Lewis, 57, 282
Johnson, Richard W., 92, 113, 168, 326–28, 353–54, 388, 393, 396, 397
Johnsonville, Tennessee, 67–68
Johnston, Albert Sidney, 7, 20, 75
Johnston, Joseph E., 19, 24–31, 40, 42, 43, 46, 428, 431, 435–36
Jones residence, Pulaski, Tennessee, 414
Jonesboro, Georgia, 34–35

Kellar, Andrew J., 377, 404
Kelley, David C., 284
Kellogg, Elijah, 248
Kellogg, Sanford, 292
Kennesaw Mountain, battle of, 27, 43, 77

Kentucky Brigade, Crossland's, 168
Kentucky Light Artillery (Federal), 193
Kilpatrick, Judson, 84
Kimball, Nathan, 107, 109, 120, 140, 143, 150, 151, 167, 171, 186, 240, 255, 341
Kingston, Georgia, 59, 60
Kirby, Isaac M., 167, 341
Knipe, Joseph F., 332–34, 393, 395, 396, 399

Lamb's Ferry Road, 414, 418
Lane, John Q., 121, 129, 132–33, 138, 172, 173, 175, 176, 186, 188, 190, 191, 207, 288
LaVergne, Tennessee, 283, 293, 314
Lawrenceburg, Tennessee, 82, 83, 89, 92
Lea, J. M., home of, 348
Lebanon, Tennessee, 298
LeDuc, William G., 274
Lee, Custis, 37, 52
Lee, Robert E., 7, 24, 37, 48, 75, 96; and Hood, 8–9, 32, 436
Lee, S. P., 284, 285, 289, 401, 421, 423
Lee, Stephen D., 34–35, 40, 66, 80, 82, 89, 94–96, 114, 141, 142, 158, 265, 269, 271, 315, 407, 427, 431, 444; Franklin battle, 182, 245–47, 255–56, 269; Nashville battle, 278–79, 282, 286–87, 330, 335, 338–39, 342, 344, 348, 360, 362, 370, 379, 382–85, 387–88; retreat, 394–97, 407, 421; Spring Hill battle, 150, 154, 156–57; views of Hood, 263, 305–7
Letters, secret, Hood to Bragg, 25–26, 45
Lewis, Mary Foreman, 38
Lewisburg pike, 103, 105, 159, 165, 168, 172, 177, 180, 217, 397
Lexington, Tennessee, 415, 424
Lightfoot, Amelia, 39
Lightfoot, Sallie, 39
Lillard's Mills, Tennessee, 405
Lincoln, Abraham, 2, 26, 346; and Sherman, 59; and Thomas, 277–78, 319
Locust thicket, 164, 234–38, 246, 258–59
Logan, John A., 312, 319
Longstreet, James, 9–10
Loring, William W., 183, 216–18, 340, 341, 377
Lotz, Albert, 233
Lovejoy's Station, Georgia, 35
Lowndes, Rawlins, 437
Lowrey, Mark, 114, 126–29, 131, 223–24, 360, 377–79
Lumsden, Charles L., 334, 336–37
Lynnville, Tennessee, 83, 92, 93, 415, 416
Lyon, Hylan B., 289

MacArthur, Arthur, Jr., 204
McArthur, John, 321, 331, 332, 334, 336, 337, 339, 351, 365–67, 373, 375, 383, 389, 441
McCook, Edward M., 289
McCornack, Andrew, 61

McCutcheon Creek, Tennessee, 126
McGavock, John, grove of, 216
McGavock, Mrs. John, 260, 264
McGavock, Randal, mansion, 165
McGavock's Ford, 168–69
Mackall, W. W., 33
McKissack, William, residence of, 144, 145
McMillan, William L., 334–37, 366, 373–76
Macon, Georgia, Davis speech, 4, 52
Macon & Western Railroad, 34
McPherson, James B., 32, 33–34
McWayne, Eugene, 42, 44
Malloy, Adam, 316
Maney, George, 377–78, 407
Maney, Mrs., residence of, 391
Mangum, L. H., 130, 264
Manigault, Arthur M., 247, 338
Marsh, John, 264
Marshall, William, 374–76
Mason, A. P., 148
"Maury Grays," 97
Meade, George M., 27, 402
Mehringer, John, 343, 352
Memories of wartime experiences, 438
Memphis & Charleston Railroad, 63, 64, 68, 69, 305
Merrill's Hill (Privet Knob), 173
Military strength of opposing armies, 3
Military unit designations, 66n
Mill Creek, Tennessee, 282
Mill Springs, Kentucky, battle of, 76
Milroy, Robert H., 293–98
Minie balls, 43
Missionary Ridge, battle of, 18, 77
Missouri, invasion of, 85
Mitchell, Milton A., 172, 173, 176, 187–88, 190
Mobile & Ohio Railroad, 68, 69, 425
Mohrmann, William O., 186
Montgomery, Alabama, 7; Davis speech, 4
Montgomery Hill, 328–29
Moons, E., 220
Moore, Jonathan B., 351–52
Moore, Orlando H., 93, 166, 239–40
Moose (gunboat), 284
Morale: Confederate, 3–4, 36–37, 44, 56, 65, 73, 261–62, 267–69, 305–6, 377–78; Union, 42
Morgan, John Hunt, 326
Morgan, Thomas J., 322, 324, 325, 357–59
Motherspaw, Thomas W., 201, 204
Mount Carmel, Tennessee, 111–12, 117, 118
Mount Pleasant, Tennessee, 91–92, 94
Mowrer, Joseph A., 365
Murfreesboro, Tennessee, 279, 281, 283–84, 293, 295–98, 313–17
Murphey, Virgil S., 229, 231, 252–53, 274
Muscle Shoals, Alabama, 65, 80, 421

Nash, Charles E., 17
Nashville, Tennessee, 79, 85–86, 95, 274–76, 278–87, 313–17; battle of, x–xi, 321–91, 425; 300–307; weather, 319–20
Nashville & Chattanooga Railroad, 293, 295, 317, 324, 357
Neeley, Green, house of, 245
Negroes. See Blacks; Black soldiers
Neilson, C. P., 440
Nelson, Noel L., 260
New Hope Church, Georgia, 27, 43
New York Herald, 40
New York Times, 311
Newspapers, and battle of Franklin, 265–67
9th Illinois Cavalry, 337, 389, 399
9th Indiana Infantry, 401
9th Tennessee Cavalry (Confederate), 97
19th Pennsylvania Cavalry, 353
19th Tennessee Infantry (Confederate), 304
96th Illinois Infantry, 150, 171, 272, 313
97th Ohio Infantry, 210, 243
Nisbet, James C., 32
Nolen's plantation, 113
North. See Union Army; United States

Officers: Confederate, 33, 238, 270, 274; Federal, and Hood, 32–33
Olmstead, Charles H., 314
Olson, Porter C., 204
100th Colored Regiment, 359–60
100th Illinois Infantry, 132–33
100th Ohio Infantry, 195, 221, 228, 379
101st Ohio Infantry, 236–37
103rd Ohio Infantry, 118, 120
104th Ohio Infantry, 185, 195, 219–21, 227, 228, 230, 249, 274
111th Ohio Infantry, 236–37
112th Illinois Infantry, 143, 212–13, 230
115th Ohio Infantry band, 283
120th Indiana Infantry, 217
124th Ohio Infantry, 166, 255, 329
125th Ohio Infantry, 165, 201–2, 208, 300–301, 318
127th Illinois Volunteer Infantry, 42, 43
129th Indiana Infantry, 239
175th Ohio Infantry, 221
183rd Ohio Infantry, 186, 191–92, 210, 236, 239
Oostanaula River, Georgia, 49, 56
Oostanaula Valley, 60
Opdycke, Emerson, 120, 121, 129, 152, 159, 287–88, 318, 329, 341, 441; Franklin battle, 171–75, 199–207, 208, 210, 213, 228, 234, 249, 254; and Wagner, 170–71, 173–75
Order of battle: Confederate, 444–47; Federal, 448–51
Overall Creek railroad blockhouse, 293–98
Overton, John, home of, 286, 307

Overton Hill, 348, 355–63, 379–85
Owen's Ford, Tennessee, 97

Palmer, William J., 432
Palmer's Brigade, 296, 298
Palmetto, Georgia, 37–38, 45–47
Paris, Lee O., 229, 248n
Peach Orchard Hill. See Overton Hill
Peachtree Creek, battle of, 33
Pennsylvania Light Artillery, 130, 239–40
Personnel decisions by Davis, 20–22, 24–25, 29, 31–33, 40, 47–48
Peters, George B., 117n
Pettus, Edmund W., 142, 383, 394
Pickett's Charge, Gettysburg, 270
Pinhook, Tennessee, 423
Pirtle, John B., 147
Plundering: Confederate, 97; Federal, 101
Polk, Andrew J., 95
Polk, Leonidas, 27, 40
Polk, Lucius J., 94, 264
Polk, William J., residence of, 264
Pontoon bridge: Duck River, 413; Tennessee River, 69, 87, 416, 420–22
Pontoon train: Confederate, 64, 95–96, 98, 432; Federal, 167, 400, 411–12
Porter, James D., 148
Post, Philip Sidney, 140–41, 329, 355, 359–62, 363
Presstman, Stephen W., 98, 240, 420–21
Preston, Caroline, 52
Preston, Jack, 434
Preston, John Smith, 58, 438; and Hood, 12
Preston, Mary "Mamie," 10, 58
Preston, Sarah Buchanan (Sally, "Buck"), 10–11; and Davis, 52; and Hood, 12–13, 30, 36, 38, 287, 434–37
Preston, Susan "Tudy," 10
Preston, Willie, 58, 435
Preston family, and Hood, 434–35
Price, Sterling, 85
Prisoners: Confederate, 206, 230–31, 274, 374, 376–77, 379, 385, 390–91, 402, 425, 426; Confederate treatment, 57; Federal, 78
Privet Knob, 173, 175, 183, 187
Pulaski, Tennessee, 2, 77, 80, 83, 92, 100, 417, 408–10, 414–15, 424

Quarles, William A., 182–83, 218–19, 334, 335, 396–97, 407
Quintard, Charles T., 94–96, 98, 113, 264, 281, 284, 307, 404–6, 408, 410, 428

Railroads, 34–35, 46, 53–57, 62, 69
Rainey, Martha, 232
Rally Hill, Tennessee, 98, 107
Rally Hill pike, 124–26, 138
Ramsey, Robert H., 400
Rawhide, Alabama, 89
Rebel yell, 191
Recruits, Confederate, in Tennessee, 315

Redoubts, Nashville battle, 316, 330, 334–39, 341–42
Reilly, James A., 142–43, 166, 195, 203, 214, 216–17, 227–28
Religion, of Hood, 96; after defeat, 410
Reports, deceptive: by Bragg, 28–29, 37; by Hood, 25–28, 45–46, 268–69, 404, 426, 427–28, 435
Resaca, Georgia, 56, 60–61
Reynolds, Daniel H., 219, 227, 339, 369, 381, 407
Richardson, T. G., 11
Richland Creek, Tennessee, 326, 416–17
Richmond, Kentucky, battle of, 17, 18
Richmond, Virginia, 7, 10, 23, 48, 436
Rifle muskets, 43, 205n
Ringgold Gap, battle of, 19
Road conditions, 69, 73, 82, 89, 91, 94; Confederate retreat, 415, 417, 418, 420
Roberts, Deering, 261
Roddey, Philip D., 416, 420, 432
Rome, Georgia, 60
Rosecrans, William Starke, 76, 85
Ross, Lawrence S., 105, 117, 145, 151–52, 241
Ross's Texas Brigade, 447
Rough and Ready, Georgia, 35
Rousseau, Lawrence, 221–22
Rousseau, Lovell H., 78, 228, 229, 293–96, 298
Rucker, Edmund W., 91, 93, 314, 326, 327, 388–90, 447
Ruger, Thomas H., 93, 108, 109, 141–44, 149, 166, 234–37, 239, 449
Rutherford Creek, Tennessee, 103, 107, 109, 117, 120, 124–26, 140, 143, 152, 407–8, 410–12

Sanford's Mississippi battery, 360
Savannah, Georgia, 58, 423
Schell, A. Buck, 137, 183, 187
Schofield, John McAllister, 27, 32, 56, 82, 83, 86, 92, 93, 95, 96, 99–109, 114–15, 129, 159–62, 166, 170, 276, 288–89, 310–12, 440–41; Franklin battle, 167–69, 171–72, 197–98, 250–53, 269, 273; Nashville battle, 321, 332, 343, 347, 351–54, 363–64, 367–68, 386; and Spring Hill battle, 129–30, 140–45, 149–50, 153; and Thomas, 273–74, 292–93, 320–21; and Wilson, 111, 277
Scofield, Levi T., 189, 190
Scott's Brigade, 216, 218
Scovill, Charles W., 208
Sears, Claudius W., 227–29, 248, 296, 342, 370, 423
2nd Iowa Cavalry, 303, 335–37, 398–99
2nd Iowa Light Battery, 334, 339
2nd Michigan Cavalry, 69, 80, 119–20, 151–52, 168–69, 264–65, 451
2nd Tennessee Cavalry (Confederate), 265
2nd U.S. Cavalry, 7, 75
Secret order of Southern soldiers, 14

Seddon, James A., 25, 306, 329–30, 404, 429, 430
Selma, Alabama, 67, 424
7th Alabama Cavalry, 327
7th Illinois Cavalry, 364, 416
7th Illinois Infantry, 59
7th Ohio Cavalry, 105
Seventeenth Corps, U.S. Army, 86
17th Alabama Infantry, 228, 252
17th U.S. Colored Troops, 318, 324
72nd Illinois Infantry, 162–63, 185, 186, 191, 193, 209–10, 212, 234, 236, 237, 246n
73rd Illinois Infantry, 118, 120, 201, 202, 208, 255
74th Illinois Infantry, 201, 248
79th Illinois Infantry, 129
Sexton, James A., 212
Shafter, William R., 318, 324–25, 357
Sharp, Jacob H., 246
Shellenberger, John K., 186, 188, 191–94, 249, 441
Shelley, Charles M., 219, 220, 221, 224–25, 370
Sheridan, Philip, 110, 402
Sherman, William Tecumseh, 4, 24, 26, 32–35, 44, 52, 79, 85, 100, 129, 402, 412, 423; Grant and, 76–77; march through Georgia, 27–28, 60–62, 72, 96; strategies, 43–44, 58–62, 70–71; and Thomas, 76, 77
Shoes, Confederate need, 305, 406, 414, 415
Shy, William M., 373–74, 442
Shy's Hill, 352, 363, 367, 369–70, 373–79, 384
6th Cavalry Division (Johnson's), 326
6th Ohio Light Battery, 130, 219, 220
6th Tennessee Infantry (Union), 340
Sixteenth Corps, U.S. Army, 85, 276
16th Illinois Cavalry, 327
16th Kentucky Infantry (Federal), 221
64th Ohio Infantry, 121, 122, 128, 176, 185, 186, 191, 254
65th Illinois Infantry, 227
65th Indiana Infantry, 218, 219
65th Ohio Infantry, 220
Smith, Andrew J., 85–86, 100, 103, 108, 160, 161, 251, 273, 276, 310, 321, 331, 411; Nashville battle, 320, 328, 331–32, 337–38, 340, 341, 343, 351, 352, 354, 367, 376, 379–80, 386
Smith, E. Kirby, 17, 19, 315
Smith, George W., 201
Smith, Gustavus Woodson, 435
Smith, James A., 407
Smith, Jim, 115
Smith, Thomas Benton, 238–39, 257, 295, 370, 372–74, 390
"Smith's Guerrillas," 320
Snyder, Carrie, 232–33, 261
Soldiers: Confederate, 32, 183–84, 422; experience of, x; Federal, 61–62, 79, 83, 162–63, 185–86, 199, 201, 204–5
South. See Confederate Army; Confederate States

Spalding, George, 389n, 420, 423
Spring Hill, Tennessee, 77, 105, 108, 113, 114, 117–23, 149–58, 397, 401
Stafford, Fountain, 211, 259–60
Stanley, David S., 83, 93, 99, 100, 106–9, 120–21, 126, 131–32, 164–65, 167, 170, 176, 206, 272, 276, 322, 440–41; Franklin battle, 171–72, 198–99, 251, 255; Spring Hill battle, 129–30, 144–45, 149–52
Stanton, Edwin M., 277–78, 289, 291, 402; and Thomas, 319, 346–47, 412, 422
Steedman, James B., 78, 273, 276–77, 288, 310, 311, 320–22, 324–26, 357–59, 384–85, 401–2, 423; Schofield and, 441
Steedman, Thomas J., 354–56
Stephenson, J. M., 159, 171
Stevenson, Carter L., 97, 383, 397–99, 407, 408, 444
Stewart, Alexander P., 40, 54, 69, 70, 74, 95, 158, 261, 265, 278–79, 313–16, 320, 444–45; Franklin battle, 177–78, 180, 182–84, 191, 207, 214, 216, 225, 227, 255–56, 266, 269; Nashville battle, 330, 332, 334–36, 338–43, 347–48, 369–72, 374–75, 382–83, 386; retreat, 407, 408, 421; Spring Hill battle, 124, 135–38, 147, 148, 152, 155
Stewart, Robert R., 340
Stewart, Samuel, 216
Stiles, Israel N., 166, 214, 254
Stockton, Joseph, 210
Stones River, battle of, 18, 20, 76, 293, 314
Stovall, Marcellus A., 360, 384, 394
Strahl, Otho F., 134, 183, 210–11, 263, 377, 407
Strange, J. P., 91
Streight, Abel D., 106, 329, 355, 361
Strickland, Silas A., 143, 166, 195, 203, 207, 209, 212, 234
Sugar Creek, 419–20
Supply system: Confederate, 65, 68–70, 73, 89–91, 305–6, 425; Federal, 34, 46–48, 53–57, 62, 411–12
Surveillance of Johnston, by Hood, 25–26
Sykes, Mrs. William, 265

Tarleton, Grace, 39
Tarleton, Robert, 39
Tarleton, Susan, 38–41, 53, 184, 264, 287, 440
Taylor, Richard, 48, 49, 67, 74, 427–29, 431
Technology of warfare, 43
Tennessee, 94, 286; invasion of, 1–2, 4, 74
Tennessee & Alabama Railroad, 77–78, 81, 165, 355
Tennessee River, 63–66, 68–69, 74, 80, 87, 401–2, 406–7, 416, 420–22
10th Minnesota Infantry, 373
Texas Brigade, 8, 88
3rd Illinois Cavalry, 118–19
3rd Mississippi regiment, 217, 225

3rd Texas Cavalry, 241
13th Colored Regiment, 359–63
13th Indiana Cavalry, 293–95
13th Ohio Infantry, 149
33rd Alabama Infantry, 224
33rd Wisconsin Infantry, 340
35th Alabama Infantry, 216
35th Tennessee Cavalry (Confederate), 305
36th Illinois Infantry, 130, 131, 201, 204–5, 341
39th Georgia Infantry, 384, 387
39th North Carolina Infantry, 421
Thoburn, Thomas C., 248
Thomas, Fanny, 75
Thomas, George H., 7, 59, 75–86, 102–3, 108, 290–93, 308–13, 317, 319, 331, 422, 425; and Confederate retreat, 400, 401, 411–13, 417, 420, 423–24; defense of Nashville, 276–78, 285–87, 289–90, 298–99; and dissension among officers, 288–89; and Franklin battle, 251, 273; Grant and, 346–47; and Nashville battle, 326, 328, 332, 343, 344, 352–55, 363, 367–68, 379–80, 386, 390, 392; and Confederate retreat, 393; report by, 424–25; and Schofield, 160–61, 171, 273–74, 288–89, 441; and Spring Hill battle, 122, 140; strategies of, 100, 107, 320–22; and Wagner, 288
Thomas, Julia, 75
Thompson, Absalom, 127; residence of, 135–36
Thompson, Charles R., 316, 324, 356–62
Thompson's Station, Tennessee, 138, 144–45, 147, 150–51, 158–59
Tower, Zealous B., 274, 276
"Traveler's Rest" (Overton home), 286
Triune, Tennessee, 113
Truett, Alpheus, 167, 197–98, 250, 252
Truett, Edwin, 197
Tucker's farmhouse, Nashville, 390
Tullahoma, Tennessee, 293
Tunnel Hill, Georgia, 39, 56, 61
Tupelo, Mississippi, 425–26, 428–29
Tuscumbia, Alabama, 63, 65, 421
12th Colored Regiment, 357–60
12th Kentucky Infantry (Federal), 221–22, 227–29, 379
12th Tennessee Cavalry (Federal), 80, 117–18, 332, 388–89, 420
20th Alabama Regiment, 383

20th Louisiana Regiment band, 87, 95
20th Ohio Battery, 208, 212, 254
20th Tennessee Infantry (Confederate), 234
21st Tennessee Cavalry (Confederate), 119–20
22nd Mississippi Regiment, 217
Twenty-third Corps, U.S. Army, 59, 83, 93–94, 99, 101, 108, 109, 161, 162–63, 166, 167, 266, 269, 276, 289, 412, 449; Nashville battle, 332, 340, 343, 351–53, 386; Schofield and, 170, 320
23rd Michigan Infantry, 144, 239–40
24th Illinois Infantry, 151
24th South Carolina Infantry, 237, 243
24th Tennessee Infantry (Confederate), 97
26th Ohio Infantry Regiment, 136–37
28th Kentucky Volunteers (Federal), 226n
28th Mississippi Cavalry, 165
29th Alabama Infantry, 224, 230, 336
Twining, William J., 140–41, 160
Tyler's Brigade, 295

Union army. See Federal army
United States, 3; war status, 1864, 26

Van Dorn, Earl, 117, 165
Van Duzer, John C., 292, 345–46
Vandalism, by Union soldiers, 301
Vaught residence, Columbia, Tennessee, 404
Veterans of Franklin battle, 440–42

Wagner, George Day, 130, 132, 167, 170–71, 253, 270, 288; Franklin battle, 172, 173–78, 189–90, 196, 220, 234, 254–55
Wagon train, Federal, 120–21, 130, 144–45, 150–51, 159–61, 167, 265
Walker, W. H. T., 19, 21
Walthall, Edward C., 426; Franklin battle, 218–20, 227, 229, 230; Nashville battle, 334–35, 339–40, 372, 374–75, 379; retreat, 407, 415, 417–19, 421–22
War: ideal, 42–43; Sherman's views, 5
Warfield, Mrs. Amos, home of, 95
Warrensburg, Missouri, 86
Warwick, Braddy, 11
Waynesboro, Tennessee, 89

Weapons, 43, 91, 92–93, 190, 226n, 241; Confederate, 136; Federal, 119
Weather, 65, 303–4, 308–10, 315, 317–21; and Confederate retreat, 397, 400–401, 406, 408–14; Nashville battle, 350, 354, 389; and Tennessee invasion, 1–2, 68–69, 71, 73, 81–83, 85, 88–89, 96, 101
West Point: Hood at, 7, 32; Schofield at, 99
Western & Atlantic Railroad, 46, 54, 60, 63
Wheeler, Joseph, 29, 34, 67, 70, 71
Whipple, William D., 311
Whitaker, Walter C., 120, 167, 171, 240
White, John S., 221, 222
Whittmore, Walter, 264
Wigfall, F. Halsey, 94, 268, 405
Wigfall, Louis T., 8, 25, 436
Wilkinson pike, 296–97
Wilkinson's Cross Roads, Tennessee, 348
Willett, James B., 400
Williamson County, Tennessee, 165
"Williamson Greys," 165
Wilson, James H., 84, 86, 102–13, 118, 145, 167–69, 277, 289–91, 298, 310–11, 318, 390, 421, 424; and Confederate retreat, 392–97, 399–401, 408, 411, 413, 417–20, 423–24; Franklin battle, 197, 241; Nashville battle, 320–21, 332–34, 343, 347, 351, 353–54, 363–64, 367–68, 385–86, 389–90
Wilson-Kautz Railroad Raid, 111
Winstead Hill, 162, 171–73, 177–78, 180, 187
Wolfe, Edward H., 341–42
Women, Confederate, 286–87
Wood, Thomas J., 101–2, 106–8, 141, 143, 151, 159, 162, 167, 276, 301, 310, 441; and Confederate retreat, 393, 400–401, 407–8, 411, 413, 424; Franklin battle, 198; Nashville battle, 320, 328–29, 341, 347, 354–56, 363, 384–85
Wounded soldiers, 242–43, 253, 260, 350, 390, 396, 402

Yell Rifles, 16
Yorkville, South Carolina, 436–37
Young, J. Morris, 105
Young, J. P., 414
Young, R. B., 264

Ziegler's Pennsylvania battery, 239–40